TEACHER'S EDITION

SENDEROS 1

Spanish for a Connected World

VISTA®
HIGHER LEARNING

Boston, Massachusetts

Publisher: José A. Blanco

Editorial Development: Armando Brito, Jhonny Alexander Calle, Deborah Coffey, María Victoria Echeverri, Jo Hanna Kurth, Megan Moran, Jaime Patiño, Raquel Rodríguez, Verónica Tejeda, Sharla Zwirek

Project Management: Cécile Engeln, Sally Giangrande

Rights Management: Ashley Dos Santos, Annie Pickert Fuller

Technology Production: Jamie Kostecki, Daniel Ospina, Paola Ríos Schaaf

Design: Radoslav Mateev, Gabriel Noreña, Andrés Vanegas

Production: Manuela Arango, Oscar Díez, Erik Restrepo

Student Text (Casebound-SIMRA) ISBN: 978-1-68005-190-2

Teacher's Edition ISBN: 978-1-68005-191-9

Library of Congress Control Number: 2016949696

1 2 3 4 5 6 7 8 9 TC 21 20 19 18 17 16

Printed in Canada.

Teacher's Edition Table of Contents

Teacher's Edition Table of Contents

The Vista Higher Learning
Difference

As a specialized publisher, we focus on what we love and do best—developing world language materials that get teachers and students as excited about language and culture as we are.

What does that mean for you?

- Unparalleled service from day one, including personalized training by nationally-renowned world language educators.

- Superior technology support to ensure that your classes run smoothly throughout the year.

- Seamless integration of technology, content, and resources to ensure success for you and your students.

"My **Vista Higher Learning rep** is absolutely fantastic. He is **responsive to the needs** of my department and colleagues."

Sally Sefami, Sage High School
Newport Coast, CA

VISTA
HIGHER LEARNING

SENDEROS

Spanish for a Connected World

At Vista Higher Learning, we recognize that proficiency is best achieved through an articulated and extended sequence of study. **Senderos 1–5** was designed with this in mind, resulting in a fully integrated and scaffolded Spanish program with a variety of print offerings and superior technology.

With powerful and easy-to-use course management tools, you can shape **Senderos** to fit your instructional goals and teaching style—all while delivering an engaging, personalized learning experience to each and every student.

What sets Senderos apart?

- Vocabulary Tutorials
- Grammar Tutorials
- News and Cultural Updates
- Multi-part Video Collection
- Video Virtual Chat activities
- Partner Chat activities
- Heritage Speaker activities

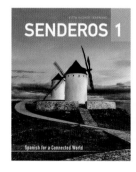    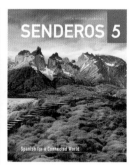

Scope & Sequence: Senderos 1

	contextos	cultura	estructura	adelante

2

Lección preliminar

A brief overview of the contexts and grammar from Level 1

Lección 1 La rutina diaria

contextos	cultura	estructura	adelante
Daily routine Personal hygiene Time expressions	**En detalle:** La siesta **Perfil:** El mate	**1.1** Reflexive verbs **1.2** Indefinite and negative words **1.3** Preterite of **ser** and **ir** **1.4** Verbs like **gustar**	**En pantalla** **Lectura:** *¡Qué día!* **Panorama:** Perú

Lección 2 La comida

contextos	cultura	estructura	adelante
Food Food descriptions Meals	**En detalle:** Frutas y verduras de América **Perfil:** Ferran Adrià: arte en la cocina	**2.1** Preterite of stem-changing verbs **2.2** Double object pronouns **2.3** Comparisons **2.4** Superlatives	**En pantalla** **Lectura:** Menú y crítica: La feria del maíz **Panorama:** Guatemala

Lección 3 Las fiestas

contextos	cultura	estructura	adelante
Parties and celebrations Personal relationships Stages of life	**En detalle:** Semana Santa: vacaciones y tradición **Perfil:** Festival de Viña del Mar	**3.1** Irregular preterites **3.2** Verbs that change meaning in the preterite **3.3** ¿**Qué**? and ¿**cuál**? **3.4** Pronouns after prepositions	**En pantalla** **Lectura:** *Vida social* **Panorama:** Chile

Lección 4 En el consultorio

contextos	cultura	estructura	adelante
Health and medical terms Parts of the body Symptoms and medical conditions Health professions	**En detalle:** Servicios de salud **Perfil:** Curanderos y chamanes	**4.1** The imperfect tense **4.2** The preterite and the imperfect **4.3** Constructions with **se** **4.4** Adverbs	**En pantalla** **Lectura:** *Libro de la semana* **Panorama:** Costa Rica

Lección 5 La tecnología

contextos	cultura	estructura	adelante
Home electronics Computers and the Internet The car and its accessories	**En detalle:** Las redes sociales **Perfil:** Los mensajes de texto	**5.1** Familiar commands **5.2** **Por** and **para** **5.3** Reciprocal reflexives **5.4** Stressed possessive adjectives and pronouns	**En pantalla** **Lectura:** *Una tira cómica* **Panorama:** Argentina

Lección 6 La vivienda

contextos	cultura	estructura	adelante
Parts of a house Household chores Table settings	**En detalle:** El patio central **Perfil:** Las islas flotantes del lago Titicaca	**6.1** Relative pronouns **6.2** Formal (**usted/ustedes**) commands **6.3** The present subjunctive **6.4** Subjunctive with verbs of will and influence	**En pantalla** **Lectura:** *Bienvenidos al Palacio de las Garzas* **Panorama:** Panamá

Scope & Sequence: Senderos 3

Scope & Sequence: Senderos 4

Scope & Sequence: Senderos 5

World-Readiness Standards for Learning Languages

Senderos blends the underlying principles of the World-Readiness Standards with features and strategies tailored specifically to build students' language and cultural competencies.

 This icon provides information on the specific standard(s) addressed in each section.

THE FIVE C'S OF FOREIGN LANGUAGE LEARNING

Communication

Students:

1. Interact and negotiate meaning in spoken, signed, or written conversations to share information, reactions, feelings, and opinions. (Interpersonal mode)
2. Understand, interpret, and analyze what is heard, read, or viewed on a variety of topics. (Interpretive mode)
3. Present information, concepts, and ideas to inform, explain, persuade, and narrate on a variety of topics using appropriate media and adapting to various audiences of listeners, readers, or viewers. (Presentational mode)

Cultures

Students use Spanish to investigate, explain, and reflect on:

1. The relationship of the practices and perspectives of the culture studied.
2. The relationship of the products and perspectives of the culture studied.

Connections

Students:

1. Build, reinforce, and expand their knowledge of other disciplines while using Spanish to develop critical thinking and to solve problems creatively.
2. Access and evaluate information and diverse perspectives that are available through Spanish and its cultures.

Comparisons

Students use Spanish to investigate, explain, and reflect on:

1. The nature of language through comparisons of the Spanish language and their own.
2. The concept of culture through comparisons of the cultures studied and their own.

Communities

Students:

1. Use Spanish both within and beyond the school to interact and collaborate in their community and the globalized world.
2. Set goals and reflect on their progress in using languages for enjoyment, enrichment, and advancement.

Adapted from ACTFL's *Standards for Foreign Language Learning in the 21st Century*

SENDEROS PRIME vs. SENDEROS (s)upersite

At Vista Higher Learning, we recognize that classrooms and districts across the country are at different stages in the implementation of technology. That's why we offer two levels of technology with **Senderos: Prime** or **Supersite**. Regardless of a school's resources and readiness, **Senderos** is the perfect fit with any curriculum and infrastructure. It meets customers where they are, and will take them where they want to be.

For the Teacher

COMPONENT	WHAT IS IT?	PRIME	(s)upersite
Teacher's Edition		•	•
Activity Pack (with Answer Key)	Supplementary activities, including: • Additional structured language practice • Additional activities using authentic sources • Communication activities for practicing interpersonal speaking • Lesson review activities • *¡Atrévete!* Board Game	•	•
Audio and Video Scripts	Scripts for all audio and video selections: • Textbook audio • Testing Program audio • Video Virtual Chat scripts • *Fotonovela, Flash cultura,* and *Panorama cultural* • Grammar Tutorials	•	•
Digital Image Bank	Images and maps from the text to use for presentation in class, plus a bank of illustrations to use with the Instructor-Created Content tool	•	•
Grammar Presentation Slides	Grammar presentation reformatted in PowerPoint	•	•
I Can Worksheets	Lesson Objectives broken down by section and written in student-friendly "I Can" statement format	•	•
Implementation Guides	In-depth support for every stage of instruction—from planning and implementation, to assessment and remediation	•	•
Learning Templates	Pre-built syllabi that provide you with flexible options to suit your On-level, Above-level, and Heritage Speaker classes	•	
Lesson Plans	Editable block and standard schedules	•	•
Middle School Activity Pack	Hands-on vocabulary and grammar practice design for younger learners, but effective for kinesthetic instruction for all level 1 students	•	•
Pacing Guides	Guidelines for how to cover the level's instructional material for a variety of scenarios (standard, block, etc.)	•	•
Teacher's DVD Set	*Flash cultura/Fotonovela/Panorama cultural* DVD, Teacher Resources DVD	•	•
Assessment Program (with Answer Key)	Quizzes, tests, and exams	•	•
Assessment Program Audio	Audio to accompany all tests	•	•

For the **Student**

COMPONENT	WHAT IS IT?	PRIME	supersite
Student Edition	Core instruction for students	•	•
Audio-synced Readings	Audio to accompany all *Lecturas*	•	•
Dictionary	Easy digital access to dictionary	•	•
eBook	Downloadable Student Edition	•	•
En pantalla Video	Authentic TV clips from across the Spanish-speaking world	•	•
Enhanced Diagnostics	Embedded assessment activities provide immediate feedback to students	•	
Flash cultura Video	Young broadcasters from the Spanish-speaking world share cultural aspects of life	•	•
Fotonovela Video	Engaging storyline video	•	•
Grammar Tutorials	Animated tutorials pair lesson concepts with fun examples and interactive questions that check for understanding		•
Grammar Tutorials with Diagnostics	Interactive tutorials featuring embedded quick checks and multi-part diagnostic with real-time feedback and remediation	•	
Learning Progression	Unique learning progression logically contextualizes lesson content	•	
My Vocabulary	A variety of tools to practice vocabulary	•	•
News and Cultural Updates	Monthly posting of authentic resource links with scaffolded activities	•	•
Online Information Gap Activities	Student pairs work synchronously to record a conversation as they negotiate for meaning to complete a task	•	
Panorama cultural Video	Short video showcases the nations of the Spanish-speaking world	•	•
Partner Chat Activities	Pairs of students work synchronously to record a conversation in the target language	•	•
Personalized Study Plan	Personalized prescriptive pathway highlights areas where students need more practice	•	
Practice Tests with Diagnostics	Students get feedback on what they need to study before a test or exam	•	•
Pronunciation Tutorials	Interactive presentation of Spanish pronunciation and spelling with Speech Recognition	•	
Speech Recognition	Innovative technology analyzes students' speech and provides real-time feedback	•	
vText	Virtual interactive textbook for browser-based exploration		•
Video Virtual Chat Activities	Students create simulated conversations by responding to questions delivered by video recordings of native speakers	•	•
Vocabulary Hotpots	Vocabulary presentation with embedded audio	•	
Vocabulary Spotlights	Automated spotlighting on images with audio	•	
Vocabulary Tutorials (Animated)	Animated tutorials allow students to practice vocabulary at their own pace		•
Vocabulary Tutorials (Interactive)	Lesson vocabulary taught in a cyclical learning sequence—Listen & repeat, Match, Say it—with Speech Recognition and diagnostics	•	
Web-enhanced Readings	Dynamic presentation with audio	•	

Teacher-Driven Technology

Senderos Prime allows your unique teaching style to shine through. With convenient, ready-made Learning Templates, you'll have the time and flexibility to create and incorporate your own activities, videos, assignments, and assessments. Adding your own voice is easy—and your students will hear your unique accent loud and clear.

So what are Learning Templates?

Learning Templates are pre-built lesson plans that provide flexible options to suit your On-level, Above-level, or Heritage Speaker Spanish classes.

Once you've selected a Learning Template as a base for your course, **Senderos Prime** will automatically set all of the assignments for the entire year, as well as create your gradebook. You can then add or delete activities, change due dates, and customize assessments. You can even add your own personal touches, including activities, videos, and notes to students.

Student-Directed Learning

To effectively learn a new language, students need opportunities for meaningful practice—both inside and outside of the classroom. **Senderos Prime** provides students with the interactive tools and engaging content they need to stay motivated and on track throughout the school year.

Senderos Prime is unique in its organization and delivery of lesson content. Each color-coded strand features a progression that contextualizes the learning experience for students by breaking lesson content into comprehensible language chunks.

Explore and Learn

Explore and Learn activities engage students, so they can actively learn and build confidence in a safe online environment. With these low-stakes activities, students receive credit for participation, not performance.

Explore

Explore activities activate students' prior knowledge and connect them with the material they are about to learn.

Contextos Explore features a multimodal presentation with audio, text, illustrations, and contemporary photos that immerses students in an engaging learning environment.

Contextos Spotlights capture and focus students' attention on key vocabulary from the lesson.

Fotonovela Explore mini video clips in an easy-to-follow storyboard format set the context for the entire episode.

Estructura Explore features carefully designed charts and diagrams that call out key grammatical structures as well as additional active vocabulary. Audio and point-of-use photos from the Vocabulary Tutorials and *Fotonovela* episode provide additional context.

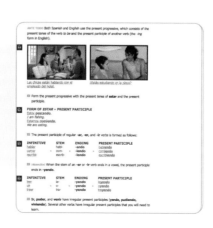

Learn

Learn activities shift from purely receptive to interactive learning, inviting students to be active participants and take ownership of their learning. Embedded quick checks give students immediate feedback, without grading or demotivating them.

Vocabulary Tutorials feature a cyclical learning sequence that optimizes comprehension and retention:

- **Listen & repeat:** How does the word look and sound?

- **Match:** Which picture represents the word?

- **Say it:** Do you recognize the picture? Do you know how to say the word?

Audio hints and cognate/false cognate icons help students understand and remember new vocabulary.

Speech Recognition, embedded in the Vocabulary Tutorials, Pronunciation Tutorials, and *Fotonovela,* identifies student utterances in real time and objectively determines whether a student knows the word.

This innovative technology increases student awareness of pronunciation through low-stakes production practice.

Learn

Pronunciation Tutorials require students to engage with the material via interactive quick checks throughout each tutorial.

Real-time feedback via embedded Speech Recognition gives students an opportunity to reflect on their language patterns and increases their awareness of pronunciation for more effective speaking and listening skills.

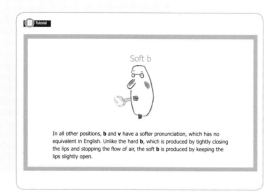

En detalle features a dynamic web-enhanced presentation of the reading with audio to engage 21st century learners.

Practice

Practice activities are carefully scaffolded—moving from discrete to open-ended—to support students as they acquire new language. This purposeful progression develops students' confidence and skills as they master new vocabulary and structures.

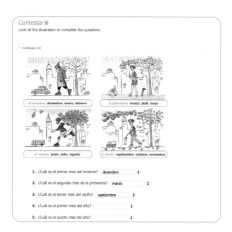

Communicate

Communicate activities provide opportunities for students to develop their oral skills and build confidence, reducing the affective filter. Scaffolded activities build on the three modes of communication: interpretive, interpersonal, and presentational.

Online Information Gap activities engage student partners in interpersonal communication as they negotiate meaning to solve a real-world task. They also provide opportunities for students to learn how to ask for clarification, request information, and use circumlocution or paraphrasing when faced with misunderstandings.

Self-check

Self-check activities support the self-directed nature of learning by enabling students to gauge their performance every step of the way. These low-stakes activities feature real-time feedback and personalized remediation that highlights areas where students may need more practice.

Autoevaluación is a Self-check activity that provides students with low-stakes diagnostic opportunities for vocabulary and each grammar point. Depending on their performance, students are provided with opportunities to review the vocabulary or each grammar point.

Assessment

A variety of formative and summative assessments allow for varied and ongoing evaluation of student learning and progress. Tailor these assessments to meet the needs of your students.

Prueba de práctica is a multi-question practice test that provides students with a low-stakes opportunity for assessing their knowledge of the vocabulary and grammar points covered in each lesson.

A **Personalized Study Plan** highlights areas where students need additional support and recommends remediation activities for completion prior to the lesson test.

Lesson Walkthrough: Senderos 1

Senderos is built around Vista Higher Learning's proven six-step instructional design. Each lesson is organized into color-coded strands that present new material in clear, comprehensible, and communicative ways. With a focus on personalization, authenticity, cultural immersion, and the seamless integration of text and technology, Spanish-language learning comes to life in ways that are meaningful to each and every student.

Contextos ensures students' understanding and application of new vocabulary by presenting new words and phrases in real-life contexts.

Fotonovela storyline videos bridge language and culture, providing a glimpse into everyday life in the Spanish-speaking world.

Pronunciación provides students with training opportunities to be accurate and effective communicators.

Cultura exposes students to different aspects of contemporary Hispanic cultures tied to the lesson theme.

Estructura provides a clear and concise presentation of relevant grammar and scaffolded activities for building confidence, fluency, and accuracy. Grammar is presented as a tool, not a topic.

Adelante synthesizes students' listening, speaking, reading, and writing skills within a culturally rich context.

Icons

Familiarize yourself with these icons that appear throughout **Senderos**.

 Listening activity/section

 Pair activity

 Group activity

 Interpretive activity

 Interpersonal activity

 Presentational activity

Walkthrough Legend

Point-of-Use Suggestions support the presentation of new material and in-class implementation of activities and group work.

Online Features describe digital material integral to the instruction of each strand.

General Suggestions describe the purpose of each instructional section and how it supports learning.

Teacher Resources

Teacher Resources provide you with a wealth of material that is ideal for communicative practice in class. Print copies of these activities or simply project them on a screen for students to see during class.

Presentation Enhance your presentations using the additional tools provided. These include digital images for vocabulary and geography, as well as Grammar Slides for step-by-step coverage of the grammar explanations.

Practice & Communicate To enhance class time with your students, choose additional activities from the Activity Pack based on their needs. For extra practice with vocabulary and grammar, or for a cumulative review of a lesson's grammar points, use the *Más práctica* worksheets. If you want to get your students talking, work with the Information Gap activities, surveys, role-plays, Integrated Performance Assessments, or the *¡Atrévete!* board game.

Assess Editable quizzes and tests in RTF (rich text format) allow you to customize assessments or administer pre-designed quizzes, tests, and exams. Corresponding audio scripts and answer keys also are provided.

Scripts and Translations Videoscripts are provided for the *Fotonovela, Flash cultura, Panorama cultural*, and *En pantalla* video programs. Depending on how you work with video and culture in your classroom, use scripts to give students additional support for comprehension of the target language or to create cloze activities for targeted listening practice. Skim the scripts for quicker course planning.

Lección 5: Teacher Resources

There is a wealth of resources online to support instruction using **Senderos**. For details on how to integrate these Teacher Resources into your lessons, see the front matter of this Teacher's Edition on pages T16 to T48.

Presentation	Practice & Communicate	Assess*	Scripts and Translations
• Digital Images: • **Las vacaciones** • **Las estaciones** • **El tiempo**	• Information Gap Activities* • Activity Pack Practice Activities (with Answer Key): **Contextos** • Additional Vocabulary (**Más vocabulario para las vacaciones**) • Digital Image Bank (Travel) • Surveys: Worksheet for classroom survey	• Vocabulary Quiz (with Answer Key)	
		• **Fotonovela** Optional Testing Sections (with Answer Key)	• **Fotonovela** Videoscript • **Fotonovela** English Translation
• **Estructura 5.1** Grammar Slides	• Information Gap Activities* • Activity Pack Practice Activities (with Answer Key): **Estar** with conditions and emotions	• Grammar 5.1 Quiz (with Answer Key)	• Tutorial Script: **Estar** with conditions and emotions
• **Estructura 5.2** Grammar Slides	• Information Gap Activities* • Activity Pack Practice Activities (with Answer Key): The present progressive	• Grammar 5.2 Quiz (with Answer Key)	• Tutorial Script: The present progressive
• **Estructura 5.3** Grammar Slides	• Activity Pack Practice Activities (with Answer Key): **Ser** and **estar**	• Grammar 5.3 Quiz (with Answer Key)	• Tutorial Script: **Ser** and **estar**
• **Estructura 5.4** Grammar Slides	• Activity Pack Practice Activities (with Answer Key): Direct object nouns and pronouns	• Grammar 5.4 Quiz (with Answer Key)	• Tutorial Script: Direct object nouns and pronouns
			• **En pantalla** Videoscript • **En pantalla** English Translation
		• **Flash cultura** Optional Testing Sections (with Answer Key)	• **Flash cultura** Videoscript • **Flash cultura** English Translation
Digital Images: • **Puerto Rico**		• **Panorama** Optional Testing Sections (with Answer Key) • **Panorama cultural** (video)	• **Panorama cultural** Videoscript • **Panorama cultural** English Translation

*Can also be assigned online.

Tabs along right edge: contextos | fotonovela | estructura | En pantalla | Flash cultura | adelante | Panorama

Las vacaciones

5

Communicative Goals

You will learn how to:
- Discuss and plan a vacation
- Describe a hotel
- Talk about how you feel
- Talk about the seasons and the weather

contextos

pages 152–157
- Travel and vacation
- Months of the year
- Seasons and weather
- Ordinal numbers

fotonovela

pages 158–161

Felipe plays a practical joke on Miguel, and the friends take a trip to the coast. They check in to their hotel and go to the beach, where Miguel gets his revenge.

cultura

pages 162–163
- **Las cataratas del Iguazú**
- **Punta del Este**

estructura

pages 164–179
- **Estar** with conditions and emotions
- The present progressive
- **Ser** and **estar**
- Direct object nouns and pronouns
- **Recapitulación**

adelante

pages 180–187

Lectura: A hotel brochure from Puerto Rico
Escritura: A travel brochure for a hotel
Escuchar: A weather report
En pantalla
Flash cultura
Panorama: Puerto Rico

A PRIMERA VISTA

¿Están ellos en una montaña o en un museo?
¿Son viejos o jóvenes?
¿Pasean o ven una película? ¿Andan en patineta o van de excursión?
¿Es posible esquiar en este lugar?

Lesson Goals

In **Lección 5**, students will be introduced to the following:
- terms for traveling and vacations
- seasons and months
- weather expressions
- ordinal numbers (1st–10th)
- **Las cataratas del Iguazú**
- **Punta del Este**, Uruguay
- **estar** with conditions and emotions
- adjectives for conditions and emotions
- present progressive of regular and irregular verbs
- comparison of the uses of **ser** and **estar**
- direct object nouns and pronouns
- personal **a**
- scanning to find specific information
- making an outline
- writing a brochure for a hotel
- listening for key words
- an ad for **LANPASS**, a Chilean airline loyalty program
- a video about **Machu Picchu**
- cultural, geographic, and historical information about Puerto Rico

A primera vista Here are some additional questions you can ask to personalize the photo: **¿Dónde te gusta pasar tus ratos libres? ¿Qué haces en tus ratos libres? ¿Te gusta explorar otras culturas? ¿Te gusta viajar a otros países? ¿Adónde quieres ir en las próximas vacaciones?**

Teaching Tip Look for these icons for additional communicative practice:

⟶🎙	Interpretive communication
⟶🎙⟶	Presentational communication
🎙↔🎙	Interpersonal communication

Lesson Openers outline the content of each lesson.

Lesson Goals provide an at-a-glance view of the vocabulary, grammar, and cultural topics covered in each lesson. Lesson strands are color-coded for easy use and navigation.

Communicative Goals introduce the lesson's learning objectives.

A primera vista questions jump-start the lesson, allowing students to use the Spanish they already know to talk about the photo.

SUPPORT FOR BACKWARD DESIGN

Lección 5 Essential Questions
- How do people discuss and plan a vacation?
- How do people talk about how they feel?
- What are some popular vacation destinations in the Spanish-speaking world and why?

Lección 5 Integrated Performance Assessment
Before teaching this chapter, review the Integrated Performance Assessment (IPA) and its accompanying scoring rubric. Use the IPA to assess students' progress toward proficiency targets at the end of the chapter. **IPA Context**: Six students from your Spanish class will be chosen to spend a week in Puerto Rico, at the **Hotel Vistahermosa** in Lajas. Students will be chosen in pairs based on their presentation to the selection committee.

Voice boards online allow you and your students to record and share up to five minutes of audio. Use voice boards for presentations, oral assessments, discussions, directions, etc.

Integrated Performance Assessments (IPAs) begin with a real-life task that engages students' interest. To complete the task, students progress through the three modes of communication: they read, view, and listen for information (interpretive mode); they talk and write with classmates about what they have experienced (interpersonal mode); and they share formally what they have learned (presentational mode).

A critical step in administering the IPA is to define and share rubrics with students before beginning the task. They need to be aware of what successful performance should look like.

Contextos

Contextos presents theme-related vocabulary through expansive, full-color illustrations and easy-to-use references.

Teacher Resources
Project digital images of the vocabulary illustrations to enhance in-class presentations.

For additional practice and variety, use the *Más práctica* worksheets from the Activity Pack.

Use the Illustration Bank to build your own image-rich activities.

Administer the Vocabulary Quiz to check comprehension.

Más vocabulario
calls out active, theme-related vocabulary in easy-to-reference Spanish-English lists. For expansion, use the Additional Vocabulary handout online.

Variación léxica
highlights linguistic diversity in the Spanish-speaking world by presenting alternate words and expressions.

Las vacaciones

Más vocabulario

la cama	bed
la habitación individual, doble	single, double room
el piso	floor (of a building)
la planta baja	ground floor
el campo	countryside
el paisaje	landscape
el equipaje	luggage
la estación de autobuses, del metro, de tren	bus, subway, train station
la llegada	arrival
el pasaje (de ida y vuelta)	(round-trip) ticket
la salida	departure; exit
la tabla de (wind)surf	surfboard/sailboard
acampar	to camp
estar de vacaciones	to be on vacation
hacer las maletas	to pack (one's suitcases)
hacer un viaje	to take a trip
hacer (wind)surf	to (wind)surf
ir de compras	to go shopping
ir de vacaciones	to go on vacation
ir en autobús (m.), auto(móvil) (m.), motocicleta (f.), taxi (m.)	to go by bus, car, motorcycle, taxi

Variación léxica

automóvil ←→ coche (*Esp.*), carro (*Amér. L.*)
autobús ←→ camión (*Méx.*), guagua (*Caribe*)
motocicleta ←→ moto (*coloquial*)

la agente de viajes

el pasaporte

Confirma una reservación. (confirmar)

En la agencia de viajes

la habitación

el ascensor

el empleado

la llave

la huésped

el huésped

En el hotel

aca/Toma fotos.
(sacar, tomar)

BIENVENIDOS

el avión

viajero

la inspectora
de aduanas

En el aeropuerto

Pesca.
(pescar)

Monta a caballo.
(montar)

Va en barco.
(ir)

mar

Juegan a las
cartas. (jugar)

la playa

En la playa

Práctica

1 **Escuchar** Indicate who would probably make each statement you hear.
Each answer is used twice.

a. el agente de viajes   1. __a__   4. __b__
b. el inspector de aduanas   2. __a__   5. __c__
c. un empleado del hotel   3. __c__   6. __b__

2 **¿Cierto o falso?** Mario and his wife, Natalia, are planning their next
vacation with a travel agent. Indicate whether each statement is **cierto**
or **falso** according to what you hear in the conversation.

	Cierto	Falso
1. Mario y Natalia están en Puerto Rico.	○	●
2. Ellos quieren hacer un viaje a Puerto Rico.	●	○
3. Natalia prefiere ir a la montaña.	○	●
4. Mario quiere pescar en Puerto Rico.	●	○
5. La agente de viajes va a confirmar la reservación.	●	○

3 **Escoger** Choose the best answer for each sentence.

1. Un huésped es una persona que __b__.
   a. toma fotos   b. está en un hotel   c. pesca en el mar
2. Abrimos la puerta con __a__.
   a. una llave   b. un caballo   c. una llegada
3. Enrique tiene __a__ porque va a viajar a otro (*another*) país.
   a. un pasaporte   b. una foto   c. una llegada
4. Antes de (*Before*) ir de vacaciones, hay que __c__.
   a. pescar   b. ir en tren   c. hacer las maletas
5. Nosotros vamos en __a__ al aeropuerto.
   a. autobús   b. pasaje   c. viajero
6. Me gusta mucho ir al campo. El __a__ es increíble.
   a. paisaje   b. pasaje   c. equipaje

4 **Analogías** Complete the analogies using the words below. Two words
will not be used.

auto	huésped	mar	sacar
empleado	llegada	pasaporte	tren

1. acampar ⟶ campo ⊜ pescar ⟶ _mar_
2. agencia de viajes ⟶ agente ⊜ hotel ⟶ _empleado_
3. llave ⟶ habitación ⊜ pasaje ⟶ _tren_
4. estudiante ⟶ libro ⊜ turista ⟶ _pasaporte_
5. aeropuerto ⟶ viajero ⊜ hotel ⟶ _huésped_
6. maleta ⟶ hacer ⊜ foto ⟶ _sacar_

1 **Expansion**
In pairs, have students
select one of the statements
they hear and then write a
conversation based on it.

1 **Script** 1. ¡Deben ir a Puerto
Rico! Allí hay unas playas muy
hermosas y pueden acampar.
2. Deben llamarme el lunes para
confirmar la reservación.
Script continues on page 154.

2 **Expansion** To challenge
students, give them these true/
false statements as items 6–9:
**6. Mario prefiere una habitación
doble. (Cierto.) 7. Natalia no
quiere ir a la playa. (Falso.)
8. El hotel está en la playa.
(Cierto.) 9. Mario va a montar
a caballo. (Falso.)**

2 **Script** MARIO: Queremos
ir de vacaciones a Puerto Rico.
AGENTE: ¿Desean hacer un viaje
al campo? NATALIA: Yo quiero
ir a la playa. M: Pues, yo prefiero
una habitación doble en un hotel
con un buen paisaje. A: Puedo
reservar para ustedes una habitación en el hotel San Juan que
está en la playa. M: Es una
buena idea, así yo voy a pescar
y tú vas a montar a caballo.
N: Muy bien, ¿puede confirmar
la reservación? A: Claro que sí.

3 **Expansion** Ask a volunteer
to help you model making
statements similar to item 1.
Say: **Un turista es una persona
que… (va de vacaciones).** Then
ask volunteers to do the same
with **una agente de viajes, una
inspectora de aduanas, un
empleado de hotel.**

4 **In-Class Tip** Present
these items using the following
formula: **Acampar** tiene la
misma relación con **campo** que
pescar tiene con… (**mar**).

Práctica begins with listening exercises and
continues with activities to practice new vocabulary
in meaningful contexts. The practice sections always
move from closed-ended and directed practice to
more open-ended activities that require students to
produce language.

Scripts are available to help you with planning.
As an alternative, read the script aloud for your
students instead of using the MP3 audio.

TEACHING OPTIONS

Small Groups Have students work in groups of three to
write a riddle about one of the people or objects in the **Contextos**
illustrations. The group must come up with at least three
descriptions of their subject. Then one of the group members
reads the description to the class and asks **¿Qué soy?** Ex: **Soy un
pequeño libro. Tengo una foto de una persona. Soy necesario si
un viajero quiere viajar a otro país. ¿Qué soy? (Soy un pasaporte.)**

Large Groups Split the class into two evenly-numbered groups.
Hand out cards at random to the members of each group. One
type of card should contain a verb or verb phrase (Ex: **confirmar
una reservación**). The other will contain a related noun (Ex: **el
agente de viajes**). The people within the groups must find their
partners.

General Suggestions for Teaching Contextos

Begin each lesson by asking students to provide from their own experience
words, concepts, categories, and opinions related to the theme. Spend quality
time generating words, images, ideas, phrases, and sentences; then group
and classify concepts.

You are giving students the "hook" for learning, focusing them on their most
interesting topic—themselves—and encouraging them to invest personally in
their learning.

Contextos

9 In-Class Tip Review weather expressions by asking students about current weather conditions around the world. Ex: ¿Hace calor en Alaska hoy? ¿Nieva en Puerto Rico?

9 Expansion Use the alternate choices in the exercise to ask students weather-related questions. Ex: No nieva en Yucatán. ¿Dónde nieva?

10 In-Class Tip Point out the words soleado, lluvia, and nieve in the key. Have students guess the meaning of these words based on the context. Finally, explain that soleado is an adjective and lluvia and nieve are nouns related to llover and nevar.

10 Expansion
- Ask students questions that compare and contrast the weather conditions presented in the activity or on the weather page of a Spanish-language newspaper. Ex: Cuando la temperatura está a 85 grados en Buenos Aires, ¿a cuánto está en Tokio?
- To challenge students, ask them to predict tomorrow's weather for these cities, based on the same cues. Have them use ir a + [infinitive]. Ex: En Montreal, mañana va a nevar y va a hacer mucho frío.

10 Partner Chat Available online.

11 In-Class Tip Model the activity by completing the first two sentences about yourself.

11 Expansion Tell students to imagine that they are six years old again. Then have them write a short paragraph repeating the activity.

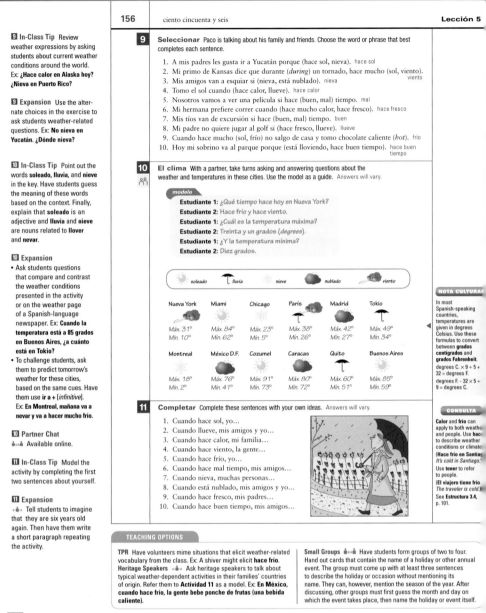

9 Seleccionar Paco is talking about his family and friends. Choose the word or phrase that best completes each sentence.

1. A mis padres les gusta ir a Yucatán porque (hace sol, nieva). hace sol
2. Mi primo de Kansas dice que durante (*during*) un tornado, hace mucho (sol, viento). viento
3. Mis amigos van a esquiar si (nieva, está nublado). nieva
4. Tomo el sol cuando (hace calor, llueve). hace calor
5. Nosotros vamos a ver una película si hace (buen, mal) tiempo. mal
6. Mi hermana prefiere correr cuando (hace mucho calor, hace fresco). hace fresco
7. Mis tíos van de excursión si hace (buen, mal) tiempo. buen
8. Mi padre no quiere jugar al golf si (hace fresco, llueve). llueve
9. Cuando hace mucho (sol, frío) no salgo de casa y tomo chocolate caliente (*hot*). frío
10. Hoy mi sobrino va al parque porque (está lloviendo, hace buen tiempo). hace buen tiempo

10 El clima With a partner, take turns asking and answering questions about the weather and temperatures in these cities. Use the model as a guide. Answers will vary.

modelo
Estudiante 1: ¿Qué tiempo hace hoy en Nueva York?
Estudiante 2: Hace frío y hace viento.
Estudiante 1: ¿Cuál es la temperatura máxima?
Estudiante 2: Treinta y un grados (*degrees*).
Estudiante 1: ¿Y la temperatura mínima?
Estudiante 2: Diez grados.

soleado   lluvia   nieve   nublado   viento

Nueva York	Miami	Chicago	París	Madrid	Tokio
Máx. 31°	Máx. 84°	Máx. 23°	Máx. 38°	Máx. 42°	Máx. 49°
Mín. 10°	Mín. 62°	Mín. 5°	Mín. 26°	Mín. 27°	Mín. 34°

Montreal	México D.F.	Cozumel	Caracas	Quito	Buenos Aires
Máx. 18°	Máx. 76°	Máx. 91°	Máx. 80°	Máx. 60°	Máx. 85°
Mín. 2°	Mín. 41°	Mín. 73°	Mín. 72°	Mín. 51°	Mín. 59°

11 Completar Complete these sentences with your own ideas. Answers will vary.

1. Cuando hace sol, yo…
2. Cuando llueve, mis amigos y yo…
3. Cuando hace calor, mi familia…
4. Cuando hace viento, la gente…
5. Cuando hace frío, yo…
6. Cuando hace mal tiempo, mis amigos…
7. Cuando nieva, muchas personas…
8. Cuando está nublado, mis amigos y yo…
9. Cuando hace fresco, mis padres…
10. Cuando hace buen tiempo, mis amigos…

NOTA CULTURAL

In most Spanish-speaking countries, temperatures are given in degrees Celsius. Use these formulas to convert between grados centígrados and grados Fahrenheit.

degrees C. × 9 ÷ 5 + 32 = degrees F.
degrees F. - 32 × 5 ÷ 9 = degrees C.

CONSULTA

Calor and frío can apply to both weather and people. Use hacer to describe weather conditions or climate. (Hace frío en Santiago. *It's cold in Santiago.*) Use tener to refer to people. (El viajero tiene frío. *The traveler is cold.*) See Estructura 3.4, p. 101.

TEACHING OPTIONS

TPR Have volunteers mime situations that elicit weather-related vocabulary from the class. Ex: A shiver might elicit hace frío.
Heritage Speakers Ask heritage speakers to talk about typical weather-dependent activities in their families' countries of origin. Refer them to Actividad 11 as a model. Ex: En México, cuando hace frío, la gente bebe ponche de frutas (una bebida caliente).

Small Groups Have students form groups of two to four. Hand out cards that contain the name of a holiday or other annual event. The group must come up with at least three sentences to describe the holiday or occasion without mentioning its name. They can, however, mention the season of the year. After discussing, other groups must first guess the month and day on which the event takes place, then name the holiday or event itself.

General Suggestions for Teaching Contextos

Encourage the exclusive use of the target language in your classroom, employing visual aids, mnemonics, circumlocution, or gestures to complement what you say. Encourage students to perceive meaning directly through careful listening and observation, and by using cognates and familiar structures and patterns to deduce meaning.

Remind students that errors are a natural part of language learning. Emphasize that their spoken and written Spanish will improve if they make the effort to practice.

Comunicación

12 **En la agencia de viajes** Listen to the conversation between Mr. Vega and a travel agent. Then indicate whether the following conclusions are **lógico** or **ilógico**, based on what you heard.

	Lógico	Ilógico
1. El señor Vega quiere visitar la Antártida.	○	☑
2. Hace calor en Puerto Rico.	☑	○
3. El señor Vega va a ver el mar en Puerto Rico.	☑	○
4. El señor Vega va a comprar un pasaje de ida y vuelta.	☑	○
5. El señor Vega viaja con su familia.	○	☑

13 **Preguntas personales** Answer your partner's questions. Answers will vary.

1. ¿Cuál es la fecha de hoy? ¿Qué estación es?
2. ¿Te gusta esta estación? ¿Por qué?
3. ¿Qué estación prefieres? ¿Por qué?
4. ¿Prefieres el mar o las montañas? ¿La playa o el campo? ¿Por qué?
5. Cuando haces un viaje, ¿qué te gusta hacer y ver?
6. ¿Piensas ir de vacaciones este verano? ¿Adónde quieres ir? ¿Por qué?
7. ¿Qué deseas ver y qué lugares quieres visitar?
8. ¿Cómo te gusta viajar? ¿En avión? ¿En motocicleta...?

14 **Itinerario** Create a trip itinerary for a friend, a relative, or someone famous. First, choose a destination. Include information about transportation and accommodations, as well as a section for each day with activities. Answers will vary.

* fechas
* lugar
* transporte
* hotel
* actividades

Síntesis

15 **Un viaje** With a partner, role-play a conversation between a travel agent and a client planning a trip. Discuss destinations, dates, transportation, hotel accommodations, and activities for the trip.
Answers will vary.

 Communication 1.1, 1.2, 1.3

12 **In-Class Tip** Ask students if they have ever been to a travel agency. Let them share their experiences before doing the activity.

12 **Script** *See the script for this activity on Interleaf page 151B.*

13 **Expansion** Have pairs imagine that one of them is a journalist and the other is a celebrity. Then have them conduct the interview using questions 3–8.

13 **Virtual Chat** Available online.

14 **In-Class Tip** Have students create a tourist brochure of the destination they selected for their trip.

15 **In-Class Tip** Encourage students to use the information they prepared in activity **14 Itinerario** as the basis of this conversation.

15 **Expansion** Divide the class in pairs and distribute the handouts for activity **Un viaje** from the online Resources (Lección 5/Activity Pack/Information Gap Activities). Ask students to read the instructions and give them ten minutes to complete the activity.

 Communication 1.1

15 **In-Class Tip** Set up the classroom chairs in two parallel rows so pairs of students face each other. The students in one row will be assigned the role of travel agents and the others will be the customers. Let them interact for two minutes and then ask one row to shift one seat to the right, and ask the new pairs to continue the role-play.

15 **Partner Chat** Available online.

157

Comunicación provides scaffolded activities built around the three modes of communication:

→🎙️← **Interpretive communication** activities target students' reading and listening comprehension skills.

🎙️↔🎙️ **Interpersonal communication** activities target the development of students' skills in real-time negotiation of meaning with one or more partners in both spoken and written communication settings.

←🎙️→ **Presentational communication** activities target students' skills in producing a variety of written and spoken language.

Teaching Options offer in-class activity ideas to reinforce new and previously taught vocabulary. Games, such as 20 questions or charades, enliven students' newly-acquired vocabulary.

Video Virtual Chat activities provide students with opportunities to develop their listening and speaking skills. They also help build students' confidence as they practice with video recordings of native speakers.

Students also benefit from nonverbal and articulatory cues that are essential for production and pronunciation.

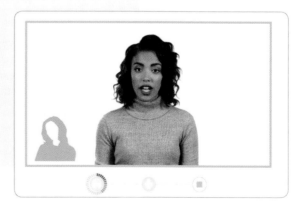

Fotonovela

Fotonovela is an episodic video series that follows the adventures of a group of students living and traveling in Mexico.

Video Recap helps students recall the events of the previous lesson's episode.

Teacher Resources

Videoscripts can be used to support comprehension or to work with listening.

Incorporate the Optional Testing Sections into a lesson test, or use them as additional practice.

Fotonovela storyline episodes combine new vocabulary and grammar with previously taught language, exposing students to a variety of authentic accents along the way.

Section Goals

In **Fotonovela**, students will:
- receive comprehensible input from free-flowing discourse
- learn functional phrases that preview lesson grammatical structures

Communication 1.2
Cultures 2.1, 2.2

Teacher Resources
Read the front matter for suggestions on how to incorporate all the program's components. See pages 151A–151B for a detailed listing of Teacher Resources online.

Video Recap: Lección 4
Review the previous episode with these questions:
1. ¿Qué prefiere hacer tía Ana María en sus ratos libres? (Ella nada, juega al tenis y al golf y va al cine y a los museos.)
2. ¿Adónde van Miguel, Maru, Marissa y Jimena? (Van a un cenote.) 3. ¿Qué van a hacer Felipe y Juan Carlos? (Van a jugar al fútbol con Eduardo y Pablo.) 4. ¿Qué quieren comer los chicos después de jugar al fútbol? (Quieren comer mole.)

Video Synopsis The friends watch the weather report on TV and discuss weather and seasons in their hometowns. **Felipe** rouses **Miguel** so they don't miss the bus to the beach. The group checks in to their hotel. At the beach, **Maru** and **Miguel** windsurf. Miguel gets back at **Felipe**.

In-Class Tips
- Have the class glance over the **Fotonovela** captions and list words and phrases related to tourism.
- Ask individuals how they are today, using **cansado/a** and **aburrido/a**.
- Ask the class: ¿**Cómo es el hotel ideal?** ¿**Cómo es la habitación de hotel perfecta?**

¡Vamos a la playa!

Los seis amigos hacen un viaje a la playa.

PERSONAJES   FELIPE   JUAN CAR

1

TÍA ANA MARÍA ¿Están listos para su viaje a la playa?
TODOS Sí.
TÍA ANA MARÍA Excelente... ¡A la estación de autobuses!
MARU ¿Dónde está Miguel?
FELIPE Yo lo traigo.

2

(se escucha un grito de Miguel)
FELIPE Ya está listo. Y tal vez enojado. Ahorita vamos.

FELIPE No está nada mal el hotel, ¿verdad? Limpio, cómodo... ¡Oye, Miguel! ¿Todavía estás enojado conmigo? *(a Juan Carlos)* Miguel está de mal humor. No me habla.
JUAN CARLOS ¿Todavía?

5

3

EMPLEADO Bienvenidas. ¿En qué puedo servirles?
MARU Hola. Tenemos una reservación para seis personas para esta noche.
EMPLEADO ¿A nombre de quién?
JIMENA ¿Díaz? ¿López? No estoy segura.

6

4

EMPLEADO No encuentro su nombre. Ah, no, ahora sí lo veo, aquí está. Díaz. Dos habitaciones en el primer piso para seis huéspedes.

EMPLEADO Aquí están las llaves de sus habitaciones.
MARU Gracias. Una cosa más. Mi novio y yo queremos hacer windsurf, pero no tenemos tablas.
EMPLEADO El botones las puede conseguir para ustedes.

TEACHING OPTIONS

Video Tips General suggestions for using video clips in the classroom can be found in the front matter of this Teacher's Edition.
¡Vamos a la playa! Before viewing the **¡Vamos a la playa!** episode of the **Fotonovela**, ask students to brainstorm a list of things that might happen in an episode in which the characters

check in to a hotel and go to the beach. Then play the **¡Vamos a la playa!** episode once without sound and have the class create a plot summary based on visual clues. Finally, show the video segment with sound and have the class correct any mistaken guesses and fill in any gaps. Ask comprehension questions as a follow-up.

ARISSA   JIMENA   MARU   MIGUEL   MAITE FUENTES   ANA MARÍA   EMPLEADO

7

JUAN CARLOS ¿Qué hace este libro aquí? ¿Estás estudiando en la playa?

JIMENA Sí, es que tengo un examen la próxima semana.

8

JUAN CARLOS Ay, Jimena. ¡No! ¿Vamos a nadar?

JIMENA Bueno, como estudiar es tan aburrido y el tiempo está tan bonito...

MARISSA Yo estoy un poco cansada. ¿Y tú? ¿Por qué no estás nadando?

FELIPE Es por causa de Miguel.

9

10

MARISSA Hmm, estoy confundida.

FELIPE Esta mañana. ¡Sigue enojado conmigo!

MARISSA No puede seguir enojado tanto tiempo.

Expresiones útiles

Talking with hotel personnel

¿En qué puedo servirles?
How can I help you?
Tenemos una reservación.
We have a reservation.
¿A nombre de quién?
In whose name?
¿Quizás López? ¿Tal vez Díaz?
Maybe López? Maybe Díaz?
Ahora lo veo, aquí está. Díaz.
Now I see it. Here it is. Díaz.
Dos habitaciones en el primer piso para seis huéspedes.
Two rooms on the first floor for six guests.
Aquí están las llaves.
Here are the keys.

Describing a hotel

No está nada mal el hotel.
The hotel isn't bad at all.
Todo está tan limpio y cómodo.
Everything is so clean and comfortable.
Es excelente/estupendo/fabuloso/ fenomenal/increíble/magnífico/ maravilloso/perfecto.
It's excellent/stupendous/fabulous/ phenomenal/incredible/magnificent/ marvelous/perfect.

Talking about how you feel

Yo estoy un poco cansado/a.
I am a little tired.
Estoy confundido/a. *I'm confused.*
Todavía estoy/Sigo enojado/a contigo.
I'm still angry with you.

Additional vocabulary

afuera *outside*
amable *nice; friendly*
el balde *bucket*
el/la botones *bellhop*
la crema de afeitar
shaving cream
el frente (frío) *(cold) front*
el grito *scream*
la temporada *period of time*
entonces *so, then*
es igual *it's the same*

Expresiones útiles Remind students that **está**, **están**, and **estoy** are present-tense forms of the verb **estar**, which is often used with adjectives that describe conditions and emotions. Remind students that **Es** is a present-tense form of the verb **ser**, which is often used to describe characteristics of people and things and to make generalizations. Draw students' attention to video stills 7 and 9. Point out that **Estás estudiando** and **estás nadando** are examples of the present progressive, which is used to emphasize an action in progress. Finally, point out the captions for video stills 1, 4, and 6 and explain that **lo** and **las** are examples of direct object pronouns. Explain that these are words that replace direct object nouns in order to avoid repetition. Tell students that they will learn more about these concepts in **Estructura**.

In-Class Tip

👤↔👤 Have students work in groups of six to read the **Fotonovela** captions aloud (have one student read the role of both **tía Ana María** and the **empleado**). Then have one group come to the front of the class and role-play the scenes. Encourage them to use props and gestures.

Nota cultural The **Yucatán** peninsula is warm year-round, but there are rainy and dry seasons. Generally, the dry season lasts from November to April and the wet season runs from May through October. Hurricanes occur in the late summer and fall. The **Yucatán's** average temperature is 25°C to 27°C (77°F to 81°F), rarely dropping below 16°C (61°F) or rising above 49°C (120°F).

Personajes show the main characters who appear in the episode.

Expresiones útiles highlight active vocabulary from the episode. Lists are organized by language function, demonstrating their real, practical use.

Pre-AP® offers ideas on how students can build the skills needed for long-term success in Spanish-language learning.

Fotonovela

¿Qué pasó? practice activities are carefully scaffolded to support students as they acquire new language, thus building their confidence, skills, and fluency.

In-Class Tips help you engage students with the *Fotonovela* episode and its corresponding textbook section to enhance their comprehension.

Notas culturales provide a wide range of cultural information relevant to the topic of an activity or section. Background information helps you expand students' knowledge about cultural products and practices.

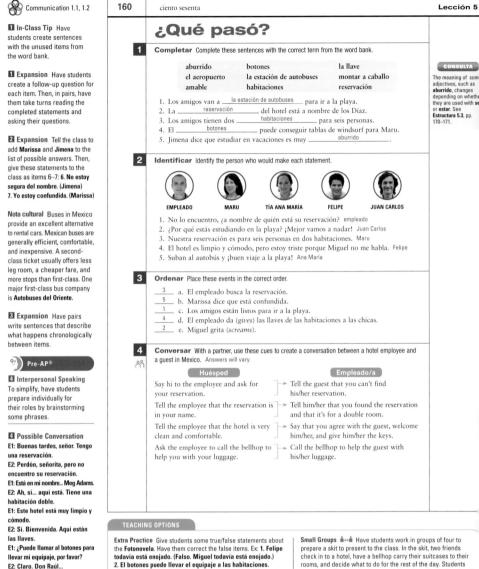

1 In-Class Tip Have students create sentences with the unused items from the word bank.

1 Expansion Have students create a follow-up question for each item. Then, in pairs, have them take turns reading the completed statements and asking their questions.

2 Expansion Tell the class to add **Marissa** and **Jimena** to the list of possible answers. Then, give these statements to the class as items 6–7: **6. No estoy segura del nombre. (Jimena) 7. Yo estoy confundida. (Marissa)**

Nota cultural Buses in Mexico provide an excellent alternative to rental cars. Mexican buses are generally efficient, comfortable, and inexpensive. A second-class ticket usually offers less leg room, a cheaper fare, and more stops than first-class. One major first-class bus company is **Autobuses del Oriente.**

3 Expansion Have pairs write sentences that describe what happens chronologically between items.

Pre-AP®

4 Interpersonal Speaking To simplify, have students prepare individually for their roles by brainstorming some phrases.

4 Possible Conversation
E1: Buenas tardes, señor. Tengo una reservación.
E2: Perdón, señorita, pero no encuentro su reservación.
E1: Está en mi nombre... Meg Adams.
E2: Ah, sí... aquí está. Tiene una habitación doble.
E1: Este hotel está muy limpio y cómodo.
E2: Sí. Bienvenida. Aquí están las llaves.
E1: ¿Puede llamar al botones para llevar mi equipaje, por favor?
E2: Claro. Don Raúl...

4 Partner Chat
Available online.

160 Teacher's Edition • Lesson Five

¿Qué pasó?

1 **Completar** Complete these sentences with the correct term from the word bank.

aburrido	botones	la llave
el aeropuerto	la estación de autobuses	montar a caballo
amable	habitaciones	reservación

1. Los amigos van a ___la estación de autobuses___ para ir a la playa.
2. La ___reservación___ del hotel está a nombre de los Díaz.
3. Los amigos tienen dos ___habitaciones___ para seis personas.
4. El ___botones___ puede conseguir tablas de windsurf para Maru.
5. Jimena dice que estudiar en vacaciones es muy ___aburrido___.

2 **Identificar** Identify the person who would make each statement.

EMPLEADO   MARU   TÍA ANA MARÍA   FELIPE   JUAN CARLOS

1. No lo encuentro, ¿a nombre de quién está su reservación? empleado
2. ¿Por qué estás estudiando en la playa? ¡Mejor vamos a nadar! Juan Carlos
3. Nuestra reservación es para seis personas en dos habitaciones. Maru
4. El hotel es limpio y cómodo, pero estoy triste porque Miguel no me habla. Felipe
5. Suban al autobús y ¡buen viaje a la playa! Ana María

3 **Ordenar** Place these events in the correct order.
___3___ a. El empleado busca la reservación.
___5___ b. Marissa dice que está confundida.
___1___ c. Los amigos están listos para ir a la playa.
___4___ d. El empleado da (*gives*) las llaves de las habitaciones a las chicas.
___2___ e. Miguel grita (*screams*).

4 **Conversar** With a partner, use these cues to create a conversation between a hotel employee and a guest in Mexico. Answers will vary.

Huésped	Empleado/a
Say hi to the employee and ask for your reservation.	→ Tell the guest that you can't find his/her reservation.
Tell the employee that the reservation is in your name.	→ Tell him/her that you found the reservation and that it's for a double room.
Tell the employee that the hotel is very clean and comfortable.	→ Say that you agree with the guest, welcome him/her, and give him/her the keys.
Ask the employee to call the bellhop to help you with your luggage.	→ Call the bellhop to help the guest with his/her luggage.

CONSULTA
The meaning of some adjectives, such as **aburrido**, changes depending on whether they are used with **ser** or **estar**. See **Estructura 5.3**, pp. 170–171.

TEACHING OPTIONS

Extra Practice Give students some true/false statements about the **Fotonovela**. Have them correct the false items. Ex: **1. Felipe todavía está enojado.** (Falso. **Miguel todavía está enojado.**) **2. El botones puede llevar el equipaje a las habitaciones.** (Cierto.) **3. La reservación es para siete huéspedes.** (Falso. Es para seis huéspedes.) **4. Felipe no está nadando porque tiene que estudiar.** (Falso. Es por causa de Miguel.)

Small Groups Have students work in groups of four to prepare a skit to present to the class. In the skit, two friends check in to a hotel, have a bellhop carry their suitcases to their rooms, and decide what to do for the rest of the day. Students should specify what city they are visiting, describe the hotel and their rooms, and explain what activities they want to do while they are visiting the city.

Using Fotonovela for grammar instruction

- Play parts of the episode that demonstrate the grammar point you are teaching.

- Show selected scenes that review known grammar topics and ask students to identify them.

- After completing the *Estructura* section, have students watch the corresponding *Resumen* section of the *Fotonovela* in its entirety for additional review.

Pronunciación

Pronunciación
Spanish **b** and **v**

bueno	vóleibol	biblioteca	vivir

There is no difference in pronunciation between the Spanish letters **b** and **v**. However, each letter can be pronounced two different ways, depending on which letters appear next to them.

bonito	viajar	también	investigar

B and **v** are pronounced like the English hard *b* when they appear either as the first letter of a word, at the beginning of a phrase, or after **m** or **n**.

deber	novio	abril	favor

In all other positions, **b** and **v** have a softer pronunciation, which has no equivalent in English. Unlike the hard **b**, which is produced by tightly closing the lips and stopping the flow of air, the soft **b** is produced by keeping the lips slightly open.

bola	vela	Caribe	declive

In both pronunciations, there is no difference in sound between **b** and **v**. The English *v* sound, produced by friction between the upper teeth and lower lip, does not exist in Spanish. Instead, the soft **b** comes from friction between the two lips.

Verónica y su esposo cantan boleros.

When **b** or **v** begins a word, its pronunciation depends on the previous word. At the beginning of a phrase or after a word that ends in **m** or **n**, it is pronounced as a hard **b**.

Benito es de Boquerón pero vive en Victoria.

Words that begin with **b** or **v** are pronounced with a soft **b** if they appear immediately after a word that ends in a vowel or any consonant other than **m** or **n**.

Práctica Read these words aloud to practice the **b** and the **v**.

1. hablamos	4. van	7. doble	10. nublado
2. trabajar	5. contabilidad	8. novia	11. llave
3. botones	6. bien	9. béisbol	12. invierno

Oraciones Read these sentences aloud to practice the **b** and the **v**.

1. Vamos a Guaynabo en autobús.
2. Voy de vacaciones a la Isla Culebra.
3. Tengo una habitación individual en el octavo piso.
4. Víctor y Eva van en avión al Caribe.
5. La planta baja es bonita también.
6. ¿Qué vamos a ver en Bayamón?
7. Beatriz, la novia de Víctor, es de Arecibo, Puerto Rico.

Refranes Read these sayings aloud to practice the **b** and the **v**.

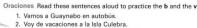

No hay mal que por bien no venga.[1]

Hombre prevenido vale por dos.[2]

1 Every cloud has a silver lining.
2 An ounce of prevention equals a pound of cure.

Section Goal

In **Pronunciación**, students will be introduced to the pronunciation of **b** and **v**.

 Comparisons 4.1

In-Class Tips
- Emphasize that **b (alta/grande)** and **v (baja/chica)** are pronounced identically in Spanish, but depending on the letter's position in a word, each can be pronounced two ways. Pronounce **vóleibol** and **vivir** and have students listen for the difference between the initial and medial sounds represented by **b** and **v**.
- Explain the cases in which **b** and **v** are pronounced like English *b* in *boy* and model the pronunciation of **bonito, viajar, también,** and **investigar**.
- Point out that before **b** or **v**, **n** is usually pronounced **m**.
- Explain that in all other positions, **b** and **v** are fricatives. Pronounce **deber, novio, abril,** and **cerveza** and stress that the friction is between the two lips.
- Remind the class that Spanish has no sound like the English **v**. Pronounce **vida, vacaciones, avión,** and **automóvil**.
- Explain that the same rules apply in connected speech. Practice with phrases like **de vacaciones** and **de ida y vuelta**.

Pronunciación helps students demonstrate the accuracy necessary for effective communication.

Refranes feature illustrated sayings and proverbs, so students can practice the pronunciation point in an entertaining cultural context.

Teaching Options provide you with in-class activity ideas for extra practice and small group work.

TEACHING OPTIONS

Extra Practice Write some additional proverbs on the board and have the class practice saying each one. Ex: **Más vale que sobre y no que falte.** (*Better too much than too little.*) **No sólo de pan vive el hombre.** (*Man doesn't live by bread alone.*) **A caballo regalado no se le ve el colmillo.** (*Don't look a gift horse in the mouth.*) **Más vale dar que recibir.** (*It's better to give than to receive.*)

Small Groups Have students work in small groups and take turns reading aloud sentences from the **Fotonovela** on pages 158–159, focusing on the correct pronunciation of **b** and **v**. If a group member has trouble pronouncing a word that contains **b** or **v**, the rest of the group should supply the rule that explains how it should be pronounced.

Pronunciación **161**

General Suggestions for Teaching Pronunciación

Have the class work in pairs to practice the pronunciation of the *Fotonovela* captions. Encourage students to help their partners if they are having trouble pronouncing a particular word or phrase.

This collaborative communication activity provides students with an opportunity to try out new rules and modify their output accordingly. Circulate around the class and model correct pronunciation as needed.

Cultura

Cultura offers theme-driven coverage of cultural products, practices, and perspectives from throughout the Spanish-speaking world.

En detalle explores the lesson's cultural topic in-depth.

Actividades comprehension activities check understanding and solidify learning.

Teaching Options include cultural notes and suggestions for homework and projects that address the needs of various learning styles, age groups, and heritage speakers.

News and Cultural Updates provide real-world connections to language and culture via authentic articles and videos. From online newspaper articles to TV news segments, each source is chosen for its age-appropriate content, currency, and high interest to students. Each selection includes scaffolded pre-, during-, and post-reading and viewing activities for a wide range of learning abilities.

Section Goals

In **Cultura**, students will:
- read about **Las cataratas del Iguazú**
- learn travel-related terms
- read about **Punta del Este**, Uruguay
- read about popular vacation destinations in the Spanish-speaking world

Communication 1.1, 1.2
Cultures 2.1, 2.2
Connections 3.1, 3.2
Comparisons 4.2

En detalle

Antes de leer Ask students what kind of travel interests them. Ex: **¿Te gusta acampar o dormir en un hotel? ¿Adónde prefieres ir: a la ciudad, a las montañas…?** Then ask students to predict what a tourist would see and do near a waterfall.

Lectura
- Explain that the **Guaraní** are an indigenous group who traditionally inhabit areas of Paraguay, northern Argentina, southern Brazil, and parts of Uruguay and Bolivia. The **Guaraní** language is one of the two official languages of Paraguay.
- The **Iguazú** Falls have been featured in many movies, most notably in *The Mission* (1986).

Después de leer Ask students through which country they would prefer to visit **Iguazú** and why.

1 Expansion Give students these true/false statements as items 11–12: 11. The **Tren Ecológico de la Selva** takes tourists to San Martín Island. (**Falso.** It takes them to the walkways.) 12. **Piedra Volada** is the tallest waterfall in Mexico. (**Cierto.**)

EN DETALLE

Las cataratas del Iguazú

Imagine the impressive and majestic **Niagara Falls**, the most powerful waterfall in North America. Now, if you can, imagine a waterfall four times as wide and almost twice as tall that caused Eleanor Roosevelt to exclaim "Poor Niagara!" upon seeing it for the first time. Welcome to **las cataratas del Iguazú!**

Iguazú is located in Iguazú National Park, an area of subtropical jungle where Argentina meets Brazil. Its name comes from the indigenous Guaraní word for "great water." A UNESCO World Heritage Site, **las cataratas del Iguazú** span three kilometers and comprise 275 cascades split into two main sections by San Martín Island. Most of the falls are about 82 meters (270 feet) high. The horseshoe-shaped cataract **Garganta del Diablo** (Devil's Throat) has the greatest water flow and is considered to be the most impressive; it also marks the border between Argentina and Brazil.

Each country offers different views and tourist options. Most visitors opt to use the numerous catwalks that are available on both sides; however, from the Argentinean side, tourists can get very close to the falls, whereas Brazil provides more panoramic views. If you don't mind getting wet, a jet boat tour is a good choice; those looking for wildlife—such as toucans, ocelots, butterflies, and jaguars—should head for San Martín Island. Brazil boasts less conventional ways to view the falls, such as helicopter rides and rappelling, while Argentina focuses on sustainability with its **Tren Ecológico de la Selva** (*Ecological Jungle Train*), an environmentally friendly way to reach the walkways.

No matter which way you choose to enjoy the falls, you are certain to be captivated.

Más cascadas° en Latinoamérica

Nombre	País	Altura°	Datos
Salto Ángel	Venezuela	979 metros	la más alta° del mundo°
Catarata del Gocta	Perú	771 metros	descubierta° en 2006
Piedra Volada	México	453 metros	la más alta de México

cascadas *waterfalls* Altura *Height* más alta *tallest* mundo *world* descubierta *discovered*

ACTIVIDADES

1 ¿Cierto o falso? Indicate whether these statements are cierto or falso. Correct the false statements.

1. Iguazú Falls is located on the border of Argentina and Brazil. Cierto.
2. Niagara Falls is four times as wide as Iguazú Falls. Falso. Iguazú is four times as wide as Niagara Falls.
3. Iguazú Falls has a few cascades, each about 82 meters. Falso. Iguazú is composed of 275 cascades about 82 meters tall.
4. Tourists visiting Iguazú can see exotic wildlife. Cierto.
5. Iguazú is the Guaraní word for "blue water." Falso. Iguazú is the Guaraní word for "great water."
6. You can access the walkways by taking the Garganta del Diablo. Falso. One way of accessing the walkways is taking the Tren Ecológico de la Selva.
7. It is possible for tourists to visit Iguazú Falls by air. Cierto.
8. Salto Ángel is the tallest waterfall in the world. Cierto.
9. There are no waterfalls in Mexico. Falso. The Piedra Volada is in Mexico.
10. For the best views of Iguazú Falls, tourists should visit the Brazilian side. Cierto.

TEACHING OPTIONS

La leyenda Share this legend of the **Iguazú** Falls with students: Many ages ago, in the **Iguazú** River there lived a god-serpent, **Mboi**, to whom the **Guaraní** tribes sacrificed a young woman during their annual gathering. At one such gathering, a young man named **Tarobá** instantly fell in love with **Naipí**, who was to be sacrificed. After pleading in vain to have her spared, one night **Tarobá** took **Naipí** and tried to flee with her in his canoe. The furious **Mboi** awoke and split the river in two, forming the waterfall and trapping the pair. He transformed **Naipí** into a rock at the base of the falls and **Tarobá** into a tree perched at the edge of the abyss. Lest the lovers try to reunite, the watchful **Mboi** keeps an eternal vigil from deep under the waters of the **Garganta del Diablo**. Now ask them to think of other creation legends they know (Ex: Paul Bunyan and the Great Lakes).

Cultura **163**

ASÍ SE DICE

Viajes y turismo

el asiento del medio, del pasillo, de la ventanilla	center, aisle, window seat
el itinerario	itinerary
media pensión	breakfast and one meal included
el ómnibus (Perú)	el autobús
pensión completa	all meals included
el puente	long weekend (lit., bridge)

EL MUNDO HISPANO

Destinos populares

- **Las playas del Parque Nacional Manuel Antonio** (Costa Rica) ofrecen° la oportunidad de nadar y luego caminar por el bosque tropical°.

- **Teotihuacán** (México) Desde antes de la época° de los aztecas, aquí se celebra el equinoccio de primavera en la Pirámide del Sol.

- **Puerto Chicama** (Perú), con sus olas° de cuatro kilómetros de largo°, es un destino para surfistas expertos.

- **Tikal** (Guatemala) Aquí puedes ver las maravillas de la selva° y ruinas de la civilización maya.

- **Las playas de Rincón** (Puerto Rico) Son ideales para descansar y observar ballenas°.

ofrecen *offer* bosque tropical *rainforest*
Desde antes de la época *Since before the time* olas *waves*
de largo *in length* selva *jungle* ballenas *whales*

PERFIL

Punta del Este

One of South America's largest and most fashionable beach resort towns is Uruguay's **Punta del Este**, a narrow strip of land containing twenty miles of pristine beaches. Its peninsular shape gives it two very different seascapes. **La Playa Mansa**, facing the bay and therefore the more protected side, has calm waters. Here, people practice water sports like swimming, water skiing, windsurfing, and diving. **La Playa Brava**, facing the east, receives the Atlantic Ocean's powerful, wave-producing winds, making it popular for surfing, body boarding, and kite surfing. Besides the beaches, posh shopping, and world-famous nightlife, **Punta** offers its 600,000 yearly visitors yacht and fishing clubs, golf courses, and excursions to observe sea lions at the **Isla de Lobos** nature reserve.

Conexión Internet

¿Cuáles son los sitios más populares para el turismo en Puerto Rico? — Use the Web to find more cultural information related to this *Cultura* section.

ACTIVIDADES

2 Comprensión Complete the sentences.

1. En las playas de Rincón puedes ver __ballenas__.
2. Cerca de 600.000 turistas visitan __Punta del Este__ cada año.
3. En el avión pides un __asiento de la ventanilla__ si te gusta ver el paisaje.
4. En Punta del Este, la gente prefiere nadar en la Playa __Mansa__.
5. El __ómnibus__ es un medio de transporte en Perú.

3 De vacaciones Spring break is coming up, and you want to go on a short vacation with your family. Decide which of the locations featured on these pages best suits your likes and interests. Come to an agreement about how you will get there, where you prefer to stay and for how long, and what each of you will do during your free time. *Answers will vary.*

Así se dice
- To challenge students, add these airport-related words to the list: **el/la auxiliar de vuelo** (*flight attendant*), **aterrizar** (*to land*), **el bolso de mano** (*carry-on bag*), **despegar** (*to take off*), **facturar** (*to check*), **hacer escala** (*to stop over*), **el retraso** (*delay*), **la tarjeta de embarque** (*boarding pass*).
- To practice vocabulary from the list, survey the class about their travel habits. Ex: **¿Prefieres el asiento de la ventanilla, del medio o del pasillo? ¿Por qué?**

Perfil **Punta del Este** is located 80 miles east of Uruguay's capital, Montevideo, on a small peninsula that separates the Atlantic Ocean and the **Río de la Plata** estuary. At the beginning of the nineteenth century, **Punta** was nearly deserted and only visited by fishermen and sailors. Its glamorous hotels, dining, nightlife, and beaches have earned it the nickname "the St. Tropez of South America."

El mundo hispano
- Add a visual aspect to this list by using a map to point out the locations of the different **destinos populares**.
- Ask students which destination interests them the most and why.

2 Expansion Ask students to write two additional cloze statements about the information on this page. Then have them exchange papers with a partner and complete the sentences.

3 In-Class Tip To simplify, make a list on the board of the vacation destinations mentioned on this spread. As a class, brainstorm tourist activities in Spanish for each location.

3 Partner Chat
🏃↔🏃 Available online.

Así se dice presents familiar words and phrases related to the lesson's theme that are used in everyday spoken Spanish.

El mundo hispano continues the exploration of the lesson's cultural theme, but with a regional focus.

Conexión Internet invites students to find additional cultural information online. Search terms guide students to sites that help them respond to the topical questions.

Estructura

Estructura provides a formal presentation of relevant grammar and scaffolded activities for building confidence, fluency, and accuracy.

Ante todo helps students ease into grammar with definitions of grammatical terms, comparisons to English grammar and syntax, and reminders of previously learned Spanish grammar.

In-Class Tips provide extensive suggestions on how to clarify the grammar point for enhanced student comprehension and to engage students with the material in class.

Teaching Options offer in-class activity ideas to reinforce new and previously taught grammar, such as working with the *Fotonovela* in order to demonstrate a grammar topic in action.

Section Goals

In **Estructura 5.2**, students will learn:
- the present progressive of regular and irregular verbs
- the present progressive versus the simple present tense in Spanish

 Comparisons 4.1

Teacher Resources
Read the front matter for suggestions on how to incorporate all the program's components. See pages 151A–151B for a detailed listing of Teacher Resources online.

In-Class Tips
- Use regular verbs to ask questions about things students are not doing. Ex: **¿Estás comiendo pizza? (No, no estoy comiendo pizza.)**
- Explain the formation of the present progressive, writing examples on the board.
- Add a visual aspect to this grammar presentation. Use photos to elicit sentences with the present progressive. Ex: **¿Qué está haciendo el hombre alto? (Está sacando fotos.)** Include present participles ending in **–yendo** as well as those with stem changes.
- Point out that the present progressive is rarely used with the verbs **ir, poder,** and **venir** since they already imply an action in progress.

5.2   The present progressive

ANTE TODO   Both Spanish and English use the present progressive, which consists of the present tense of the verb *to be* and the present participle of another verb (the *-ing* form in English).

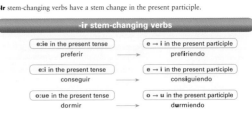

Las chicas están hablando con el empleado del hotel.

¿Estás estudiando en la playa?

▶ Form the present progressive with the present tense of **estar** and a present participle.

FORM OF ESTAR + PRESENT PARTICIPLE		FORM OF ESTAR + PRESENT PARTICIPLE	
Estoy	**pescando.**	**Estamos**	**comiendo.**
I am	*fishing.*	*We are*	*eating.*

▶ The present participle of regular **-ar**, **-er**, and **-ir** verbs is formed as follows:

INFINITIVE	STEM	ENDING	PRESENT PARTICIPLE
hablar	habl-	**-ando**	habl**ando**
comer	com-	**-iendo**	com**iendo**
escribir	escrib-	**-iendo**	escrib**iendo**

▶ **¡Atención!** When the stem of an **-er** or **-ir** verb ends in a vowel, the present participle ends in **-yendo**.

INFINITIVE	STEM	ENDING	PRESENT PARTICIPLE
leer	le-	**-yendo**	le**yendo**
oir	o-	**-yendo**	o**yendo**
traer	tra-	**-yendo**	tra**yendo**

▶ **Ir, poder,** and **venir** have irregular present participles (**yendo, pudiendo, viniendo**). Several other verbs have irregular present participles that you will need to learn.

▶ **-Ir** stem-changing verbs have a stem change in the present participle.

-ir stem-changing verbs

e:ie in the present tense	e → i in the present participle
preferir	→ prefiriendo

e:i in the present tense	e → i in the present participle
conseguir	→ consiguiendo

o:ue in the present tense	o → u in the present participle
dormir	→ durmiendo

TEACHING OPTIONS

TPR Divide the class into three groups. Appoint leaders and give them a list of verbs. Leaders call out a verb and a subject (Ex: **seguir/yo**), then toss a ball to someone in the group. That student says the appropriate present progressive form of the verb (Ex: **estoy siguiendo**) and tosses the ball back. Leaders should use all the verbs on the list and be sure to toss the ball to each member of the group.

TPR Play charades. In groups of four, have students take turns miming actions for the rest of the group to guess. Ex: Student pretends to read a newspaper. (**Estás leyendo el periódico.**) For incorrect guesses, the student should respond negatively. Ex: **No, no estoy estudiando.**

COMPARE & CONTRAST

The use of the present progressive is much more restricted in Spanish than in English. In Spanish, the present progressive is mainly used to emphasize that an action is in progress at the time of speaking.

Maru **está escuchando** música latina **ahora mismo.**
Maru is listening to Latin music right now.

Felipe y su amigo **todavía están jugando** al fútbol.
Felipe and his friend are still playing soccer.

In English, the present progressive is often used to talk about situations and actions that occur over an extended period of time or in the future. In Spanish, the simple present tense is often used instead.

Xavier **estudia** computación este semestre.
Xavier is studying computer science this semester.

Marissa **sale** mañana para los Estados Unidos.
Marissa is leaving tomorrow for the United States.

¿Está pensando en su futuro?
Nosotros, sí.

🏛 BANCO **CONGRESO** 🏛

Preparándolo para el mañana

¡INTÉNTALO!

Create complete sentences by putting the verbs in the present progressive.

1. mis amigos / descansar en la playa ___Mis amigos están descansando en la playa.___
2. nosotros / practicar deportes ___Estamos practicando deportes.___
3. Carmen / comer en casa ___Carmen está comiendo en casa.___
4. nuestro equipo / ganar el partido ___Nuestro equipo está ganando el partido.___
5. yo / leer el periódico ___Estoy leyendo el periódico.___
6. él / pensar comprar una bicicleta ___Está pensando comprar una bicicleta.___
7. ustedes / jugar a las cartas ___Ustedes están jugando a las cartas.___
8. José y Francisco / dormir ___José y Francisco están durmiendo.___
9. Marisa / leer correo electrónico ___Marisa está leyendo correo electrónico.___
10. yo / preparar sándwiches ___Estoy preparando sándwiches.___
11. Carlos / tomar fotos ___Carlos está tomando fotos.___
12. ¿dormir / tú? ___¿Estás durmiendo?___

TEACHING OPTIONS

Pairs Have students write eight sentences in Spanish modeled after the examples in the **Compare & Contrast** box. There should be two sentences modeled after each example. Ask students to replace the verbs with blanks. Then, have students exchange papers with a partner and complete the sentences.

Extra Practice ←👤→ For homework, ask students to find five photos from a magazine or create five simple drawings of people performing different activities. For each image, have them write one sentence telling where the people are, one explaining what they are doing, and one describing how they feel. Ex: **Juan está en la biblioteca. Está estudiando. Está cansado.**

In-Class Tips

- Discuss each point in the **Compare & Contrast** box.
- Write these statements on the board and ask students if they would use the present or the present progressive in Spanish for each item. 1. I'm going on vacation tomorrow. 2. She's packing her suitcase right now. 3. They are fishing in Puerto Rico this week. 4. Roberto is still working. Then ask students to translate the items. **(1. Voy de vacaciones mañana. 2. Está haciendo la maleta ahora mismo. 3. Pescan en Puerto Rico esta semana. 4. Roberto todavía está trabajando.)**
- In this lesson, students learn **todavía** to mean *still* in the present progressive tense. You may want to point out that **todavía** also means *yet*. They will be able to use that meaning in later lessons as they learn the past tenses.
- Have students rewrite the sentences in the **¡Inténtalo!** activity using the simple present. Ask volunteers to explain how the sentences change depending on whether the verb is in the present progressive or the simple present.

¡Inténtalo! is a brief activity that practices the grammar forms that have just been presented. It is a quick way to check student accuracy.

Teacher Resources

Grammar Slides can be used as an additional in-class presentation tool.

For extra directed practice, use the *Más práctica* activities from the Activity Pack. An answer key is provided in PDF format.

Scripts for the interactive Grammar Tutorials are available to help you plan.

The *¡Atrévete!* Board Game in the Activity Pack is a fun and interactive way for students to practice and apply the grammar and vocabulary they've learned.

Quizzes for each grammar point may be assigned online or printed for in-class use. Either way, you can edit the assessments to address your exact needs.

Grammar Tutorials feature guided instruction to keep students on track and ensure comprehension. *El profesor* provides a humorous, engaging, and relatable approach to grammar instruction.

Estructura

Práctica guided exercises weave current and previously learned vocabulary together with the current grammar point.

In-Class Tips give you detailed ideas of how to make each activity work in your classroom, including ideas for simplifying an activity, challenging your students, and creating variations to provide more practice.

---

1 Expansion Ask students comprehension questions that elicit the present progressive. Ex: ¿Quién está buscando información? (Marta y José Luis están buscando información.) ¿Qué información están buscando? (Están buscando información sobre San Juan.)

2 In-Class Tips
- Use the **Lección 5 Estructura** online Resources to assist with the presentation of this activity.
- Before starting the activity, ask students questions about each drawing to elicit a description of what they see. Ex: ¿Quién está en el dibujo número 5? (Samuel está en el dibujo.) ¿Dónde está Samuel? (Está en la playa.) ¿Qué más ven en el dibujo? (Vemos una silla y el mar.)

3 In-Class Tip To simplify, first read through the names in column A as a class. Point out the profession clues in the **Ayuda** box, then guide students in matching each name with an infinitive. Finally, have students form sentences.

3 Expansion
↔ Have students choose five more celebrities and write descriptions of what they are doing at this moment.

Práctica

1 Completar Alfredo's Spanish class is preparing to travel to Puerto Rico. Use the present progressive of the verb in parentheses to complete Alfredo's description of what everyone is doing.

1. Yo _estoy investigando_ (investigar) la situación política de la isla (*island*).
2. La esposa del profesor _está haciendo_ (hacer) las maletas.
3. Marta y José Luis _están buscando_ (buscar) información sobre San Juan en Internet.
4. Enrique y yo _estamos leyendo_ (leer) un correo electrónico de nuestro amigo puertorriqueño.
5. Javier _está aprendiendo_ (aprender) mucho sobre la cultura puertorriqueña.
6. Y tú _estás practicando_ (practicar) el español, ¿verdad?

2 ¿Qué están haciendo? María and her friends are vacationing at a resort in San Juan, Puerto Rico. Complete her description of what everyone is doing right now.

CONSULTA
For more information about Puerto Rico, see **Panorama,** pp. 186–187.

1. Yo
estoy escribiendo una carta.

2. Javier
está buceando en el mar.

3. Alejandro y Rebeca
están jugando a las cartas.

4. Celia y yo
estamos tomando el sol.

5. Samuel
está escuchando música.

6. Lorenzo
está durmiendo.

3 Personajes famosos Say what these celebrities are doing right now, using the cues provided. Answers will vary.

modelo
Shakira
Shakira está cantando una canción ahora mismo.

A		B	
Isabel Allende	Nelly Furtado	bailar	hacer
Rachael Ray	Dwight Howard	cantar	jugar
James Cameron	Las Rockettes de	correr	preparar
Venus y Serena	Nueva York	escribir	¿?
Williams	¿?	hablar	¿?
Joey Votto	¿?		

AYUDA
Isabel Allende: **novelas**
Rachael Ray: **televisión, negocios** (*business*)
James Cameron: **cine**
Venus y Serena Williams: **tenis**
Joey Votto: **béisbol**
Nelly Furtado: **canciones**
Dwight Howard: **baloncesto**
Las Rockettes de Nueva York: **baile**

TEACHING OPTIONS

Pairs ↔ Have students bring in photos from a vacation. Ask them to describe the photos to a partner. Students should explain what the weather is like, who is in the photo, and what they are doing. The partner should try to guess the location the student is describing. Students can ask additional questions until they guess correctly.

Game Have the class form a circle. Appoint one student to be the starter, who will mime an action (Ex: eating) and say what he or she is doing (Ex: **Estoy comiendo.**). The next student mimes the same action, says what that person is doing (_____ **está comiendo.**), and then mimes and states a different action (Ex: sleeping/**Estoy durmiendo.**). Have students continue until the chain breaks. Have students see how long the chain can get in three minutes.

Comunicación

4   Las vacaciones   Read Elena's description of her family vacation. Then indicate whether these conclusions are **lógico** or **ilógico**, based on what you read.

> Está lloviendo. Mis tres hermanos están jugando a las cartas. Mi hermana está leyendo una revista. Mi madre está buscando la llave de la habitación. Mi padre está durmiendo. ¿Y yo? Estoy escribiendo este mensaje electrónico...

	Lógico	Ilógico
1. Hace mal tiempo.	☑	○
2. La familia es pequeña.	○	☑
3. La madre está contenta.	○	☑
4. El padre está en la cama.	☑	○
5. La familia está en un hotel.	☑	○

5   Preguntar   Answer your partner's questions about what you are doing at these times.   Answers will vary.

> **modelo**
> 8:00 a.m.
> **Estudiante 1:** Son las ocho de la mañana. ¿Qué estás haciendo?
> **Estudiante 2:** Estoy desayunando.

1. 5:00 a.m.	3. 11:00 a.m.	5. 2:00 p.m.	7. 9:00 p.m.
2. 9:30 a.m.	4. 12:00 p.m.	6. 5:00 p.m.	8. 11:30 p.m.

6   Describir   Use the present progressive to write a description of what is happening in this Spanish beach scene.   Answers will vary.

Síntesis

7   ¿Qué están haciendo?   With a partner, take turns asking each other what people are doing right now. You could ask about other students, professors, or even celebrities.   Answers will vary.

bailar	comer	escribir	estudiar	leer
cantar	enseñar	escuchar	jugar	mirar

Estructura   **169**

Communication 1.1,
1.2, 1.3
Comparisons 4.1

4   Expansion   After checking students' answers, ask volunteers to change the activities so they would be true for their family on a rainy day on vacation. Ex: **Está lloviendo. Mis hermanos están jugando a los videojuegos. Mi hermana está escuchando música en su habitación…**

5   Expansion Reverse the activity by having students state what they are doing. Their partner should guess the time of day. Alternatively, students could say that they are doing season-specific activities (Ex: **Estoy tomando el sol.**) and their partner will guess the month.

5   Virtual Chat Available online.

6   In-Class Tip   Use the online Resources (Lección 5/ Digital Image Bank/ Estructura 5.2 Present Progessive) to assist with the presentation of this activity.

6   Expansion In pairs, have students write a conversation between two or more of the people in the drawing. Conversations should consist of at least three exchanges.

Communication 1.1

7   Expansion   Divide the class in pairs and distribute the handouts for the activity **¿Qué están haciendo?** from the online Resources (Lección 5/Activity Pack/ Information Gap Activities). Ask students to read the instructions and give them ten minutes to complete the activity. Have volunteers report their findings to the class.

7   Partner Chat Available online.

Comunicación provides scaffolded activities built around the three modes of communication:

→ **Interpretive communication** activities target students' reading and listening comprehension skills.

↔ **Interpersonal communication** activities target the development of students' skills in real-time negotiation of meaning with one or more partners in both spoken and written communication settings.

← **Presentational communication** activities target students' skills in producing a variety of written and spoken language.

Notas culturales and **¡Lengua viva!** boxes appear when there's an interesting cultural or linguistic note to give students even more real-world context as they communicate.

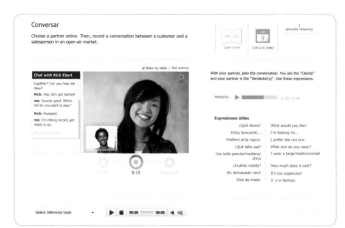

Conversar

Choose a partner online. Then, record a conversation between a customer and a salesperson in an open-air market.

Partner Chat activities allow students to work in pairs to synchronously record a conversation in the target language. This collaborative activity allows for spontaneous and creative communication in a safe environment.

Adelante: Lectura

Lectura develops reading skills in the context of the lesson theme.

Context-based readings pull all of the lesson elements together, recycling vocabulary and grammar that students have learned.

Charts, graphic organizers, photos, and other visual elements support reading comprehension.

Estrategia features reading strategies and pre-reading activities that strengthen students' reading abilities in Spanish.

Examinar el texto prompts students to take an initial bird's-eye view of the reading and draw assumptions based on its format, photos, title, and other readily apparent elements.

Lectura readings provide students with an opportunity to listen to native speakers as auto-sync highlighting of sentences guides their eyes.

Section Goals

In **Lectura**, students will:
- learn the strategy of scanning to find specific information in reading matter
- read a brochure about ecotourism in Puerto Rico

 Communication 1.1, 1.2
Cultures 2.1, 2.2, 2.3
Connections 3.1, 3.2
Comparisons 4.2

Pre-AP®

Interpretive Reading: Estrategia Explain to students that a good way to improve reading comprehension and to get an idea of what an article or other text is about is to scan it before reading. Scanning means running one's eyes over a text in search of specific information that can be used to infer the content of the text.

The Affective Dimension Point out to students that becoming familiar with cognates will help them feel less overwhelmed when they encounter new Spanish texts.

Examinar el texto Do the activity orally as a class. Some cognates that give a clue to the content of the text are: **turismo ecológico, teléfono, TV por cable, Internet, hotel, aire acondicionado, perfecto, Parque Nacional Foresta, Museo de Arte Nativo, Reserva, Biosfera, Santuario**. These clues should tell a reader scanning the text that it is about a hotel promoting ecotourism.

Preguntas Ask the questions orally of the class. Possible responses: 1. travel brochure 2. Puerto Rico 3. photos of beautiful tropical beaches, bays, and forests; The document is trying to attract the reader. 4. **Hotel Vistahermosa** in Lajas, Puerto Rico; attract guests

---

Lectura
Antes de leer

Estrategia
Scanning

Scanning involves glancing over a document in search of specific information. For example, you can scan a document to identify its format, to find cognates, to locate visual clues about the document's content, or to find specific facts. Scanning allows you to learn a great deal about a text without having to read it word for word.

Examinar el texto

Scan the reading selection for cognates and write down a few of them. Answers will vary.

1. _____   4. _____
2. _____   5. _____
3. _____   6. _____

Based on the cognates you found, what do you think this document is about?
_____

Preguntas

Read these questions. Then scan the document again to look for answers. Answers will vary.

1. What is the format of the reading selection?
_____

2. Which place is the document about?
_____

3. What are some of the visual cues this document provides? What do they tell you about the content of the document?
_____

4. Who produced the document, and what do you think it is for?
_____

Turismo ecológico en Puerto Rico

Hotel Vistahermosa
~ Lajas, Puerto Rico ~

- 40 habitaciones individuales
- 15 habitaciones dobles
- Teléfono/TV por cable/Internet
- Aire acondicionad
- Restaurante (Bar)
- Piscina
- Área de juegos
- Cajero automático

El hotel está situado en Playa Grande, un pequeño pueblo de pescadores del mar Caribe. Es el lugar perfecto para el viajero que viene de vacaciones. Las playas son seguras y limpias, ideales para tomar el sol, descansar, tomar fotografías y nadar. Está abierto los 365 días del año. Hay una rebaja° especial para estudiantes universitarios.

DIRECCIÓN: Playa Grande 406, Lajas, PR 00667, cerca del Parque Nacional Foresta.

Cajero automático *ATM* rebaja *discount*

TEACHING OPTIONS

Heritage Speakers Ask heritage speakers of Puerto Rican descent who have lived on or visited the island to talk briefly about any experiences they have had with the beaches, nature preserves, or wildlife of Puerto Rico.
Small Groups Have students work in small groups to research and prepare a short presentation about the climate, geography, or people of Puerto Rico. If possible, ask them to

illustrate their presentations with photos or illustrations.
Small Groups Lead a discussion about vacations. Have students work in groups to brainstorm what are important aspects of an "ideal" vacation. Each student should contribute at least one idea. When each group has its list, ask for volunteers to share the information with the rest of the class. How do the groups differ? How are they similar?

Atracciones cercanas

Playa Grande ¿Busca la playa perfecta? Playa Grande es la playa que está buscando. Usted puede pescar, sacar fotos, nadar y pasear en bicicleta. Playa Grande es un paraíso para el turista que quiere practicar deportes acuáticos. El lugar es bonito e interesante y usted va a tener muchas oportunidades para descansar y disfrutar en familia.

Valle Niebla Ir de excursión, tomar café, montar a caballo, caminar, hacer picnics. Más de cien lugares para acampar.

Bahía Fosforescente Sacar fotos, salidas de noche, excursión en barco. Una maravillosa experiencia llena de luz°.

Arrecifes de Coral Sacar fotos, bucear, explorar. Es un lugar único en el Caribe.

Playa Vieja Tomar el sol, pasear en bicicleta, jugar a las cartas, escuchar música. Ideal para la familia.

Parque Nacional Foresta Sacar fotos, visitar el Museo de Arte Nativo. Reserva Mundial de la Biosfera.

Santuario de las Aves Sacar fotos, observar aves°, seguir rutas de excursión.

llena de luz *full of light* aves *birds*

Después de leer

Listas
Which amenities of Hotel Vistahermosa would most interest these potential guests? Explain your choices. Answers will vary.
1. dos padres con un hijo de seis años y una hija de ocho años
2. un hombre y una mujer en su luna de miel (*honeymoon*)
3. una persona en un viaje de negocios (*business trip*)

Conversaciones
Answer your partner's questions. Answers will vary.
1. ¿Quieres visitar el Hotel Vistahermosa? ¿Por qué?
2. Tienes tiempo de visitar sólo tres de las atracciones turísticas que están cerca del hotel. ¿Cuáles vas a visitar? ¿Por qué?
3. ¿Qué prefieres hacer en Valle Niebla? ¿En Playa Vieja? ¿En el Parque Nacional Foresta?

Situaciones
You have just arrived at Hotel Vistahermosa. Your partner is the concierge. Use the phrases below to express your interests and ask for suggestions about where to go. Answers will vary.
1. montar a caballo
2. bucear
3. pasear en bicicleta
4. pescar
5. observar aves

Contestar
Answer these questions. Answers will vary.
1. ¿Quieres visitar Puerto Rico? Explica tu respuesta.
2. ¿Adónde quieres ir de vacaciones el verano que viene? Explica tu respuesta.

Listas
- Ask these comprehension questions. 1. ¿El Hotel Vistahermosa está situado cerca de qué mar? (el mar Caribe) 2. ¿Qué playa es un paraíso para el turista? (la Playa Grande) 3. ¿Dónde puedes montar a caballo? (en el Valle Niebla)
- 👥 Encourage discussion of each of the items by asking questions such as: En tu opinión, ¿qué tipo de atracciones buscan los padres con hijos de seis y ocho años? ¿Qué esperan de un hotel? Y una pareja en su luna de miel, ¿qué tipo de atracciones espera encontrar en un hotel? En tu opinión, ¿qué busca una persona en un viaje de negocios?

Conversaciones Ask individuals about what their partners said. Ex: ¿Por qué (no) quiere _____ visitar el Hotel Vistahermosa? ¿Qué atracciones quiere ver? Ask other students: Y tú, ¿quieres visitar el Parque Nacional Foresta o prefieres visitar otro lugar?

Conversaciones
👥 Available online as **Virtual Chat**

Situaciones
- Give students a couple of minutes to review **Más vocabulario** on page 152 and **Expresiones útiles** on page 159.
- To challenge students, add to the list activities such as **sacar fotos, correr, nadar,** and **ir de excursión.**

Situaciones
👥 Available online as **Partner Chat**

Contestar Have volunteers explain how the reading selection might influence their choice of a vacation destination for next summer.

TEACHING OPTIONS

Pairs Have pairs of students work together to read the brochure aloud and write three questions about it. After they have finished, ask pairs to exchange papers with another pair, who will work together to answer them. Alternatively, you might pick pairs to read their questions to the class. Ask volunteers to answer them.

Small Groups 👥 To practice scanning written material to infer its content, bring in short, simple Spanish-language magazine or newspaper articles you have read. Have small groups scan the articles to determine what they are about. Have them write down all the clues that help them. When each group has come to a decision, ask it to present its findings to the class. Confirm the accuracy of the inferences.

Después de leer includes scaffolded post-reading activities that check students' comprehension.

Teaching Options provide information about lexical variations that are touched upon in the reading.

General Suggestions: Reading

- Remind students to look over pre-reading activities or strategies and post-reading activities to anticipate the context.
- Ask students to read the selection once, focusing on the gist, *not* looking up words, but taking notes as needed.
- Ask students to read the selection a second time, consulting glosses for unfamiliar terms. Have students revisit post-reading activities to answer as many items as possible.
- Students will benefit from reading the selection a third time before you lead the class in a discussion of the topic, details, and real-world application.

Adelante: Escritura

Escritura helps students develop writing skills in the context of the lesson theme.

Estrategia offers strategies for preparing and executing the writing task related to the lesson theme. This writing task allows students to present information, concepts, and ideas to inform, explain, or persuade on a variety of topics.

Tema provides a writing topic and includes suggestions for approaching it.

Evaluation provides a sample rubric for the writing task. Consider sharing this criteria with your students as a tool for self-assessment.

Section Goals

In **Escritura**, students will:
• write a brochure for a hotel or resort
• integrate travel-related vocabulary and structures taught in **Lección 5**

Communication 1.3

Pre-AP®

Interpersonal Writing: Estrategia
Explain that outlines are a great way for a writer to think about what a piece of writing will be like before actually expending much time and effort on writing. An outline is also a great way of keeping a writer on track while composing the piece and helps the person keep the whole project in mind as he or she focuses on a specific part.

Tema Discuss the hotel or resort brochure students are to write. Go over the list of information that they might include. You might indicate a specific number of the points that should be included in the brochure. Tell students that the brochure for **Hotel Vistahermosa** in **Lectura**, pages 180–181, can serve as a model for their writing. Remind them that they are writing with the purpose of attracting guests to the hotel or resort. Suggest that, as they begin to think about writing, students should brainstorm as many details as they can remember about the hotel they are going to describe. Tell them to do this in Spanish.

In-Class Tip Have students write each of the individual items of their brainstorm lists on index cards so that they can arrange and rearrange them into different idea maps as they plan their brochures.

Escritura

Estrategia
Making an outline

When we write to share information, an outline can serve to separate topics and subtopics, providing a framework for the presentation of data. Consider the following excerpt from an outline of the tourist brochure on pages 180–181.

IV. Descripción del sitio (con foto)
  A. Playa Grande
    1. Playas seguras y limpias
    2. Ideal para tomar el sol, descansar, tomar fotografías, nadar
  B. El hotel
    1. Abierto los 365 días del año
    2. Rebaja para estudiantes universitarios

Mapa de ideas
Idea maps can be used to create outlines. The major sections of an idea map correspond to the Roman numerals in an outline. The minor idea map sections correspond to the outline's capital letters, and so on. Examine the idea map that led to the outline above.

Tema

Escribir un folleto
Write a tourist brochure for a hotel or resort you have visited. If you wish, you may write about an imaginary location. You may want to include some of this information in your brochure:

▶ the name of the hotel or resort
▶ phone and fax numbers that tourists can use to make contact
▶ the hotel website that tourists can consult
▶ an e-mail address that tourists can use to request information
▶ a description of the exterior of the hotel or resort
▶ a description of the interior of the hotel or resort, including facilities and amenities
▶ a description of the surrounding area, including its climat
▶ a listing of nearby scenic natural attractions
▶ a listing of nearby cultural attractions
▶ a listing of recreational activities that tourists can pursue in the vicinity of the hotel or resort

EVALUATION: Folleto

Criteria	Scale
Appropriate details	1 2 3 4 5
Organization	1 2 3 4 5
Use of vocabulary	1 2 3 4 5
Grammatical accuracy	1 2 3 4 5

Scoring	
Excellent	18–20 points
Good	14–17 points
Satisfactory	10–13 points
Unsatisfactory	< 10 points

General Suggestions: Writing

Presentational writing serves to communicate meaning, and students must ensure that their audience can understand their message. Remind students to take into account spelling, mechanics, and the logical sequencing of their work.

Remember that activities in other strands such as *Cultura* and *Estructura* provide writing practice with shorter tasks.

Adelante: Escuchar

Escuchar

Estrategia
Listening for key words

By listening for key words or phrases, you can identify the subject and main ideas of what you hear, as well as some of the details.

 To practice this strategy, you will now listen to a short paragraph. As you listen, jot down the key words that help you identify the subject of the paragraph and its main ideas.

Preparación

Based on the illustration, who do you think Hernán Jiménez is, and what is he doing? What key words might you listen for to help you understand what he is saying?

Ahora escucha 🔊

Now you are going to listen to a weather report by Hernán Jiménez. Note which phrases are correct according to the key words and phrases you hear.

Santo Domingo
1. hace sol ✔
2. va a hacer frío
3. una mañana de mal tiempo
4. va a estar nublado ✔
5. buena tarde para tomar el sol
6. buena mañana para la playa ✔

San Francisco de Macorís
1. hace frío ✔
2. hace sol
3. va a nevar
4. va a llover ✔
5. hace calor
6. mal día para excursiones ✔

Comprensión

¿Cierto o falso?
Indicate whether each statement is **cierto** or **falso**, based on the weather report. Correct the false statements.

1. Según el meteorólogo, la temperatura en Santo Domingo es de 26 grados.
   Cierto.

2. La temperatura máxima en Santo Domingo hoy va a ser de 30 grados.
   Cierto.

3. Está lloviendo ahora en Santo Domingo.
   Falso. Hace sol.

4. En San Francisco de Macorís la temperatura mínima de hoy va a ser de 20 grados.
   Falso. La temperatura mínima va a ser de 18 grados.

5. Va a llover mucho hoy en San Francisco de Macorís.
   Cierto.

Preguntas
Answer these questions about the weather report.

1. ¿Hace viento en Santo Domingo ahora?
   Sí, hace viento en Santo Domingo.
2. ¿Está nublado en Santo Domingo ahora?
   No, no está nublado ahora en Santo Domingo.
3. ¿Está nevando ahora en San Francisco de Macorís?
   No, no está nevando ahora en San Francisco de Macorís.
4. ¿Qué tiempo hace en San Francisco de Macorís?
   Hace frío.

---

18 grados. Va a llover casi todo el día. ¡No es buen día para excursiones a las montañas!

Hasta el noticiero del mediodía, me despido de ustedes. ¡Que les vaya bien!

Section Goals
In **Escuchar**, students will:
- learn the strategy of listening for key words
- listen to a short paragraph and note the key words
- answer questions based on the content of a recorded conversation

🌐 Communication 1.2

Estrategia
Script Aquí está la foto de mis vacaciones en la playa. Ya lo sé; no debo pasar el tiempo tomando el sol. Es que vivo en una ciudad donde llueve casi todo el año y mis actividades favoritas son bucear, pescar en el mar y nadar.

In-Class Tip Have students look at the drawing and describe what they see. Guide them in saying what **Hernán Jiménez** is like and what he is doing.

Preguntas
👥↔👥 Available online as **Virtual Chat**

Ahora escucha
Script Buenos días, queridos televidentes, les saluda el meteorólogo Hernán Jiménez, con el pronóstico del tiempo para nuestra bella isla.

Hoy, 17 de octubre, a las diez de la mañana, la temperatura en Santo Domingo es de 26 grados. Hace sol con viento del este a 10 kilómetros por hora.

En la tarde, va a estar un poco nublado con la posibilidad de lluvia. La temperatura máxima del día va a ser de 30 grados. Es una buena mañana para ir a la playa.

En las montañas hace bastante frío ahora, especialmente en el área de San Francisco de Macorís. La temperatura mínima de estas 24 horas va a ser de

(Script continues at far left in the bottom panels.)

Escuchar builds students' listening skills with a recorded conversation and narration.

Ahora escucha offers a variety of scaffolded activities to support listening comprehension. These activities provide students with an opportunity to understand, interpret, and analyze what they hear on a variety of engaging topics.

Scripts for listening activities are available to help you with planning. As an alternative, read the script aloud for your students instead of using the MP3 audio.

Adelante: En pantalla

En pantalla presents TV clips from around the Spanish-speaking world connected to the language, vocabulary, and theme of the lesson. These clips include commercials, newscasts, and TV shows.

A complete instructional sequence engages students through personal reflection, discussion, and real-world application of what they have seen and heard.

Conversación discussion questions invite student partners to expand on the themes explored in the TV clip and to make connections with their own experiences and opinions.

Aplicación activities engage students with interesting and personal applications of the topics covered in the TV clip.

Teacher Resources include Videoscripts, English Translations, and Optional Testing Sections.

En pantalla clips are a great tool for exposing students to target language discourse. This authentic input provides evidence of the correct formulations of the language so that students can form hypotheses about how it works.

Section Goals

In **En pantalla**, students will:
- read about airline travel in Latin America
- watch an ad for **LANPASS**, a Chilean airline loyalty program

 Communication 1.1, 1.2, 1.3
Cultures 2.2
Connections 3.2
Comparisons 4.2
Communities 5.2

Teacher Resources Read the front matter for suggestions on how to incorporate all the program's components. See pages 151A–151B for a detailed listing of Teacher Resources online.

El arte de viajar Check comprehension: 1. How will airline travel evolve in Latin America by the year 2034? 2. What is LAN? 3. What is LANPASS and what is its goal?

Pre-AP®

Audiovisual Interpretive Communication
Antes de ver Strategy Remind students to focus first on familiar words to identify the purpose of the video.

Comprensión Once students have marked the items they hear in the ad, ask them to make a list of other ways everyday life is different when we travel.

Aplicación Encourage students to use photos or videos of their own family trips when presenting their ad to the class.

en pantalla

Anuncio de Santander LANPASS

Con lo que realmente nos importa°.

Preparación

Answer these questions in Spanish. Answers will vary.

1. ¿Te gusta viajar? ¿Por qué? ¿Adónde te gusta viajar?
2. ¿Qué te gusta hacer cuando estás de vacaciones?
3. ¿Qué modo de transporte prefieres usar? ¿Por qué?

El arte de viajar

Millions of people travel on airlines every year for business and pleasure. The number of airline passengers is expected to double between 2014 and 2034 worldwide. This is true for Latin America, too, as airlines are looking at how to attract all those customers to their planes. The airline of Chile, LAN, has partnered with the international bank Santander to create the loyalty program LANPASS to encourage frequent travel on LAN. What does an airline say to travelers that captures their attention and makes their business seem like your pleasure?

importa matters

Comprensión

Mark an X next to the phrases you hear in the ad. Irse es volver a....

x cambiar de piel	__ trabajar	__ la oficina
x desconectarnos	x castillos de arena	x sentirse vivo
__ estudiar mucho	__ destinos exóticos	x las siestas
x un mundo sin Internet	x la esencia de todo	__ tiempo en familia

Conversación

Answer these questions with a classmate. *Answers will vary.*

1. Según el anuncio, ¿cuáles son algunas cosas positivas de viajar?
2. ¿Cuáles de estas cosas positivas son importantes para ti? ¿Por qué?
3. Para tener experiencias positivas, ¿a dónde viajas tú? ¿A dónde viaja tu familia? ¿Y tus amigos?

Vocabulario útil

arena	sand
cambiar	to change
destino	destination
medir	to measure
mismo/a	itself
piel	skin
puestas de sol	sunsets
recuerdos	memories
sentirse	to feel
sino	but

Aplicación

With a classmate, prepare an ad inviting other peo[ple] to travel to a special place. Explain why it is a per[fect] or ideal place. What evocative words and images w[ill] you use? Present your ad to the class. Answers will v[ary]

EXPANSION

Culture Note Although airline travel is becoming more popular throughout Latin America, in some countries people still use other means of transportation for their trips, especially intercity buses. This is in part a custom and in part due to the high costs of airline tickets. However, low-cost airlines have recently started operations in some countries.

Small Groups Have small groups of students research and create an oral presentation about other big airline companies in the Spanish-speaking world. Encourage them to include information on the alliances they have with other companies and the way they attract customers.

Adelante: Flash cultura

etween 1438 and 1533, when the vast and owerful Incan Empire was at its height, the Incas uilt an elaborate network of **caminos** (*trails*) that aversed the Andes Mountains and converged on e empire's capital, Cuzco. Today, hundreds of ousands of tourists come to Peru annually to walk e surviving trails and enjoy the spectacular scenery. e most popular trail, **el Camino Inca**, leads from uzco to **Intipunku** (*Sun Gate*), the entrance to the ncient mountain city of Machu Picchu.

Vocabulario útil

ciudadela	*citadel*
de cultivo	*farming*
el/la guía	*guide*
maravilla	*wonder*
quechua	*Quechua (indigenous Peruvian)*
sector (urbano)	*(urban) sector*

reparación

ave you ever visited an archeological or historic site? here? Why did you go there? Answers will vary.

ompletar

omplete these sentences. Make the necessary changes.

. Las ruinas de Machu Picchu son una antigua
<u>ciudadela</u> inca.

. La ciudadela estaba (*was*) dividida en tres sectores:
<u>urbano</u> , religioso y de cultivo.

. Cada año los <u>guías</u> reciben a cientos (*hundreds*) de turistas de diferentes países.

. Hoy en día, la cultura <u>quechua</u> está presente en las comunidades andinas (*Andean*) de Perú.

ncuentra aislada sobre *it is isolated on* siempre he querido *I have*
ays wanted Me encantan *I love* antiguas *ancient*

¡Vacaciones en Perú!

Machu Picchu [...] se encuentra aislada sobre° esta montaña...

... siempre he querido° venir [...] Me encantan° las civilizaciones antiguas°.

Somos una familia francesa [...] Perú es un país muy, muy bonito de verdad.

Adelante **185**

Flash cultura videos feature young broadcasters from across the Spanish-speaking world sharing aspects of life related to each lesson's theme.

Preparación activities activate students' knowledge by asking about their own experience with topics related to the *Flash cultura* segment.

Teaching Options Go deeper into the content with activities that expand on the themes explored in the *Flash cultura*. Build student excitement around contemporary culture in Spanish-speaking countries.

Flash cultura videos provide valuable cultural insights as well as linguistic input, while introducing students to a variety of accents and vocabulary.

The similarities and differences among Spanish-speaking countries that come up through their adventures will challenge students to think about their own cultural practices and values.

Panorama

Panorama showcases the nations of the Spanish-speaking world with short features about each country's culture—history, places, fine arts, literature, and aspects of everyday life.

El país en cifras presents almanac information that orients students to key facts for each country or region, offering opportunities for comparison to their own community. Comprehension questions (with answers) are provided to check students' understanding.

¡Increíble pero cierto! highlights an intriguing, and often little-known fact about the featured country or its people.

Section Goal
In **Panorama**, students will read about the geography, history, and culture of Puerto Rico.

Communication 1.3
Cultures 2.1, 2.2
Connections 3.1, 3.2
Comparisons 4.2

Teacher Resources
Read the front matter for suggestions on how to incorporate all the program's components. See pages 151A–151B for a detailed listing of Teacher Resources online.

In-Class Tips
• Use the **Lección 5 Panorama** online Resources to assist with this presentation.
• Discuss Puerto Rico's location in relation to the U.S. mainland and the other Caribbean islands. Encourage students to describe what they see in the photos on this page.

El país en cifras After reading **Puertorriqueños célebres**, ask volunteers who are familiar with these individuals to tell a little more about each one. For example, **José Rivera** is a playwright and screenwriter who was nominated for an Academy Award for his screenplay of *Diarios de motocicleta* (2004). You might also mention **Rita Moreno**, the only Hispanic female performer to have won an Oscar, a Tony, an Emmy, and a Grammy, and novelist **Rosario Ferré**, whose *House on the Lagoon* (**La casa de la laguna**) gives a fictional portrait of a large part of Puerto Rican history.

¡Increíble pero cierto! The **río Camuy** caves are actually a series of karstic sinkholes, formed by water sinking into and eroding limestone. Another significant cave in this system is **Cueva Clara**, located in the **Parque de las Cavernas del Río Camuy**.

---

5 | panorama

Puerto Rico

El país en cifras

► **Área:** 8.959 km² (3.459 millas²) *menor° que el área de Connecticut*
► **Población:** 3.667.084
Puerto Rico es una de las islas más densamente pobladas° del mundo. Más de la mitad de la población vive en San Juan, la capital.
► **Capital:** San Juan—2.730.000
► **Ciudades principales:** Arecibo, Bayamón, Fajardo, Mayagüez, Ponce
► **Moneda:** dólar estadounidense
► **Idiomas:** español (oficial); inglés (oficial)
Aproximadamente la cuarta parte de la población puertorriqueña habla inglés, pero en las zonas turísticas este porcentaje es mucho más alto. El uso del inglés es obligatorio para documentos federales.

Bandera de Puerto Rico

Puertorriqueños célebres

► **Raúl Juliá,** actor (1940–1994)
► **Roberto Clemente,** beisbolista (1934–1972)
► **Julia de Burgos,** escritora (1914–1953)
► **Benicio del Toro,** actor y productor (1967–)
► **Rosie Pérez,** actriz y bailarina (1964–)
► **José Rivera,** dramaturgo y guionista (1955–)

menor *less* pobladas *populated* río subterráneo *underground river* más largo *longest* cuevas *caves* bóveda *vault* fortaleza *fort* caber *fit*

Faro en Arecibo
Playa en San Juan
Océano Atlántico
Arecibo
San Jua...
Río Grande de Añasco
Bayamón
Mayagüez
Cordillera Central
Sierra de Cay...
Ponce
Mar Cari...
Iglesia en Ponce
Pescadores en Mayagüez

OCÉ...
ATL...
PUE...
OCÉANO PACÍFICO

¡Increíble pero cierto!

El río Camuy es el tercer río subterráneo° más largo° del mundo y tiene el sistema de cuevas° más grande del hemisferio occidental. La Cueva de los Tres Pueblos es una gigantesca bóveda°, tan grande que toda la fortaleza° del Morro puede caber° en su interior.

TEACHING OPTIONS

Heritage Speakers Encourage heritage speakers of Puerto Rican descent who have visited or lived on the island to share their impressions of it with the class. Ask them to describe people they knew or met, places they saw, and experiences they had. Have the class ask follow-up questions.
El béisbol Baseball is a popular sport in Puerto Rico, home of the Winter League. **Roberto Clemente**, a player with the Pittsburgh

Pirates who died tragically in a plane crash, was the first Latino to be inducted into the Baseball Hall of Fame. He is venerated all over the island with buildings and monuments. There are numerous Major League Baseball players that were born in Puerto Rico, such as **Carlos Beltrán, Iván Rodríguez, Jorge Posada, Carlos Delgado,** and **Yadier Molina.**

Lugares • El Morro

El Morro es una fortaleza que se construyó para proteger° la bahía° de San Juan desde principios del siglo° XVI hasta principios del siglo XX. Hoy día muchos turistas visitan este lugar, convertido en un museo. Es el sitio más fotografiado de Puerto Rico. La arquitectura de la fortaleza es impresionante. Tiene misteriosos túneles, oscuras mazmorras° y vistas fabulosas de la bahía.

Artes • Salsa

La salsa, un estilo musical de origen puertorriqueño y cubano, nació° en el barrio latino de la ciudad de Nueva York. Dos de los músicos de salsa más famosos son Tito Puente y Willie Colón, los dos de Nueva York. Las estrellas° de la salsa en Puerto Rico son Felipe Rodríguez y Héctor Lavoe. Hoy en día, Puerto Rico es el centro internacional de este estilo musical. El Gran Combo de Puerto Rico es una de las orquestas de salsa más famosas del mundo°.

Ciencias • El Observatorio de Arecibo

El Observatorio de Arecibo tiene uno de los radiotelescopios más grandes del mundo. Gracias a este telescopio, los científicos° pueden estudiar las propiedades de la Tierra°, la Luna° y otros cuerpos celestes. También pueden analizar fenómenos celestiales como los quasares y pulsares, y detectar emisiones de radio de otras galaxias, en busca de inteligencia extraterrestre.

Isla de Culebra

Fajardo

Isla de Vieques

Historia • Relación con los Estados Unidos

Puerto Rico pasó a ser° parte de los Estados Unidos después de° la guerra° de 1898 y se hizo° un estado libre asociado en 1952. Los puertorriqueños, ciudadanos° estadounidenses desde° 1917, tienen representación política en el Congreso, pero no votan en las elecciones presidenciales y no pagan impuestos° federales. Hay un debate entre los puertorriqueños: ¿debe la isla seguir como estado libre asociado, hacerse un estado como los otros° o volverse° independiente?

¿Qué aprendiste? Contesta las preguntas con una oración completa.

1. ¿Cuál es la moneda de Puerto Rico? La moneda de Puerto Rico es el dólar estadounidense.
2. ¿Qué idiomas se hablan (*are spoken*) en Puerto Rico? Se hablan español e inglés en Puerto Rico.
3. ¿Cuál es el sitio más fotografiado de Puerto Rico? El Morro es el sitio más fotografiado de Puerto Rico.
4. ¿Qué es el Gran Combo? Es una orquesta de Puerto Rico.
5. ¿Qué hacen los científicos en el Observatorio de Arecibo? Los científicos estudian las propiedades de la Tierra y la Luna y detectan emisiones de otras galaxias.

Conexión Internet Investiga estos temas en Internet.

1. Describe a dos puertorriqueños famosos. ¿Cómo son? ¿Qué hacen? ¿Dónde viven? ¿Por qué son célebres?
2. Busca información sobre lugares en los que se puede hacer ecoturismo en Puerto Rico.

proteger *protect* bahía *bay* siglo *century* mazmorras *dungeons* nació *was born* estrellas *stars* mundo *world* científicos *scientists* Tierra *Earth* Luna *Moon* pasó a ser *become* después de *after* guerra *war* se hizo *become* ciudadanos *citizens* desde *since* pagan impuestos *pay taxes* otros *others* volverse *to become*

Variación léxica When the first Spanish colonists arrived on the island they were to name Puerto Rico, they found it inhabited by the Taínos, who called the island **Boriquen**. Puerto Ricans still use **Boriquen** to refer to the island, and they frequently call themselves **boricuas**. The Puerto Rican national anthem is *La borinqueña*. Some other Taíno words that have entered Spanish (and English) are **huracán, hamaca, canoa,** and **iguana**. **Juracán** was the name of the

Taíno god of the winds whose anger stirred up the great storms that periodically devastated the island. The hammock, of course, was the device the Taínos slept in, and canoes were the boats made of great hollowed-out logs with which they paddled between islands. The Taíno language also survives in many Puerto Rican place names: **Arecibo, Bayamón, Guayama, Sierra de Cayey, Yauco,** and **Coamo.**

El Morro

- Remind students that at the time **El Morro** was built, piracy was a major concern for Spain and its Caribbean colonies. If possible, show other photos of **El Morro**, San Juan Bay, and **Viejo San Juan**.
- For additional information about **El Morro** and **Viejo San Juan**, you may want to play the *Panorama cultural* video footage for this lesson.

Salsa With students, listen to **salsa** or **merengue** from the Dominican Republic, and **rumba** or **mambo** from Cuba. Encourage them to identify common elements in the music (strong percussion patterns rooted in African traditions, alternating structure of soloist and ensemble, incorporation of Western instruments and musical vocabulary). Then, have them point out contrasts.

El Observatorio de Arecibo The Arecibo Ionospheric Observatory has the world's most sensitive radio telescope. It can detect objects up to 13 billion light years away. The telescope dish is 1,000 feet in diameter and covers 20 acres. The dish is made of about 40,000 aluminum mesh panels. The Arecibo Observatory celebrated its 50th anniversary in 2013.

Relación con los Estados Unidos Point out that only Puerto Ricans living on the island vote in plebiscites (or referenda) on the question of the island's political relationship with the United States.

Teaching Options provide expansion activities and additional culture notes.

Teacher Resources include Videoscripts, English Translations, Digital Image Bank, and Optional Testing Sections.

Panorama cultural videos present authentic documentary and travelogue footage of the featured Spanish-speaking country, exposing students to the sights and sounds of an aspect of its culture.

Here are the countries represented in each lesson in Panorama:

Lesson 1 USA and Canada   **Lesson 3** Ecuador   **Lesson 5** Puerto Rico
Lesson 2 Spain   **Lesson 4** Mexico   **Lesson 6** Cuba

Recapitulación

Recapitulación provides diagnostic, scaffolded activities for targeted review of the lesson's key grammar points.

Expansion activities offer suggestions for more complex communication. Pair and group activities engage students as they collaborate and build fluency, while individual activities extend application.

Resumen gramatical provides a handy summary of the grammatical points presented in the lesson.

Recapitulación

Review the grammar concepts you have learned in this lesson by completing these activities.

1 **Completar** Complete the chart with the correct present participle of these verbs. **16 pts.**

Infinitive	Present participle	Infinitive	Present participle
hacer	haciendo	estar	estando
acampar	acampando	ser	siendo
tener	teniendo	vivir	viviendo
venir	viniendo	estudiar	estudiando

2 **Vacaciones en París** Complete this paragraph about Julia's trip to Paris with the correct form of **ser** or **estar**. **24 pts.**

Hoy (1) __es__ (es/está) el 3 de julio y voy a París por tres semanas. (Yo) (2) __Estoy__ (Soy/Estoy) muy feliz porque voy a ver a mi mejor amiga. Ella (3) __es__ (es/está) de Puerto Rico, pero ahora (4) __está__ (es/está) viviendo en París. También (yo) (5) __estoy__ (soy/estoy) un poco nerviosa porque (6) __es__ (es/está) mi primer viaje a Francia. El vuelo (*flight*) (7) __es__ (es/está) hoy por la tarde, pero ahora (8) __está__ (es/está) lloviendo. Por eso (9) __estamos__ (somos/estamos) preocupadas, porque probablemente el avión va a salir tarde. Mi equipaje ya (10) __está__ (es/está) listo. (11) __Es__ (Es/Está) tarde y me tengo que ir. ¡Va a (12) __ser__ (ser/estar) un viaje fenomenal!

3 **¿Qué hacen?** Respond to these questions by indicating what people do with the items mentioned. Use direct object pronouns. **20 pts.**

modelo
¿Qué hacen ellos con la película? (ver)
La ven.

1. ¿Qué haces tú con el libro de viajes? (leer) __Lo leo.__
2. ¿Qué hacen los turistas en la ciudad? (explorar) __La exploran.__
3. ¿Qué hace el botones con el equipaje? (llevar) __Lo lleva (a la habitación).__
4. ¿Qué hace la agente con las reservaciones? (confirmar) __Las confirma.__
5. ¿Qué hacen ustedes con los pasaportes? (mostrar) __Los mostramos.__

RESUMEN GRAMATICAL

5.1 Estar with conditions and emotions *p. 16*
► Yo estoy aburrido/a, feliz, nervioso/a.
► El cuarto está desordenado, limpio, ordenado.
► Estos libros están abiertos, cerrados, sucios.

5.2 The present progressive *pp. 166–167*
► The present progressive is formed with the present tense of estar plus the present participle.

Forming the present participle

infinitive	stem	ending	present participle
hablar	habl-	-ando	hablando
comer	com-	-iendo	comiendo
escribir	escrib-	-iendo	escribiendo

-ir stem-changing verbs

	infinitive	present participle
e:ie	preferir	prefiriendo
e:i	conseguir	consiguiendo
o:ue	dormir	durmiendo

► Irregular present participles: yendo (ir), pudiend (poder), viniendo (venir)

5.3 Ser and estar *pp. 170–171*
► Uses of ser: nationality, origin, profession or occupation, characteristics, generalizations, possession, what something is made of, time and date, time and place of events
► Uses of estar: location, health, physical states and conditions, emotional states, weather expressions, ongoing actions
► Many adjectives can be used with both ser and estar, but the meaning of the adjectives will change.

Juan es delgado.	Juan está más delgado hoy.
Juan is thin.	Juan looks thinner today.

4 **Opuestos** Complete these sentences with the appropriate form of the verb **estar** and an antonym for the underlined adjective.

Modelo: Mis respuestas están bien, pero las de Susana están mal.

1. Las tiendas están abiertas, pero la agencia de viajes
2. No me gustan las habitaciones desordenadas. Incluso (*Even*) mi habitación de hotel
3. Nosotras estamos tristes cuando trabajamos. Hoy comienzan las vacaciones y
4. En esta ciudad los autobuses están sucios, pero los taxis
5. —El avión sale a las 5:30, ¿verdad?
   —No, estás confundida. Yo _____ de que el avión sale a las 5:00.

5 **En la playa** Describe what these people are doing. Complete the sentences using the present progressive tense.

Sr. Camacho   Leo
nosotros

1. El Sr. Camacho
2. Felicia
3. Leo
4. Nosotros

Recapitulación is an auto-gradable cumulative grammar section available for every lesson. The series of activities, moving from discrete to open-ended, systematically tests students' understanding of the lesson's grammar.

Students can choose to improve their score by watching the Grammar Tutorial again or by completing additional practice activities.

Vocabulario

Comparisons 4.1

Resources
e front matter for
tions on how to
rate all the program's
ents. See pages
1B for a detailed listing
her Resources online.

s Tip Ask students
are a list of the three
s or perspectives
rned about in this
to share with the class.
y ask them to focus
ally on the **Cultura**
orama sections.

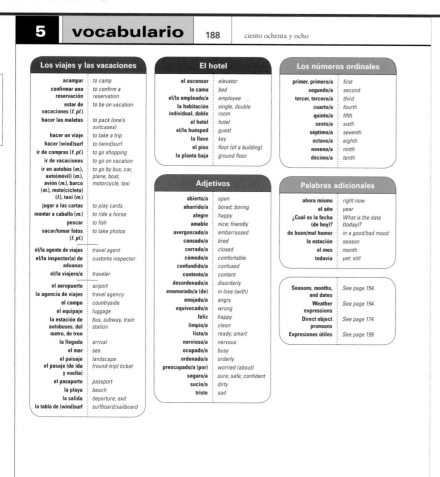

Los viajes y las vacaciones

acampar	to camp
confirmar una reservación	to confirm a reservation
estar de vacaciones (f. pl.)	to be on vacation
hacer las maletas	to pack (one's suitcases)
hacer un viaje	to take a trip
hacer (wind)surf	to (wind)surf
ir de compras (f. pl.)	to go shopping
ir de vacaciones	to go on vacation
ir en autobús (m.), auto(móvil) (m.), avión (m.), barco (m.), moto(cicleta) (f.), taxi (m.)	to go by bus, car, plane, boat, motorcycle, taxi
jugar a las cartas	to play cards
montar a caballo (m.)	to ride a horse
pescar	to fish
sacar/tomar fotos (f. pl.)	to take photos
el/la agente de viajes	travel agent
el/la inspector(a) de aduanas	customs inspector
el/la viajero/a	traveler
el aeropuerto	airport
la agencia de viajes	travel agency
el campo	countryside
el equipaje	luggage
la estación de autobuses, del metro, de tren	bus, subway, train station
la llegada	arrival
el mar	sea
el paisaje	landscape
el pasaje (de ida y vuelta)	(round-trip) ticket
el pasaporte	passport
la playa	beach
la salida	departure; exit
la tabla de (wind)surf	surfboard/sailboard

El hotel

el ascensor	elevator
la cama	bed
el/la empleado/a	employee
la habitación individual, doble	single, double room
el hotel	hotel
el/la huésped	guest
la llave	key
el piso	floor (of a building)
la planta baja	ground floor

Adjetivos

abierto/a	open
aburrido/a	bored; boring
alegre	happy
amable	nice; friendly
avergonzado/a	embarrassed
cansado/a	tired
cerrado/a	closed
cómodo/a	comfortable
confundido/a	confused
contento/a	content
desordenado/a	disorderly
enamorado/a (de)	in love (with)
enojado/a	angry
equivocado/a	wrong
feliz	happy
limpio/a	clean
listo/a	ready; smart
nervioso/a	nervous
ocupado/a	busy
ordenado/a	orderly
preocupado/a (por)	worried (about)
seguro/a	sure; safe; confident
sucio/a	dirty
triste	sad

Los números ordinales

primer, primero/a	first
segundo/a	second
tercer, tercero/a	third
cuarto/a	fourth
quinto/a	fifth
sexto/a	sixth
séptimo/a	seventh
octavo/a	eighth
noveno/a	ninth
décimo/a	tenth

Palabras adicionales

ahora mismo	right now
el año	year
¿Cuál es la fecha (de hoy)?	What is the date (today)?
de buen/mal humor	in a good/bad mood
la estación	season
el mes	month
todavía	yet; still

Seasons, months, and dates	See page 154.
Weather expressions	See page 154.
Direct object pronouns	See page 174.
Expresiones útiles	See page 159.

cher's Edition • Lesson Five

Vocabulario summarizes all the active vocabulary in the lesson that may appear in quizzes or tests.

Vocabulary lists are categorized by topic for efficient study. This organization provides a handy way for students to find the right word as they complete activities.

Students are responsible for words and expressions taught in the illustrations and *Más vocabulario* lists, as well as the *¡Atención!* sidebars. Encourage students to review vocabulary within the context of the lesson, as well as in these categorized lists to solidify acquisition of the words and phrases.

References are made at the end of the list to the *Expresiones útiles* from *Fotonovela* and grammar charts. Students are also responsible for learning these terms for formative assessment.

My Vocabulary enables students to identify, practice, and retain vocabulary for each lesson.

Students can print bilingual word lists. They can also create personalized word lists.

Interactive Flashcards featuring the Spanish word or expression (with audio) and the English translation are available for fast and effective review and practice.

Assessment: Options

Tailor a variety of formative and summative assessments to meet the needs of your students. Assessments include downloadable and printable grammar and vocabulary quizzes, lesson tests, and multi-lesson exams.

Minipruebas assess students' knowledge of lesson vocabulary and each grammar point. These open-ended quizzes provide students with an opportunity to demonstrate their understanding and proficiency with the lesson content.

Pruebas focus on the grammar, vocabulary, and theme of a lesson. These formal assessments consist of three different sets of testing material per lesson, with two versions per set.

PRUEBAS A & B	PRUEBAS C & D	PRUEBAS E & F
• Open-ended question format requiring students to write sentences and paragraphs. • Discrete question format. • The listening activity consists of narrations (commercials, radio broadcasts, etc.) and focuses on global comprehension, as well as key details.	• Briefer versions of **Prueba A**. • Open-ended question format. • The listening activity consists of personalized questions, designed to incorporate the lesson's vocabulary and grammar.	• Test students' mastery of lesson vocabulary and grammar. • Discrete question format. • Completely auto-gradable. • Same listening activity type as **Pruebas A** and **B**.

Note: All versions are interchangeable.

Exámenes are cumulative assessments that encompass the vocabulary, grammar points, and language functions. Each *Examen* begins with a listening comprehension, continues with achievement and proficiency-oriented vocabulary and grammar checks, and ends with a reading activity and a personalized writing task.

General Suggestions for Assessment

Writing Assessment

In each lesson, the *Adelante* section includes an *Escritura* page that introduces a writing strategy, which students apply as they complete the writing activity. The Teacher's Edition contains suggested rubrics for evaluating students' written work.

These activities also include suggestions for peer- and self-editing that will focus students' attention on what is important for attaining clarity in written communication.

The tests are also available on the Teacher Resources DVD and in the Resources library so that you can customize them by adding, eliminating, or moving items according to your classroom and student needs.

Portfolio Assessment

Portfolios can provide further valuable evidence of your students' learning. They are useful tools for evaluating students' progress in Spanish and also suggest to students how they are likely to be assessed in the real world. Since portfolio activities often comprise classroom tasks that you would assign as part of a lesson or as homework, you should think of the planning, selecting, recording, and interpreting of information about individual performance as a way of blending assessment with instruction.

You may find it helpful to refer to portfolio contents, such as drafts, essays, and samples of presentations when writing student reports and conveying the status of a student's progress to his or her parents.

Ask students regularly to consider which pieces of their own work they would like to share with family and friends, and help them develop criteria for selecting representative samples of essays, stories, poems, recordings of plays or interviews, mock documentaries, and so on. Prompt students to choose a variety of media in their activities wherever possible to demonstrate development in all four language skills. Encourage them to seek peer and parental input as they generate and refine criteria to help them organize and reflect on their own work.

Strategies for Differentiating Assessment

Here are some strategies for modifying tests and other forms of assessment according to your students' needs and for your own purposes in administering the assessment.

Adjust Questions Direct complex or higher-level questions to students who are equipped to answer them adequately and modify questions for students with greater needs. Always ask questions that elicit thinking, but keep in mind students' abilities.

Provide Tiered Assignments Assign tasks of varying complexity depending on individual student needs. Appealing to learners of different abilities and learning styles will allow you to foster a positive teaching environment.

Promote Flexible Grouping Encourage movement among groups of students so that all learners are appropriately challenged. Group students according to interest, oral proficiency levels, or learning styles.

Adjust Pacing Pace the sequence and speed of assessments to suit your students' learning needs. Time advanced learners to challenge them and allow slower-paced learners more time to complete tasks or answer questions.

"I Can" Statements

Students can assess their own progress by using "I Can" (or "Can-Do") Statements. The template below may be customized with the Student Objectives found in **Senderos** to guide student learning and to train students to assess their progress.

Editable worksheets are available in the Resources library.

"I Can" Statements

STUDENT OBJECTIVES
Lección 5 Senderos 1

Nombre _____   Fecha _____

Objetivos: Contextos	Fecha	¿Cómo voy?
1. I can discuss trips and tourist attractions with others.		
2. I can describe lodging and accommodations in Spanish.		
3. I can talk about security measures.		
4. I can exchange some information with others about accidents.		

¿Cómo voy?

4 ¡Excelente!: I know this well enough to teach it to someone.

3 Muy bien: I can do this with almost no mistakes.

2 Más o menos: I can do much of this but I have questions.

1 Es difícil: I can do this only with help.

0 ¡Ayúdame!: I can't do this, even with help.

Notas: _____

_____

_____

SENDEROS 1

Spanish for a Connected World

VISTA®
HIGHER LEARNING

Boston, Massachusetts

Publisher: José A. Blanco

Editorial Development: Armando Brito, Jhonny Alexander Calle, Deborah Coffey, María Victoria Echeverri, Jo Hanna Kurth, Megan Moran, Jaime Patiño, Raquel Rodríguez, Verónica Tejeda, Sharla Zwirek

Project Management: Cécile Engeln, Sally Giangrande

Rights Management: Ashley Dos Santos, Annie Pickert Fuller

Technology Production: Jamie Kostecki, Daniel Ospina, Paola Ríos Schaaf

Design: Radoslav Mateev, Gabriel Noreña, Andrés Vanegas

Production: Manuela Arango, Oscar Díez, Erik Restrepo

Student Text (Casebound-SIMRA) ISBN: 978-1-68005-190-2

Teacher's Edition ISBN: 978-1-68005-191-9

Library of Congress Control Number: 2016949696

1 2 3 4 5 6 7 8 9 TC 21 20 19 18 17 16

Printed in Canada.

SENDEROS 1

Spanish for a Connected World

Table of Contents

	Contextos	**Fotonovela**

Table of Contents

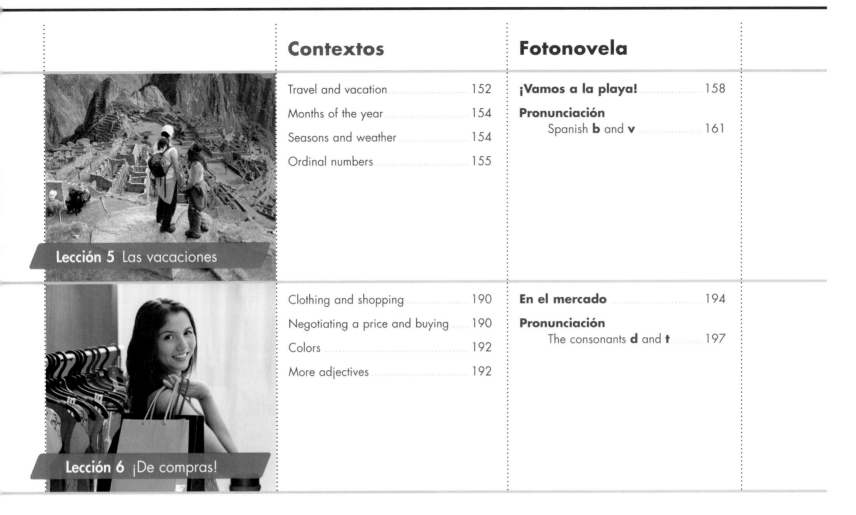

Icons

Familiarize yourself with these icons
that appear throughout **Senderos**.

◁))   Listening activity/section

⋔   Pair activity

The Spanish-Speaking World

OCÉANO ÁRTICO

Mar de Siberia Oriental

Mar de Beaufort

Bahía de Baffin

GROENLANDIA (DINAMARCA)

R U S I A

Alaska (EE.UU.)

60N

Mar de Bering

CANADÁ

Bahía de Hudson

Mar del Labrador

30N

ESTADOS UNIDOS

OCÉANO ATLÁNTICO

Trópico de Cáncer

MÉXICO

Golfo de México

ISLAS BAHAMAS

REPÚBLICA DOMINICANA

Islas Hawái (EE.UU.)

CUBA

PUERTO RICO (EE.UU.)

BELICE

HAITÍ

SAN CRISTÓBAL Y NIEVES

ISLAS MARSHALL

JAMAICA

SAN VICENTE Y LAS GRANADINAS

ANTIGUA Y BARBUDA

GUADALUPE (FRANCIA)

DOMINICA

GUATEMALA

EL SALVADOR

Mar Caribe

MARTINICA (FRANCIA)

HONDURAS

GRANADA

BARBADOS

SANTA LUCÍA

ESTADOS FEDERADOS DE MICRONESIA

OCÉANO PACÍFICO

NICARAGUA

COSTA RICA

PANAMÁ

VENEZUELA

TRINIDAD Y TOBAGO

GUAYANA FRANCESA (FRANCIA)

KIRIBATI

COLOMBIA

GUYANA

NAURU

Islas Galápagos (Ecuador)

ECUADOR

SURINAM

ISLAS SALOMÓN

ISLAS TUVALU

SAMOA OCCIDENTAL

PERÚ

BRASIL

VANUATU

FIYI

SAMOA ORIENTAL (EE.UU.)

BOLIVIA

APIA

Trópico de Capricornio

PARAGUAY

NUEVA CALEDONIA (FRANCIA)

Isla de Pascua (CHILE)

30S

URUGUAY

NUEVA ZELANDA

CHILE ARGENTINA

Islas Malvinas

El mundo

● Países hispanohablantes

● Países con alto número de hispanohablantes

60S

ANTÁRTIDA

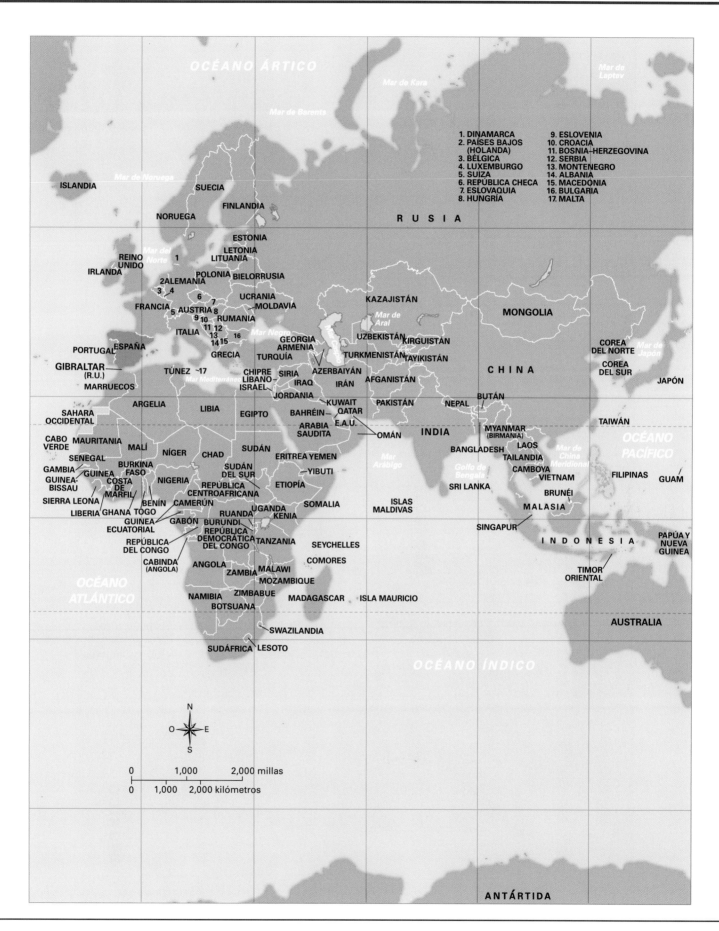

OCÉANO ÁRTICO

Mar de Kara

Mar de Laptev

Mar de Barents

Mar de Noruega

ISLANDIA

SUECIA

1. DINAMARCA
2. PAÍSES BAJOS (HOLANDA)
3. BÉLGICA
4. LUXEMBURGO
5. SUIZA
6. REPÚBLICA CHECA
7. ESLOVAQUIA
8. HUNGRÍA

9. ESLOVENIA
10. CROACIA
11. BOSNIA–HERZEGOVINA
12. SERBIA
13. MONTENEGRO
14. ALBANIA
15. MACEDONIA
16. BULGARIA
17. MALTA

NORUEGA

FINLANDIA

RUSIA

ESTONIA
LETONIA
LITUANIA

Mar del Norte

REINO UNIDO

IRLANDA

1

POLONIA
BIELORRUSIA

2 ALEMANIA

KAZAJISTÁN

MONGOLIA

3 4

6

UCRANIA

FRANCIA

7

5 AUSTRIA 8
9 10

MOLDAVIA

Mar de Aral

RUMANIA

11 12

UZBEKISTÁN
KIRGUISTÁN

COREA DEL NORTE

Mar de Japón

ITALIA

13
14 15

16

Mar Negro

GEORGIA
ARMENIA

Mar Caspio

TURKMENISTÁN
TAYIKISTÁN

CHINA

COREA DEL SUR

PORTUGAL

ESPAÑA

GRECIA

TURQUÍA

AZERBAIYÁN

JAPÓN

GIBRALTAR (R.U.)

TÚNEZ ~17

CHIPRE
LÍBANO

SIRIA

IRÁN

AFGANISTÁN

MARRUECOS

Mar Mediterráneo

ISRAEL

IRAQ

JORDANIA

KUWAIT

PAKISTÁN

NEPAL

BUTÁN

SAHARA OCCIDENTAL

ARGELIA

LIBIA

EGIPTO

BAHRÉIN

QATAR

E.A.U.

OMÁN

INDIA

TAIWÁN

ARABIA SAUDITA

MYANMAR (BIRMANIA)

OCÉANO PACÍFICO

CABO VERDE

MAURITANIA

MALÍ

NÍGER

CHAD

SUDÁN

ERITREA

YEMEN

Mar Arábigo

BANGLADESH

LAOS

Mar de China Meridional

SENEGAL

BURKINA FASO

SUDÁN DEL SUR

YIBUTI

TAILANDIA

GAMBIA

GUINEA

NIGERIA

CAMBOYA

FILIPINAS

GUAM

GUINEA-BISSAU

COSTA DE MARFIL

REPÚBLICA CENTROAFRICANA

ETIOPÍA

SRI LANKA

VIETNAM

SIERRA LEONA

BENÍN

CAMERÚN

SOMALIA

BRUNÉI

LIBERIA

GHANA TOGO

RUANDA

UGANDA

ISLAS MALDIVAS

MALASIA

GUINEA ECUATORIAL

GABÓN

BURUNDI

KENIA

REPÚBLICA DEL CONGO

REPÚBLICA DEMOCRÁTICA DEL CONGO

TANZANIA

SEYCHELLES

SINGAPUR

INDONESIA

PAPÚA Y NUEVA GUINEA

CABINDA (ANGOLA)

ANGOLA

ZAMBIA

MALAWI

COMORES

TIMOR ORIENTAL

MOZAMBIQUE

OCÉANO ATLÁNTICO

NAMIBIA

ZIMBABUE

MADAGASCAR

ISLA MAURICIO

BOTSUANA

AUSTRALIA

SWAZILANDIA

SUDÁFRICA

LESOTO

OCÉANO ÍNDICO

N

O   E

S

0   1,000   2,000 millas

0   1,000   2,000 kilómetros

ANTÁRTIDA

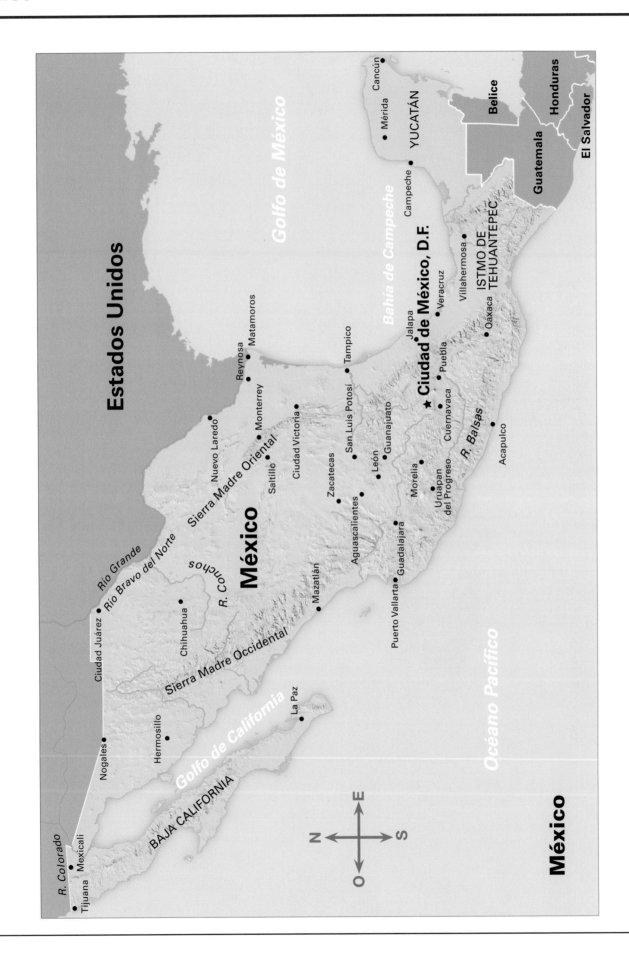

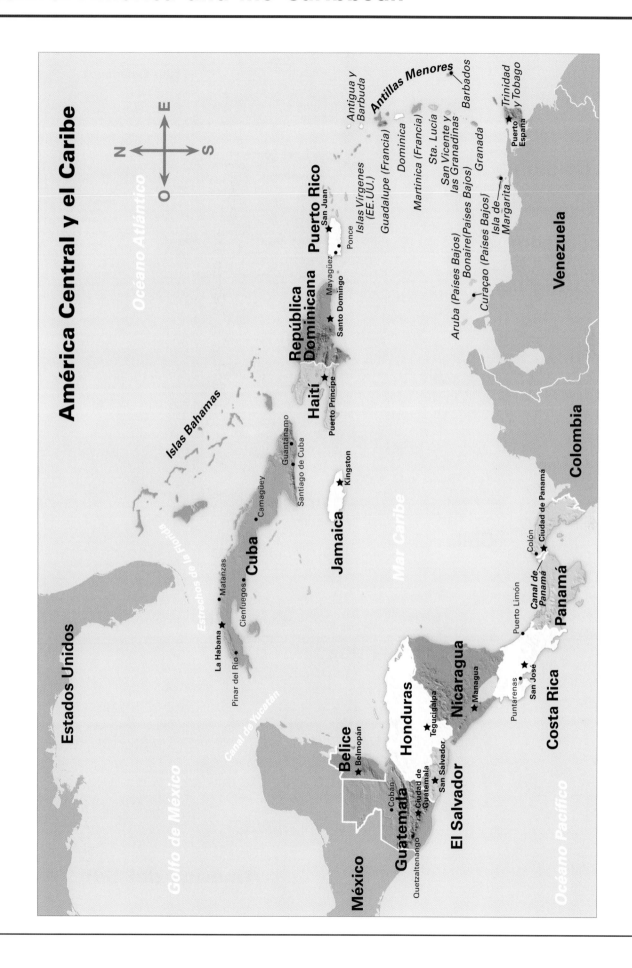

América Central y el Caribe

Estados Unidos

Golfo de México

Océano Atlántico

Islas Bahamas

Estrechos de la Florida

Canal de Yucatán

La Habana
Pinar del Río
Matanzas
Cienfuegos
Cuba
Camagüey
Santiago de Cuba
Guantánamo

México

Belice
Belmopán
Cobán
Ciudad de Guatemala
Guatemala
Quetzaltenango
San Salvador
El Salvador
Honduras
Tegucigalpa
Nicaragua
Managua

Costa Rica
San José
Puntarenas

Panamá
Puerto Limón
Colón
Ciudad de Panamá
Canal de Panamá

Océano Pacífico

Mar Caribe

Jamaica
Kingston

Haití
Puerto Príncipe

República Dominicana
Santo Domingo

Puerto Rico
San Juan
Ponce
Mayagüez

Islas Vírgenes (EE.UU.)

Antillas Menores

Antigua y Barbuda

Guadalupe (Francia)

Dominica

Martinica (Francia)

Sta. Lucía

San Vicente y las Granadinas

Granada

Barbados

Trinidad y Tobago
Puerto España

Aruba (Países Bajos)
Bonaire (Países Bajos)
Curaçao (Países Bajos)
Isla de Margarita

Colombia

Venezuela

N
E
O
S

South America

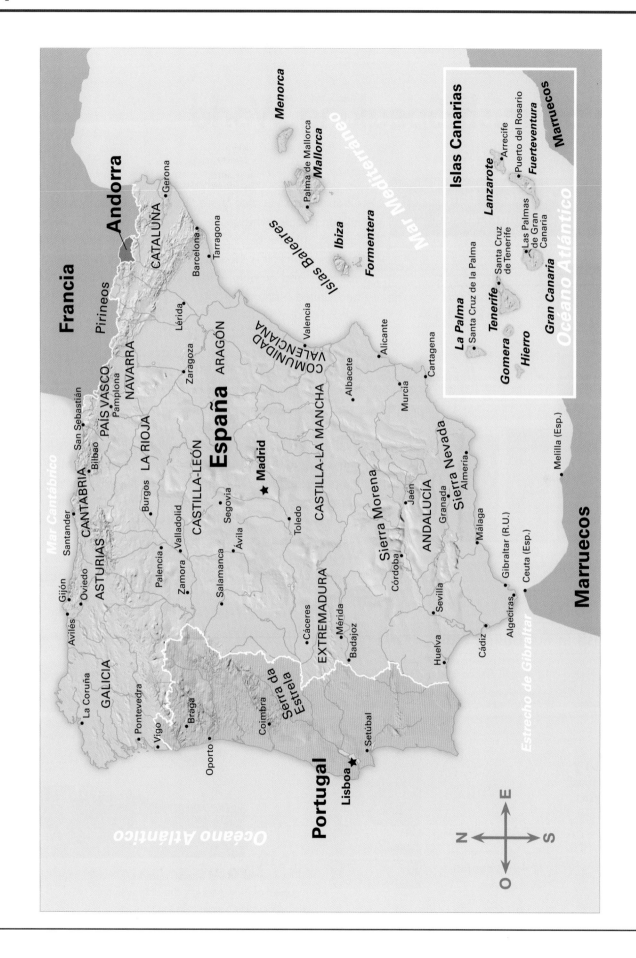

The Spanish-Speaking World

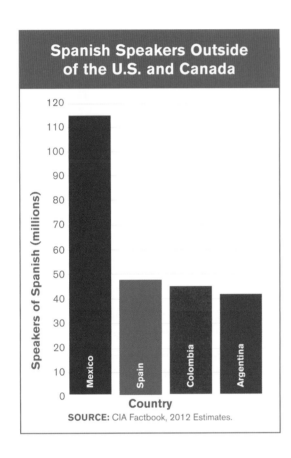

Spanish Speakers Outside of the U.S. and Canada

Speakers of Spanish (millions)

Country

SOURCE: CIA Factbook, 2012 Estimates.

Do you know someone whose first language is Spanish? Chances are you do! More than approximately forty million people living in the U.S. speak Spanish; after English, it is the second most commonly spoken language in this country. It is the official language of twenty-two countries and an official language of the European Union and United Nations.

The Growth of Spanish

Have you ever heard of a language called Castilian? It's Spanish! The Spanish language as we know it today has its origins in a dialect called Castilian (castellano in Spanish). Castilian developed in the 9th century in north-central Spain, in a historic provincial region known as Old Castile. Castilian gradually spread towards the central region of New Castile, where it was adopted as the main language of commerce. By the 16th century, Spanish had become the official language of Spain and eventually, the country's role in exploration, colonization, and overseas trade led to its spread across Central and South America, North America, the Caribbean, parts of North Africa, the Canary Islands, and the Philippines.

Spanish in the United States

1500   **1600**   **1700**

16th Century
Spanish is the official language of Spain.

1565
The Spanish arrive in Florida and found St. Augustine.

1610
The Spanish found Santa Fe, today's capital of New Mexico, the state with the most Spanish speakers in the U.S.

Spanish in the United States

Spanish came to North America in the 16th century with the Spanish who settled in St. Augustine, Florida. Spanish-speaking communities flourished in several parts of the continent over the next few centuries. Then, in 1848, in the aftermath of the Mexican-American War, Mexico lost almost half its land to the United States, including portions of modern-day Texas, New Mexico, Arizona, Colorado, California, Wyoming, Nevada, and Utah. Overnight, hundreds of thousands of Mexicans became citizens of the United States, bringing with them their rich history, language, and traditions.

This heritage, combined with that of the other Hispanic populations that have immigrated to the United States over the years, has led to the remarkable growth of Spanish around the country. After English, it is the most commonly spoken language in 43 states. More than 12 million people in California alone claim Spanish as their first or "home" language.

You've made a popular choice by choosing to take Spanish in school. Not only is Spanish found and heard almost everywhere in the United States, but it is the most commonly taught foreign language in classrooms throughout the country! Have you heard people speaking Spanish in your community? Chances are that you've come across an advertisement, menu, or magazine that is in Spanish. If you look around, you'll find that Spanish can be found in some pretty common places. For example, most ATMs respond to users in both English and Spanish. News agencies and television stations such as CNN and Telemundo provide Spanish-language broadcasts. When you listen to the radio or download music from the Internet, some of the most popular choices are Latino artists who perform in Spanish. Federal government agencies such as the Internal Revenue Service and the Department of State provide services in both languages. Even the White House has an official Spanish-language webpage! Learning Spanish can create opportunities within your everyday life.

1800   1900   2015

1848
Mexicans who choose to stay in the U.S. after the Mexican-American War become U.S. citizens.

1959
After the Cuban Revolution, thousands of Cubans emigrate to the U.S.

2015
Spanish is the 2nd most commonly spoken language in the U.S., with more than approximately 52.5 million speakers.

Why Study Spanish?

Learn an International Language

There are many reasons to learn Spanish, a language that has spread to many parts of the world and has along the way embraced words and sounds of languages as diverse as Latin, Arabic, and Nahuatl. Spanish has evolved from a medieval dialect of north-central Spain into the fourth most commonly spoken language in the world. It is the second language of choice among the majority of people in North America.

Understand the World Around You

Knowing Spanish can also open doors to communities within the United States, and it can broaden your understanding of the nation's history and geography. The very names Colorado, Montana, Nevada, and Florida are Spanish in origin. Just knowing their meanings can give you some insight into the landscapes for which the states are renowned. Colorado means "colored red;" Montana means "mountain;" Nevada is derived from "snow-capped mountain;" and Florida means "flowered." You've already been speaking Spanish whenever you talk about some of these states!

Connect with the World

Learning Spanish can change how you view the world. While you learn Spanish, you will also explore and learn about the origins, customs, art, music, and literature of people in close to two dozen countries. When you travel to a Spanish-speaking country, you'll be able to converse freely with the people you meet. And whether in the U.S., Canada, or abroad, you'll find that speaking to people in their native language is the best way to bridge any culture gap.

State Name	Meaning in Spanish
Colorado	"colored red"
Florida	"flowered"
Montana	"mountain"
Nevada	"snow-capped mountain"

Why Study Spanish?

Expand Your Skills

Studying a foreign language can improve your ability to analyze and interpret information and help you succeed in many other subject areas. When you first begin learning Spanish, your studies will focus mainly on reading, writing, grammar, listening, and speaking skills. You'll be amazed at how the skills involved with learning how a language works can help you succeed in other areas of study. Many people who study a foreign language claim that they gained a better understanding of English. Spanish can even help you understand the origins of many English words and expand your own vocabulary in English. Knowing Spanish can also help you pick up other related languages, such as Italian, Portuguese, and French. Spanish can really open doors for learning many other skills in your school career.

Explore Your Future

How many of you are already planning your future careers? Employers in today's global economy look for workers who know different languages and understand other cultures. Your knowledge of Spanish will make you a valuable candidate for careers abroad as well as in the United States or Canada. Doctors, nurses, social workers, hotel managers, journalists, businessmen, pilots, flight attendants, and many other professionals need to know Spanish or another foreign language to do their jobs well.

How to Learn Spanish

Start with the Basics!

As with anything you want to learn, start with the basics and remember that learning takes time! The basics are vocabulary, grammar, and culture.

Vocabulary | Every new word you learn in Spanish will expand your vocabulary and ability to communicate. The more words you know, the better you can express yourself. Focus on sounds and think about ways to remember words. Use your knowledge of English and other languages to figure out the meaning of and memorize words like **conversación, teléfono, oficina, clase,** and **música**.

Grammar | Grammar helps you put your new vocabulary together. By learning the rules of grammar, you can use new words correctly and speak in complete sentences. As you learn verbs and tenses, you will be able to speak about the past, present, or future, express yourself with clarity, and be able to persuade others with your opinions. Pay attention to structures and use your knowledge of English grammar to make connections with Spanish grammar.

Culture | Culture provides you with a framework for what you may say or do. As you learn about the culture of Spanish-speaking communities, you'll improve your knowledge of Spanish. Think about a word like **salsa**, and how it connects to both food and music. Think about and explore customs observed on **Nochevieja** (New Year's Eve) or at a **fiesta de quince años** (a girl's fifteenth birthday party). Watch people greet each other or say good-bye. Listen for idioms and sayings that capture the spirit of what you want to communicate!

Teenagers celebrating at a **fiesta de quince años.**

Listen, Speak, Read, and Write

Listening | Listen for sounds and for words you can recognize. Listen for inflections and watch for key words that signal a question such as **cómo** (*how*), **dónde** (*where*), or **qué** (*what*). Get used to the sound of Spanish. Play Spanish pop songs or watch Spanish movies. Borrow audiobooks from your local library, or try to visit places in your community where Spanish is spoken. Don't worry if you don't understand every single word. If you focus on key words and phrases, you'll get the main idea. The more you listen, the more you'll understand!

Speaking | Practice speaking Spanish as often as you can. As you talk, work on your pronunciation, and read aloud texts so that words and sentences flow more easily. Don't worry if you don't sound like a native speaker, or if you make some mistakes. Time and practice will help you get there. Participate actively in Spanish class. Try to speak Spanish with classmates, especially native speakers (if you know any), as often as you can.

Reading | Pick up a Spanish-language newspaper or a pamphlet on your way to school, read the lyrics of a song as you listen to it, or read books you've already read in English translated into Spanish. Use reading strategies that you know to understand the meaning of a text that looks unfamiliar. Look for cognates, or words that are related in English and Spanish, to guess the meaning of some words. Read as often as you can, and remember to read for fun!

Writing | It's easy to write in Spanish if you put your mind to it. And remember that Spanish spelling is phonetic, which means that once you learn the basic rules of how letters and sounds are related, you can probably become an expert speller in Spanish! Write for fun—make up poems or songs, write e-mails or instant messages to friends, or start a journal or blog in Spanish.

Tips for Learning Spanish

- Listen to Spanish radio shows and podcasts. Write down words that you can't recognize or don't know and look up the meaning.

- Watch Spanish TV shows, movies, or YouTube clips. Read subtitles to help you grasp the content.

- Read Spanish-language newspapers, magazines, or blogs.

- Listen to Spanish songs that you like —anything from Shakira to a traditional mariachi melody. Sing along and concentrate on your pronunciation.

- Seek out Spanish speakers. Look for neighborhoods, markets, or cultural centers where Spanish might be spoken in your community. Greet people, ask for directions, or order from a menu at a Mexican restaurant in Spanish.

- Pursue language exchange opportunities **(intercambio cultural)** in your school or community. Try to join language clubs or

Practice, practice, practice!

Seize every opportunity you find to listen, speak, read, or write Spanish. Think of it like a sport or learning a musical instrument—the more you practice, the more you will become comfortable with the language and how it works. You'll marvel at how quickly you can begin speaking Spanish and how the world that it transports you to can change your life forever!

cultural societies, and explore opportunities for studying abroad or hosting a student from a Spanish-speaking country in your home or school.

- Connect your learning to everyday experiences. Think about naming the ingredients of your favorite dish in Spanish. Think about the origins of Spanish place names in the U.S., like Cape Canaveral and Sacramento, or of common English words like *adobe*, *chocolate*, *mustang*, *tornado*, and *patio*.

- Use mnemonics, or a memorizing device, to help you remember words. Make up a saying in English to remember the order of the days of the week in Spanish (L, M, M, J, V, S, D).

- Visualize words. Try to associate words with images to help you remember meanings. For example, think of a **paella** as you learn the names of different types of seafood or meat. Imagine a national park and create mental pictures of the landscape as you learn names of animals, plants, and habitats.

- Enjoy yourself! Try to have as much fun as you can learning Spanish. Take your knowledge beyond the classroom and make the learning experience your own.

Useful Spanish Expressions

The following expressions will be very useful in getting you started learning Spanish. You can use them in class to check your understanding or to ask and answer questions about the lessons. Read En las **instrucciones** ahead of time to help you understand direction lines in Spanish, as well as your teacher's instructions. Remember to practice your Spanish as often as you can!

En las instrucciones *In direction lines*

Cierto o falso	*True or false*
Completa las oraciones de una manera lógica.	*Complete the sentences logically.*
Con un(a) compañero/a...	*With a classmate...*
Contesta las preguntas.	*Answer the questions.*
Corrige la información falsa.	*Correct the false information.*
Di/Digan...	*Say...*
En grupos...	*In groups...*
En parejas...	*In pairs...*
Entrevista...	*Interview...*
Forma oraciones completas.	*Create/Make complete sentences.*
Háganse preguntas.	*Ask each other questions.*
Haz el papel de...	*Play the role of...*
Haz los cambios necesarios.	*Make the necessary changes.*
Indica/Indiquen si las oraciones...	*Indicate if the sentences...*
Lee/Lean en voz alta.	*Read aloud.*
...que mejor completa...	*...that best completes...*
Toma nota...	*Take note...*
Tomen apuntes.	*Take notes.*
Túrnense...	*Take turns...*

Expresiones útiles *Useful expressions*

¿Cómo se dice _____ en español?	*How do you say _____ in Spanish?*
¿Cómo se escribe _____?	*How do you spell _____?*
¿Comprende(n)?	*Do you understand?*
Con permiso.	*Excuse me.*
De acuerdo.	*Okay.*
De nada.	*You're welcome.*
¿De veras?	*Really?*
¿En qué página estamos?	*What page are we on?*
Enseguida.	*Right away.*
Más despacio, por favor.	*Slower, please.*
Muchas gracias.	*Thanks a lot.*
No entiendo.	*I don't understand.*
No sé.	*I don't know.*
Perdone.	*Excuse me.*
Pista	*Clue*
Por favor.	*Please.*
Por supuesto.	*Of course.*
¿Qué significa _____?	*What does _____ mean?*
Repite, por favor.	*Please repeat.*
Tengo una pregunta.	*I have a question.*
¿Tiene(n) alguna pregunta?	*Do you have questions?*
Vaya(n) a la página dos.	*Go to page 2.*

Common Names

Get started learning Spanish by using a Spanish name in class. You can choose from the lists on these pages, or you can find one yourself. How about learning the Spanish equivalent of your name? The most popular Spanish female names are Lucía, María, Paula, Sofía, and Valentina. The most popular male names in Spanish are Alejandro, Daniel, David, Mateo, and Santiago. Is your name, or that of someone you know, in the Spanish top five?

Más nombres masculinos	Más nombres femeninos
Alfonso	Alicia
Antonio (Toni)	Beatriz (Bea, Beti, Biata)
Carlos	Blanca
César	Carolina (Carol)
Diego	Claudia
Ernesto	Diana
Felipe	Emilia
Francisco (Paco)	Irene
Guillermo	Julia
Ignacio (Nacho)	Laura
Javier (Javi)	Leonor
Leonardo	Liliana
Luis	Lourdes
Manolo	Margarita (Marga)
Marcos	Marta
Oscar (Óscar)	Noelia
Rafael (Rafa)	Patricia
Sergio	Rocío
Vicente	Verónica

Los 5 nombres masculinos más populares	Los 5 nombres femeninos más populares
Alejandro	Lucía
Daniel	María
David	Paula
Mateo	Sofía
Santiago	Valentina

Lección 1: Teacher Resources

There is a wealth of resources online to support instruction using **Senderos**. For details on how to integrate these Teacher Resources into your lessons, see the front matter of this Teacher's Edition on pages T16 to T48.

Presentation	Practice & Communicate	Assess*	Scripts and Translations	
• Digital Images: • **Hola, ¿qué tal?**	• Audio files for **Contextos** listening activities • Information Gap Activities* • Activity Pack Practice Activities (with Answer Key): **Contextos** • Additional Vocabulary (**Más vocabulario para la clase de español; Más vocabulario para los países**) • Digital Image Bank (Personal Interactions)	• Vocabulary Quiz (with Answer Key)		**contextos**
		• **Fotonovela** Optional Testing Sections (with Answer Key)	• **Fotonovela** Videoscript • **Fotonovela** English Translation	**fotonovela**
• **Estructura 1.1** Grammar Slides	• Activity Pack Practice Activities (with Answer Key): Nouns and articles • Surveys: Worksheet for survey	• Grammar 1.1 Quiz (with Answer Key)	• Tutorial Script: Nouns and articles	**estructura**
• **Estructura 1.2** Grammar Slides	• Activity Pack Practice Activities (with Answer Key): Numbers 0–30	• Grammar 1.2 Quiz (with Answer Key)	• Tutorial Script: Numbers 0–30	
• **Estructura 1.3** Grammar Slides	• Information Gap Activities* • Activity Pack Practice Activities (with Answer Key): Present tense of **ser**	• Grammar 1.3 Quiz (with Answer Key)	• Tutorial Script: Present tense of **ser**	
• **Estructura 1.4** Grammar Slides • Digital Images: • Telling time	• Information Gap Activities* • Activity Pack Practice Activities (with Answer Key): Telling time	• Grammar 1.4 Quiz (with Answer Key)	• Tutorial Script: Telling time	
			• **En pantalla** Videoscript • **En pantalla** English Translation	**En pantalla** / **adelante**
		• **Flash cultura** Optional Testing Sections (with Answer Key)	• **Flash cultura** Videoscript • **Flash cultura** English Translation	**Flash cultura**
Digital Images: • **Estados Unidos y Canadá**		• **Panorama** Optional Testing Sections (with Answer Key) • **Panorama cultural** (video)	• **Panorama cultural** Videoscript • **Panorama cultural** English Translation	**Panorama**

*Can also be assigned online.

Lección 1: Teacher Resources

Pulling It All Together

Practice and Communicate
- Role-plays
- Activity Pack Practice Activities (¡A repasar!) (with Answer Key)

Assessment

Tests and Exams*
- **Prueba A** with audio
- **Prueba B** with audio
- **Prueba C** with audio
- **Prueba D** with audio
- **Prueba E** with audio
- **Prueba F** with audio
- Tests Answer Key
- Oral Testing Suggestions

- **Examen A** with audio (lessons 1-3)
- **Examen B** with audio (lessons 1-3)
- Exams Answer Key

Audioscripts
- Tests and Exams Audioscripts
- Alternative Listening Sections Audioscript

Additional Tools for Planning and Teaching

- Essential Questions
- I Can Worksheets
- IPAs & Rubrics
- Lesson Plans
- Middle School Activity Pack
- Pacing Guides

Audio MP3s for Classroom Activities

- **Contextos. Práctica**: Activities 1 and 2 (p. 3)
- **Estructura** 1.4. **Comunicación**: Activity 4 (p. 27)
- **Escuchar** (p. 33)

Script for Comunicación: Actividad 4 (p. 27)

Laura   ¿A qué hora es la clase de español?
David   Es a las once y media.
Laura   ¿Y, a qué hora es la clase de historia?
David   Es a la una y cuarto.
Laura   Sí. Y la fiesta, ¿a qué hora es?
David   ¿La fiesta? ¿Hay una fiesta?
Laura   Sí. La fiesta de Rafael.
David   ¡Ah, sí! ¡Rafael! El chico de la clase de biología. La fiesta de Rafael es a las ocho.

*Tests and Exams can also be assigned online.

Hola, ¿qué tal?

1

Communicative Goals

You will learn how to:
- Greet people in Spanish
- Say goodbye
- Identify yourself and others
- Talk about the time of day

A PRIMERA VISTA
- Guess what the people on the photo are saying:
  a. Adiós. b. Hola. c. salsa
- Most likely they would also say:
  a. Gracias. b. fiesta c. Buenos días.
- The women are:
  a. amigas b. chicos c. señores

Lesson Goals

In **Lección 1**, students will be introduced to the following:
- terms for greetings and goodbyes
- identifying where one is from
- courtesy expressions
- greetings in the Spanish-speaking world
- the **plaza principal**
- nouns and articles (definite and indefinite)
- numbers 0–30
- present tense of **ser**
- telling time
- recognizing cognates
- reading a comic strip
- writing a telephone/address list in Spanish
- listening for known vocabulary
- a television commercial for MasterCard
- a video about **plazas** and greetings
- demographic and cultural information about Hispanics in the United States and Canada

A primera vista Have students look at the photo and ask them what they think the young people are doing. Explain that it is common in Hispanic cultures for friends to greet each other with one or two kisses on the cheek. As a class, discuss how friends typically greet each other in North America.

Teaching Tip You will see a series of icons pointing out communicative expansions, activities, and teaching tips in the teacher annotations. Follow this key:

→👤	**Interpretive communication**
←👤→	**Presentational communication**
👤↔👤	**Interpersonal communication**

SUPPORT FOR BACKWARD DESIGN

Lección 1 Essential Questions
1. How do people greet one another?
2. How do people make introductions?
3. What influence do Spanish speakers have in the U.S. and Canada?

Lección 1 Integrated Performance Assessment
Before teaching this chapter, review the Integrated Performance Assessment (IPA) and its accompanying scoring rubric. Use the IPA to assess students' progress toward proficiency targets at the end of the chapter.
IPA Context: You are meeting many students in Spanish class for the first time. You will prepare a brief presentation to introduce yourself to the class.

Voice boards online allow you and your students to record and share up to five minutes of audio. Use voice boards for presentations, oral assessments, discussions, directions, etc.

Section Goals

In **Contextos**, students will learn and practice:
• basic greetings
• introductions
• courtesy expressions

Communication 1.2
Comparisons 4.1

Teacher Resources
Read the front matter for suggestions on how to incorporate all the program's components. See pages 1A–1B for a detailed listing of Teacher Resources online.

In-Class Tips
• To familiarize students with lesson headings and vocabulary for classroom interactions, hand out **Vocabulario adicional: Más vocabulario para la clase de español** from the online Resources.
• Editable Lesson Plans are available in the online Resources.
• Use the **Lección 1 Contextos** vocabulary presentation online or the digital images in the Resources online to assist with this presentation.
• Write a few greetings, farewells, and courtesy expressions on the board, explain their meaning, and model their pronunciation. Circulate around the class, greeting students, making introductions, and encouraging responses. Then have students open to pages 2–3 and ask them to identify which conversations seem to be exchanges between friends and which seem more formal. Draw attention to the use of **usted** vs. **tú** in these conversations. Explain situations in which each form is appropriate.

Hola, ¿qué tal?

Más vocabulario

Buenos días.	*Good morning.*
Buenas noches.	*Good evening; Good night.*
Hasta la vista.	*See you later.*
Hasta pronto.	*See you soon.*
¿Cómo se llama usted?	*What's your name? (form.)*
Le presento a…	*I would like to introduce you to (name). (form.)*
Te presento a…	*I would like to introduce you to (name). (fam.)*
el nombre	*name*
¿Cómo estás?	*How are you? (fam.)*
No muy bien.	*Not very well.*
¿Qué pasa?	*What's happening?; What's going on?*
por favor	*please*
De nada.	*You're welcome.*
No hay de qué.	*You're welcome.*
Lo siento.	*I'm sorry.*
Gracias.	*Thank you; Thanks.*
Muchas gracias.	*Thank you very much; Thanks a lot.*

Variación léxica

Items are presented for recognition purposes only.

Buenos días.	⟷	Buenas.
De nada.	⟷	A la orden.
Lo siento.	⟷	Perdón.
¿Qué tal?	⟷	¿Qué hubo? (*Col.*)
Chau	⟷	Ciao; Chao

1

ELENA Patricia, le presento a Jorge Perales.
PATRICIA Encantada.
SEÑOR PERALES Igualmente. ¿De dónde es usted, señorita?
PATRICIA Soy de México. ¿Y usted?
SEÑOR PERALES De Puerto Rico.

2

TOMÁS ¿Qué tal, Alberto?
ALBERTO Regular. ¿Y tú?
TOMÁS Bien. ¿Qué hay de nuevo?
ALBERTO Nada.

3

SEÑOR VARGAS Buenas tardes, señora Wong. ¿Cómo está usted?
SEÑORA WONG Muy bien, gracias. ¿Y usted, señor Vargas?
SEÑOR VARGAS Bien, gracias.
SEÑORA WONG Hasta mañana, señor Vargas. Saludos a la señora Vargas.
SEÑOR VARGAS Adiós.

TEACHING OPTIONS

Extra Practice Bring in photos or magazine images of people greeting each other or saying goodbye. Ask pairs to write dialogue captions for each photo. Remind students to use formal and informal expressions as appropriate.

Groups Write questions and possible answers from the new set of expressions in **Contextos** on separate note cards. Give each student one note card and have them find the student with the matching card that completes their question/answer. Then have students work with other pairs to see if they can create a longer dialogue with their expressions.

Extra Practice Prepare name tags with a variety of different names, titles, and ages. Ex: **señora Lopez, 63; Carlos de la Vega, 22,** etc. Each student should wear a name tag and greet their peers according to the information on their tags.

Práctica

1 Escuchar Listen to each question or statement, then choose the correct response.

1. a. Muy bien, gracias.   b. Me llamo Graciela. b
2. a. Lo siento.   b. Mucho gusto. b
3. a. Soy de Puerto Rico.   b. No muy bien. a
4. a. No hay de qué.   b. Regular. a
5. a. Mucho gusto.   b. Hasta pronto. b
6. a. Nada.   b. Igualmente. a
7. a. Me llamo Guillermo Montero. b. Muy bien, gracias. b
8. a. Buenas tardes. ¿Cómo estás? b. El gusto es mío. a
9. a. Saludos a la Sra. Ramírez.   b. Encantada. b
10. a. Adiós.   b. Regular. b

2 Identificar You will hear a series of expressions. Identify the expression (**a**, **b**, **c**, or **d**) that does not belong in each series.

1. __c__   3. __b__
2. __a__   4. __c__

3 Escoger For each expression, write another word or phrase that expresses a similar idea.

> **modelo**
> ¿Cómo estás? *¿Qué tal?*

1. De nada. No hay de qué.   4. Hasta la vista. Hasta luego.
2. Encantado. Mucho gusto.   5. Mucho gusto. El gusto es mío.
3. Adiós. Chau o Hasta luego/mañana/pronto.

4 Ordenar Put this scrambled conversation in order.

—Muy bien, gracias. Soy Rosabel.
—Soy de México. ¿Y tú?
—Mucho gusto, Rosabel.
—Hola. Me llamo Carlos. ¿Cómo estás?
—Soy de Argentina.
—Igualmente. ¿De dónde eres, Carlos?

CARLOS   Hola. Me llamo Carlos. ¿Cómo estás?
ROSABEL   Muy bien, gracias. Soy Rosabel.
CARLOS   Mucho gusto, Rosabel.
ROSABEL   Igualmente. ¿De dónde eres, Carlos?
CARLOS   Soy de México. ¿Y tú?
ROSABEL   Soy de Argentina.

BERTA Hasta luego, Tere.
TERESA Chau, Berta. Nos vemos mañana.

CARMEN Buenas tardes. Me llamo Carmen. ¿Cómo te llamas tú?
ANTONIO Buenas tardes. Me llamo Antonio. Mucho gusto.
CARMEN El gusto es mío. ¿De dónde eres?
ANTONIO Soy de los Estados Unidos, de California.

5 In-Class Tip Have pairs share their responses with the class.

5 Expansion
👤↔👤 Have pairs or small groups create conversations that include the expressions used in **Actividad 5**. Ask volunteers to present their conversations to the class.

6 In-Class Tips
• Discuss the **modelo** before assigning the activity to pairs.
• 👤↔👤 After students have completed the activity, have pairs role-play the corrected mini-conversations. Ask them to substitute their own names and personal information where possible.
• Have volunteers write each mini-conversation on the board. Work as a class to identify and explain any errors.

¡Lengua viva! Have students locate examples of the titles in **Actividad 6**. Then ask them to create short sentences in which they use the titles with people they know.

5 **Completar** Complete these dialogues. Some answers will vary. Suggested answers:

> **modelo**
> ¿Cómo estás?
> Muy bien, gracias.

1. — Buenos días.
   — Buenos días. ¿Qué tal?

2. — ¿Cómo te llamas?
   — Me llamo Carmen Sánchez.

3. — ¿De dónde eres?
   — De Canadá.

4. — Te presento a Marisol.
   — Encantado/a.

5. — Gracias.
   — De nada.

6. — ¿Qué tal?
   — Regular.

7. — ¿Qué pasa?
   — Nada.

8. — ¡Hasta la vista!
   — Answers will vary.

6 **Cambiar** Correct the second part of each conversation to make it logical. Answers will vary.

> **modelo**
> ¿Qué tal?
> ~~No hay de qué.~~ Bien. ¿Y tú?

1. — Hasta mañana, señora Ramírez. Saludos al señor Ramírez.
   — *Muy bien, gracias.*

2. — ¿Qué hay de nuevo, Alberto?
   — *Sí, me llamo Alberto. ¿Cómo te llamas tú?*

3. — Gracias, Tomás.
   — *Regular. ¿Y tú?*

4. — Miguel, te presento a la señorita Perales.
   — *No hay de qué, señorita.*

5. — ¿De dónde eres, Antonio?
   — *Muy bien, gracias. ¿Y tú?*

6. — ¿Cómo se llama usted?
   — *El gusto es mío.*

7. — ¿Qué pasa?
   — *Hasta luego, Alicia.*

8. — Buenas tardes, señor. ¿Cómo está usted?
   — *Soy de Puerto Rico.*

◄ **¡LENGUA VIVA!**

The titles **señor**, **señora**, and **señorita** are abbreviated **Sr.**, **Sra.**, and **Srta.** Note that these abbreviations are capitalized, while the titles themselves are not.

•••

There is no Spanish equivalent for the English title *Ms.*; women are addressed as **señora** or **señorita**.

Comunicación

7 **Diálogos** With a partner, complete and role-play these conversations. Answers will vary.

Conversación 1

—Hola. Me llamo Teresa. ¿Cómo te llamas tú?

—_____

—Soy de Puerto Rico. ¿Y tú?

—_____

Conversación 2

—_____

—Muy bien, gracias. ¿Y usted, señora López?

—_____

—Hasta luego, señora. Saludos al señor López.

—_____

Conversación 3

—_____

—Regular. ¿Y tú?

—_____

—Nada.

8 **Conversaciones** This is the first day of class. Write four short conversations based on what the people in this scene would say. Answers will vary.

9 **Situaciones** With a partner, role-play these situations. Answers will vary.

1. On your way to the library, you strike up a conversation with another student. You find out the student's name and where he or she is from before you say goodbye.
2. At the library you meet up with a friend and find out how he or she is doing.
3. As you're leaving the library, you see your friend's father, Mr. Sánchez. You say hello and send greetings to Mrs. Sánchez.
4. Make up a real-life situation that you and your partner can role-play with the language you've learned.

TEACHING OPTIONS

Extra Practice ♦↔♦ Have students circulate around the classroom and conduct unrehearsed mini-conversations in Spanish with other students, using the words and expressions that they learned on pages 2–3. Monitor students' work and offer assistance if requested.

Heritage Speakers Ask heritage speakers to role-play some of the conversations and situations in these **Comunicación** activities, modeling correct pronunciation and intonation for the class. Remind students that, just as in English, there are regional differences in the way Spanish is pronounced. Help clarify unfamiliar vocabulary as necessary.

---

7 **Expansion**
• ←♦→ Have students work in small groups to write a few mini-conversations modeled on this activity. Then ask them to copy the dialogues, omitting a few words or phrases. Have groups exchange papers and fill in the blanks.
• Have students rewrite **Conversaciones 1** and **3** in the formal register and **Conversación 2** in the informal register.

7 **Virtual Chat**
♦↔♦ Available online.

8 **In-Class Tip** To simplify, have students brainstorm who the people in the illustration are and what they are talking about. Ask students which groups would be speaking to each other in the **usted** form, and which would be using the **tú** form.

8 **Expansion**
♦↔♦ In pairs, have students take turns selecting a person from the drawing and providing 2-3 statements that he or she might be saying. The partner will try to guess who it is.

9 **In-Class Tip**
♦↔♦ To challenge students, have each group pick a situation to write and perform. Tell groups not to memorize every word of the conversation, but rather to re-create it.

9 **Partner Chat**
♦↔♦ Available online.

The Affective Dimension
Have students rehearse the situations a few times, so that they will feel more comfortable with the material and less anxious when presenting it before the class.

Video Synopsis **Marissa**, an American college student, arrives in Mexico City for a year abroad. She meets her Mexican hosts, **Carolina** and **Roberto Díaz**, and their doorman, **Don Diego**. As **Marissa** unpacks, the **Díaz** children, **Felipe** and **Jimena**, take away her English-Spanish dictionary as a joke. **Marissa** accepts the challenge and leaves the dictionary with **Carolina**.

In-Class Tips
- In small groups, have students cover the captions and guess the plot based on the video stills. Write their predictions on the board. After students have watched the video, compare their predictions to what actually happened in the episode.
- Point out that **don** is a title of respect and neither equivalent nor related to the English name *Don*. Students will learn more about the titles **don** and **doña** on page 8.
- Tell students that all items in **Expresiones útiles** on page 7 are active vocabulary. Model the pronunciation of each item and have the class repeat.
- ♦↔♦ You can also practice the **Expresiones útiles** by using them in short conversations with individual students.

Bienvenida, Marissa

Marissa llega a México para pasar un año con la familia Díaz.

PERSONAJES   MARISSA   SRA. DÍAZ

MARISSA ¿Usted es de Cuba?

SRA. DÍAZ Sí, de La Habana. Y Roberto es de Mérida. Tú eres de Wisconsin, ¿verdad?

MARISSA Sí, de Appleton, Wisconsin.

MARISSA ¿Quiénes son los dos chicos de las fotos? ¿Jimena y Felipe?

SRA. DÍAZ Sí. Ellos son estudiantes.

DON DIEGO ¿Cómo está usted hoy, señora Carolina?

SRA. DÍAZ Muy bien, gracias. ¿Y usted?

DON DIEGO Bien, gracias.

DON DIEGO Buenas tardes, señora. Señorita, bienvenida a la Ciudad de México.

MARISSA ¡Muchas gracias!

SRA. DÍAZ Ahí hay dos maletas. Son de Marissa.

DON DIEGO Con permiso.

MARISSA ¿Cómo se llama usted?

DON DIEGO Yo soy Diego. Mucho gusto.

MARISSA El gusto es mío, don Diego.

DON DIEGO   **SR. DÍAZ**   **FELIPE**   **JIMENA**

SR. DÍAZ ¿Qué hora es?

FELIPE Son las cuatro y veinticinco.

SRA. DÍAZ Marissa, te presento a Roberto, mi esposo.

SR. DÍAZ Bienvenida, Marissa.

MARISSA Gracias, señor Díaz.

JIMENA ¿Qué hay en esta cosa?

MARISSA Bueno, a ver, hay tres cuadernos, un mapa... ¡Y un diccionario!

JIMENA ¿Cómo se dice mediodía en inglés?

FELIPE "Noon".

FELIPE Estás en México, ¿verdad?

MARISSA ¿Sí?

FELIPE Nosotros somos tu diccionario.

Expresiones útiles

Identifying yourself and others

¿Cómo se llama usted?
What's your name?
Yo soy Diego, el portero. Mucho gusto.
I'm Diego, the doorman. Nice to meet you.
¿Cómo te llamas?
What's your name?
Me llamo Marissa.
My name is Marissa.
¿Quién es...? / ¿Quiénes son...?
Who is...? / Who are...?
Es mi esposo.
He's my husband.
Tú eres..., ¿verdad?/¿cierto?/¿no?
You are..., right?

Identifying objects

¿Qué hay en esta cosa?
What's in this thing?
Bueno, a ver, aquí hay tres cuadernos...
Well, let's see, here are three notebooks...
Oye/Oiga, ¿cómo se dice *suitcase* en español?
Hey, how do you say suitcase in Spanish?
Se dice *maleta*.
You say maleta.

Saying what time it is

¿Qué hora es?
What time is it?
Es la una. / Son las dos.
It's one o'clock. / It's two o'clock.
Son las cuatro y veinticinco.
It's four twenty-five.

Polite expressions

Con permiso.
Pardon me; Excuse me.
(to request permission)
Perdón.
Pardon me; Excuse me. (to get someone's attention or excuse yourself)
¡Bienvenido/a! *Welcome!*

Expresiones útiles Identify forms of the verb **ser** and point out some subject pronouns. Identify time-telling expressions. Point out the verb form **hay** and explain that it means *there is/are*. Tell students that they will learn more about these concepts in **Estructura**.

In-Class Tip
👤↔👤 Have volunteers read individual parts of the **Fotonovela** captions aloud. Then have students work in groups of six to role-play the episode, ad-libbing when possible. Have one or two groups present the episode to the class.

Successful Language Learning Tell students that their conversational skills will grow more quickly as they learn each lesson's **Expresiones útiles**. This feature is designed to teach phrases that will be useful in conversation, and it will also help students understand key phrases in each **Fotonovela**.

Nota cultural Mexico City's metropolitan area is the largest in the hemisphere, with about 21 million people. This number is still only a fraction of Mexico's total population of 125 million. It is the most highly populated Spanish-speaking country in the world.

Extra Practice →👤← Photocopy pages 6–7 or the **Fotonovela** Videoscript (Supersite) and white out some key words. Play the episode once, and then distribute the photocopied scripts. Play the video a second time and ask students to fill in the missing words. Go over the answers as a class.

Extra Practice Write questions and phrases from **Expresiones útiles** on the board. Ex: **Es la una. Con permiso. ¿Cómo te llamas?**

With their books closed, have students describe a context in which each question or phrase could be used.

Pairs In pairs, have students predict whom **Marissa** will get along with better: **Felipe** or **Jimena**. Have them support their opinions with specific scenes from the episode.

¿Qué pasó?

1 **¿Cierto o falso?** Indicate if each statement is **cierto** or **falso**. Then correct the false statements.

		Cierto	Falso	
1.	La Sra. Díaz es de Caracas.	○	✓	La Sra. Díaz es de La Habana.
2.	El Sr. Díaz es de Mérida.	✓	○	
3.	Marissa es de Los Ángeles, California.	○	✓	Marissa es de Appleton, Wisconsin.
4.	Jimena y Felipe son profesores.	○	✓	Jimena y Felipe son estudiantes.
5.	Las dos maletas son de Jimena.	○	✓	Las dos maletas son de Marissa.
6.	El Sr. Díaz pregunta "¿qué hora es?".	✓	○	
7.	Hay un diccionario en la mochila (*backpack*) de Marissa.	✓	○	

2 **Identificar** Indicate which person would make each statement. One name will be used twice.

1. Son las cuatro y veinticinco, papá.   Felipe
2. Roberto es mi esposo.   Sra. Díaz
3. Yo soy de Wisconsin, ¿de dónde es usted?   Marissa
4. ¿Qué hay de nuevo, doña Carolina?   don Diego
5. Yo soy de Cuba.   Sra. Díaz
6. ¿Qué hay en la mochila, Marissa?   Jimena

MARISSA   FELIPE   SRA. DÍAZ

DON DIEGO   JIMENA

¡LENGUA VIVA!

In Spanish-speaking countries, **don** and **doña** are used with first names to show respect: **don Diego**, **doña Carolina**. Note that these titles, like **señor** and **señora**, are not capitalized.

3 **Completar** Complete the conversation between Don Diego and Marissa.

DON DIEGO Hola, (1)___señorita___.
MARISSA Hola, señor. ¿Cómo se (2)___llama___ usted?
DON DIEGO Yo me llamo Diego, ¿y (3)___usted___?
MARISSA Yo me llamo Marissa. (4)___Encantada___.
DON DIEGO (5)___Igualmente___, señorita Marissa.
MARISSA Nos (6)___vemos___, don Diego.
DON DIEGO Hasta (7)___luego/pronto/la vista___, señorita Marissa.

4 **Conversar** Imagine that you are chatting with a traveler you just met at the airport. With a partner, prepare a conversation using these cues. Some answers will vary.

Estudiante 1	Estudiante 2
Say "good afternoon" to your partner and ask for his or her name.	→ Say hello and what your name is. Then ask what your partner's name is.
Say what your name is and that you are glad to meet your partner.	→ Say that the pleasure is yours.
Ask how your partner is.	→ Say that you're doing well, thank you.
Ask where your partner is from.	→ Say where you're from.
Say it's one o'clock and say goodbye.	→ Say goodbye.

Teacher's notes (left margin):

1 Expansion Give students these true/false statements as items 8–10: **8. En la mochila de Marissa hay una foto de Jimena y Felipe. (Cierto.) 9. No hay cuadernos en la mochila de Marissa. (Falso.) 10. Hay cuatro personas en la familia Díaz. (Cierto.)**

2 Expansion Ask volunteers to call out additional statements that were made in the **Fotonovela**. The class should guess which character made each statement.

¡Lengua viva! Ask students how they might address **Sr. Díaz** (**don Roberto**).

Nota cultural Señor(a) and **señorita** may also be used with a person's first name as a sign of respect. Using these titles with a first name also shows a greater level of intimacy or warmth; **señor Díaz** sounds more formal than **señor Roberto**.

3 In-Class Tip Go over the activity by asking volunteers to take the roles of **don Diego** and **Marissa**.

4 Possible Conversation
E1: Buenas tardes. ¿Cómo te llamas?
E2: Hola. Me llamo Felipe. Y tú, ¿cómo te llamas?
E1: Me llamo Luisa. Mucho gusto.
E2: El gusto es mío.
E1: ¿Cómo estás?
E2: Bien, gracias.
E1: ¿De dónde eres?
E2: Soy de Venezuela.
E2: ¡Uf! Es la una. ¡Adiós!
E2: Chau.

4 Partner Chat
♟↔♟ Available online.

The Affective Dimension
Point out that many people feel nervous when speaking in front of a group. Encourage students to think of anxious feelings as extra energy that will help them accomplish their goals.

TEACHING OPTIONS

Small Groups ♟↔♟ Ask students to work in small groups to ad-lib the exchanges between **Marissa** and **Sra. Díaz**, **Marissa** and **don Diego**, and **Marissa, Felipe,** and **Jimena.** Tell them to convey the general meaning using vocabulary and expressions they know, and assure them that they do not have to stick to the original dialogues word for word. Then, ask volunteers to present their exchanges to the class.

Extra Practice →♟← Choose four or five lines of the **Fotonovela** to use as a dictation. Read the lines twice slowly to give students sufficient time to write. Then read them again at normal speed to allow students to correct any errors or fill in any gaps. You may have students correct their own work by checking it against the **Fotonovela** text and ask follow-up questions to test comprehension.

Pronunciación
The Spanish alphabet

Section Goals

In **Pronunciación**, students will be introduced to:
• the Spanish alphabet
• the names of the letters

Comparisons 4.1

The Spanish and English alphabets are almost identical, with a few exceptions. For example, the Spanish letter **ñ (eñe)** doesn't occur in the English alphabet. Furthermore, the letters **k (ka)** and **w (doble ve)** are used only in words of foreign origin. Examine the chart below to find other differences.

In-Class Tip Point out that the **Real Academia Española** has decided that **ch** and **ll** are no longer letters. In 2010 the **Real Academia** recommended the use of a unified naming convention for the alphabet. The suggested names for **r, v, w,** and **y** are **erre, uve, doble uve,** and **ye**. However, most Spanish speakers tend to use the traditional naming conventions followed in their countries.

¡LENGUA VIVA!

Note that **ch** and **ll** are digraphs, or two letters that together produce one sound. Conventionally they have been considered part of the alphabet, but **ch** and **ll** do not have their own entries when placing words in alphabetical order, as in a glossary.

AYUDA

The letter combination **rr** produces a strong trilled sound which does not have an English equivalent. English speakers commonly make this sound when imitating the sound of a motor. This sound occurs with the **rr** between vowels and with the **r** at the beginning of a word: **puertorriqueño, terrible, Roberto,** etc. See **Lección 7,** p. 233 for more information.

Letra	Nombre(s)	Ejemplos	Letra	Nombre(s)	Ejemplos
a	a	adiós	m	eme	mapa
b	be	bien, problema	n	ene	nacionalidad
c	ce	cosa, cero	ñ	eñe	mañana
ch	che	chico	o	o	once
d	de	diario, nada	p	pe	profesor
e	e	estudiante	q	cu	qué
f	efe	foto	r	ere	regular, señora
g	ge	gracias, Gerardo, regular	s	ese	señor
h	hache	hola	t	te	tú
i	i	igualmente	u	u	usted
j	jota	Javier	v	ve	vista, nuevo
k	ka, ca	kilómetro	w	doble ve	walkman
l	ele	lápiz	x	equis	existir, México
ll	elle	llave	y	i griega, ye	yo
			z	zeta, ceta	zona

El alfabeto Repeat the Spanish alphabet and example words after your teacher.

Práctica Spell these words aloud in Spanish.

1. nada
2. maleta
3. quince
4. muy
5. hombre
6. por favor
7. San Fernando
8. Estados Unidos
9. Puerto Rico
10. España
11. Javier
12. Ecuador
13. Maite
14. gracias
15. Nueva York

Refranes Read these sayings aloud

Ver es creer.[1]

En boca cerrada no entran moscas.[2]

1 Seeing is believing.
2 Silence is golden.

TEACHING OPTIONS

Extra Practice Do a dictation activity in which you spell aloud Spanish words (e.g., world capitals and countries). Spell each word twice to allow students sufficient time to write. After you have finished, write your list on the board or project it on a transparency and have students check their work. You can also have students spell their names in Spanish.

Extra Practice Here are four additional **refranes** to practice the alphabet: **De tal palo, tal astilla** (*A chip off the old block*); **Los ojos son el espejo del alma** (*Eyes are the window to the soul*); **El rayo nunca cae dos veces en el mismo lugar** (*Lightning never strikes twice in the same place*); **No dejes para mañana lo que puedas hacer hoy** (*Don't put off until tomorrow what you can do today*).

Section Goals

In **Cultura**, students will:
• read about greetings in Spanish-speaking countries
• learn informal greetings and leave-takings
• read about the **plaza principal**
• read about famous friends and couples

Communication 1.1, 1.2
Cultures 2.1, 2.2
Connections 3.1, 3.2
Comparisons 4.2

En detalle

Antes de leer Ask students to share how they would normally greet a friend or family member.

Lectura
• Linguists have determined that, in the U.S., friends generally remain at least eighteen inches apart while chatting. Hispanic friends would probably deem eighteen inches to be excessive.
• Show students the locations mentioned here by referring them to the maps in their textbooks. Explain that there may be regional variations within each country.
• Explain that an "air kiss" is limited to a grazing of cheeks.

Después de leer Call on two volunteers to stand in front of the class. Point out the natural distance between them. Then demonstrate reduced personal space in Hispanic cultures by having the volunteers face each other with their toes touching and start a conversation. Tell the rest of the class to do the same. Ask students to share their feelings on this change in personal space.

1 Expansion Ask students to write three more true/false statements for a classmate to complete.

EN DETALLE

Saludos y besos en los países hispanos

In Spanish-speaking countries, kissing on the cheek is a customary way to greet friends and family members. Even when people are introduced for the first time, it is common for them to kiss, particularly in non-business settings. Whereas North Americans maintain considerable personal space when greeting, Spaniards and Latin Americans tend to decrease their personal space and give one or two kisses (**besos**) on the cheek, sometimes accompanied by a handshake or a hug. In formal business settings, where associates do not know one another on a personal level, a simple handshake is appropriate.

Greeting someone with a **beso** varies according to gender and region. Men generally greet each other with a hug or warm handshake, with the exception of Argentina, where male friends and relatives lightly kiss on the cheek. Greetings between men and women, and between women, generally include kissing, but can differ depending on the country and context. In Spain, it is customary to give **dos besos**, starting with the right cheek first. In Latin American countries, including Mexico, Costa Rica, Colombia, and Chile, a greeting consists of a single "air kiss" on the right cheek. Peruvians also "air kiss," but  strangers will simply shake hands. In Colombia, female acquaintances tend to simply pat each other on the right forearm or shoulder.

Tendencias

País	Beso	País	Beso
Argentina	💋	España	💋💋
Bolivia	💋	México	💋
Chile	💋	Paraguay	💋💋
Colombia	💋	Puerto Rico	💋
El Salvador	💋	Venezuela	💋/💋💋

ACTIVIDADES

1 **¿Cierto o falso?** Indicate whether these statements are true (cierto) or false (falso). Correct the false statements.

1. In Spanish-speaking countries, people use less personal space when greeting than in the U.S. **Cierto.**

2. Men never greet with a kiss in Spanish-speaking countries. **Falso.** Argentine men can greet with a light kiss.

3. Shaking hands is not appropriate for a business setting in Latin America. **Falso.** In most business settings, people greet one another by shaking hands.

4. Spaniards greet with one kiss on the right cheek. **Falso.** They greet with one kiss on each cheek.

5. In Mexico, people greet with an "air kiss." **Cierto.**

6. Gender can play a role in the type of greeting given. **Cierto.**

7. If two women acquaintances meet in Colombia, they should exchange two kisses on the cheek. **Falso.** They pat one another on the right forearm or shoulder.

8. In Peru, a man and a woman meeting for the first time would probably greet each other with an "air kiss." **Falso.** They would probably shake hands.

TEACHING OPTIONS

Game Divide the class into two teams. Give situations in which people greet one another, and have one member from each team identify the appropriate way to greet. Ex: Two male friends in Argentina. (light kiss on the cheek) Give one point for each correct answer. The team with the most points at the end wins.

Un beso Kisses are not only a form of greeting in Hispanic cultures. It is also common to end phone conversations and close letters or e-mails with the words **un beso** or **besos**. Additionally, friends may use **un abrazo** to end a written message. In a more formal e-mail, one can write **un saludo (cordial)** or **saludos**.

ASÍ SE DICE

Saludos y despedidas

¿Cómo te/le va?	How are things going (for you)?
¡Cuánto tiempo!	It's been a long time!
Hasta ahora.	See you soon.
¿Qué hay?	What's new?
¿Qué onda? (Méx., Arg., Chi.); ¿Qué más? (Ven., Col.)	What's going on?

EL MUNDO HISPANO

Parejas y amigos famosos

Here are some famous couples and friends from the Spanish-speaking world.

- **Penélope Cruz** (España) y **Javier Bardem** (España) Both Oscar-winning actors, the couple married in 2010. They starred together in *Vicky Cristina Barcelona* (2008).

- **Gael García Bernal** (México) y **Diego Luna**  (México) These lifelong friends became famous when they starred in the 2001 Mexican film *Y tu mamá también*. They continue to work together on projects, such as the 2012 film *Casa de mi padre.*

- **Salma Hayek** (México) y **Penélope Cruz** (España) These two close friends developed their acting skills in their home countries before meeting in Hollywood.

PERFIL

La plaza principal

In the Spanish-speaking world, public space is treasured. Small city and town life revolves around the **plaza principal**. Often surrounded by cathedrals or municipal buildings like the **ayuntamiento** (*city hall*), the pedestrian **plaza** is designated as a central meeting place for family and friends. During warmer months, when outdoor cafés usually line the **plaza**, it is

La Plaza Mayor de Salamanca

a popular spot to have a leisurely cup of coffee, chat, and people watch. Many town festivals, or **ferias**, also take place in this space. One of the most famous town squares

is the **Plaza Mayor** in the university town of Salamanca, Spain. Students gather underneath its famous clock tower to meet up with friends or simply take a coffee break.

La Plaza de Armas, Lima, Perú

Conexión Internet

What are the plazas principales in large cities such as Mexico City and Caracas?

Use the Web to find more cultural information related to this **Cultura** section.

ACTIVIDADES

2 **Comprensión** Answer these questions. *Some answers may vary. Suggested answers:*
1. What are two types of buildings found on the **plaza principal?** *municipal buildings and cathedrals*
2. What two types of events or activities are common at a **plaza principal?** *meeting with friends and festivals*
3. How would Diego Luna greet his friends? *¿Qué onda?*
4. Would Salma Hayek and Gael García Bernal greet each other with one kiss or two? *one*

3 **Saludos** Role-play these greetings with a partner. *Role-plays will vary according to student gender.*
1. friends in Mexico
2. business associates at a conference in Chile
3. friends meeting in Madrid's Plaza Mayor
4. Peruvians meeting for the first time
5. relatives in Argentina

Section Goals

In **Estructura 1.1**, students will be introduced to:
- gender of nouns
- definite and indefinite articles

 Comparisons 4.1

Teacher Resources
Read the front matter for suggestions on how to incorporate all the program's components. See pages 1A–1B for a detailed listing of Teacher Resources online.

In-Class Tips
- Write these nouns from the **Fotonovela** on the board: **chicos, diccionario, estudiantes, maleta.** Ask volunteers what each means. Point out the different endings and introduce grammatical gender in Spanish. Explain what a noun is and give examples of people (**chicos**), places (**comunidad**), things (**documentos**), and ideas (**nacionalidad**). Ask volunteers to point out which of these nouns are singular or plural and why.
- Point out that while nouns for male beings are generally masculine and those for female beings are generally feminine, grammatical gender does not necessarily correspond to the actual gender of the being.
- Point out patterns of noun endings **–o, –a; –or, –ora.** Stress that **–ista** can refer to males or females, and give additional examples: **el/la artista, el/la dentista.**

1.1 Nouns and articles

Spanish nouns

ANTE TODO A noun is a word used to identify people, animals, places, things, or ideas. Unlike English, all Spanish nouns, even those that refer to non-living things, have gender; that is, they are considered either masculine or feminine. As in English, nouns in Spanish also have number, meaning that they are either singular or plural.

Nouns that refer to living things

Masculine nouns		Feminine nouns	
el hombre	*the man*	**la mujer**	*the woman*
ending in –o		*ending in –a*	
el chico	*the boy*	**la chica**	*the girl*
el pasajero	*the (male) passenger*	**la pasajera**	*the (female) passenger*
ending in –or		*ending in –ora*	
el conductor	*the (male) driver*	**la conductora**	*the (female) driver*
el profesor	*the (male) teacher*	**la profesora**	*the (female) teacher*
ending in –ista		*ending in –ista*	
el turista	*the (male) tourist*	**la turista**	*the (female) tourist*

▶ Generally, nouns that refer to males, like **el hombre**, are masculine, while nouns that refer to females, like **la mujer**, are feminine.

▶ Many nouns that refer to male beings end in **–o** or **–or.** Their corresponding feminine forms end in **–a** and **–ora**, respectively.

el conductor

la profesora

▶ The masculine and feminine forms of nouns that end in **–ista**, like **turista**, are the same, so gender is indicated by the article **el** (masculine) or **la** (feminine). Some other nouns have identical masculine and feminine forms.

el joven	**la** joven
the young man	*the young woman*
el estudiante	**la** estudiante
the (male) student	*the (female) student*

¡LENGUA VIVA!

Profesor(a) and **turista** are *cognates*— words that share similar spellings and meanings in Spanish and English. Recognizing cognates will help you determine the meaning of many Spanish words. Here are some other cognates:
**la administración,
el animal,
el apartamento,
el cálculo, el color,
la decisión, la historia,
la música,
el restaurante,
el/la secretario/a.**

AYUDA

Cognates can certainly be very helpful in your study of Spanish. Beware, however, of "false" cognates, those that have similar spellings in Spanish and English, but different meanings:
la carpeta *folder*
el/la conductor(a) *driver*
el éxito *success*
la fábrica *factory*

TEACHING OPTIONS

Extra Practice Write ten singular nouns on the board. Make sure the nouns represent a mix of the different types of noun endings. In a rapid-response drill, call on students to give the appropriate gender. For **–ista** words, accept either masculine or feminine, but clarify that both are used. You may also do this as a completely oral drill by not writing the words on the board.

Game Divide the class into teams of three or four. Bring in photos or magazine pictures showing objects or people. Hold up each photo and say the Spanish noun without the article. Call on teams to indicate the noun's gender. Give one point for each correct answer. Deduct one point for each incorrect answer. The team with the most points at the end wins.

Nouns that refer to non-living things

Masculine nouns

ending in –o

el cuaderno	the notebook
el diario	the diary
el diccionario	the dictionary
el número	the number
el video	the video

ending in –ma

| el problema | the problem |
| el programa | the program |

ending in –s

| el autobús | the bus |
| el país | the country |

Feminine nouns

ending in –a

la computadora	the computer
la cosa	the thing
la escuela	the school
la maleta	the suitcase
la palabra	the word

ending in –ción

| la lección | the lesson |
| la conversación | the conversation |

ending in –dad

| la nacionalidad | the nationality |
| la comunidad | the community |

¡LENGUA VIVA!

The Spanish word for *video* can be pronounced with the stress on the **i** or the **e**. For that reason, you might see the word written with or without an accent: **video** or **vídeo**.

▶ As shown above, certain noun endings are strongly associated with a specific gender, so you can use them to determine if a noun is masculine or feminine.

▶ Because the gender of nouns that refer to non-living things cannot be determined by foolproof rules, you should memorize the gender of each noun you learn. It is helpful to learn each noun with its corresponding article, **el** for masculine and **la** for feminine.

▶ Another reason to memorize the gender of every noun is that there are common exceptions to the rules of gender. For example, **el mapa** (*map*) and **el día** (*day*) end in **–a**, but are masculine. **La mano** (*hand*) ends in **–o**, but is feminine.

Plural of nouns

▶ To form the plural, add **–s** to nouns that end in a vowel. For nouns that end in a consonant, add **–es**. For nouns that end in **z**, change the **z** to **c**, then add **–es**.

el chic**o** ⟶ los chic**os**   la nacionalida**d** ⟶ las nacionalida**des**

el diari**o** ⟶ los diari**os**   el paí**s** ⟶ los país**es**

el problem**a** ⟶ los problem**as**   el lápi**z** (*pencil*) ⟶ los lápi**ces**

CONSULTA

You will learn more about accent marks in **Lección 4, Pronunciación**, p. 123.

▶ In general, when a singular noun has an accent mark on the last syllable, the accent is dropped from the plural form.

la lecci**ón** ⟶ las lecci**ones**   el autob**ús** ⟶ los autob**uses**

▶ Use the masculine plural form to refer to a group that includes both males and females.

1 pasajer**o** + 2 pasajer**as** = 3 pasajer**os**   2 chic**os** + 2 chic**as** = 4 chic**os**

In-Class Tips

• Work through the list of nouns, modeling their pronunciation. Point out patterns of gender, including word endings **–ma**, **–ción**, and **–dad**. Give cognate nouns with these endings and ask students to indicate the gender. Ex: **diagrama**, **acción**, **personalidad**. Point out common exceptions to gender agreement rules for **el mapa, el día**, and **la mano**.

• Stress the addition of **–s** to nouns that end in vowels and **–es** to nouns that end in consonants. Write ten nouns on the board and ask volunteers to give the plural forms, along with the appropriate articles.

• Point to three male students and ask if the group is **los** or **las estudiantes** (**los**). Next, point to three female students and ask the same question (**las**). Then indicate a group of males and females and ask for the correct term to refer to them (**los estudiantes**). Stress that even if a group contains 100 women and one man, the masculine plural form and article are used.

• Point out that words like **lección** and **autobús** lose the written accent in the plural form in order to keep the stress on the same syllable as in the singular noun.

The Affective Dimension
Tell students that many people feel anxious when learning grammar. Tell them that grammar will seem less intimidating if they think of it as a description of how the language works instead of a list of strict rules.

TEACHING OPTIONS

TPR Give four students each a card with a different definite article. Give the other students each a card with a noun (include a mix of masculine, feminine, singular, and plural). Have students form a circle; each student's card should be visible to others. Call out one of the nouns; that student must step forward. The student with the corresponding article has five seconds to join the noun student.

Game Divide the class into two teams, A and B. Point to a member of team A and say a singular noun. The student repeats the noun with the definite article, and then spells it. Then point to a team B member, who will supply the plural form and spell it. Award one point per correct answer and deduct one point for each wrong answer. Make sure to give each team a variety of both plural and singular nouns. The team with the most points wins.

Spanish articles

ANTE TODO   As you know, English often uses definite articles (*the*) and indefinite articles (*a, an*) before nouns. Spanish also has definite and indefinite articles. Unlike English, Spanish articles vary in form because they agree in gender and number with the nouns they modify.

Definite articles

▶ Spanish has four forms that are equivalent to the English definite article *the*. Use definite articles to refer to specific nouns.

Masculine		Feminine	
SINGULAR	PLURAL	SINGULAR	PLURAL
el diccionario	**los** diccionarios	**la** computadora	**las** computadoras
the dictionary	*the dictionaries*	*the computer*	*the computers*

Indefinite articles

▶ Spanish has four forms that are equivalent to the English indefinite article, which according to context may mean *a, an,* or *some*. Use indefinite articles to refer to unspecified persons or things.

Masculine		Feminine	
SINGULAR	PLURAL	SINGULAR	PLURAL
un pasajero	**unos** pasajeros	**una** fotografía	**unas** fotografías
a (one) passenger	*some passengers*	*a (one) photograph*	*some photographs*

¡INTÉNTALO!   Provide a definite article for each noun in the first column and an indefinite article for each noun in the second column.

¿el, la, los o las?	¿un, una, unos o unas?
1. _la_ chica	1. _un_ autobús
2. _el_ chico	2. _unas_ escuelas
3. _la_ maleta	3. _una_ computadora
4. _los_ cuadernos	4. _unos_ hombres
5. _el_ lápiz	5. _una_ señora
6. _las_ mujeres	6. _unos_ lápices

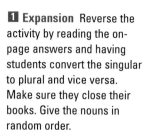

Práctica

1 **¿Singular o plural?** If the word is singular, make it plural. If it is plural, make it singular.

1. el número los números
2. un diario unos diarios
3. la estudiante las estudiantes
4. el conductor los conductores
5. el país los países
6. las cosas la cosa
7. unos turistas un turista
8. las nacionalidades la nacionalidad
9. unas computadoras una computadora
10. los problemas el problema
11. una fotografía unas fotografías
12. los profesores el profesor
13. unas señoritas una señorita
14. el hombre los hombres
15. la maleta las maletas
16. la señora las señoras

1 Expansion Reverse the activity by reading the on-page answers and having students convert the singular to plural and vice versa. Make sure they close their books. Give the nouns in random order.

2 **Identificar** For each drawing, provide the noun with its corresponding definite and indefinite articles.

 modelo
las maletas, unas maletas

1. la computadora, una computadora

2. los cuadernos, unos cuadernos

3. las mujeres, unas mujeres

4. el chico, un chico

5. la escuela, una escuela

6. las fotos, unas fotos

7. los autobuses, unos autobuses

8. el diario, un diario

2 Expansion As an additional visual exercise, bring in photos or magazine pictures that illustrate items whose names students know. Ask students to indicate the definite article and the noun. Include a mix of singular and plural nouns. Repeat the exercise with indefinite articles.

Comunicación

3 **Un juego** With a partner, play a game in which one of you names a noun and the other says a related noun (**un chico; un estudiante**). Keep the chain going until one of you can't think of another noun.

 Communication 1.1

3 Expansion
• Split the class into two teams to act out a game of charades using the vocabulary from the lesson. Give a point to each team for correctly guessing the charade. The team with the most points wins.
• Model the game by writing some new cognates on the board (Ex: **la guitarra, el teléfono, la televisión**). Emphasize that the students acting out the charade must not speak and that he or she may show the number of syllables using his/her fingers.

3 Partner Chat
🏃↔🏃 Available online.

TEACHING OPTIONS

Video →🏃← Show the **Fotonovela** episode again to offer more input on singular and plural nouns and articles. With their books closed, have students write down every noun and article that they hear. After viewing the video, ask volunteers to list the nouns and articles they heard. Explain that the **las** used when telling time refers to **las horas** (Ex: **Son las cinco = Son las cinco horas**).

Extra Practice →🏃← To challenge students, slowly read aloud a short passage from a novel, story, poem, or newspaper article written in Spanish, preferably one with a great number of nouns and articles. As a listening exercise, have students write down every noun and article they hear, even unfamiliar ones (the articles may cue when nouns appear).

Section Goals

In **Estructura 1.2**, students will be introduced to:
- numbers 0–30
- the verb form **hay**

 Comparisons 4.1

Teacher Resources
Read the front matter for suggestions on how to incorporate all the program's components. See pages 1A–1B for a detailed listing of Teacher Resources online.

In-Class Tips
- Introduce numbers by asking students if they can count to ten in Spanish. Model the pronunciation of each number. Write individual numbers on the board and call on students at random to say the number.
- Say numbers aloud at random and have students hold up the appropriate number of fingers. Then reverse the drill; hold up varying numbers of fingers at random and ask students to shout out the corresponding number in Spanish.
- Emphasize the variable forms of **uno** and **veintiuno**, giving examples of each. Ex: **veintiún profesores, veintiuna profesoras.**
- Ask questions like these: **¿Cuántos estudiantes hay en la clase? (Hay ____ estudiantes en la clase.)**

1.2 Numbers 0–30

Los números 0 a 30

0	cero				
1	uno	11	once	21	veintiuno
2	dos	12	doce	22	veintidós
3	tres	13	trece	23	veintitrés
4	cuatro	14	catorce	24	veinticuatro
5	cinco	15	quince	25	veinticinco
6	seis	16	dieciséis	26	veintiséis
7	siete	17	diecisiete	27	veintisiete
8	ocho	18	dieciocho	28	veintiocho
9	nueve	19	diecinueve	29	veintinueve
10	diez	20	veinte	30	treinta

AYUDA

Though it is less common, the numbers 16 through 29 (except 20) can also be written as three words: **diez y seis, diez y siete…**

▶ The number **uno** (*one*) and numbers ending in **–uno**, such as **veintiuno**, have more than one form. Before masculine nouns, **uno** shortens to **un**. Before feminine nouns, **uno** changes to **una**.

un hombre ⟶ veinti**ún** hombres   una mujer ⟶ veinti**una** mujeres

▶ **¡Atención!** The forms **uno** and **veintiuno** are used when counting (**uno, dos, tres… veinte, veintiuno, veintidós…**). They are also used when the number *follows* a noun, even if the noun is feminine: **la lección uno.**

▶ To ask *how many people* or *things* there are, use **cuántos** before masculine nouns and **cuántas** before feminine nouns.

▶ The Spanish equivalent of both *there is* and *there are* is **hay**. Use **¿Hay…?** to ask *Is there…?* or *Are there…?* Use **no hay** to express *there is not* or *there are not*.

—**¿Cuántos** estudiantes **hay**?
How many students are there?

—**Hay** seis estudiantes en la foto.
There are six students in the photo.

—**¿Hay** chicos en la fotografía?
Are there guys in the picture?

—**Hay** tres chicas y **no hay** chicos.
There are three girls, and there are no guys.

¡INTÉNTALO!   Provide the Spanish words for these numbers.

1. **7** _siete_
2. **16** _dieciséis_
3. **29** _veintinueve_
4. **1** _uno_
5. **0** _cero_
6. **15** _quince_
7. **21** _veintiuno_
8. **9** _nueve_
9. **23** _veintitrés_
10. **11** _once_
11. **30** _treinta_
12. **4** _cuatro_
13. **12** _doce_
14. **28** _veintiocho_
15. **14** _catorce_
16. **10** _diez_

TEACHING OPTIONS

TPR Assign ten students a number from 0–30 and line them up in front of the class. Call out one of the numbers at random, and have the student assigned that number step forward. When two students have stepped forward, ask them to repeat their numbers. Then ask individuals to add (Say: **Suma**) or subtract (Say: **Resta**) the two numbers, giving the result in Spanish.

Game Ask students to write B-I-N-G-O across the top of a blank piece of paper. Have them draw five squares vertically under each letter and randomly fill in the squares with numbers from 0–30, without repeating any numbers. Draw numbers from a hat and call them out in Spanish. The first student to mark five in a row (horizontally, vertically, or diagonally) yells **¡Bingo!** and wins. Have the winner confirm the numbers for you in Spanish.

Práctica

1 **Contar** Following the pattern, write out the missing numbers in Spanish.

1. 1, 3, 5, ..., 29　7, 9, 11, 13, 15, 17, 19, 21, 23, 25, 27
2. 2, 4, 6, ..., 30　8, 10, 12, 14, 16, 18, 20, 22, 24, 26, 28
3. 3, 6, 9, ..., 30　12, 15, 18, 21, 24, 27
4. 30, 28, 26, ..., 0　24, 22, 20, 18, 16, 14, 12, 10, 8, 6, 4, 2
5. 30, 25, 20, ..., 0　15, 10, 5
6. 28, 24, 20, ..., 0　16, 12, 8, 4

2 **Resolver** Solve these math problems.

> **modelo**
> 5 + 3 =
> *Cinco más tres son ocho.*

AYUDA

+　→　**más**
−　→　**menos**
=　→　**son**

1. **2 + 15 =** Dos más quince son diecisiete.
2. **20 − 1 =** Veinte menos uno son diecinueve.
3. **5 + 7 =** Cinco más siete son doce.
4. **18 + 12 =** Dieciocho más doce son treinta.
5. **3 + 22 =** Tres más veintidós son veinticinco.
6. **6 − 3 =** Seis menos tres son tres.
7. **11 + 12 =** Once más doce son veintitrés.
8. **7 − 2 =** Siete menos dos son cinco.
9. **8 + 5 =** Ocho más cinco son trece.
10. **23 − 14 =** Veintitrés menos catorce son nueve.

3 **¿Cuántos hay?** How many persons or things are there in these drawings?

> **modelo**
> Hay tres maletas.

1. Hay veinte lápices.

2. Hay un hombre.

Chicos

3. Hay veinticinco chicos.

4. Hay una conductora.

5. Hay cuatro fotos.

6. Hay treinta cuadernos.

7. Hay seis turistas.

Chicas

8. Hay diecisiete chicas.

TEACHING OPTIONS

TPR Give ten students each a card that contains a different number from 0–30. The cards should be visible to the other students. Then call out simple math problems (addition or subtraction) involving the assigned numbers. When the first two numbers are called, each student steps forward. The student whose assigned number completes the math problem then has five seconds to join them.

Extra Practice Ask questions about your school and the town or city in which it is located. Ex: **¿Cuántos profesores hay en el departamento de español? ¿Cuántas escuelas hay en _____? ¿Cuántas pizzerías hay en _____?** Encourage students to guess the number. If a number exceeds 30, write that number on the board and model its pronunciation.

---

1 In-Class Tips
• Before beginning the activity, make sure students know each pattern: odds (**los números impares**), evens (**los números pares**), count by threes (**contar de tres en tres**).
• To simplify, write complete patterns out on the board.

1 Expansion Explain that a prime number (**un número primo**) is any number that can only be divided by itself and 1. To challenge students, ask the class to list the prime numbers up to 30. (They are: 1, 2, 3, 5, 7, 11, 13, 17, 19, 23, 29.)

2 Expansion Do simple multiplication problems. Introduce the phrases **multiplicado por** and **dividido por**. Ex: **Cinco multiplicado por cinco son...** (veinticinco). **Veinte dividido por cuatro son...** (cinco).

3 In-Class Tip Have students read the directions and the model. Cue student responses by asking questions related to the drawings. Ex: **¿Cuántos lápices hay? (Hay veinte lápices.)**

3 Expansion Add an additional visual aspect to this activity. Hold up or point to classroom objects and ask how many there are. Since students will not know the names of many items, a simple number or **hay** + the number will suffice to signal comprehension. Ex: —**¿Cuántas plumas hay aquí?** —**(Hay) Dos.**

Comunicación

4 **¿Cuántos?** Answer your partner's questions about the place where you study.   Answers will vary.

1. ¿Cuántos estudiantes hay?   6. ¿Cuántos lápices hay?

2. ¿Hay un video?   7. ¿Hay cuadernos?

3. ¿Hay una computadora?   8. ¿Cuántos diccionarios hay?

4. ¿Hay una maleta?   9. ¿Hay un diario?

5. ¿Cuántos mapas hay?   10. ¿Cuántas fotografías hay?

5 **Preguntas** With a partner, take turns asking and answering questions about the drawing.
Talk about: Answers will vary.

1. how many children there are   6. if there is a bus

2. how many women there are   7. if there are tourists

3. if there are some photographs   8. how many pencils there are

4. if there is a boy   9. if there is a man

5. how many notebooks there are   10. how many computers there are

---

4 **In-Class Tip** For items 3, 4, 7, and 9, ask students: **¿Cuántos/as hay?** If there are no examples of the item listed, students should say: **No hay _____.**

4 **Expansion** After completing the activity, call on individuals to give rapid responses for the same items. To challenge students, mix up the order of items.

4 **Virtual Chat**
👤↔👤 Available online.

5 **In-Class Tip** Remind students that they will be forming sentences with **hay** and a number. Give them four minutes to do the activity. You might also have students write out their answers.

5 **Expansion** After pairs have finished analyzing the drawing, call on individuals to respond. Convert the statements into questions in Spanish. Ask: **¿Cuántos chicos hay? ¿Cuántas mujeres hay?**

5 **Expansion**
👤↔👤 Have students work in pairs to role-play conversations between one of the family members in the drawing and an exchange student that has come to live with them. Encourage students to use phrases they learned in **Contextos**, as well as simple questions about the host family, such as **¿Cuántas personas hay en la casa?**

5 **Partner Chat**
👤↔👤 Available online.

Pairs 👤↔👤 Have each student draw a scene similar to the one on this page. Of course, stick figures are perfectly acceptable! Give them three minutes to draw the scene. Encourage students to include multiple numbers of particular items (**cuadernos, maletas, lápices**). Then have pairs take turns describing what is in their partner's picture. The student who created the drawing should ask questions to verify the accuracy of the description.

Pairs Divide the class into pairs. Give half of the pairs magazine pictures that contain images of familiar words or cognates. Give the other half written descriptions of the pictures, using **hay**. Ex: **En la foto hay dos mujeres, un chico y una chica.** Have pairs circulate around the room to match the descriptions with the corresponding pictures.

1.3 | # Present tense of *ser*

Subject pronouns

ANTE TODO In order to use verbs, you will need to learn about subject pronouns. A subject pronoun replaces the name or title of a person and acts as the subject of a verb.

Subject pronouns

SINGULAR		PLURAL	
yo	*I*	**nosotros**	*we* (masculine)
		nosotras	*we* (feminine)
tú	*you* (familiar)	**vosotros**	*you* (masc., fam.)
usted (Ud.)	*you* (formal)	**vosotras**	*you* (fem., fam.)
		ustedes (Uds.)	*you*
él	*he*	**ellos**	*they* (masc.)
ella	*she*	**ellas**	*they* (fem.)

¡LENGUA VIVA!

In Latin America, **ustedes** is used as the plural for both **tú** and **usted**. In Spain, however, **vosotros** and **vosotras** are used as the plural of **tú**, and **ustedes** is used only as the plural of **usted**.

• • •

Usted and **ustedes** are abbreviated as **Ud.** and **Uds.**, or occasionally as **Vd.** and **Vds.**

▶ Spanish has two subject pronouns that mean *you* (singular). Use **tú** when addressing a friend, a family member, or a child you know well. Use **usted** to address a person with whom you have a formal or more distant relationship, such as a superior at work, a teacher, or an older person.

Tú eres de Canadá, ¿verdad, David?
You are from Canada, right, David?

¿**Usted** es la profesora de español?
Are you the Spanish teacher?

▶ The masculine plural forms **nosotros**, **vosotros**, and **ellos** refer to a group of males or to a group of males and females. The feminine plural forms **nosotras**, **vosotras**, and **ellas** can refer only to groups made up exclusively of females.

nosotros, vosotros, ellos   nosotros, vosotros, ellos   nosotras, vosotras, ellas

▶ There is no Spanish equivalent of the English subject pronoun *it*. Generally *it* is not expressed in Spanish.

Es un problema.
It's a problem.

Es una computadora.
It's a computer.

Section Goals

In **Estructura 1.3**, students will be introduced to:
• subject pronouns
• the present tense of the verb **ser**
• the uses of **ser** (to identify, to indicate possession, to describe origin, and to talk about professions or occupations)

 Comparisons 4.1

Teacher Resources
Read the front matter for suggestions on how to incorporate all the program's components. See pages 1A–1B for a detailed listing of Teacher Resources online.

In-Class Tips
• Point to yourself and say: **Yo soy profesor(a)**. Then point to a student and ask: ¿**Tú eres profesor(a) o estudiante?** (estudiante) Say: **Sí, tú eres estudiante**. Indicate the whole class and tell them: **Ustedes son estudiantes**. Once the pattern has been established, include other subject pronouns and forms of **ser** while indicating other students. Ex: **Él es...**, **Ella es...**, **Ellos son...**
• Review familiar and formal forms of address students learned in **Contextos**.
• You may want to point out that while **usted** and **ustedes** are second person forms of address equivalent to the English *you*, they take third person verb forms.

Note: While the **vosotros/as** forms are listed in verb paradigms in **Senderos**, they will not be actively practiced.

TEACHING OPTIONS

Extra Practice Indicate people in the classroom and have students give subject pronouns based on their point of view. Ex: Point to yourself (**usted**), a female student (**ella**), everyone in the class (**nosotros**).

Extra Practice Ask students to indicate whether certain people would be addressed as **tú** or **usted**. Ex: A roommate, a friend's grandfather, a doctor, a neighbor's child.

Heritage Speakers Ask heritage speakers how they address elder members of their family, such as parents, grandparents, aunts, and uncles—whether they use **tú** or **usted**. Also ask them if they use **vosotros/as** (they typically will not unless they or their family are from Spain) or **voseo**. Explain that **voseo** is the use of the second-person subject pronoun **vos** instead of **tú**. It is used extensively in much of Latin America, including Argentina, Uruguay, and Costa Rica.

The present tense of ser

ANTE TODO   In **Contextos** and **Fotonovela**, you have already used several present-tense forms of **ser** (*to be*) to identify yourself and others, and to talk about where you and others are from. **Ser** is an irregular verb; its forms do not follow the regular patterns that most verbs follow. You need to memorize the forms, which appear in this chart.

The verb ser (*to be*)

SINGULAR FORMS	yo	**soy**	*I am*
	tú	**eres**	*you are* (fam.)
	Ud./él/ella	**es**	*you are* (form.); *he/she is*
PLURAL FORMS	nosotros/as	**somos**	*we are*
	vosotros/as	**sois**	*you are* (fam.)
	Uds./ellos/ellas	**son**	*you are; they are*

Uses of *ser*

▶ Use **ser** to identify people and things.

—¿Quién **es** él?
Who is he?

—**Es** Felipe Díaz Velázquez.
He's Felipe Díaz Velázquez.

—¿Qué **es**?
What is it?

—**Es** un mapa de España.
It's a map of Spain.

Es Marissa.

Es una maleta.

▶ **Ser** also expresses possession, with the preposition **de**. There is no Spanish equivalent of the English construction [*noun*] + 's (*Maru's*). In its place, Spanish uses [*noun*] + **de** + [*owner*].

—¿**De** quién **es**?
Whose is it?

—**Es** el diario **de** Maru.
It's Maru's diary.

—¿**De** quién **son**?
Whose are they?

—**Son** los lápices **de** la chica.
They are the girl's pencils.

▶ When **de** is followed by the article **el**, the two combine to form the contraction **del**. **De** does *not* contract with **la**, **las**, or **los**.

—**Es** la computadora **del** conductor.
It's the driver's computer.

—**Son** las maletas **del** chico.
They are the boy's suitcases.

▶ **Ser** also uses the preposition **de** to express origin.

¿De dónde eres?

Yo soy de Wisconsin.

¿De dónde es usted?

Yo soy de Cuba.

—¿**De** dónde **es** Juan Carlos?
Where is Juan Carlos from?

—Es **de** Argentina.
He's from Argentina.

—¿**De** dónde **es** Maru?
Where is Maru from?

—Es **de** Costa Rica.
She's from Costa Rica.

▶ Use **ser** to express profession or occupation.

Don Francisco **es conductor**.
Don Francisco is a driver.

Yo **soy estudiante**.
I am a student.

▶ Unlike English, Spanish does not use the indefinite article (**un, una**) after **ser** when referring to professions, unless accompanied by an adjective or other description.

Marta **es** profesora.
Marta is a teacher.

Marta **es una** profesora excelente.
Marta is an excellent teacher.

Somos Perú

LanPerú

¡INTÉNTALO!   Provide the correct subject pronouns and the present forms of **ser**.

1. Gabriel — él — es
2. Juan y yo — nosotros — somos
3. Óscar y Flora — ellos — son
4. Adriana — ella — es
5. las turistas — ellas — son
6. el chico — él — es
7. los conductores — ellos — son
8. los señores Ruiz — ellos — son

1 **In-Class Tip** Review **tú** and **usted**, asking students which pronoun they would use in a formal situation and which they would use in an informal situation.

1 **Expansion** Once students have identified the correct subject pronouns, ask them to give the form of **ser** they would use when *addressing* each person and when *talking about* each person.

2 **Expansion** Give additional names of well-known Spanish speakers and ask students to tell where they are from. Have students give the country names in English if they do not know the Spanish equivalent. Ex: **¿De dónde es Javier Bardem? (Es de España.)**

3 **In-Class Tips**
- To simplify, before beginning the activity, guide students in identifying the objects.
- You might tell students to answer the second part of the question (**¿De quién es?**) with any answer they wish. Have students take turns asking and answering questions.

Práctica

1 **Pronombres** What subject pronouns would you use to (a) talk *to* these people directly and (b) talk *about* them to others?

> **modelo**
> un joven   tú, él

1. una chica   tú, ella
2. el presidente de México   Ud., él
3. tres chicas y un chico   Uds., ellos
4. un estudiante   tú, él
5. la señora Ochoa   Ud., ella
6. dos profesoras   Uds., ellas

2 **Identidad y origen** Answer these questions about the people indicated: **¿Quién es?/¿Quiénes son?** and **¿De dónde es?/¿De dónde son?**

> **modelo**
> Selena Gomez (Estados Unidos)
> ¿Quién es?   ¿De dónde es?
> Es Selena Gomez.   Es de los Estados Unidos.

1. Enrique Iglesias (España)
   ¿Quién es? Es Enrique Iglesias. ¿De dónde es? Es de España.
2. Robinson Canó (República Dominicana)
   ¿Quién es? Es Robinson Canó. ¿De dónde es? Es de (la) República Dominicana.
3. Eva Mendes y Marc Anthony (Estados Unidos)
   ¿Quiénes son? Son Eva Mendes y Marc Anthony. ¿De dónde son? Son de (los) Estados Unidos.
4. Carlos Santana y Salma Hayek (México)
   ¿Quiénes son? Son Carlos Santana y Salma Hayek. ¿De dónde son? Son de México.
5. Shakira (Colombia)
   ¿Quién es? Es Shakira. ¿De dónde es? Es de Colombia.
6. Antonio Banderas y Penélope Cruz (España)
   ¿Quiénes son? Son Antonio Banderas y Penélope Cruz. ¿De dónde son? Son de España.
7. Taylor Swift y Demi Lovato (Estados Unidos)
   ¿Quiénes son? Son Taylor Swift y Demi Lovato. ¿De dónde son? Son de (los) Estados Unidos.
8. Daisy Fuentes (Cuba)
   ¿Quién es? Es Daisy Fuentes. ¿De dónde es? Es de Cuba.

3 **¿Qué es?** Indicate what each object is and to whom it belongs.

> **modelo**
> ¿Qué es?   ¿De quién es?
> Es un diccionario.   Es del profesor Núñez.

1.   2.   3.   4.

1. ¿Qué es?
   Es una maleta.
   ¿De quién es?
   Es de la Sra. Valdés.

2. ¿Qué es?
   Es un cuaderno.
   ¿De quién es?
   Es de Gregorio.

3. ¿Qué es?
   Es una computadora.
   ¿De quién es?
   Es de Rafael.

4. ¿Qué es?
   Es un diario.
   ¿De quién es?
   Es de Marisa.

TEACHING OPTIONS

Video ➡🎞➡ Replay the **Fotonovela**, having students focus on subject pronouns and the verb **ser**. Ask them to copy down as many examples of sentences that use forms of **ser** as they can. Stop the video where appropriate to ask comprehension questions on what the characters said.

Heritage Speakers ↤🎞↦ Encourage heritage speakers to describe themselves and their family briefly. Make sure they use the cognates **familia**, **mamá**, and **papá**. Call on students to report the information given. Ex: **Francisco es de la Florida. La mamá de Francisco es de España. Ella es profesora. El papá de Francisco es de Cuba. Él es dentista.**

Comunicación

4 La clase Read Stephanie's description of one of her classes. Then indicate whether the following conclusions are **lógico** or **ilógico**, based on what you read.

> Yo soy Stephanie. Soy estudiante de la clase de la señora Rodríguez. Ella es de Uruguay y yo soy de los Estados Unidos. En la clase de la señora Rodríguez hay diez diccionarios de español y una computadora. Los diccionarios son de los estudiantes y la computadora es de la señora Rodríguez.

		Lógico	Ilógico
1.	La señora Rodríguez es profesora.	☑	○
2.	Stephanie es de Madrid.	○	☑
3.	Es una clase de español.	☑	○
4.	Hay dos estudiantes en la clase.	○	☑
5.	La señora Rodríguez es de Miami.	○	☑

5 Famosos Describe several famous people using the vocabulary and grammar you have learned. Use the list of professions to think of people from a variety of backgrounds. Answers will vary.

actor *actor*	cantante *singer*	escritor(a) *writer*
actriz *actress*	deportista *athlete*	músico/a *musician*

> **modelo**
> John Leguizamo es actor. Es de Colombia...

5 Preguntas Using the items in the word bank, ask your partner questions about the ad. Answers will vary.

¿Cuántas?	¿De dónde?	¿Qué?
¿Cuántos?	¿De quién?	¿Quién?

SOMOS ECOTURISTA, S.A.
Los autobuses oficiales de la Ruta Maya
- 25 autobuses en total
- 30 conductores del área
- pasajeros internacionales
- mapas de la región
¡Todos a bordo!

1.4 Telling time

ANTE TODO In both English and Spanish, the verb *to be* (**ser**) and numbers are used to tell time.

▶ To ask what time it is, use **¿Qué hora es?** When telling time, use **es + la** with **una** and **son + las** with all other hours.

Es la una.　　　**Son las** dos.　　　**Son las** seis.

▶ As in English, you express time in Spanish from the hour to the half hour by adding minutes.

Son las cuatro **y cinco**.　　　Son las once **y veinte**.

▶ You may use either **y cuarto** or **y quince** to express fifteen minutes or quarter past the hour. For thirty minutes or half past the hour, you may use either **y media** or **y treinta**.

Es la una **y cuarto**.　　Son las nueve **y quince**.　　Son las doce **y media**.　　Son las siete **y treinta**.

▶ You express time from the half hour to the hour in Spanish by subtracting minutes or a portion of an hour from the next hour.

Es la una **menos cuarto**.　　Son las tres **menos quince**.　　Son las ocho **menos veinte**.　　Son las tres **menos diez**.

▶ To ask at what time a particular event takes place, use the phrase **¿A qué hora (...)?**
   To state at what time something takes place, use the construction **a la(s)** + *time*.

¿A qué hora es la clase de biología?   La clase es **a las dos**.
(At) what time is biology class?   *The class is at two o'clock.*

¿A qué hora es la fiesta?   **A las ocho**.
(At) what time is the party?   *At eight.*

▶ Here are some useful words and phrases associated with telling time.

Son las ocho **en punto**.   Son las nueve **de la mañana**.
It's 8 o'clock on the dot/sharp.   *It's 9 a.m./in the morning.*

Es **el mediodía**.   Son las cuatro y cuarto **de la tarde**.
It's noon.   *It's 4:15 p.m./in the afternoon.*

Es **la medianoche**.   Son las diez y media **de la noche**.
It's midnight.   *It's 10:30 p.m./at night.*

¡LENGUA VIVA!

Other useful expressions for telling time:

Son las doce (del día).
It is twelve o'clock (p.m.).

Son las doce (de la noche).
It is twelve o'clock (a.m.).

¿Qué hora es?

Son las cuatro menos diez.

¿Qué hora es?

Son las cuatro y veinticinco.

¡INTÉNTALO!   Practice telling time by completing these sentences.

1. (1:00 a.m.) Es la _____una_____ de la mañana.
2. (2:50 a.m.) Son las tres _____menos_____ diez de la mañana.
3. (4:15 p.m.) Son las cuatro y ___cuarto/quince___ de la tarde.
4. (8:30 p.m.) Son las ocho y ___media/treinta___ de la noche.
5. (9:15 a.m.) Son las nueve y quince de la _____mañana_____.
6. (12:00 p.m.) Es el _____mediodía_____.
7. (6:00 a.m.) Son las seis de la _____mañana_____.
8. (4:05 p.m.) Son las cuatro y cinco de la _____tarde_____.
9. (12:00 a.m.) Es la _____medianoche_____.
10. (3:45 a.m.) Son las cuatro menos ___cuarto/quince___ de la mañana.
11. (2:15 a.m.) Son las _____dos_____ y cuarto de la mañana.
12. (1:25 p.m.) Es la una y ___veinticinco___ de la tarde.
13. (6:50 a.m.) Son las _____siete_____ menos diez de la mañana.
14. (10:40 p.m.) Son las once menos veinte de la _____noche_____.

In-Class Tips

• Review **¿Qué hora es?** and introduce **¿A qué hora?** and make sure students know the difference between them. Ask a few questions to contrast the constructions. Ex: **¿Qué hora es? ¿A qué hora es la clase de español?** Emphasize the difference between the questions by looking at your watch as you ask **¿Qué hora es?** and shrugging your shoulders with a quizzical look when asking **¿A qué hora es?**

• Go over **en punto, mediodía,** and **medianoche.** Explain that **medio/a** means *half.*

• Go over **de la mañana/tarde/noche.** Ask students what time it is now.

• You may wish to explain that Spanish speakers tend to view times of day differently than English speakers do. In many countries, only after someone has eaten lunch does one say **Buenas tardes.** Similarly, with the evening, Spanish speakers tend to view 6:00 and even 7:00 as **de la tarde**, not **de la noche.**

¡Lengua viva! Introduce the Spanish equivalents for noon **(las doce del día)** and midnight **(las doce de la noche).**

TEACHING OPTIONS

Extra Practice Give half of the class slips of paper with clock faces depicting certain times. Give the corresponding times written out in Spanish to the other half of the class. Have students circulate around the room to match their times. To increase difficulty, include duplicates of each time with **de la mañana** or **de la tarde/noche** on the written-out times and a sun or a moon on the clock faces.

Heritage Speakers Ask heritage speakers if they generally tell time as presented in the text. If they use different constructions, ask them to share these with the class. Some ways Hispanics use time constructions include (1) stating the hour and the minute (**Son las diez cuarenta**) rather than using **menos**, and (2) asking the question **¿Qué horas son?** Stress, however, that the constructions presented in the text are the ones students should focus on.

Práctica

1 **Ordenar** Put these times in order, from the earliest to the latest.

a. Son las dos de la tarde. 4
b. Son las once de la mañana. 2
c. Son las siete y media de la noche. 6
d. Son las seis menos cuarto de la tarde. 5
e. Son las dos menos diez de la tarde. 3
f. Son las ocho y veintidós de la mañana. 1

2 **¿Qué hora es?** Give the times shown on each clock or watch.

> **modelo**
> Son las cuatro y cuarto/quince de la tarde.

 p.m.   a.m.   p.m.   p.m.   a.m.

1. Son las doce y media/treinta de la tarde.
2. Es la una de la mañana.
3. Son las cinco y cuarto/quince de la tarde.
4. Son las ocho y diez de la noche.
5. Son las cinco y media/treinta de la mañana.

> **NOTA CULTURAL**
> Many Spanish-speaking countries use both the 12-hour clock and the 24-hour clock (that is, military time). The 24-hour clock is commonly used in written form on signs and schedules. For example, 1 p.m. is **13h**, 2 p.m. is **14h** and so on. See the photo on p. 33 for a sample schedule.

 a.m.   a.m.    a.m.   p.m.

6. Son las once menos cuarto/quince de la mañana.
7. Son las dos y doce de la tarde.
8. Son las siete y cinco de la mañana.
9. Son las cuatro menos cinco de la tarde.
10. Son las doce menos veinticinco de la noche.

3 **¿A qué hora?** Indicate at what time these events take place.

> **modelo**
> la clase de matemáticas (2:30 p.m.)
> La clase de matemáticas es a las dos y media de la tarde.

1. el programa *Las cuatro amigas* (11:30 a.m.)
2. el drama *La casa de Bernarda Alba* (7:00 p.m.)
3. el programa *Las computadoras* (8:30 a.m.)
4. la clase de español (10:30 a.m.)
5. la clase de biología (9:40 a.m.)
6. la clase de historia (10:50 a.m.)
7. el partido (*game*) de béisbol (5:15 p.m.)
8. el partido de tenis (12:45 p.m.)
9. el partido de baloncesto (*basketball*) (7:45 p.m.)

1. El programa *Las cuatro amigas* es a las once y media/treinta de la mañana.
2. El drama *La casa de Bernarda Alba* es a las siete de la noche.
3. El programa *Las computadoras* es a las ocho y media/treinta de la mañana.
4. La clase de español es a las diez y media/treinta de la mañana.
5. La clase de biología es a las diez menos veinte de la mañana.
6. La clase de historia es a las once menos diez de la mañana.
7. El partido de béisbol es a las cinco y cuarto/quince de la tarde.
8. El partido de tenis es a la una menos cuarto/quince de la tarde.
9. El partido de baloncesto es a las ocho menos cuarto/quince de la noche.

> **NOTA CULTURAL**
> *La casa de Bernarda Alba* is a famous play by Spanish poet and playwright **Federico García Lorca** (1898–1936). Lorca was one of the most famous writers of the 20th century and a close friend of Spain's most talented artists, including the painter Salvador Dalí and the filmmaker Luis Buñuel.

Sidebar (left margin)

1 **In-Class Tip** To add a visual aspect to this activity, have students draw clock faces showing the times presented in the activity. Have them compare drawings with a partner to verify accuracy.

2 **In-Class Tip** Read aloud the two ways of saying *4:15* in the model sentence. Point out that the clocks and watches indicate the part of day (morning, afternoon, or evening) as well as the hour. Have students include this information in their responses.

2 **Expansion** At random, say aloud times shown in the activity. Students must give the number of the clock or watch you describe.
Ex: **Es la una de la mañana. (Es el número 2.)**

3 **In-Class Tips**
• To simplify, go over new vocabulary introduced in this activity and model pronunciation. Have students repeat the items after you to build confidence.
• Have partners switch roles and ask and answer the questions again.

3 **Expansion**
♣↔♣ Have students come up with three additional items to ask their partner, who should respond with actual times.
Ex: —¿**A qué hora es el programa *Modern Family*?**
—**Es a las nueve de la noche.**

TEACHING OPTIONS

Pairs ♣↔♣ Have students work with a partner to create an original conversation in which they: (1) greet each other appropriately, (2) ask for the time, (3) ask what time a particular class is, and (4) say goodbye. Have pairs role-play their conversations for the class.
Game Divide the class into two teams and have each team form a line. Write two city names on the board. (Ex: **Los Ángeles** and **Miami**) Check that students know the time difference and then list a time underneath the first city. (Ex: **10:30 a.m.**) Point to the first member of each team and ask: **En Los Ángeles son las diez y media de la mañana. ¿Qué hora es en Miami?** The first student to write the correct time in Spanish under the second column earns a point for their team. Vary the game with different times and cities. The team with the most points wins.

Comunicación

4 **Escuchar** Laura and David are taking the same courses and are checking to see if they have the same schedule. Listen as they confirm the times of several of their classes.

	Lógico	Ilógico
1. La clase es a las once y media de la mañana.	☑	○
2. La clase de historia es a las once y cuarto.	○	☑
3. La fiesta es a las ocho de la noche.	☑	○
4. Rafael es estudiante.	☑	○

5 **Preguntas** Answer your partner's questions based on your own knowledge. Some answers will vary.

1. Son las tres de la tarde en Nueva York. ¿Qué hora es en Los Ángeles?
Es el mediodía./ Son las doce.
2. Son las ocho y media en Chicago. ¿Qué hora es en Miami?
Son las nueve y media/treinta.
3. Son las dos menos cinco en San Francisco. ¿Qué hora es en San Antonio?
Son las cuatro menos cinco.
4. ¿A qué hora es el programa *Saturday Night Live*?; ¿A qué hora es el programa *American Idol*? Es a las once y media/treinta de la noche.; Es a las ocho de la noche.

6 **Horas** Write sentences about the times that your favorite TV shows are on. Mention at least three shows. Answers will vary.

Síntesis

7 **Situación** With a partner, play the roles of a student reporter interviewing the new Spanish teacher (**profesor(a) de español**) from Venezuela. Answers will vary.

Estudiante	Profesor(a) de literatura
Ask the teacher his/her name.	→ Ask the student his/her name.
Ask the teacher what time his/her literature class is.	→ Ask the student where he/she is from.
Ask how many students are in his/her class.	→ Ask to whom the notebook belongs.
Say thank you and goodbye.	→ Say thank you and you are pleased to meet him/her.

4 **In-Class Tip** Have students listen to the audio once. Ask them to write down as many words as they understand. Help students by clarifying the meaning and spelling of the words they catch, and ask them to predict the situation.

4 **Script** *See the script for this activity on Interleaf page 1B.*

5 **In-Class Tip** Remind students that there are four time zones in the continental United States, and that when it is noon in the Eastern Time zone, it is three hours earlier in the Pacific Time zone.

5 **Virtual Chat**
👤↔👤 Available online.

6 **Expansion** Ask students to write a question for each sentence they have written, and partner students to ask and answer questions about their favorite TV shows. Provide examples: —¿A qué hora es el programa *The Daily Show* with Trevor Noah? —Es a las once.

 Communication 1.1

7 **In-Class Tip** Point out that this activity synthesizes everything students have learned in this lesson: greetings and leave-takings, nouns and articles, numbers 0–30 and **hay**, the verb **ser**, and telling time. Spend a few moments reviewing these topics.

7 **Partner Chat**
👤↔👤 Available online.

TEACHING OPTIONS

Small Groups 👤↔👤 Have small groups prepare skits. Students can choose any situation they wish, provided that they use material presented in the **Contextos** and **Estructura** sections. Possible situations include: meeting to go on an excursion, meeting between classes, and introducing friends to teachers.

Heritage Speakers 👤→👤 Ask heritage speakers to describe popular shows that are currently featured on Spanish-language television, noting the type of show (**telenovela, reality**, etc.), the channel (**canal**), and time when they are shown. As a class, try to think of English-language versions or similar programs. Examples may include *American Idol, Big Brother, Dancing with the Stars,* and their respective Latin American counterparts.

Recapitulación

SUBJECT Javier | CONJUGATED FORM empiezo | Main clause | Dudan

1 In-Class Tips
- Before beginning the activity, remind students that nouns ending in -**ma** tend to be masculine, despite ending in an -**a**.
- To add an auditory aspect to this activity, read aloud a masculine or feminine noun, then call on individuals to supply the other form. Do the same for plural and singular nouns. Keep a brisk pace.

1 Expansion Have students identify the corresponding definite and indefinite articles in both singular and plural forms for all of the nouns.

2 In-Class Tips
- Have students explain why they chose their answers. Ex: 1. **Cuántas** is feminine and modifies **chicas**.
- Ask students to explain the difference between **¿Tienes un diccionario?** and **¿Tienes el diccionario?** (general versus specific).

2 Expansion
- ←**👤**→ Ask students to rewrite the dialogue with information from one of their own classes.
- **👤**↔**👤** Have volunteers ask classmates questions using possessives with **ser**. Ex:
  —**¿De quién es esta mochila?**
  —**Es de ella.**

Review the grammar concepts you have learned in this lesson by completing these activities.

1 Completar Complete the charts according to the models. **28 pts.**

Masculino	Femenino
el chico	la chica
el profesor	**la profesora**
el amigo	**la amiga**
el señor	la señora
el pasajero	**la pasajera**
el estudiante	la estudiante
el turista	**la turista**
el joven	la joven

Singular	Plural
una cosa	unas cosas
un libro	unos libros
una clase	**unas clases**
una lección	unas lecciones
un conductor	unos conductores
un país	**unos países**
un lápiz	**unos lápices**
un problema	unos problemas

2 En la clase Complete each conversation with the correct word. **22 pts.**

 César   Beatriz

CÉSAR ¿(1) _Cuántas_ (Cuántos/Cuántas) chicas hay en la (2) _clase_ (maleta/clase)?

BEATRIZ Hay (3) _catorce_ (catorce/cuatro) [14] chicas.

CÉSAR Y, ¿(4) _cuántos_ (cuántos/cuántas) chicos hay?

BEATRIZ Hay (5) _trece_ (tres/trece) [13] chicos.

CÉSAR Entonces (*Then*), en total hay (6) _veintisiete_ (veintiséis/veintisiete) (7) _estudiantes_ (estudiantes/chicas) en la clase.

 Ariana   Daniel

ARIANA ¿Tienes (*Do you have*) (8) _un_ (un/una) diccionario?

DANIEL No, pero (*but*) aquí (9) _hay_ (es/hay) uno.

ARIANA ¿De quién (10) _es_ (son/es)?

DANIEL (11) _Es_ (Son/Es) de Carlos.

1.1 Nouns and articles *pp. 12–14*

Gender of nouns

Nouns that refer to living things

	Masculine		Feminine
-o	el chico	-a	la chica
-or	el profesor	-ora	la profesora
-ista	el turista	-ista	la turista

Nouns that refer to non-living things

	Masculine		Feminine
-o	el libro	-a	la cosa
-ma	el programa	-ción	la lección
-s	el autobús	-dad	la nacionalidad

Plural of nouns
- ending in vowel + -*s*   la chica → las chicas
- ending in consonant + -*es*   el señor → los señores
  (-z → -ces un lápiz → unos lápices)
- Definite articles: el, la, los, las
- Indefinite articles: un, una, unos, unas

1.2 Numbers 0–30 *p. 16*

0	cero	8	ocho	16	dieciséis
1	uno	9	nueve	17	diecisiete
2	dos	10	diez	18	dieciocho
3	tres	11	once	19	diecinueve
4	cuatro	12	doce	20	veinte
5	cinco	13	trece	21	veintiuno
6	seis	14	catorce	22	veintidós
7	siete	15	quince	30	treinta

1.3 Present tense of *ser* *pp. 19–21*

yo	soy	nosotros/as	somos
tú	eres	vosotros/as	sois
Ud./él/ella	es	Uds./ellos/ellas	son

TEACHING OPTIONS

Extra Practice To add a visual aspect to this grammar review, bring in pictures from newspapers, magazines, or the Internet of nouns that students have learned. Ask them to identify the people or objects using **ser**. As a variation, ask students questions about the photos, using **hay**. Ex: **¿Cuántos/as _____ hay en la foto?**

TPR Give certain times of day and night and ask students to identify who would be awake: **vigilante** (*night watchman*), **estudiante**, or **los dos**. Have students raise their left hand for the **vigilante**, right hand for the **estudiante**, and both hands for **los dos**. Ex: **Son las cinco menos veinte de la mañana.** (left hand) **Es la medianoche.** (both hands)

3 **Presentaciones** Complete this conversation with the correct form of the verb **ser**. [18 pts.]

JUAN   ¡Hola! Me llamo Juan. (1) _____Soy_____ estudiante en la clase de español.

DANIELA ¡Hola! Mucho gusto. Yo (2) _____soy_____ Daniela y ella (3) _____es_____ Mónica. ¿De dónde (4) _____eres_____ (tú), Juan?

JUAN   De California. Y ustedes, ¿de dónde (5) _____son_____ ?

MÓNICA Nosotras (6) _____somos_____ de Florida.

1.4	Telling time	*pp. 24–25*
Es la una.	It's 1:00.
Son las dos.	It's 2:00.
Son las tres y diez.	It's 3:10.
Es la una y cuarto/quince.	It's 1:15.
Son las siete y media/treinta.	It's 7:30.
Es la una menos cuarto/quince.	It's 12:45.
Son las once menos veinte.	It's 10:40.
Es el mediodía.	It's noon.
Es la medianoche.	It's midnight.

4 **¿Qué hora es?** Write out in words the following times, indicating whether it's morning, noon, afternoon, or night. [28 pts.]

1. It's 12:00 p.m.
Es el mediodía./Son las doce del día.

2. It's 7:05 a.m.
Son las siete y cinco de la mañana.

3. It's 9:35 p.m.
Son las diez menos veinticinco de la noche.

4. It's 5:15 p.m.
Son las cinco y cuarto/quince de la tarde.

5. It's 1:30 p.m.
Es la una y media/treinta de la tarde.

6. It's 11:50 a.m.
Son las doce menos diez de la mañana.

7. It's 3:10 p.m.
Son las tres y diez de la tarde.

5 **Canción** Use the two appropriate words from the list to complete this children's song. [4 pts.]

| cinco | cuántas | cuatro | media | quiénes |

" _____Cuántas_____ patas° tiene un gato°? Una, dos, tres y _____cuatro_____ . "

patas *legs*   tiene un gato *does a cat have*

---

3 **In-Class Tip** Before beginning the activity, orally review the conjugation of **ser**.

3 **Expansion** Ask questions about the characters in the dialogue. Ex: **¿Quién es Juan? (Juan es un estudiante en la clase de español.) ¿De dónde es? (Es de California.)**

4 **In-Class Tip** Go over the answers with the class and point out that items 1, 4, and 5 may be written two ways.

4 **Expansion** To challenge students, give them these times as items 6–10: **6. It's 3:13 p.m., 7. It's 4:29 a.m., 8. It's 1:04 a.m., 9. It's 10:09 a.m., 10. It's 12:16 a.m.**

4 **Expansion** Have students write down five additional times in Spanish. Then have them get together with a partner and take turns reading the times aloud. The partner will draw a clock showing the appropriate time, plus a sun or moon to indicate a.m. or p.m. Students should check each other's drawings to verify accuracy.

5 **In-Class Tip** Point out the word **Una** in line 3 of the song. To challenge students, have them work in pairs to come up with an explanation for why **Una** is used. (It refers to **pata** [una pata, dos patas…]).

Game →👤← Have students make a five-column, five-row chart with B-I-N-G-O written across the top of the columns. Tell them to fill in the squares at random with different times of day. (Remind them to use only full, quarter, or half hours.) Draw times from a hat and call them out in Spanish. The first student to mark five in a row (horizontally, vertically, or diagonally) yells **¡Bingo!** and wins.

Extra Practice ←👤← Have students imagine they have a new pen pal in a Spanish-speaking country. Ask them to write a short e-mail in which they introduce themselves, state where they are from, and give information about their class schedule. (You may want to give students the verb form **tengo** and class subjects vocabulary.) Encourage them to finish the message with questions about their pen pal.

Section Goals

In **Lectura**, students will:
- learn to recognize cognates
- use prefixes and suffixes to recognize cognates
- read a biography on **Joaquín Salvador Lavado (Quino)**
- read a comic strip

Communication 1.1, 1.2
Cultures 2.1, 2.2
Connections 3.1, 3.2
Comparisons 4.2

 Pre-AP®

Interpretive Reading: Estrategia
Have students look at the cognates in the **Estrategia** box. Write some of the common suffix correspondences between Spanish and English on the board: **–ción/–sión** = *–tion/–sion* (**nación, decisión**); **–ante/–ente** = *–ant/–ent* (**importante, inteligente, elegante**); **–ia/–ía** = *–y* (**farmacia, sociología, historia**); **–dad** = *–ty* (**oportunidad, universidad**).

The Affective Dimension
Tell students that reading in Spanish will be less anxiety-provoking if they follow the advice in the **Estrategia** sections, which are designed to reinforce and improve reading comprehension skills.

Examinar el texto Ask students to tell you what type of text this is and how they can tell. *(It is a comic strip and it consists of a series of drawings with speech bubbles.)*

Cognados Ask students to mention any cognates that they see in the author's biography or the comic strip. Discuss the cognates and ask students to look for other examples of words with suffixes that have correspondence to English. Ex: **protagonista; -ista** = *-ist*

Lectura

Antes de leer

Estrategia
Recognizing cognates

As you learned earlier in this lesson, cognates are words that share similar meanings and spellings in two or more languages. When reading in Spanish, it's helpful to look for cognates and use them to guess the meaning of what you're reading. But watch out for false cognates. For example, **librería** means *bookstore*, not *library*, and **embarazada** means *pregnant*, not *embarrassed*. Look at this list of Spanish words, paying special attention to prefixes and suffixes. Can you guess the meaning of each word?

importante	oportunidad
farmacia	cultura
inteligente	activo
dentista	sociología
decisión	espectacular
televisión	restaurante
médico	policía

Examinar el texto
Glance quickly at the reading selection and guess what type of document it is. Explain your answer.

Cognados
Read the document and make a list of the cognates you find. Guess their English equivalents.

Joaquín Salvador Lavado nació (*was born*) en Argentina en 1932 (mil novecientos treinta y dos). Su nombre profesional es **Quino**. Es muy popular en Latinoamérica, Europa y Canadá por sus tiras cómicas (*comic strips*). Mafalda es su serie más famosa. La protagonista, Mafalda, es una chica muy inteligente de seis años (*years*). La tira cómica ilustra las aventuras de ella y su grupo de amigos. Las anécdotas de Mafalda y los chicos también presentan temas (*themes*) importantes como la paz (*peace*) y los derechos humanos (*human rights*).

Después de leer

Preguntas

Answer these questions. Some answers may vary. Suggested answers:
1. What is Joaquín Salvador Lavado's pen name?
   Quino
2. What is Mafalda like?
   She is a precocious six-year-old.
3. Where is Mafalda in panel 1? What is she doing?
   She is in bed, counting sheep in order to fall asleep.
4. What happens to the sheep in panel 3? Why?
   It is left balancing on the hurdle because Mafalda falls asleep.
5. Why does Mafalda wake up?
   The sheep says ¡Béeee!
6. What number corresponds to the sheep in panel 5?
   veintiséis
7. In panel 6, what is Mafalda doing? How do you know?
   She is sleeping; the Zs indicate this.

Preguntas Have students work in pairs to answer the questions. Then check the answers as a class.

Los animales
- Have a volunteer read aloud the animal names in group A.
- Model the animal sounds in group B and have students repeat them so that they become comfortable making these sounds.
- Review the answers as a class. Then, ask students if any of the animal/sound combinations were surprising to them and why.
- Write the names of a few more animals (Ex: **pollito, búho, pavo**) accompanied by simple drawings on the board and have students try to guess what the sound would be in Spanish (**pío pío, uu uu, gluglú**).

Los animales

This comic strip uses a device called onomatopoeia: a word that represents the sound that it stands for. Did you know that many common instances of onomatopoeia are different from language to language? The noise a sheep makes is *baaaah* in English, but in Mafalda's language it is **béeeee**.

Do you think you can match these animals with their Spanish sounds? First, practice saying aloud each animal sound in group B. Then, match each animal with its sound in Spanish. If you need help remembering the sounds the alphabet makes in Spanish, see p. 9.

A

 1. _f_ **gato**   2. _d_ **perro**   3. _b_ **vacas**   4. _a_ **gallo**

 5. _c_ **rana**   6. _e_ **pato**   7. _g_ **cerdo**

B

a. kikirikí   b. muuu   c. croac   d. guau

e. cuac cuac   f. miau   g. oinc

TEACHING OPTIONS

Small Groups In small groups, have students create an alternate ending for the *Mafalda* comic above. Ask them to create new content for panels 3 through 6. When they are finished, have groups share their comic strips, and have the class vote for the funniest or most creative.

Heritage Speakers Ask heritage speakers if they are familiar with any other classic Spanish-language comic strips, such as *Condorito*. Have them describe the general characteristics of the main character. As a class, compare this character to *Mafalda*.

Section Goals

In **Escritura**, students will:
- learn to write a telephone/address list in Spanish
- integrate lesson vocabulary, including cognates and structures

 Communication 1.3

 Pre-AP®

Estrategia
Go over the strategy as a class. Encourage students to give examples of how they will use the suggestions for this activity.

Tema Introduce students to standard headings (**Nombre, Teléfono, Dirección electrónica**) used in a telephone/address list. They may wish to add notes pertaining to home (**número de casa**), cellular (**número de celular/móvil**), or office (**número de oficina**) phone numbers, fax numbers (**número de fax**), or office hours (**horas de oficina**).

The Affective Dimension
Tell the class that they will feel less anxious about writing in a foreign language if they follow the step-by-step advice in the **Estrategia** and **Tema** sections.

In-Class Tip Tell students to consult the **Plan de escritura** on page A-2 for step-by-step writing instructions.

Spanish Characters in Word Processing

Macintosh

á **Á**, etc.	*option* + *e* then *a* or *A*, etc.
ñ **Ñ**	*option* + *n* then *n* or *N*
ü **Ü**	*option* + *u* then *u* or *U*
¿	*option* + *shift* + *?*
¡	*option* + *!*

PC (Windows)

á **Á**, etc.	*ctrl* + *'* then *a* or *A*, etc.
ñ **Ñ**	*ctrl* + *shift* + *~* then *n* or *N*
ü **Ü**	*ctrl* + *shift* + *:* then *u* or *U*
¿	*ctrl* + *alt* + *shift* + *?*
¡	*ctrl* + *alt* + *shift* + *!*

Escritura

Estrategia
Writing in Spanish

Why do we write? All writing has a purpose. For example, we may write an e-mail to share important information or compose an essay to persuade others to accept a point of view. Proficient writers are not born, however. Writing requires time, thought, effort, and a lot of practice. Here are some tips to help you write more effectively in Spanish.

DO

▶ Try to write your ideas in Spanish

▶ Use the grammar and vocabulary that you know

▶ Use your textbook for examples of style, format, and expression in Spanish

▶ Use your imagination and creativity

▶ Put yourself in your reader's place to determine if your writing is interesting

AVOID

▶ Translating your ideas from English to Spanish

▶ Simply repeating what is in the textbook or on a web page

▶ Using a dictionary until you have learned how to use foreign language dictionaries

Tema

Hacer una lista

Create a telephone/address list that includes important names, numbers, and websites that will be helpful to you in your study of Spanish. Make whatever entries you can in Spanish without using a dictionary. You might want to include this information:

▶ The names, phone numbers, and e-mail addresses of at least four other students

▶ Your teacher's name, e-mail address, and office hours

▶ Three phone numbers and e-mail addresses of campus offices or locations related to your study of Spanish

▶ Five electronic resources for students of Spanish, such as chat rooms and sites dedicated to the study of Spanish as a second language

Nombre *Sally (la chica de Indiana)* ☎
Teléfono 655-8888 ✉
Dirección electrónica *sally@uru.edu*

Nombre *Profesor José Ramón Casas*
Teléfono 655-8090
Dirección electrónica *jrcasas@uru.edu*
Horas de oficina 12 a 12:30

Nombre *Biblioteca* 655-7000
Dirección electrónica *library@uru.edu*

EVALUATION: Lista

Criteria	Scale
Content	1 2 3 4 5
Organization	1 2 3 4 5
Accuracy	1 2 3 4 5
Creativity	1 2 3 4 5

Scoring	
Excellent	18–20 points
Good	14–17 points
Satisfactory	10–13 points
Unsatisfactory	< 10 points

Escuchar

Estrategia

Listening for words you know

You can get the gist of a conversation by listening for words and phrases you already know.

🔊 To help you practice this strategy, listen to the following sentence and make a list of the words you have already learned.

Preparación

Based on the photograph, what do you think Dr. Cavazos and Srta. Martínez are talking about? How would you get the gist of their conversation, based on what you know about Spanish?
Answers will vary.

Ahora escucha 🔊

Now you are going to hear Dr. Cavazos's conversation with Srta. Martínez. List the familiar words and phrases each person says.
Answers will vary.

Dr. Cavazos	Srta. Martínez
1. _____	9. _____
2. _____	10. _____
3. _____	11. _____
4. _____	12. _____
5. _____	13. _____
6. _____	14. _____
7. _____	15. _____
8. _____	16. _____

Use your lists of familiar words as a guide to come up with a summary of what happened in the conversation.. Answers will vary.

Comprensión

Identificar
Who would say the following things, Dr. Cavazos or Srta. Martínez?

1. Me llamo… Dr. Cavazos
2. De nada. Srta. Martínez
3. Gracias. Muchas gracias. Dr. Cavazos
4. Aquí tiene usted los documentos de viaje (*trip*), señor. Srta. Martínez
5. Usted tiene tres maletas, ¿no? Srta. Martínez
6. Tengo dos maletas. Dr. Cavazos
7. Hola, señor. Srta. Martínez
8. ¿Viaja usted a Buenos Aires? Srta. Martínez

Contestar

1. Does this scene take place in the morning, afternoon, or evening? How do you know? The scene takes place in the morning, as indicated by **Buenos días**.
2. How many suitcases does Dr. Cavazos have? two
3. Using the words you already know to determine the context, what might the following words and expressions mean? Answers will vary.
   - boleto
   - pasaporte
   - un viaje de ida y vuelta
   - ¡Buen viaje!

M: ¿Un viaje de ida y vuelta a Quito?
C: Sí.
M: ¿Cuántas maletas tiene usted? ¿Tres?
C: Dos.

M: Bueno, aquí tiene usted su boleto.
C: Muchas gracias.
M: No hay de qué, doctor Cavazos. ¡Buen viaje!
C: Gracias. ¡Adiós!

Section Goals

In **Escuchar**, students will:
• listen to sentences containing familiar and unfamiliar vocabulary
• learn the strategy of listening for known vocabulary
• answer questions based on the content of a recorded conversation

♋ Communication 1.2

Estrategia
Script Creo que hay… este… treinta pasajeros en el autobús que va a Guayaquil.

The Affective Dimension
Tell students that many people feel nervous about their ability to comprehend what they hear in a foreign language. Tell them that they will probably feel less anxious if they follow the advice for increasing listening comprehension in the **Estrategia** sections.

In-Class Tip Have students look at the photo. Guide them to guess where **Dr. Cavazos** and **Srta. Martínez** are and what they are talking about.

Ahora escucha
In-Class Tip To simplify, give students a list of the familiar words and phrases from the conversation. As you play the audio, have students indicate who says each one.

Script DR. CAVAZOS: Buenos días.
SRTA. MARTÍNEZ: Buenos días, señor. ¿En qué le puedo servir?
C: Yo soy el doctor Alejandro Cavazos. Voy a Quito. Aquí tiene mi boleto. Deseo facturar mis maletas.
M: ¿Alejandro Cavazos? ¿C-A-V-A-Z-O-S?
C: Sí.

(Script continues at far left in the bottom panels.)

Section Goals

In **En pantalla**, students will:
- read about advertising geared toward Hispanics in the United States
- watch a television commercial for MasterCard

Communication 1.2, 1.3
Cultures 2.1, 2.2
Connections 3.2
Comparisons 4.2

Teacher Resources
Read the front matter for suggestions on how to incorporate all the program's components. See pages 1A–1B for a detailed listing of Teacher Resources online.

Anuncios para los latinos
To check comprehension, ask these questions: 1. By which year will Hispanic population double? (2050) 2. What are the two major Spanish-language TV stations? (**Univisión** and **Telemundo**) 3. Why are marketing campaigns targeting Spanish-speaking audiences? (Spending power of $1.7 trillion in 2017)

Antes de ver
Read through the **Vocabulario útil** with students. Assure students that they do not have to understand every word they hear in the video. Tell them to rely on visual clues, cognates, and the **Vocabulario útil**.

 Pre-AP®

Audiovisual Interpretive Communication
Antes de ver strategy
Invite students to identify the key words in each entry in the **Vocabulario útil**. Then have them infer Spanish word order compared to that of English.

Preparación
Answer these questions in English. Answers will vary.
1. Name some foods your family buys at the supermarket.
2. What is something you consider precious that cannot be bought?

Anuncios para los latinos
Latinos form the fastest-growing minority group in the United States; Census Bureau projections show Hispanic populations doubling from 2015–2050, to 106 million. Viewership of the two major Spanish language TV stations, **Univisión** and **Telemundo**, has skyrocketed, sometimes surpassing that of the four major English-language networks. With Latino purchasing power estimated at $1.7 trillion for 2017, many companies have responded by adapting successful marketing campaigns to target a Spanish-speaking audience. Along with the change in language, there often come cultural adaptations important to Latino viewers.

Comprensión
Complete the chart below based on what you see in the video.

aperitivo	salami	$8
plato principal	carne en salsa	$15
postre	copa de helado	$6

Conversación
Based on the video, discuss in English the following questions with a partner. Answers will vary.
1. In what ways do the food purchasing choices of this family differ from your own? In what ways are they alike?
2. How does the role of the pet in this video reflect that of your family or culture? How is it different?

Anuncio de MasterCard

Un domingo en familia...

Vocabulario útil	
aperitivo	*appetizer*
carne en salsa	*beef with sauce*
copa de helado	*cup of ice cream*
no tiene precio	*priceless*
plato principal	*main dish*
postre	*dessert*
un domingo en familia	*Sunday with the family*

Aplicación
With a partner, use a dictionary to prepare an ad in Spanish like that in the video. Present your ad to the class. How did your food choices vary from the ad? What was your "priceless" item? Answers will vary.

The **Plaza de Mayo** in Buenos Aires, Argentina, is perhaps best known as a place of political protest. Aptly nicknamed **Plaza de Protestas** by the locals, it is the site of weekly demonstrations. Despite this reputation, for many it is also a traditional **plaza**, a spot to escape from the hustle of city life. In warmer months, office workers from neighboring buildings flock to the plaza during lunch hour. **Plaza de Mayo** is also a favorite spot for families, couples, and friends to gather, stroll, or simply sit and chat. Tourists come year-round to take in the iconic surroundings: **Plaza de Mayo** is flanked by the rose-colored presidential palace (**Casa Rosada**), city hall (**municipalidad**), a colonial era museum (**Cabildo**), and a spectacular cathedral (**Catedral Metropolitana**).

Vocabulario útil

abrazo	*hug*
¡Cuánto tiempo!	*It's been a long time!*
encuentro	*encounter*
plaza	*city or town square*
¡Qué bueno verte!	*It's great to see you!*
¡Qué suerte verlos!	*How lucky to see you!*

Preparación

Where do you and your friends usually meet? Are there public places where you get together? What activities do you take part in there? Answers will vary.

Identificar

Identify the person or people who make(s) each of these statements.

1. ¿Cómo están ustedes? d   a. Gonzalo
2. ¡Qué bueno verte! b   b. Mariana
3. Bien, ¿y vos? a   c. Mark
4. Hola. a, b, c, d   d. Silvina
5. ¡Qué suerte verlos! d

Encuentros en la plaza

Today we are at the Plaza de Mayo.

People come to walk and get some fresh air...

And children come to play...

Introduction To check comprehension, ask: 1. Is the **Plaza de Mayo** located in a large city or small town? (in a large city) 2. Why is it nicknamed **Plaza de Protestas**? (It is the site of weekly demonstrations.) 3. What are some leisure activities that people do there? (have lunch, stroll, sit and chat, sightsee) 4. What landmarks surround the **plaza**? (**Casa Rosada**, **municipalidad**, **Cabildo**, **Catedral Metropolitana**)

Antes de ver
- Read through the **Vocabulario útil** with students. Explain that **¡Qué bueno verte!** would be used with someone you refer to with **tú**; you might use **¡Qué suerte verlos!** when speaking to a group.
- Assure students that they do not need to understand every Spanish word they hear in the video. Tell them to rely on visual cues and to listen for cognates and words from **Vocabulario útil**.

Preparación Have students answer the questions in pairs. Then survey the class and write the most common answers on the board.

Identificar Play the video a second time and pause to point out each character as he or she appears.

Section Goal

In **Panorama**, students will read demographic and cultural information about Hispanics in the United States and Canada.

Communication 1.2, 1.3
Cultures 2.1, 2.2
Connections 3.1, 3.2
Comparisons 4.2

Teacher Resources

Read the front matter for suggestions on how to incorporate all the program's components. See pages 1A–1B for a detailed listing of Teacher Resources online.

In-Class Tips

- Use **Lección 1 Panorama** online Resources to assist with this presentation.
- Have students look at the map. Have volunteers read aloud the labeled cities and geographic features. Model Spanish pronunciation of names as necessary. Have students jot down as many names of places and geographic features with Spanish origins as they can.

El país en cifras Have volunteers read the bulleted headings in **El país en cifras**. Point out cognates and clarify unfamiliar words. Explain that numerals in Spanish have a comma where English would use a decimal point (**3,5%**) and have a period where English would use a comma (**14.013.719**). Explain that **EE.UU.** is the abbreviation of **Estados Unidos**, and the doubling of the initial letters indicates plural. Model the pronunciation of **Florida** (accent on the second syllable) and point out that it is often used with an article (**la Florida**) by Spanish speakers. For perspective, give the total populations for the five states: California, 37,253,956; Texas, 25,145,561; Florida, 18,801,310; New York, 19,378,102; Illinois, 12,830,632.

Estados Unidos

El país en cifras°

▶ **Población° de los EE.UU.:** 317 millones
▶ **Población de origen hispano:** 50 millones
▶ **País de origen de hispanos en los EE.UU.:**

3,5% Cuba — 10,9% otros — 9,2% Puerto Rico
13,4% Centroamérica y Suramérica
63,0% México

SOURCE: U.S. Census Bureau

▶ **Estados con la mayor° población hispana:**

California 14.013.719
Texas 9.460.921
Florida 4.223.806
Nueva York 3.416.922
Illinois 2.027.578

SOURCE: U.S. Census Bureau

Canadá

El país en cifras

▶ **Población de Canadá:** 35 millones
▶ **Población de origen hispano:** 700.000
▶ **País de origen de hispanos en Canadá:**

12,4% México
11,6% Chile
67% otros
9% El Salvador

SOURCE: Statistics Canada

▶ **Ciudades° con la mayor población hispana:**
Montreal, Toronto, Vancouver

en cifras *by the numbers* Población *Population* mayor *largest*
Ciudades *Cities* creció *grew* más *more* cada *every* niños *children*
Se estima *It is estimated* va a ser *it is going to be*

¡Increíble pero cierto!

La población hispana en los EE.UU. creció° un 48% entre los años 2000 (dos mil) y 2011 (dos mil once) (16,7 millones de personas más°). Hoy, uno de cada° cinco niños° en los EE.UU. es de origen hispano. Se estima° que en el año 2034 va a ser° uno de cada tres.

Mission District, en San Francisco

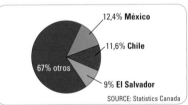

AK   HI

CANADÁ

Vancouver • Calgary

Ottawa ★
Toronto • Montreal
Chicago • Nueva York •

San Francisco
Las Vegas
Los Ángeles
San Diego

EE.UU.

Washington, D.C ★

San Antonio

Océano Atlántico

Miami

MÉXICO

Golfo de México

El Álamo, en San Antonio, Texas

Mar Caribe

Comida • La comida mexicana

La comida° mexicana es muy popular en los Estados Unidos. Los tacos, las enchiladas, las quesadillas y los frijoles frecuentemente forman parte de las comidas de muchos norteamericanos. También° son populares las variaciones de la comida mexicana en los Estados Unidos: el tex-mex y el cali-mex.

Lugares • La Pequeña Habana

La Pequeña Habana° es un barrio° de Miami, Florida, donde viven° muchos cubanoamericanos. Es un lugar° donde se encuentran° las costumbres° de la cultura cubana, los aromas y sabores° de su comida y la música salsa. La Pequeña Habana es una parte de Cuba en los Estados Unidos.

Costumbres • Desfile puertorriqueño

Cada junio, desde° 1958 (mil novecientos cincuenta y ocho), los puertorriqueños celebran su cultura con un desfile° en Nueva York. Es un gran espectáculo con carrozas° y música salsa, merengue y hip-hop. Muchos espectadores llevan° la bandera° de Puerto Rico en su ropa° o pintada en la cara°.

Comunidad • Hispanos en Canadá

En Canadá viven° muchos hispanos. Toronto y Montreal son las ciudades° con mayor° población hispana. Muchos de ellos tienen estudios universitarios° y hablan° una de las lenguas° oficiales: inglés o francés°. Los hispanos participan activamente en la vida cotidiana° y profesional de Canadá.

¿Qué aprendiste? Completa las oraciones con la información adecuada (*appropriate*).

1. Hay __50 millones__ de personas de origen hispano en los Estados Unidos.
2. Los cuatro estados con las poblaciones hispanas más grandes son (en orden) __California__, Texas, Florida y __Nueva York__.
3. Toronto, Montreal y __Vancouver__ son las ciudades con más población hispana de Canadá.
4. Las quesadillas y las enchiladas son platos (*dishes*) __mexicanos__.
5. La Pequeña __Habana__ es un barrio de Miami.
6. En Miami hay muchas personas de origen __cubano__.
7. Cada junio se celebra en Nueva York un gran desfile para personas de origen __puertorriqueño__.
8. Muchos hispanos en Canadá hablan __inglés__ o francés.

Conexión Internet Investiga estos temas en Internet.

1. Haz (*Make*) una lista de seis hispanos célebres de los EE.UU. o Canadá. Explica (*Explain*) por qué (*why*) son célebres.
2. Escoge (*Choose*) seis lugares en los Estados Unidos con nombres hispanos e investiga sobre el origen y el significado (*meaning*) de cada nombre.

....

comida *food* También *Also* La Pequeña Habana *Little Havana* barrio *neighborhood* viven *live* lugar *place* se encuentran *are found* costumbres *customs* sabores *flavors* Cada junio desde *Each June since* desfile *parade* con carrozas *with floats* llevan *wear* bandera *flag* ropa *clothing* cara *face* viven *live* ciudades *cities* mayor *most* tienen estudios universitarios *have a degree* hablan *speak* lenguas *languages* inglés o francés *English or French* vida cotidiana *daily life*

In-Class Tip Ask volunteers to read sentences from **¡Increíble pero cierto!**, **Comida**, **Lugares**, **Costumbres**, and **Comunidad**. As necessary, model pronunciation, pause to point out cognates, and clarify unfamiliar words.

La comida mexicana Ask students if they have tried these dishes. Have students look at illustrated cookbooks or recipes to identify the ingredients and variations of the dishes mentioned in the paragraph.

La Pequeña Habana Many large cities in the United States have neighborhoods where people of Hispanic origin predominate. Encourage students to talk about the neighborhoods they know.

Desfile puertorriqueño The Puerto Rican Day Parade takes place on the weekend nearest the feast day of St. John the Baptist (**San Juan Bautista**), the patron saint of San Juan, capital of Puerto Rico.

Hispanos en Canadá The Canadian Hispanic Business Association holds a national awards program every year that honors the ten most influential Hispanic Canadians. Nominees represent countries from all over the Spanish-speaking world. Past winners have included researchers, corporate executives, judges, lawyers, entrepreneurs, musicians, artists, and politicians.

In-Class Tip You may want to wrap up this section by playing the *Panorama cultural* video footage for this lesson.

TEACHING OPTIONS

Variación léxica Hispanic groups in the United States refer to themselves with various names. The most common of these terms, **hispano** and **latino**, refer to all people who come from Hispanic backgrounds, regardless of the country of origin of their ancestors. **Puertorriqueño**, **cubanoamericano**, and **mexicoamericano** refer to Hispanics whose ancestors came from Puerto Rico, Cuba, and Mexico, respectively.

Many Mexican Americans also refer to themselves as **chicanos**. This word has stronger socio-political connotations than **mexicoamericano**. Use of the word **chicano** implies identification with Mexican Americans' struggle for civil rights and equal opportunity in the United States. It also suggests an appreciation of the indigenous aspects of Mexican and Mexican-American culture.

 Comparisons 4.1

Teacher Resources
Read the front matter for suggestions on how to incorporate all the program's components. See pages 1A–1B for a detailed listing of Teacher Resources online.

In-Class Tip Tell students that this is active vocabulary for which they are responsible and that it will appear on tests and exams.

Saludos

Hola.	Hello; Hi.
Buenos días.	Good morning.
Buenas tardes.	Good afternoon.
Buenas noches.	Good evening; Good night.

Despedidas

Adiós.	Goodbye.
Nos vemos.	See you.
Hasta luego.	See you later.
Hasta la vista.	See you later.
Hasta pronto.	See you soon.
Hasta mañana.	See you tomorrow.
Saludos a...	Greetings to…
Chau.	Bye.

¿Cómo está?

¿Cómo está usted?	How are you? (form.)
¿Cómo estás?	How are you? (fam.)
¿Qué hay de nuevo?	What's new?
¿Qué pasa?	What's happening?; What's going on?
¿Qué tal?	How are you?; How is it going?
(Muy) bien, gracias.	(Very) well, thanks.
Nada.	Nothing.
No muy bien.	Not very well.
Regular.	So-so; OK.

Expresiones de cortesía

Con permiso.	Pardon me; Excuse me.
De nada.	You're welcome.
Lo siento.	I'm sorry.
(Muchas) gracias.	Thank you (very much); Thanks (a lot).
No hay de qué.	You're welcome.
Perdón.	Pardon me; Excuse me.
por favor	please

Títulos

señor (Sr.); don	Mr.; sir
señora (Sra.); doña	Mrs.; ma'am
señorita (Srta.)	Miss

Presentaciones

¿Cómo se llama usted?	What's your name? (form.)
¿Cómo te llamas?	What's your name? (fam.)
Me llamo...	My name is…
¿Y usted?	And you? (form.)
¿Y tú?	And you? (fam.)
Mucho gusto.	Pleased to meet you.
El gusto es mío.	The pleasure is mine.
Encantado/a.	Delighted; Pleased to meet you.
Igualmente.	Likewise.
Le presento a...	I would like to introduce you to (name). (form.)
Te presento a...	I would like to introduce you to (name). (fam.)
el nombre	name

¿De dónde es?

¿De dónde es usted?	Where are you from? (form.)
¿De dónde eres?	Where are you from? (fam.)
Soy de...	I'm from…

Palabras adicionales

¿cuánto(s)/a(s)?	how much/many?
¿de quién...?	whose…? (sing.)
¿de quiénes...?	whose…? (plural)
(no) hay	there is (not); there are (not)

Sustantivos

el autobús	bus
el chico	boy
la chica	girl
la computadora	computer
la comunidad	community
el/la conductor(a)	driver
la conversación	conversation
la cosa	thing
el cuaderno	notebook
el día	day
el diario	diary
el diccionario	dictionary
la escuela	school
el/la estudiante	student
la foto(grafía)	photograph
el hombre	man
el/la joven	young person
el lápiz	pencil
la lección	lesson
la maleta	suitcase
la mano	hand
el mapa	map
la mujer	woman
la nacionalidad	nationality
el número	number
el país	country
la palabra	word
el/la pasajero/a	passenger
el problema	problem
el/la profesor(a)	teacher
el programa	program
el/la turista	tourist
el video	video

Verbo

ser	to be

Numbers 0–30	See page 16.
Telling time	See pages 24–25.
Expresiones útiles	See page 7.

Lección 2: Teacher Resources

There is a wealth of resources online to support instruction using **Senderos**. For details on how to integrate these Teacher Resources into your lessons, see the front matter of this Teacher's Edition on pages T16 to T48.

Presentation	Practice & Communicate	Assess*	Scripts and Translations	
• Digital Images: • **En la clase**	• Information Gap Activities* • Activity Pack Practice Activities (with Answer Key): **Contextos** • Additional Vocabulary (**Más vocabulario para las clases**) • Digital Image Bank (School and University)	• Vocabulary Quiz (with Answer Key)		contextos
		• **Fotonovela** Optional Testing Sections (with Answer Key)	• **Fotonovela** Videoscript • **Fotonovela** English Translation	fotonovela
• **Estructura 2.1** Grammar Slides	• Activity Pack Practice Activities (with Answer Key): Present tense of **-ar** verbs	• Grammar 2.1 Quiz (with Answer Key)	• Tutorial Script: Present tense of **-ar** verbs	
• **Estructura 2.2** Grammar Slides	• Information Gap Activities* • Activity Pack Practice Activities (with Answer Key): Forming questions in Spanish • Surveys: Worksheet for survey	• Grammar 2.2 Quiz (with Answer Key)	• Tutorial Script: Forming questions in Spanish	estructura
• **Estructura 2.3** Grammar Slides • Digital Images: • Present tense of **estar**	• Activity Pack Practice Activities (with Answer Key): Present tense of **estar**	• Grammar 2.3 Quiz (with Answer Key)	• Tutorial Script: Present tense of **estar**	
• **Estructura 2.4** Grammar Slides	• Information Gap Activities* • Activity Pack Practice Activities (with Answer Key): Numbers 31 and higher	• Grammar 2.4 Quiz (with Answer Key)	• Tutorial Script: Numbers 31 and higher	
			• **En pantalla** Videoscript • **En pantalla** English Translation	En pantalla
		• **Flash cultura** Optional Testing Sections (with Answer Key)	• **Flash cultura** Videoscript • **Flash cultura** English Translation	Flash cultura / adelante
Digital Images: • **España**		• **Panorama** Optional Testing Sections (with Answer Key) • **Panorama cultural** (video)	• **Panorama cultural** Videoscript • **Panorama cultural** English Translation	Panorama

*Can also be assigned online.

Lección 2: Teacher Resources

Pulling It All Together

Practice and Communicate
- Role-plays
- Activity Pack Practice Activities (¡A repasar!) (with Answer Key)

Assessment

Tests and Exams*
- **Prueba A** with audio
- **Prueba B** with audio
- **Prueba C** with audio
- **Prueba D** with audio
- **Prueba E** with audio
- **Prueba F** with audio
- Tests Answer Key
- Oral Testing Suggestions

- **Examen A** with audio (lessons 1-3)
- **Examen B** with audio (lessons 1-3)
- Exams Answer Key

Audioscripts
- Tests and Exams Audioscripts
- Alternative Listening Sections Audioscript

Additional Tools for Planning and Teaching

- Essential Questions
- I Can Worksheets
- IPAs & Rubrics
- Lesson Plans
- Middle School Activity Pack
- Pacing Guides

Audio MP3s for Classroom Activities

- **Contextos. Práctica**: Activities 1 and 2 (p. 41)
- **Estructura** 2.2. **Comunicación**: Activity 4 (p. 58)
- **Escuchar** (p. 71)

Script for Comunicación: Actividad 4 (p. 58)

Manuel	Ana, ¿qué clases tomas?
Ana	Tomo computación, español y biología.
Manuel	¿A qué hora es la clase de computación?
Ana	La clase de computación es a las dos de la tarde.
Manuel	¿De dónde es la profesora de español?
Ana	Es de España.
Manuel	¿Hay mucha tarea en la clase de biología?
Ana	Sí, hay mucha tarea.
Manuel	Diana y tú trabajan, ¿verdad?
Ana	No, no trabajamos.
Manuel	¿Por qué Diana no toma la clase de computación?
Ana	Porque ella necesita tomar la clase de química a las dos... Cuántas preguntas, ¿no?

*Tests and Exams can also be assigned online.

En la clase

2

Communicative Goals

You will learn how to:

- Talk about your classes and school life
- Discuss everyday activities
- Ask questions in Spanish
- Describe the location of people and things

A PRIMERA VISTA

- ¿Hay un chico y una chica en la foto?
- ¿Hay una computadora o dos?
- ¿Son turistas o estudiantes?
- ¿Qué hora es, la una de la mañana o de la tarde?

Lesson Goals

In **Lección 2**, students will be introduced to the following:

- classroom- and school-related words
- names of academic courses and fields of study
- class schedules
- days of the week
- universities and majors in the Spanish-speaking world
- the **Universidad de Salamanca**
- present tense of regular –**ar** verbs
- forming negative sentences
- the verb **gustar**
- forming questions
- the present tense of **estar**
- prepositions of location
- numbers 31 and higher
- using text formats to predict content
- brainstorming and organizing ideas for writing
- writing descriptions of themselves
- listening for cognates
- a television commercial for **Jumbo**, a Chilean superstore chain
- a video about the **Universidad Nacional Autónoma de México (UNAM)**
- cultural, geographic, and economic information about Spain

A primera vista Have students look at the photo. Say: **Es una foto de dos jóvenes en la clase.** Then ask: **¿Qué son los jóvenes? (Son estudiantes.) ¿Qué hay en la mano del chico? (Hay una computadora.)**

Teaching Tip Look for these icons for additional communicative practice:

➡️👤	**Interpretive communication**
↔️👤	**Presentational communication**
👤↔️👤	**Interpersonal communication**

SUPPORT FOR BACKWARD DESIGN

Lección 2 **Essential Questions**
1. How do students talk about their classes and school life?
2. How do people ask and answer questions about their daily activities?
3. How is school in Latin America the same as and different from school in the U.S.?

Lección 2 **Integrated Performance Assessment**
Before teaching this chapter, review the Integrated Performance Assessment (IPA) and its accompanying scoring rubric. Use the IPA to assess students' progress toward proficiency targets at the end of the chapter.
IPA Context: You and your classmates want to know about each others' class schedules and your opinions about the classes you take. First, you will interview one of your classmates to find out about his/her classes. Then you will present your own schedule to the class.

VOICE BOARD

Voice boards online allow you and your students to record and share up to five minutes of audio. Use voice boards for presentations, oral assessments, discussions, directions, etc.

En la clase

Más vocabulario

la biblioteca	*library*
la cafetería	*cafeteria*
la casa	*house; home*
la escuela	*school*
el estadio	*stadium*
el laboratorio	*laboratory*
la librería	*bookstore*
la universidad	*university; college*
el/la compañero/a de clase	*classmate*
la clase	*class*
el curso	*course*
el examen	*test; exam*
el horario	*schedule*
la prueba	*test; quiz*
el semestre	*semester*
la tarea	*homework*
el trimestre	*trimester; quarter*
el arte	*art*
la biología	*biology*
las ciencias	*sciences*
la computación	*computer science*
la contabilidad	*accounting*
la economía	*economics*
el español	*Spanish*
la física	*physics*
la geografía	*geography*
la música	*music*

Variación léxica

pluma ⟷ bolígrafo
pizarra ⟷ tablero (*Col.*)

el reloj · la ventana · la puerta · la profesora · el estudiante · la mesa · la calculadora · el libro · la pluma

Labels on image: el mapa, la pizarra, LAS MATERIAS / COURSES, el papel, el borrador, la tiza, la papelera, el escritorio, la mochila, la estudiante, la silla

LAS MATERIAS — COURSES

LAS MATERIAS	COURSES
la historia	history
las humanidades	humanities
el inglés	English
las lenguas extranjeras	foreign languages
la literatura	literature
las matemáticas	mathematics
el periodismo	journalism
la psicología	psychology
la química	chemistry
la sociología	sociology

Práctica

1 **Escuchar** Listen to Ms. Morales talk about her Spanish classroom, then check the items she mentions.

puerta	☑	tiza	☑	plumas	☑
ventanas	☑	escritorios	☑	mochilas	○
pizarra	☑	sillas	○	papel	☑
borrador	○	libros	☑	reloj	☑

2 **Identificar** You will hear a series of words. Write each one in the appropriate category.

Personas	Lugares	Materias
el estudiante	el estadio	la química
la profesora	la biblioteca	las lenguas extranjeras
el compañero de clase		el inglés

3 **Emparejar** Match each question with its most logical response. **¡Ojo!** (*Careful!*) One response will not be used.

1. ¿Qué clase es? d
2. ¿Quiénes son? g
3. ¿Quién es? e
4. ¿De dónde es? c
5. ¿A qué hora es la clase de inglés? f
6. ¿Cuántos estudiantes hay? a

a. Hay veinticinco.
b. Es un reloj.
c. Es de Perú.
d. Es la clase de química.
e. Es el señor Bastos.
f. Es a las nueve en punto.
g. Son los profesores.

4 **Escoger** Identify the word that does not belong in each group.

1. examen • casa • tarea • prueba casa
2. literatura • matemáticas • biblioteca • historia biblioteca
3. pizarra • tiza • borrador • librería librería
4. lápiz • cafetería • papel • cuaderno cafetería
5. veinte • diez • pluma • treinta pluma
6. conductor • laboratorio • autobús • pasajero laboratorio

5 **¿Qué clase es?** Name the class associated with the subject matter.

> **modelo**
> los elementos, los átomos Es la clase de química.

1. Abraham Lincoln, Winston Churchill Es la clase de historia.
2. Picasso, Leonardo da Vinci Es la clase de arte.
3. Newton, Einstein Es la clase de física.
4. África, el océano Pacífico Es la clase de geografía.
5. la cultura de España, verbos Es la clase de español.
6. Hemingway, Shakespeare Es la clase de literatura.
7. geometría, calculadora Es la clase de matemáticas.

1 **Expansion** Have students circle the items that they see in their own classroom.

1 **Script** ¿Qué hay en mi clase de español? ¡Muchas cosas! Hay una puerta y cinco ventanas. Hay una pizarra con tiza. Hay muchos escritorios para los estudiantes. En los escritorios de los estudiantes hay libros y plumas. En la mesa de la profesora hay papel. Hay un mapa y un reloj en la clase también.

2 **In-Class Tip** To simplify, have students prepare for listening by predicting a few words for each category.

2 **Script** el estudiante, la química, el estadio, las lenguas extranjeras, la profesora, la biblioteca, el inglés, el compañero de clase

3 **Expansion** Have student pairs ask each other the questions and answer truthfully, based on your class. Ex: **1. ¿Qué clase es? (Es la clase de español.)** For items 2–4, the questioner should indicate specific people in the classroom.

4 **Expansion** Have students write four additional items for a partner to complete.

5 **Expansion** Have the class associate famous people with these fields: **química, computación, música.** Then have them guess the fields associated with these people: Socrates (**filosofía**), Charles Darwin (**biología**).

TEACHING OPTIONS

Extra Practice Ask students what phrases or vocabulary words they associate with these items: **1. la pizarra** (Ex: **la tiza, el borrador**), **2. el reloj** (Ex: **¿Qué hora es?, Son las…, Es la…**), **3. la biblioteca** (Ex: **los libros, los exámenes, las materias**).

Extra Practice 🔁 On the board, write **¿Qué clases tomas?** and **Tomo…** Explain the meaning of these phrases and ask students to circulate around the classroom and imagine that they are meeting their classmates for the first time. Tell them to introduce themselves, find out where each person is from, and ask what classes they are taking. Follow up by asking individual students what their classmates are taking.

- Write these questions and answers on the board, explaining their meaning as you do so:
  —**¿Qué día es hoy?**
  —**Hoy es ____.**
  —**¿Qué día es mañana?**
  (Students learned **mañana** in **Lección 1**.)
  —**Mañana es ____.**
  —**¿Cuándo es la prueba?**
  —**Es el ____.**
  Then ask students the questions on the board.
- Explain that Monday is considered the first day of the week in the Spanish-speaking world and usually appears as such on calendars.

⑥ Expansion To challenge students, ask them questions such as: **Mañana es viernes… ¿qué día fue ayer? (miércoles); Ayer fue domingo… ¿qué día es mañana? (martes)**

⑦ In-Class Tip To simplify, before doing this activity, have students review the list of **sustantivos** on page 38 and numbers 0–30 on page 16.

Los días de la semana

¿Qué día es hoy (today)?

Hoy es martes.

¿Cuándo (When) es el examen?

Es el viernes.

septiembre

lunes	martes	miércoles	jueves	viernes	sábado	domingo
	1	2	3	4	5	6
7	8	9	10			

6 ¿Qué día es hoy? Complete each statement with the correct day of the week.

1. Hoy es martes. Mañana es ___miércoles___. Ayer fue (*Yesterday was*) ___lunes___.
2. Ayer fue sábado. Mañana es ___lunes___. Hoy es ___domingo___.
3. Mañana es viernes. Hoy es ___jueves___. Ayer fue ___miércoles___.
4. Ayer fue domingo. Hoy es ___lunes___. Mañana es ___martes___.
5. Hoy es jueves. Ayer fue ___miércoles___. Mañana es ___viernes___.
6. Mañana es lunes. Hoy es ___domingo___. Ayer fue ___sábado___.

7 Analogías Use these words to complete the analogies. Some words will not be used.

arte	día	martes	pizarra
biblioteca	domingo	matemáticas	profesor
catorce	estudiante	mujer	reloj

1. maleta ⟷ pasajero ⊜ mochila ⟷ ___estudiante___
2. chico ⟷ chica ⊜ hombre ⟷ ___mujer___
3. pluma ⟷ papel ⊜ tiza ⟷ ___pizarra___
4. inglés ⟷ lengua ⊜ miércoles ⟷ ___día___
5. papel ⟷ cuaderno ⊜ libro ⟷ ___biblioteca___
6. quince ⟷ dieciséis ⊜ lunes ⟷ ___martes___
7. Cervantes ⟷ literatura ⊜ Dalí ⟷ ___arte___
8. autobús ⟷ conductor ⊜ clase ⟷ ___profesor___
9. los EE.UU. ⟷ mapa ⊜ hora ⟷ ___reloj___
10. veinte ⟷ veintitrés ⊜ jueves ⟷ ___domingo___

Communication 1.1, 1.2, 1.3

Comunicación

8 **Horario** Read Cristina's description of her schedule. Then indicate whether the following conclusions are **lógico** or **ilógico**, based on what you read.

> Las clases de inglés, matemáticas, español, e historia son a la misma (*same*) hora cada (*each*) día, de lunes a viernes. El profesor Núñez enseña (*teaches*) la clase de inglés. Empieza (*It starts*) a las ocho. Tomo (*I take*) matemáticas a las nueve menos diez, y español a las diez menos veinte. Me gusta (*I like*) la profesora Salazar que enseña la clase de historia. Los lunes y miércoles, voy (*I go*) al laboratorio para biología a la una. Los martes, jueves y viernes, tomo la clase de música. ¡Me gusta mucho la clase de música!

	Lógico	Ilógico
1. Cristina es estudiante.	☑	○
2. Cristina toma seis clases durante la semana.	☑	○
3. Cristina toma una clase los lunes a las tres de la tarde.	○	☑
4. La profesora Salazar enseña la clase de historia.	☑	○
5. El profesor Núñez enseña la clase de español.	○	☑
6. Cristina toma clase de música los sábados.	○	☑

9 **La semana** Write a paragraph about what a typical week looks like for you. Describe your schedule for the week, including classes, times, and teachers. Answers will vary.

> *modelo*
>
> *El lunes tomo la clase de matemáticas a las nueve con el profesor Smith. A las diez...*

10 **Nuevos amigos** During the first week of class, you meet a new student in the cafeteria. With a partner, prepare a conversation using these cues. Answers will vary.

Estudiante 1		**Estudiante 2**
Greet your new acquaintance.	→	Introduce yourself.
Find out about him or her.	→	Tell him or her about yourself.
Ask about your partner's class schedule.	→	Compare your schedule to your partner's.
Say nice to meet you and goodbye.	→	Say nice to meet you and goodbye.

PERSONAJES   MARISSA   FELIPE

Section Goals

In **Fotonovela**, students will:
• receive comprehensible input from free-flowing discourse
• learn functional phrases that preview lesson grammatical structures

 Communication 1.2
Cultures 2.1, 2.2

Teacher Resources

Read the front matter for suggestions on how to incorporate all the program's components. See pages 39A–39B for a detailed listing of Teacher Resources online.

Video Recap: Lección 1

Before doing this **Fotonovela** section, review the previous episode with these questions:
1. En la familia Díaz, ¿quiénes son estudiantes? (Felipe y Jimena son estudiantes.)
2. ¿Quién es Roberto? (Es el esposo de Carolina.) 3. ¿De dónde es Marissa? (Es de Wisconsin.) 4. ¿De dónde es la señora Díaz? (Es de Cuba.) 5. ¿Es de Felipe el diccionario? (No, es de Marissa.)

Video Synopsis
Felipe takes **Marissa** around Mexico City. Along the way, they meet some friends, **Juan Carlos** and **Miguel. Felipe, Marissa,** and **Juan Carlos** compare schedules for the upcoming semester, while **Miguel** rushes off to meet **Maru.**

In-Class Tips

• Have students cover up the **Expresiones útiles.** Have them scan the **Fotonovela** captions to find phrases about classes and then phrases that express what people like.
• Ask a few basic questions that use the **Expresiones útiles.** Ex: **¿Cuántas clases tomas? ¿Te gusta la clase de _____?**

¿Qué estudias?

Felipe, Marissa, Juan Carlos y Miguel visitan Chapultepec y hablan de las clases.

1   FELIPE Dos boletos, por favor.

2   EMPLEADO Dos boletos son 64 pesos.
FELIPE Aquí están 100 pesos.
EMPLEADO 100 menos 64 son 36 pesos de cambio.

MIGUEL Marissa, hablas muy bien el español... ¿Y dónde está tu diccionario?
MARISSA En casa de los Díaz. Felipe necesita practicar inglés.
MIGUEL ¡Ay, Maru! Chicos, nos vemos más tarde.

3   FELIPE Ésta es la Ciudad de México.

4   FELIPE Oye, Marissa, ¿cuántas clases tomas?
MARISSA Tomo cuatro clases: español, historia, literatura y también geografía. Me gusta mucho la cultura mexicana.

FELIPE Juan Carlos, ¿quién enseña la clase de química este semestre?
JUAN CARLOS El profesor Morales. Ah, ¿por qué tomo química y computación?
FELIPE Porque te gusta la tarea.

TEACHING OPTIONS

Video Tips General suggestions for using video clips in the classroom can be found in the front matter of this Teacher's Edition.
¿Qué estudias? 👤↔👤 Play the **¿Qué estudias?** episode of the **Fotonovela** and have students give you a "play-by-play" description of the action. Write their descriptions on the board.

Give the class a moment to read the descriptions you have written and then play the episode a second time so that students can add more details to the descriptions or consolidate information. Finally, discuss the material on the board with the class and call attention to any incorrect information. Help students prepare a brief plot summary.

JUAN CARLOS **MIGUEL** **EMPLEADO** **MARU**

7

FELIPE Los lunes y los miércoles, economía a las 2:30. Tú tomas computación los martes en la tarde, y química, a ver... Los lunes, los miércoles y los viernes ¿a las 10? ¡Uf!

8

FELIPE Y Miguel, ¿cuándo regresa?

JUAN CARLOS Hoy estudia con Maru.

MARISSA ¿Quién es Maru?

9

MIGUEL ¿Hablas con tu mamá?

MARU Mamá habla. Yo escucho. Es la 1:30.

MIGUEL Ay, lo siento. Juan Carlos y Felipe...

MARU Ay, Felipe.

10

MARU Y ahora, ¿adónde? ¿A la biblioteca?

MIGUEL Sí, pero primero a la librería. Necesito comprar unos libros.

Expresiones útiles

Talking about classes

¿Cuántas clases tomas?
How many classes are you taking?
Tomo cuatro clases.
I'm taking four classes.
Este año, espero sacar buenas notas y, por supuesto, viajar por el país.
This year, I hope / I'm hoping to get good grades. And, of course, travel through the country.

Talking about likes/dislikes

Me gusta mucho la cultura mexicana.
I like Mexican culture a lot.
Me gustan las ciencias ambientales.
I like environmental science.
Me gusta dibujar.
I like to draw.
¿Te gusta este lugar?
Do you like this place?

Paying for tickets

Dos boletos, por favor.
Two tickets, please.
Dos boletos son sesenta y cuatro pesos.
Two tickets are sixty-four pesos.
Aquí están cien pesos.
Here's a hundred pesos.
Son treinta y seis pesos de cambio.
That's thirty-six pesos change.

Talking about location and direction

¿Dónde está tu diccionario?
Where is your dictionary?
Está en casa de los Díaz.
It's at the Díaz house.
Y ahora, ¿adónde? ¿A la biblioteca?
And now, where to? To the library?
Sí, pero primero a la librería. Está al lado.
Yes, but first to the bookstore. It's next door.

Expresiones útiles Identify forms of **tomar** and **estar**. Point out the questions and interrogative words. Tell students that they will learn more about these concepts in **Estructura**. Point out that **gusta** is used when what is liked is singular, and **gustan** when what is liked is plural. A detailed discussion of the **gustar** construction (see **Estructura 2.1**, page 52) is unnecessary here. Emphasize the **me/te gusta(n)** forms, as these are the only ones that will appear on tests until **Lección 7**.

In-Class Tip Have the class read through the entire **Fotonovela**, with volunteers playing the parts of **Felipe, Marissa, Juan Carlos, Miguel, Maru,** and the **empleado**.

¿Qué pasó?

1 **Escoger** Choose the answer that best completes each sentence.

1. Marissa toma (*is taking*) _____c_____ en la universidad.
   a. español, inglés, economía y música   b. historia, inglés, sociología y periodismo
   c. español, historia, literatura y geografía
2. El profesor Morales enseña (*teaches*) _____a_____.
   a. química   b. matemáticas   c. historia
3. Juan Carlos toma química _____b_____.
   a. los miércoles, jueves y viernes   b. los lunes, miércoles y viernes
   c. los lunes, martes y jueves
4. Miguel necesita ir a (*needs to go to*) _____c_____.
   a. la biblioteca   b. la cafetería   c. la librería

2 **Identificar** Indicate which person would make each statement. The names may be used more than once.

1. ¿Maru es compañera de ustedes? __Marissa__
2. Mi mamá habla mucho. __Maru__
3. El profesor Morales enseña la clase de química este semestre. __Juan Carlos__
4. Mi diccionario está en casa de Felipe y Jimena. __Marissa__
5. Necesito estudiar con Maru. __Miguel__
6. Yo tomo clase de computación los martes por la tarde. __Juan Carlos__

MARU

JUAN CARLOS   MARISSA

MIGUEL

3 **Completar** These sentences are similar to things said in the **Fotonovela**. Complete each sentence with the correct word(s).

Castillo de Chapultepec	estudiar	miércoles
clase	inglés	tarea

1. Marissa, éste es el __Castillo de Chapultepec__.
2. Felipe tiene (*has*) el diccionario porque (*because*) necesita practicar __inglés__.
3. A Juan Carlos le gusta mucho la __tarea__.
4. Hay clase de economía los lunes y __miércoles__.
5. Miguel está con Maru para __estudiar__.

4 **Preguntas personales** Answer your partner's questions about your classes. Answers will vary.

1. ¿Qué clases tomas?
2. ¿Qué clases tomas los martes?
3. ¿Qué clases tomas los viernes?
4. ¿Quién enseña la clase de español?
5. ¿Te gusta la clase de español?

Pronunciación
Spanish vowels

a   **e**   **i**   **o**   **u**

Spanish vowels are never silent; they are always pronounced in a short, crisp way without the glide sounds used in English.

Álex	**clase**	**nada**	**encantada**

The letter **a** is pronounced like the *a* in *father*, but shorter.

el	**ene**	**mesa**	**elefante**

The letter **e** is pronounced like the *e* in *they*, but shorter.

Inés	**chica**	**tiza**	**señorita**

The letter **i** sounds like the *ee* in *beet*, but shorter.

hola	**con**	**libro**	**don Francisco**

The letter **o** is pronounced like the *o* in *tone*, but shorter.

uno	**regular**	**saludos**	**gusto**

The letter **u** sounds like the *oo* in *room*, but shorter.

Práctica Practice the vowels by saying the names of these places in Spain.

1. Madrid
2. Alicante
3. Tenerife
4. Toledo
5. Barcelona
6. Granada
7. Burgos
8. La Coruña

Oraciones Read the sentences aloud, focusing on the vowels.

1. Hola. Me llamo Ramiro Morgado.
2. Enseño español en la escuela secundaria.
3. Tomo también literatura y contabilidad.
4. Ay, tengo clase de biología. ¡Nos vemos!

Refranes Practice the vowels by reading these sayings aloud.

Del dicho al hecho hay un gran trecho.[1]

Cada loco con su tema.[2]

1 *Easier said than done.*
2 *To each his own.*

Section Goals

In **Cultura**, students will:
- learn how Mexican students choose their courses to determine their career or university-level studies
- learn school-related terms
- read about the **Instituto Nacional Franciso Menéndez**
- read about Latin American school systems

Communication 1.1, 1.2
Cultures 2.1, 2.2
Connections 3.1, 3.2
Comparisons 4.2

En detalle

Antes de leer Ask students about how they choose their classes. Who or what influences their choices?

Lectura

- Explain that students often choose their high school based on its programs.
- In Mexico, **preparatoria** is optional, but all students are legally required to finish **escuela secundaria**.

Después de leer Ask students what they think of the Mexican school system and how it differs from that of the U.S.

1 Expansion Give students these sentences as items 9–10:
9. Students in Mexico take courses in foreign languages every year. (**Cierto.**) 10. Students enrolled in **Ciencias Biológicas** are not expected to continue studying. (**Falso.**)

EN DETALLE

La escuela
secundaria

Manuel, a 15-year-old student in Mexico, is taking an intense third level course focused on **la química**. This is a typical part of the studies for his grade. **Escuela secundaria** (*secondary school*), which in Mexico begins after six years of **escuela primaria** (*primary school*), has three grades for students between the ages of 12 and 15.

Students like Manuel must study courses in mathematics, science, Spanish, foreign languages (English or French), music, and more every year. After that, students choose a **plan de estudio** (*program of study*) in **preparatoria**, the three years (or two, depending on the program) of school after **escuela secundaria** and before university studies. The program of study that students choose requires them to study specific **materias** that are needed in preparation for their future career.

Some **bachilleratos** (*high school degrees*) are **terminales**, which means that when students graduate they are prepared with all of the skills and requirements to begin their field of work.

These students are not expected to continue studying. Some **modalidades** (*programs of study*) that are terminal include:
- **Educación Tecnológica Agropecuaria** (*Agriculture and Fishing*)
- **Comercio y Administración** (*Commerce, for administrative work*)

Other programs are designed for students who plan to continue their studies in a **carrera universitaria** (*college major*). Some programs that prepare students for university studies are:
- **Ciencias Biológicas**
- **Ciencias Contables, Económicas y Bancarias** (*Economic and Banking Sciences*)
- **Música y Arte**

Each program has courses that are designed for a specific career. This means that although all high school students may take a mathematics course, the type of mathematics studied varies according to the needs of each degree.

La escuela y la universidad

Some Mexican high schools are designed and managed by universities as well as by the Secretary of Education. One university that directs such schools is the **Universidad Nacional Autónoma de México (UNAM),** Mexico's largest university.

ACTIVIDADES

1 **¿Cierto o falso?** Indicate whether each statement is **cierto** or **falso**. Correct the false statements.

1. High schools are specialized in certain areas of study. **Cierto.**
2. Students in Mexico cannot study art in school. **Falso. Música y arte** is a **preparatoria** program of study.
3. Students do not need to complete primary school before going to **escuela secundaria**. **Falso.** Students must complete primary school as a prerequisite for **escuela secundaria**.
4. The length of high school **planes de estudio** in Mexico varies between two and three years. **Cierto.**
5. Students need to go to college to study to do administrative work. **Falso. Comercio y Administración** is a **terminal** program of study.
6. All students must take the same mathematics courses at the high school level. **Falso.** Mathematics courses differ depending on the program of study a student follows.
7. **La escuela secundaria** is for students from the ages of 16 to 18 years old. **Falso. Escuela secundaria** primarily serves students who are 12 to 15 years old, followed by the **preparatoria**.
8. All students in Mexico complete university studies. **Falso.** Some students do not study beyond **preparatoria**.

TEACHING OPTIONS

Small Groups In groups of three, have students discuss their favorite course in which they are currently enrolled. Ask them to write several sentences in Spanish about why they like the course and whether or not it is a **curso electivo** (*elective*).

PRE-AP®

Presentational Speaking with Cultural Comparison Ask student pairs to decide whether or not they would prefer to study in a school program similar to Manuel's program in Mexico. Ask them to explain their choice based on the aspects included in the reading, such as programs of study, courses offered, and future plans. Tally their choices and make a bar graph of the results to hang in the classroom.

ASÍ SE DICE

Clases y exámenes

aprobar	to pass
el colegio/la escuela	school
la escuela secundaria/ la preparatoria (Méx.)/ el liceo (Ven.)/ el instituto (Esp.)	high school
el examen parcial	midterm exam
el horario	schedule
la matrícula	enrollment (in school)
reprobar	to fail
sacar buenas/ malas notas	to get good/ bad grades

EL MUNDO HISPANO

La escuela en Latinoamérica

- **In Latin America**, public secondary schools are free of charge. Private schools, however, can be quite costly. At **la Escuela Campo Alegre** in Venezuela, annual tuition is about $25,000 a year.

- **Argentina** and **Chile** are the two Latin American countries with the most years of required schooling at 13 years each.

- **In Chile**, students begin the school year in March and finish in December. Of course—Chile lies south of the equator, so while it is winter in the United States, Chilean students are on their summer break!

PERFIL

El INFRAMEN

La ciudad de San Salvador

The **Instituto Nacional Francisco Menéndez (INFRAMEN)** is the largest public high school in El Salvador. So it should be: it is named after General Francisco Menéndez, an ex-president of the country who was the founder of **enseñanza secundaria** (*secondary studies*) for the entire country! The 1,900 students at the INFRAMEN can choose to complete one of four kinds of diplomas: general studies, health care, tourism, and business. The institution has changed locales (and even cities) many times since it was founded in 1885 and is currently located in the capital city of San Salvador. Students at the INFRAMEN begin their school year in mid January and finish in early November.

Conexión Internet

How do dress codes vary in schools across Latin America?

Go to **vhlcentral.com** to find more cultural information related to this **Cultura** section.

ACTIVIDADES

2 **Comprensión** Complete these sentences.
1. The INFRAMEN was founded in _____.
2. The programs of study available in the INFRAMEN are _____.
3. There are _____ students in the INFRAMEN.
4. General Francisco Menéndez was a _____ of El Salvador.
5. El _____ is a student's schedule.

3 **¡A estudiar!** All students have classes they like and classes they don't. What are your favorite classes? Which are your least favorite? With a partner, discuss what you like and don't like about your classes and make a short list of what could be done to improve the classes you don't like.

2.1 Present tense of -ar verbs

ANTE TODO In order to talk about activities, you need to use verbs. Verbs express actions or states of being. In English and Spanish, the infinitive is the base form of the verb. In English, the infinitive is preceded by the word *to*: *to study, to be*. The infinitive in Spanish is a one-word form and can be recognized by its endings: **-ar**, **-er**, or **-ir**.

-*ar* verb	-*er* verb	-*ir* verb
estudiar *to study*	**comer** *to eat*	**escribir** *to write*

▶ In this lesson, you will learn the forms of regular **-ar** verbs.

The verb estudiar (*to study*)

SINGULAR FORMS	yo	estudi**o**	*I study*
	tú	estudi**as**	*you* (fam.) *study*
	Ud./él/ella	estudi**a**	*you* (form.) *study; he/she studies*
PLURAL FORMS	nosotros/as	estudi**amos**	*we study*
	vosotros/as	estudi**áis**	*you* (fam.) *study*
	Uds./ellos/ellas	estudi**an**	*you study; they study*

Juan Carlos estudia ciencias ambientales.

Y tú, ¿qué estudias, Miguel?

▶ To create the forms of most regular verbs in Spanish, drop the infinitive endings (**-ar**, **-er**, **-ir**). You then add to the stem the endings that correspond to the different subject pronouns. This diagram will help you visualize verb conjugation.

Conjugation of -*ar* verbs

INFINITIVE	VERB STEM	CONJUGATED FORM
estudi**ar**	estudi-	yo estudi**o**
bail**ar**	bail-	tú bail**as**
trabaj**ar**	trabaj-	nosotros trabaj**amos**

TEACHING OPTIONS

Extra Practice Do a pattern practice drill. Write an infinitive from the list of common –**ar** verbs on page 51 on the board and ask individual students to provide conjugations for the subject pronouns and names you suggest. Reverse the activity by saying a conjugated form and asking students to give the corresponding subject pronoun. Allow multiple answers for the third-person singular and plural.

Extra Practice 👤↔👤 Ask questions using **estudiar, bailar,** and **trabajar.** Students should answer in complete sentences. Ask additional questions to get more information. Ex: —_____, **¿trabajas? —Sí, trabajo. —¿Dónde trabajas? —Trabajo en _____.**
- —**¿Quién baila los sábados? —Yo bailo los sábados. —¿Bailas merengue?** • —**¿Estudian mucho ustedes? —¿Quién estudia más? —¿Cuántas horas estudias los lunes? ¿Y los sábados?**

Common -ar verbs

bailar	to dance	**estudiar**	to study
buscar	to look for	**explicar**	to explain
caminar	to walk	**hablar**	to talk; to speak
cantar	to sing	**llegar**	to arrive
cenar	to have dinner	**llevar**	to carry
comprar	to buy	**mirar**	to look (at); to watch
contestar	to answer	**necesitar (+ inf.)**	to need
conversar	to converse, to chat	**practicar**	to practice
desayunar	to have breakfast	**preguntar**	to ask (a question)
descansar	to rest	**preparar**	to prepare
desear (+ inf.)	to desire; to wish	**regresar**	to return
dibujar	to draw	**terminar**	to end; to finish
enseñar	to teach	**tomar**	to take; to drink
escuchar	to listen (to)	**trabajar**	to work
esperar (+ inf.)	to wait (for); to hope	**viajar**	to travel

▶ **¡Atención!** Unless referring to a person, the Spanish verbs **buscar, escuchar, esperar,** and **mirar** do not need to be followed by prepositions as they do in English.

Busco la tarea.
I'm looking for the homework.

Escucho la música.
I'm listening to the music.

Espero el autobús.
I'm waiting for the bus.

Miro la pizarra.
I'm looking at the blackboard.

COMPARE & CONTRAST

English uses three sets of forms to talk about the present: (1) the simple present (*Paco works*), (2) the present progressive (*Paco is working*), and (3) the emphatic present (*Paco does work*). In Spanish, the simple present can be used in all three cases.

Paco **trabaja** en la cafetería.
1. *Paco works in the cafeteria.*
2. *Paco is working in the cafeteria.*
3. *Paco does work in the cafeteria.*

In Spanish and English, the present tense is also sometimes used to express future action.

Marina **viaja** a Madrid mañana.
1. *Marina travels to Madrid tomorrow.*
2. *Marina will travel to Madrid tomorrow.*
3. *Marina is traveling to Madrid tomorrow.*

▶ When two verbs are used together with no change of subject, the second verb is generally in the infinitive. To make a sentence negative in Spanish, the word **no** is placed before the conjugated verb. In this case, **no** means *not*.

Deseo hablar con el señor Díaz.
I want to speak with Mr. Díaz.

Alicia **no** desea bailar ahora.
Alicia doesn't want to dance now.

In-Class Tips

- Remind students that **vosotros/as** forms will not be practiced actively in **Senderos**.
- Model the pronunciation of each infinitive and have students repeat it after you.
- Model the **yo** form of several verbs, creating simple sentences about yourself (Ex: **Bailo con mis amigos.**) and asking students if they do the same activities (Ex: **¿Bailas mucho con los amigos?**). Restate students' answers using the **él/ella** forms of the –ar verbs and then ask them to verify their classmates' answers. Ex: ¿_____ baila mucho? No, _____ no baila.
- 👤↔👤 To personalize the information presented here, have students ask each other about the activities they do on a typical day of the week (e.g., Friday). Write on the board **¿A qué hora...?** and underneath list **desayunar, terminar las clases,** and **cenar.** Model question and answer formation with your own information. Have students interview each other in pairs and then report back to the class.
- Explain that the simple present tense in Spanish is the equivalent of the three present tense forms of English. Model sentences and give a few additional examples.
- Write additional examples of a conjugated verb followed by an infinitive on the board.
- Explain that, when answering questions negatively, **no** must be used twice. To practice this construction, ask questions of students that will most likely result in negative answers. Ex: —_____, ¿bailas tango? —**No, no bailo tango.**

TEACHING OPTIONS

Heritage Speakers ←👤→ Have heritage speakers talk about their current semester: what they study, if/where they work, which television programs they watch, etc. Ask the rest of the class comprehension questions.

Extra Practice 👤↔👤 Ask students to create a two-column chart with the heads **Necesito...** and **Espero...**, and have them complete it with six things they need to do this week, and six

things they hope to do after the semester is over. Ex: **Necesito estudiar. Espero viajar.** Then have them interview a classmate and report back to the class.

Pairs ←👤→ Ask student pairs to write ten sentences using the verbs presented in this section. Point out that students can use vocabulary words from **Contextos** with these verbs. Have pairs share their sentences with the class.

In-Class Tips

• Model clarification/contrast sentences. Ask several students: **¿Dónde desayunas?** Then, pointing to two students who answered differently, ask the class: **¿Dónde desayunan? (Él desayuna en la cafetería y ella desayuna en su casa.)** Then show how to use subject pronouns to give emphasis. Ex: —____, **¿te gusta bailar?** —**No, no me gusta bailar.** —____ **no baila. Yo bailo.**

• Point out the position of subjects and subject pronouns with regard to the verbs in affirmative and negative sentences.

• Stress that subject pronouns are never used with **gustar**. They appear in the grammar explanation only for guidance.

• Point out that, just as subject pronouns can be used for clarification or emphasis, students should use the prepositional phrases **a mí, a ti,** etc., with the verb **gustar** to clarify or give emphasis. Also point out the written accent on **mí** and the lack of an accent on **ti**.

• Point out that, even when two or more infinitives are used, the form remains singular: **gusta**.

• Divide the board into two columns. On the left side, list the indirect object pronouns (**me, te**). On the right side, provide a mix of infinitives and plural and singular nouns, and have students supply **gusta** or **gustan** for each one. Then call on volunteers to combine elements from each column to form sentences.

• If you wish to practice the third person, write the headings **Gustos** and **Disgustos** on the board. Have the class brainstorm likes and dislikes among the students at your school, including classes, pastimes, music, and movies. Use the lists to form statements and questions.

▶ Spanish speakers often omit subject pronouns because the verb endings indicate who the subject is. In Spanish, subject pronouns are used for emphasis, clarification, or contrast.

—¿Qué enseñan?
What do they teach?

—**Ella** enseña arte y **él** enseña física.
She teaches art, and he teaches physics.

—¿Quién desea trabajar hoy?
Who wants to work today?

—**Yo** no deseo trabajar hoy.
I don't want to work today.

The verb gustar

▶ **Gustar** is different from other **-ar** verbs. To express your likes and dislikes, use the expression **(no) me gusta + el/la** + [*singular noun*] or **(no) me gustan + los/las** + [*plural noun*]. Note: You may use the phrase **a mí** for emphasis, but never the subject pronoun **yo**.

Me gusta la música clásica.
I like classical music.

Me gustan las clases de español y biología.
I like Spanish and biology classes.

A mí me gustan las artes.
I like the arts.

A mí no me gusta el programa.
I don't like the program.

▶ To talk about what you like and don't like to do, use **(no) me gusta** + [*infinitive(s)*]. Note that the singular **gusta** is always used, even with more than one infinitive.

No me gusta viajar en autobús.
I don't like to travel by bus.

Me gusta cantar y bailar.
I like to sing and dance.

▶ To ask a friend about likes and dislikes, use the pronoun **te** instead of **me**. Note: You may use **a ti** for emphasis, but never the subject pronoun **tú**.

—**¿Te gusta la geografía?**
Do you like geography?

—**Sí, me gusta. Y a ti, ¿te gusta el inglés?**
Yes, I like it. And you, do you like English?

▶ You can use this same structure to talk about other people by using the pronouns **nos, le,** and **les**.

Nos gusta dibujar. (nosotros)
We like to draw.

Nos gustan las clases de español e inglés. (nosotros)
We like Spanish class and English class.

No le gusta trabajar. (usted, él, ella)
You don't like to work.
He/She doesn't like to work.

Les gusta el arte. (ustedes, ellos, ellas)
You like art.
They like art.

¡ATENCIÓN!

Note that **gustar** does not behave like other **-ar** verbs. You must study its use carefully and pay attention to prepositions, pronouns, and agreement.

AYUDA

Use the construction **a** + [*name/pronoun*] to clarify to whom you are referring. This construction is not always necessary.
A Gabriela le gusta bailar.
A Sara y a él les gustan los animales.
A mí me gusta viajar.
¿A ti te gustan las clases?

¡INTÉNTALO!   Provide the present tense forms of these verbs. The first items have been done for you.

hablar

1. Yo ___hablo___ español.
2. Ellos ___hablan___ español.
3. Inés ___habla___ español.
4. Nosotras ___hablamos___ español.
5. Tú ___hablas___ español.

gustar

1. ___Me gusta___ el café. (a mí)
2. ¿___Te gustan___ las clases? (a ti)
3. No ___te gusta___ el café. (a ti)
4. No ___me gustan___ las clases. (a mí)
5. No ___me gusta___ el café. (a mí)

TEACHING OPTIONS

Video → Show the **Fotonovela** again and stop the video where appropriate to discuss how certain verbs were used and to ask questions.

Pairs ← Write five word pairs (mix of infinitives and plural and singular nouns) on the board. Ex: **la *Coca-Cola*/la *Pepsi*** Have student pairs take turns asking each other what they like better: **¿Qué te gusta más…?** Then have them write a summary of what each of them likes to share with the class.

Game Divide the class into two teams. Call on one team member at a time, alternating between teams. Give an **–ar** verb in its infinitive form and name a subject pronoun. The team member should say the corresponding present tense verb form. Give one point per correct answer. Deduct one point for each wrong answer. The team with the most points at the end wins.

Communication 1.1
Comparisons 4.1

Práctica

1 **Completar** Complete the conversation with the appropriate forms of the verbs in parentheses.

JUAN   ¡Hola, Linda! ¿Qué (1)___*llevas*___ (llevar) en la mochila?

LINDA   (2)___*llevo*___ (llevar) las cosas que (3)___*necesito*___ (necesitar) para la clase de español.

JUAN   (4)___*necesitas*___ (necesitar) el libro de español?

LINDA   Claro que sí.

JUAN   ¿Los estudiantes en tu clase de español (5)___*estudian*___ (estudiar) mucho?

LINDA   Sí, nosotros (6)___*practicamos*___ (practicar) y (7)___*conversamos*___ (conversar) en español treinta minutos todos los días (*every day*).

2 **Oraciones** Form sentences using the words provided. Remember to conjugate the verbs and add any other necessary words.

1. ustedes / practicar / vocabulario   Ustedes practican el vocabulario.
2. ¿preparar (tú) / tarea?   ¿Preparas la tarea?
3. clase de español / terminar / once   La clase de español termina a las once.
4. ¿qué / buscar / ustedes?   ¿Qué buscan ustedes?
5. (nosotros) buscar / pluma   Buscamos una pluma.
6. (yo) comprar / calculadora   Compro una calculadora.

3 **Gustos** Read what these people do. Then use the information in parentheses to tell what they like.

> **modelo**
>
> Yo enseño en la escuela. (las clases)   Me gustan las clases.

1. Tú deseas mirar cuadros (*paintings*) de Picasso. (el arte)   Te gusta el arte.
2. Soy estudiante de química. (estudiar)   Me gusta estudiar.
3. Tú estudias italiano y español. (las lenguas extranjeras)   Te gustan las lenguas extranjeras.
4. No descansas los sábados. (cantar y bailar)   Te gusta cantar y bailar.
5. Busco una computadora. (la computación)   Me gusta la computación.

4 **Actividades** Get together with a classmate and take turns asking each other if you do these activities. Which activities does your classmate like? Which do you both like?   Answers will vary.

> **modelo**
>
> tomar el autobús
>
> **Estudiante 1:** ¿Tomas el autobús?
>
> **Estudiante 2:** Sí, tomo el autobús, pero (*but*) no me gusta./ No, no tomo el autobús.

bailar merengue	escuchar música rock	practicar el español
cantar en público	estudiar física	hablar italiano
dibujar bien	mirar la televisión	viajar a Europa

1 **In-Class Tip** To simplify, guide the class to first identify the subject and verb ending for each item.

1 **Expansion** Go over the answers quickly as a class. Then ask volunteers to role-play the dialogue.

2 **In-Class Tip** Point out that students will need to conjugate the verbs and add missing articles and other words to complete these dehydrated sentences. Tell them that subject pronouns in parentheses are not necessary in the completed sentences. Model completion of the first sentence for the class.

2 **Expansion** Give these dehydrated sentences to the class as items 7–10: **7. (yo) desear / practicar / verbos / hoy** (Deseo practicar los verbos hoy.) **8. mi hermano / regresar / lunes** (Mi hermano regresa el lunes.) **9. ella / cantar / y / bailar / muy bien** (Ella canta y baila muy bien.) **10. jóvenes / necesitar / descansar / ahora** (Los jóvenes necesitan descansar ahora.)

3 **In-Class Tip** After reading the model aloud, ask students why **me** is used in the answer (the first-person singular is used in the example sentence) and why **gustan** is needed (**las clases** is plural). Have students identify the indirect object pronoun and choose **gusta** or **gustan** for each item, then complete the activity.

3 **Expansion** If you wish to practice the third-person forms, repeat the activity, providing different subjects for each item. Ex: **1. Deseamos mirar cuadros de Picasso. (Nos gusta el arte.)**

4 **In-Class Tip** Before beginning the activity, give a two- to three-minute oral rapid-response drill. Provide infinitives and subjects, and call on students to give the conjugated form.

Pairs Have individual students write five dehydrated sentences and exchange them with a partner, who will complete them. After pairs have completed their sentences, ask volunteers to share some of their dehydrated sentences. Write them on the board and have the class "hydrate" them.

Game Divide the class into two teams. Prepare brief descriptions of easily recognizable people, using –ar verbs. Write each name on a card, and give each team a set of names. Then read the descriptions aloud. The first team to hold up the correct name earns a point. Ex: **Ella canta, baila y viaja a muchos países. (Jennifer López)**

In-Class Tips

5 **In-Class Tips**
- Give students time to write the list of activities in advance.
- Model the activity by talking about your own favorite activities during the week.

6 **In-Class Tip** To challenge students, make copies of this activity with the text removed so that students can only see the illustrations. Pass out the copies and have students close their books. Write all the verbs of the activity in one list on the board. Tell students to complete the activity using three of the verbs from the board for each drawing.

6 **Expansion**
↞🯅→ Ask students to write additional descriptions of the drawings. Ex: **La profesora habla en clase. Hay números y letras en la pizarra. Ella explica la tarea.** Have volunteers share their descriptions with the class.

6 **Game** Have groups of three students play a game of charades using the verbs given with the pictures. The first student to guess correctly acts out the next charade.

7 **In-Class Tip** Point out that, in addition to practicing **–ar** verbs, this activity recycles and reviews material from **Lección 1**: greetings, leave-takings, and telling time. Allow students several minutes to plan their conversation before they begin speaking.

7 **Partner Chat**
🯅↔🯅 Available online.

Comunicación

5 **Actividades** Talk about the different activities you and your friends do in your daily life. Then specify which of those activities you like to do and which you don't. Use at least five of the **-ar** verbs you have learned. Answers will vary.

> **modelo**
> Yo bailo hip hop en una academia. Mary dibuja...
> Me gusta bailar. No me gusta dibujar.

6 **Describir** Write a description of what you see in each picture using the given verbs. Also mention whether or not you like the activities. Answers will vary.

> **modelo**
> enseñar
> La profesora enseña química. A mí me gusta la química.

1. caminar, hablar, llevar

2. buscar, descansar, estudiar

3. dibujar, cantar, escuchar

4. llevar, tomar, viajar

Síntesis

7 **Conversación** With a classmate, pretend that you are friends who have not seen each other for a few days. Have a conversation in which you catch up on things. Mention how you're feeling, what classes you're taking, which teachers teach those classes, and which classes you like and don't like.
Answers will vary.

TEACHING OPTIONS

Extra Practice ↞🯅→ Have students write a description of themselves made up of activities they like or do not like to do, using sentences containing **(no) me gusta…** Collect the descriptions and read them aloud. Have the class guess who wrote each description.
Game To add a visual aspect to this grammar practice, play **Concentración**. Choose eight infinitives taught in this section, and write each one on a separate card. On another eight cards, draw or paste a picture that illustrates the action of each infinitive. Randomly place the cards facedown in four rows of four. Play with even-numbered groups of students. In pairs, students select two cards. If the two cards match, the pair keeps them. If the cards do not match, students return them to their original position. The pair that finishes with the most cards wins.

[2.2] Forming questions in Spanish

ANTE TODO   There are three basic ways to ask questions in Spanish. Can you guess what they are by looking at the photos and photo captions on this page?

> Te gusta mucho la tarea, ¿no?

> ¿Hablas con tu mamá?

> ¿Estudia Maru?

▶ One way to form a question is to raise the pitch of your voice at the end of a declarative sentence. When writing any question in Spanish, be sure to use an upside-down question mark (¿) at the beginning and a regular question mark (?) at the end of the sentence.

Statement	Question
Ustedes trabajan los sábados.	¿Ustedes trabajan los sábados?
You work on Saturdays.	*Do you work on Saturdays?*
Carlota busca un mapa.	¿Carlota busca un mapa?
Carlota is looking for a map.	*Is Carlota looking for a map?*

▶ You can also form a question by inverting the order of the subject and the verb of a declarative statement. The subject may even be placed at the end of the sentence.

Statement	Question
SUBJECT VERB	VERB SUBJECT
Ustedes trabajan los sábados.	¿**Trabajan ustedes** los sábados?
You work on Saturdays.	*Do you work on Saturdays?*
SUBJECT VERB	VERB SUBJECT
Carlota regresa a las seis.	¿**Regresa** a las seis **Carlota**?
Carlota returns at six.	*Does Carlota return at six?*

▶ Questions can also be formed by adding the tags **¿no?** or **¿verdad?** at the end of a statement.

Statement	Question
Ustedes trabajan los sábados.	Ustedes trabajan los sábados, **¿no?**
You work on Saturdays.	*You work on Saturdays, don't you?*
Carlota regresa a las seis.	Carlota regresa a las seis, **¿verdad?**
Carlota returns at six.	*Carlota returns at six, right?*

Question words

Interrogative words

¿Adónde?	Where (to)?	**¿De dónde?**	From where?
¿Cómo?	How?	**¿Dónde?**	Where?
¿Cuál?, ¿Cuáles?	Which?; Which one(s)?	**¿Por qué?**	Why?
¿Cuándo?	When?	**¿Qué?**	What?; Which?
¿Cuánto/a?	How much?	**¿Quién?**	Who?
¿Cuántos/as?	How many?	**¿Quiénes?**	Who (plural)?

▶ To ask a question that requires more than a *yes* or *no* answer, use an interrogative word.

¿Cuál de ellos estudia en la biblioteca?
Which of them studies in the library?

¿Adónde caminamos?
Where are we walking (to)?

¿Cuántos estudiantes hablan español?
How many students speak Spanish?

¿Por qué necesitas hablar con ella?
Why do you need to talk to her?

¿Dónde trabaja Ricardo?
Where does Ricardo work?

¿Quién enseña la clase de arte?
Who teaches the art class?

¿Qué clases tomas?
What classes are you taking?

¿Cuánta tarea hay?
How much homework is there?

▶ When pronouncing this type of question, the pitch of your voice falls at the end of the sentence.

¿Cómo llegas a clase?
How do you get to class?

¿Por qué necesitas estudiar?
Why do you need to study?

▶ Notice the difference between **¿por qué?**, which is written as two words and has an accent, and **porque**, which is written as one word without an accent.

¿Por qué estudias español?
Why do you study Spanish?

¡Porque es divertido!
Because it's fun!

▶ In Spanish **no** can mean both *no* and *not*. Therefore, when answering a yes/no question in the negative, you need to use **no** twice.

¿Caminan a la escuela?
Do you walk to school?

No, no caminamos a la escuela.
No, we do not walk to the school.

¡INTÉNTALO! Make questions out of these statements. Use the intonation method in column 1 and the tag **¿no?** method in column 2.

Statement	Intonation	Tag questions
1. Hablas inglés.	¿Hablas inglés?	Hablas inglés, ¿no?
2. Trabajamos mañana.	¿Trabajamos mañana?	Trabajamos mañana, ¿no?
3. Ustedes desean bailar.	¿Ustedes desean bailar?	Ustedes desean bailar, ¿no?
4. Raúl estudia mucho.	¿Raúl estudia mucho?	Raúl estudia mucho, ¿no?
5. Enseño a las nueve.	¿Enseño a las nueve?	Enseño a las nueve, ¿no?
6. Luz mira la televisión.	¿Luz mira la televisión?	Luz mira la televisión, ¿no?

Práctica

1 **Preguntas** Change these sentences into questions by inverting the word order.

> **modelo**
>
> Ernesto habla con su compañero de clase.
>
> *¿Habla Ernesto con su compañero de clase? /*
>
> *¿Habla con su compañero de clase Ernesto?*

1. La profesora Cruz prepara la prueba.
   ¿Prepara la profesora Cruz la prueba? / ¿Prepara la prueba la profesora Cruz?
2. Sandra y yo necesitamos estudiar.
   ¿Necesitamos Sandra y yo estudiar? / ¿Necesitamos estudiar Sandra y yo?
3. Los chicos practican el vocabulario.
   ¿Practican los chicos el vocabulario? / ¿Practican el vocabulario los chicos?
4. Jaime termina la tarea.
   ¿Termina Jaime la tarea? / ¿Termina la tarea Jaime?
5. Tú trabajas en la biblioteca. *¿Trabajas tú en la biblioteca? / ¿Trabajas en la biblioteca tú?*

2 **Completar** Irene and Manolo are chatting in the library. Complete their conversation with the appropriate questions. Answers will vary.

IRENE Hola, Manolo. (1)_¿Cómo estás? / ¿Qué tal?_

MANOLO Bien, gracias. (2)_¿Y tú?_

IRENE Muy bien. (3)_¿Qué hora es?_

MANOLO Son las nueve.

IRENE (4)_¿Qué estudias?_

MANOLO Estudio historia.

IRENE (5)_¿Por qué?_

MANOLO Porque hay un examen mañana.

IRENE (6)_¿Te gusta la clase?_

MANOLO Sí, me gusta mucho la clase.

IRENE (7)_¿Quién enseña la clase?_

MANOLO El profesor Padilla enseña la clase.

IRENE (8)_¿Tomas biología?_

MANOLO No, no tomo biología.

IRENE (9)_¿A qué hora regresas a tu casa?_

MANOLO Regreso a mi casa a las tres.

IRENE (10)_¿Deseas tomar una soda?_

MANOLO No, no deseo tomar una soda. ¡Deseo estudiar!

3 **Dos profesores** Create a dialogue, similar to the one in **Actividad 2**, between two teachers, Mr. Padilla and his colleague Mrs. Martínez. Use question words. Answers will vary.

> **modelo**
>
> **Prof. Padilla:** *¿Qué enseñas este semestre?*
>
> **Prof. Martínez:** Enseño matemáticas.

1 **In-Class Tip** Ask students to give both ways of forming questions for each item. Then have student pairs take turns making the statements and converting them into questions.

1 **Expansion** Make the even statements negative. Then have students add tag questions to the statements.

2 **Expansion**
🔺↔🔺 Have pairs of students create a similar conversation, replacing Manolo's answers with information that is true for them. Then ask volunteers to role-play their conversations for the class.

3 **In-Class Tip** To prepare students for the activity, have them brainstorm possible topics of conversation.

TEACHING OPTIONS

Heritage Speakers ←🔺→ Ask students to interview heritage speakers, whether in the class or outside. Students should prepare questions about who the person is, if he or she works and when/where, what he or she studies and why, and so forth. Have students use the information they gather in the interviews to write a brief profile of the person.

Large Groups Divide the class into two groups, A and B. To each member of group A give a strip of paper with a question on it. Ex: **¿Cuántos estudiantes hay en la clase?** Give an answer to each member of group B. Ex: **Hay veinte estudiantes en la clase.** Have students find their partners. Be sure that each question has only one possible answer.

Comunicación

4 Muchas preguntas Listen to the conversation between Manuel and Ana. Then indicate whether the following conclusions are **lógico** or **ilógico**, based on what you heard.

	Lógico	Ilógico
1. Ana es profesora.	○	☑
2. Diana es estudiante.	☑	○
3. La profesora de español es de España.	☑	○
4. Diana no toma la clase de computación porque hay mucha tarea.	○	☑
5. Ana toma la clase de química.	○	☑

5 Un juego With a classmate, play a game (**un juego**) of Jeopardy®. Remember to phrase your answers in the form of a question. Answers will vary.

Es algo que... It's something that...   **Es un lugar donde...** It's a place where...   **Es una persona que...** It's a person that...

modelo
Estudiante 1: Es un lugar donde estudiamos.
Estudiante 2: ¿Qué es la biblioteca?

Estudiante 2: Es algo que escuchamos.
Estudiante 1: ¿Qué es la música?

Estudiante 1: Es un director de España.
Estudiante 2: ¿Quién es Pedro Almodóvar?

6 El nuevo estudiante Imagine you are a transfer student and today is your first day of Spanish class. Ask your partner questions to find out all you can about the class, your classmates, and the school. Then switch roles. Answers will vary.

modelo
Estudiante 1: Hola, me llamo Samuel. ¿Cómo te llamas?
Estudiante 2: Me llamo Laura.
Estudiante 1: ¿Quiénes son ellos?
Estudiante 2: Son Melanie y Lucas.
Estudiante 1: En la escuela hay cursos de artes, ¿verdad?
Estudiante 2: Sí, hay clases de música y dibujo.
Estudiante 1: ¿Cuántos exámenes hay en esta clase?
Estudiante 2: Hay dos.

Síntesis

7 Entrevista Write an article about school life in your community. Write five questions you would ask students about their academic life. Answers will vary.

NOTA CULTURAL
Pedro Almodóvar is an award-winning film director from Spain. His films are full of both humor and melodrama, and their controversial subject matter has often sparked great debate. His film **Hable con ella** won the Oscar for Best Original Screenplay in 2002. His 2006 hit **Volver** was nominated for numerous awards, and won the Best Screenplay and Best Actress award for the entire female cast at the Cannes Film Festival.

4 Expansion Ask students to create two new items for the **lógico** or **ilógico** reading comprehension activity. Ex: —**La clase de computación es a las cuatro. (ilógico)**

4 Script See the script for this activity on Interleaf page 39B.

5 Expansion Play this game with the entire class. Select a few students to play the contestants and to "buzz in" their answers.

5 Virtual Chat  Available online.

6 In-Class Tip Write **la clase, los compañeros de clase,** and **la escuela** on the board. Guide students in brainstorming questions and write each one in the appropriate column.

6 Partner Chat Available online.

Communication 1.3

7 In-Class Tip Brainstorm ideas for interview questions and write them on the board, or have students prepare their questions as homework for an in-class interview session.

TEACHING OPTIONS

Extra Practice Have students go back to the **Fotonovela** on pages 44–45 and write as many questions as they can about what they see in the photos. Ask volunteers to share their questions as you write them on the board. Then call on individual students to answer them.

Extra Practice Prepare eight questions and answers. Write only the answers on the board in random order. Then read the questions aloud and have students identify the appropriate answer. Ex: ¿**Cuándo es la clase de español?** (**Es los lunes, miércoles y viernes.**)

2.3 Present tense of estar

CONSULTA

To review the forms of **ser**, see **Estructura 1.3**, pp. 19–21.

ANTE TODO In **Lección 1**, you learned how to conjugate and use the verb **ser** (*to be*). You will now learn a second verb which means *to be*, the verb **estar**. Although **estar** ends in **-ar**, it does not follow the pattern of regular **-ar** verbs. The **yo** form (**estoy**) is irregular. Also, all forms have an accented **á** except the **yo** and **nosotros/as** forms.

The verb estar (*to be*)

SINGULAR FORMS			
	yo	est**oy**	*I am*
	tú	est**ás**	*you* (fam.) *are*
	Ud./él/ella	est**á**	*you* (form.) *are; he/she is*

PLURAL FORMS			
	nosotros/as	est**amos**	*we are*
	vosotros/as	est**áis**	*you* (fam.) *are*
	Uds./ellos/ellas	est**án**	*you are; they are*

¡Estamos en Perú!

María está en la biblioteca.

COMPARE & CONTRAST

Compare the uses of the verb **estar** to those of the verb **ser**.

Uses of *estar*	Uses of *ser*
Location **Estoy** en casa. *I am at home.* Marissa **está** al lado de Felipe. *Marissa is next to Felipe.*	**Identity** Hola, **soy** Maru. *Hello, I'm Maru.*
Health Juan Carlos **está** enfermo hoy. *Juan Carlos is sick today.*	**Occupation** **Soy** estudiante. *I'm a student.*
Well-being —¿Cómo **estás**, Jimena? *How are you, Jimena?* —**Estoy** muy bien, gracias. *I'm very well, thank you.*	**Origin** —¿**Eres** de México? *Are you from Mexico?* —Sí, **soy** de México. *Yes, I'm from Mexico.*
	Telling time **Son** las cuatro. *It's four o'clock.*

AYUDA

Use **la casa** to express *the house*, but **en casa** to express *at home*.

CONSULTA

To learn more about the difference between **ser** and **estar**, see **Estructura 5.3**, pp. 170–171.

Section Goals

In **Estructura 2.3**, students will be introduced to:
• the present tense of **estar**
• contrasts between **ser** and **estar**
• prepositions of location used with **estar**

 Comparisons 4.1

Teacher Resources
Read the front matter for suggestions on how to incorporate all the program's components. See pages 39A–39B for a detailed listing of Teacher Resources online.

In-Class Tips
• Point out that only the **yo** and **nosotros/as** forms do not have a written accent.
• Emphasize that the principal distinction between **estar** and **ser** is that **estar** is generally used to express temporary conditions (**Juan Carlos está enfermo hoy**) and **ser** is generally used to express inherent qualities (**Juan Carlos es inteligente**).
• On the board, make a chart similar to the one in **Compare & Contrast**, but create sample sentences using the names of your students and information about them.
• Students will learn to compare **ser** and **estar** formally in **Estructura 5.3**.

TEACHING OPTIONS

TPR Have students write **ser** and **estar** on separate sheets of paper. Give statements in English and have students indicate if they would use **ser** or **estar** in each by holding up the appropriate paper. Ex: *I'm at home.* (estar) *I'm a student.* (ser) *I'm tired.* (estar) *I'm glad.* (estar) *I'm generous.* (ser)
Extra Practice Ask students to tell where certain people are or probably are at this moment. Ex: **¿Dónde estás? (Estoy en**

la clase.) ¿Dónde está el presidente/la presidenta? (Está en Washington, D.C.)
Heritage Speakers Ask heritage speakers to name instances where either **ser** or **estar** may be used. They may point out more advanced uses, such as with certain adjectives: **Es aburrido** vs. **Está aburrido**. This may help to compare and contrast inherent qualities and temporary conditions.

In-Class Tips
- Explain that prepositions typically indicate where one thing or person is in relation to another thing or person: *near, far, on, between, below.*
- Point out that **estar** is used in the model sentences to indicate presence or existence in a place.
- Take a book or other object and place it in various locations in relation to your desk or a student's. Ask individual students about its location. Ex: **¿Dónde está el libro? ¿Está cerca o lejos del escritorio de ____? ¿Qué objeto está al lado del libro?** Work through various locations, eliciting all of the prepositions of location.
- Ask where students are in relation to one another. Ex: **____, ¿dónde está ____? Está al lado (a la derecha/ izquierda, delante, detrás) de ____.**
- Describe students' locations in relation to each other. Ex: **Esta persona está lejos de ____. Está delante de ____. Está al lado de ____ ...** Have the class call out the student you identify. Ex: **Es ____.** Then have students describe other students' locations for a partner to guess.

▶ **Estar** is often used with certain prepositions and adverbs to describe the location of a person or an object.

Prepositions and adverbs often used with estar

al lado de	next to	**delante de**	in front of
a la derecha de	to the right of	**detrás de**	behind
a la izquierda de	to the left of	**en**	in; on
allá	over there	**encima de**	on top of
allí	there	**entre**	between
cerca de	near	**lejos de**	far from
con	with	**sin**	without
debajo de	below	**sobre**	on; over

La tiza **está al lado de** la pluma.
The chalk is next to the pen.

Los libros **están encima del** escritorio.
The books are on top of the desk.

El laboratorio **está cerca de** la clase.
The lab is near the classroom.

Maribel **está delante de** José.
Maribel is in front of José.

La maleta **está allí**.
The suitcase is there.

El estadio no **está lejos de** la librería.
The stadium isn't far from the bookstore.

El mapa **está entre** la pizarra y la puerta.
The map is between the blackboard and the door.

Los estudiantes **están en** la clase.
The students are in class.

La calculadora **está sobre** la mesa.
The calculator is on the table.

Los turistas **están allá**.
The tourists are over there.

Estamos lejos de casa.

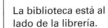
La biblioteca está al lado de la librería.

¡INTÉNTALO! Provide the present tense forms of **estar**.

1. Ustedes __están__ en la clase.
2. José __está__ en la biblioteca.
3. Yo __estoy__ bien, gracias.
4. Nosotras __estamos__ en la cafetería.
5. Tú __estás__ en el laboratorio.
6. Elena __está__ en la librería.
7. Ellas __están__ en la clase.
8. Ana y yo __estamos__ en la clase.
9. ¿Cómo __está__ usted?
10. Javier y Maribel __están__ en el estadio.
11. Nosotros __estamos__ en la cafetería.
12. Yo __estoy__ en el laboratorio.
13. Carmen y María __están__ enfermas.
14. Tú __estás__ en la clase.

TEACHING OPTIONS

Extra Practice Name various places at your school and ask students to describe their location in relation to other buildings. Model sample sentences so students will know how to answer. You may wish to write **el aula de...** on the board and explain its meaning.

TPR Have students remain seated. One student starts with a ball. Identify another student by his or her location with reference to other students. Ex: **Es la persona a la derecha de ____.** The student with the ball has to throw it to the student you described. The latter student must then toss the ball to the next person you identify.

Práctica

1 **Completar** Daniela has just returned home from the library. Complete this conversation with the appropriate forms of **ser** or **estar**.

MAMÁ   Hola, Daniela. ¿Cómo (1)___estás___?

DANIELA   Hola, mamá. (2)___Estoy___ bien. ¿Dónde (3)___está___ papá?
¡Ya (*Already*) (4)___son___ las ocho de la noche!

MAMÁ   No (5)___está___ aquí. (6)___Está___ en la oficina.

DANIELA   Y Andrés y Margarita, ¿dónde (7)___están___ ellos?

MAMÁ   (8)___Están___ en el restaurante La Palma con Martín.

DANIELA   ¿Quién (9)___es___ Martín?

MAMÁ   (10)___Es___ un compañero de clase. (11)___Es___ de México.

DANIELA   Ah. Y el restaurante La Palma, ¿dónde (12)___está___?

MAMÁ   (13)___Está___ cerca de la Plaza Mayor, en San Modesto.

DANIELA   Gracias, mamá. Voy (*I'm going*) al restaurante. ¡Hasta pronto!

2 **Escoger** Choose the preposition that best completes each sentence.

1. La pluma está (encima de / detrás de) la mesa. encima de
2. La ventana está (a la izquierda de / debajo de) la puerta. a la izquierda de
3. La pizarra está (debajo de / delante de) los estudiantes. delante de
4. Las sillas están (encima de / detrás de) los escritorios. detrás de
5. Los estudiantes llevan los libros (en / sobre) la mochila. en
6. La biblioteca está (sobre / al lado de) la cafetería. al lado de
7. España está (cerca de / lejos de) Puerto Rico. lejos de
8. México está (cerca de / lejos de) los Estados Unidos. cerca de
9. Felipe trabaja (con / en) Ricardo en la cafetería. con

3 **La librería** Indicate the location of five items in the drawing. Answers will vary.

 modelo

   Los diccionarios están debajo de los libros de literatura.

---

4 Expansion Have students write a short paragraph describing their Spanish classroom. Remind them to use Camila's description as a model.

Comunicación

4 En la clase Read Camila's e-mail to her friend, in which she describes her new school. Then, indicate whether each statement is **lógico** or **ilógico**, based on what you read.

Para: Andrés	Asunto:

Hola Andrés,
¿Cómo estás? Yo estoy muy bien, ¡adoro la nueva escuela!
Hay dos cafeterías, una gran biblioteca y un laboratorio de
biología. ¡Y mi salón de clases (*classroom*) está genial! Está
cerca de la biblioteca. Tiene una puerta y dos ventanas, una
mesa y una computadora para mí. También hay un reloj al lado
de la puerta, y hay muchos escritorios y sillas para los
estudiantes. ¿Y tú cómo estás? ¿Te gusta tu nueva escuela?
¿Cuántos estudiantes hay en tus clases de matemáticas?
¡Hasta pronto!
Camila

1. Camila es una estudiante de la clase de matemáticas. ilógico
2. El salón de clases está cerca del laboratorio de biología. ilógico
3. Hay una computadora en el salón de clases. lógico
4. Camila y Andrés son profesores en la escuela. lógico
5. Andrés es profesor de biología. ilógico

5 In-Class Tips
• Ask two volunteers to read the model aloud.
• Have students scan the days and times and ask you for any additional vocabulary.

5 Expansion After students have completed the activity, ask the same questions of selected individuals. Then expand on their answers by asking additional questions. Ex: —**¿Dónde estás los sábados a las seis de la mañana?** —**Estoy en casa.** —**¿Dónde está la casa?**

5 Partner Chat
 Available online.

Communication 1.1

6 Expansion Call on students to share the information they obtained with the class.

6 Virtual Chat
Available online.

5 ¿Dónde estás...? With a partner, take turns asking each other where you normally are at these times. Answers will vary.

> **modelo**
> lunes / 10:00 a.m.
> **Estudiante 1:** *¿Dónde estás los lunes a las diez de la mañana?*
> **Estudiante 2:** *Estoy en la biblioteca.*

1. sábados / 6:00 a.m.
2. miércoles / 9:15 a.m.
3. lunes / 11:10 a.m.
4. jueves / 12:30 a.m.

5. viernes / 2:25 p.m.
6. martes / 3:50 p.m.
7. jueves / 5:45 p.m.
8. miércoles / 8:20 p.m.

Síntesis

6 Entrevista Answer your partner's questions. Answers will vary.

1. ¿Cómo estás?
2. ¿Dónde estás ahora?
3. ¿Dónde está tu (*your*) diccionario de español?
4. ¿Dónde está tu casa?
5. ¿Cuándo hay un examen?
6. ¿Estudias mucho?
7. ¿Cuántas horas estudias para (*for*) una prueba?

TEACHING OPTIONS

Video Show the **Fotonovela** again to give students more input. Stop the video where appropriate to discuss how **estar** and prepositions were used and to ask comprehension questions.
Pairs Write a list of well-known monuments, places, and people on the board. Ex: **el Space Needle, Bill Gates, las Cataratas del Niágara, Jessica Alba.** Have student pairs take turns asking each other the location of each item. Ex: —**¿Dónde está el**

Space Needle? —Está en Seattle, Washington.
Game Divide the class into two teams. Select a student from team A to think of an item in the classroom. Team B can ask five questions about where this item is. The first student can respond only with **sí**, **no**, **caliente** (*hot*), or **frío** (*cold*). If a team guesses the item within five tries, award it a point. If not, give the other team a point. The team with the most points wins.

2.4 # Numbers 31 and higher

ANTE TODO   You have already learned numbers 0–30. Now you will learn the rest of the numbers.

Numbers 31–100

▶ Numbers 31–99 follow the same basic pattern as 21–29.

	Numbers 31–100				
31	treinta y uno	40	cuarenta	50	cincuenta
32	treinta y dos	41	cuarenta y uno	51	cincuenta y uno
33	treinta y tres	42	cuarenta y dos	52	cincuenta y dos
34	treinta y cuatro	43	cuarenta y tres	60	sesenta
35	treinta y cinco	44	cuarenta y cuatro	63	sesenta y tres
36	treinta y seis	45	cuarenta y cinco	64	sesenta y cuatro
37	treinta y siete	46	cuarenta y seis	70	setenta
38	treinta y ocho	47	cuarenta y siete	80	ochenta
39	treinta y nueve	48	cuarenta y ocho	90	noventa
		49	cuarenta y nueve	100	cien, ciento

▶ **Y** is used in most numbers from **31** through **99**. Unlike numbers 21–29, these numbers must be written as three separate words.

Hay **noventa y dos** exámenes.
There are ninety-two exams.

Hay **cuarenta y dos** estudiantes.
There are forty-two students.

Hay cuarenta y siete estudiantes en la clase de geografía.

Cien menos sesenta y cuatro son treinta y seis pesos de cambio.

▶ With numbers that end in **uno** (31, 41, etc.), **uno** becomes **un** before a masculine noun and **una** before a feminine noun.

Hay **treinta y un** chicos.
There are thirty-one guys.

Hay **treinta y una** chicas.
There are thirty-one girls.

▶ **Cien** is used before nouns and in counting. The words **un, una,** and **uno** are never used before **cien** in Spanish. Use **cientos** to say *hundreds*.

Hay **cien** libros y **cien** sillas.
There are one hundred books and one hundred chairs.

¿Cuántos libros hay? **Cientos.**
How many books are there?
Hundreds.

Numbers 101 and higher

▶ As shown in the chart, Spanish uses a period to indicate thousands and millions, rather than a comma, as is used in English.

Numbers 101 and higher			
101	ciento uno	**1.000**	mil
200	doscientos/as	**1.100**	mil cien
300	trescientos/as	**2.000**	dos mil
400	cuatrocientos/as	**5.000**	cinco mil
500	quinientos/as	**100.000**	cien mil
600	seiscientos/as	**200.000**	doscientos/as mil
700	setecientos/as	**550.000**	quinientos/as cincuenta mil
800	ochocientos/as	**1.000.000**	un millón (de)
900	novecientos/as	**8.000.000**	ocho millones (de)

▶ Notice that you should use **ciento**, not **cien**, to count numbers over 100.

110 = **ciento diez**   118 = **ciento dieciocho**   150 = **ciento cincuenta**

▶ The numbers 200 through 999 agree in gender with the nouns they modify.

324 plum**as**
trescient**as** veinticuatro plum**as**

3.505 libr**os**
tres mil quinient**os** cinco libr**os**

▶ The word **mil**, which can mean *a thousand* and *one thousand*, is not usually used in the plural form to refer to an exact number, but it can be used to express the idea of *a lot*, *many*, or *thousands*. **Cientos** can also be used to express *hundreds* in this manner.

¡Hay **miles** de personas en el estadio!
There are thousands of people in the stadium!

Hay **cientos** de libros en la biblioteca.
There are hundreds of books in the library.

▶ To express a complex number (including years), string together all of its components.

55.422   cincuenta y cinco mil cuatrocientos veintidós

¡INTÉNTALO!   Write out the Spanish equivalent of each number.

1. **102** _ciento dos_
2. **5.000.000** _cinco millones_
3. **201** _doscientos uno_
4. **76** _setenta y seis_
5. **92** _noventa y dos_
6. **550.300** _quinientos cincuenta mil trescientos_
7. **235** _doscientos treinta y cinco_
8. **79** _setenta y nueve_
9. **113** _ciento trece_
10. **88** _ochenta y ocho_
11. **17.123** _diecisiete mil ciento veintitrés_
12. **497** _cuatrocientos noventa y siete_

Práctica y Comunicación

1 **Baloncesto** Provide these basketball scores in Spanish.

1. Ohio State 76, Michigan 65
2. Florida 92, Florida State 104
3. Stanford 83, UCLA 89
4. Purdue 81, Indiana 78
5. Princeton 67, Harvard 55
6. Duke 115, Virginia 121

1. setenta y seis, sesenta y cinco   3. ochenta y tres, ochenta y nueve   5. sesenta y siete, cincuenta y cinco
2. noventa y dos, ciento cuatro   4. ochenta y uno, setenta y ocho   6. ciento quince, ciento veintiuno

1 **Expansion** In pairs, have each student write three additional basketball scores and dictate them to his or her partner, who writes them down.

2 **Completar** Following the pattern, write out the missing numbers in Spanish.

1. 50, 150, 250 … 1.050 trescientos cincuenta, cuatrocientos cincuenta, quinientos cincuenta, seiscientos cincuenta, setecientos cincuenta, ochocientos cincuenta, novecientos cincuenta
2. 5.000, 20.000, 35.000 … 95.000
cincuenta mil, sesenta y cinco mil, ochenta mil
3. 100.000, 200.000, 300.000 … 1.000.000
cuatrocientos mil, quinientos mil, seiscientos mil, setecientos mil, ochocientos mil, novecientos mil
4. 100.000.000, 90.000.000, 80.000.000 … 0 setenta millones, sesenta millones, cincuenta millones, cuarenta millones, treinta millones, veinte millones, diez millones

2 **In-Class Tip** To simplify, have students identify the pattern of each sequence. Ex: 1. Add one hundred.

3 **Resolver** Solve the math problems. Write out the numbers in Spanish.

> **modelo**
> 200 + 300 =
> *Doscientos más trescientos son quinientos.*

AYUDA
+ → **más**
− → **menos**
= → **son**

1. 1.000 + 753 = Mil más setecientos cincuenta y tres son mil setecientos cincuenta y tres.
2. 1.000.000 − 30.000 = Un millón menos treinta mil son novecientos setenta mil.
3. 10.000 + 555 = Diez mil más quinientos cincuenta y cinco son diez mil quinientos cincuenta y cinco.
4. 15 + 150 = Quince más ciento cincuenta son ciento sesenta y cinco.
5. 100.000 + 205.000 = Cien mil más doscientos cinco mil son trescientos cinco mil.
6. 29.000 − 10.000 = Veintinueve mil menos diez mil son diecinueve mil.

3 **Expansion** To challenge students, have them create four additional math problems for a partner to solve.

4 **Los números de teléfono** Write a list of telephone numbers that are important to you. Write out the numbers. Answers will vary.

> **modelo**
> mi celular: 635-1951 seis-tres-cinco-diecinueve-cincuenta y uno

4 **Expansion**
👤↔👤 Have pairs continue practicing by dictating the phone numbers they wrote down to each other.

Síntesis

5 **Preguntas** With a classmate, ask each other questions that require numbers in the answers. The questions could be about phone numbers, the number of people in your city or state, the year you finish school, etc. Answers will vary.

> **modelo**
> **Estudiante 1:** ¿Cuándo terminas la escuela?
> **Estudiante 2:** Termino la escuela en dos mil veintiuno.

5 **In-Class Tips**
• If this is the first time students are completing an activity from the Activity Pack, explain that they will need a handout.
• 👤↔👤 Divide the class into pairs and distribute the handouts for the activity **¿A qué distancia…?** from the online Resources (Lección 2/Activity Pack/ Information Gap Activities). Ask students to read the instructions and give them ten minutes to complete the activity. Have volunteers report their findings to the class.

5 **Partner Chat**
👤↔👤 Available online.

TEACHING OPTIONS

Small Groups ←👤→ In groups of three or four, ask students to think of a city or town within a 100-mile radius of your school. Have them find out the distance in miles (**Está a ____ millas de la escuela.**) and what other cities or towns are nearby (**Está cerca de…**). Then have groups read their descriptions for the class to guess.

Game Ask for two volunteers and station them at opposite ends of the board so neither one can see what the other is writing. Say a number for them to write on the board. If both students are correct, continue to give numbers until one writes an incorrect number. The winner continues on to play against another student.

Section Goal

In **Recapitulación**, students will review the grammar concepts from this lesson.

1 In-Class Tips
- To simplify, ask students to identify the infinitive of the verb in each row.
- Complete this activity orally as a class. Write each form on the board as students call them out.

1 Expansion Ask students to provide the third-person singular (**Ud./él/ella**) conjugations.

2 Expansion
- Ask students to write five more numbers above 31. Have them read the numbers to a partner, who will jot them down. Remind students to check each other's answers.
- To challenge students, have them complete the activity and then say what they can buy with that amount of money. Model the first item for the class. Ex: **Con 49 dólares, compro una mochila.**

3 In-Class Tips
- Remind students that all question words should carry accent marks.
- Remind students that verbs in Spanish do not require subject pronouns; they are used for emphasis or clarification.

Recapitulación

RESUMEN GRAMATICAL

Review the grammar concepts you have learned in this lesson by completing these activities.

1 Completar Complete the chart with the correct verb forms. **24 pts.**

yo	tú	nosotros	ellas
compro	compras	compramos	compran
deseo	**deseas**	deseamos	desean
miro	miras	**miramos**	miran
pregunto	preguntas	preguntamos	**preguntan**

2 Números Write these numbers in Spanish. **16 pts.**

modelo
645: seiscientos cuarenta y cinco

1. **49:** cuarenta y nueve
2. **97:** noventa y siete
3. **113:** ciento trece
4. **632:** seiscientos treinta y dos
5. **1.781:** mil setecientos ochenta y uno
6. **3.558:** tres mil quinientos cincuenta y ocho
7. **1.006.015:** un millón seis mil quince
8. **67.224.370:** sesenta y siete millones doscientos veinticuatro mil trescientos setenta

3 Preguntas Write questions for these answers. **12 pts.**

1. —¿ De dónde es _____ Patricia?
   —Patricia es de Colombia.
2. —¿ Quién es _____ él?
   —Él es mi amigo (*friend*).
3. —¿ Cuántos idiomas hablas _____ (tú)?
   —Hablo dos idiomas (*languages*).
4. —¿ Qué desean (tomar) _____ (ustedes)?
   —Deseamos tomar café.
5. —¿ Por qué tomas biología _____?
   —Tomo biología porque me gustan las ciencias.
6. —¿ Cuándo descansa Camilo _____?
   —Camilo descansa por las mañanas.

2.1 Present tense of -ar verbs pp. 50–52

estudiar	
estudio	estudiamos
estudias	estudiáis
estudia	estudian

The verb gustar

(no) me gusta + el/la + [*singular noun*]
(no) me gustan + los/las + [*plural noun*]
(no) me gusta + [*infinitive(s)*]

Note: You may use a mí for emphasis, but never yo.

To ask a friend about likes and dislikes, use te instead of me, but never tú.

¿Te gusta la historia?

2.2 Forming questions in Spanish pp. 55–56

▸ **¿Ustedes trabajan los sábados?**
▸ **¿Trabajan ustedes los sábados?**
▸ **Ustedes trabajan los sábados, ¿verdad?/¿no?**

Interrogative words		
¿Adónde?	¿Cuánto/a?	¿Por qué?
¿Cómo?	¿Cuántos/as?	¿Qué?
¿Cuál(es)?	¿De dónde?	¿Quién(es)?
¿Cuándo?	¿Dónde?	

2.3 Present tense of estar pp. 59–60

▸ estar: estoy, estás, está, estamos, estáis, están

2.4 Numbers 31 and higher pp. 63–64

31	treinta y uno	101	ciento uno
32	treinta y dos	200	doscientos/as
	(and so on)	500	quinientos/as
40	cuarenta	700	setecientos/as
50	cincuenta	900	novecientos/as
60	sesenta	1.000	mil
70	setenta	2.000	dos mil
80	ochenta	5.100	cinco mil cien
90	noventa	100.000	cien mil
100	cien, ciento	1.000.000	un millón (de)

TEACHING OPTIONS

Pairs Have students write ten questions using the interrogative words from **Estructura 2.2** to ask their partner about his/her family, house, friends, etc. Remind students that ¿Cuánto/a? and ¿Cuántos/as? should agree with their corresponding nouns. Then have students exchange papers with a classmate and answer the questions. Finally, have pairs work together to review the answers. Have them write sentences using **nosotros/as** about any items they have in common.

Extra Practice On the board, write a list of landmarks (libraries, parks, churches, restaurants, hotels, and so forth) in the community. Have students choose a landmark and write a short paragraph describing its location. Ex: **El Hotel Plaza está al lado de la biblioteca. Está cerca de la catedral y delante de Sebastian's Café. Está lejos de mi casa.**

4 **Al teléfono** Complete this telephone conversation with the correct forms of the verb **estar**.

`16 pts.`

MARÍA TERESA	Hola, señora López. (1) ¿ _____Está_____ Elisa en casa?
SRA. LÓPEZ	Hola, ¿quién es?
MARÍA TERESA	Soy María Teresa. Elisa y yo (2) _____estamos_____ en la misma (*same*) clase de literatura.
SRA. LÓPEZ	¡Ah, María Teresa! ¿Cómo (3) _____estás_____ ?
MARÍA TERESA	(4) _____Estoy_____ muy bien, gracias. Y usted, ¿cómo (5) _____está_____ ?
SRA. LÓPEZ	Bien, gracias. Pues, no, Elisa no (6) _____está_____ en casa. Ella y su hermano (*her brother*) (7) _____están_____ en la Biblioteca Cervantes.
MARÍA TERESA	¿Cervantes?
SRA. LÓPEZ	Es la biblioteca que (8) _____está_____ al lado del café Bambú.
MARÍA TERESA	¡Ah, sí! Gracias, señora López.
SRA. LÓPEZ	Hasta luego, María Teresa.

5 **¿Qué te gusta?** Form complete sentences with the information provided to indicate what is liked. `28 pts.`

> *modelo*
>
> yo: las ciencias
> *Me gustan las ciencias.*

1. yo: la clase de música   _Me gusta la clase de música. / A mí me gusta la clase de música._
2. tú: las lenguas extranjeras   _Te gustan las lenguas extranjeras. / A ti te gustan las lenguas extranjeras._
3. yo: escuchar la radio   _Me gusta escuchar la radio. / A mí me gusta escuchar la radio._
4. tú: la historia   _Te gusta la historia. / A ti te gusta la historia._
5. yo: las matemáticas   _Me gustan las matemáticas. / A mí me gustan las matemáticas._
6. tú: viajar   _Te gusta viajar. / A ti te gusta viajar._
7. yo: el arte   _Me gusta el arte. / A mí me gusta el arte._

6 **Canción** Use the appropriate forms of the verb **gustar** to complete the beginning of a popular song by Manu Chao. `4 pts.`

> ❝ Me _____gustan_____ los aviones°,
> me gustas tú,
> me _____gusta_____ viajar,
> me gustas tú,
> me gusta la mañana,
> me gustas tú. ❞

aviones *airplanes*

Pairs Write **más, menos, multiplicado por,** and **dividido por** on the board. Model a few simple problems using numbers 31 and higher. Ex: **Cien mil trescientos menos diez mil son noventa mil trescientos. Mil dividido por veinte son cincuenta.** Then ask students to write two math problems of each type for a classmate to solve. Have partners verify each other's work.

Small Groups 👥 Tell students to think of a famous person and write five statements about their likes and dislikes from that person's point of view. Tell them to progressively give more clues to the person's identity and to end with **¿Quién soy?** Then, in small groups, have students read their statements aloud for their partners to guess. Have them respond to the guesses with more information as necessary.

---

4 **Expansion**
👥↔👥 Ask student pairs to write a brief phone conversation based on the one in **Actividad 4.** Have volunteers role-play their dialogues for the class.

5 **In-Class Tips**
- Before writing their paragraphs, have students brainstorm a list of words or phrases related to universities.
- Remind students of when to use **gusta** versus **gustan.** Write a few example sentences on the board.
- Have students exchange papers with a partner to peer-edit each other's paragraphs.

6 **In-Class Tips** Point out the form **gustas** in lines 2, 4, and 6, and ask students to guess the translation of the phrase **me gustas tú** (*I like you,* literally, *you are pleasing to me*). Tell students that **me gustas** and **le gustas** are not used as much as their English counterparts. Most often they are used in romantic situations.

6 **Canción** **Manu Chao** (born 1961) is a French singer of Spanish origin. In the 80's he and his brother started the band **Mano Negra.** Since the band's breakup in 1995, he has led a successful solo career. His music, which draws on diverse influences such as punk, ska, reggae, salsa, and Algerian raï, is popular throughout Europe and Latin America. **Chao** often mixes several languages in one song.

Lectura

Antes de leer

Estrategia
Predicting content through formats

Recognizing the format of a document can help you to predict its content. For instance, invitations, greeting cards, and classified ads follow an easily identifiable format, which usually gives you a general idea of the information they contain. Look at the text and identify it based on its format.

Período	Hora	Clase
1	7:45 – 8:37	Matemáticas
2	8:43 – 9:30	Español
3	9:36 – 10:23	Inglés
4	10:29 – 11:16	Historia
Almuerzo	11:16 – 12:06	
5	12:12 – 12:59	Biología
6	1:05 – 1:52	Arte
7	1:58 – 2:45	Música

If you guessed that this is a page from a student's schedule, you are correct. You can now infer that the document contains information about a student's weekly schedule, including days, times, and activities.

Cognados
Make a list of the cognates in the text and guess their English meanings. What do cognates reveal about the content of the document?

Examinar el texto
Look at the format of the document entitled **¡Español en Madrid!** What type of text is it? What information do you expect to find in this type of document?

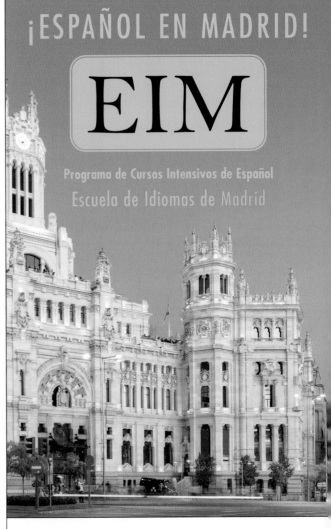

¡ESPAÑOL EN MADRID!

EIM

Programa de Cursos Intensivos de Español
Escuela de Idiomas de Madrid

Después de leer

Correspondencias
Provide the letter of each item in Column B that matches the words in Column A. Two items will not be used.

 A   **B**

1. profesores f
2. vivienda h
3. Madrid d
4. número de teléfono a
5. Español 2B c
6. número de fax g

a. (34) 91 523 4500
b. (34) 91 524 0210
c. 23 junio–30 julio
d. capital cultural de Europa
e. 16 junio–22 julio
f. especializados en enseñar español como lengua extranjera
g. (34) 91 523 4623
h. familias españolas

Escuela de Idiomas de Madrid

Madrid, la capital cultural de Europa, y la EIM te ofrecen cursos intensivos de verano° para aprender° español.

¿Dónde?
En el edificio de la EIM, cerca a la Plaza de Cibeles.

¿Quiénes son los profesores?
Son todos hablantes nativos del español especializados en enseñar el español como lengua extranjera.

¿Qué niveles se ofrecen?
Se ofrecen tres niveles° básicos:
1. Español Elemental, A, B y C
2. Español Intermedio, A y B
3. Español Avanzado, A y B

Viviendas
Para estudiantes extranjeros se ofrece vivienda° con familias españolas.

¿Cuándo?
Este verano desde° el 16 de junio hasta el 10 de agosto. Los cursos tienen una duración de 6 semanas.

Cursos	Empieza°	Termina
Español 1A	16 junio	22 julio
Español 1B	23 junio	30 julio
Español 1C	30 junio	10 agosto
Español 2A	16 junio	22 julio
Español 2B	23 junio	30 julio
Español 3A	16 junio	22 julio
Español 3B	23 junio	30 julio

Información
Para mayor información, sirvan comunicarse con la siguiente° oficina:

Escuela de Idiomas de Madrid
Programa de Español como Lengua Extranjera
Calle del Barquillo 1, 28005, 28039 Madrid, España
Tel. (34) 91 523 4500, **Fax** (34) 91 523 4623
www.uae.es

verano *summer* aprender *to learn* edificio *building* niveles *levels* vivienda *housing* desde *from* Empieza *Begins* siguiente *following*

¿Cierto o falso?
Indicate whether each statement is **cierto** or **falso**.
Then correct the false statements.

          Cierto   Falso

1. La Escuela de Idiomas de Madrid ofrece (*offers*) cursos intensivos de italiano.   ○   ⊘
   Ofrece cursos intensivos de español.

2. La lengua nativa de los profesores del programa es el inglés.   ○   ⊘
   La lengua nativa de los profesores es el español.

3. Se ofrecen dos niveles básicos de español.   ○   ⊘
   Se ofrecen tres niveles básicos.

4. Los estudiantes pueden vivir (*can live*) con familias españolas.   ⊘   ○

          Cierto   Falso

5. La escuela de idiomas que ofrece los cursos intensivos está en Salamanca.   ○   ⊘
   Está en Madrid.

6. Español 3B termina en agosto.   ○   ⊘
   Termina en julio.

7. Si deseas información sobre (*about*) los cursos intensivos de español, es posible llamar al (34) 91 523 4500.   ⊘   ○

8. Español 1A empieza en julio.   ○   ⊘
   Empieza en junio.

Correspondencias Go over the answers as a class or assign pairs of students to work together to check each other's answers.

¿Cierto o falso? Give students these true-false statements as items 9–16: **9. El edificio de la EIM está en la Ciudad de México. (Falso; está en Madrid.) 10. Los cursos terminan en junio. (Falso; terminan en julio y agosto.) 11. Hay un curso de español intermedio. (Falso; hay dos cursos.) 12. Los cursos se ofrecen en el verano. (Cierto) 13. Hay vivienda con familias españolas para estudiantes extranjeros. (Cierto) 14. Hay un número de teléfono para más información. (Cierto) 15. Todos los profesores son hablantes nativos. (Cierto) 16. Los cursos tienen una duración de doce semanas. (Falso; tienen una duración de seis semanas.)**

Expansion
←🛉→ Divide the class into pairs. Instruct one student to research a Spanish-language summer program in Spain and the other student a program in Mexico. Tell them to compile information on the program's dates, fees, housing options, teachers or professors, and courses offered. Then, have pairs compare their findings and decide which program they prefer. Have volunteers describe to the class the program they chose.

Language Notes Explain that in Spanish dates are usually written in the order of day/month/year rather than month/day/year, as they are in the United States and Canada. Someone from Mexico with a birthdate of July 5, 2003, would write his or her birthdate as 5/7/03.

Pairs ←🛉→ Provide pairs of students with Spanish-language magazines and newspapers. Ask them to look for documents with easily recognizable formats, such as classified ads or advertisements. Ask them to use cognates and other context clues to predict the content. Then have partners present their examples and findings to the class.

Section Goals

In **Escritura**, students will:
• brainstorm and organize their ideas for writing
• write a description of themselves
• incorporate lesson vocabulary and structures

 Communication 1.3

 Pre-AP®

Interpretative Reading: Estrategia
Discuss information students might want to include in a self-description. Record their suggestions in Spanish on the board. Quickly review structures students will include in their writing, such as **me gusta** and **no me gusta** as well as the first-person singular of several verbs, for example: **soy, estoy, tomo, trabajo, estudio.**

Tema Copy on the board the brief forum description for Alicia Roberts, leaving blanks where her name, courses, and preferences appear. At the end, add the sentences **Me gusta _____.** and **No me gusta _____.** Model completing the description orally with your information and then ask volunteers to complete it with their information.

 Pre-AP®

Presentational Writing: Estrategia
Remind students that the audience for this description is Spanish-speaking teens. Encourage them to think of likes and dislikes that they might have in common.

Escritura

Estrategia
Brainstorming

How do you find ideas to write about? In the early stages of writing, brainstorming can help you generate ideas on a specific topic. You should spend ten to fifteen minutes brainstorming and jotting down any ideas about the topic. Whenever possible, try to write your ideas in Spanish. Express your ideas in single words or phrases, and jot them down in any order. While brainstorming, don't worry about whether your ideas are good or bad. Selecting and organizing ideas should be the second stage of your writing. Remember that the more ideas you write down while you're brainstorming, the more options you'll have to choose from later when you start to organize your ideas.

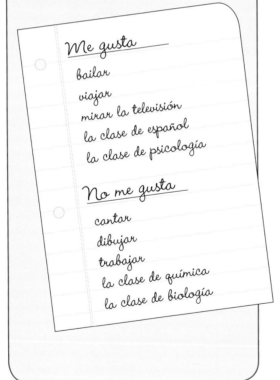

Me gusta
bailar
viajar
mirar la televisión
la clase de español
la clase de psicología

No me gusta
cantar
dibujar
trabajar
la clase de química
la clase de biología

Tema
Una descripción

Write a description of yourself to post in a forum on a website in order to meet Spanish-speaking people. Include this information in your description:

▶ your name and where you are from, and a photo (optional) of yourself
▶ where you go to school
▶ the courses you are taking
▶ where you work (if you have a job)
▶ some of your likes and dislikes

¡Hola! Me llamo Alicia Roberts. Estudio matemáticas y economía. Me gusta dibujar, cantar y viajar.

EVALUATION: Descripción

Criteria	Scale
Content	1 2 3 4 5
Organization	1 2 3 4 5
Use of vocabulary	1 2 3 4 5
Grammatical accuracy	1 2 3 4 5

Scoring	
Excellent	18–20 points
Good	14–17 points
Satisfactory	10–13 points
Unsatisfactory	< 10 points

Escuchar

Estrategia

Listening for cognates

You already know that cognates are words that have similar spellings and meanings in two or more languages: for example, *group* and **grupo** or *stereo* and **estéreo**. Listen for cognates to increase your comprehension of spoken Spanish.

 To help you practice this strategy, you will now listen to two sentences. Make a list of all the cognates you hear.

Preparación

Based on the photograph, who do you think Armando and Julia are? What do you think they are talking about? Answers will vary.

Ahora escucha

Now you are going to hear Armando and Julia's conversation. Make a list of the cognates they use.

Armando	Julia
clases, biología	inglés
matemáticas, música	química, italiano
italiano	historia, clase
_____	_____

Based on your knowledge of cognates, decide whether the following statements are **cierto** or **falso**.

	Cierto	Falso
1. Armando y Julia hablan de la familia.	○	☑
2. Armando y Julia toman una clase de italiano.	☑	○
3. Julia toma clase de historia.	☑	○
4. Armando estudia lenguas extranjeras.	☑	○
5. Julia toma una clase de religión.	○	☑

Comprensión

Preguntas

Answer these questions about Armando and Julia's conversation.

1. ¿Qué clases toma Armando?
   Toma italiano, músca y matemáticas.

2. ¿Qué clases toma Julia?
   Toma química, inglés, historia e italiano.

Seleccionar

Choose the answer that best completes each sentence.

1. Armando toma ____b____ clases.
   a. cuatro   b. tres   c. seis
2. Julia toma dos clases de ____c____.
   a. matemáticas   b. ciencias   c. idiomas
3. Armando toma italiano y ____b____.
   a. historia   b. música   c. química

Preguntas personales   Answers will vary.

1. ¿Cuántas clases tomas?
2. ¿Qué clases tomas?
3. ¿Qué clases te gustan y qué clases no te gustan?

Section Goals

In **Escuchar**, students will:
- listen for cognates in a short paragraph
- answer questions based on the content of a recorded conversation

Communication 1.2

Estrategia
Script 1. La democracia es una forma de gobierno. 2. A mí me gustan los conciertos, las obras de teatro y la danza.

In-Class Tip Invite students to look at the photo and describe what they see. Guide them to guess where they think **Julia** and **Armando** are and what they are talking about.

Ahora escucha
Script ARMANDO: ¡Hola Julia! ¿Cómo estás?
JULIA: Bien. ¿Y tú, Armando?
ARMANDO: Bien, gracias. ¿Qué tal tus clases?
JULIA: Van bien.
ARMANDO: ¿Tomas biología?
JULIA: No. Pero sí tomo química.
ARMANDO: ¿Qué otras clases tomas?
JULIA: Tomo inglés a las ocho con la señora O'Connor e historia a las nueve con el señor Vélez. ¿Y tú?
ARMANDO: Tomo italiano, música y matemáticas.
JULIA: ¿A qué hora es tu clase de italiano?
ARMANDO: A las nueve, con la señora Menotti.
JULIA: Yo también tomo italiano con la señora Menotti, pero a la una.

Preguntas personales
👥↔👥 Available online as **Virtual Chat**.

Section Goals

In **En pantalla**, students will:
- read about the seasons in Chile
- watch a television commercial for **Jumbo**, a Chilean superstore chain

 Communication 1.1, 1.2, 1.3
Cultures 2.1, 2.2
Connections 3.2
Comparisons 4.2

Teacher Resources
Read the front matter for suggestions on how to incorporate all the program's components. See pages 39A–39B for a detailed listing of Teacher Resources online.

Calendarios Check comprehension: 1. What is the weather like in the southern hemisphere when it is cold and snowy in North America? 2. How long is summer in Chile? 3. What months are included in Chile's scholastic calendar?

 Pre-AP®

Audiovisual Interpretive Communication
Antes de ver strategy
Show the clip without sound to focus students' attention on the concept being presented. Ask: What can observation alone allow them to predict about its content and purpose?

Comprensión To challenge students, have them write a list in Spanish of objects they see as they watch the ad.

Preparación
Answer the following questions in English. Answers will vary.

1. For what occasions do you give and get gifts?
2. When did you get a very special or needed gift? What was the gift?

Calendarios

During the months of cold weather and snow in North America, the southern hemisphere enjoys warm weather and longer days. Since Chile's summer lasts from December to February, school vacation coincides with these months. In Chile, the school year starts in early March and finishes toward the end of December. All schools, from preschools to universities, observe this scholastic calendar, with only a few days' variation between institutions.

Viejito Pascuero *Santa Claus (Chile)*

Comprensión
Answer the following questions, using both English and Spanish as directed.

1. In the video, what was the young boy doing?
   Writing a letter to Santa Claus.
2. Who else is in the video? How do you know who he is?
   His father. The boy says, "Papá."
3. What did the boy ask? Give both the Spanish and the English equivalent. He asked "¿Cómo se escribe *mountain bike*?" In English: How do you spell "mountain bike"?
4. What answer was he given? Give both the Spanish and the English equivalent.
   He was told "mochila." In English: "backpack."

Conversación
With a partner, take turns asking for something and being sure of the spelling. Each of you should ask for four different things. Follow the model. Answers will vary.

> **modelo**
> **Estudiante 1:** ¿Qué quieres?
> **Estudiante 2:** Quiero un diccionario.
> **Estudiante 1:** ¿Cómo se escribe "diccionario"?
> **Estudiante 2:** D-I-C-C-I-O-N-A-R-I-O

Anuncio de Jumbo

Viejito Pascuero°...

Vocabulario útil

ahorrar	to save (money)
Navidad	Christmas
pedirte	to ask you
quería	I wanted
te preocupa	it worries you

Aplicación
With a partner, describe your school calendar and vacations. Then research and describe the same for a Spanish-speaking culture. Include the following elements: at what age students start school, the first and last days of the school year, and the dates of school vacations. Present your descriptions to the class, comparing the two as you present.
Answers will vary.

EXPANSION

Culture Note Latin American supermarkets differ from those in the U.S.; they are similar to a Wal-Mart superstore. **Jumbo** is an **hipermercado** that sells groceries, televisions, clothing, and school supplies.
Culture Note The idea of Santa Claus differs throughout the Spanish-speaking world. In Chile, he is referred to as **Viejito Pascuero** or **Viejo Pascuero**. In other countries, such as

HERITAGE SPEAKERS

Colombia, young people expect gifts from **El Niño Jesús**. In Spain and Argentina, **Los Reyes Magos** deliver gifts on January 6.
Heritage Speakers Ask heritage speakers in the class to describe a typical school experience in their culture. Which aspects do they find to be significantly different from the experience of their current school and classmates? Which do they find to be similar? Why might these differences and similarities exist?

Mexican author and diplomat Octavio Paz (March 31, 1914–April 19, 1998) studied both law and literature at the **Universidad Nacional Autónoma de México (UNAM)**, but after graduating he immersed himself in the art of writing. An incredibly prolific writer of novels, poetry, and essays, Paz solidified his prestige as Mexico's preeminent author with his 1950 book ***El laberinto de la soledad***, a fundamental study of Mexican identity. Among the many awards he received in his lifetime are the **Premio Miguel de Cervantes** (1981) and Nobel Prize for Literature (1990). Paz foremost considered himself a poet and affirmed that poetry constitutes "**la religión secreta de la edad° moderna**".

Vocabulario útil

¿Cuál es tu materia favorita?	*What is your favorite subject?*
¿Cuántos años tienes?	*How old are you?*
¿Qué estudias?	*What do you study?*
el/la alumno/a	*student*
la carrera (de medicina)	*(medical) degree program, major*
derecho	*law*
reconocido	*well-known*

Preparación

What is the name of your school? What classes are you taking this semester? Answers will vary.

Emparejar

Match the first part of the sentence in the left column with the appropriate ending in the right column.

1. Los estudiantes Mexicanos de la UNAM viven en c
2. México, D.F. es d
3. La UNAM es a
4. La UNAM ofrece b

   a. una universidad muy grande.
   b. 74 carreras de estudio.
   c. sus casas con sus padres.
   d. la ciudad más grande (*biggest*) de Hispanoamérica.

edad *age* ¿Conoces a algún...? *Do you know any...?* que dé *that teaches*

Los estudios

—¿Qué estudias?
—Ciencias de la comunicación.

Estudio derecho en la UNAM.

¿Conoces a algún° profesor famoso que dé° clases... en la UNAM?

Section Goals

In **Flash cultura**, students will:
• read about **Octavio Paz**
• watch a video about the **Universidad Nacional Autónoma de México (UNAM)**

Communication 1.2
Cultures 2.1, 2.2
Comparisons 4.2

Teacher Resources

Read the front matter for suggestions on how to incorporate all the program's components. See pages 39A–39B for a detailed listing of Teacher Resources online.

Introduction Check comprehension: 1. Where and what did Octavio Paz study? 2. What is *El laberinto de la soledad* and what does it deal with? 3. What type of literature did Paz prefer, and why?

Antes de ver
• Explain to students that **tienes** means *you have* and **tener... años** means *to be... years old*.
• Assure students that they do not need to understand every Spanish word they hear in the video. Tell them to rely on visual cues and to listen for cognates and words from **Vocabulario útil**.

Preparación
🔲↔🔲 Have students write down the answers in Spanish using complete sentences. Then, using words and phrases from **Vocabulario útil** and **Contextos**, have them interview a partner. Ask a few volunteers to report their findings.

Emparejar Ask students to share their impressions of the **UNAM**. Have them name some advantages and disadvantages of studying at such a large university.

España

El país en cifras

▶ **Área:** 505.370 km² (kilómetros cuadrados) o 195.124 millas cuadradas°, incluyendo las islas Baleares y las islas Canarias

▶ **Población:** 47.043.000

▶ **Capital:** Madrid—5.762.000

▶ **Ciudades° principales:** Barcelona—5.029.000, Valencia—812.000, Sevilla, Zaragoza

▶ **Moneda°:** euro

▶ **Idiomas°:** español o castellano, catalán, gallego, valenciano, euskera

Regiones lingüísticas

Bandera de España

Españoles célebres

▶ **Miguel de Cervantes,** escritor° (1547–1616)
▶ **Pedro Almodóvar,** director de cine° (1949–)
▶ **Rosa Montero,** escritora y periodista° (1951–)
▶ **Fernando Alonso,** corredor de autos° (1981–)
▶ **Paz Vega,** actriz° (1976–)
▶ **Severo Ochoa,** Premio Nobel de Medicina, 1959; doctor y científico (1905–1993)

millas cuadradas *square miles* Ciudades *Cities* Moneda *Currency* Idiomas *Languages* escritor *writer* cine *film* periodista *reporter* corredor de autos *race car driver* actriz *actress* pueblo *town* Cada año *Every year* Durante todo un día *All day long* se tiran *throw at each other* varias toneladas *many tons*

¡Increíble pero cierto!

En Buñol, un pueblo° de Valencia, la producción de tomates es un recurso económico muy importante. Cada año° se celebra el festival de *La Tomatina*. Durante todo un día°, miles de personas se tiran° tomates. Llegan turistas de todo el país, y se usan varias toneladas° de tomates.

Plaza Mayor en Madrid

La Sagrada Familia en Barcelona

El baile flamenco

Islas Canarias

TEACHING OPTIONS

Heritage Speakers ◄▪► **Paella,** the national dish of Spain, is the ancestor of the popular Latin American dish **arroz con pollo**. Ask heritage speakers if they know of any traditional dishes in their families that have their roots in Spanish cuisine. Invite them to describe the dish(es) to the class.

Variación léxica Tell students that they may also see the word **euskera** spelled **euskara** and **eusquera**. The letter **k** is used in Spanish only in words of foreign origin. **Euskara** is the Basque name of the Basque language, which linguists believe is unrelated to any other known language. The Spanish name for *Basque* is **vascuence** or **vasco**.

Gastronomía • **José Andrés**

José Andrés es un chef español famoso internacionalmente°. Le gusta combinar platos° tradicionales de España con las técnicas de cocina más innovadoras°. Andrés vive° en Washington, DC, es dueño° de varios restaurantes en los EE.UU. y presenta° un programa en PBS (foto, izquierda). También° ha estado° en *Late Show with David Letterman* y *Top Chef.*

Cultura • **La diversidad**

La riqueza° cultural y lingüística de España refleja la combinación de las diversas culturas que han habitado° en su territorio durante siglos°. El español es la lengua oficial del país, pero también son oficiales el catalán, el gallego, el euskera y el valenciano.

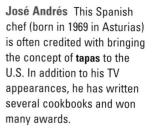

Póster en catalán

Artes • **Velázquez y el Prado**

El Prado, en Madrid, es uno de los museos más famosos del mundo°. En el Prado hay pinturas° importantes de Botticelli, de El Greco y de los españoles Goya y Velázquez. *Las meninas* es la obra° más conocida° de Diego Velázquez, pintor° oficial de la corte real° durante el siglo° XVII.

Las meninas,
Diego Velázquez, 1656

Comida • **La paella**

La paella es uno de los platos más típicos de España. Siempre se prepara° con arroz° y azafrán°, pero hay diferentes recetas°. La paella valenciana, por ejemplo, es de pollo° y conejo°, y la paella marinera es de mariscos°.

La costa de Ibiza

¿Qué aprendiste? Completa las oraciones con la información adecuada.
1. El chef español __José Andrés__ es muy famoso.
2. El arroz y el azafrán son ingredientes básicos de la ___paella___.
3. El Prado está en ___Madrid___.
4. José Andrés vive en ___Washington, DC/EE.UU.___.
5. El chef José Andrés tiene un ___programa___ de televisión en PBS.
6. El gallego es una de las lenguas oficiales de ___España___.

Conexión Internet Investiga estos temas en Internet.
1. Busca información sobre la Universidad de Salamanca u otra universidad española. ¿Qué cursos ofrece (*does it offer*)?
2. Busca información sobre un español o una española célebre (por ejemplo, un[a] político/a, un actor, una actriz, un[a] artista). ¿De qué parte de España es y por qué es célebre?

....

internacionalmente *internationally* platos *dishes* más innovadoras *most innovative* vive *lives* dueño *owner* presenta *hosts* También *Also*
ha estado *has been* riqueza *richness* han habitado *have lived* durante siglos *for centuries* mundo *world* pinturas *paintings* obra *work*
más conocida *best-known* pintor *painter* corte real *royal court* siglo *century* Siempre se prepara *It is always prepared* arroz *rice*
azafrán *saffron* recetas *recipes* pollo *chicken* conejo *rabbit* mariscos *seafood*

La clase

el/la compañero/a de clase	classmate
el/la estudiante	student
el/la profesor(a)	teacher
el borrador	eraser
la calculadora	calculator
el escritorio	desk
el libro	book
el mapa	map
la mesa	table
la mochila	backpack
el papel	paper
la papelera	wastebasket
la pizarra	blackboard
la pluma	pen
la puerta	door
el reloj	clock; watch
la silla	seat
la tiza	chalk
la ventana	window
la biblioteca	library
la cafetería	cafeteria
la casa	house; home
el estadio	stadium
el laboratorio	laboratory
la librería	bookstore
la universidad	university; college
la clase	class
el curso, la materia	course
el examen	test; exam
el horario	schedule
la prueba	test; quiz
el semestre	semester
la tarea	homework
el trimestre	trimester; quarter

Las materias

la arqueología	archeology
el arte	art
la biología	biology
las ciencias	sciences
la computación	computer science
la contabilidad	accounting
la economía	economics
el español	Spanish
la física	physics
la geografía	geography
la historia	history
las humanidades	humanities
el inglés	English
las lenguas extranjeras	foreign languages
la literatura	literature
las matemáticas	mathematics
la música	music
el periodismo	journalism
la psicología	psychology
la química	chemistry
la sociología	sociology

Preposiciones y adverbios

al lado de	next to
a la derecha de	to the right of
a la izquierda de	to the left of
allá	over there
allí	there
cerca de	near
con	with
debajo de	below
delante de	in front of
detrás de	behind
en	in; on
encima de	on top of
entre	between
lejos de	far from
sin	without
sobre	on; over

Palabras adicionales

¿Adónde?	Where (to)?
ahora	now
¿Cuál?, ¿Cuáles?	Which?; Which one(s)?
¿Por qué?	Why?
porque	because

Verbos

bailar	to dance
buscar	to look for
caminar	to walk
cantar	to sing
cenar	to have dinner
comprar	to buy
contestar	to answer
conversar	to converse, to chat
desayunar	to have breakfast
descansar	to rest
desear	to wish; to desire
dibujar	to draw
enseñar	to teach
escuchar la radio/ música	to listen (to) the radio/music
esperar (+ *inf.*)	to wait (for); to hope
estar	to be
estudiar	to study
explicar	to explain
gustar	to like
hablar	to talk; to speak
llegar	to arrive
llevar	to carry
mirar	to look (at); to watch
necesitar (+ *inf.*)	to need
practicar	to practice
preguntar	to ask (a question)
preparar	to prepare
regresar	to return
terminar	to end; to finish
tomar	to take; to drink
trabajar	to work
viajar	to travel

Los días de la semana

¿Cuándo?	When?
¿Qué día es hoy?	What day is it?
Hoy es…	Today is…
la semana	week
lunes	Monday
martes	Tuesday
miércoles	Wednesday
jueves	Thursday
viernes	Friday
sábado	Saturday
domingo	Sunday

Numbers 31 and higher	See pages 63–64.
Expresiones útiles	See page 45.

Lección 3: Teacher Resources

There is a wealth of resources online to support instruction using **Senderos**. For details on how to integrate these Teacher Resources into your lessons, see the front matter of this Teacher's Edition on pages T16 to T48.

Presentation	Practice & Communicate	Assess*	Scripts and Translations	

• Digital Images:
  • **La familia de José Miguel Pérez Santoro**
  • **Una familia**
	• Activity Pack Practice Activities (with Answer Key): **Contextos**
	• Additional Vocabulary **Más vocabulario relacionado con las nacionalidades y las mascotas; Más adjetivos**
	• Digital Image Bank (Family)
		• Vocabulary Quiz (with Answer Key)		**contextos**

		• **Fotonovela** Optional Testing Sections (with Answer Key)	• **Fotonovela** Videoscript • **Fotonovela** English Translation	**fotonovela**
• **Estructura 3.1** Grammar Slides	• Information Gap Activities* • Activity Pack Practice Activities (with Answer Key): Descriptive adjectives • Surveys: Worksheet for survey	• Grammar 3.1 Quiz (with Answer Key)	• Tutorial Script: Descriptive adjectives	**estructura**
• **Estructura 3.2** Grammar Slides	• Activity Pack Practice Activities (with Answer Key): Possessive adjectives	• Grammar 3.2 Quiz (with Answer Key)	• Tutorial Script: Possessive adjectives	
• **Estructura 3.3** Grammar Slides	• Information Gap Activities* • Activity Pack Practice Activities (with Answer Key): Present tense of **-er** and **-ir** verbs	• Grammar 3.3 Quiz (with Answer Key)	• Tutorial Script: Present tense of **-er** and **-ir** verbs	
• **Estructura 3.4** Grammar Slides	• Activity Pack Practice Activities (with Answer Key): Present tense of **tener** and **venir**	• Grammar 3.4 Quiz (with Answer Key)	• Tutorial Script: Present tense of **tener** and **venir**	
			• **En pantalla** Videoscript • **En pantalla** English Translation	**En pantalla**
		• **Flash cultura** Optional Testing Sections (with Answer Key)	• **Flash cultura** Videoscript • **Flash cultura** English Translation	**Flash cultura** / **adelante**
Digital Images: • **Ecuador**		• **Panorama** Optional Testing Sections (with Answer Key) • **Panorama cultural** (video)	• **Panorama cultural** Videoscript • **Panorama cultural** English Translation	**Panorama**

*Can also be assigned online.

Lección 3: Teacher Resources

Pulling It All Together

Practice and Communicate
- Role-plays
- Activity Pack Practice Activities (**¡A repasar!**) (with Answer Key)

Assessment

Tests and Exams*
- **Prueba A** with audio
- **Prueba B** with audio
- **Prueba C** with audio
- **Prueba D** with audio
- **Prueba E** with audio
- **Prueba F** with audio
- Tests Answer Key
- Oral Testing Suggestions

- **Examen A** with audio (lessons 1-3)
- **Examen B** with audio (lessons 1-3)
- Exams Answer Key

Audioscripts
- Tests and Exams Audioscripts
- Alternative Listening Sections Audioscript

Additional Tools for Planning and Teaching

- Essential Questions
- I Can Worksheets
- IPAs & Rubrics
- Lesson Plans
- Middle School Activity Pack
- Pacing Guides

Audio MP3s for Classroom Activities

- **Contextos. Práctica**: Activities 1 and 2 (p. 79)
- **Estructura** 3.2. **Comunicación**: Activity 4 (p.95)
- **Estructura** 3.4. **Comunicación**: Activity 4 (p.103)
- **Escuchar** (p. 109)

Script for Comunicación: Actividad 4 (p. 95)

Ana María Mi primo está en nuestra casa. Él es alemán. Está aquí, en Bogotá, porque desea aprender español. Él es un médico muy importante en su ciudad. Es rubio y muy simpático. Su novia espera estar aquí el jueves. Ella termina sus clases el lunes. Ella estudia psicología.

Script for Comunicación: Actividad 4 (p. 103)

Francisco ¡Hola! Me llamo Francisco Acosta y soy puertorriqueño. Tengo veinte años y asisto a la Universidad de Nueva York donde estudio economía. Mi familia vive en San Juan, la capital de Puerto Rico. Mi padre, Carlos, tiene cuarenta y cinco años. Es ingeniero. Mi madre, Dolores, enseña inglés en un instituto de idiomas. Mi hermana Maricarmen asiste a la escuela secundaria. Tiene dieciséis años.

*Tests and Exams can also be assigned online.

La familia

Communicative Goals

You will learn how to:
- Talk about your family and friends
- Describe people and things
- Express possession

Lesson Goals

In **Lección 3**, students will be introduced to the following:
- terms for family relationships
- names of various professions
- surnames and families in the Spanish-speaking world
- Spain's Royal Family
- descriptive adjectives
- possessive adjectives
- the present tense of common regular –**er** and –**ir** verbs
- the present tense of **tener** and **venir**
- context clues to unlock meaning of unfamiliar words
- using idea maps when writing
- how to write a friendly letter
- strategies for asking clarification in oral communication
- the television commercial *Diminutivo*
- a video about two Ecuadorian families
- geographical and cultural information about Ecuador

A primera vista Here are some additional questions you can ask to personalize the photo: **¿Cuántas personas hay en tu familia? ¿De qué conversas con ellos? ¿Viajas mucho con ellos?**

Teaching Tip Look for these icons for additional communicative practice:

→👤	Interpretive communication
←👤	Presentational communication
👤↔👤	Interpersonal communication

A PRIMERA VISTA
- ¿Cuántos chicos hay en la foto?
- ¿Hay una mujer detrás de la chica? ¿Y a la izquierda?
- ¿Hay una cosa en la mano del chico?
- ¿Conversan ellos? ¿Trabajan? ¿Descansan?
- ¿Están en su casa?

SUPPORT FOR BACKWARD DESIGN

Lección 3 Essential Questions
1. How do people describe their families and family members?
2. How do people talk about how they spend their time?
3. How are a person's surnames determined in the Spanish-speaking world?

Lección 3 Integrated Performance Assessment
Before teaching this chapter, review the Integrated Performance Assessment (IPA) and its accompanying scoring rubric. Use the IPA to assess students' progress toward proficiency targets at the end of the chapter.
IPA Context: You and a classmate are spending Spring vacation in a Spanish-speaking country, and the coordinator of the trip needs to place you with host families. You are going to read about six different people. Decide which person is the best host for your classmate. Then, present your recommendation to the class, describing your classmate and explaining your choice of host.

VOICE BOARD

Voice boards online allow you and your students to record and share up to five minutes of audio. Use voice boards for presentations, oral assessments, discussions, directions, etc.

La familia

La familia de José Miguel Pérez Santoro

Más vocabulario

los abuelos	*grandparents*
el/la bisabuelo/a	*great-grandfather/ great-grandmother*
el/la gemelo/a	*twin*
el/la hermanastro/a	*stepbrother/stepsister*
el/la hijastro/a	*stepson/stepdaughter*
la madrastra	*stepmother*
el medio hermano/ la media hermana	*half-brother/ half-sister*
el padrastro	*stepfather*
los padres	*parents*
los parientes	*relatives*
el/la cuñado/a	*brother-in-law/ sister-in-law*
la nuera	*daughter-in-law*
el/la suegro/a	*father-in-law/ mother-in-law*
el yerno	*son-in-law*
el/la amigo/a	*friend*
el apellido	*last name*
la gente	*people*
el/la muchacho/a	*boy/girl*
el/la niño/a	*child*
el/la novio/a	*boyfriend/girlfriend*
la persona	*person*
el/la artista	*artist*
el/la ingeniero/a	*engineer*
el/la doctor(a), el/la médico/a	*doctor; physician*
el/la periodista	*journalist*
el/la programador(a)	*computer programmer*

Variación léxica

madre ⟷ mamá, mami (*colloquial*)
padre ⟷ papá, papi (*colloquial*)
muchacho/a ⟷ chico/a

Juan Santoro Sánchez

mi abuelo (*my grandfather*)

Ernesto Santoro González

mi tío (*uncle*)
hijo (*son*) de Juan y Socorro

Marina Gutiérrez de Santoro

mi tía (*aunt*)
esposa (*wife*) de Ernesto

Silvia Socorro Santoro Gutiérrez

mi prima (*cousin*)
hija (*daughter*) de Ernesto y Marina

Héctor Manuel Santoro Gutiérrez

mi primo (*cousin*)
nieto (*grandson*) de Juan y Socorro

Carmen Santoro Gutiérrez

mi prima
hija de Ernesto y Marina

¡LENGUA VIVA!

In Spanish-speaking countries, it is common for people to go by both their first name and middle name, such as **José Miguel** or **Juan Carlos.** You will learn more about names and naming conventions on p. 86.

Práctica

1 Escuchar
Listen to each statement made by José Miguel Pérez Santoro, then indicate whether it is **cierto** or **falso**, based on his family tree.

	Cierto	Falso			Cierto	Falso
1.	●	○		6.	●	○
2.	●	○		7.	●	○
3.	○	●		8.	○	●
4.	●	○		9.	○	●
5.	○	●		10.	●	○

2 Personas
Indicate each word that you hear mentioned in the narration.

1. _____ cuñado   4. ✔ niño   7. _____ ingeniera
2. ✔ tía   5. ✔ esposo   8. ✔ primo
3. ✔ periodista   6. _____ abuelos

3 Emparejar
Provide the letter of the phrase that matches each description. Two items will not be used.

1. Mi hermano programa las computadoras. c
2. Son los padres de mi esposo. e
3. Son los hijos de mis (*my*) tíos. h
4. Mi tía trabaja en un hospital. a
5. Es el hijo de mi madrastra y el hijastro de mi padre. b
6. Es el esposo de mi hija. l
7. Es el hijo de mi hermana. k
8. Mi primo dibuja y pinta mucho. i
9. Mi hermanastra enseña en la universidad. j
10. Mi padre trabaja con planos (*blueprints*). d

a. Es médica.
b. Es mi hermanastro.
c. Es programador.
d. Es ingeniero.
e. Son mis suegros.
f. Es mi novio.
g. Es mi padrastro.
h. Son mis primos.
i. Es artista.
j. Es profesora.
k. Es mi sobrino.
l. Es mi yerno.

4 Definiciones
Define these family terms in Spanish. Some answers may vary.

> **modelo**
> hijastro Es el hijo de mi esposo/a, pero no es mi hijo.

1. abuela   5. suegra
2. bisabuelo   6. cuñado
3. tío   7. nietos
4. primas   8. medio hermano

1. la madre de mi madre/padre
2. el abuelo de mi madre/padre
3. el hermano de mi madre/padre
4. las hijas de mis tíos/as
5. la madre de mi esposo/a
6. el esposo de mi hermana
7. los hijos de mis hijos
8. el hijo de mi padre pero no de mi madre

Family tree (left column):

Socorro González de Santoro
mi abuela (*my grandmother*)

Mirta Santoro de Pérez
mi madre (*mother*)
hija de Juan y Socorro

Rubén Ernesto Pérez Gómez
mi padre (*father*)
esposo de mi madre

José Miguel Pérez Santoro
hijo de Rubén y Mirta

Beatriz Alicia Pérez de Morales
mi hermana (*sister*)

Felipe Morales Zapata
esposo (*husband*) **de Beatriz Alicia**

Víctor Miguel Morales Pérez
mi sobrino (*nephew*)
hermano (*brother*) **de Anita**

Anita Morales Pérez
mi sobrina (*niece*)
nieta (*granddaughter*) **de mis padres**

los hijos (*children*) **de Beatriz Alicia y Felipe**

---

1 Expansion To challenge students, write the false statements on the board and have students correct them by referring to the family tree.

1 Script 1. Beatriz Alicia es mi hermana. 2. Rubén es el abuelo de Víctor Miguel. 3. Silvia es mi sobrina. 4. Mirta y Rubén son los tíos de Héctor Manuel. 5. Anita es mi prima. 6. Ernesto es el hermano de mi madre. 7. Soy el tío de Anita. 8. Víctor Miguel es mi nieto. 9. Carmen, Beatriz Alicia y Marina son los nietos de Juan y Socorro. 10. El hijo de Juan y Socorro es el tío de Beatriz Alicia.

2 In-Class Tips
- To simplify, read through the list as a class before playing the audio. Remind students to focus only on these words as they listen.
- Tell students that the words, if they appear in the narration, will not follow the sequence in the list.

2 Script Julia y Daniel son mis abuelos. Ellos viven en Montreal con mi tía Leti, que es periodista, y con mi primo César. César es un niño muy bueno y dibuja muy bien. Hoy voy a hablar por teléfono con todos ellos y con el esposo de Leti. Él es de Canadá.

3 Expansion After students finish, ask volunteers to provide complete sentences combining elements from the numbered and lettered lists. Ex: **Los padres de mi esposo son mis suegros. Mis primos son los hijos de mis tíos.**

4 Expansion Have student pairs write five additional definitions following the pattern of those in the activity.

• To challenge students, ask them to provide other possible responses for items 2, 4, 5, and 8. Ex: **2. esposos 4. tío/sobrino, hijastro/padrastro 5. niños, muchachos, amigos, primos, chicos, hermanastros, medios hermanos 8. bisabuelo, tío, padre, padrastro**

• Ask the class questions about the photos and captions in the textbook. Ex: **¿Quién es artista? (Elena Vargas Soto es artista.) ¿Trabaja Irene? (Sí, es ingeniera.)**

5 Expansion

• ←**👥**→ Have pairs of students create an additional sentence for each of the photos on this page. Ask one student to write sentences for the first four photos and the other student to write sentences for the remainder. Then have them exchange papers and check each other's work.

• Bring family-related photos to class. Prepare a fill-in-the-blank sentence for each. Talk about the photos, and ask volunteers to complete the sentences.

6 In-Class Tips

• Tell students to take notes on their partner's responses. When they are finished, ask students questions about their partner's answers.

• As an alternative, first read through the questions as a class. Tell students to select a partner that they have not worked with before. Individually, have them jot down guesses to their partner's responses for a few of the questions. Students can write down any other predictions they may have about their partner's family. Then have pairs get together and complete the activity. Survey the class to find out the accuracy of the predictions.

5 **Escoger** Complete the description of each photo using words you have learned in **Contextos**.
Some answers will vary. Possible answers:

1. La ___familia___ de Sara es grande.

2. Héctor y Lupita son ___novios___.

3. Maira Díaz es ___periodista___.

4. Rubén habla con su ___hijo/padre___.

5. Los dos ___hermanos___ están en el parque.

6. Irene es ___ingeniera___.

7. Elena Vargas Soto es ___artista___.

8. Don Manuel es el ___abuelo___ de Martín.

TEACHING OPTIONS

Extra Practice Add an additional visual aspect to this vocabulary practice. Ask students to bring in a family-related photo of their own or a photo from the Internet or a magazine. Have them write several fill-in-the-blank sentences to go with it. Working in pairs, have them guess what is happening in each other's photo and complete the sentences.

Pairs 👤↔👤 In pairs, have students take turns assuming the identity of a person pictured in **Actividad 5** and making statements using **gustar** and **-ar** verbs. Encourage them to be creative. (Ex: **Me gusta cenar con mi novio.**) Their partner will try to guess the person's identity (**Eres Lupita.**).

Comunicación

6 **Preguntas personales** Answer your partner's questions. *Answers will vary.*

1. ¿Cuántas personas hay en tu familia?
2. ¿Cómo se llaman tus padres? ¿De dónde son? ¿Dónde trabajan?
3. ¿Cuántos hermanos tienes? ¿Cómo se llaman? ¿Dónde estudian o trabajan?
4. ¿Cuántos primos tienes? ¿Cuáles son los apellidos de ellos? ¿Cuántos son niños y cuántos son adultos? ¿Hay más chicos o más chicas en tu familia?
5. ¿Eres tío/a? ¿Cómo se llaman tus sobrinos/as? ¿Dónde estudian o trabajan?
6. ¿Quién es tu pariente favorito?
7. ¿Tienes un mejor amigo? ¿Cómo se llama?

7 **Árbol genealógico** Write about a family tree. Use your own family or invent a family.
Answers will vary.

> *modelo*
>
> El abuelo se llama Robert Lange. Es de Nebraska...

6 **Una familia** With a partner, identify the members in the family tree by asking questions about how each family member is related to Graciela Vargas García.

> *modelo*
>
> **Estudiante 1:** ¿Quién es Beatriz Pardo de Vargas?
> **Estudiante 2:** Es la abuela de Graciela.

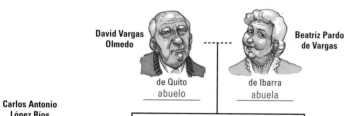

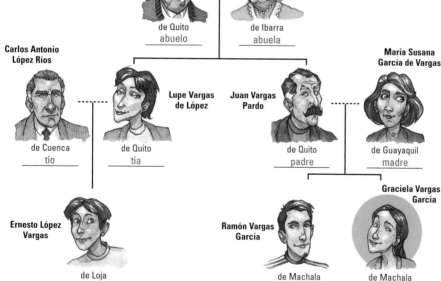

David Vargas Olmedo — de Quito — abuelo

Beatriz Pardo de Vargas — de Ibarra — abuela

Carlos Antonio López Ríos — de Cuenca — tío

Lupe Vargas de López — de Quito — tía

Juan Vargas Pardo — de Quito — padre

María Susana García de Vargas — de Guayaquil — madre

Ernesto López Vargas — de Loja — primo

Ramón Vargas García — de Machala — hermano

Graciela Vargas García — de Machala

---

6 **Virtual Chat** 👥 Available online.

7 **Expansion**
• 👥 Have students bring in pictures of their family or of a famous family. Turn the writing activity into an oral one by letting them present their family pictures in small groups.
• Encourage students to ask their classmates questions about their family members. Ex: **¿Quién es él? ¿Cómo se llama tu mamá? ¿Cuántos años tiene tu hermana? ¿Qué le gusta a tu papá?**

8 **In-Class Tip** Remind students that it is common for Spanish speakers to go by two names (like **Carlos Antonio** in this chart). Students will learn about surnames on page 86; however, you may want to preview that information by pointing out how **Graciela** and her brother got their last names.

8 **Expansion**
• 👥 Ask students to write five statements about people in the chart (Ex: **Es la prima de Ernesto; Es una mujer de Quito.**). Then, in pairs, have them take turns reading their statements aloud. The other student should identify the person (**Es Graciela; Es Lupe**).
• Model the pronunciation of the Ecuadorian cities mentioned. Ask students to locate each on the map of Ecuador, page 112. Ask students to talk about each city based on the map. Ex: **Guayaquil y Machala son ciudades de la costa del Pacífico. Quito, Loja y Cuenca son ciudades de la cordillera de los Andes. Quito es la capital de Ecuador.**

8 **Partner Chat** 👥 Available online.

Un domingo en familia

Marissa pasa el día en Xochimilco con la familia Díaz.

PERSONAJES FELIPE TÍA NAYELI

JIMENA Hola, tía Nayeli.
TÍA NAYELI ¡Hola, Jimena! ¿Cómo estás?
JIMENA Bien, gracias. Y, ¿dónde están mis primas?
TÍA NAYELI No sé. ¿Dónde están mis hijas? ¡Ah!

MARISSA ¡Qué bonitas son tus hijas! Y ¡qué simpáticas!

MARISSA La verdad, mi familia es pequeña.
SRA. DÍAZ ¿Pequeña? Yo soy hija única. Bueno, y ¿qué más? ¿Tienes novio?
MARISSA No. Tengo mala suerte con los novios.

FELIPE Soy guapo y delgado.
JIMENA Ay, ¡por favor! Eres gordo, antipático y muy feo.

TÍO RAMÓN ¿Tienes una familia grande, Marissa?
MARISSA Tengo dos hermanos mayores, Zack y Jennifer, y un hermano menor, Adam.

MARISSA Tía Nayeli, ¿cuántos años tienen tus hijas?
TÍA NAYELI Marta tiene ocho años y Valentina doce.

JIMENA   **MARTA**   **VALENTINA**   **SRA. DÍAZ**   **TÍO RAMÓN**   **SR. DÍAZ** **MARISSA**

7

SRA. DÍAZ Chicas, ¿compartimos una trajinera?

MARISSA ¡Claro que sí! ¡Qué bonitas son!

SRA. DÍAZ ¿Vienes, Jimena?

JIMENA No, gracias. Tengo que leer.

8

MARISSA Me gusta mucho este sitio. Tengo ganas de visitar otros lugares en México.

SRA. DÍAZ ¡Debes viajar a Mérida!

TÍA NAYELI ¡Sí, con tus amigos! Debes visitar a Ana María, la hermana de Roberto y de Ramón.

9

(*La Sra. Díaz habla por teléfono con la tía Ana María.*)

SRA. DÍAZ ¡Qué bien! Excelente. Sí, la próxima semana. Muchísimas gracias.

10

MARISSA ¡Gracias, Sra. Díaz!
SRA. DÍAZ Tía Ana María.
MARISSA Tía Ana María.
SRA. DÍAZ ¡Un beso, chau!
MARISSA Bye!

Expresiones útiles

Talking about your family

¿Tienes una familia grande?
Do you have a big family?
Tengo dos hermanos mayores y un hermano menor.
I have two older siblings and a younger brother.
La verdad, mi familia es pequeña.
The truth is, my family is small.
¿Pequeña? Yo soy hija única.
Small? I'm an only child.

Describing people

¡Qué bonitas son tus hijas!
Y ¡qué simpáticas!
Your daughters are so pretty!
And so nice!
Soy guapo y delgado.
I'm handsome and slim.
¡Por favor! Eres gordo, antipático y muy feo.
Please! You're fat, unpleasant, and very ugly.

Talking about plans

¿Compartimos una trajinera?
Shall we share a trajinera*?*
¡Claro que sí! ¡Qué bonitas son!
Of course! They're so pretty!
¿Vienes, Jimena?
Are you coming, Jimena?
No, gracias. Tengo que leer.
No, thanks. I have to read.

Saying how old people are

¿Cuántos años tienen tus hijas?
How old are your daughters?
Marta tiene ocho años y Valentina doce.
Marta is eight and Valentina twelve.

Additional vocabulary

ensayo *essay*
pobrecito/a *poor thing*
próxima *next*
sitio *place*
todavía *still*
trajinera *type of barge*

Expresiones útiles Draw attention to the descriptive and possessive adjectives and the present tense forms of **tener** in the **Fotonovela** captions, **Expresiones útiles**, and as they occur in your conversation with the students. Point out that this material will be formally presented in **Estructura**. If students make errors of noun-adjective agreement or with verb conjugations, provide correct forms as needed, but do not expect them to be able to produce the forms accurately at this time.

In-Class Tip
🧍↔🧍 Ask students to read aloud the **Fotonovela** captions in groups of six, with one person assigned to each character. Then ask one or two groups to role-play the conversation for the class.

Nota cultural The **Xochimilcas** arrived in the Valley of Mexico around 900 A.D. and settled on the hill of **Cuahilama**, southeast of present-day Mexico City. From the 14th century the **Xochimilcas** were in conflict with the Aztecs, and were finally conquered by them in the mid-15th century.

TEACHING OPTIONS

TPR →🧍← As you play the **Fotonovela** episode, have students raise their right hand when they hear family-related vocabulary and their left hand when they hear a word or phrase related to professions.
Extra Practice As a preview to **Estructura 3.1**, have students scan pages 82–83, and guide them in identifying the descriptive adjectives. Then ask students to rephrase the sentences to reflect their own families. Ex: **Mi papá es hijo único.**

Pairs 🧍↔🧍 Have students create a two-column chart with the heads *Marissa* and *Roberto*. Play the **Fotonovela** episode and have students jot down the names and family-related words they hear in the appropriate column. Then have them use the chart to create simple family trees for **Marissa** and **Roberto**. Finally, in pairs, have students examine the trees for accuracy and make statements describing the familial relationships.

1 Expansion Give these true/false statements to the class as items 7–10: **7. Jimena dice que Felipe es feo. (Cierto.) 8. Marissa tiene un novio. (Falso. Tiene mala suerte con los novios.) 9. Valentina tiene una hermana menor. (Cierto.) 10. Jimena no comparte la trajinera porque tiene que asistir a clase. (Falso. Tiene que leer.)**

2 Expansion **Sra. Díaz** is the only person not associated with a statement. Ask students to look at the **Fotonovela** captions and **Expresiones útiles** on pages 82–83 and invent a statement for her. Remind them not to use her exact words. Ex: **Hablo por teléfono con mi cuñada.**

Nota cultural In the 19th century, the **chinampas** fulfilled agricultural purposes. At that time, **trajineras** were used to transport crops from the islands of **Xochimilco** to markets in Mexico City.

3 Expansion Have pairs who wrote about the same family exchange papers and compare their descriptions. Ask them to share the differences with the class.

4 In-Class Tip Model the activity by providing answers based on your own family.

4 Expansion Ask volunteers to share their partners' answers with the rest of the class.

4 Virtual Chat Available online.

¿Qué pasó?

1 ¿Cierto o falso? Indicate whether each sentence is **cierto** or **falso**. Correct the false statements.

	Cierto	Falso	
1. Marissa dice que (*says that*) tiene una familia grande.	○	✓	Marissa dice que tiene una familia pequeña.
2. La Sra. Díaz tiene dos hermanos.	○	✓	La señora Díaz es hija única.
3. Marissa no tiene novio.	✓	○	
4. Valentina tiene veinte años.	○	✓	Valentina tiene doce años.
5. Marissa comparte una trajinera con la Sra. Díaz y la tía Nayeli.	✓	○	
6. A Marissa le gusta mucho Xochimilco.	✓	○	

NOTA CULTURAL

Xochimilco is famous for its system of canals and **chinampas**, or artificial islands, which have been used for agricultural purposes since Pre-Hispanic times. In 1987, UNESCO declared **Xochimilco** a World Heritage Site.

2 Identificar Indicate which person would make each statement. The names may be used more than once. **¡Ojo!** One name will not be used.

1. Felipe es antipático y feo. Jimena
2. Mis hermanos se llaman Jennifer, Adam y Zack. Marissa
3. ¡Soy un joven muy guapo! Felipe
4. Mis hijas tienen ocho y doce años. tía Nayeli
5. ¡Qué bonitas son las trajineras! Marissa
6. Ana María es la hermana de Ramón y Roberto. tía Nayeli
7. No puedo (*I can't*) compartir una trajinera porque tengo que leer. Jimena
8. Tus hijas son bonitas y simpáticas, tía Nayeli. Marissa

SRA. DÍAZ

JIMENA

MARISSA

FELIPE

TÍA NAYELI

NOTA CULTURAL

Trajineras are large passenger barges that you can rent in **Xochimilco**. Each boat is named and decorated and has a table and chairs so passengers can picnic while they ride.

3 Escribir Choose Marissa, Sra. Díaz, or tía Nayeli and write a brief description of her family. Be creative! Answers will vary.

MARISSA

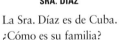

Marissa es de los EE.UU. ¿Cómo es su familia?

SRA. DÍAZ

La Sra. Díaz es de Cuba. ¿Cómo es su familia?

TÍA NAYELI

La tía Nayeli es de México. ¿Cómo es su familia?

4 Conversar Answer your partner's questions. Answers will vary.

1. ¿Cuántos años tienes?
2. ¿Tienes una familia grande?
3. ¿Tienes hermanos o hermanas?
4. ¿Cuántos años tiene tu abuelo (tu hermana, tu primo, etc.)?
5. ¿De dónde son tus padres?

AYUDA

Here are some expressions to help you talk about age.

Yo tengo... años.
I am... years old.
Mi abuelo tiene... años.
My grandfather is... years old.

PRE-AP®

Extra Practice Ask volunteers to reenact the **Fotonovela** episode for the class. Assure them that it is not necessary to memorize the script or stick strictly to its content. They should try to get the general meaning across with the vocabulary and expressions they know, and they also should feel free to be creative. Give students time to prepare.

TEACHING OPTIONS

Small Groups Have groups of three interview each other about their families. Assign one person as the interviewer, one the interviewee, and the third person as the note taker. At three-minute intervals, have students switch roles. When everyone has been interviewed, have students report back to the class.

Pronunciación

Diphthongs and linking

hermano	**niña**	**cuñado**

In Spanish, **a**, **e**, and **o** are considered strong vowels. The weak vowels are **i** and **u**.

ruido	**parientes**	**periodista**

A diphthong is a combination of two weak vowels or of a strong vowel and a weak vowel. Diphthongs are pronounced as a single syllable.

mi hijo	**una clase excelente**

Two identical vowel sounds that appear together are pronounced like one long vowel.

la abuela

con Natalia	**sus sobrinos**	**las sillas**

Two identical consonants together sound like a single consonant.

es ingeniera	**mis abuelos**	**sus hijos**

A consonant at the end of a word is linked with the vowel sound at the beginning of the next word.

mi hermano	**su esposa**	**nuestro amigo**

A vowel at the end of a word is linked with the vowel sound at the beginning of the next word.

Práctica Say these words aloud, focusing on the diphthongs.

1. historia
2. nieto
3. parientes
4. novia
5. residencia
6. prueba
7. puerta
8. ciencias
9. lenguas
10. estudiar
11. izquierda
12. ecuatoriano

Oraciones Read these sentences aloud to practice diphthongs and linking words.

1. Hola. Me llamo Anita Amaral. Soy del Ecuador.
2. Somos seis en mi familia.
3. Tengo dos hermanos y una hermana.
4. Mi papá es del Ecuador y mi mamá es de España.

Refranes Read these sayings aloud to practice diphthongs and linking sounds.

Cuando una puerta se cierra, otra se abre.[1]

Hablando del rey de Roma, por la puerta se asoma.[2]

1 When one door closes, another opens.
2 Speak of the devil and he will appear.

Section Goals

In **Pronunciación**, students will be introduced to:
• the strong and weak vowels
• common diphthongs
• linking in pronunciation

Comparisons 4.1

In-Class Tips
• Write **hermano, niña**, and **cuñado** on the board. Ask students to identify the strong and weak vowels.
• Pronounce **ruido, parientes**, and **periodista**, and have students identify the diphthong in each word. Point out that the strong vowels (**a, e, o**) do not combine with each other to form diphthongs. When two strong vowels come together, they remain in different syllables.
• Pronounce **mi hermano** and **su esposa** and ask volunteers to write them on the board. Point out that the linked vowels form a diphthong and are pronounced as one syllable.
• Follow the same procedure with **es ingeniera** and **mis abuelos**. You may want to introduce linking involving the other final consonants (**l, n, r, z**). Ex: **Son hermanos. El hermano mayor está aquí. ¿Cuál es tu hermana?**
• Ask students to provide words they learned in **Lecciones 1** and **2** and **Contextos** and **Fotonovela** of this lesson that exemplify each point.

TEACHING OPTIONS

Heritage Speakers Ask heritage speakers if they know of other **refranes**. Write each **refrán** on the board and have the student who volunteered it explain what it means. Ex: **A quien Dios no le dio hijos, el diablo le da sobrinos. Más sabe el diablo por viejo que por diablo.**

Video ➡📹⬅ Add an additional auditory aspect to this **Pronunciación** presentation. Play the **Fotonovela** segment and

have students identify diphthongs and linking words.
Extra Practice Here are additional sentences for extra practice with diphthongs and linking: **Los estudiantes extranjeros hablan inglés. Mi abuela Ana tiene ochenta años. Juan y Enrique son hermanos. ¿Tu esposa aprende una lengua extranjera? Tengo un examen en la clase de español hoy.** Read them aloud and have students identify diphthongs and linking words.

¿Cómo te llamas?

In the Spanish-speaking world, it is common to have two last names: one paternal and one maternal. In some cases, the conjunctions **de** or **y** are used to connect the two. For example, in the name **Juan Martínez Velasco**, *Martínez* is the paternal surname (**el apellido paterno**), and *Velasco* is the maternal surname (**el apellido materno**). This convention of using two last names (**doble apellido**) is a European tradition that Spaniards brought to the Americas. It continues to be practiced in many countries, including Chile, Colombia, Mexico, Peru, and Venezuela. There are exceptions, however. In Argentina, the prevailing custom is for children to inherit only the father's last name.

When a woman marries in a country where two last names are used, legally she retains her two maiden surnames. However, socially she may take her husband's paternal surname in place of her inherited maternal surname. For example, **Karen Martínez Insignares**, the wife of Colombian singer

José Martínez García

Mercedes Velasco Pérez

Juan Martínez Velasco

Juanes (**Juan Esteban Aristizábal Vásquez**), might use the names **Karen Martínez Aristizábal** or **Karen Martínez de Aristizábal** in social situations (although officially her name remains **Karen Martínez Insignares**). Adopting a husband's last name for social purposes, though widespread, is only legally recognized in Ecuador and Peru.

Most parents do not break tradition upon naming their children; regardless of the surnames the mother uses, they use the father's first surname followed by the mother's first surname, as in the name **Juan Martínez Velasco**. However, one should note that both surnames come from the grandfathers, and therefore all **apellidos** are effectively paternal.

Hijos en la casa

In Spanish-speaking countries, family and society place very little pressure on young adults to live on their own (**independizarse**), and children often live with their parents well into their thirties. For example, about 60% of Spaniards under 34 years of age live at home with their parents. This delay in moving out is both cultural and economic—lack of job security or low wages coupled with a high cost of living may make it impractical for young adults to live independently before they marry.

ACTIVIDADES

1 **¿Cierto o falso?** Indicate whether these statements are cierto or falso. Correct the false statements.

1. Most Spanish-speaking people have three last names. **Falso.** Most people have two last names.
2. Hispanic last names generally consist of the paternal last name followed by the maternal last name. **Cierto.**
3. It is common to see **de** or **y** used in a Hispanic last name. **Cierto.**
4. Someone from Argentina would most likely have two last names. **Falso.** They would use only the father's last name.
5. Generally, married women legally retain two maiden surnames. **Cierto.**
6. In social situations, a married woman often uses her husband's last name in place of her inherited paternal surname. **Falso.** She often uses it in place of her inherited maternal surname.
7. Adopting a husband's surname is only legally recognized in Peru and Ecuador. **Cierto.**
8. Hispanic last names are effectively a combination of the maternal surnames from the previous generation. **Falso.** They are a combination of the paternal surnames from the previous generation.

Así se dice
- To challenge students, add these words to the list: **el/la enamorado/a (Ecu., Perú), el/la pololo/a (Chi.)** (*boyfriend/girlfriend*); **el/la novio/a, el/la comprometido/a (Méx.), el/la prometido/a (Amér. L.)** (*fiancé/fiancée*); **el/la tutor(a)** (*[legal] guardian*).
- Ask simple questions using the terms. Ex: **¿Cómo se llama tu abuelo?**

Perfil In addition to **Leonor** and **Sofía**, Spain's royal couple has six other grandchildren. Their daughter **Elena** has a son and a daughter, **don Felipe** and **doña Victoria**. Their other daughter, **Cristina**, has three sons and a daughter: **don Juan, don Pablo, don Miguel**, and **doña Irene**. However, it is **Leonor** who is next in the succession to the Spanish throne, after her father, **Felipe**.

El mundo hispano
- Remind students that in Spanish a comma is often used instead of a period to indicate a decimal. In spite of this, it is possible to use **punto** or **coma** when saying these numbers (Ex: **México, cuatro coma cero** or **cuatro punto cero**).
- If time permits, find the average family size of other Spanish-speaking countries. Ask students if any of the statistics are surprising to them.

2 Expansion Ask students to write two additional fill-in-the-blank statements. Then have them exchange papers with a partner and complete the sentences.

3 In-Class Tip
←👤→ To challenge students, have them prepare a list of questions in Spanish about their partner's genealogical tree.

ASÍ SE DICE

Familia y amigos

el/la bisnieto/a	*great-grandson/daughter*
el/la chamaco/a (Méx.); el/la chamo/a (Ven.); el/la chaval(a) (Esp.); el/la pibe/a (Arg.)	el/la muchacho/a
mi colega (Esp.); mi cuate (Méx.); mi parcero/a (Col.); mi pana (Ven., P. Rico, Rep. Dom.)	*my pal; my buddy*
la madrina	*godmother*
el padrino	*godfather*
el/la tatarabuelo/a	*great-great-grandfather/great-great-grandmother*

EL MUNDO HISPANO

Las familias

Although worldwide population trends show a decrease in average family size, households in many Spanish-speaking countries are still larger than their U.S. counterparts.

- **México** 4,0 personas
- **Colombia** 3,9 personas
- **Argentina** 3,6 personas
- **Uruguay** 3,0 personas
- **España** 2,9 personas
- **Estados Unidos** 2,6 personas

PERFIL

La familia real española

Undoubtedly, Spain's most famous family is **la familia real** (*Royal*). In 1962, the then prince **Juan Carlos de Borbón** married Princess **Sofía** of Greece. In the 1970s, **el Rey** (*King*) **Juan Carlos** and **la Reina** (*Queen*) **Sofía** helped transition Spain to democracy after a forty-year dictatorship. The royal couple has three children: las **infantas** (*Princesses*) **Elena** and **Cristina**, and a son, **el príncipe** (*Prince*) **Felipe**, whose official title was **el Príncipe de Asturias**. In 2004, Felipe married **Letizia Ortiz Rocasolano**, a journalist and TV presenter. They have two daughters, **las infantas Leonor** (born in 2005) and **Sofía** (born in 2007). In 2014, Juan Carlos decided to abdicate the throne in favor of his son.

Conexión Internet

What role do **padrinos** and **madrinas** have in today's Hispanic family?

Use the Web to find more cultural information related to this **Cultura** section.

ACTIVIDADES

2 Comprensión Complete these sentences.
1. Spain's royals were responsible for guiding in <u>democracy</u>.
2. In Spanish, your godmother is called <u>la madrina</u>.
3. Princess Leonor is the <u>granddaughter</u> of Queen Sofía.
4. Uruguay's average household has <u>3.0</u> people.
5. If a Venezuelan calls you **mi pana**, you are that person's <u>friend</u>.

3 Una familia famosa Create a genealogical tree of a famous family, using photos or drawings labeled with names and ages. Explain who the people are and their relationships to each other. Answers will vary.

PRE-AP®

Cultural Comparison Have student pairs research a famous English-speaking family (such as the Kennedys) and write a brief comparison with the Spanish Royal Family. Ask students to include information about their prominence in the media, involvement in politics, and general popularity. This activity may have to be done using English.

TEACHING OPTIONS

La familia hispana Explain to students that the concept **la familia** in Spanish-speaking countries is somewhat more inclusive than it is in English. When people say **la familia**, the majority of them are referring to their extended family. Extended families, if they do not live in the same dwelling, tend to live in closer geographical proximity in Latin America than they do in the U.S. and Canada.

Section Goals

In **Estructura 3.1**, students will learn:
• forms, agreement, and position of adjectives ending in –o/–a, –e, or a consonant
• high-frequency descriptive adjectives and some adjectives of nationality

 Comparisons 4.1

Teacher Resources
Read teaching suggestions incorporating all components of **Senderos** in the front matter. See pages 77A–77B for a detailed listing of Teacher Resources online.

In-Class Tips
• Write these adjectives on the board: **ecuatoriana, alto, bonito, viejo, trabajador.** Ask what each means and whether it is masculine or feminine. Model one of the adjectives in a sentence and ask volunteers to use the others in sentences.
• Work through the discussion of adjective forms point by point, writing examples on the board. Test comprehension as you proceed by asking volunteers to supply the correct form of adjectives for nouns you suggest. Remind students that grammatical gender does not necessarily reflect actual gender.
• Drill gender by pointing to individuals and asking the class to supply the correct form. Ex: (Pointing to male student) **¿Guapo o guapa?** (Pointing to female) **¿Simpático o simpática?** Then use adjectives ending in –e. Point to a male and say **inteligente**, then point to a female and have students provide the correct form. Continue with plurals. Keep a brisk pace.

3.1 Descriptive adjectives

ANTE TODO Adjectives are words that describe people, places, and things. In Spanish, descriptive adjectives are used with the verb **ser** to point out characteristics such as nationality, size, color, shape, personality, and appearance.

Forms and agreement of adjectives

COMPARE & CONTRAST

In English, the forms of descriptive adjectives do not change to reflect the gender (masculine/feminine) and number (singular/plural) of the noun or pronoun they describe.

*Juan is **nice**.*   *Elena is **nice**.*   *They are **nice**.*

In Spanish, the forms of descriptive adjectives agree in gender and/or number with the nouns or pronouns they describe.

Juan es simpátic**o**.   Elena es simpátic**a**.   Ellos son simpátic**os**.

▶ Adjectives that end in **-o** have four different forms. The feminine singular is formed by changing the **-o** to **-a**. The plural is formed by adding **-s** to the singular forms.

Masculine		**Feminine**	
SINGULAR	PLURAL	SINGULAR	PLURAL
el muchach**o** alt**o**	los muchach**os** alt**os**	la muchach**a** alt**a**	las muchach**as** alt**as**

¡Qué bonitas son tus hijas, tía Nayeli!

Felipe es gordo, antipático y muy feo.

▶ Adjectives that end in **-e** or a consonant have the same masculine and feminine forms.

Masculine		**Feminine**	
SINGULAR	PLURAL	SINGULAR	PLURAL
el chico inteligent**e**	los chicos inteligent**es**	la chica inteligent**e**	las chicas inteligent**es**
el examen difíci**l**	los exámenes difíci**les**	la clase difíci**l**	las clases difíci**les**

▶ Adjectives that end in **-or** are variable in both gender and number.

Masculine		**Feminine**	
SINGULAR	PLURAL	SINGULAR	PLURAL
el hombre trabajad**or**	los hombres trabajad**ores**	la mujer trabajad**ora**	las mujeres trabajad**oras**

Extra Practice Have pairs of students write sentences using adjectives such as **inteligente, alto, joven**. When they have finished, ask volunteers to dictate their sentences to you to write on the board. After you have written a sentence and corrected any errors, ask volunteers to suggest a sentence that uses the antonym of the adjective.

Variación léxica Clarify that the adjective **americano/a** applies to all inhabitants of North and South America, not just citizens of the United States. Residents of the United States usually are referred to with the adjective **norteamericano/a**. In more formal contexts, such as official documents, the adjective **estadounidense** is used.

AYUDA

Many adjectives are cognates, that is, words that share similar spellings and meanings in Spanish and English.

A cognate can be a noun like **profesor** or a descriptive adjective like **interesante**.

¡ATENCIÓN!

Note that **joven** takes an accent in its plural form. **Los jóvenes estudian mucho.**

▶ Use the masculine plural form to refer to groups that include males and females.

Manuel es alt**o**.   Lola es alt**a**.   Manuel y Lola son alt**os**.

Common adjectives

alto/a	tall	**gordo/a**	fat	**mucho/a**	much; many;
antipático/a	unpleasant	**grande**	big		a lot of
bajo/a	short (in	**guapo/a**	good-looking	**pelirrojo/a**	red-haired
	height)	**importante**	important	**pequeño/a**	small
bonito/a	pretty	**inteligente**	intelligent	**rubio/a**	blond(e)
bueno/a	good	**interesante**	interesting	**simpático/a**	nice; likeable
delgado/a	thin	**joven**	young	**tonto/a**	foolish
difícil	difficult	**malo/a**	bad	**trabajador(a)**	hard-working
fácil	easy	**mismo/a**	same	**viejo/a**	old
feo/a	ugly	**moreno/a**	brunet(te)		

Adjectives of nationality

▶ Unlike in English, Spanish adjectives of nationality are **not** capitalized. Proper names of countries, however, are capitalized.

Some adjectives of nationality

alemán, alemana	German	**francés, francesa**	French
argentino/a	Argentine	**inglés, inglesa**	English
canadiense	Canadian	**italiano/a**	Italian
chino/a	Chinese	**japonés, japonesa**	Japanese
costarricense	Costa Rican	**mexicano/a**	Mexican
cubano/a	Cuban	**norteamericano/a**	(North) American
ecuatoriano/a	Ecuadorian	**puertorriqueño/a**	Puerto Rican
español(a)	Spanish	**ruso/a**	Russian
estadounidense	from the U.S.		

▶ Adjectives of nationality are formed like other descriptive adjectives. Those that end in **-o** change to **-a** when forming the feminine.

chin**o** ⟶ chin**a**   mexican**o** ⟶ mexican**a**

The plural is formed by adding an **-s** to the masculine or feminine form.

argentin**o** ⟶ argentin**os**   cuban**a** ⟶ cuban**as**

▶ Adjectives of nationality that end in **-e** have only two forms, singular and plural.

canadiens**e** ⟶ canadiens**es**   estadounidens**e** ⟶ estadounidens**es**

▶ To form the feminine of adjectives of nationality that end in a consonant, add **–a**.

alem**án** ⟶ alema**na**   españo**l** ⟶ españo**la**
japoné**s** ⟶ japone**sa**   inglé**s** ⟶ ingle**sa**

¡ATENCIÓN!

Note that adjectives with an accent on the last syllable drop the accent in the feminine and plural forms.
inglés → inglesa
alemán → alemanes

In-Class Tips

• Point out that when referring to people, **bonito/a** can only be used for females, but **guapo/a** can be used for both males and females. Some heritage speakers may use **moreno/a** to refer to someone with dark skin, and **rubio/a** for someone with light brown hair.

• Use pictures or names of celebrities to teach descriptive adjectives in semantic pairs. Ex: **¿Marc Gasol es alto o bajo? (Es alto.) ¿Salma Hayek es fea? (No, es bonita.)**

• Use names of celebrities to practice adjectives of nationality. Ex: **Daniel Craig, ¿es canadiense? (No, es inglés.) Hillary Clinton, ¿es francesa? (No, es norteamericana.)**

• Point out that adjectives with an accent mark on the last syllable drop the accent mark in the feminine and plural forms. Ex: **inglés, inglesa, ingleses, inglesas**

• Point out that adjectives of nationality also can be used as nouns. Ex: **La chica rusa es guapa. La rusa es guapa.** Like adjectives, nouns of nationality are not capitalized.

• At this point you may want to present *Vocabulario adicional: Más adjetivos* and *Más vocabulario relacionado con las nacionalidades y las mascotas* from the online Resources.

• You may want to add to the list of nationalities. Ex: **¿Kylie Minogue es australiana? (Sí, es australiana.) ¿Cuáles son las formas plurales de** *australiano*? **(australianos/australianas)**

TEACHING OPTIONS

Pairs 👤↔👤 If the majority of your students are **norteamericanos**, have pairs ask each other their family's origin. Write **¿Cuál es el origen de tu familia?** and **Mi familia es de origen...** on the board. Brainstorm other adjectives of nationality as necessary (Ex: **galés, indígena, nigeriano, polaco**). Point out that since **el origen** is masculine and singular, any adjectives they use will be as well.

TPR 👤↔👤 Create two sets of note cards with a city and a corresponding adjective of nationality. Shuffle the cards and distribute them. Have students circulate around the room to find the person who shares their nationality. Ex: **¿De dónde eres? Soy de Toronto. Soy canadiense.** Then students should arrange themselves in a "map," finding their place by asking other pairs' nationality (**¿De dónde son ustedes? Somos cubanos.**).

In-Class Tips

- Introduce the position of descriptive adjectives and adjectives of nationality. Ask simple questions, such as: **¿Tienes amigos inteligentes? ¿Tomas clases difíciles? ¿Tienes profesores simpáticos o antipáticos?**
- To practice position of descriptive adjectives, write simple sentences (similar to the example sentences on this page) on paper and cut them into strips, one word per strip. In pairs, have students arrange the words in the correct order.
- Practice adjectives of quantity by saying: **Hay mucha tarea en esta clase, ¿verdad?** You may want to introduce **poco/a** for contrast. Survey the class: **¿En qué clases hay mucha tarea? ¿En qué clases hay poca tarea?**
- Introduce **bueno/a, malo/a,** and **grande,** and explain the process by which they get shortened. Clarify that **bueno** and **malo** are shortened only before masculine singular nouns and their meaning does not change. However, **grande** is shortened before any singular noun, regardless of gender, and there is a change in meaning.
- To practice **bueno/a, malo/a,** and **grande,** write a series of cloze sentences on the board. In pairs, have students fill in the blanks.

Position of adjectives

▶ Descriptive adjectives and adjectives of nationality generally follow the nouns they modify.

El niño **rubio** es de España.
The blond boy is from Spain.

La mujer **española** habla inglés.
The Spanish woman speaks English.

▶ Unlike descriptive adjectives, adjectives of quantity precede the modified noun.

Hay **muchos** libros en la biblioteca.
There are many books in the library.

Hablo con **dos** turistas puertorriqueños.
I am talking with two Puerto Rican tourists.

▶ **Bueno/a** and **malo/a** can appear before or after a noun. When placed before a masculine singular noun, the forms are shortened: **bueno → buen; malo → mal**.

Joaquín es un **buen** amigo.
Joaquín es un amigo **bueno**.
→ *Joaquín is a good friend.*

Hoy es un **mal** día.
Hoy es un día **malo**.
→ *Today is a bad day.*

▶ When **grande** appears before a singular noun, it is shortened to **gran**, and the meaning of the word changes: **gran** = *great* and **grande** = *big, large*.

Don Francisco es un **gran** hombre.
Don Francisco is a great man.

La familia de Inés es **grande**.
Inés' family is large.

¡INTÉNTALO! Provide the appropriate forms of the adjectives.

simpático

1. Mi hermano es _simpático_.
2. La profesora Martínez es _simpática_.
3. Rosa y Teresa son _simpáticas_.
4. Nosotros somos _simpáticos_.

alemán

1. Hans es _alemán_.
2. Mis primas son _alemanas_.
3. Marcus y yo somos _alemanes_.
4. Mi tía es _alemana_.

difícil

1. La química es _difícil_.
2. El curso es _difícil_.
3. Las pruebas son _difíciles_.
4. Los libros son _difíciles_.

guapo

1. Su esposo es _guapo_.
2. Mis sobrinas son _guapas_.
3. Los padres de ella son _guapos_.
4. Marta es _guapa_.

TEACHING OPTIONS

Video Show the **Fotonovela** episode again, stopping where appropriate to discuss how certain adjectives were used.
TPR Divide the class into two teams and have them line up. Point to a member from each team and give a certain form of an adjective (Ex: **rubios**). Then name another form that you want students to provide (Ex: feminine singular) and have them race to the board. The first student who writes the correct form earns

one point for his or her team. Deduct one point for each wrong answer. The team with the most points at the end wins.
Extra Practice Create sentences similar to those in **¡Inténtalo!** Say the sentence, have students repeat it, then say a different subject. Have students say the sentence with the new subject, changing adjectives and verbs as necessary.

Práctica

1 **Emparejar** Find the words in column B that are the opposite of the words in column A. One word in B will not be used.

Marcos

Jorge

A		**B**
1. guapo	d	a. delgado
2. moreno	f	b. pequeño
3. alto	h	c. malo
4. gordo	a	d. feo
5. joven	e	e. viejo
6. grande	b	f. rubio
7. simpático	g	g. antipático
		h. bajo

2 **Completar** Indicate the nationalities of these people by selecting the correct adjectives and changing their forms when necessary.

1. Penélope Cruz es ___española___.
2. Alfonso Cuarón es un gran director de cine de México; es ___mexicano___.
3. Ellen Page y Avril Lavigne son ___canadienses___.
4. Giorgio Armani es un diseñador de modas (*fashion designer*) ___italiano___.
5. Daisy Fuentes es de La Habana, Cuba; ella es ___cubana___.
6. Emma Watson y Daniel Radcliffe son actores ___ingleses___.
7. Heidi Klum y Michael Fassbender son ___alemanes___.
8. Serena Williams y Michael Phelps son ___estadounidenses___.

3 **Describir** Look at the drawing and describe each family member using as many adjectives as possible. Some answers will vary. Possible answers:

Carlos Romero Sandoval — Josefina Barcos de Romero — Susana Romero Barcos — Tomás Romero Barcos — Alberto Romero Pereda

1. Susana Romero Barcos es ___delgada, rubia, alta___
2. Tomás Romero Barcos es ___pelirrojo, inteligente, gordo___
3. Los dos hermanos son ___jóvenes___
4. Josefina Barcos de Romero es ___alta, bonita, rubia___
5. Carlos Romero Sandoval es ___bajo, gordo, pelirrojo___
6. Alberto Romero Pereda es ___viejo, bajo, gordo___
7. Tomás y su (*his*) padre son ___pelirrojos, gordos___
8. Susana y su (*her*) madre son ___altas, delgadas, rubias___

Comunicación

4 **Busco novio** Read Cecilia's personal profile. Then indicate whether these conclusions are **lógico** or **ilógico**, based on what you read.

SOY ALTA, morena y bonita. Soy cubana, de Holguín. Me gusta mucho el arte. Busco una amiga similar. Mi amiga ideal es alta, morena, inteligente y muy simpática.

	Lógico	Ilógico
1. Cecilia es profesora.	○	⊘
2. Cecilia desea ser artista.	⊘	○
3. Cecilia dibuja.	⊘	○
4. Cecilia es tonta.	○	⊘
5. La amiga ideal de Cecilia es interesante.	⊘	○

5 **Preguntas** Answer your partner's questions. Answers will vary.

1. ¿Cómo eres tú?
2. ¿Cómo es tu casa?
3. ¿Cómo es tu escuela?
4. ¿Cómo es tu ciudad?
5. ¿Cómo es tu país?
6. ¿Cómo son tus amigos?

6 **Anuncio personal** Write a personal profile for your school newspaper. Describe yourself and your ideal best friend. Then compare you profile with a classmate's. How are you similar and how are you different? Are you looking for the same things in a best friend? Answers will vary.

Síntesis

7 **¿Cómo es?** With a partner, take turns describing people, places, and things. You may want to use the items on the list. Tell your partner whether you agree (**Estoy de acuerdo**) or disagree (**No estoy de acuerdo**) with his/her descriptions.
Answers will vary.

> **modelo**
> San Francisco
> **Estudiante 1:** *San Francisco es una ciudad (city) muy bonita.*
> **Estudiante 2:** *No estoy de acuerdo. Es muy fea.*

Nueva York	los periodistas
Chicago	las clases de español/física/
George Clooney	matemáticas/química
Taylor Swift	el/la presidente/a de los
los médicos	Estados Unidos

Sidebar (left column)

5 **In-Class Tips**

• Divide the class into pairs and distribute the handouts for the activity **Diferencias** from the online Resources (Lección 3/Activity Pack/ Information Gap Activities). Ask students to read the instructions and give them ten minutes to complete the activity. Have volunteers report their findings to the class.

• To simplify, have students brainstorm a list of adjectives for each person in their drawing, then have them proceed with the activity.

5 **Virtual Chat**
▲↔▲ Available online.

6 **In-Class Tip** Have students divide a sheet of paper into two columns, labeling one **Yo** and the other **Mi amigo/a ideal**. Have them brainstorm Spanish adjectives for each column. Ask them to rank each adjective in the second column in terms of its importance to them.

 Communication 1.1

7 **Expansion**
▲↔▲ Have student pairs brainstorm a list of additional famous people, places, and things. Ask them to include some plural items. Then ask students to exchange papers with another pair and discuss the people, places, and things on the lists they receive.

7 **Partner Chat**
▲↔▲ Available online.

TEACHING OPTIONS

Heritage Speakers ←▲→ Ask heritage speakers to describe members of their extended families. Ask the rest of the class comprehension questions.
Extra Practice Research zodiac signs on the Internet and prepare a simple personality description for each sign, using cognates and adjectives from this lesson. Divide the class into pairs and distribute the descriptions. Have students guess their partners' sign. Ex: —**Eres Aries, ¿verdad?** —**No, no soy Aries. No soy impulsiva y no soy aventurera.**
Extra Practice ←▲→ Encourage students to collect pictures of people from the Internet, magazines, or newspapers. Have them prepare a description of one of the pictures. Invite students to display their pictures and give their descriptions orally. The class should guess which picture is being described.

3.2 # Possessive adjectives

ANTE TODO   Possessive adjectives, like descriptive adjectives, are words that are used to qualify people, places, or things. Possessive adjectives express the quality of ownership or possession.

Forms of possessive adjectives

SINGULAR FORMS	PLURAL FORMS	
mi	**mis**	*my*
tu	**tus**	*your* (fam.)
su	**sus**	*his, her, its, your* (form.)
nuestro/a	**nuestros/as**	*our*
vuestro/a	**vuestros/as**	*your* (fam.)
su	**sus**	*their, your*

COMPARE & CONTRAST

In English, possessive adjectives are invariable; that is, they do not agree in gender and number with the nouns they modify. Spanish possessive adjectives, however, do agree in number with the nouns they modify.

my cousin	*my cousins*	*my aunt*	*my aunts*
mi primo	**mis** primos	**mi** tía	**mis** tías

The forms **nuestro** and **vuestro** agree in both gender and number with the nouns they modify.

nuestr**o** prim**o**	nuestr**os** prim**os**	nuestr**a** tía	nuestr**as** tías

▶ Possessive adjectives are always placed before the nouns they modify.

—¿Está **tu novio** aquí?   —No, **mi novio** está en la biblioteca.
Is your boyfriend here?   *No, my boyfriend is in the library.*

▶ Because **su** and **sus** have multiple meanings (*your, his, her, their, its*), you can avoid confusion by using this construction instead: [*article*] + [*noun*] + **de** + [*subject pronoun*].

AYUDA
Look at the context, focusing on nouns and pronouns, to help you determine the meaning of **su(s)**.

sus parientes ◀ | los parientes **de él/ella** | *his/her relatives* |
| los parientes **de Ud./Uds.** | *your relatives* |
| los parientes **de ellos/ellas** | *their relatives* |

¡INTÉNTALO!   Provide the appropriate form of each possessive adjective.

Singular

1. Es ___mi___ (*my*) libro.
2. ___Mi___ (*My*) familia es ecuatoriana.
3. ___Tu___ (*Your*, fam.) esposo es italiano.
4. ___Nuestro___ (*Our*) profesor es español.
5. Es ___su___ (*her*) reloj.
6. Es ___tu___ (*your*, fam.) mochila.
7. Es ___su___ (*your*, form.) maleta.
8. ___Su___ (*Their*) sobrina es alemana.

Plural

1. ___Sus___ (*Her*) primos son franceses.
2. ___Nuestros___ (*Our*) primos son canadienses.
3. Son ___sus___ (*their*) lápices.
4. ___Sus___ (*Their*) nietos son japoneses.
5. Son ___nuestras___ (*our*) plumas.
6. Son ___mis___ (*my*) papeles.
7. ___Mis___ (*My*) amigas son inglesas.
8. Son ___sus___ (*his*) cuadernos.

Section Goals
In **Estructura 3.2**, students will be introduced to:
• possessive adjectives
• ways of clarifying **su(s)** when the referent is ambiguous

 Comparisons 4.1

Teacher Resources
Read teaching suggestions incorporating all components of **Senderos** in the front matter. See pages 77A–77B for a detailed listing of Teacher Resources online.

In-Class Tips
• Introduce the concept of possessive adjectives. Hold up your book, jacket, or other personal possession and ask individuals: **¿Es *tu* libro? (No.)** Then, as you point to one student, ask the class: **¿Es el libro de ____? ¿Es *su* libro?** Link arms with another student and ask the class: **¿Es *nuestro* libro?** Indicate the whole class and ask: **¿Es el libro de ustedes? ¿Es *su* libro?** Finally, hug the object dramatically and say: **No. Es *mi* libro.** Then ask volunteers personalized questions. Ex: **¿Es simpática tu madre?**
• Use each possessive adjective with a noun to illustrate agreement. Point out that all agree in number with the noun they modify but that only **nuestro/a** and **vuestro/a** show gender. Point out that **tú** (subject) has an accent mark; **tu** (possessive) does not.
• Ask students to give plural or singular possessive adjectives with nouns. Say: **Da el plural: nuestra clase. (nuestras clases)** Say: **Da el singular: mis manos. (mi mano)**
• Write **su familia** and **sus amigos** on the board and ask volunteers to supply all possible equivalent phrases using **de**.

Práctica

1 **La familia de Manolo** Complete each sentence with the correct possessive adjective from the options in parentheses. Use the subject of each sentence as a guide.

1. Me llamo Manolo, y _____mi_____ (nuestro, mi, sus) hermano es Federico.
2. _____Nuestra_____ (Nuestra, Sus, Mis) madre Silvia es profesora y enseña química.
3. Ella admira a _____sus_____ (tu, nuestro, sus) estudiantes porque trabajan mucho.
4. Yo estudio en la misma escuela, pero no tomo clases con _____mi_____ (mi, nuestras, tus) madre.
5. Federico trabaja en una oficina con _____nuestro_____ (mis, tu, nuestro) padre.
6. _____Su_____ (Mi, Su, Tu) oficina está en el centro de la Ciudad de México.
7. Javier y Óscar son _____mis_____ (mis, mi, sus) tíos de Oaxaca.
8. ¿Y tú? ¿Cómo es _____tu_____ (mi, su, tu) familia?

2 **Clarificar** Clarify each sentence with a prepositional phrase. Follow the model.

> **modelo**
> Su hermana es muy bonita. (ella)
> *La hermana de ella es muy bonita.*

1. Su casa es muy grande. (ellos) La casa de ellos es muy grande.
2. ¿Cómo se llama su hermano? (ellas) ¿Cómo se llama el hermano de ellas?
3. Sus padres trabajan en el centro. (ella) Los padres de ella trabajan en el centro.
4. Sus abuelos son muy simpáticos. (él) Los abuelos de él son muy simpáticos.
5. Maribel es su prima. (ella) Maribel es la prima de ella.
6. Su primo lee los libros. (ellos) El primo de ellos lee los libros.

3 **¿Dónde está?** Look at the drawings and indicate where your belongings are. Answers will vary. ◀

> **modelo**
> *Mi mochila está encima del escritorio.*

1.   2.   3.

4.   5.   6.

AYUDA

Remember that possessive adjectives don't agree in number or gender with the owner of an item; they always agree with the item(s) being possessed.

CONSULTA

For a list of useful prepositions, refer to the table *Prepositions often used with* **estar**, in **Estructura 2.3**, p. 60.

---

1 **In-Class Tip** Point out the **Ayuda** sidebar and guide students in applying this information to item 1. (**Manolo** is the possessor and **hermano/ Federico** is what is possessed.)

1 **Expansion**
- Have students change the number and gender of the nouns in items 1–7. Then have them say each new sentence, changing the possessives as necessary.
- Have students respond to the question in item 8.

2 **Expansion**
- Change the subject pronouns in parentheses and have the class provide new answers. Then have groups of students provide new nouns and the corresponding answers.
- Give the class sentences such as **Es su libro** and have volunteers rephrase them with a clarifying prepositional phrase.

3 **In-Class Tips**
- Before doing the activity, quickly review **estar** by writing the present-tense forms on the board.
- Remind students that **estar** is used to indicate location.

3 **Expansion** Ask questions about objects that are in the classroom. Ex: **¿Dónde está mi escritorio? ¿Dónde está el libro de ____? ¿Dónde están las plumas de ____? ¿Dónde están tus lápices?**

TEACHING OPTIONS

Extra Practice ←👤→ Ask students a few questions about the members of their immediate and extended families. Ex: **¿Cómo son tus padres? ¿Cómo se llama tu tío favorito? ¿Es el hermano de tu madre o de tu padre? ¿Tienes muchos primos? ¿Cómo se llaman tus primos? ¿De dónde son tus abuelos? ¿Hablas mucho con tus abuelos?**

Heritage Speakers ←👤→ Ask heritage speakers to talk briefly about a favorite relative. Have them include the characteristics that make that relative their favorite. Ask the rest of the class comprehension questions.

Comunicación

4 **Noticias de familia** Listen to Ana María talk about some family news. Then indicate whether the following conclusions are **lógico** or **ilógico**, based on what you heard.

		Lógico	Ilógico
1.	Ana María es rubia.	○	⊘
2.	Sus padres están en Bogotá.	⊘	○
3.	Su primo es inteligente.	⊘	○
4.	Su primo habla español.	○	⊘
5.	La novia de su primo es argentina.	○	⊘

5 **Describir** With a partner, describe the people and places listed below. Answers will vary.

> **modelo**
> la biblioteca de su escuela
> La biblioteca de nuestra escuela es muy grande. Hay muchos libros
> en la biblioteca.

1. tu profesor favorito
2. tu profesora favorita
3. tu clase favorita
4. la cafetería de su escuela
5. tus padres
6. tus abuelos
7. tu mejor (*best*) amigo
8. tu mejor amiga

6 **Una familia famosa** Assume the identity of a member of a famous family, real or fictional (the Obamas, Clintons, Bushes, Kardashians, Simpsons, etc.), and write a description of "your" family. Reveal your identity at the end of your description. Answers will vary.

> **modelo**
> Hay cuatro personas en mi familia. Mi padre es delgado y simpático. Él es de
> Philadelphia. Mi madre es muy inteligente y guapa. Mis padres son actores. Tengo
> una hermana menor. Nosotros también somos actores... Soy Jaden Smith.

Síntesis

7 **Describe a tu familia** With a partner, take turns asking each other questions about your families. Answers will vary.

> **modelo**
> **Estudiante 1:** ¿Cómo es tu padre?
> **Estudiante 2:** Mi padre es alto, guapo y muy inteligente.

Extra Practice ←👤→ Have students work in small groups to prepare a description of a famous person, such as a politician, a movie star, or a sports figure, and his or her extended family. Tell them to feel free to invent family members as necessary. Have groups present their descriptions to the class.

Heritage Speakers ←👤→ Ask heritage speakers to describe their families' home countries (**países de origen**) to the class. As they are giving their descriptions, ask them questions that elicit more information. Clarify for the class any unfamiliar words and expressions they may use.

---

4 **In-Class Tip**
Have students listen once and ask them to write as many words as they understand. Help them clarify the meaning and spelling of the words they catch.

4 **Script** *See the script for this activity on Interleaf page 77B.*

5 **In-Class Tips** Ask students to suggest a few more details to add to the **modelo**.

5 **Virtual Chat**
👤↔👤 Available online.

6 **In-Class Tip**
Quickly review the descriptive adjectives on page 89. You can do this by saying an adjective and having a volunteer give its antonym (**antónimo**).

6 **Expansion**
→👤← Have each group choose their favorite description and share it with the class.

 Communication 1.1

7 **Expansion**
• Review the family vocabulary on pages 78–79.
• Divide the class into groups of three. One student will describe his or her own family (using **mi**), and then the other two will describe the first student's family to one another (using **su**) and ask for clarification as necessary (using **tu**).
• Before beginning, ask students to list the family members they plan to describe.

7 **Partner Chat**
👤↔👤 Available online.

3.3 Present tense of -er and -ir verbs

ANTE TODO In **Lección 2**, you learned how to form the present tense of regular **-ar** verbs. You also learned about the importance of verb forms, which change to show who is performing the action. The chart below shows the forms from two other important groups, **-er** verbs and **-ir** verbs.

		comer (to eat)	**escribir** (to write)
SINGULAR FORMS	yo	com**o**	escrib**o**
	tú	com**es**	escrib**es**
	Ud./él/ella	com**e**	escrib**e**
PLURAL FORMS	nosotros/as	com**emos**	escrib**imos**
	vosotros/as	com**éis**	escrib**ís**
	Uds./ellos/ellas	com**en**	escrib**en**

▶ **-Er** and **-ir** verbs have very similar endings. Study the preceding chart to detect the patterns that make it easier for you to use them to communicate in Spanish.

Felipe y su tío comen.

Jimena lee.

▶ Like **-ar** verbs, the **yo** forms of **-er** and **-ir** verbs end in **-o**.

Yo com**o**.   Yo escrib**o**.

▶ Except for the **yo** form, all of the verb endings for **-er** verbs begin with **-e**.

-es   -emos   -en
-e   -éis

▶ **-Er** and **-ir** verbs have the exact same endings, except in the **nosotros/as** and **vosotros/as** forms.

nosotros ◀ com**emos** / escrib**imos**   vosotros ◀ com**éis** / escrib**ís**

CONSULTA

To review the conjugation of **-ar** verbs, see **Estructura 2.1**, p. 50.

AYUDA

Here are some tips on learning Spanish verbs:

1) Learn to identify the verb's stem, to which all endings attach.

2) Memorize the endings that go with each verb and verb tense.

3) As often as possible, practice using different forms of each verb in speech and writing.

4) Devote extra time to learning irregular verbs, such as **ser** and **estar**.

Common -er and -ir verbs

-er verbs	
aprender (a + *inf.*)	to learn
beber	to drink
comer	to eat
comprender	to understand
correr	to run
creer (en)	to believe (in)
deber (+ *inf.*)	should
leer	to read

-ir verbs	
abrir	to open
asistir (a)	to attend
compartir	to share
decidir (+ *inf.*)	to decide
describir	to describe
escribir	to write
recibir	to receive
vivir	to live

Ellos **corren** en el parque.

Él **escribe** una carta.

¡INTÉNTALO!   Provide the appropriate present tense forms of these verbs.

correr

1. Graciela ____ *corre* ____.
2. Tú ____ *corres* ____.
3. Yo ____ *corro* ____.
4. Sara y Ana ____ *corren* ____.
5. Usted ____ *corre* ____.
6. Ustedes ____ *corren* ____.
7. La gente ____ *corre* ____.
8. Marcos y yo ____ *corremos* ____.

abrir

1. Ellos ____ *abren* ____ la puerta.
2. Carolina ____ *abre* ____ la maleta.
3. Yo ____ *abro* ____ las ventanas.
4. Nosotras ____ *abrimos* ____ los libros.
5. Usted ____ *abre* ____ el cuaderno.
6. Tú ____ *abres* ____ la ventana.
7. Ustedes ____ *abren* ____ las maletas.
8. Los muchachos ____ *abren* ____ los cuadernos.

aprender

1. Él ____ *aprende* ____ español.
2. Maribel y yo ____ *aprendemos* ____ inglés.
3. Tú ____ *aprendes* ____ japonés.
4. Tú y tu hermanastra ____ *aprenden* ____ francés.
5. Mi hijo ____ *aprende* ____ chino.
6. Yo ____ *aprendo* ____ alemán.
7. Usted ____ *aprende* ____ inglés.
8. Nosotros ____ *aprendemos* ____ italiano.

Práctica

1 **Completar** Complete Susana's sentences about her family with the correct forms of the verbs in parentheses. One of the verbs will remain in the infinitive.

1. Mi familia y yo ___vivimos___ (vivir) en Mérida, Yucatán.
2. Tengo muchos libros. Me gusta ___leer___ (leer).
3. Mi hermano Alfredo es muy inteligente. Alfredo ___asiste___ (asistir) a clases los lunes, miércoles y viernes.
4. Los martes y jueves Alfredo y yo ___corremos___ (correr) en el Parque del Centenario.
5. Mis padres ___comen___ (comer) mucha lasaña los domingos y se quedan dormidos (*they fall asleep*).
6. Yo ___creo___ (creer) que (*that*) mis padres deben comer menos (*less*).

2 **Oraciones** Juan is talking about what he and his friends do after school. Form complete sentences by adding any other necessary elements.

> **modelo**
> yo / correr / amigos / lunes y miércoles
> *Yo corro con mis amigos los lunes y miércoles.*

1. Manuela / asistir / clase / yoga   Manuela asiste a la clase de yoga.
2. Eugenio / abrir / correo electrónico (*e-mail*)   Eugenio abre su correo electrónico.
3. Isabel y yo / leer / biblioteca   Isabel y yo leemos en la biblioteca.
4. Sofía y Roberto / aprender / hablar / inglés   Sofía y Roberto aprenden a hablar inglés.
5. tú / comer / cafetería / escuela   Tú comes en la cafetería de la escuela.
6. mi novia y yo / compartir / libro de historia   Mi novia y yo compartimos el libro de historia.

3 **Consejos** Mario and his family are spending a year abroad to learn Japanese. Use the words below to indicate what he and/or his family members are doing or should do to adjust to life in Japan. Then, create one more sentence using a verb not on the list.   Answers will vary.

> **modelo**
> recibir libros / deber practicar japonés
> *Mario y su esposa reciben muchos libros en japonés.*
> *Los hijos deben practicar japonés.*

aprender japonés	decidir explorar el país
asistir a clases	escribir listas de palabras en japonés
beber té (*tea*)	leer novelas japonesas
deber comer cosas nuevas	vivir con una familia japonesa
¿?	¿?

Comunicación

4   **Entrevista** Answer your partner's questions.   Answers will vary.

1. ¿Dónde comes al mediodía? ¿Comes mucho?
2. ¿Dónde vives?
3. ¿Con quién vives?
4. ¿Qué cursos debes tomar el próximo (*next*) semestre?
5. ¿Lees el periódico (*newspaper*)? ¿Qué periódico lees y cuándo?
6. ¿Recibes muchos mensajes de texto (*text messages*)? ¿De quién(es)?
7. ¿Escribes poemas?
8. ¿Crees en fantasmas (*ghosts*)?

5   **Deberes** Talk about at least five things you should do to improve your life and the lives of others. Use **deber** (+ *inf.*) and other **-er** or **-ir** verbs.   Answers will vary.

> **modelo**
> Yo debo correr más...

6   **Descripción** With a partner, take turns choosing an action from the list. Then give a description. Your partner will have to guess the action you are describing.   Answers will vary.

abrir (un libro, una puerta, una mochila)	correr (en el parque, en un maratón)
aprender (a bailar, a hablar francés, a dibujar)	escribir (una composición, un mensaje de texto [*text message*], con lápiz)
asistir (a una clase de yoga, a un concierto de rock, a una clase interesante)	leer (una carta [*letter*] de amor, un mensaje electrónico [*e-mail message*], un periódico [*newspaper*])
beber (agua, limonada)	recibir un regalo (*gift*)
comer (pasta, un sándwich, pizza)	¿?
compartir (un libro, un sándwich)	

> **modelo**
> **Estudiante 1:** Soy estudiante y tomo muchas clases. Vivo en Roma.
> **Estudiante 2:** ¿Comes pasta?
> **Estudiante 1:** No, no como pasta.
> **Estudiante 2:** ¿Aprendes a hablar italiano?
> **Estudiante 1:** ¡Sí!

Síntesis

7   **Un día típico** Write a description of a typical day in your life. Include at least six verbs.
Answers will vary.

> **modelo**
> A las nueve de la mañana mis amigas y yo bebemos un café.
> Asisto a la clase de yoga a las nueve y media.....

Communication 1.1
Comparisons 4.1

4 In-Class Tip
Students should complete their interviews before switching roles.

4 Virtual Chat
👤↔👤 Available online.

5 In-Class Tip
Review the conjugation of verb **deber** and emphasize its structure (**deber** + *inf.*). You may also suggest them to use **tener que** as alternative vocabulary to express obligation. Ex:
—**Tengo que comer saludablemente.**
—**Tengo que ser más simpático.**
—**Tengo que asistir a la clase de español.**

6 In-Class Tip Make sure that students understand that they have the option of acting out an activity or describing it in a creative way. Model both methods. Ex: Write on the board **beber té** (*tea*). First, act out sitting primly in a chair, serving tea from a teapot, stirring in sugar, and holding the cup daintily while taking small sips. Then give a description: **Estoy en Londres. Son las cuatro de la tarde. Deseo tomar algo** (*something*).

6 Expansion Write **asociación** on the board. Have students repeat the activity, but this time they must make associations with the verbs instead of acting them out or describing them. Ex: **Santa Claus/Papá Noel (recibir un regalo); clases de tango (aprender a bailar)**

6 Partner Chat
👤↔👤 Available online.

Communication 1.3

7 Expansion Challenge students to write about the typical day of another person, and ask them to share their description with the class.

Section Goals

In **Estructura 3.4**, students will:
- learn the present tense forms of **tener** and **venir**
- learn several common expressions with **tener**

 Comparisons 4.1

Teacher Resources
Read teaching suggestions incorporating all components of **Senderos** in the front matter. See pages 77A–77B for a detailed listing of Teacher Resources online.

In-Class Tips

- Model **tener** by asking volunteers questions. Ex: **¿Tienes una familia grande? ¿Tienes hermanos? ¿Cuántos tíos tiene ____? ¿Tienes muchos primos?** Point out that students have been using forms of **tener** since the beginning of the lesson.
- Point out that the **yo** form of **tener** is irregular and ends in **–go**. Begin a paradigm for **tener** by writing **tengo** on the board. Ask volunteers questions that elicit **tengo** such as: **Tengo una pluma, ¿quién tiene un lápiz?**
- Write **tienes, tiene, tienen** in the paradigm. Point out that in the **tú, usted**, and **ustedes** forms, the **–e–** of the verb stem changes to **–ie–**.
- Write **tenemos** in the paradigm and point out that this form is regular.
- Follow the same procedure to present **venir**. Have students give you the **nosotros** forms of **comer** and **escribir** for comparison.

3.4 Present tense of **tener** and **venir**

> **ANTE TODO** The verbs **tener** (*to have*) and **venir** (*to come*) are among the most frequently used in Spanish. Because most of their forms are irregular, you will have to learn each one individually.

The verbs tener and venir

		tener	venir
SINGULAR FORMS	yo	ten**go**	ven**go**
	tú	tien**es**	vien**es**
	Ud./él/ella	tien**e**	vien**e**
PLURAL FORMS	nosotros/as	ten**emos**	ven**imos**
	vosotros/as	ten**éis**	ven**ís**
	Uds./ellos/ellas	tien**en**	vien**en**

▶ The endings are the same as those of regular **-er** and **-ir** verbs, except for the **yo** forms, which are irregular: **tengo, vengo**.

▶ In the **tú, Ud.**, and **Uds.** forms, the **e** of the stem changes to **ie**, as shown below.

INFINITIVE	VERB STEM	VERB FORM
tener →	ten- →	tú t**ie**nes
		Ud./él/ella t**ie**ne
		Uds./ellos/ellas t**ie**nen
venir →	ven- →	tú v**ie**nes
		Ud./él/ella v**ie**ne
		Uds./ellos/ellas v**ie**nen

¿Tienes una familia grande, Marissa?

No, tengo una familia pequeña.

▶ Only the **nosotros** and **vosotros** forms are regular. Compare them to the forms of **comer** and **escribir** that you learned on page 96.

	tener	comer	venir	escribir
nosotros/as	ten**emos**	com**emos**	ven**imos**	escrib**imos**
vosotros/as	ten**éis**	com**éis**	ven**ís**	escrib**ís**

▶ In certain idiomatic or set expressions in Spanish, you use the construction **tener** + [*noun*] to express *to be* + [*adjective*]. This chart contains a list of the most common expressions with **tener**.

Expressions with tener

tener... años	*to be... years old*	**tener (mucha) prisa**	*to be in a (big) hurry*
tener (mucho) calor	*to be (very) hot*	**tener razón**	*to be right*
tener (mucho) cuidado	*to be (very) careful*	**no tener razón**	*to be wrong*
tener (mucho) frío	*to be (very) cold*	**tener (mucha) sed**	*to be (very) thirsty*
tener (mucha) hambre	*to be (very) hungry*	**tener (mucho) sueño**	*to be (very) sleepy*
tener (mucho) miedo (de)	*to be (very) afraid/ scared (of)*	**tener (mucha) suerte**	*to be (very) lucky*

—¿**Tienen** hambre ustedes?
Are you hungry?

—Sí, y **tenemos** sed también.
Yes, and we're thirsty, too.

▶ To express an obligation, use **tener que** (*to have to*) + [*infinitive*].

—¿Qué **tienes que** estudiar hoy?
What do you have to study today?

—**Tengo que** estudiar biología.
I have to study biology.

▶ To ask people if they feel like doing something, use **tener ganas de** (*to feel like*) + [*infinitive*].

—¿**Tienes ganas de** comer?
Do you feel like eating?

—No, **tengo ganas de** dormir.
No, I feel like sleeping.

MICIUDAD.COM
Usted tiene que visitarnos.

¡INTÉNTALO! Provide the appropriate forms of **tener** and **venir**.

tener

1. Ellos ___tienen___ dos hermanos.
2. Yo ___tengo___ una hermana.
3. El artista ___tiene___ tres primos.
4. Nosotros ___tenemos___ diez tíos.
5. Eva y Diana ___tienen___ un sobrino.
6. Usted ___tiene___ cinco nietos.
7. Tú ___tienes___ dos hermanastras.
8. Ustedes ___tienen___ cuatro hijos.
9. Ella ___tiene___ una hija.

venir

1. Mis padres ___vienen___ de México.
2. Tú ___vienes___ de España.
3. Nosotras ___venimos___ de Cuba.
4. Pepe ___viene___ de Italia.
5. Yo ___vengo___ de Francia.
6. Ustedes ___vienen___ de Canadá.
7. Alfonso y yo ___venimos___ de Portugal.
8. Ellos ___vienen___ de Alemania.
9. Usted ___viene___ de Venezuela.

Práctica

1 Go over the activity with the class, reading a statement in column A and having volunteers give the corresponding phrase in column B. Note that option **e** (tener ganas de) does not match any items in column A. Help students think of a word or phrase that would match it. Ex: **comer una pizza, asistir a un concierto**

1 **Emparejar** Find the expression in column B that best matches an item in column A. Then, come up with a new item that corresponds with the leftover expression in column B.

A		B
1. el Polo Norte	c	a. tener calor
2. una sauna	a	b. tener sed
3. la comida salada (*salty food*)	b	c. tener frío
4. una persona muy inteligente	d	d. tener razón
5. un abuelo	g	e. tener ganas de
6. una dieta	f	f. tener hambre
		g. tener 75 años

1 Expansion Have pairs of students write sentences by combining elements from the two columns. Ex: **Sonia está en el Polo Norte y tiene mucho frío. José es una persona muy inteligente pero no tiene razón.**

2 **Completar** Complete the sentences with the correct forms of **tener** or **venir**.

1. Hoy nosotros ___tenemos___ una reunión familiar (*family reunion*).
2. Yo ___vengo___ en autobús del aeropuerto de Quito.
3. Todos mis parientes ___vienen___, excepto mi tío Manolo y su esposa.
4. Ellos no ___tienen___ ganas de venir porque viven en Portoviejo.
5. Mi prima Susana y su novio no ___vienen___ hasta las ocho porque ella ___tiene___ que trabajar.
6. En las fiestas, mi hermana siempre (*always*) ___viene___ muy tarde (*late*).
7. Nosotros ___tenemos___ mucha suerte porque las reuniones son divertidas (*fun*).
8. Mi madre cree que mis sobrinos son muy simpáticos. Creo que ella ___tiene___ razón.

2 Expansion Have students write the questions that would elicit the sentences in this activity. Ex: **¿Qué tienen ellos hoy? ¿Cómo viene el narrador a la reunión? ¿Quién no viene?**

3 In-Class Tip Before doing this activity as a class, have students identify which picture is referred to in each of these questions. Have them answer: **La(s) persona(s) del dibujo número ____.** Ask: **¿Quién bebe agua? (6), ¿Quién asiste a una fiesta? (3), ¿Quiénes comen pizza? (4), ¿Quiénes esperan el autobús? (5), ¿Quién corre a la oficina? (1), ¿Quién hace ejercicio en una bicicleta? (2)**

3 **Describir** Describe what these people are doing or feeling using an expression with **tener**.

1. ___Tiene (mucha) prisa.___

2. ___Tiene (mucho) calor.___

3. ___Tiene veintiún años.___

4. ___Tienen (mucha) hambre.___

5. ___Tienen (mucho) frío.___

6. ___Tiene (mucha) sed.___

3 Expansion Describe different situations and have students respond using **tener** expressions. Ex: **Pedro come mucho. ¿Por qué? (Porque tiene hambre.)**

Communication 1.1, 1.2

Comunicación

4 🔊 **Mi familia** Listen to Francisco's description of his family. Then indicate whether the following conclusions are **lógico** or **ilógico**, based on what you heard.

	Lógico	Ilógico
1. Francisco tiene una familia grande.	○	⦿
2. A Francisco le gustan los números.	⦿	○
3. Francisco vive en la casa de sus padres durante el semestre.	○	⦿
4. Francisco desea ser artista.	○	⦿
5. Carlos y Dolores tienen gemelos.	○	⦿

5 👥 **Preguntas** Answer your partner's questions.   Answers will vary.

1. ¿Tienes que estudiar hoy?
2. ¿Cuántos años tienes? ¿Y tus hermanos/as?
3. ¿Cuándo vienes a la escuela?
4. ¿Cuándo vienen tus amigos a tu casa o apartamento?
5. ¿De qué tienes miedo? ¿Por qué?
6. ¿Qué tienes ganas de hacer el sábado?

6 **Obligaciones** Talk about five things that you have to do but cannot do for various reasons, such as fear, lack of motivation, or being in a rush. Use expressions with **tener**.   Answers will vary.

> *modelo*
>
> Tengo que estudiar, pero no tengo ganas.

Síntesis

7 👥 **Minidrama** Role-play this situation with a partner: you are introducing your best friend to your extended family. To avoid any surprises before you go, talk about who is coming and what each family member is like. Switch roles.   Answers will vary.

TEACHING OPTIONS

Small Groups 👥↔👥 Have small groups prepare skits in which one person takes a few friends to a family reunion. Students play the roles of host and other family members. The student playing the host should make polite introductions and tell the people he or she is introducing a few facts about each other. All the people involved should attempt to make small talk.

Pairs 👥↔👥 Give pairs of students five minutes to write a conversation in which they use as many **tener** expressions as they can in a logical manner. Have the top three pairs perform their conversations for the class.

---

4 In-Class Tip
Before starting the activity, ensure students understand the following words:
- **asistir (a)** – false cognate
- **economía**
- **escuela secundaria**
- **ingeniero**
- **instituto de idiomas**
- **puertorriqueño**
- **San Juan**

4 Script *See the script for this activity on Interleaf page 77B.*

5 In-Class Tips
- You may want to provide additional vocabulary for item 5.
- Ask volunteers to summarize the responses. Record these responses on the board as a survey about the class's characteristics.

5 Virtual Chat
👤↔👤 Available online.

 Communication 1.1

6 Expansion Give students enough time to use the dictionary and write the expressions in advance. If they find the activity difficult, allow them to work in pairs or small groups first.

7 In-Class Tip Before doing **Síntesis**, have students quickly review this material: family vocabulary on pages 78–79; descriptive adjectives on pages 88–90; possessive adjectives on page 93; and the forms of **tener** and **venir** on pages 100–101.

7 Partner Chat
👤↔👤 Available online.

SUBJECT CONJUGATED FORM Main clause
Javier empiezo
Dudan

Recapitulación

Section Goal

In **Recapitulación**, students will review the grammar concepts from this lesson.

RESUMEN GRAMATICAL

Review the grammar concepts you have learned in this lesson by completing these activities.

---

1 **Adjetivos** Complete each phrase with the appropriate adjective from the list. Make all necessary changes. **18 pts.**

| antipático | interesante | mexicano |
| difícil | joven | moreno |

1. Mi tía es ___mexicana___. Vive en Guadalajara.
2. Mi primo no es rubio, es ___moreno___.
3. Mi amigo cree que la clase no es fácil; es ___difícil___.
4. Los libros son ___interesantes___; me gustan mucho.
5. Mis hermanos son ___antipáticos___; no tienen muchos amigos.
6. Las gemelas tienen nueve años. Son ___jóvenes___.

---

2 **Completar** For each set of sentences, provide the appropriate form of the verb **tener** and the possessive adjective. Follow the model. **36 pts.**

> **modelo**
> Él tiene un libro. Es su libro.

1. Esteban y Julio ___tienen___ una tía. Es ___su___ tía.
2. Yo ___tengo___ muchos amigos. Son ___mis___ amigos.
3. Tú ___tienes___ tres primas. Son ___tus___ primas.
4. María y tú ___tienen___ un hermano. Es ___su/vuestro___ hermano.
5. Nosotras ___tenemos___ unas mochilas. Son ___nuestras___ mochilas.
6. Usted ___tiene___ dos sobrinos. Son ___sus___ sobrinos.

---

3 **Oraciones** Arrange the words in the correct order to form complete logical sentences. ¡Ojo! Don't forget to conjugate the verbs. **20 pts.**

1. libros / unos / tener / interesantes / tú / muy
Tú tienes unos libros muy interesantes.

2. dos / leer / fáciles / compañera / tu / lecciones
Tu compañera lee dos lecciones fáciles.

3. mi / francés / ser / amigo / buen / Hugo
Hugo es mi buen amigo francés./Mi buen amigo francés es Hugo.

4. ser / simpáticas / dos / personas / nosotras
Nosotras somos dos personas simpáticas.

5. a / clases / menores / mismas / sus / asistir / hermanos / las
Sus hermanos menores asisten a las mismas clases.

RESUMEN GRAMATICAL (sidebar)

3.1 Descriptive adjectives pp. 88–90

Forms and agreement of adjectives

Masculine		Feminine	
Singular	Plural	Singular	Plural
alto	altos	alta	altas
inteligente	inteligentes	inteligente	inteligentes
trabajador	trabajadores	trabajadora	trabajadoras

▶ Descriptive adjectives follow the noun:
el chico rubio

▶ Adjectives of nationality also follow the noun:
la mujer española

▶ Adjectives of quantity precede the noun:
muchos libros, dos turistas

▶ When placed before a singular masculine noun, these adjectives are shortened.
bueno → buen   malo → mal

▶ When placed before a singular noun, **grande** is shortened to **gran**.

3.2 Possessive adjectives p. 93

Singular		Plural	
mi	nuestro/a	mis	nuestros/as
tu	vuestro/a	tus	vuestros/as
su	su	sus	sus

3.3 Present tense of -er and -ir verbs pp. 96–97

comer		escribir	
como	comemos	escribo	escribimos
comes	coméis	escribes	escribís
come	comen	escribe	escriben

3.4 Present tense of tener and venir pp. 100–101

tener		venir	
tengo	tenemos	vengo	venimos
tienes	tenéis	vienes	venís
tiene	tienen	viene	vienen

Teacher's notes (left column)

1 In-Class Tips
• To add an auditory aspect to the activity, have students read their answers aloud, emphasizing the adjective ending sounds **–a(s)** and **–o(s)**.
• Remind students that some adjectives have the same masculine and feminine forms.

1 Expansion Ask students to rewrite the sentences to convey an opposite or different meaning. Ex: **1. Mi tía es francesa. Vive en París. 2. Mi primo no es moreno, es rubio.**

2 In-Class Tip Remind students that possessive adjectives agree in number (and in gender for **nuestro/a** and **vuestro/a**) with the nouns they modify, not with the subject. Therefore, in item 1, even though **Esteban y Julio** is a plural subject, **su** is singular to agree with **tía**.

2 Expansion
←👤→ Have students rewrite the sentences using different subjects. Encourage them to add additional sentences to each item using any of the **-er/-ir** verbs they have learned in this chapter. Ex: **Yo tengo una tía. Es mi tía. Ella vive en Nueva York.**

3 In-Class Tip To simplify, have students circle the subject and underline the verb before forming the sentences.

3 Expansion Have pairs create two additional dehydrated sentences for another pair to write out.

TEACHING OPTIONS

TPR Make sets of cards containing **–er** and **–ir** infinitives that are easy to act out. Divide the class into groups of five. Have students take turns drawing a card and acting out the verb for the group. Once someone has correctly guessed the verb, the group members must take turns providing the conjugated forms.

Extra Practice ←👤→ To add a visual aspect to this grammar review, bring in magazine or newspaper photos of people and places. Have students describe the people and places using descriptive adjectives.

4 **Carta** Complete this letter with the appropriate forms of the verbs in the word list. Not all verbs will be used. **22 pts.**

abrir	correr	recibir
asistir	creer	tener
compartir	escribir	venir
comprender	leer	vivir

Hola, Ángel:

¿Qué tal? (Yo) (1) <u>Escribo</u> esta carta (*this letter*) en la biblioteca. Todos los días (2) <u>vengo</u> aquí y (3) <u>leo</u> un buen libro. Yo (4) <u>creo</u> que es importante leer por diversión. Mi hermano no (5) <u>comprende</u> por qué me gusta leer. Él sólo (6) <u>abre/lee</u> los libros de texto. Pero nosotros (7) <u>compartimos</u> unos intereses. Por ejemplo, los dos somos atléticos; por las mañanas nosotros (8) <u>corremos</u>. También nos gustan las ciencias; por las tardes (9) <u>asistimos</u> a nuestra clase de biología. Nosotros (10) <u>vivimos</u> en un apartamento que está cerca de la escuela. Y tú, ¿cómo estás? ¿(Tú) (11) <u>Tienes</u> mucho trabajo (*work*)?

5 **Proverbio** Complete this proverb with the correct forms of the verbs in parentheses. **4 pts.**

❝ Dos andares° <u>tiene</u> (tener) el dinero°, <u>viene</u> (venir) despacio° y se va° ligero°. ❞

andares *speeds* dinero *money* despacio *slowly*
se va *it leaves* ligero *quickly*

4 **Expansion**
• Ask students to create a sentence with the verb not used (**recibir**).
• Ask students questions using vocabulary and sentence structures from the letter. Ex: **¿Compartes muchos intereses con tus hermanos? ¿Lees en la biblioteca todos los días? ¿Crees que es importante leer aparte de las clases?**
• ←👥→ To challenge students, ask them to write a response from **Ángel**. Encourage them to use lesson vocabulary.

5 **In-Class Tips**
• Have a volunteer read the proverb aloud. Help students understand the inverted word order in the first line. Explain that this is a common literary technique. Have a volunteer restate the first line in a colloquial manner (**El dinero tiene dos andares**).
• Have students discuss their interpretation of the proverb. Ask heritage speakers if they have heard this proverb or if they know of similar ones.

TEACHING OPTIONS

Game Create two *Mad-Libs*-style paragraphs that have blanks where the nouns and descriptive adjectives should be. Underneath each blank, indicate the type of word needed. Ex: ____ (*singular, feminine adjective*) Give each pair a set of paragraphs and have them take turns asking their partner to supply the missing words. Tell them they can use any nouns or adjectives that they have learned up to this point. When

students have finished, ask them to read their paragraphs aloud. Have the class vote for the funniest one.
Extra Practice Name **tener** expressions and have students say what they or their family members do in that situation. Ex: **tener hambre (Cuando tengo hambre, como pizza. Cuando mis hermanos tienen hambre, comen en McDonald's.); tener prisa (Cuando mi padre tiene prisa, toma el autobús.)**

Section Goals

In **Lectura**, students will:
- learn to use context clues in reading
- read context-rich selections about Hispanic families

Communication 1.2
Cultures 2.1, 2.2
Connections 3.1, 3.2
Comparisons 4.2

Pre-AP®

Interpretive Reading: Estrategia
Tell students that they can often infer the meaning of an unfamiliar Spanish word by looking at the word's context and by using common sense. Five types of context clues are:
- synonyms
- antonyms
- clarifications
- definitions
- additional details

Have students read the sentence **Ayer fui a ver a mi tía abuela, la hermana de mi abuela** from the letter. Point out that the meaning of **tía abuela** can be inferred from its similarity to the known word **abuela** and from the clarification that follows (**la hermana de mi abuela**).

Examinar el texto Have students read Paragraph 1 silently, without looking up the glossed words. Point out the phrase **salgo a pasear** and ask a volunteer to explain how the context might give clues to the meaning. Afterward, point out that **salgo** is the first-person singular form of **salir** (*to go out*). Tell students they will learn all the forms of **salir** in **Lección 4**.

Examinar el formato Guide students to see that the photos and captions reveal that the paragraphs are about several different families.

Lectura
Antes de leer

Estrategia
Guessing meaning from context

As you read in Spanish, you'll often come across words you haven't learned. You can guess what they mean by looking at the surrounding words and sentences. Look at the following text and guess what **tía abuela** means, based on the context.

¡Hola, Claudia!
  ¿Qué hay de nuevo?
¿Sabes qué? Ayer fui a ver a mi tía abuela, la hermana de mi abuela. Tiene 85 años, pero es muy independiente. Vive en un apartamento en Quito con su prima Lorena, quien también tiene 85 años.

If you guessed *great-aunt*, you are correct, and you can conclude from this word and the format clues that this is a letter about someone's visit with his or her great-aunt.

Examinar el texto
Quickly read through the paragraphs and find two or three words you don't know. Using the context as your guide, guess what these words mean. Then glance at the paragraphs where these words appear and try to predict what the paragraphs are about.

Examinar el formato
Look at the format of the reading. What clues do the captions, photos, and layout give you about its content?

Gente... Las familias

1. Me llamo Armando y tengo setenta años, pero no me considero viejo. Tengo seis nietas y un nieto. Vivo con mi hija y tengo la oportunidad de pasar mucho tiempo con ella y con mi nieto. Por las tardes salgo a pasear° por el parque con él y por la noche le leo cuentos°.

Armando. Tiene seis nietas y un nieto.

2. Mi prima Victoria y yo nos llevamos muy bien. Estudiamos juntas° en la universidad y compartimos un apartamento. Ella es muy inteligente y me ayuda° con los estudios. Además°, es muy simpática y generosa. Si necesito cualquier° cosa, ¡ella me la compra!

Diana. Vive con su prima.

3. Me llamo Ramona y soy paraguaya, aunque° ahora vivo en los Estados Unidos. Tengo tres hijos, uno de nueve años, uno de doce y el mayor de quince. Es difícil a veces, pero mi esposo y yo tratamos° de ayudarlos y comprenderlos siempre°.

Ramona. Sus hijos son muy importantes para ella.

TEACHING OPTIONS

Extra Practice Ask students to use the paragraphs in **Gente... Las familias** as models for writing paragraphs about their families, but from the perspective of another family member (e.g., their mother). Have volunteers read their paragraphs aloud.

Extra Practice Use these items, each of which contains an unfamiliar word or phrase, to practice using context clues. **1. Mi tío Daniel es maestro en una escuela secundaria; enseña ciencias. 2. No, Daniel no es antipático, ¡es un cariño! 3. Por favor, ¿tienes un boli o un lápiz? Te escribo su número de teléfono.**

4. Tengo mucha suerte. Aunque mis padres están divorciados, tengo una familia muy unida. Tengo dos hermanos y dos hermanas. Me gusta hablar y salir a fiestas con ellos. Ahora tengo novio en la universidad y él no conoce a mis hermanos. ¡Espero que se lleven bien!

Ana María. Su familia es muy unida.

5. Antes quería° tener hermanos, pero ya no° es tan importante. Ser hijo único tiene muchas ventajas°: no tengo que compartir mis cosas con hermanos, no hay discusiones° y, como soy nieto único también, ¡mis abuelos piensan° que soy perfecto!

Fernando. Es hijo único.

6. Como soy joven todavía°, no tengo ni esposa ni hijos. Pero tengo un sobrino, el hijo de mi hermano, que es muy especial para mí. Se llama Benjamín y tiene diez años. Es un muchacho muy simpático. Siempre tiene hambre y por lo tanto vamos° frecuentemente a comer hamburguesas. Nos gusta también ir al cine° a ver películas de acción. Hablamos de todo. ¡Creo que ser tío es mejor que ser padre!

Santiago. Cree que ser tío es divertido.

salgo a pasear *I go take a walk* cuentos *stories* juntas *together* me ayuda *she helps me* Además *Besides* cualquier *any* aunque *although* tratamos *we try* siempre *always* quería *I wanted* ya no *no longer* ventajas *advantages* discusiones *arguments* piensan *think* todavía *still* vamos *we go* ir al cine *to go to the movies*

Después de leer

Emparejar
Glance at the paragraphs and see how the words and phrases in column A are used in context. Then find their definitions in column B.

A		B
1. me la compra	d	a. the oldest
2. nos llevamos bien	h	b. movies
3. no conoce	g	c. the youngest
4. películas	b	d. buys it for me
5. mejor que	j	e. borrows it from me
6. el mayor	a	f. we see each other
		g. doesn't know
		h. we get along
		i. portraits
		j. better than

Seleccionar
Choose the sentence that best summarizes each paragraph.

1. Párrafo 1 a
   a. Me gusta mucho ser abuelo.
   b. No hablo mucho con mi nieto.
   c. No tengo nietos.

2. Párrafo 2 c
   a. Mi prima es antipática.
   b. Mi prima no es muy trabajadora.
   c. Mi prima y yo somos muy buenas amigas.

3. Párrafo 3 a
   a. Tener hijos es un gran sacrificio, pero es muy bonito también.
   b. No comprendo a mis hijos.
   c. Mi esposo y yo no tenemos hijos.

4. Párrafo 4 c
   a. No hablo mucho con mis hermanos.
   b. Comparto mis cosas con mis hermanos.
   c. Mis hermanos y yo somos como (*like*) amigos.

5. Párrafo 5 a
   a. Me gusta ser hijo único.
   b. Tengo hermanos y hermanas.
   c. Vivo con mis abuelos.

6. Párrafo 6 b
   a. Mi sobrino tiene diez años.
   b. Me gusta mucho ser tío.
   c. Mi esposa y yo no tenemos hijos.

Escritura

Estrategia
Using idea maps

How do you organize ideas for a first draft? Often, the organization of ideas represents the most challenging part of the process. Idea maps are useful for organizing pertinent information. Here is an example of an idea map you can use:

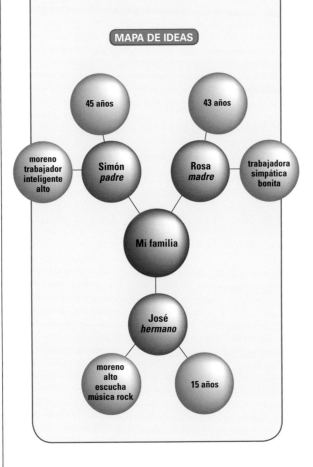

MAPA DE IDEAS

- 45 años
- 43 años
- moreno trabajador inteligente alto
- Simón *padre*
- Rosa *madre*
- trabajadora simpática bonita
- Mi familia
- José *hermano*
- moreno alto escucha música rock
- 15 años

Tema

Escribir un mensaje electrónico

A friend you met in a chat room for Spanish speakers wants to know about your family. Using some of the verbs and adjectives you have learned in this lesson, write a brief e-mail describing your family or an imaginary family, including:

▶ Names and relationships
▶ Physical characteristics
▶ Hobbies and interests

Here are some useful expressions for writing an e-mail or letter in Spanish:

Salutations

Estimado/a Julio/Julia:	*Dear Julio/Julia,*
Querido/a Miguel/Ana María:	*Dear Miguel/Ana María,*

Closings

Un abrazo,	*A hug,*
Abrazos,	*Hugs,*
Con cariño,	*Affectionately,*
¡Hasta pronto!	*See you soon!*
¡Hasta la próxima semana!	*See you next week!*

EVALUATION: Mensaje electrónico

Criteria	Scale
Appropriate salutations/closings	1 2 3 4 5
Appropriate details	1 2 3 4 5
Organization	1 2 3 4 5
Accuracy	1 2 3 4 5

Scoring	
Excellent	18–20 points
Good	14–17 points
Satisfactory	10–13 points
Unsatisfactory	< 10 points

Escuchar

Estrategia

Asking for repetition/ Replaying the recording

Sometimes it is difficult to understand what people say, especially in a noisy environment. During a conversation, you can ask someone to repeat by saying **¿Cómo?** (*What?*) or **¿Perdón?** (*Pardon me?*). In class, you can ask your teacher to repeat by saying **Repita, por favor** (*Repeat, please*). If you don't understand a recorded activity, you can simply replay it.

◁)) To help you practice this strategy, you will listen to a short paragraph. Ask your teacher to repeat it or replay the recording, and then summarize what you heard.

Preparación

Based on the photograph, where do you think Cristina and Laura are? What do you think Laura is saying to Cristina?

Ahora escucha

Now you are going to hear Laura and Cristina's conversation. Use **R** to indicate which adjectives describe Cristina's boyfriend, Rafael. Use **E** for adjectives that describe Laura's boyfriend, Esteban. Some adjectives will not be used.

____ rubio	E	interesante
____ feo	____	antipático
R	alto	R	inteligente
E	trabajador	R	moreno
E	un poco gordo	____	viejo

Comprensión

Identificar

Which person would make each statement: Cristina or Laura?

	Cristina	Laura
1. Mi novio habla sólo de fútbol y de béisbol.	☑	○
2. Tengo un novio muy interesante y simpático.	○	☑
3. Mi novio es alto y moreno.	☑	○
4. Mi novio trabaja mucho.	○	☑
5. Mi amiga no tiene buena suerte con los muchachos.	○	☑
6. El novio de mi amiga es un poco gordo, pero guapo.	☑	○

¿Cierto o falso?

Indicate whether each sentence is **cierto** or **falso**, then correct the false statements.

	Cierto	Falso
1. Esteban es un chico interesante y simpático.	☑	○
2. Laura tiene mala suerte con los chicos. Cristina tiene mala suerte con los chicos.	○	☑
3. Rafael es muy interesante. Esteban es muy interesante.	○	☑
4. Laura y su novio hablan de muchas cosas.	☑	○

Section Goals

In **Escuchar**, students will:
- listen to and summarize a short paragraph
- learn strategies for asking for clarification in oral communication
- answer questions based on the content of a recorded conversation

⊗ Communication 1.2

Estrategia
Script La familia de María Dolores es muy grande. Tiene dos hermanos y tres hermanas. Su familia vive en España. Pero la familia de Alberto es muy pequeña. No tiene hermanos ni hermanas. Alberto y sus padres viven en el Ecuador.

Ahora escucha
Script LAURA: ¿Qué hay de nuevo, Cristina?
CRISTINA: No mucho… sólo problemas con mi novio.
L: ¿Perdón?
C: No hay mucho de nuevo… sólo problemas con mi novio, Rafael.
L: ¿Qué les pasa?
C: Bueno, Rafael es alto y moreno… es muy guapo. Y es buena gente. Es inteligente también… pero es que no lo encuentro muy interesante.
L: ¿Cómo?
C: No es muy interesante. Sólo habla del fútbol y del béisbol. No me gusta hablar del fútbol las veinticuatro horas al día. No comprendo a los muchachos. ¿Cómo es tu novio, Laura?

(Script continues at far left in the bottom panels.)

L: Esteban es muy simpático. Es un poco gordo, pero creo que es muy guapo. También es muy trabajador.
C: ¿Es interesante?

L: Sí. Hablamos dos o tres horas cada día. Hablamos de muchas cosas… las clases, los amigos… de todo.
C: ¡Qué bien! Siempre tengo mala suerte con los novios.

Section Goals

In **En pantalla**, students will:
- read about the use of diminutives in Spanish
- watch the television commercial for **Banco Galicia**, *Diminutivo*

Communication 1.2, 1.3
Cultures 2.1, 2.2
Connections 3.2
Comparisons 4.2

Teacher Resources
Read teaching suggestions incorporating all components of **Senderos** in the front matter. See pages 77A–77B for a detailed listing of Teacher Resources online.

Introduction Ask students when they use diminutives in English and how they are formed. You may need to prompt them with some examples: **Scott/Scotty; bus/minibus; book/booklet**. After reading about **diminutivos** in Spanish, ask them to compare their use in English and Spanish.

Pre-AP®

Antes de ver **Strategy**
- Have students guess what the commercial is about, based on the video still and caption.
- Explain to students that they do not need to understand every word they hear. Tell them to rely on visual cues and to listen for cognates and words from **Vocabulario útil**.

Aplicación Whether the ad is print or video, have students provide lots of visual support for the product. Help and encourage students to use short, clear sentences and phrases that focus on diminutives.

Diminutivo

¡Oh! ¡Un saquito te compró mamá!

Preparación
How do you feel about shopping sprees? Do you like spending time in shopping malls? What would you rather do: buy things for yourself or gifts for others?
Answers will vary.

Diminutivos are suffixes used to indicate a small size, young age, or to express affection. They are also used to talk to babies and toddlers, and to communicate that something is cute. The most commonly used diminutive suffix in Spanish is **–ito/ita**, which can be used with nouns and names (**niñito/a, Miguelito, Susanita**), adjectives (**pequeñito/a**), and adverbs (**lueguito, ahorita**). When words end in consonants like n, r, or z, such as in **lápiz** and **lección**, -ito/ita becomes **–cito/cita**; for example: **lapicito** and **leccioncita**. However, there are many exceptions, such as **novio/a**, which diminutive is **noviecito/a**. Diminutives can also be created using the suffix **–illo/illa** (**cuadernillo, problemilla**).

Vocabulario útil
¿Te falta mucho?	*Have you got long to go?*
apurarse	*to hurry*
saquito	*small/cute coat*
par de zapatitos	*pair of small shoes*
conjuntito	*small outfit*
cerrar	*to close*

Comprensión
Fill in the blanks, choosing the correct option from the word bank.

| hija/a | prisa | su | cierra |
| regresar | esposo | zapatos | |

1. Marcos es el __esposo__ de Claudia.
2. Claudia compra __zapatos__ y otras cosas para ella en el centro comercial (*shopping mall*).
3. Marcos y Claudia tienen una __hija__.
4. El centro comercial __cierra__ en diez minutos.
5. Claudia busca un regalo (*gift*) para __su__ hija.
6. Claudia tiene __prisa__ porque debe __regresar__ pronto a casa.

Conversación
Talk with a classmate about these questions:
1. In the video, why did the man think the woman was buying presents for their baby daughter? Because she used diminutives, so he thought his wife was buying clothes for the baby.
2. Why do you think the woman was using diminutives such as **saquito, zapatitos**, and **conjuntito**? Because she thought what she had bought was very cute.

Aplicación
Work in small groups to create an ad for **Banco Galicia**, using adjectives from this lesson and applying different diminutives to nouns you include in the ad. Present it to the class, and discuss afterward which ads seem most effective and why.
Answers will vary.

Language Notes In some countries like Colombia and Cuba, diminutives with the endings **–tito/tita** are replaced by **–tico/tica**; for example the diminutive for **pato** (*duck*)—**patito** (*duckling*)—becomes **patico**. More examples: **gotita** and **gotica** (*droplet*); **zapatito** and **zapatico**.

Extra Practice Give students the following words and have them practice forming diminutives: **papá, mamá, hermano/a, primo/a, gemelo/a, alto/a, bajo/a, viejo/a, joven, jóvenes**.

If a Spanish-speaking friend told you he was going to a **reunión familiar,** what type of event would you picture? Most likely, your friend would not be referring to an annual event reuniting family members from far-flung cities. In Hispanic culture, family gatherings are often more frequent and relaxed, and thus do not require intensive planning or juggling of schedules. Some families gather every Sunday afternoon to enjoy a leisurely meal; others may prefer to hold get-togethers on a Saturday evening, with food, music, and dancing. In any case, gatherings tend to be laid-back events in which family members spend hours chatting, sharing stories, and telling jokes.

Vocabulario útil

el Día de la Madre	*Mother's Day*
estamos celebrando	*we are celebrating*
familia grande y feliz	*a big, happy family*
familia numerosa	*a large family*
hacer (algo) juntos	*to do (something) together*
el patio interior	*courtyard*
pelear	*to fight*
reuniones familiares	*family gatherings, reunions*

Preparación

What is a "typical family" like where you live? Is there such a thing? What members of a family usually live together?
Answers will vary.

Completar

Complete this paragraph with the correct options.

Los Valdivieso y los Bolaños son dos ejemplos de familias en Ecuador. Los Valdivieso son una familia (1) _numerosa_ (difícil/numerosa). Viven en una casa (2) _grande_ (grande/buena). En el patio, hacen (*they do*) muchas reuniones (3) _familiares_ (familiares/con amigos). Los Bolaños son una familia pequeña. Ellos comen (4) _juntos_ (separados/juntos) y preparan canelazo, una bebida (*drink*) típica ecuatoriana.

tan *so*

La familia

—Érica, ¿y cómo se llaman tus padres?
—Mi mamá, Lorena y mi papá, Miguel.

¡Qué familia tan° grande tiene!

Te presento a la familia Bolaños.

Section Goals

In **Flash cultura**, students will:
• read about **reuniones familiares**
• watch a video about two Ecuadorian families

  Communication 1.2
Cultures 2.1, 2.2
Comparisons 4.2

Instructional Resources
See front matter and pages 77A–77B for a detailed listing of Instructor Resources available online.

Introduction Ask: 1. How do you say **reunión familiar** in English? (*family gathering*) 2. In Hispanic culture, what are family gatherings like and how often do they occur? (*They are relaxed and happen frequently, perhaps once a week.*) 3. What might a Saturday evening gathering involve? (*food, music, dancing*)

Antes de ver
• Have students look at the video stills, read the captions, and predict the content of the video.
• Read through **Vocabulario útil** with students. Model the pronunciation.
• Explain to students that they do not need to understand every word they hear. Tell them to rely on visual cues, cognates, and words from **Vocabulario útil**.

Preparación Survey the class. Ask students if they think there is such a thing as a "typical" family. If so, what does it look like?

Completar Make copies of this activity with the options in parentheses removed. Pass out the copies and have students close their books. Write all the possible options on the board. Tell students to complete the activity using one word from the board for each item.

Section Goal

In **Panorama**, students will receive comprehensible input by reading about the geography and culture of Ecuador.

Communication 1.2
Cultures 2.1, 2.2
Connections 3.1, 3.2
Comparisons 4.2

Teacher Resources

Read teaching suggestions incorporating all components of **Senderos** in the front matter. See pages 77A–77B for a detailed listing of Teacher Resources online.

In-Class Tip

- Have students examine the map of Ecuador and look at the call-out photos and read the captions. Encourage students to mention anything they may know about Ecuador.
- Use the **Lección 3 Panorama** online Resources to assist with this presentation.

El país en cifras

- Ask students to glance at the headings. Establish the kind of information contained in each and clarify unfamiliar words. Point out the words in the headings that have an English cognate.
- Point out that in September 2000, the U.S. dollar became the official currency of Ecuador.

¡Increíble pero cierto!

Mt. St. Helens in Washington and **Cotopaxi** in Ecuador are just two of a chain of volcanoes that stretches along the entire Pacific coast of North and South America, from Mt. McKinley in Alaska to **Monte Sarmiento** in the **Tierra del Fuego** of southern Chile.

Ecuador

El país en cifras

- **Área:** 283.560 km² (109.483 millas²), *incluyendo las islas Galápagos, aproximadamente el área de Colorado*
- **Población:** 15.439.000
- **Capital:** Quito — 1.622.000
- **Ciudades° principales:**
  Guayaquil — 2.634.000, Cuenca, Machala, Portoviejo
- **Moneda:** dólar estadounidense
- **Idiomas:** español (oficial), quichua

La lengua oficial de Ecuador es el español, pero también se hablan° otras° lenguas en el país. Aproximadamente unos 4.000.000 de ecuatorianos hablan lenguas indígenas; la mayoría° de ellos habla quichua. El quichua es el dialecto ecuatoriano del quechua, la lengua de los incas.

Bandera de Ecuador

Ecuatorianos célebres

- **Francisco Eugenio de Santa Cruz y Espejo,** médico, periodista y patriota (1747–1795)
- **Juan León Mera,** novelista (1832–1894)
- **Eduardo Kingman,** pintor° (1913–1997)
- **Rosalía Arteaga,** abogada°, política y ex vicepresidenta (1956–)
- **Iván Vallejo Ricafuerte,** montañista (1959–)

Ciudades *cities* se hablan *are spoken* otras *other* mayoría *majority*
pintor *painter* abogada *lawyer* sur *south* mundo *world* pies *feet*
dos veces más alto que *twice as tall as*

¡Increíble pero cierto!

El volcán Cotopaxi, situado a unos 60 kilómetros al sur° de Quito, es considerado el volcán activo más alto del mundo°. Tiene una altura de 5.897 metros (19.340 pies°). Es dos veces más alto que° el monte Santa Elena (2.550 metros o 9.215 pies) en el estado de Washington.

Muchos indígenas de Ecuador hablan quichua.

Las islas Galápagos

COLOMBIA

Indígenas del Amazonas

ESTADOS UNIDOS
OCÉANO PACÍFICO
OCÉANO ATLÁNTICO
ECUADOR
AMÉRICA DEL SUR

Río Esmeraldas

• Ibarra

Quito ☆

Volcán Cotopaxi
Río Napo

Portoviejo •
Río Daule

Volcán Tungurahua

Río Pastaza

Cordillera de los Andes

Guayaquil •

Volcán Chimborazo

Océano Pacífico

Cuenca •

Machala •

Loja •

La ciudad de Quito y la Cordillera de los Andes

PERÚ

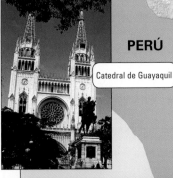

Catedral de Guayaquil

TEACHING OPTIONS

Heritage Speakers ←👤→ If a heritage speaker is of Ecuadorian origin or has visited Ecuador, ask him or her to share some of his or her favorite experiences there. Encourage the rest of the class to ask follow-up questions, and if a particular topic piques their interest, to find out more online.

Language Notes Remind students that **km²** is the abbreviation for **kilómetros cuadrados** and that **millas²** is the abbreviation for **millas cuadradas**. Ask a volunteer to explain why **kilómetros** takes **cuadrados** and **millas** takes **cuadradas**.

Lugares • **Las islas Galápagos**

Muchas personas vienen de lejos a visitar las islas Galápagos porque son un verdadero tesoro° ecológico. Aquí Charles Darwin estudió° las especies que inspiraron° sus ideas sobre la evolución. Como las Galápagos están lejos del continente, sus plantas y animales son únicos. Las islas son famosas por sus tortugas° gigantes.

Artes • **Oswaldo Guayasamín**

Oswaldo Guayasamín fue° uno de los artistas latinoamericanos más famosos del mundo. Fue escultor° y muralista. Su expresivo estilo viene del cubismo y sus temas preferidos son la injusticia y la pobreza° sufridas° por los indígenas de su país.

Deportes • **El *trekking***

El sistema montañoso de los Andes cruza° y divide Ecuador en varias regiones. La Sierra, que tiene volcanes, grandes valles y una variedad increíble de plantas y animales, es perfecta para el *trekking*. Muchos turistas visitan Ecuador cada° año para hacer° *trekking* y escalar montañas°.

Lugares • **Latitud 0**

Hay un monumento en Ecuador, a unos 22 kilómetros (14 millas) de Quito, donde los visitantes están en el hemisferio norte y el hemisferio sur a la vez°. Este monumento se llama la Mitad del Mundo° y es un destino turístico muy popular.

Explosión del volcán
Tungurahua

¿Qué aprendiste? Completa las oraciones con la información correcta.

1. La ciudad más grande (*biggest*) de Ecuador es ___Guayaquil___.
2. La capital de Ecuador es ___Quito___.
3. Unos 4.000.000 de ecuatorianos hablan ___lenguas indígenas___
4. Darwin estudió el proceso de la evolución en ___las islas Galápagos___.
5. Dos temas del arte de ___Guayasamín___ son la pobreza y la ___injusticia___.
6. Un monumento muy popular es ___la Mitad del Mundo___.
7. La Sierra es un lugar perfecto para el ___trekking___.
8. El volcán ___Cotopaxi___ es el volcán activo más alto del mundo.

Conexión Internet Investiga estos temas en Internet.

1. Busca información sobre una ciudad de Ecuador. ¿Te gustaría (*Would you like*) visitar la ciudad? ¿Por qué?
2. Haz una lista de tres animales o plantas que viven sólo en las islas Galápagos. ¿Dónde hay animales o plantas similares?

....

verdadero tesoro *true treasure* **estudió** *studied* **inspiraron** *inspired* **tortugas** *tortoises* **fue** *was* **escultor** *sculptor* **pobreza** *poverty* **sufridas** *suffered* **cruza** *crosses* **cada** *every* **hacer** *to do* **escalar montañas** *to climb mountains* **a la vez** *at the same time* **Mitad del Mundo** *Equatorial Line Monument (lit. Midpoint of the World)*

Las islas Galápagos →🔊← Bring in books, magazines, or Internet articles about the Galapagos Islands for students to read. For more information about **las islas Galápagos**, you may want to play the *Panorama cultural* video footage for this lesson.

Oswaldo Guayasamín The name **Guayasamín** means *white bird* in Quichua. The artist took this name out of solidarity with his Incan ancestors. If possible, bring reproductions of some of **Guayasamín's** work to class. Show a variety of his paintings and encourage students to talk about what the artist's social and political stance might be.

El *trekking* Although the word **senderismo** is widely used, *trekking* is one of many English words that have been incorporated into Spanish. Generally, these are words for phenomena whose popularity originated in the English-speaking world. Some words enter Spanish without much change: **camping**, **marketing**. Others are modified to match Spanish spelling patterns, as **líder** (*leader*) or **mitin** (*meeting*).

Latitud 0 Bring in a globe and have students find Ecuador and point out its location on the equator.

TEACHING OPTIONS

Variación léxica A word that the Quichua language has contributed to English is *jerky* (salted, dried meat), which comes from the Quichua word **charqui**. The Quichua-speaking peoples of the Andean highlands had perfected techniques for "freeze-drying" both vegetable tubers and meat before the first Spaniards arrived in the region. (Freeze-dried potatoes, called **chuño**, are a staple in the diet of the inhabitants of the Andes.)

In Ecuador and throughout the rest of South America, **charqui** is the word used to name meat preserved by drying. **Charqui** is an important component in the national cuisines of South America, and in Argentina, Uruguay, and Brazil, its production is a major industry. In other parts of the Spanish-speaking world, you may hear the terms **tasajo** or **carne seca** used instead of **charqui**.

 Comparisons 4.1

Teacher Resources
Read teaching suggestions incorporating all components of **Senderos** in the front matter. See pages 77A–77B for a detailed listing of Teacher Resources online.

La familia

el/la abuelo/a	grandfather/grandmother
los abuelos	grandparents
el apellido	last name
el/la bisabuelo/a	great-grandfather/great-grandmother
el/la cuñado/a	brother-in-law/sister-in-law
el/la esposo/a	husband/wife; spouse
la familia	family
el/la gemelo/a	twin
el/la hermanastro/a	stepbrother/stepsister
el/la hermano/a	brother/sister
el/la hijastro/a	stepson/stepdaughter
el/la hijo/a	son/daughter
los hijos	children
la madrastra	stepmother
la madre	mother
el/la medio/a hermano/a	half-brother/half-sister
el/la nieto/a	grandson/granddaughter
la nuera	daughter-in-law
el padrastro	stepfather
el padre	father
los padres	parents
los parientes	relatives
el/la primo/a	cousin
el/la sobrino/a	nephew/niece
el/la suegro/a	father-in-law/mother-in-law
el/la tío/a	uncle/aunt
el yerno	son-in-law

Otras personas

el/la amigo/a	friend
la gente	people
el/la muchacho/a	boy/girl
el/la niño/a	child
el/la novio/a	boyfriend/girlfriend
la persona	person

Profesiones

el/la artista	artist
el/la doctor(a), el/la médico/a	doctor; physician
el/la ingeniero/a	engineer
el/la periodista	journalist
el/la programador(a)	computer programmer

Adjetivos

alto/a	tall
antipático/a	unpleasant
bajo/a	short (in height)
bonito/a	pretty
buen, bueno/a	good
delgado/a	thin
difícil	difficult
fácil	easy
feo/a	ugly
gordo/a	fat
grande	big
guapo/a	good-looking
importante	important
inteligente	intelligent
interesante	interesting
joven (sing.), jóvenes (pl.)	young
mal, malo/a	bad
mismo/a	same
moreno/a	brunet(te)
mucho/a	much; many; a lot of
pelirrojo/a	red-haired
pequeño/a	small
rubio/a	blond(e)
simpático/a	nice; likeable
tonto/a	foolish
trabajador(a)	hard-working
viejo/a	old

Nacionalidades

alemán, alemana	German
argentino/a	Argentine
canadiense	Canadian
chino/a	Chinese
costarricense	Costa Rican
cubano/a	Cuban
ecuatoriano/a	Ecuadorian
español(a)	Spanish
estadounidense	from the U.S.
francés, francesa	French
inglés, inglesa	English
italiano/a	Italian
japonés, japonesa	Japanese
mexicano/a	Mexican
norteamericano/a	(North) American
puertorriqueño/a	Puerto Rican
ruso/a	Russian

Verbos

abrir	to open
aprender (a + *inf.*)	to learn
asistir (a)	to attend
beber	to drink
comer	to eat
compartir	to share
comprender	to understand
correr	to run
creer (en)	to believe (in)
deber (+ *inf.*)	should
decidir (+ *inf.*)	to decide
describir	to describe
escribir	to write
leer	to read
recibir	to receive
tener	to have
venir	to come
vivir	to live

Possessive adjectives	See page 93.
Expressions with *tener*	See page 101.
Expresiones útiles	See page 83.

Lección 4: Teacher Resources

There is a wealth of resources online to support instruction using **Senderos**. For details on how to integrate these Teacher Resources into your lessons, see the front matter of this Teacher's Edition on pages T16 to T48.

Presentation	Practice & Communicate	Assess*	Scripts and Translations	
• Digital Images: • **Los pasatiempos** • **En el centro**	• Information Gap Activity • Activity Pack Practice Activities (with Answer Key): **Contextos** • Additional Vocabulary (**Más vocabulario para el fin de semana**) • Digital Image Bank: • Leisure and Entertainment • Sports and Outdoor Activities	• Vocabulary Quiz (with Answer Key)		contextos
		• **Fotonovela** Optional Testing Sections (with Answer Key)	• **Fotonovela** Videoscript • **Fotonovela** English Translation	fotonovela
• **Estructura 4.1** Grammar Slides	• Information Gap Activity* • Activity Pack Practice Activities (with Answer Key): Present tense of **ir** • Surveys: Worksheet for classroom survey	• Grammar 4.1 Quiz (with Answer Key)	• Tutorial Script: Present tense of **ir**	
• **Estructura 4.2** Grammar Slides	• Information Gap Activity* • Activity Pack Practice Activities (with Answer Key): Stem-changing verbs: **e→ie, o→ue** • Surveys: Worksheet for classroom survey	• Grammar 4.2 Quiz (with Answer Key)	• Tutorial Script: Stem-changing verbs: **e→ie, o→ue**	estructura
• **Estructura 4.3** Grammar Slides	• Activity Pack Practice Activities (with Answer Key): Stem-changing verbs: **e→i**	• Grammar 4.3 Quiz (with Answer Key)	• Tutorial Script: Stem-changing verbs: **e→i**	
• **Estructura 4.4** Grammar Slides	• Activity Pack Practice Activities (with Answer Key): Verbs with irregular **yo** forms	• Grammar 4.4 Quiz (with Answer Key)	• Tutorial Script: Verbs with irregular **yo** forms	
			• **En pantalla** Videoscript • **En pantalla** English Translation	En pantalla
		• **Flash cultura** Optional Testing Sections (with Answer Key)	• **Flash cultura** Videoscript • **Flash cultura** English Translation	Flash cultura
Digital Images: • **México**		• **Panorama** Optional Testing Sections (with Answer Key) • **Panorama cultural** (video)	• **Panorama cultural** Videoscript • **Panorama cultural** English Translation	Panorama

*Can also be assigned online.

Lección 4: Teacher Resources

Pulling It All Together

Practice and Communicate
- Role-plays
- Activity Pack Practice Activities (¡A repasar!) (with Answer Key)

Assessment

Tests and Exams*
- **Prueba A** with audio
- **Prueba B** with audio
- **Prueba C** with audio
- **Prueba D** with audio
- **Prueba E** with audio
- **Prueba F** with audio
- Tests Answer Key
- Oral Testing Suggestions

- **Examen A** with audio (lessons 4-6)
- **Examen B** with audio (lessons 4-6)
- Exams Answer Key

Audioscripts
- Tests and Exams Audioscripts
- Alternative Listening Sections Audioscript

Additional Tools for Planning and Teaching

- Essential Questions
- I Can Worksheets
- IPAs & Rubrics
- Lesson Plans
- Middle School Activity Pack
- Pacing Guides

Audio MP3s for Classroom Activities

- **Contextos**. Activities 1 and 2 (p. 117)
- **Estructura 4.1. Comunicación**: Activity 4 (p.128)
- **Estructura 4.4. Comunicación**: Activity 4 (p. 139)
- **Escuchar** (p. 145)

Script for Comunicación: Actividad 4 (p. 128)

Enrique	Hola, Rosa. ¿Adónde vas esta noche?
Rosa	Voy al cine con Mercedes. ¿Quieres venir?
Enrique	No, gracias. Pedro y yo vamos al partido de béisbol.
Rosa	¡Oh! Fenomenal. Va a ser un partido muy bueno.
Enrique	¡Sí! Y después vamos a ir a un restaurante. ¿Quieren venir después de la película?
Rosa	Voy a hablar con Mercedes. ¿A qué restaurante van?
Enrique	Vamos a Osaka, el restaurante japonés del centro.
Rosa	¡Oh! Es mi restaurante favorito.
Enrique	¡Tienen que venir! Vamos a estar en el restaurante a las nueve y media.

Script for Comunicación: Actividad 4 (p. 139)

Francisco	Salgo de casa a las siete y media de la mañana después de desayunar. Comienzo el día con mi clase favorita, la de matemáticas, a las siete y cuarenta y cinco. Almuerzo a las once y cuarto, y salgo de mi clase de arte a las dos y cuarenta y cinco de la tarde. Después de clases, practico baloncesto con el equipo escolar. A las cinco, llego a casa y uso mi tableta. Veo mis programas favoritos y hago mi tarea. Por la noche oigo un poco de música y leo mi blog favorito antes de ir a dormir.

*Tests and Exams can also be assigned online.

Los pasatiempos

4

contextos

fotonovela

cultura

estructura

adelante

A PRIMERA VISTA
- ¿Es esta persona un atleta o un artista?
- ¿En qué tiene interés, en el ciclismo o en el tenis?
- ¿Es viejo? ¿Es delgado?
- ¿Tiene frío o calor?

Lesson Goals

In **Lección 4**, students will be introduced to the following:
- names of sports and other pastimes
- names of places in a city
- soccer rivalries
- Mexican diver **Paola Espinosa** and Venezuelan baseball player **Miguel Cabrera**
- present tense of **ir**
- the contraction **al**
- **ir a** + [*infinitive*]
- present tense of common stem-changing verbs
- verbs with irregular **yo** forms
- predicting content from visual elements
- using a Spanish-English dictionary
- writing an events pamphlet
- listening for the gist
- an excerpt of a documentary about skateboarding and BMX
- a video about soccer in Spain
- cultural, historical, economic, and geographic information about Mexico

A primera vista Ask these additional questions to personalize the photo: **¿Te gusta practicar los deportes? ¿Crees que son importantes los pasatiempos? ¿Estudias mucho los sábados y domingos? ¿Bailas? ¿Lees? ¿Escuchas música?**

Teaching Tip Look for these icons for additional communicative practice:

→👤←	Interpretive communication
←👤→	Presentational communication
👤↔👤	Interpersonal communication

SUPPORT FOR BACKWARD DESIGN

Lección 4 Essential Questions
1. How do people talk about pastimes, weekend activities, and sports?
2. How do people make plans and extend invitations?
3. What sports and sports figures are popular in the Spanish-speaking world?

Lección 4 Integrated Performance Assessment
Before teaching this chapter, review the Integrated Performance Assessment (IPA) and its accompanying scoring rubric. Use the IPA to assess students' progress toward proficiency targets at the end of the chapter. **IPA Context:** Your school is having an election for student council, and you need to decide what attributes are important in the person you elect. You are going to listen to two people describe themselves. Then, you and a partner will talk about the characteristics that would make each of them a better candidate. Finally, you will describe the characteristics of your ideal candidate to the class.

VOICE BOARD
Voice boards online allow you and your students to record and share up to five minutes of audio. Use voice boards for presentations, oral assessments, discussions, directions, etc.

4 | **contextos**

Section Goals

In **Contextos**, students will learn and practice:
• names of sports and other pastimes
• names of places in a city

 Communication 1.2
Comparisons 4.1

Teacher Resources
Read the front matter for suggestions on how to incorporate all the program's components. See pages 115A–115B for a detailed listing of Teacher Resources online.

In-Class Tips
• Write **practicar un deporte** on the board and explain what it means. Ask: **¿Qué deportes practicas?** Offer some cognates as suggestions: **¿Practicas el béisbol? ¿El vóleibol? ¿El tenis? ¿El golf?** After the student answers, ask another student: **¿Qué deporte practica _____?**
• Use the **Lección 4 Contextos** vocabulary presentation online or the digital images in the Resources online to assist with this presentation.
• Ask true/false questions about the illustration. Ex: **¿Cierto o falso? Una chica nada en la piscina. (Falso. Es un chico.)** Next, name famous athletes and have students give the sports they play. Ex: **¿Qué deporte practica Novak Djokovic?**
• Point out that, except for the **nosotros/as** and **vosotros/as** forms, all present tense forms of **esquiar** carry an accent over the **i**: **esquío, esquías, esquía, esquían.**

Note: At this point you may want to present **Vocabulario adicional: Más vocabulario para el fin de semana** from the online Resources.

Los pasatiempos

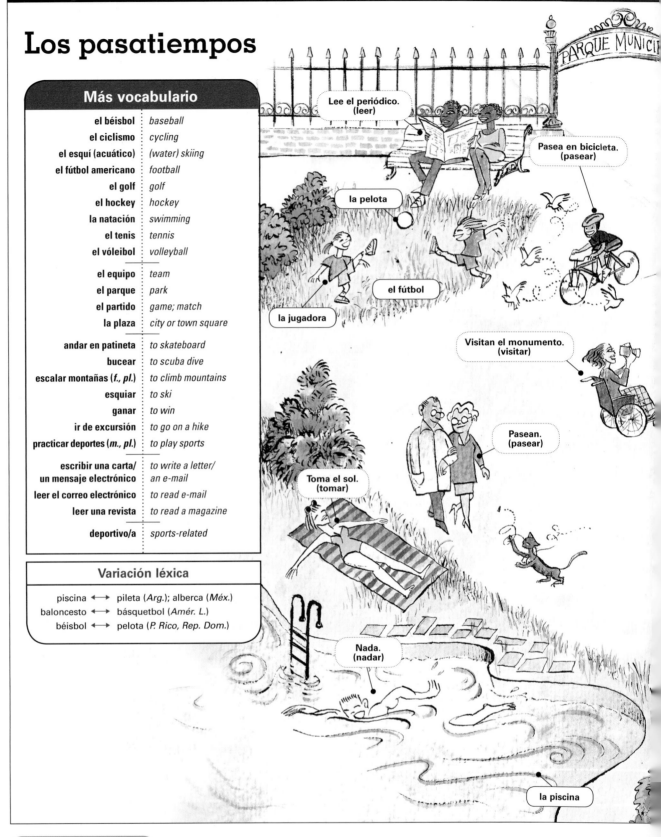

Más vocabulario

el béisbol	baseball
el ciclismo	cycling
el esquí (acuático)	(water) skiing
el fútbol americano	football
el golf	golf
el hockey	hockey
la natación	swimming
el tenis	tennis
el vóleibol	volleyball
el equipo	team
el parque	park
el partido	game; match
la plaza	city or town square
andar en patineta	to skateboard
bucear	to scuba dive
escalar montañas (f., pl.)	to climb mountains
esquiar	to ski
ganar	to win
ir de excursión	to go on a hike
practicar deportes (m., pl.)	to play sports
escribir una carta/ un mensaje electrónico	to write a letter/ an e-mail
leer el correo electrónico	to read e-mail
leer una revista	to read a magazine
deportivo/a	sports-related

Variación léxica

piscina	⟷	pileta (*Arg.*); alberca (*Méx.*)
baloncesto	⟷	básquetbol (*Amér. L.*)
béisbol	⟷	pelota (*P. Rico, Rep. Dom.*)

Captions within illustration: Lee el periódico. (leer) • Pasea en bicicleta. (pasear) • la pelota • Visitan el monumento. (visitar) • el fútbol • la jugadora • Pasean. (pasear) • Toma el sol. (tomar) • Nada. (nadar) • la piscina

TEACHING OPTIONS

Pairs Ask students to write down in Spanish their three favorite sports or leisure activities. Have students pair up and share the information using complete sentences. Ex: **Me gusta practicar la natación. Es un deporte divertido. Nado en mi piscina. ¿Qué deportes practicas?** As a class, call on individuals to report their partners' favorite pastimes. Partners will confirm or correct the information.

Variación léxica Point out that many sports in Spanish are referred to by names derived from English (**básquetbol, béisbol, fútbol**), including many in **Más vocabulario: el golf, el hockey, el vóleibol.** Ask students to guess the meaning of these activities (be sure to use Spanish pronunciation): **el footing** (*jogging*), **el camping, el surf(ing), el windsurf.**

Communication 1.1

Práctica

1 Escuchar Indicate the letter of the activity in Column B that best corresponds to each statement you hear. Two items in Column B will not be used.

A	B
1. __b__	a. leer el correo electrónico
2. __d__	b. tomar el sol
3. __f__	c. pasear en bicicleta
4. __c__	d. ir a un partido de fútbol americano
5. __g__	e. escribir una carta
6. __h__	f. practicar muchos deportes
	g. nadar
	h. ir de excursión

2 Ordenar Order these activities according to what you hear in the narration.

__5__	a. pasear en bicicleta	__3__	d. tomar el sol
__1__	b. nadar	__6__	e. practicar deportes
__4__	c. leer una revista	__2__	f. patinar en línea

3 ¿Cierto o falso? Indicate whether each statement is **cierto** or **falso** based on the illustration.

	Cierto	Falso
1. Un hombre nada en la piscina.	⊘	○
2. Un hombre lee una revista.	○	⊘
3. Un chico pasea en bicicleta.	⊘	○
4. Dos muchachos esquían.	○	⊘
5. Una mujer y dos niños visitan un monumento.	⊘	○
6. Un hombre bucea.	○	⊘
7. Hay un equipo de hockey.	○	⊘
8. Una mujer toma el sol.	⊘	○

4 Clasificar Fill in the chart below with as many terms from **Contextos** as you can. Answers will vary.

Actividades	Deportes	Personas

Patina en línea. (patinar)

el jugador

el baloncesto

TEACHING OPTIONS

Extra Practice →📖← Add an auditory aspect to this vocabulary practice. Prepare short descriptions of different places you need to visit using the vocabulary from the chapter. Read each description aloud and have students name an appropriate location. Ex: **Necesito estudiar en un lugar tranquilo. También deseo leer una revista y unos periódicos. Aquí la gente no debe comer ni beber ni hablar por teléfono. (la biblioteca)**

Game 📖↔📖 Play a modified version of **20 Preguntas**. Ask a volunteer to choose an activity, person, or place from the illustration or **Más vocabulario** that other students will take turns guessing by asking yes/no questions. Limit the attempts to ten questions, after which the volunteer will reveal the item. You may need to provide some phrases on the board.

---

1 In-Class Tip Have students check their answers with a partner before going over **Actividad 1** with the class.

1 Script 1. No me gusta nadar pero paso mucho tiempo al lado de la piscina. 2. Alicia y yo vamos al estadio a las cuatro. Creemos que nuestro equipo va a ganar. 3. Me gusta patinar en línea, esquiar y practicar el tenis. 4. El ciclismo es mi deporte favorito. 5. Me gusta mucho la natación. Paso mucho tiempo en la piscina. 6. Mi hermana es una gran excursionista.

2 In-Class Tips
• To simplify, prepare the class for listening by having students read the list aloud.
• Ask students if the verbs in the list are conjugated or if they are infinitives. Tell them that the verbs they hear in the audio recording may be in the infinitive or conjugated form.

2 Script Hoy es sábado y mis amigos y yo estamos en el parque. Todos tenemos pasatiempos diferentes. Clara y Daniel nadan en la piscina. Luis patina en línea. Sergio y Paco toman el sol. Dalia lee una revista. Rosa y yo paseamos en bicicleta. Y tú, ¿practicas deportes?

3 Expansion Ask students to write three additional true/false sentences based on the illustration. Have volunteers read sentences aloud for the rest of the class to answer.

4 Expansion
←📖→ Ask students to write three sentences using the words they listed in each category. You can cue students to elicit more responses. Ex: **¿Qué es la natación? (La natación es un deporte.)**

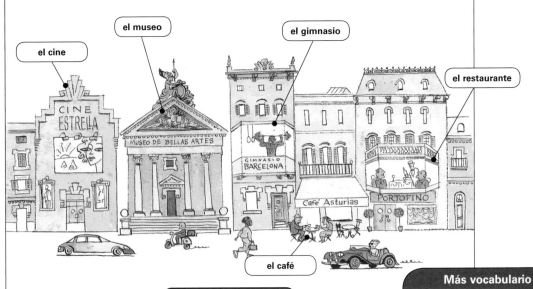

el cine • el museo • el gimnasio • el restaurante • el café

En el centro

5 **Identificar** Identify the place where these activities would take place.

> **modelo**
> Esquiamos. **Es una montaña.**

1. Tomamos una limonada. **Es un café./Es un restaurante.**
2. Vemos una película. **Es un cine.**
3. Nadamos y tomamos el sol. **Es una piscina./Es un parque.**
4. Hay muchos monumentos. **Es un parque./Es una plaza.**
5. Comemos tacos y fajitas. **Es un restaurante.**
6. Miramos pinturas (*paintings*) de Diego Rivera y Frida Kahlo. **Es un museo.**
7. Hay mucho tráfico. **Es el centro.**
8. Practicamos deportes. **Es un gimnasio./Es un parque.**

6 **Lugares** Indicate what you do in the places mentioned below. **Answers will vary.**

> **modelo**
> una plaza
> *Camino por la plaza y miro a las personas.*

beber	escalar	mirar	practicar
caminar	escribir	nadar	tomar
correr	leer	patinar	visitar

1. una biblioteca
2. un estadio
3. una plaza
4. una piscina
5. las montañas
6. un parque
7. un café
8. un museo

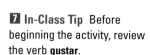
Comunicación

7 Guadalajara Read this description of Guadalajara. Then indicate whether the following conclusions are **lógico** or **ilógico**, based on what you read.

> Guadalajara es una gran ciudad del estado de Jalisco, México. ¿Te gustan los parques? El Parque Mirador Independencia es un buen lugar para pasear en bicicleta, andar en patineta o tomar el sol. ¿Te gusta el cine? Guadalajara es un importante centro cultural, famosa por el Festival de Cine de Guadalajara. ¿Tienes hambre? Hay fabulosos restaurantes por toda la ciudad. ¿Te gustan los deportes? Debes asistir a un partido del Club Deportivo Guadalajara, uno de los equipos de fútbol más populares de México. ¿Te gusta el arte? Guadalajara es también muy famosa por sus museos y sus monumentos.

	Lógico	Ilógico
1. En el Parque Mirador Independencia, hay lugar para la diversión.	⊘	○
2. Asistes al Festival de Cine de Guadalajara para ver películas.	⊘	○
3. En Guadalajara, la gente come bien.	⊘	○
4. No hay estadios de fútbol en Guadalajara.	○	⊘
5. En Guadalajara, los turistas visitan monumentos.	⊘	○

8 Entrevista Answer your partner's questions. Answers will vary.

1. ¿Hay un café cerca de tu casa?
2. ¿Cuál es tu restaurante favorito?
3. ¿Te gusta viajar y visitar monumentos?
4. ¿Te gusta ir al cine los fines de semana?
5. ¿Cuáles son tus películas favoritas?
6. ¿Te gusta practicar deportes?
7. ¿Cuáles son tus deportes favoritos?
8. ¿Cuáles son tus pasatiempos favoritos?

CONSULTA
To review expressions with **gustar**, see **Estructura 2.1**, p. 52.

9 Pasatiempos Write a paragraph about the pastimes three of your friends and family members enjoy. Answers will vary.

modelo
Mi hermana pasea mucho en bicicleta, pero mis padres practican la natación.
Mi hermano no nada, pero visita muchos museos.

10 Conversación Using the words and expressions provided, work with a partner to prepare a short conversation about pastimes. Answers will vary.

| ¿a qué hora? | ¿con quién(es)? | ¿dónde? |
| ¿cómo? | ¿cuándo? | ¿qué? |

modelo
Estudiante 1: ¿Cuándo patinas en línea?
Estudiante 2: Patino en línea los domingos. Y tú, ¿patinas en línea?
Estudiante 1: No, no me gusta patinar en línea. Me gusta practicar el béisbol.

7 In-Class Tip Before beginning the activity, review the verb **gustar**.

7 Expansion Have pairs or groups of students create a video ad promoting activities and interesting places to visit in their community. Then, ask students to present their ads to the class.

8 Expansion Have the same pairs ask each other additional questions. Then ask volunteers to share their mini-conversations with the class.

8 Virtual Chat Available online.

9 Expansion
• Ask volunteers to share any pastimes they and their partners, friends, and families have in common.
• In pairs, have students write sentences about the pastimes of a famous person without using their name. Encourage them to also recycle the descriptive adjectives and adjectives of nationality they learned in Lesson 3. Then have them work with another pair, asking questions as necessary, to guess the identity of the person being described.

10 In-Class Tip After students have asked and answered questions, ask volunteers to report their partners' activities back to the class. The partners should verify the information and provide at least one additional detail.

10 Partner Chat Available online.

Fútbol, cenotes y mole

Maru, Miguel, Jimena y Marissa visitan un cenote, mientras Felipe y Juan Carlos van a un partido de fútbol.

PERSONAJES   MIGUEL   PABLO

MIGUEL Buenos días a todos.

TÍA ANA MARÍA Hola, Miguel. Maru, ¿qué van a hacer hoy?

MARU Miguel y yo vamos a llevar a Marissa a un cenote.

MARISSA ¿No vamos a nadar? ¿Qué es un cenote?

MIGUEL Sí, sí vamos a nadar. Un cenote... difícil de explicar. Es una piscina natural en un hueco profundo.

MARU ¡Ya vas a ver! Seguro que te va a gustar.

ANA MARÍA Marissa, ¿qué te gusta hacer? ¿Escalar montañas? ¿Ir de excursión?

MARISSA Sí, me gusta ir de excursión y practicar el esquí acuático. Y usted, ¿qué prefiere hacer en sus ratos libres?

PABLO Mi mamá tiene muchos pasatiempos y actividades.

EDUARDO Sí. Ella nada y juega al tenis y al golf.

PABLO Va al cine y a los museos.

ANA MARÍA Sí, salgo mucho los fines de semana

(unos minutos después)

EDUARDO Hay un partido de fútbol en el parque. ¿Quieren ir conmigo?

PABLO Y conmigo. Si no consigo más jugadores, nuestro equipo va a perder.

FELIPE ¿Recuerdas el restaurante del mole?

EDUARDO ¿Qué restaurante?

JIMENA El mole de mi tía Ana María es mi favorito.

MARU Chicos, ya es hora. ¡Vamos!

ANA MARÍA   **MARU**   **MARISSA**   **EDUARDO**   **FELIPE**   **JUAN CARLOS**   **JIMENA**   **DON GUILLERMO**

7

(*más tarde, en el parque*)

PABLO No puede ser. ¡Cinco a uno!

FELIPE ¡Vamos a jugar! Si perdemos, compramos el almuerzo. Y si ganamos...

EDUARDO ¡Empezamos!

8

(*mientras tanto, en el cenote*)

MARISSA ¿Hay muchos cenotes en México?

MIGUEL Sólo en la península de Yucatán.

MARISSA ¡Vamos a nadar!

9

(*Los chicos visitan a don Guillermo, un vendedor de paletas heladas.*)

JUAN CARLOS Don Guillermo, ¿dónde podemos conseguir un buen mole?

FELIPE Eduardo y Pablo van a pagar el almuerzo. Y yo voy a pedir un montón de comida.

10

FELIPE Sí, éste es el restaurante. Recuerdo la comida.

EDUARDO Oye, Pablo... No tengo...

PABLO No te preocupes, hermanito.

FELIPE ¿Qué buscas? (*muestra la cartera de Pablo*) ¿Esto?

Expresiones útiles

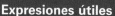

Making invitations

Hay un partido de fútbol en el parque. ¿Quieren ir conmigo?
There's a soccer game in the park. Do you want to come with me?
¡Yo puedo jugar!
I can play!
Mmm... no quiero.
Hmm... I don't want to.
Lo siento, pero no puedo.
I'm sorry, but I can't.
¡Vamos a nadar!
Let's go swimming!
Sí, vamos.
Yes, let's go.

Making plans

¿Qué van a hacer hoy?
What are you going to do today?
Vamos a llevar a Marissa a un cenote.
We are taking Marissa to a cenote.
Vamos a comprar unas paletas heladas.
We're going to buy some popsicles.
Vamos a jugar. Si perdemos, compramos el almuerzo.
Let's play. If we lose, we'll buy lunch.

Talking about pastimes

¿Qué te gusta hacer? ¿Escalar montañas? ¿Ir de excursión?
What do you like to do? Mountain climbing? Hiking?
Sí, me gusta ir de excursión y practicar esquí acuático.
Yes, I like hiking and water skiing.
Y usted, ¿qué prefiere hacer en sus ratos libres?
And you, what do you like to do in your free time?
Salgo mucho los fines de semana.
I go out a lot on the weekends.
Voy al cine y a los museos.
I go to the movies and to museums.

Additional vocabulary

el/la aficionado/a *fan*
la cartera *wallet*   **el hueco** *hole*
un montón de *a lot of*

¿Qué pasó?

1 **Escoger** Choose the answer that best completes each sentence.

1. Marissa, Maru y Miguel desean _____a____.
   a. nadar   b. correr por el parque   c. leer el periódico

2. A Marissa le gusta _____c____.
   a. el tenis   b. el vóleibol   c. ir de excursión y practicar esquí acuático

3. A la tía Ana María le gusta _____b____.
   a. jugar al hockey   b. nadar y jugar al tenis y al golf   c. hacer ciclismo

4. Pablo y Eduardo pierden el partido de _____a____.
   a. fútbol   b. béisbol   c. baloncesto

5. Juan Carlos y Felipe desean _____c____.
   a. patinar   b. esquiar   c. comer mole

2 **Identificar** Identify the person who would make each statement.

1. A mí me gusta nadar, pero no sé qué es un cenote. _Marissa_

2. Mamá va al cine y al museo en sus ratos libres. _Pablo/Eduardo_

3. Yo voy a pedir mucha comida. _Felipe_

4. ¿Quieren ir a jugar al fútbol con nosotros en el parque? _Pablo/Eduardo_

5. Me gusta salir los fines de semana. _tía Ana María_

 MARISSA

 FELIPE

EDUARDO

 PABLO

TÍA ANA MARÍA

3 **Preguntas** Answer the questions using the information from the **Fotonovela**.

1. ¿Qué van a hacer Miguel y Maru?
   Miguel y Maru van a llevar a Marissa a un cenote.
2. ¿Adónde van Felipe y Juan Carlos mientras sus amigos van al cenote?
   Felipe y Juan Carlos van a jugar al fútbol con Pablo y Eduardo.
3. ¿Quién gana el partido de fútbol?
   Felipe y Juan Carlos ganan el partido de fútbol.
4. ¿Quiénes van al cenote con Maru y Miguel?
   Marissa y Jimena van al cenote con Maru y Miguel.

4 **Conversación** With a partner, prepare a conversation in which you talk about pastimes and invite each other to do some activity together. Use these expressions and also look at **Expresiones útiles** on the previous page. Answers will vary.

¿A qué hora?	¿Dónde? *Where?*	Nos vemos a las siete.
(At) What time?	No puedo porque...	*See you at seven.*
contigo *with you*	*I can't because...*	

▶ ¿Eres aficionado/a a...?   ▶ ¿Por qué no...?   ▶ ¿Qué vas a hacer esta noche?
▶ ¿Te gusta...?   ▶ ¿Quieres... conmigo?

TEACHING OPTIONS

Small Groups 👤↔👤 Have the class quickly glance at frames 7, 8, and 10 of the **Fotonovela**. Then have students work in groups of three to ad-lib what transpires between the friends. Assure them that it is not necessary to follow the **Fotonovela** word for word. Students should be creative while getting the general meaning across with the vocabulary and expressions they know.

Extra Practice Have students close their books and complete these statements with words from the **Fotonovela**. 1. ¿Qué prefiere _____ usted en sus ratos libres? (hacer) 2. ¿Dónde _____ conseguir un buen mole? (podemos) 3. ¿Nosotros _____ a nadar? (vamos) 4. Eduardo y Pablo _____ a pagar el almuerzo. (van) 5. ¿Ustedes _____ ir conmigo al partido de fútbol? (quieren)

Pronunciación
Word stress and accent marks

pe-lí-cu-la	**e-di-fi-cio**	**ver**	**yo**

Every Spanish syllable contains at least one vowel. When two vowels are joined in the same syllable they form a **diphthong***. A **monosyllable** is a word formed by a single syllable.

bi-blio-te-ca	**vi-si-tar**	**par-que**	**fút-bol**

The syllable of a Spanish word that is pronounced most emphatically is the "stressed" syllable.

pe-lo-ta	**pis-ci-na**	**ra-tos**	**ha-blan**

Words that end in **n**, **s**, or a **vowel** are usually stressed on the next-to-last syllable.

na-ta-ción	**pa-pá**	**in-glés**	**Jo-sé**

If words that end in **n**, **s**, or a **vowel** are stressed on the last syllable, they must carry an accent mark on the stressed syllable.

bai-lar	**es-pa-ñol**	**u-ni-ver-si-dad**	**tra-ba-ja-dor**

Words that do not end in **n**, **s**, or a **vowel** are usually stressed on the last syllable.

béis-bol	**lá-piz**	**ár-bol**	**Gó-mez**

If words that do not end in **n**, **s**, or a **vowel** are stressed on the next-to-last syllable, they must carry an accent mark on the stressed syllable.

*The two vowels that form a diphthong are either both weak or one is weak and the other is strong.

Práctica Pronounce each word, stressing the correct syllable. Then give the word stress rule for each word.

1. profesor
2. Puebla
3. ¿Cuántos?
4. Mazatlán
5. examen
6. ¿Cómo?
7. niños
8. Guadalajara
9. programador
10. México
11. están
12. geografía

Oraciones Read the conversation aloud to practice word stress.

MARINA Hola, Carlos. ¿Qué tal?
CARLOS Bien. Oye, ¿a qué hora es el partido de fútbol?
MARINA Creo que es a las siete.
CARLOS ¿Quieres ir?
MARINA Lo siento, pero no puedo. Tengo que estudiar biología.

Refranes Read these sayings aloud to practice word stress.

En la unión está la fuerza.[2]

Quien ríe de último, ríe mejor.[1]

1 He who laughs last, laughs best.
2 United we stand.

EN DETALLE

Real Madrid y Barça: rivalidad total

Soccer in Spain is a force to be reckoned with, and no two teams draw more attention than **Real Madrid** and the **Fútbol Club Barcelona.** Whether the venue is Madrid's **Santiago Bernabéu** or Barcelona's **Camp Nou**, the two cities shut down for the showdown, paralyzed by **fútbol** fever. A ticket to the actual game is always the hottest ticket in town.

The rivalry between **Real Madrid** and **Barça** is about more than soccer. As the two biggest, most powerful cities in Spain, Barcelona and Madrid are constantly compared to one another and have a natural rivalry. There is also a political component to the dynamic. Barcelona, with its distinct language and culture, has long struggled for increased autonomy from Madrid's centralized government. Under Francisco Franco's rule (1939–1975), when repression of the Catalan identity was at its height, a game between **Real Madrid** and **FC Barcelona** was wrapped up with all the symbolism of the regime versus the resistance, even though both teams suffered casualties in Spain's civil war and the subsequent Franco dictatorship.

Although the dictatorship is long over, the momentum of all those decades of competition still transforms both cities into a frenzied, tense panic leading up to the game. Once the final score is announced, one of those cities is transformed again, this time into the best party in the country.

Rivalidades del fútbol

Argentina: Boca Juniors vs River Plate
México: Águilas del América vs Chivas del Guadalajara
Chile: Colo Colo vs Universidad de Chile
Guatemala: Comunicaciones vs Municipal
Uruguay: Peñarol vs Nacional
Colombia: Millonarios vs Independiente Santa Fe

ACTIVIDADES

1 ¿Cierto o falso? Indicate whether each statement is cierto or falso. Correct the false statements.

1. People from Spain don't like soccer. **Falso.** People from Spain like soccer very much.
2. Madrid and Barcelona are the most important cities in Spain. **Cierto.**
3. Santiago Bernabéu is a stadium in Barcelona. **Falso.** It is a stadium in Madrid.
4. The rivalry between Real Madrid and FC Barcelona is not only in soccer. **Cierto.**
5. Barcelona has resisted Madrid's centralized government. **Cierto.**
6. Only the FC Barcelona team was affected by the civil war. **Falso.** Both teams were affected by the civil war.
7. During Franco's regime, the Catalan culture thrived. **Falso.** Catalan culture was repressed during Franco's regime.
8. There are many famous rivalries between soccer teams in the Spanish-speaking world. **Cierto.**
9. River Plate is a popular team from Argentina. **Cierto.**
10. Comunicaciones and Peñarol are famous rivals in Guatemala. **Falso.** Comunicaciones and Municipal are important rivals in Guatemala.

Así se dice
- Model the pronunciation of each term and have students repeat it.
- To challenge students, add these words to the list: **el atletismo** (*track and field*); **el/la golfista** (*golfer*); **marcar un gol** (*to score a goal*); **el palo de golf** (*golf club*); **el/la portero/a** (*goalie*).

ASÍ SE DICE

Los deportes

el/la árbitro/a	referee
el/la atleta	athlete
la bola; el balón	**la pelota**
el campeón/ la campeona	champion
la carrera	race
competir	to compete
empatar	to tie
la medalla	medal
el/la mejor	the best
mundial	worldwide
el torneo	tournament

EL MUNDO HISPANO

Atletas importantes

World-renowned Hispanic athletes:

- **Rafael Nadal** (España) has won 14 Grand Slam singles titles and the 2008 Olympic gold medal in singles tennis.

- **Lionel Andrés Messi** (Argentina) is one of the world's top soccer players. He plays for **FC Barcelona** and for the Argentine national team.

- **Mireia Belmonte García** (España) won two silver medals in swimming at the 2012 Olympics.

- **Lorena Ochoa** (México) was the top-ranked female golfer in the world when she retired in 2010 at the age of 28. She still hosts an LPGA golf tournament, the Lorena Ochoa Invitational, every year.

PERFILES

Miguel Cabrera y Paola Espinosa

Miguel Cabrera, considered one of the best hitters in baseball, now plays first base for the Detroit Tigers. Born in Venezuela in 1983, he made his Major League debut at the age of 20. Cabrera has been selected for both the National League and American League All-Star Teams. In 2012, he became the first player since 1967 to win the Triple Crown.

Mexican diver **Paola Milagros Espinosa Sánchez**, born in 1986, has competed in three Olympics (2004, 2008, and 2012). She and her partner Tatiana Ortiz took home a bronze medal in 2008. In 2012, she won a silver medal with partner Alejandra Orozco. She won three gold medals at the Pan American Games in 2007 and again in 2011.

Conexión Internet

¿Qué deportes son populares en los países hispanos?

Use the Web to find more cultural information related to this **Cultura** section.

Perfiles
- Miguel Cabrera has played left field, right field, third base, and first base. In 2012, he led the American League with a .330 batting average, 44 home runs, and 139 runs batted in. Cabrera was named the American League's Most Valuable Player in 2012 and 2013.
- **Paola Espinosa**'s Olympic medals are in the 10m platform synchronized diving event. She won gold medals at the Pan American Games for individual and synchronized events.

El mundo hispano Have students write three true/false sentences about this section. Then have them get together with a classmate and take turns reading and correcting their statements.

ACTIVIDADES

2 **Comprensión** Write the name of the athlete described in each sentence.

1. Es un jugador de fútbol de Argentina. <u>Lionel Messi</u>
2. Es una mujer que practica el golf. <u>Lorena Ochoa</u>
3. Es un jugador de béisbol de Venezuela. <u>Miguel Cabrera</u>
4. Es una mujer mexicana que practica un deporte en la piscina. <u>Paola Milagros Espinosa Sánchez</u>

3 **¿Quién es?** Write a short paragraph describing an athlete that you like. What does he/she look like? What sport does he/she play? Where does he/she live? Answers will vary.

2 **Expansion** Give students these sentences as items 5–6:
5. ____ es una mujer española que practica la natación. (**Mireia Belmonte García**)
6. El ____ es el deporte favorito de Rafael Nadal. (tenis)

3 **In-Class Tip**
→👤← Have students get together with a classmate and peer edit each other's paragraphs, paying close attention to gender agreement.

PRE-AP®

Presentational Speaking ←👤→ For homework, ask students to research one of the athletes from **El mundo hispano**. They should write five Spanish sentences about the athlete's life and career, and bring in a photo from the Internet. Have students who researched the same person work as a group to present that athlete to the class.

TEACHING OPTIONS

Heritage Speakers ←👤→ Ask heritage speakers to describe sports preferences in their families' countries of origin, especially ones that are not widely known in the United States, such as **jai-alai**. What well-known athletes in the U.S. are from their families' countries of origin?

Section Goals

In **Estructura 4.1**, students will learn:
- the present tense of **ir**
- the contraction **al**
- **ir a** + [*infinitive*] to express future events
- **vamos a** to express *let's...*

 Communication 1.1
Comparisons 4.1

Teacher Resources
Read the front matter for suggestions on how to incorporate all the program's components. See pages 115A–115B for a detailed listing of Teacher Resources online.

In-Class Tips
- Write your next day's schedule on the board. Ex: **8:00—la biblioteca; 12:00—comer**. Explain where you are going or what you are going to do, using the verb **ir**. Ask volunteers about their schedules, using forms of **ir**.
- Add a visual aspect to this grammar presentation. Write names of Spanish-speaking countries on construction paper, and pin up the papers at different points around the classroom in order to make a "map." Point to your destination "country," and as you pantomime flying there, ask students: **¿Adónde voy? (Vas a Chile.)** Once there, act out an activity, asking: **¿Qué voy a hacer? (Vas a esquiar.)**
- Practice **vamos a** to express the idea of *let's* by asking volunteers to suggest things to do. Ex: **Tengo hambre. (Vamos a la cafetería.)**

Ayuda Point out the difference in usage between **dónde** and **adónde**. Ask: **¿Adónde va el/la presidente/a de los Estados Unidos para descansar? (Va a Camp David.) ¿Dónde está Camp David? (Está en Maryland.)**

4.1 Present tense of ir

ANTE TODO The verb **ir** (*to go*) is irregular in the present tense. Note that, except for the **yo** form (**voy**) and the lack of a written accent on the **vosotros** form (**vais**), the endings are the same as those for regular present tense **-ar** verbs.

The verb ir (to go)

Singular forms		Plural forms	
yo	**voy**	nosotros/as	**vamos**
tú	**vas**	vosotros/as	**vais**
Ud./él/ella	**va**	Uds./ellos/ellas	**van**

▶ **Ir** is often used with the preposition **a** (*to*). If **a** is followed by the definite article **el**, they combine to form the contraction **al**. If **a** is followed by the other definite articles (**la, las, los**), there is no contraction.

a + el = al

Voy **al** parque con Juan.
I'm going to the park with Juan.

Mis amigos van **a las** montañas.
My friends are going to the mountains.

▶ The construction **ir a** + [*infinitive*] is used to talk about actions that are going to happen in the future. It is equivalent to the English *to be going* + [*infinitive*].

Va a leer el periódico.
He is going to read the newspaper.

Van a pasear por el pueblo.
They are going to walk around town.

¡Voy a ir con ellos!

Ella va al cine y a los museos.

AYUDA
When asking a question that contains a form of the verb **ir**, remember to use **adónde**:
¿Adónde vas? *(To) Where are you going?*

▶ **Vamos a** + [*infinitive*] can also express the idea of *let's (do something)*.

Vamos a pasear.
Let's take a walk.

¡Vamos a comer!
Let's eat!

¡INTÉNTALO! Provide the present tense forms of **ir**.

1. Ellos ___van___.
2. Yo ___voy___.
3. Tu amigo ___va___.
4. Adela ___va___.
5. Mi prima y yo ___vamos___.
6. Tú ___vas___.
7. Ustedes ___van___.
8. Nosotros ___vamos___.
9. Usted ___va___.
10. Nosotras ___vamos___.
11. Miguel ___va___.
12. Ellas ___van___.

TEACHING OPTIONS

TPR Invent gestures to act out the activities mentioned in **Lección 4**. Ex: **leer el periódico** (act out reading and holding a newspaper), **patinar** (skate), **nadar** (move arms as if swimming). Signal individuals to gesture appropriately as you cue activities with **Vamos a**. Keep a brisk pace.

Pairs ←🔹→ Have students form pairs, and tell them they are going somewhere with a friend. On paper strips, write varying dollar amounts, ranging from three dollars to five thousand. Have each pair draw out a dollar amount at random and tell the class where they will go and what they will do with the money they've drawn. Encourage creativity. Ex: **Tenemos seis dólares. Vamos a McDonald's para comer. Ella va a cenar, pero yo voy a beber agua porque no tenemos más dinero./Tenemos cinco mil dólares. Vamos a cenar en París…**

Práctica

1 **¿Adónde van?** Everyone in your neighborhood is dashing off to various places. Say where they are going.

1. la señora Castillo / el centro   La señora Castillo va al centro.
2. las hermanas Gómez / la piscina   Las hermanas Gómez van a la piscina.
3. tu tío y tu papá / el partido de fútbol   Tu tío y tu papá van al partido de fútbol.
4. yo / el Museo de Arte Moderno   (Yo) Voy al Museo de Arte Moderno.
5. nosotros / el restaurante Miramar   (Nosotros) Vamos al restaurante Miramar.

2 **¿Qué van a hacer?** These sentences describe what several students in a college hiking club are doing today. Use **ir a** + [*infinitive*] to say that they are also going to do the same activities tomorrow.

> **modelo**
>
> Martín y Rodolfo nadan en la piscina.
> *Van a nadar en la piscina mañana también.*

1. Sara lee una revista.   Va a leer una revista mañana también.
2. Yo practico deportes.   Voy a practicar deportes mañana también.
3. Ustedes van de excursión.   Van a ir de excursión mañana también.
4. El presidente del club patina.   Va a patinar mañana también.
5. Tú tomas el sol.   Vas a tomar el sol mañana también.
6. Paseamos con nuestros amigos.   Vamos a pasear con nuestros amigos mañana también.

3 **Actividades** Indicate where the people are going and what they are going to do there. Some answers will vary.

> **modelo**
>
> Estela va a la Librería Sol.
> *Va a comprar un libro.*

Estela

1. Álex y Miguel
Álex y Miguel van al parque.
Van a…

2. mi amigo
Mi amigo va al gimnasio.
Va a…

3. tú
Voy al restaurante. Voy a…

4. los estudiantes
Los estudiantes van al estadio.
Van a…

5. la profesora Torres
La profesora Torres va a la
Biblioteca Nacional. Va a…

6. ustedes
Vamos a la piscina.
Vamos a…

1 **In-Class Tip** To add a visual aspect to this exercise, bring in photos of people dressed for a particular activity. As you hold up each photo, have the class say where they are going, using the verb **ir**. Ex: Show a photo of a basketball player. (**Va al gimnasio./Va a un partido.**)

1 **Expansion** After completing the activity, extend each answer with **pero** and a different name or pronoun, and have students complete the sentence. Ex: **La señora Castillo va al centro, pero el señor Castillo... (va al trabajo).**

2 **Expansion**
• Show the same photos you used for **Actividad 1** and ask students to describe what the people are going to do. Ex: **Va a jugar al baloncesto.**
• Ask students about tomorrow's activities. Ex: **¿Qué van a hacer tus amigos mañana? ¿Qué va a hacer tu hermano/hermana mañana?**

3 **Expansion**
↤👤↦ Ask pairs to write a riddle using **ir a** + [*infinitive*]. Ex: **Ángela, Laura, Tomás y Manuel van a hacer cosas diferentes. Tomás va a nadar y Laura va a comer, pero no en casa. Uno de los chicos y una de las chicas van a ver una película. ¿Adónde van todos?** Then have pairs exchange papers to solve the riddles.

TEACHING OPTIONS

Heritage Speakers ↤👤↦ Ask heritage speakers to write six sentences with the verb **ir** indicating places they go on weekends either by themselves or with friends and family. Ex: **Mi familia y yo vamos a visitar a mi abuela los domingos…** Share the descriptions with the class and ask comprehension questions.
Game 👤↔👤 Have students work in teams to write a brief description of a well-known fictional character's activities for

tomorrow, using the verb **ir**. Ex: **Mañana va a dormir de día. Va a caminar de noche. Va a buscar una muchacha bonita. La muchacha va a tener mucho miedo.** Have each team read their description aloud without naming the character. Teams can ask for and share more details about the person as needed. The first team to correctly identify the person (**Es Drácula.**) receives a point. The team with the most points at the end wins.

Comunicación

4 **Esta noche** Listen to the conversation between Enrique and Rosa. Then indicate whether the following conclusions are **lógico** or **ilógico**, based on what you heard.

	Lógico	Ilógico
1. Rosa y Mercedes van a ver una película esta noche.	☑	○
2. A Enrique le gustan los deportes.	☑	○
3. Enrique va a ir al estadio esta noche.	☑	○
4. Enrique y Pedro van a cenar mientras (*while*) miran el partido.	○	☑
5. A Rosa no le gustan los restaurantes japoneses.	○	☑
6. Rosa y Enrique conversan en el cine.	○	☑

5 **Situaciones** Work with a partner and say where you and your friends go in these situations. Answers will vary.

1. Cuando deseo descansar…
2. Cuando mi mejor amigo/a tiene que estudiar…
3. Si deseo hablar con mis amigos…
4. Cuando mis amigos y yo tenemos hambre…
5. En mis ratos libres…
6. Cuando mis amigos desean esquiar…
7. Si estoy de vacaciones…
8. Si tengo ganas de leer…

6 **Entrevista** With a partner, take turns asking each other where you are going and what you are going to do on your next vacation. Answers will vary.

> **modelo**
> **Estudiante 1:** ¿Adónde vas de vacaciones (*on vacation*)?
> **Estudiante 2:** Voy a Guadalajara con mi familia.
> **Estudiante 1:** ¿Y qué van a hacer (*to do*) ustedes en Guadalajara?
> **Estudiante 2:** Vamos a visitar unos monumentos y museos. ¿Y tú?

Síntesis

7 **Planes** Make a schedule of your activities for the weekend. Answers will vary.

▶ For each day, list at least three things you have to do.
▶ For each day, list at least two things you will do for fun.

---

4 In-Class Tip Have students listen to the audio once and ask for the global idea of the text. Then, ask more specific questions, such as: **¿Cómo se llaman los participantes de la conversación? ¿A dónde van por la noche? ¿A qué hora van al restaurante?**

4 Script *See the script for this activity on Interleaf page 115B.*

5 Expansion Have students make the phrases negative and then provide a new appropriate ending. Ex: **Cuando no deseo descansar, voy al gimnasio.**

5 Virtual Chat ▸↔▸ Available online.

6 In-Class Tip Add a visual aspect to this activity. Ask students to use an idea map to brainstorm a trip they would like to take. Have them write **lugar** in the central circle, and in the surrounding ones: **visitar, deportes, otras actividades, comida, compañeros/as.**

6 Partner Chat ▸↔▸ Available online.

Communication 1.1

7 In-Class Tips
• To simplify, have students make two columns on a sheet of paper. The first one should be headed **El fin de semana tengo que…** and the other **El fin de semana tengo ganas de…** Give students a few minutes to brainstorm about their activities for the weekend.
• Before students begin the last step, brainstorm a list of expressions as a class. Ex: **—¿Quieres jugar al tenis conmigo? —Lo siento, pero no puedo./Sí, vamos.**

TEACHING OPTIONS

Pairs Write these times on the board: **8:00 a.m., 12:00 p.m., 12:45 p.m., 4:00 p.m., 6:00 p.m., 10:00 p.m.** Have student pairs take turns reading a time and suggesting an appropriate activity or place. Ex: **E1: Son las ocho de la mañana. E2: Vamos a correr./Vamos al gimnasio.**
Game Divide the class into teams. Name a category (Ex: **lugares públicos**) and set a time limit of two minutes. The first team

member will write down one answer on a piece of paper and pass it to the next person. The paper will continue to be passed from student to student until the two minutes are up. The team with the most words wins.
Video →▪← Show the **Fotonovela** episode again to give students more input containing the verb **ir.** Stop the video where appropriate to discuss how **ir** is used to express different ideas.

4.2 Stem-changing verbs:
e→ie, o→ue

 ANTE TODO   Stem-changing verbs deviate from the normal pattern of regular verbs. When stem-changing verbs are conjugated, they have a vowel change in the last syllable of the stem.

CONSULTA

To review the present tense of regular -**ar** verbs, see **Estructura 2.1**, p. 50.

• • •

To review the present tense of regular -**er** and -**ir** verbs, see **Estructura 3.3**, p. 96.

INFINITIVE	VERB STEM	STEM CHANGE	CONJUGATED FORM
empezar	empez-	emp**ie**z-	emp**ie**zo
volver	v**o**lv-	v**ue**lv-	v**ue**lvo

▶ In many verbs, such as **empezar** (*to begin*), the stem vowel changes from **e** to **ie**. Note that the **nosotros/as** and **vosotros/as** forms don't have a stem change.

The verb empezar (e:ie) (*to begin*)

Singular forms		Plural forms	
yo	emp**ie**zo	nosotros/as	empezamos
tú	emp**ie**zas	vosotros/as	empezáis
Ud./él/ella	emp**ie**za	Uds./ellos/ellas	emp**ie**zan

Los chicos empiezan a hablar de su visita al cenote.

Ellos vuelven a comer en el restaurante.

▶ In many other verbs, such as **volver** (*to return*), the stem vowel changes from **o** to **ue**. The **nosotros/as** and **vosotros/as** forms have no stem change.

The verb volver (o:ue) (*to return*)

Singular forms		Plural forms	
yo	v**ue**lvo	nosotros/as	volvemos
tú	v**ue**lves	vosotros/as	volvéis
Ud./él/ella	v**ue**lve	Uds./ellos/ellas	v**ue**lven

▶ To help you identify stem-changing verbs, they will appear as follows throughout the text:

> empezar (e:ie), volver (o:ue)

Section Goals
In **Estructura 4.2**, students will be introduced to:
• present tense of stem-changing verbs: **e → ie**; **o → ue**
• common stem-changing verbs

 Comparisons 4.1

Teacher Resources
Read the front matter for suggestions on how to incorporate all the program's components. See pages 115A–115B for a detailed listing of Teacher Resources online.

In-Class Tips
• Take a survey of students' habits. Ask: **¿A qué hora comienzan las clases?** Make a chart with students' names on the board. Ask: **¿Quiénes vuelven a casa a las seis?** Then create sentences based on the chart. Ex: **Tú vuelves a casa a las siete, pero Amanda vuelve a las seis. Daniel y yo volvemos a las cinco.**
• Copy the forms of **empezar** and **volver** on the board. Reiterate that the personal endings for the present tense of all the verbs listed in **Estructura 4.2** are the same as those for the present tense of regular –**ar**, –**er**, and –**ir** verbs.
• Explain that an easy way to remember which forms of these verbs have stem changes is to think of them as boot verbs. Draw a line around the stem-changing forms in each paradigm to show the boot-like shape.

TEACHING OPTIONS

Extra Practice Write a pattern sentence on the board. Ex: **Ella empieza una carta**. Have students write down the model, and then dictate a list of subjects (Ex: **Carmen, nosotras, don Miguel**), pausing after each one to allow students to write a complete sentence using the model verb. Ask volunteers to read their sentences aloud.

Heritage Speakers 👥↔👤 Ask heritage speakers to work in pairs to write a mock interview with a Spanish-speaking celebrity such as **Lorena Ochoa, Salma Hayek, Manu Ginóbili,** or **Benicio del Toro,** in which they use the verbs **empezar, volver, querer,** and **recordar**. Ask them to role-play their interview for the class, who will write down the forms of **empezar, volver, querer,** and **recordar** that they hear.

In-Class Tips

- Write **e:ie** and **o:ue** on the board and explain that some very common verbs have these types of stem changes. Point out that all the verbs listed are conjugated like **empezar** or **volver**. Model the pronunciation of the verbs and ask students a few questions using verbs of each type. Have them answer in complete sentences. Ex: **¿A qué hora cierra la biblioteca? ¿Duermen los estudiantes hasta tarde, por lo general? ¿Qué piensan hacer este fin de semana? ¿Quién quiere comer en un restaurante esta noche?**

- Point out the structure **jugar al** used with sports. Practice it by asking students about the sports they play. Have them answer in complete sentences. Ex: ____, **¿te gusta jugar al fútbol? Y tú, ____, ¿juegas al fútbol? ¿Prefieres jugar al fútbol o ver un partido en el estadio? ¿Cuántos juegan al tenis? ¿Qué prefieres, ____, jugar al tenis o jugar al fútbol?**

- Prepare a few dehydrated sentences. Ex: **Raúl / empezar / la lección; ustedes / mostrar / los trabajos; nosotros / jugar / al fútbol** Write them on the board one at a time, and ask students to form complete sentences based on the cues.

Common stem-changing verbs

e:ie		o:ue	
cerrar	to close	almorzar	to have lunch
comenzar (a + *inf.*)	to begin	contar	to count; to tell
empezar (a + *inf.*)	to begin	dormir	to sleep
entender	to understand	encontrar	to find
pensar	to think	mostrar	to show
perder	to lose; to miss	poder (+ *inf.*)	to be able to; can
preferir (+ *inf.*)	to prefer	recordar	to remember
querer (+ *inf.*)	to want; to love	volver	to return

▶ **Jugar** (*to play a sport or a game*) is the only Spanish verb that has a **u:ue** stem change. **Jugar** is followed by **a** + [*definite article*] when the name of a sport or game is mentioned.

Ella juega al tenis y al golf.

Los chicos juegan al fútbol.

▶ **Comenzar** and **empezar** require the preposition **a** when they are followed by an infinitive.

Comienzan a jugar a las siete.
They begin playing at seven.

Ana **empieza** a escribir una postal.
Ana is starting to write a postcard.

▶ **Pensar** + [*infinitive*] means *to plan* or *to intend to do something*. **Pensar en** means *to think about someone* or *something*.

¿Piensan ir al gimnasio?
Are you planning to go to the gym?

¿En qué **piensas**?
What are you thinking about?

¡INTÉNTALO! Provide the present tense forms of these verbs.

cerrar (e:ie)

1. Ustedes _cierran_.
2. Tú _cierras_.
3. Nosotras _cerramos_.
4. Mi hermano _cierra_.
5. Yo _cierro_.
6. Usted _cierra_.
7. Los chicos _cierran_.
8. Ella _cierra_.

dormir (o:ue)

1. Mi abuela no _duerme_.
2. Yo no _duermo_.
3. Tú no _duermes_.
4. Mis hijos no _duermen_.
5. Usted no _duerme_.
6. Nosotros no _dormimos_.
7. Él no _duerme_.
8. Ustedes no _duermen_.

TEACHING OPTIONS

TPR Add an auditory aspect to this grammar presentation. At random, call out infinitives of regular and **e:ie** stem-changing verbs. Have students raise their hands if the verb has a stem change. Repeat for **o:ue** stem-changing verbs.
Extra Practice For additional drills of stem-changing verbs, do the **¡Inténtalo!** activity orally using infinitives other than **cerrar** and **dormir**. Keep a brisk pace.

TPR Have the class stand in a circle. As you toss a ball to a student, call out the infinitive of a stem-changing verb, followed by a pronoun. (Ex: **querer, tú**) The student should say the appropriate verb form (**quieres**), then name a different pronoun (Ex: **usted**) and throw the ball to another student. When all subject pronouns have been covered, start over with another infinitive.

Práctica

1 **Completar** Complete this conversation with the appropriate forms of the verbs.

PABLO Óscar, voy al centro ahora.

ÓSCAR ¿A qué hora (1)___piensas___ (pensar) volver? El partido de fútbol (2)___empieza___ (empezar) a las dos.

PABLO (3)___Vuelvo___ (Volver) a la una. (4)___Quiero___ (Querer) ver el partido.

ÓSCAR (5)¿___Recuerdas___ (Recordar) que (*that*) nuestro equipo es muy bueno? (6)¡___Puede___ (Poder) ganar!

PABLO No, (7)___pienso___ (pensar) que va a (8)___perder___ (perder). Los jugadores de Guadalajara son salvajes (*wild*) cuando (9)___juegan___ (jugar).

2 **Preferencias** Indicate what these people want to do, using the cues provided.

> **modelo**
> Guillermo: estudiar / pasear en bicicleta
> *Guillermo no quiere estudiar. Prefiere pasear*
> *en bicicleta.*

1. tú: trabajar / dormir
   Tú no quieres trabajar. Prefieres dormir.
▶ 2. ustedes: mirar la televisión / jugar al dominó
   Ustedes no quieren mirar la televisión. Prefieren jugar al dominó.
3. tus amigos: ir de excursión / descansar
   Tus amigos no quieren ir de excursión. Prefieren descansar.
4. tú: comer en la cafetería / ir a un restaurante
   Tú no quieres comer en la cafetería. Prefieres ir a un restaurante.
5. Elisa: ver una película / leer una revista
   Elisa no quiere ver una película. Prefiere leer una revista.
6. María y su hermana: tomar el sol / practicar el esquí acuático
   María y su hermana no quieren tomar el sol. Prefieren practicar el esquí acuático.

3 **Describir** Use a verb from the list to describe what these people are doing.

almorzar   cerrar   contar   dormir   encontrar   mostrar

1. las niñas   Las niñas duermen.   2. yo   (Yo) Cierro la ventana.   3. nosotros (Nosotros) Almorzamos.

4. tú   (Tú) Encuentras una maleta.   5. Pedro   Pedro muestra una foto.   6. Teresa   Teresa cuenta.

TEACHING OPTIONS

TPR Brainstorm gestures for stem-changing verbs. Have students act out the activity you mention. Tell them that only male students should respond to **él/ellos** and only females to **ella/ellas**. Everyone should respond to **nosotros**.
Game Arrange students in rows of five (or six if you use **vosotros**). Give the first person in each row a piece of paper and tell the class they should be silent while they are completing

this activity. Call out the infinitive of a stem-changing verb. The first person writes down the **yo** form and gives the paper to the next student, who writes the **tú** form and passes the paper on. The last person in the row holds up the paper and says, **¡Terminamos!** The first team to finish the conjugation correctly gets a point. Have students rotate positions in their row before calling out another infinitive.

---

1 **In-Class Tip**
Divide the class into pairs and give them three minutes to role-play the conversation. Then have partners switch roles. Encourage students to ad-lib as they go.

1 **Expansion**
- To challenge students, supply them with short-answer prompts based on the conversation. They should provide questions that would elicit the answers. Ex: **A las dos. (¿A qué hora empieza el partido de fútbol?) Porque quiere ver el partido. (¿Por qué vuelve Pablo a la una?)**
- Ask questions using **pensar** + [*infinitive*], **pensar en**, and **perder** (in both senses). Ex: **¿Qué piensas hacer mañana? ¿En qué piensas ahora? ¿Cuándo pierdes las cosas?**

2 **In-Class Tip** Have pairs of students take turns asking and answering questions using the cues provided. To challenge students, have them be creative and use other stem-changing verbs in their responses. For example, in the model, students could also respond: **No, no puede porque va a pasear en bicicleta** or **No, porque piensa pasear en bicicleta.**

2 **Expansion**
Have students ask each other questions of their own using the same pattern. Ex:
—**¿Quieres jugar al baloncesto?**
—**No, prefiero jugar al tenis.**
—**¿Por qué? —¡Porque no puedo encontrar la pelota de baloncesto!**

3 **Expansion** Bring in photos or magazine pictures to extend this activity. Choose images that are easy to describe with common stem-changing verbs.

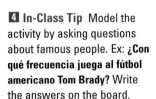
4 In-Class Tip Model the activity by asking questions about famous people. Ex: **¿Con qué frecuencia juega al fútbol americano Tom Brady?** Write the answers on the board.

4 Expansion Have pairs of students record their responses in a chart, and then tally the results on the board.

5 In-Class Tips
• Model the activity by stating two programs from the listing that you want to watch and asking the class to react.
• Remind students that the 24-hour clock is often used for schedules. Model a few of the program times. Then ask: **Quiero ver *Héroes* y mi amigo prefiere ver *Elsa y Fred*. ¿Hay un conflicto?** (No.) **¿Por qué?** (Porque *Héroes* es a las 15:00 y *Elsa y Fred* es a las 22:00.)

5 Partner Chat
👤↔👤 Available online.

5 Expansion
👤↔👤 First, guide students in identifying the shows and movies that have versions in English: **Yo soy Betty, la fea; Héroes; Hermanos y hermanas; El padrastro; 60 Minutos.** Then, have students personalize the activity by choosing their favorite programs from the list. Divide the class into pairs and have them compare and contrast their reasons for their choices.

 Communication 1.3

6 In-Class Tip
←👤→ Before assessing the writing activity, have pairs of students exchange their compositions and peer-edit their classmate's texts.

6 Expansion Have students read their composition aloud for the class.

Comunicación

4 Frecuencia Use the verbs from the list and other stem-changing verbs you know to explain which activities you do daily (**todos los días**), which you do once a month (**una vez al mes**), and which you do once a year (**una vez al año**). Answers will vary.

> **modelo**
> Yo recuerdo a mi familia todos los días. Yo pierdo uno de mis libros una vez al año...

cerrar	encontrar	poder	recordar
dormir	jugar	preferir	¿?
empezar	perder	querer	

5 En la televisión Read the television listings for Saturday. With a partner, role-play a conversation between two siblings arguing about what to watch. Answers will vary.

> **modelo**
> **Hermano:** *Podemos ver la Copa Mundial.*
> **Hermana:** *¡No, no quiero ver la Copa Mundial! Prefiero ver...*

	13:00	14:00	15:00	16:00	17:00	18:00	19:00	20:00	21:00	22:00	23:00
7	Copa Mundial (*World Cup*) de fútbol			República Deportiva		Campeonato (*Championship*) Mundial de Vóleibol: México-Argentina				Torneo de Natación	
8	Abierto (*Open*) Mexicano de Tenis: Santiago González (México) vs. Nicolás Almagro (España). Semifinales			Campeonato de baloncesto: Los Correcaminos de Tampico vs. los Santos de San Luis				Aficionados al buceo		Cozumel: Aventuras	
12	Yo soy Betty, la fea		Héroes		Hermanos y hermanas			Película: **Sin nombre**		Película: **El coronel no tiene quien le escriba**	
13	El padrastro			60 Minutos				El esquí acuático		Patinaje artístico	
17	Biografías: La artista Frida Kahlo			Música de la semana			Entrevista del día: Iker Casillas y su pasión por el fútbol			Cine de la noche: **Elsa y Fred**	

NOTA CULTURAL

Iker Casillas Fernández is a famous goalkeeper for **Real Madrid**. A native of Madrid, he is among the best goalkeepers of his generation.

Síntesis

6 Deportes Write a paragraph about your favorite sport. Mention why you like it, and whether you practice it or watch it on TV. Include some facts you know about the sport. Use at least three stem-changing verbs. Answers will vary.

> **modelo**
> Mi deporte favorito es el béisbol porque es un deporte interesante.
> Esta noche pienso ver el partido de los Padres en la televisión.
> Empieza a las siete...

TEACHING OPTIONS

Small Groups ←👤→ Have students choose their favorite pastime and work in small groups with other students who have chosen that same activity. Have each group write six sentences about the activity, using a different stem-changing verb in each.

Pairs Ask students to write incomplete dehydrated sentences (only subjects and infinitives) about people and groups at the school. Ex: **el equipo de béisbol / perder / ¿?** Then have them exchange papers with a classmate, who will form a complete sentence by conjugating the verb and inventing an appropriate ending. Ask volunteers to write sentences on the board.

(4.3) Stem-changing verbs: e→i

ANTE TODO   You've already seen that many verbs in Spanish change their stem vowel when conjugated. There is a third kind of stem-vowel change in some verbs, such as **pedir** (*to ask for; to request*). In these verbs, the stressed vowel in the stem changes from **e** to **i**, as shown in the diagram.

INFINITIVE	VERB STEM	STEM CHANGE	CONJUGATED FORM
pedir ▶	p**e**d- ▶	p**i**d- ▶	p**i**do

▶ As with other stem-changing verbs you have learned, there is no stem change in the **nosotros/as** or **vosotros/as** forms in the present tense.

The verb **pedir** (e:i) (*to ask for; to request*)

Singular forms		Plural forms	
yo	p**i**do	nosotros/as	pedimos
tú	p**i**des	vosotros/as	pedís
Ud./él/ella	p**i**de	Uds./ellos/ellas	p**i**den

▶ To help you identify verbs with the **e:i** stem change, they will appear as follows throughout the text:

> **pedir (e:i)**

▶ These are the most common **e:i** stem-changing verbs:

conseguir	**decir**	**repetir**	**seguir**
to get; to obtain	*to say; to tell*	*to repeat*	*to follow; to continue; to keep (doing something)*

Pido favores cuando es necesario.
I ask for favors when it's necessary.

Javier **dice** la verdad.
Javier is telling the truth.

Sigue con su tarea.
He continues with his homework.

Consiguen ver buenas películas.
They get to see good movies.

▶ **¡Atención!** The verb **decir** is irregular in its **yo** form: **yo digo**.

▶ The **yo** forms of **seguir** and **conseguir** have a spelling change in addition to the stem change **e:i**.

Sigo su plan.
I'm following their plan.

Consigo novelas en la librería.
I get novels at the bookstore.

¡INTÉNTALO!   Provide the correct forms of the verbs.

repetir (e:i)	**decir (e:i)**	**seguir (e:i)**
1. Arturo y Eva _repiten_.	1. Yo _digo_.	1. Yo _sigo_.
2. Yo _repito_.	2. Él _dice_.	2. Nosotros _seguimos_.
3. Nosotros _repetimos_.	3. Tú _dices_.	3. Tú _sigues_.
4. Julia _repite_.	4. Usted _dice_.	4. Los chicos _siguen_.
5. Sofía y yo _repetimos_.	5. Ellas _dicen_.	5. Usted _sigue_.

TEACHING OPTIONS

Game Divide the class into two teams. Name an infinitive and a subject pronoun (Ex: **decir / yo**). Have the first member of team A give the appropriate conjugated form of the verb. If the team member answers correctly, team A gets one point. If not, give the first member of team B the same example. If he or she does not know the answer, give the correct verb form and move on. The team with the most points at the end wins.

Extra Practice ←🖐→ Add a visual aspect to this grammar presentation. Bring in magazine pictures or photos of parks and city centers where people are doing fun activities. In small groups, have students describe the photos using as many stem-changing verbs from **Estructura 4.2** and **4.3** as they can. Give points to the groups who use the most stem-changing verbs.

Section Goal

In **Estructura 4.3**, students will learn the present tense of stem-changing verbs: **e → i**.

Communication 1.1
Comparisons 4.1

Teacher Resources
Read the front matter for suggestions on how to incorporate all the program's components. See pages 115A–115B for a detailed listing of Teacher Resources online.

In-Class Tips
• Take a survey of students' habits. Ask questions like: **¿Quiénes piden limonada?** Make a chart on the board. Then form sentences based on the chart.
• Ask volunteers to answer questions using **conseguir, decir, pedir, repetir,** and **seguir**.
• Reiterate that the personal endings for the present tense of all the verbs listed are the same as those for the present tense of regular –**ir** verbs.
• Point out the spelling changes in the **yo** forms of **seguir** and **conseguir**.
• Prepare dehydrated sentences and write them on the board one at a time. Ex: **1. tú / pedir / café 2. usted / repetir / la pregunta 3. nosotros / decir / la verdad** Have students form complete sentences based on the cues.
• For additional drills with stem-changing verbs, do the **¡Inténtalo!** activity orally using other infinitives, such as **conseguir, impedir, pedir,** and **servir**. Keep a brisk pace.

Note: Students will learn more about **decir** with indirect object pronouns in **Estructura 6.2**.

Práctica

1 **Completar** Complete these sentences with the correct form of the verb provided.

1. Cuando mi familia pasea por la ciudad, mi madre siempre (*always*) va a un café y _____pide_____ (pedir) una soda.
2. Pero mi padre _____dice_____ (decir) que perdemos mucho tiempo. Tiene prisa por llegar al Bosque de Chapultepec.
3. Mi padre tiene suerte, porque él siempre _____consigue_____ (conseguir) lo que (*that which*) desea.
4. Cuando llegamos al parque, mis hermanos y yo _____seguimos_____ (seguir) conversando (*talking*) con nuestros padres.
5. Mis padres siempre _____repiten_____ (repetir) la misma cosa: "Nosotros tomamos el sol aquí sin ustedes".
6. Yo siempre _____pido_____ (pedir) permiso para volver a casa un poco más tarde porque me gusta mucho el parque.

NOTA CULTURAL

A popular weekend destination for residents and tourists, **el Bosque de Chapultepec** is a beautiful park located in Mexico City. It occupies over 1.5 square miles and includes lakes, wooded areas, several museums, and a botanical garden. You may recognize this park from **Fotonovela, Lección 2.**

2 **Combinar** Combine words from the two columns to create sentences about yourself and people you know. Answers will vary.

A	B
yo	(no) pedir muchos favores
mi madre	nunca (*never*) pedir perdón
mi mejor (*best*) amigo/a	nunca seguir las instrucciones
mi familia	siempre seguir las instrucciones
mis amigos/as	conseguir libros en Internet
mis amigos/as y yo	repetir el vocabulario
mis padres	poder hablar dos lenguas
mi hermano/a	dormir hasta el mediodía
mi profesor(a) de español	siempre perder sus libros

3 **¿Sí o no?** Indicate whether you do the following. Answers will vary.

> **modelo**
> pedir consejos con frecuencia
> *Pido consejos con frecuencia./No pido consejos con frecuencia.*

1. conseguir libros en la librería
2. almorzar en casa
3. perder cosas con frecuencia
4. pedir favores
5. seguir las instrucciones de un manual
6. volver tarde a casa
7. dormir mucho
8. jugar al tenis

---

1 Expansion
← 👥 → Have students use **conseguir, decir, pedir, repetir,** and **seguir** to write sentences about their own family members. Then have them exchange papers with a partner for peer editing.

Nota cultural
→ 👥 ← Have students read about **El Bosque de Chapultepec** in Spanish in either the library or on the Internet and bring a photo of the park to class. Ask them to share one new fact they learned about the park.

2 In-Class Tips
- Before beginning the activity, point out that not all verbs in column B have an **e:i** stem change. Have students identify those that do not (**poder, dormir, perder**).
- In pairs, have students decide which activities in column B are characteristic of a good student. Ex: **Un buen estudiante repite el vocabulario.**

2 Expansion In pairs, have students read their sentences aloud. Their partner must decide if they are true or false.

3 Expansion Have students create a survey using the list of activities provided or new ones. Let them walk around the class asking their classmates if they are going to do those activities that day. Tell them to be prepared to report their findings to the class.

Model the activity with volunteers:
—**¿Vas a leer el periódico hoy?**
—**Sí, voy a leer el periódico hoy.**
—**No, no voy a leer el periódico hoy.**

TEACHING OPTIONS

Pairs Ask students to write four simple statements using **e:i** verbs. Then have them read their sentences to a partner, who will guess where the situation takes place. Ex: **Consigo libros para las clases. (Estás en la biblioteca.)** Then reverse the activity, allowing them to answer with verbs from **Estructura 4.2.**

Small Groups Explain to students that movie titles for English-language films are frequently not directly translated into Spanish and that titles may vary from country to country. Bring in a list of movie titles in Spanish. Ex: *La guerra de las galaxias* (*Star Wars*); *Lo que el viento se llevó* (*Gone with the Wind*). In groups, have students guess the movies based on the Spanish titles. Then ask them to state which movies they'd prefer to watch.

Comunicación

4 **Una entrevista** Read this interview with actress Andrea de la Palma. Then indicate whether the following conclusions are **lógico** or **ilógico**, based on what you read.

MANUEL   Andrea, ¿qué tipo de persona eres?

ANDREA   Creo que soy una persona introvertida. No les pido demasiados favores a mis amigos. En general, pienso que soy una buena amiga; siempre digo la verdad.

MANUEL   ¿Qué pides en un restaurante?

ANDREA   Siempre (*Always*) pido comida (*food*) vegetariana. Hay un restaurante español muy bueno. Siempre pido tortilla española (*potato omelet*) y ¡siempre repito!

MANUEL   ¿Qué deportes sigues?

ANDREA   Sigo el béisbol, pero no consigo entender bien los partidos.

MANUEL   Sí, ¡pueden ser muy complicados! Andrea, muchas gracias por la entrevista y por ser tan buena actriz. Siempre veo tus películas.

ANDREA   El gusto es mío. ¡Muchas gracias!

	Lógico	Ilógico
1. Andrea es honesta.	⊘	○
2. Andrea siempre come en casa.	○	⊘
3. Andrea pide pollo (*chicken*) en los restaurantes.	○	⊘
4. A Manuel le gustan las películas.	⊘	○
5. Manuel sigue la carrera de Andrea.	⊘	○

5 **Las películas** Answer your partner's questions. Answers will vary.

1. ¿Prefieres las películas románticas, las películas de acción o las películas de terror? ¿Por qué?

2. ¿Dónde consigues información sobre (*about*) cine y televisión?

3. ¿Dónde consigues las entradas (*tickets*) para el cine?

4. Para decidir qué películas vas a ver, ¿sigues las recomendaciones de los críticos de cine? ¿Qué dicen los críticos en general?

5. ¿Qué cines de tu comunidad muestran las mejores (*best*) películas?

6. ¿Vas a ver una película esta semana? ¿A qué hora empieza la película?

6 **El cine** With a partner, discuss good and bad movies you have seen. Use stem-changing verbs in your conversation. Answers will vary.

> **modelo**
>
> **Estudiante 1:** *Pienso que* Gravedad *es una película muy buena. Los efectos especiales son excelentes.*
>
> **Estudiante 2:** *Sí. Digo que Sandra Bullock es la mejor actriz...*

Síntesis

7 **Mi película favorita** Write a paragraph about your favorite movie. Use stem-changing verbs in your description. Answers will vary.

TEACHING OPTIONS

Small Groups 👥↔👥 Select a few scenes from different Spanish-language films or plays that contain stem-changing verbs. White out the verbs and have students work in small groups to complete each dialogue. Ask them to try to identify the genre and, if possible, the title of each work. Then have volunteers act out each scene for the class, ad-libbing as appropriate.

Heritage Speakers 👥↔👥 Ask heritage speakers to start a discussion with the rest of the class about popular Spanish-language films. Brainstorm with the class a list of questions about the films, using stem-changing verbs from **Estructura 4.2** and **4.3**. Have students ask the heritage speakers the questions. Ex: **¿Dónde podemos conseguir la película aquí? ¿Dices que es tu película favorita? ¿Prefieres las películas en inglés?**

---

4 **Expansion** 👥↔👥 Have students reenact the interview in pairs using their own personal information.

5 **In-Class Tip** Have students report to the class what their partner said. After the presentation, encourage them to ask each other questions.

5 **Virtual Chat** 👥↔👥 Available online.

5 **Expansion** To challenge students, write some key movie-related words on the board, such as **actor, actriz, argumento,** and **efectos especiales**. Explain how to use **mejor** and **peor** as adjectives. Have student pairs say which movies this year they think should win Oscars. Model by telling them: **Pienso que_____ es la mejor película del año. Debe ganar porque...** Then ask students to nominate the year's worst. Have them share their opinions with the class.

6 **Expansion** 👥↔👥 In pairs, have students write a dramatic dialogue about their favorite movies using stem-changing verbs. Have volunteers role-play their dialogues for the class.

6 **Partner Chat** 👥↔👥 Available online.

 Communication 1.3

7 **Expansion** ↔👥↔ Ask students to include a drawing or a poster with their text. Transform the classroom into a gallery to exhibit students' work where they can see their classmates' drawings and read the paragraphs.

4.4 Verbs with irregular yo forms

ANTE TODO In Spanish, several verbs have irregular **yo** forms in the present tense. You have already seen three verbs with the -**go** ending in the **yo** form: **decir → digo, tener → tengo**, and **venir → vengo**.

▶ Here are some common expressions with **decir**.

decir la verdad *to tell the truth*	**decir mentiras** *to tell lies*
decir que *to say that*	**decir la respuesta** *to say the answer*

▶ The verb **hacer** is often used to ask questions about what someone does. Note that when answering, **hacer** is frequently replaced with another, more specific action verb.

Verbs with irregular yo forms

	hacer *(to do; to make)*	**poner** *(to put; to place)*	**salir** *(to leave)*	**suponer** *(to suppose)*	**traer** *(to bring)*
SINGULAR FORMS	**hago** haces hace	**pongo** pones pone	**salgo** sales sale	**supongo** supones supone	**traigo** traes trae
PLURAL FORMS	hacemos hacéis hacen	ponemos ponéis ponen	salimos salís salen	suponemos suponéis suponen	traemos traéis traen

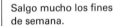
Salgo mucho los fines de semana.

Yo no salgo, yo hago la tarea y veo películas en la televisión.

▶ **Poner** can also mean to *turn on* a household appliance.

Carlos **pone** la radio. *Carlos turns on the radio.*	María **pone** la televisión. *María turns on the television.*

▶ **Salir de** is used to indicate that someone is leaving a particular place.

Hoy **salgo del** hospital. *Today I leave the hospital.*	**Sale de** la clase a las cuatro. *He leaves class at four.*

▶ **Salir para** is used to indicate someone's destination.

Mañana **salgo para** México.   Hoy **salen para** España.
Tomorrow I leave for Mexico.   *Today they leave for Spain.*

▶ **Salir con** means *to leave with someone* or *something*, or *to date someone*.

Alberto **sale con** su mochila.   Margarita **sale con** Guillermo.
Alberto is leaving with his backpack.   *Margarita is going out with Guillermo.*

The verbs **ver** and **oír**

▶ The verb **ver** (*to see*) has an irregular **yo** form. The other forms of **ver** are regular.

The verb ver (*to see*)

Singular forms		Plural forms	
yo	**veo**	nosotros/as	vemos
tú	ves	vosotros/as	veis
Ud./él/ella	ve	Uds./ellos/ellas	ven

▶ The verb **oír** (*to hear*) has an irregular **yo** form and the spelling change **i:y** in the **tú**, **usted/él/ella**, and **ustedes/ellos/ellas** forms. The **nosotros/as** and **vosotros/as** forms have an accent mark.

The verb oír (*to hear*)

Singular forms		Plural forms	
yo	**oigo**	nosotros/as	oímos
tú	oyes	vosotros/as	oís
Ud./él/ella	oye	Uds./ellos/ellas	oyen

▶ While most commonly translated as *to hear*, **oír** is also used in contexts where the verb *to listen* would be used in English.

Oigo a unas personas en la otra sala.   ¿**Oyes** la radio por la mañana?
I hear some people in the other room.   *Do you listen to the radio in the morning?*

¡INTÉNTALO!   Provide the appropriate forms of these verbs.

1. salir   Isabel ___sale___.   Nosotros ___salimos___.   Yo ___salgo___.
2. ver   Yo ___veo___.   Uds. ___ven___.   Tú ___ves___.
3. poner   Rita y yo ___ponemos___.   Yo ___pongo___.   Los niños ___ponen___.
4. hacer   Yo ___hago___.   Tú ___haces___.   Ud. ___hace___.
5. oír   Él ___oye___.   Nosotros ___oímos___.   Yo ___oigo___.
6. traer   Ellas ___traen___.   Yo ___traigo___.   Tú ___traes___.
7. suponer   Yo ___supongo___.   Mi amigo ___supone___.   Nosotras ___suponemos___.

In-Class Tips

- Point out that **oír** is irregular in all forms. Write a model sentence on the board. Ex: **Ustedes oyen el programa de radio todos los viernes.** Then change the subject, and have students give the new sentence. Ex: **tú (Tú oyes el programa de radio todos los viernes.)**
- Call out different forms of the verbs in **Estructura 4.4** and have volunteers say the infinitive. Ex: **oyen (oír).** Keep a brisk pace.
- Do a chain drill. Start by writing ¿**Qué haces los sábados?** on the board. Model an appropriate answer, such as **Salgo con mis amigos.** Ask one student to respond (Ex: **Veo una película.**). The next student you call on should repeat what the first said and add on (Ex: **Cindy ve una película y yo salgo con...**). Continue until the chain becomes too long; then start with a new question. Keep a brisk pace.
- Write these phrases on the board: **ver la tele, traer un sándwich a la escuela, salir con amigos,** and **hacer yoga.** Model the question and possible answers for each phrase. Then elicit follow-up questions (Ex: ¿**Dónde ves la tele?**). Have student pairs take turns asking and answering the questions. They should be prepared to report to the class about their partners' habits.
- Explain to students that the **i → y** spelling change strengthens the **i** sound between vowels, which clarifies to the ear that the verb is **oír**.
- Explain the difference between **escuchar** (*to listen*) and **oír** (*to hear*). Ex: **Escucho la radio. No oigo el perro.**

TEACHING OPTIONS

Extra Practice Add an auditory aspect to this grammar presentation. Call out subject pronouns and titles of songs or movies (Ex: **ustedes,** *Gravedad*). Have students respond with a complete sentence, using **ver** or **oír**. (Ex: **Ustedes ven** *Gravedad*.)

Pairs 🔺↔🔺 Have pairs create questions using the vocabulary of the chapter to ask each other about their habits. Ex: ¿**Sales a comer a restaurantes con tus padres? ¿Ves la televisión en español? ¿Supones que una clase de matemáticas es muy difícil?** Have students record their partner's answers and be prepared to share the information with the class.

Práctica

1 **Completar** Complete this conversation with the appropriate forms of the verbs.

ERNESTO David, ¿qué (1)___haces___ (hacer) hoy?
DAVID Ahora estudio biología, pero esta noche (2)___salgo___ (salir) con Luisa. Vamos al cine. Los críticos (3)___dicen___ (decir) que la nueva (*new*) película de Almodóvar es buena.
ERNESTO ¿Y Diana? ¿Qué (4)___hace___ (hacer) ella?
DAVID (5)___Sale___ (Salir) a comer con sus padres.
ERNESTO ¿Qué (6)___hacen___ (hacer) Andrés y Javier?
DAVID Tienen que (7)___hacer___ (hacer) las maletas. (8)___Salen___ (Salir) para Monterrey mañana.
ERNESTO Pues, ¿qué (9)___hago___ (hacer) yo?
DAVID Yo (10)___supongo___ (suponer) que puedes estudiar o (11)___ver___ (ver) la televisión.
ERNESTO No quiero estudiar. Mejor (12)___pongo___ (poner) la televisión. Mi programa favorito empieza en unos minutos.

2 **Oraciones** Form sentences using the cues provided and verbs from **Estructura 4.4**.

> **modelo**
> tú / _____ / cosas / en / su lugar / antes de (*before*) / salir
> *Tú pones las cosas en su lugar antes de salir.*

1. mis amigos / _____ / conmigo / centro Mis amigos salen conmigo al centro.
2. tú / _____ / mentiras / pero / yo _____ / verdad Tú dices mentiras, pero yo digo la verdad.
3. Alberto / _____ / música del café Pasatiempos Alberto oye la música del café Pasatiempos.
4. yo / no / _____ / muchas películas Yo no veo muchas películas.
5. domingo / nosotros / _____ / mucha / tarea El domingo nosotros hacemos mucha tarea.
6. si / yo _____ / que / yo querer / ir / cine / mis amigos / ir / también Si yo digo que quiero ir al cine, mis amigos van también.

3 **Describir** Use the verbs from **Estructura 4.4** to describe what these people are doing.

1. Fernán Fernán pone la mochila en el escritorio/trae una mochila.
2. los aficionados Los aficionados salen del estadio/para sus casas.
3. yo Yo traigo/salgo con una cámara.

4. nosotros Nosotros vemos el monumento.
5. la señora Vargas La señora Vargas no oye bien.
6. el estudiante El estudiante hace su tarea.

Comunicación

4 **El día de Francisco** Listen to Francisco's description of his day. Then indicate whether the following conclusions are **lógico** or **ilógico**, based on what you heard.

	Lógico	Ilógico
1. Francisco duerme hasta (*until*) el mediodía.	○	⦿
2. A Francisco no le gustan las matemáticas.	○	⦿
3. Francisco almuerza en casa.	○	⦿
4. A Francisco le gustan los deportes.	⦿	○
5. Francisco sale para la casa antes de las cinco.	⦿	○

5 **Tu rutina** Answer your partner's questions. Answers will vary.

1. ¿Siempre (*Always*) pones tus cosas en su lugar?
2. ¿Qué prefieres hacer, oír la radio o ver la televisión?
3. ¿Oyes música cuando estudias?
4. ¿Ves películas en casa o prefieres ir al cine?
5. ¿Haces mucha tarea los fines de semana?
6. ¿Sales con tus amigos los fines de semana? ¿A qué hora? ¿Qué hacen?

6 **Un día típico** Write a short paragraph about what you do on a typical day. Use at least six of the verbs you have learned in this lesson. Answers will vary.

> **modelo**
> Hola, me llamo Julia y vivo en Houston. Por la mañana, yo...

Síntesis

7 **Situación** Imagine that you are speaking with a member of your family. With a partner, prepare a conversation using these cues. Answers will vary.

Estudiante 1	**Estudiante 2**
Ask your partner what he or she is doing.	→ Tell your partner that you are watching TV.
Say what you suppose he or she is watching.	→ Say that you like the show _____. Ask if he or she wants to watch.
Say no, because you are going out with friends, and tell where you are going.	→ Say you think it's a good idea, and ask what your partner and his or her friends are doing there.
Say what you are going to do, and ask your partner whether he or she wants to come along.	→ Say no and tell your partner what you prefer to do.

TEACHING OPTIONS

Pairs 👤↔👤 Have pairs of students role-play an awful first date. Students should write their script first, then present it to the class. Encourage students to use descriptive adjectives as well as the new verbs learned in **Estructura 4.4**.
Heritage Speakers ↔👤↔ Ask heritage speakers to talk about a social custom in their cultural community. Remind them to use familiar vocabulary and simple sentences.

Charades 👤↔👤 Divide the class into small groups and have each group choose one student act out everyday actions. (You will need to provide cards or slips of paper with the actions.) The rest of the group will have a limited amount of time to guess the activities.

4 **In-Class Tip** Have students listen once and ask them to list the activities they hear. Let them compare their answers with a classmate and then check their lists by listening again.

4 **Script** *See the script for this activity on Interleaf page 115B.*

5 **Virtual Chat**
👤↔👤 Available online.

5 **Expansion**
👤↔👤 Ask volunteers to call out some of their answers. The class should speculate about the reason behind each answer and offer more information. Have the volunteer confirm or deny the speculation.
Ex: —**Traigo mi tarea a clase.**
—**Eres un(a) buen(a) estudiante.**
—**Sí, soy un(a) buen(a) estudiante porque hago mi tarea.**

6 **In-Class Tip** Before assigning the activity, provide an example of your own routine as a teacher, asking the students to help you write it.

6 **Expansion** Have students write reading comprehension questions about their paragraph. Have pairs of students read their routines to each other and then ask their questions.

 Communication 1.1

7 **Possible Conversation**
E1: ¿Qué haces?
E2: Veo la tele.
E1: Supongo que ves *Los Simpson*.
E2: Sí. Me gusta el programa. ¿Quieres ver la tele conmigo?
E1: No puedo. Salgo con mis amigos a la plaza.
E2: Buena idea. ¿Qué hacen en la plaza?
E1: Vamos a escuchar música y a pasear. ¿Quieres venir?
E2: No. Prefiero descansar.

7 **Partner Chat**
👤↔👤 Available online.

Recapitulación

SUBJECT Javier → *CONJUGATED FORM* empiezo — **Main clause**

Dudan

Review the grammar concepts you have learned in this lesson by completing these activities.

1 Completar
Complete the chart with the correct verb forms. **30 pts.**

Infinitive	yo	nosotros/as	ellos/as
volver	**vuelvo**	volvemos	vuelven
comenzar	comienzo	**comenzamos**	comienzan
hacer	hago	**hacemos**	**hacen**
ir	voy	vamos	van
jugar	**juego**	jugamos	juegan
repetir	repito	repetimos	**repiten**

2 Un día típico
Complete the paragraph with the appropriate forms of the verbs in the word list. Not all verbs will be used. Some may be used more than once. **30 pts.**

almorzar	ir	salir
cerrar	jugar	seguir
empezar	mostrar	ver
hacer	querer	volver

¡Hola! Me llamo Cecilia y vivo en Puerto Vallarta, México. ¿Cómo es un día típico en mi vida (*life*)? Por la mañana bebo café con mis padres y juntos (*together*) (1) ___vemos___ las noticias (*news*) en la televisión. A las siete y media, (yo) (2) ___salgo___ de mi casa y tomo el autobús. Me gusta llegar temprano (*early*) a la escuela porque siempre (*always*) (3) ___veo___ a mis amigos en la cafetería. Tomamos jugo y planeamos lo que (4) ___queremos___ hacer cada (*each*) día. A las ocho y cuarto, mi amiga Sandra y yo (5) ___vamos___ al laboratorio de lenguas. La clase de francés (6) ___empieza___ a las ocho y media. ¡Es mi clase favorita! A las doce y media (yo) (7) ___almuerzo___ en la cafetería con mis amigos. Después (*Afterwards*), yo (8) ___sigo___ con mis clases. Por las tardes, mis amigos (9) ___vuelven___ a sus casas, pero yo (10) ___juego___ al vóleibol con mi amigo Tomás.

4.1 Present tense of ir *p. 126*

yo	voy	nos.	vamos
tú	vas	vos.	vais
él	va	ellas	van

► ir a + [*infinitive*] = to be going + [*infinitive*]
► a + el = al
► vamos a + [*infinitive*] = let's (do something)

4.2 Stem-changing verbs e:ie, o:ue, u:ue *pp. 129–130*

	empezar	volver	jugar
yo	empiezo	vuelvo	juego
tú	empiezas	vuelves	juegas
él	empieza	vuelve	juega
nos.	empezamos	volvemos	jugamos
vos.	empezáis	volvéis	jugáis
ellas	empiezan	vuelven	juegan

► Other e:ie verbs: cerrar, comenzar, entender, pensar, perder, preferir, querer
► Other o:ue verbs: almorzar, contar, dormir, encontrar, mostrar, poder, recordar

4.3 Stem-changing verbs e:i *p. 133*

	pedir		
yo	pido	nos.	pedimos
tú	pides	vos.	pedís
él	pide	ellas	piden

► Other e:i verbs: conseguir, decir, repetir, seguir

4.4 Verbs with irregular yo forms *pp. 136–137*

hacer	poner	salir	suponer	traer
hago	pongo	salgo	supongo	traigo

► ver: veo, ves, ve, vemos, veis, ven
► oír: oigo, oyes, oye, oímos, oís, oyen

Section Goal

In **Recapitulación**, students will review the grammar concepts from this lesson.

1 In-Class Tips
• To simplify, before students begin the activity, have them identify the stem change (if any) in each row.
• Complete this activity orally as a class.

1 Expansion
Ask students to provide the remaining forms of the verbs.

2 In-Class Tip
To challenge students, ask them to provide alternative verbs for the blanks. Ex: **1. vemos/miramos** Then ask: Why can't **ir** be used for item 4? (needs **a**)

2 Expansion
• Ask questions about **Cecilia's** typical day. Have students answer with complete sentences. **¿Qué hace Cecilia a las siete y media? ¿Por qué le gusta llegar temprano?**
• Write on the board the verb phrases about **Cecilia's** day. (Ex: **ver la televisión por la mañana, almorzar a las 12:30, jugar al vóleibol por la tarde**) Brainstorm a few more entries. (Ex: **hacer la tarea por la noche**) Ask students to make a two-column chart, labeled **yo** and **compañero/a**. They should initial each activity they perform. Then have them interview a partner and report back to the class.

Pairs Pair weaker students with more advanced students. Give each pair a numbered list of the target verbs from **Resumen gramatical** and a small plastic bag containing subject pronouns written on strips of paper. Model the first verb for students by drawing out a subject pronoun at random and conjugating the verb on the board. Ask: **¿Correcto o incorrecto?** Have students take turns and correct each other's work. Keep a brisk pace.

Extra Practice Introduce the word **nunca** and have students write a short description about things they never do. Have them use as many target verbs from this lesson as possible. Ex: **Nunca veo películas románticas. Nunca pongo la televisión cuando estudio…** Collect the descriptions, shuffle them, and read them aloud. Have the class guess the person that is being described.

3 **Oraciones** Arrange the cues provided in the correct order to form complete sentences. Make all necessary changes. **36 pts.**

1. tarea / los / hacer / sábados / nosotros / la
   Los sábados nosotros hacemos la tarea./Nosotros hacemos la tarea los sábados.

2. en / pizza / Andrés / una / restaurante / el / pedir
   Andrés pide una pizza en el restaurante.

3. a / ? / museo / ir / ¿ / el / (tú)
   ¿(Tú) Vas al museo?

4. de / oír / amigos / bien / los / no / Elena
   Los amigos de Elena no oyen bien./ No oímos bien a los amigos de Elena.

5. libros / traer / yo / clase / mis / a
   Yo traigo mis libros a clase.

6. película / ver / en / Jorge y Carlos / pensar / cine / una / el
   Jorge y Carlos piensan ver una película en el cine.

7. unos / escribir / Mariana / electrónicos / querer / mensajes
   Mariana quiere escribir unos mensajes electrónicos.

8. centro / conseguir / en / nosotros / el / videojuegos
   Nosotros conseguimos videojuegos en el centro.

9. tú / favores / el / pedir / tiempo / todo
   Tú pides favores todo el tiempo.

4 **Rima** Complete the rhyme with the appropriate forms of the correct verbs from the list. **4 pts.**

contar	poder
oír	suponer

❝Si no ___puedes___ dormir
y el sueño deseas,
lo vas a conseguir
si ___cuentas___ ovejas°.**❞**

ovejas *sheep*

---

3 In-Class Tip To simplify, provide the first word for each sentence.

3 Expansion Give students these sentences as items 8–11: **8. la / ? / ustedes / cerrar / ventana / ¿ / poder (¿Pueden ustedes cerrar la ventana?) 9. cine / del / tú / las / salir / once / a (Tú sales del cine a las once.) 10. el / conmigo / a / en / ellos / tenis / el / jugar / parque (Ellos juegan al tenis conmigo en el parque.) 11. que / partido / mañana / un / decir / hay / Javier (Javier dice que hay un partido mañana.)**

4 In-Class Tip Point out the inverted word order in line 2 of the rhyme and ask students what the phrase would be in everyday Spanish (**y deseas el sueño**).

4 Expansion Come up with similar rhymes and have students complete them. Ex: **Si no ____ descansar y diversión deseas, lo vas a encontrar si ____ con ellas. (quieres, juegas)**

TEACHING OPTIONS

Game ▲↔▲ Make a *Bingo* card of places at school or around town, such as libraries, cafeterias, movie theaters, and cafés. Give each student a card and model possible questions (Ex: for a cafetería, **¿Almuerzas en _____?/¿Dónde almuerzas?**). Encourage them to circulate around the room, asking only one question per person; if they get an affirmative answer, they should write that person's name in the square. The first student

to complete a horizontal, vertical, or diagonal row and yell **¡Bingo!** is the winner.

Heritage Speakers ↔▲↔ Ask heritage speakers if counting sheep is common advice for sleeplessness in their families. Have them describe other insomnia remedies they have heard of or practiced.

Section Goals

In **Lectura**, students will:
• learn the strategy of predicting content by surveying the graphic elements in reading matter
• read a magazine article containing graphs and charts

Communication 1.1, 1.2, 1.3
Cultures 2.1, 2.2
Connections 3.1, 3.2
Comparisons 4.2

 Pre-AP®

Interpretive Reading:
Estrategia Tell students that they can infer a great deal of information about the content of an article by surveying its graphic elements. They should look for such things as: headlines or headings, bylines, photos, photo captions, and graphs and tables.

Examinar el texto Give students two minutes to write down their ideas.

Contestar Ask students how accurate their predictions were from **Examinar el texto**.

Evaluación y predicción Write two headings on the board: **Entre los jóvenes del mundo hispano** and **Entre los jóvenes de nuestra escuela**. Ask for a show of hands to respond to your questions about the ranking of each sporting event. Tally the responses as you proceed. Ask: **¿Quiénes creen que entre los jóvenes hispanos la Copa Mundial de Fútbol es el evento más popular? ¿Quiénes creen que los Juegos Olímpicos son el evento más popular?** Then ask: **Entre los jóvenes de nuestra escuela, ¿quiénes de ustedes creen que la Copa Mundial de Fútbol es el evento más popular?** Briefly discuss the differences indicated by student responses.

Lectura
Antes de leer

Estrategia
Predicting content from visuals

When you are reading in Spanish, be sure to look for visual clues that will orient you as to the content and purpose of what you are reading. Photos and illustrations, for example, will often give you a good idea of the main points that the reading covers. You may also encounter very helpful visuals that are used to summarize large amounts of data in a way that is easy to comprehend; these include bar graphs, pie charts, flow charts, lists of percentages, and other sorts of diagrams.

Examinar el texto
Take a quick look at the visual elements of the magazine article in order to generate a list of ideas about its content.

Contestar
Read the list of ideas you wrote in **Examinar el texto**, and look again at the visual elements of the magazine article. Then answer these questions:

1. Who is the woman in the photo, and what is her role? María Úrsula Echevarría is the author of this article.
2. What is the article about? The article is about sports in the Hispanic world.
3. What is the subject of the pie chart? The most popular sports among college students.
4. What is the subject of the bar graph? Hispanic countries in world soccer championships.

por María Úrsula Echevarría

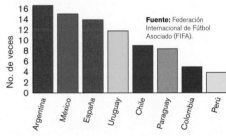

El fútbol es el deporte más popular en el mundo° hispano, según° una encuesta° reciente realizada entre estudiantes de secundaria. Mucha gente practica este deporte y tiene un equipo de fútbol favorito. Cada cuatro años se realiza la Copa Mundial°. Argentina y Uruguay han ganado° este campeonato° más de una vez°. Los aficionados siguen los partidos de fútbol en casa por tele y en muchos otros lugares como bares, restaurantes, estadios y clubes deportivos. Los jóvenes juegan al fútbol con sus amigos en parques y gimnasios.

Países hispanos en campeonatos mundiales de fútbol (1930–2014)

(Bar graph: No. de veces vs. Argentina, México, España, Uruguay, Chile, Paraguay, Colombia, Perú; values 16 to 0 scale)

Fuente: Federación Internacional de Fútbol Asociado (FIFA).

Pero, por supuesto°, en los países de habla hispana también hay otros deportes populares. ¿Qué deporte sigue al fútbol en estos países? Bueno, ¡depende del país y de otros factores!

Después de leer
Evaluación y predicción

Which of the following sporting events would be most popular among the high school students surveyed? Rate them from one (most popular) to five (least popular). Which would be the most popular at your school?
Answers will vary.

_____ 1. la Copa Mundial de Fútbol
_____ 2. los Juegos Olímpicos
_____ 3. el Campeonato de Wimbledon
_____ 4. la Serie Mundial de Béisbol
_____ 5. el Tour de Francia

TEACHING OPTIONS

Variación léxica Remind students that the term **fútbol** in the Hispanic world refers to soccer, and that in the English-speaking world outside of the United States and Canada, soccer is called *football*. The game that English speakers call *football* is **fútbol americano** in the Spanish-speaking world.

Extra Practice Ask questions that require students to refer to the article. Model the use of the definite article with percentages. **¿Qué porcentaje prefiere el fútbol? (el 69 por ciento) ¿Qué porcentaje prefiere el vóleibol? (el 2 por ciento)**

No sólo el fútbol

En Colombia, el béisbol también es muy popular después del fútbol, aunque° esto varía según la región del país. En la costa del norte de Colombia, el béisbol es una pasión. Y el ciclismo también es un deporte que los colombianos siguen con mucho interés.

Donde el béisbol es más popular

En los países del Caribe, el béisbol es el deporte predominante. Éste es el caso en Puerto Rico, Cuba y la República Dominicana. Los niños empiezan a jugar cuando son muy pequeños. En Puerto Rico y la República Dominicana, la gente también quiere participar en otros deportes, como el baloncesto, o ver los partidos en la tele. Y para los espectadores aficionados del Caribe, el boxeo es número dos.

Deportes más populares

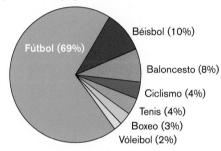

- Béisbol (10%)
- Baloncesto (8%)
- Ciclismo (4%)
- Tenis (4%)
- Boxeo (3%)
- Vóleibol (2%)
- Fútbol (69%)

Donde el fútbol es más popular

En México, el béisbol es el segundo° deporte más popular después° del fútbol. Pero en Argentina, después del fútbol, el rugby tiene mucha importancia. En Perú a la gente le gusta mucho ver partidos de vóleibol. ¿Y en España? Muchas personas prefieren el baloncesto, el tenis y el ciclismo.

mundo *world* según *according to* encuesta *survey* se realiza la Copa Mundial *the World Cup is held* han ganado *have won* campeonato *championship* más de una vez *more than once* por supuesto *of course* segundo *second* después *after* aunque *although*

¿Cierto o falso?

Indicate whether each sentence is **cierto** or **falso**, then correct the false statements.

	Cierto	Falso
1. El vóleibol es el segundo deporte más popular en México. Es el béisbol.	○	⊘
2. En España a la gente le gustan varios deportes como el baloncesto y el ciclismo.	⊘	○
3. En la costa del norte de Colombia, el tenis es una pasión. El béisbol es una pasión.	○	⊘
4. En el Caribe, el deporte más popular es el béisbol.	⊘	○

Preguntas

Answer these questions in Spanish. Answers will vary.

1. ¿Dónde ven el fútbol los aficionados? Y tú, ¿cómo ves tus deportes favoritos?

2. ¿Te gusta el fútbol? ¿Por qué?

3. ¿Miras la Copa Mundial en la televisión?

4. ¿Qué deportes miras en la televisión?

5. En tu opinión, ¿cuáles son los tres deportes más populares en tu escuela? ¿En tu comunidad? ¿En tu país?

6. ¿Practicas deportes en tus ratos libres?

¿Cierto o falso? After completing the activity, ask students to write an additional sentence about sports in each country or region mentioned. Ex: **El fútbol es el deporte más popular en México.**

Preguntas Give students these questions as items 7–10: **7. ¿Cuál es el deporte más popular en el mundo hispano? (el fútbol) 8. ¿En qué países es el béisbol el deporte más popular? (en los países del Caribe) 9. ¿Pueden nombrar algunos jugadores de béisbol hispanos en los Estados Unidos?** (Answers will vary.) **10. ¿Participan muchos países hispanos en campeonatos mundiales de fútbol? (sí)**

Section Goals

In **Escritura**, students will:
- write a pamphlet listing different events in their area
- integrate recreation-related vocabulary and structures taught in **Lección 4**

 Communication 1.3

Estrategia Explain that when students look up an English word in a Spanish-English dictionary, they will frequently find more than one definition. They must decide which one best fits the context. Discuss the meanings of *racket* that might be found in a Spanish-English dictionary and how the explanatory notes and abbreviations can be useful. Tell students that a good way to verify the meaning of a Spanish translation is to look it up and see the English translation.

Tema Discuss the three topics. You may want to introduce terms like **comité**, **guía de orientación**. Remind students of some common graphic features used in pamphlets: headings, times and places, brief events descriptions, and prices.

Successful Language Learning Tell students that they should resist the temptation to look up every unknown word. Advise them to guess the word's meaning based on context clues.

 Pre-AP®

Presentational Writing Remind students that they are writing with the purpose of attracting attendees to events and activities. Encourage them to brainstorm in Spanish as many details as possible about the activities that they are going to describe.

Escritura

Estrategia
Using a dictionary

A common mistake made by beginning language learners is to embrace the dictionary as the ultimate resource for reading, writing, and speaking. While it is true that the dictionary is a useful tool that can provide valuable information about vocabulary, using the dictionary correctly requires that you understand the elements of each entry.

If you glance at a Spanish-English dictionary, you will notice that its format is similar to that of an English dictionary. The word is listed first, usually followed by its pronunciation. Then come the definitions, organized by parts of speech. Sometimes the most frequently used definitions are listed first.

To find the best word for your needs, you should refer to the abbreviations and the explanatory notes that appear next to the entries. For example, imagine that you are writing about your pastimes. You want to write, "I want to buy a new racket for my match tomorrow," but you don't know the Spanish word for "racket." In the dictionary, you may find an entry like this:

> **racket** *s* **1**. alboroto; **2**. raqueta (*dep.*)

The abbreviation key at the front of the dictionary says that *s* corresponds to **sustantivo** (*noun*). Then, the first word you see is **alboroto**. The definition of **alboroto** is *noise* or *racket*, so **alboroto** is probably not the word you're looking for. The second word is **raqueta**, followed by the abbreviation *dep.*, which stands for **deportes**. This indicates that the word **raqueta** is the best choice for your needs.

Tema
Escribir un folleto

Choose one topic to write a brochure.   Answers will vary.

1. You are the head of the Homecoming Committee at your school this year. Create a pamphlet that lists events for Friday night, Saturday, and Sunday. Include a brief description of each event and its time and location. Include activities for different age groups, since some alumni will bring their families.

2. You are on the Freshman Student Orientation Committee and are in charge of creating a pamphlet for new students that describes the sports offered at your school. Write the flyer and include activities for both men and women.

3. You volunteer at your community's recreation center. It is your job to market your community to potential residents. Write a brief pamphlet that describes the recreational opportunities your community provides, the areas where the activities take place, and the costs, if any. Be sure to include activities that will appeal to singles as well as couples and families; you should include activities for all age groups and for both men and women.

EVALUATION: Folleto

Criteria	Scale
Appropriate details	1 2 3 4
Organization	1 2 3 4
Use of vocabulary	1 2 3 4
Grammatical accuracy	1 2 3 4
Mechanics	1 2 3 4

Scoring	
Excellent	18–20 points
Good	14–17 points
Satisfactory	10–13 points
Unsatisfactory	< 10 points

Escuchar

Estrategia
Listening for the gist

Listening for the general idea, or gist, can help you follow what someone is saying even if you can't hear or understand some of the words. When you listen for the gist, you simply try to capture the essence of what you hear without focusing on individual words.

 To help you practice this strategy, you will listen to a paragraph made up of three sentences. Jot down a brief summary of what you hear.

Preparación

Based on the photo, what do you think Anabela is like? Do you and Anabela have similar interests?
Answers will vary.

Ahora escucha

You will hear first José talking, then Anabela. As you listen, check off each person's favorite activities.

Pasatiempos favoritos de José

1. ✔ leer el correo electrónico
2. _____ jugar al béisbol
3. ✔ ver películas de acción
4. ✔ ir al café
5. ✔ ir a partidos de béisbol
6. _____ ver películas románticas
7. ✔ dormir la siesta
8. ✔ escribir mensajes electrónicos

Pasatiempos favoritos de Anabela

9. ✔ esquiar
10. ✔ nadar
11. ✔ practicar el ciclismo
12. ✔ jugar al golf
13. _____ jugar al baloncesto
14. _____ ir a ver partidos de tenis
15. ✔ escalar montañas
16. _____ ver televisión

Comprensión

Preguntas
Answer these questions about José's and Anabela's pastimes.

1. ¿Quién practica más deportes?
   Anabela
2. ¿Quién piensa que es importante descansar?
   José
3. ¿A qué deporte es aficionado José?
   Le gusta el béisbol.
4. ¿Por qué Anabela no practica el baloncesto?
   Ella no es alta.
5. ¿Qué películas le gustan a la novia de José?
   Le gustan las películas románticas.
6. ¿Cuál es el deporte favorito de Anabela?
   el ciclismo

Seleccionar
Which person do these statements best describe?

1. Le gusta practicar deportes. Anabela
2. Prefiere las películas de acción. José
3. Le gustan las computadoras. José
4. Le gusta nadar. Anabela
5. Siempre (*Always*) duerme una siesta por la tarde. José
6. Quiere ir de vacaciones a las montañas. Anabela

pero también estudio mucho y necesito diversión. Aunque prefiero practicar el ciclismo, me gustan mucho la natación, el tenis, el golf... bueno, en realidad todos los deportes. No, eso no

es cierto; no juego al baloncesto porque no soy alta. Para mis vacaciones, quiero esquiar o escalar la montaña, depende si nieva. Suena divertido, ¿no?

Section Goals

In **Escuchar**, students will:
- listen to and summarize a short paragraph
- learn the strategy of listening for the gist
- answer questions based on the content of a recorded conversation

Communication 1.2

Estrategia
Script Buenas tardes y bienvenidos a la clase de español. En esta clase van a escuchar, escribir y conversar en cada clase, y ustedes también deben estudiar y practicar todos los días. Ahora encuentran el español difícil, pero cuando termine el curso van a comprender y comunicarse bien en español.

In-Class Tip
↩👤 Have students look at the photo and write a short paragraph describing what they see. Guide them in saying what **Anabela** is like and guessing what her favorite pastimes might be.

Preguntas Students can submit this activity online. Their paragraphs will appear in your gradebook.

Ahora escucha
Script JOSÉ: No me gusta practicar deportes, pero sí tengo muchos pasatiempos. Me gusta mucho escribir y recibir correo electrónico. Me gusta también ir con mis amigos a mi café favorito. Siempre duermo una siesta por la tarde. A veces voy a ver un partido de béisbol. Me gusta mucho ver películas de acción pero mi novia prefiere las de romance... y por lo tanto veo muchas películas de romance.
ANABELA: Todos mis parientes dicen que soy demasiado activa. Soy aficionada a los deportes,

(Script continues at far left in the bottom panels.)

en pantalla

Ejes

A mí me gusta la bici y me quedo con la bici°.

Preparación
Answer these questions in English. Answers will vary.

1. What role do sports play in your life? Which sports do you enjoy? Why?
2. Is there a sport you enjoy with other members of your family? With a group of friends? Is there a special season for that sport?

Más que un deporte
For many, extreme sports aren't just games but an art form and a lifestyle. BMX, skateboarding, surfing, and other sports are passions for many young men and women who, in search of speed and adrenaline, make their bikes and boards the center of their lives. Communities around the world are responding to the demand for extreme sports by constructing bike and skate parks, and Spanish-speaking countries are no exception. The UCI BMX World Championship was held in Medellín in 2016. Colombian Olympic Gold Medalist Mariana Pajón has won gold at the games three times (2011, 2014, 2016). Argentinian professional BMX cyclist Gabriela Díaz won the championship in 2001, 2002, and 2004.

Me quedo con la bici *I stay with the bike*

Vocabulario útil

andar	*go*
bici	*bike*
callejón	*alley*
campeonato	*championship*
conocer	*to be acquainted with*
molar	*be cool*
rampas	*ramps*

Comprensión
Indicate whether each statement is **cierto** or **falso**.

	Cierto	Falso
1. A Diego le gusta la bici.	○	⊘
2. Sarini cree que patinar es un arte.	⊘	○
3. Pequesaurio prefiere la patineta.	○	⊘
4. A Pequesaurio le gusta la rampa.	⊘	○

 **Conversación**
Answers will vary.
With a partner, discuss these questions in Spanish.

1. ¿Qué deportes se pueden practicar fácilmente en tu comunidad? ¿Qué deportes son fomentados (*encouraged*) en tu comunidad?
2. ¿Cuál es la diferencia entre un deporte y un juego? ¿Cuál es la diferencia entre un deporte y un deporte extremo?

Aplicación
Participation in sports and other physical activities is important for one's well-being. With two classmates, prepare an oral presentation for your community. Your objective is to convince families and communities to encourage participation in sports among kids from an early age. Include illustrations in your presentation. Answers will vary.

TEACHING OPTIONS

Language Notes In its normal usage, **andar** means *to walk*. However, in many cases, **andar** can mean *to travel* or *to go*: **Ando en bicicleta para ir a la escuela**. In some cases, **andar** can be followed by a gerund to form a continuous tense: **Mi hermano anda estudiando mucho**. Sometimes it is a synonym of **estar**: **Mi** **madre siempre anda muy ocupada**. Note that **andar** is irregular in the indicative preterite and the past subjunctive tenses. The verb **molar** is used to express that something is cool: **La bici mola**. It can also be conjugated like the verb **gustar**: **¿Te mola el rap?** It is mainly used in Spain. **¡Cómo mola!**

The rivalry between the teams **Real Madrid** and **FC Barcelona** is perhaps the fiercest in all of soccer—just imagine if they occupied the same city! Well, each team also has competing clubs within its respective city: Spain's capital has the **Club Atlético de Madrid**, and Barcelona is home to **Espanyol**. In fact, across the Spanish-speaking world, it is common for a city to have more than one professional team, often with strikingly dissimilar origins, identity, and fan base. For example, in Bogotá, the **Millonarios** were so named for the large sums spent on players, while the **Santa Fe** team is one of the most traditional in Colombian soccer. **River Plate** and **Boca Juniors**, who enjoy a famous rivalry, are just two of twenty-four clubs in Buenos Aires—the city with the most professional soccer teams in the world.

Vocabulario útil

afición	*fans*
celebran	*they celebrate*
preferido/a	*favorite*
rivalidad	*rivalry*
se junta con	*it's tied up with*

Preparación

What is the most popular sport at your school? What teams are your rivals? How do students celebrate a win?
Answers will vary.

Escoger

Select the correct answer.

1. Un partido entre el Barça y el Real Madrid es un ____evento____ (deporte/evento) importante en toda España.

2. Los aficionados ____celebran____ (miran/celebran) las victorias de sus equipos en las calles (*streets*).

3. La rivalidad entre el Real Madrid y el Barça está relacionada con la ____política____ (religión/política).

¡Fútbol en España!

(Hay mucha afición al fútbol en España.)

¿Y cuál es vuestro jugador favorito?

—**¿Y quién va a ganar?**
—**El Real Madrid.**

Section Goals

In **Flash cultura**, students will:
• read about soccer rivalries in the Spanish-speaking world
• watch a video about soccer in Spain

Communication 1.2
Cultures 2.1, 2.2
Comparisons 4.2

Teacher Resources
Read the front matter for suggestions on how to incorporate all the program's components. See pages 115A–115B for a detailed listing of Teacher Resources online.

Introduction To check comprehension, ask these questions. 1. What are the two main soccer clubs in Madrid? 2. What are the two main soccer teams in Barcelona? 3. How did the team **Millonarios** get its name? 4. How many professional soccer teams are there in Buenos Aires?

Antes de ver
• Have students look at the video stills, read the captions, and predict the content of the video.
• Read through **Vocabulario útil** with students. Model the pronunciation.
• Explain that students do not need to understand every word they hear. Tell them to rely on visual cues, cognates, and words from **Vocabulario útil**.

Preparación Survey the class to find out what sport is the most popular and who the main rivals are.

Escoger Make copies of this activity with the words in parentheses removed. Pass out the copies and have students close their books. Write all the possible answers for the activity in one list on the board and tell students to fill in the blanks using these words.

TEACHING OPTIONS

Small Groups ←👤→ In small groups, have students research one of the teams on this page. Have them focus on the team's key players, colors, team song (**himno**), any historical or political points of interest, and its fan base. Have groups present their findings to the class.

Heritage Speakers ←👤→ Ask heritage speakers to share their experiences with soccer as they were growing up. Ask them to discuss whether they played/watched formal or informal matches, whether girls were allowed or expected to play, and if they would watch soccer in their household and celebrate wins.

México

El país en cifras

▶ **Área:** 1.972.550 km^2 (761.603 millas^2), *casi*° *tres veces*° *el área de Texas*

La situación geográfica de México, al sur° *de los Estados Unidos, ha influido en*° *la economía y la sociedad de los dos países. Una de las consecuencias es la emigración de la población mexicana al país vecino*°. *Hoy día, más de 33 millones de personas de ascendencia mexicana viven en los Estados Unidos.*

▶ **Población:** 118.818.000

▶ **Capital:** México, D.F. (y su área metropolitana)—19.319.000

▶ **Ciudades principales:** Guadalajara —4.338.000, Monterrey—3.838.000, Puebla—2.278.000, Ciudad Juárez—1.321.000

▶ **Moneda:** peso mexicano

▶ **Idiomas:** español (oficial), náhuatl, otras lenguas indígenas

Bandera de México

Mexicanos célebres

▶ **Benito Juárez,** héroe nacional (1806–1872)

▶ **Octavio Paz,** poeta (1914–1998)

▶ **Elena Poniatowska,** periodista y escritora (1932–)

▶ **Mario Molina,** Premio Nobel de Química, 1995; químico (1943–)

▶ **Paulina Rubio,** cantante (1971–)

casi *almost* veces *times* sur *south* ha influido en *has influenced* vecino *neighboring* se llenan de luz *get filled with light* flores *flowers* Muertos *Dead* se ríen *laugh* muerte *death* lo cual se refleja *which is reflected* calaveras de azúcar *sugar skulls* pan *bread* huesos *bones*

Cabo San Lucas

ESTADOS UNIDOS

Autorretrato con mono (*Self-portrait with monkey*), 1938, Frida Kahlo

Ciudad Juárez

Río Grande
Río Bravo del Norte
Golfo de California
Baja California
Sierra Madre Oriental
Sierra Madre Occidental
Monterrey

ESTADOS UNIDOS
MÉXICO
OCÉANO ATLÁNTICO
OCÉANO PACÍFICO
AMÉRICA DEL SUR

Océano Pacífico

Puerto Vallarta
Ciudad de México
Guadalajara
Puebla
Acapulco

Artesanías en Taxco, Guerrero

Pirámide de Kukulcán en Chichén Itzá

¡Increíble pero cierto!

Cada dos de noviembre los cementerios de México se llenan de luz°, música y flores°. El Día de Muertos° no es un evento triste; es una fiesta en honor a las personas muertas. En ese día, los mexicanos se ríen° de la muerte°, lo cual se refleja° en detalles como las calaveras de azúcar° y el pan° de muerto —pan en forma de huesos°.

Ciudades • México, D.F.

La Ciudad de México, fundadaº en 1525, también se llama el D.F. o Distrito Federal. Muchos turistas e inmigrantes vienen a la ciudad porque es el centro cultural y económico del país. El crecimientoº de la población es de los más altosº del mundo. El D.F. tiene una población mayor que las de Nueva York, Madrid o París.

Artes • Diego Rivera y Frida Kahlo

Frida Kahlo y Diego Rivera eranº artistas mexicanos muy famosos. Se casaronº en 1929. Los dos se interesaronº en las condiciones sociales de la gente indígena de su país. Puedes ver algunasº de sus obrasº en el Museo de Arte Moderno de la Ciudad de México.

Historia • Los aztecas

Los aztecas dominaronº en México del sigloº XIV al siglo XVI. Sus canales, puentesº y pirámides con templos religiosos eran muy importantes.
El fin del imperio azteca comenzóº con la llegadaº de los españoles en 1519, pero la presencia azteca sigue hoy. La Ciudad de México está situada en la capital azteca de Tenochtitlán, y muchos turistas van a visitar sus ruinas.

Golfo de México

Península de Yucatán

Bahía de Campeche

Mérida

Cancún

Veracruz

Istmo de Tehuantepec

BELICE

GUATEMALA

Economía • La plata

México es el mayor productor de plataº del mundoº. Estados como Zacatecas y Durango tienen ciudades fundadas cerca de los más grandes yacimientosº de plata del país. Estas ciudades fueronº en la época colonial unas de las más ricas e importantes. Hoy en día, aúnº conservan mucho de su encantoº y esplendor.

¿Qué aprendiste? Responde a cada pregunta con una oración completa.

1. ¿Qué lenguas hablan los mexicanos?
   Los mexicanos hablan español y lenguas indígenas.

2. ¿Cómo es la población del D.F. en comparación con la de otras ciudades?
   La población del D.F. es mayor.

3. ¿En qué se interesaron Frida Kahlo y Diego Rivera? Se interesaron en las condiciones sociales de la gente indígena de su país.

4. Nombra algunas de las estructuras de la arquitectura azteca. Hay canales, puentes y pirámides con templos religiosos.

5. ¿Dónde está situada la capital de México?
   Está situada en la capital azteca de Tenochtitlán.

6. ¿Qué estados de México tienen los mayores yacimientos de plata? Zacatecas y Durango tienen los mayores yacimientos de plata.

Conexión Internet Investiga estos temas en Internet.

1. Busca información sobre dos lugares de México. ¿Te gustaría (*Would you like*) vivir allí? ¿Por qué?

2. Busca información sobre dos artistas mexicanos. ¿Cómo se llaman sus obras más famosas?

....

fundada *founded* crecimiento *growth* más altos *highest* eran *were* Se casaron *They got married* se interesaron *were interested* algunas *some* obras *works* dominaron *dominated* siglo *century* puentes *bridges* comenzó *started* llegada *arrival* plata *silver* mundo *world* yacimientos *deposits* fueron *were* aún *still* encanto *charm*

Variación léxica Over 52 languages are spoken by indigenous communities in Mexico today; of these, Mayan languages are the most prevalent. Also, **náhuatl**, the language of the Aztecs, is spoken by a significant part of the population. Some **náhuatl** words have entered Mexican Spanish, such as **aguacate** (*avocado*), **guajolote** (*turkey*), **cacahuate** (*peanut*), **ejote** (*green bean*), **chile** (*chili pepper*), and **elote** (*corn*). Two food names of **náhuatl** origin that are now used in world languages are *tomato* and *chocolate*, as these foods are native to Mexico and were brought to Europe in the sixteenth century.

México, D.F. Mexicans usually refer to their capital as **México** or **el D.F.** The monument pictured here is **El Ángel de la Independencia**, located on the **Paseo de la Reforma** in **el D.F.**

Diego Rivera y Frida Kahlo Show students paintings by **Rivera** and **Kahlo**, and discuss the indigenous Mexican themes that dominate their works: **Rivera's** murals have largely proletarian and political messages, while **Kahlo** incorporated indigenous motifs in her portrayals of suffering.

Los aztecas Explain that the coat of arms on the Mexican flag represents an Aztec prophecy. Legend states that nomadic Aztecs wandered present-day Mexico in search of a place to establish a city. According to their gods, the precise location would be indicated by an eagle devouring a snake while perched atop a nopal cactus. The Aztecs saw this sign on an island in Lake Texcoco, where they founded Tenochtitlán.

La plata Taxco, in the state of Guerrero, is the home to the annual **Feria Nacional de la Plata**. Although Taxco has exploited its silver mines since pre-Columbian days, the city did not have a native silvermaking industry until American William Spratling founded his workshop there in the 1930s. Spratling, known as the father of contemporary Mexican silver, incorporated indigenous Mexican motifs in his innovative silver designs.

In-Class Tip You may want to wrap up this section by playing the *Panorama cultural* video footage for this lesson.

Comparisons 4.1

Teacher Resources
Read the front matter for suggestions on how to incorporate all the program's components. See pages 115A -115B for a detailed listing of Teacher Resources online.

In-Class Tip Ask students to prepare a list of the three products or perspectives they learned about in this lesson to share with the class. You may ask them to focus specifically on the **Cultura** and **Panorama** sections.

Pasatiempos

andar en patineta	to skateboard
bucear	to scuba dive
escalar montañas (f., pl.)	to climb mountains
escribir una carta	to write a letter
escribir un mensaje electrónico	to write an e-mail
esquiar	to ski
ganar	to win
ir de excursión	to go on a hike
leer el correo electrónico	to read e-mail
leer un periódico	to read a newspaper
leer una revista	to read a magazine
nadar	to swim
pasear	to take a walk
pasear en bicicleta	to ride a bicycle
patinar (en línea)	to (inline) skate
practicar deportes (m., pl.)	to play sports
tomar el sol	to sunbathe
ver películas (f., pl.)	to watch movies
visitar monumentos (m., pl.)	to visit monuments
la diversión	fun activity; entertainment; recreation
el fin de semana	weekend
el pasatiempo	pastime; hobby
los ratos libres	spare (free) time
el videojuego	video game

Deportes

el baloncesto	basketball
el béisbol	baseball
el ciclismo	cycling
el equipo	team
el esquí (acuático)	(water) skiing
el fútbol	soccer
el fútbol americano	football
el golf	golf
el hockey	hockey
el/la jugador(a)	player
la natación	swimming
el partido	game; match
la pelota	ball
el tenis	tennis
el vóleibol	volleyball

Adjetivos

deportivo/a	sports-related
favorito/a	favorite

Lugares

el café	café
el centro	downtown
el cine	movie theater
el gimnasio	gymnasium
la iglesia	church
el lugar	place
el museo	museum
el parque	park
la piscina	swimming pool
la plaza	city or town square
el restaurante	restaurant

Verbos

almorzar (o:ue)	to have lunch
cerrar (e:ie)	to close
comenzar (e:ie)	to begin
conseguir (e:i)	to get; to obtain
contar (o:ue)	to count; to tell
decir (e:i)	to say; to tell
dormir (o:ue)	to sleep
empezar (e:ie)	to begin
encontrar (o:ue)	to find
entender (e:ie)	to understand
hacer	to do; to make
ir	to go
jugar (u:ue)	to play (a sport or a game)
mostrar (o:ue)	to show
oír	to hear
pedir (e:i)	to ask for; to request
pensar (e:ie)	to think
pensar (+ inf.)	to intend
pensar en	to think about
perder (e:ie)	to lose; to miss
poder (o:ue)	to be able to; can
poner	to put; to place
preferir (e:ie)	to prefer
querer (e:ie)	to want; to love
recordar (o:ue)	to remember
repetir (e:i)	to repeat
salir	to leave
seguir (e:i)	to follow; to continue
suponer	to suppose
traer	to bring
ver	to see
volver (o:ue)	to return

Decir expressions	See page 136.
Expresiones útiles	See page 121.

Lección 5: Teacher Resources

There is a wealth of resources online to support instruction using **Senderos**. For details on how to integrate these Teacher Resources into your lessons, see the front matter of this Teacher's Edition on pages T16 to T48.

Presentation	Practice & Communicate	Assess*	Scripts and Translations	
• Digital Images: • **Las vacaciones** • **Las estaciones** • **El tiempo**	• Information Gap Activities* • Activity Pack Practice Activities (with Answer Key): **Contextos** • Additional Vocabulary (**Más vocabulario para las vacaciones**) • Digital Image Bank (Travel) • Surveys: Worksheet for classroom survey	• Vocabulary Quiz (with Answer Key)		contextos
		• **Fotonovela** Optional Testing Sections (with Answer Key)	• **Fotonovela** Videoscript • **Fotonovela** English Translation	fotonovela
• **Estructura 5.1** Grammar Slides	• Information Gap Activities* • Activity Pack Practice Activities (with Answer Key): **Estar** with conditions and emotions	• Grammar 5.1 Quiz (with Answer Key)	• Tutorial Script: **Estar** with conditions and emotions	
• **Estructura 5.2** Grammar Slides	• Information Gap Activities* • Activity Pack Practice Activities (with Answer Key): The present progressive	• Grammar 5.2 Quiz (with Answer Key)	• Tutorial Script: The present progressive	estructura
• **Estructura 5.3** Grammar Slides	• Activity Pack Practice Activities (with Answer Key): **Ser** and **estar**	• Grammar 5.3 Quiz (with Answer Key)	• Tutorial Script: **Ser** and **estar**	
• **Estructura 5.4** Grammar Slides	• Activity Pack Practice Activities (with Answer Key): Direct object nouns and pronouns	• Grammar 5.4 Quiz (with Answer Key)	• Tutorial Script: Direct object nouns and pronouns	
			• **En pantalla** Videoscript • **En pantalla** English Translation	En pantalla
		• **Flash cultura** Optional Testing Sections (with Answer Key)	• **Flash cultura** Videoscript • **Flash cultura** English Translation	Flash cultura
Digital Images: • **Puerto Rico**		• **Panorama** Optional Testing Sections (with Answer Key) • **Panorama cultural** (video)	• **Panorama cultural** Videoscript • **Panorama cultural** English Translation	Panorama

*Can also be assigned online.

151A

Lección 5: Teacher Resources

Script for Comunicación: Actividad 12 (p. 157)

Agente de viajes	Buenas tardes. ¿Qué desea?
Sr. Vega	Quiero ir de vacaciones a un lugar interesante y bonito.
Agente de viajes	¿Qué le gusta hacer? ¿Acampar? ¿Esquiar? ¿Bucear?
Sr. Vega	Me gusta pescar y montar a caballo.
Agente de viajes	¿Por qué no va a las montañas?
Sr. Vega	No, gracias. Prefiero ir a un lugar donde hace calor.
Agente de viajes	¿Qué tal Puerto Rico? Puerto Rico tiene muchas playas bonitas. Puede pescar, montar a caballo, nadar, bucear e ir de compras.
Sr. Vega	¿Cuánto cuesta el hotel en Puerto Rico?
Agente de viajes	Voy a ver en la computadora. ¿Cuándo quiere ir?
Sr. Vega	La primera semana de marzo.
Agente de viajes	Pues, hay Las Tres Palmas. Es un hotel de segunda categoría. Tiene restaurante, piscina y jacuzzi. También está muy cerca a la playa. Una habitación individual cuesta ochenta y cinco dólares la noche. ¿Hago una reservación?
Sr. Vega	Sí, por favor, por cinco noches.

Script for Comunicación: Actividad 4 (p. 173)

¡Hola! Me llamo Carolina y ahora estoy de vacaciones en Ponce. Ponce es la segunda ciudad más grande de Puerto Rico. Está cerca del mar Caribe y es una ciudad muy bonita. Hoy no voy a la playa porque está lloviendo. Esperaba visitar el Parque de Bombas, que es ahora un museo, pero hoy es martes y está cerrado. Así que voy a visitar el Museo de Arte. Oigo que tiene una colección fenomenal de pinturas.

Script for Comunicación: Actividad 4 (p. 177)

Mercedes	Gabriel, ¿necesitas un pasaporte para tu viaje?
Gabriel	No, no lo necesito.
Mercedes	¿Tienes que comprar un pasaje de ida y vuelta?
Gabriel	Sí, tengo que comprarlo.
Mercedes	¿Vas a llevar tu tabla de surf?
Gabriel	Sí, la voy a llevar.
Mercedes	¿Qué más vas a hacer?
Gabriel	Voy a nadar en el mar y tomar el sol.
Mercedes	Ah, tienes suerte. Aquí va a nevar.

*Tests and Exams can also be assigned online.

Las vacaciones

5

Communicative Goals

You will learn how to:

- Discuss and plan a vacation
- Describe a hotel
- Talk about how you feel
- Talk about the seasons and the weather

A PRIMERA VISTA

- ¿Están ellos en una montaña o en un museo?
- ¿Son viejos o jóvenes?
- ¿Pasean o ven una película? ¿Andan en patineta o van de excursión?
- ¿Es posible esquiar en este lugar?

Lesson Goals

In **Lección 5**, students will be introduced to the following:
- terms for traveling and vacations
- seasons and months
- weather expressions
- ordinal numbers (1st–10th)
- **Las cataratas del Iguazú**
- **Punta del Este**, Uruguay
- **estar** with conditions and emotions
- adjectives for conditions and emotions
- present progressive of regular and irregular verbs
- comparison of the uses of **ser** and **estar**
- direct object nouns and pronouns
- personal **a**
- scanning to find specific information
- making an outline
- writing a brochure for a hotel
- listening for key words
- an ad for **LANPASS**, a Chilean airline loyalty program
- a video about **Machu Picchu**
- cultural, geographic, and historical information about Puerto Rico

A primera vista Here are some additional questions you can ask to personalize the photo: **¿Dónde te gusta pasar tus ratos libres? ¿Qué haces en tus ratos libres? ¿Te gusta explorar otras culturas? ¿Te gusta viajar a otros países? ¿Adónde quieres ir en las próximas vacaciones?**

Teaching Tip Look for these icons for additional communicative practice:

→■·	Interpretive communication
·■·	Presentational communication
■↔■	Interpersonal communication

SUPPORT FOR BACKWARD DESIGN

Lección 5 Essential Questions
1. How do people discuss and plan a vacation?
2. How do people talk about how they feel?
3. What are some popular vacation destinations in the Spanish-speaking world and why?

Lección 5 Integrated Performance Assessment
Before teaching this chapter, review the Integrated Performance Assessment (IPA) and its accompanying scoring rubric. Use the IPA to assess students' progress toward proficiency targets at the end of the chapter. **IPA Context**: Six students from your Spanish class will be chosen to spend a week in Puerto Rico, at the **Hotel Vistahermosa** in Lajas. Students will be chosen in pairs based on their presentation to the selection committee.

VOICE BOARD

Voice boards online allow you and your students to record and share up to five minutes of audio. Use voice boards for presentations, oral assessments, discussions, directions, etc.

Section Goals

In **Contextos**, students will learn and practice:
- travel- and vacation-related vocabulary
- seasons and months of the year
- weather expressions
- ordinal numbers

 Communication 1.2
Comparisons 4.1

Teacher Resources
Read the front matter for suggestions on how to incorporate all the program's components. See pages 151A–151B for a detailed listing of Teacher Resources online.

In-Class Tips
- Ask: **¿A quién le gusta mucho viajar? ¿Cómo prefieres viajar?** Introduce cognates as suggestions: **¿Te gusta viajar en auto?** Write each term on the board as you say it. Ask: **¿Adónde te gusta viajar? ¿A México?** Ask students about their classmates' statements: **¿Adónde le gusta viajar a _____? ¿Cómo puede viajar?**
- Ask questions about transportation in your community. Ex: **Si quiero ir de la escuela al aeropuerto, ¿cómo puedo ir?** Ask what type of transportation students use to go home on school break.
- Use the **Lección 5 Contextos** vocabulary presentation online or the digital images in the Resources online to assist with this presentation.
- Give students two minutes to review the four scenes and then ask questions. Ex: **¿Quién trabaja en una agencia de viajes? (el/la agente de viajes)**

Note: At this point you may want to present **Vocabulario adicional: Más vocabulario para las vacaciones** from the online Resources.

Las vacaciones

Más vocabulario

la cama	bed
la habitación individual, doble	single, double room
el piso	floor (of a building)
la planta baja	ground floor
el campo	countryside
el paisaje	landscape
el equipaje	luggage
la estación de autobuses, del metro, de tren	bus, subway, train station
la llegada	arrival
el pasaje (de ida y vuelta)	(round-trip) ticket
la salida	departure; exit
la tabla de (wind)surf	surfboard/sailboard
acampar	to camp
estar de vacaciones	to be on vacation
hacer las maletas	to pack (one's suitcases)
hacer un viaje	to take a trip
hacer (wind)surf	to (wind)surf
ir de compras	to go shopping
ir de vacaciones	to go on vacation
ir en autobús (m.), auto(móvil) (m.), motocicleta (f.), taxi (m.)	to go by bus, car, motorcycle, taxi

Variación léxica

automóvil	⟷	coche (Esp.), carro (Amér. L.)
autobús	⟷	camión (Méx.), guagua (Caribe)
motocicleta	⟷	moto (coloquial)

la agente de viajes

el pasaporte

Confirma una reservación. (confirmar)

En la agencia de viajes

la habitación

el ascensor

el empleado

la llave

la huésped

el huésped

En el hotel

TEACHING OPTIONS

Extra Practice 👤↔👤 Ask questions about the people, places, and activities in **Contextos**. Ex: **¿Qué actividades pueden hacer los turistas en una playa? ¿Pueden nadar? ¿Tomar el sol? ¿Sacar fotos?** Then expand questions to ask students what they specifically do at these places. **_____, ¿qué haces tú cuando vas a la playa?** Students should respond in complete sentences.

Variación léxica Point out that these are just some of the different Spanish names for vehicles. Ask heritage speakers if they are familiar with other terms. While some of these terms are mutually understood in different regions (**el coche, el carro, el auto, el automóvil**), others are specific to a region and may not be understood by others (**la guagua, el camión**). Stress that the feminine article **la** is used with the abbreviation **moto**.

Práctica

1 Escuchar Indicate who would probably make each statement you hear. Each answer is used twice.

a. el agente de viajes
b. el inspector de aduanas
c. un empleado del hotel

1. ___a___   4. ___b___
2. ___a___   5. ___c___
3. ___c___   6. ___b___

2 ¿Cierto o falso? Mario and his wife, Natalia, are planning their next vacation with a travel agent. Indicate whether each statement is **cierto** or **falso** according to what you hear in the conversation.

	Cierto	Falso
1. Mario y Natalia están en Puerto Rico.	○	⊘
2. Ellos quieren hacer un viaje a Puerto Rico.	⊘	○
3. Natalia prefiere ir a la montaña.	○	⊘
4. Mario quiere pescar en Puerto Rico.	⊘	○
5. La agente de viajes va a confirmar la reservación.	⊘	○

3 Escoger Choose the best answer for each sentence.

1. Un huésped es una persona que ___b___.
   a. toma fotos   b. está en un hotel   c. pesca en el mar
2. Abrimos la puerta con ___a___.
   a. una llave   b. un caballo   c. una llegada
3. Enrique tiene ___a___ porque va a viajar a otro (*another*) país.
   a. un pasaporte   b. una foto   c. una llegada
4. Antes de (*Before*) ir de vacaciones, hay que ___c___.
   a. pescar   b. ir en tren   c. hacer las maletas
5. Nosotros vamos en ___a___ al aeropuerto.
   a. autobús   b. pasaje   c. viajero
6. Me gusta mucho ir al campo. El ___a___ es increíble.
   a. paisaje   b. pasaje   c. equipaje

4 Analogías Complete the analogies using the words below. Two words will not be used.

auto	huésped	mar	sacar
empleado	llegada	pasaporte	tren

1. acampar → campo ⊜ pescar → _mar_
2. agencia de viajes → agente ⊜ hotel → _empleado_
3. llave → habitación ⊜ pasaje → _tren_
4. estudiante → libro ⊜ turista → _pasaporte_
5. aeropuerto → viajero ⊜ hotel → _huésped_
6. maleta → hacer ⊜ foto → _sacar_

Illustrations:

Saca/Toma fotos. (sacar, tomar)
BIENVENIDOS
el avión
el viajero
la inspectora de aduanas

En el aeropuerto

Pesca. (pescar)
Monta a caballo. (montar)
Va en barco. (ir)
el mar
Juegan a las cartas. (jugar)
la playa

En la playa

---

1 Expansion In pairs, have students select one of the statements they hear and then write a conversation based on it.

1 Script 1. ¡Deben ir a Puerto Rico! Allí hay unas playas muy hermosas y pueden acampar. 2. Deben llamarme el lunes para confirmar la reservación. *Script continues on page 154.*

2 Expansion To challenge students, give them these true/false statements as items 6–9: **6. Mario prefiere una habitación doble. (Cierto.) 7. Natalia no quiere ir a la playa. (Falso.) 8. El hotel está en la playa. (Cierto.) 9. Mario va a montar a caballo. (Falso.)**

2 Script MARIO: Queremos ir de vacaciones a Puerto Rico. AGENTE: ¿Desean hacer un viaje al campo? NATALIA: Yo quiero ir a la playa. M: Pues, yo prefiero una habitación doble en un hotel con un buen paisaje. A: Puedo reservar para ustedes una habitación en el hotel San Juan que está en la playa. M: Es una buena idea, así yo voy a pescar y tú vas a montar a caballo. N: Muy bien, ¿puede confirmar la reservación? A: Claro que sí.

3 Expansion Ask a volunteer to help you model making statements similar to item 1. Say: **Un turista es una persona que… (va de vacaciones).** Then ask volunteers to do the same with **una agente de viajes, una inspectora de aduanas, un empleado de hotel.**

4 In-Class Tip Present these items using the following formula: *Acampar* tiene la misma relación con *campo* que *pescar* tiene con… (*mar*).

TEACHING OPTIONS

Small Groups Have students work in groups of three to write a riddle about one of the people or objects in the **Contextos** illustrations. The group must come up with at least three descriptions of their subject. Then one of the group members reads the description to the class and asks ¿Qué soy? Ex: **Soy un pequeño libro. Tengo una foto de una persona. Soy necesario si un viajero quiere viajar a otro país. ¿Qué soy? (Soy un pasaporte.)**

Large Groups Split the class into two evenly-numbered groups. Hand out cards at random to the members of each group. One type of card should contain a verb or verb phrase (Ex: **confirmar una reservación**). The other will contain a related noun (Ex: **el agente de viajes**). The people within the groups must find their partners.

In-Class Tips

- Use the **Lección 5 Contextos** online Resources to assist with this presentation.
- Point out that the names of months are not capitalized.
- Have students look over the seasons and months of the year. Call out the names of holidays or campus events and ask students to say when they occur.
- Use magazine pictures to cover as many weather conditions as possible from this page. Begin describing one of the pictures. Then, ask volunteers questions to elicit other weather expressions. Point out the use of **mucho/a** before nouns and **muy** before adjectives.
- Drill months by calling out a month and having students name the two that follow. Ex: **abril (mayo, junio).**
- Point out the use of **primero** for the first day of the month.
- Ask volunteers to associate seasons (or months) and general weather patterns. Ex: **En invierno, hace frío/ nieva. En marzo, hace viento.**
- Review the shortened forms **buen** and **mal** before **tiempo.**
- Point out that **Llueve** and **Nieva** can also mean *It rains* and *It snows.* **Está lloviendo** and **Está nevando** emphasize *at this moment.* Students will learn more about this concept in **Estructura 5.2.**

Las estaciones y los meses del año

el invierno: **diciembre, enero, febrero**

la primavera: **marzo, abril, mayo**

el verano: **junio, julio, agosto**

el otoño: **septiembre, octubre, noviembre**

—**¿Cuál es la fecha de hoy?** *What is today's date?*
—**Es el primero de octubre.** *It's the first of October.*
—**Es el dos de marzo.** *It's March 2nd.*
—**Es el diez de noviembre.** *It's November 10th.*

El tiempo

—**¿Qué tiempo hace?** *How's the weather?*
—**Hace buen/mal tiempo.** *The weather is good/bad.*

Hace (mucho) calor.
It's (very) hot.

Hace (mucho) frío.
It's (very) cold.

Llueve. (llover o:ue)
It's raining.

Está lloviendo.
It's raining.

Nieva. (nevar e:ie)
It's snowing.

Está nevando.
It's snowing.

Más vocabulario

Está (muy) nublado.	*It's (very) cloudy.*
Hace fresco.	*It's cool.*
Hace (mucho) sol.	*It's (very) sunny.*
Hace (mucho) viento.	*It's (very) windy.*

TEACHING OPTIONS

Pairs ←👤→ Have pairs of students write descriptions for each of the drawings on this page. Ask one student to write sentences for the first four drawings and the other to write sentences for the next four. When finished, ask them to check their partner's work. **TPR** Introduce the question **¿Cuándo es tu cumpleaños?** and the phrase **Mi cumpleaños es...** Allow students five minutes to ask questions and line up according to their birthdays.

Extra Practice Create a series of cloze sentences about the weather in a certain place. Ex: **En Puerto Rico _____ mucho calor. (hace) No _____ muy nublado cuando _____ sol. (está; hace) No _____ frío pero a veces _____ fresco. (hace; hace) Cuando _____ mal tiempo, _____ y _____ viento pero nunca _____. (hace; llueve; hace; nieva)**

5 **El Hotel Regis** Label the floors of the hotel.

Números ordinales	
primer (before a masculine singular noun), **primero/a**	first
segundo/a	second
tercer (before a masculine singular noun), **tercero/a**	third
cuarto/a	fourth
quinto/a	fifth
sexto/a	sixth
séptimo/a	seventh
octavo/a	eighth
noveno/a	ninth
décimo/a	tenth

a. ___séptimo___ piso
b. ___sexto___ piso
c. ___quinto___ piso
d. ___cuarto___ piso
e. ___tercer___ piso
f. ___segundo___ piso
g. ___primer___ piso
h. ___planta___ baja

6 **Contestar** Look at the illustrations of the months and seasons on the previous page. Then answer these questions.

> **modelo**
> **Estudiante 1:** ¿Cuál es el primer mes de la primavera?
> **Estudiante 2:** marzo

1. ¿Cuál es el primer mes del invierno? diciembre
2. ¿Cuál es el segundo mes de la primavera? abril
3. ¿Cuál es el tercer mes del otoño? noviembre
4. ¿Cuál es el primer mes del año? enero
5. ¿Cuál es el quinto mes del año? mayo
6. ¿Cuál es el octavo mes del año? agosto
7. ¿Cuál es el décimo mes del año? octubre
8. ¿Cuál es el segundo mes del verano? julio
9. ¿Cuál es el tercer mes del invierno? febrero
10. ¿Cuál es el sexto mes del año? junio

7 **Las estaciones** Name the season that applies to the description. Some answers may vary.

1. Las clases terminan. la primavera
2. Vamos a la playa. el verano
3. Acampamos. el verano
4. Nieva mucho. el invierno
5. Las clases empiezan. el otoño
6. Hace mucho calor. el verano
7. Llueve mucho. la primavera
8. Esquiamos. el invierno
9. el entrenamiento (training) de béisbol la primavera
10. el Día de Acción de Gracias (Thanksgiving) el otoño

8 **¿Cuál es la fecha?** Give the dates for these holidays.

> **modelo**
> el día de San Valentín   14 de febrero

1. el día de San Patricio 17 de marzo
2. el día de Halloween 31 de octubre
3. el primer día de verano 20–23 de junio
4. el Año Nuevo primero de enero
5. mi cumpleaños (birthday) Answers will vary.
6. mi día de fiesta favorito Answers will vary.

TEACHING OPTIONS

TPR Ask ten volunteers to line up facing the class. Make sure students know the starting point and what number in line they are. At random, call out ordinal numbers. The student to which each ordinal number corresponds has three seconds to step forward. If the student does not, he or she sits down and the order changes for the rest of the students further down the line. Who will be the last student(s) standing?

Game Ask four or five volunteers to come to the front of the room and hold races. (Make it difficult to reach the finish line; for example, have students hop on one foot or recite the ordinal numbers backwards.) Teach the words **llegó** and **fue** and, after each race, ask the class to summarize the results. Ex: _____ **llegó en quinto lugar.** _____ **fue la tercera persona (en llegar).**

---

5 **In-Class Tips**
• Point out that for numbers greater than ten, Spanish speakers tend to use cardinal numbers instead: **Está en el piso veintiuno.**
• Add a visual aspect to this vocabulary presentation. Write out each ordinal number on a separate sheet of paper and distribute them at random among ten students. Ask them to go to the front of the class, hold up their signs, and stand in the correct order.

5 **Expansion** Ask students questions about their lives, using ordinal numbers. Ex: **¿En qué piso vives? ¿En qué piso está tu clase de español?**

6 **In-Class Tip** Before beginning this activity, have students close their books. Review seasons and months of the year by asking questions. Ex: **¿Qué estación tiene los meses de junio, julio y agosto?**

6 **Expansion** Ask a student which month his or her birthday is in. Ask another student to give the season the first student's birthday falls in.

7 **Expansion**
↤♦↦ Ask volunteers to describe events, situations, or holidays that are important to them or their families. Have the class guess the event and name the season that applies.

8 **In-Class Tip** Bring in a Spanish-language calendar. Ask students to name the important events and their scheduled dates.

8 **Expansion**
• Give these holidays to students as items 7–10:
7. Independencia de los EE.UU. (4 de julio) 8. Navidad (25 de diciembre) 9. Día de Acción de Gracias (cuarto jueves de noviembre) 10. Día de los Inocentes (primero de abril)
• Ask heritage speakers to provide other important holidays, such as saints' days.

9 **Seleccionar** Paco is talking about his family and friends. Choose the word or phrase that best completes each sentence.

1. A mis padres les gusta ir a Yucatán porque (hace sol, nieva). hace sol
2. Mi primo de Kansas dice que durante (*during*) un tornado, hace mucho (sol, viento). viento
3. Mis amigos van a esquiar si (nieva, está nublado). nieva
4. Tomo el sol cuando (hace calor, llueve). hace calor
5. Nosotros vamos a ver una película si hace (buen, mal) tiempo. mal
6. Mi hermana prefiere correr cuando (hace mucho calor, hace fresco). hace fresco
7. Mis tíos van de excursión si hace (buen, mal) tiempo. buen
8. Mi padre no quiere jugar al golf si (hace fresco, llueve). llueve
9. Cuando hace mucho (sol, frío) no salgo de casa y tomo chocolate caliente (*hot*). frío
10. Hoy mi sobrino va al parque porque (está lloviendo, hace buen tiempo). hace buen tiempo

10 **El clima** With a partner, take turns asking and answering questions about the weather and temperatures in these cities. Use the model as a guide. Answers will vary.

> **modelo**
> **Estudiante 1:** ¿Qué tiempo hace hoy en Nueva York?
> **Estudiante 2:** Hace frío y hace viento.
> **Estudiante 1:** ¿Cuál es la temperatura máxima?
> **Estudiante 2:** Treinta y un grados (*degrees*).
> **Estudiante 1:** ¿Y la temperatura mínima?
> **Estudiante 2:** Diez grados.

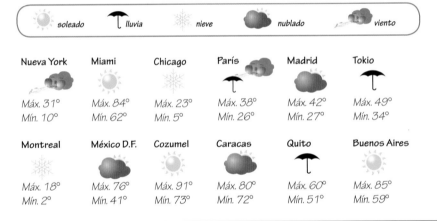

soleado   lluvia   nieve   nublado   viento

Nueva York	Miami	Chicago	París	Madrid	Tokio
Máx. 31°	Máx. 84°	Máx. 23°	Máx. 38°	Máx. 42°	Máx. 49°
Mín. 10°	Mín. 62°	Mín. 5°	Mín. 26°	Mín. 27°	Mín. 34°

Montreal	México D.F.	Cozumel	Caracas	Quito	Buenos Aires
Máx. 18°	Máx. 76°	Máx. 91°	Máx. 80°	Máx. 60°	Máx. 85°
Mín. 2°	Mín. 41°	Mín. 73°	Mín. 72°	Mín. 51°	Mín. 59°

11 **Completar** Complete these sentences with your own ideas. Answers will vary.

1. Cuando hace sol, yo…
2. Cuando llueve, mis amigos y yo…
3. Cuando hace calor, mi familia…
4. Cuando hace viento, la gente…
5. Cuando hace frío, yo…
6. Cuando hace mal tiempo, mis amigos…
7. Cuando nieva, muchas personas…
8. Cuando está nublado, mis amigos y yo…
9. Cuando hace fresco, mis padres…
10. Cuando hace buen tiempo, mis amigos…

NOTA CULTURAL

In most Spanish-speaking countries, temperatures are given in degrees Celsius. Use these formulas to convert between **grados centígrados** and **grados Fahrenheit**.
degrees C. × 9 ÷ 5 + 32 = degrees F.
degrees F. - 32 × 5 ÷ 9 = degrees C.

CONSULTA

Calor and **frío** can apply to both weather and people. Use **hacer** to describe weather conditions or climate.
(**Hace frío en Santiago.** *It's cold in Santiago.*)
Use **tener** to refer to people.
(**El viajero tiene frío.** *The traveler is cold.*)
See **Estructura 3.4**, p. 101.

Comunicación

12

En la agencia de viajes Listen to the conversation between Mr. Vega and a travel agent. Then indicate whether the following conclusions are **lógico** or **ilógico**, based on what you heard.

	Lógico	Ilógico
1. El señor Vega quiere visitar la Antártida.	○	⊘
2. Hace calor en Puerto Rico.	⊘	○
3. El señor Vega va a ver el mar en Puerto Rico.	⊘	○
4. El señor Vega va a comprar un pasaje de ida y vuelta.	⊘	○
5. El señor Vega viaja con su familia.	○	⊘

13

Preguntas personales Answer your partner's questions. *Answers will vary.*

1. ¿Cuál es la fecha de hoy? ¿Qué estación es?
2. ¿Te gusta esta estación? ¿Por qué?
3. ¿Qué estación prefieres? ¿Por qué?
4. ¿Prefieres el mar o las montañas? ¿La playa o el campo? ¿Por qué?
5. Cuando haces un viaje, ¿qué te gusta hacer y ver?
6. ¿Piensas ir de vacaciones este verano? ¿Adónde quieres ir? ¿Por qué?
7. ¿Qué deseas ver y qué lugares quieres visitar?
8. ¿Cómo te gusta viajar? ¿En avión? ¿En motocicleta...?

14

Itinerario Create a trip itinerary for a friend, a relative, or someone famous. First, choose a destination. Include information about transportation and accommodations, as well as a section for each day with activities. *Answers will vary.*

- fechas
- lugar
- transporte
- hotel
- actividades

Síntesis

15

Un viaje With a partner, role-play a conversation between a travel agent and a client planning a trip. Discuss destinations, dates, transportation, hotel accommodations, and activities for the trip.

Answers will vary.

¡Vamos a la playa!

Los seis amigos hacen un viaje a la playa.

PERSONAJES   FELIPE   JUAN CARLOS

TÍA ANA MARÍA ¿Están listos para su viaje a la playa?
TODOS Sí.
TÍA ANA MARÍA Excelente... ¡A la estación de autobuses!
MARU ¿Dónde está Miguel?
FELIPE Yo lo traigo.

FELIPE No está nada mal el hotel, ¿verdad? Limpio, cómodo... ¡Oye, Miguel! ¿Todavía estás enojado conmigo? (a Juan Carlos) Miguel está de mal humor. No me habla.
JUAN CARLOS ¿Todavía?

(se escucha un grito de Miguel)
FELIPE Ya está listo. Y tal vez enojado. Ahorita vamos.

EMPLEADO Bienvenidas. ¿En qué puedo servirles?
MARU Hola. Tenemos una reservación para seis personas para esta noche.
EMPLEADO ¿A nombre de quién?
JIMENA ¿Díaz? ¿López? No estoy segura.

EMPLEADO No encuentro su nombre. Ah, no, ahora sí lo veo, aquí está. Díaz. Dos habitaciones en el primer piso para seis huéspedes.

EMPLEADO Aquí están las llaves de sus habitaciones.
MARU Gracias. Una cosa más. Mi novio y yo queremos hacer windsurf, pero no tenemos tablas.
EMPLEADO El botones las puede conseguir para ustedes.

MARISSA   **JIMENA**   **MARU**   **MIGUEL**   **MAITE FUENTES**   **ANA MARÍA** **EMPLEADO**

JUAN CARLOS ¿Qué hace este libro aquí? ¿Estás estudiando en la playa?

JIMENA Sí, es que tengo un examen la próxima semana.

JUAN CARLOS Ay, Jimena. ¡No! ¿Vamos a nadar?

JIMENA Bueno, como estudiar es tan aburrido y el tiempo está tan bonito...

MARISSA Yo estoy un poco cansada. ¿Y tú? ¿Por qué no estás nadando?

FELIPE Es por causa de Miguel.

MARISSA Hmm, estoy confundida.

FELIPE Esta mañana. ¡Sigue enojado conmigo!

MARISSA No puede seguir enojado tanto tiempo.

Expresiones útiles

Talking with hotel personnel

¿En qué puedo servirles?
How can I help you?
Tenemos una reservación.
We have a reservation.
¿A nombre de quién?
In whose name?
¿Quizás López? ¿Tal vez Díaz?
Maybe López? Maybe Díaz?
Ahora lo veo, aquí está. Díaz.
Now I see it. Here it is. Díaz.
Dos habitaciones en el primer piso para seis huéspedes.
Two rooms on the first floor for six guests.
Aquí están las llaves.
Here are the keys.

Describing a hotel

No está nada mal el hotel.
The hotel isn't bad at all.
Todo está tan limpio y cómodo.
Everything is so clean and comfortable.
Es excelente/estupendo/fabuloso/ fenomenal/increíble/magnífico/ maravilloso/perfecto.
It's excellent/stupendous/fabulous/ phenomenal/incredible/magnificent/ marvelous/perfect.

Talking about how you feel

Yo estoy un poco cansado/a.
I am a little tired.
Estoy confundido/a. *I'm confused.*
Todavía estoy/Sigo enojado/a contigo.
I'm still angry with you.

Additional vocabulary

afuera *outside*
amable *nice; friendly*
el balde *bucket*
el/la botones *bellhop*
la crema de afeitar
shaving cream
el frente (frío) *(cold) front*
el grito *scream*
la temporada *period of time*
entonces *so, then*
es igual *it's the same*

Expresiones útiles Remind students that **está**, **están**, and **estoy** are present-tense forms of the verb **estar**, which is often used with adjectives that describe conditions and emotions. Remind students that **Es** is a present-tense form of the verb **ser**, which is often used to describe characteristics of people and things and to make generalizations. Draw students' attention to video stills 7 and 9. Point out that **Estás estudiando** and **estás nadando** are examples of the present progressive, which is used to emphasize an action in progress. Finally, point out the captions for video stills 1, 4, and 6 and explain that **lo** and **las** are examples of direct object pronouns. Explain that these are words that replace direct object nouns in order to avoid repetition. Tell students that they will learn more about these concepts in **Estructura**.

In-Class Tip
👤↔👤 Have students work in groups of six to read the **Fotonovela** captions aloud (have one student read the role of both **tía Ana María** and the **empleado**). Then have one group come to the front of the class and role-play the scenes. Encourage them to use props and gestures.

Nota cultural The **Yucatán** peninsula is warm year-round, but there are rainy and dry seasons. Generally, the dry season lasts from November to April and the wet season runs from May through October. Hurricanes occur in the late summer and fall. The **Yucatán's** average temperature is 25°C to 27°C (77°F to 81°F), rarely dropping below 16°C (61°F) or rising above 49°C (120°F).

TEACHING OPTIONS

Pairs Ask pairs to write five true/false statements based on the **¡Vamos a la playa!** captions. Then have them exchange papers with another pair, who will complete the activity and correct the false statements. Ask volunteers to read a few statements for the class, who will answer and point out the caption that contains the information.

PRE-AP®

Interpersonal Speaking 👤↔👤 Ask students to work in groups to rewrite the **¡Vamos a la playa!** episode using a different ending or location. Suggest new locations such as a ski resort, a big city, or a campground. Allow groups time to prepare, and ask them to ad-lib their new versions for the class. You may want to assign this activity as homework and have students present it in the next class period for review.

1 **In-Class Tip** Have students create sentences with the unused items from the word bank.

1 **Expansion** Have students create a follow-up question for each item. Then, in pairs, have them take turns reading the completed statements and asking their questions.

2 **Expansion** Tell the class to add **Marissa** and **Jimena** to the list of possible answers. Then, give these statements to the class as items 6–7: **6. No estoy segura del nombre. (Jimena) 7. Yo estoy confundida. (Marissa)**

Nota cultural Buses in Mexico provide an excellent alternative to rental cars. Mexican buses are generally efficient, comfortable, and inexpensive. A second-class ticket usually offers less leg room, a cheaper fare, and more stops than first-class. One major first-class bus company is **Autobuses del Oriente.**

3 **Expansion** Have pairs write sentences that describe what happens chronologically between items.

Pre-AP®

4 **Interpersonal Speaking** To simplify, have students prepare individually for their roles by brainstorming some phrases.

4 **Possible Conversation**
E1: Buenas tardes, señor. Tengo una reservación.
E2: Perdón, señorita, pero no encuentro su reservación.
E1: Está en mi nombre... Meg Adams.
E2: Ah, sí... aquí está. Tiene una habitación doble.
E1: Este hotel está muy limpio y cómodo.
E2: Sí. Bienvenida. Aquí están las llaves.
E1: ¿Puede llamar al botones para llevar mi equipaje, por favor?
E2: Claro. Don Raúl...

4 **Partner Chat**
Available online.

¿Qué pasó?

1 **Completar** Complete these sentences with the correct term from the word bank.

aburrido	botones	la llave
el aeropuerto	la estación de autobuses	montar a caballo
amable	habitaciones	reservación

1. Los amigos van a ___la estación de autobuses___ para ir a la playa.
2. La ___reservación___ del hotel está a nombre de los Díaz.
3. Los amigos tienen dos ___habitaciones___ para seis personas.
4. El ___botones___ puede conseguir tablas de windsurf para Maru.
5. Jimena dice que estudiar en vacaciones es muy ___aburrido___.

CONSULTA

The meaning of some adjectives, such as **aburrido**, changes depending on whether they are used with **ser** or **estar**. See **Estructura 5.3**, pp. 170–171.

2 **Identificar** Identify the person who would make each statement.

EMPLEADO   **MARU**   **TÍA ANA MARÍA**   **FELIPE**   **JUAN CARLOS**

1. No lo encuentro, ¿a nombre de quién está su reservación? empleado
2. ¿Por qué estás estudiando en la playa? ¡Mejor vamos a nadar! Juan Carlos
3. Nuestra reservación es para seis personas en dos habitaciones. Maru
4. El hotel es limpio y cómodo, pero estoy triste porque Miguel no me habla. Felipe
5. Suban al autobús y ¡buen viaje a la playa! Ana María

3 **Ordenar** Place these events in the correct order.

___3___ a. El empleado busca la reservación.
___5___ b. Marissa dice que está confundida.
___1___ c. Los amigos están listos para ir a la playa.
___4___ d. El empleado da (*gives*) las llaves de las habitaciones a las chicas.
___2___ e. Miguel grita (*screams*).

4 **Conversar** With a partner, use these cues to create a conversation between a hotel employee and a guest in Mexico. Answers will vary.

Huésped	Empleado/a
Say hi to the employee and ask for your reservation.	Tell the guest that you can't find his/her reservation.
Tell the employee that the reservation is in your name.	Tell him/her that you found the reservation and that it's for a double room.
Tell the employee that the hotel is very clean and comfortable.	Say that you agree with the guest, welcome him/her, and give him/her the keys.
Ask the employee to call the bellhop to help you with your luggage.	Call the bellhop to help the guest with his/her luggage.

TEACHING OPTIONS

Extra Practice Give students some true/false statements about the **Fotonovela**. Have them correct the false items. Ex: **1. Felipe todavía está enojado. (Falso. Miguel todavía está enojado.) 2. El botones puede llevar el equipaje a las habitaciones. (Cierto.) 3. La reservación es para siete huéspedes. (Falso. Es para seis huéspedes.) 4. Felipe no está nadando porque tiene que estudiar. (Falso. Es por causa de Miguel.)**

Small Groups Have students work in groups of four to prepare a skit to present to the class. In the skit, two friends check in to a hotel, have a bellhop carry their suitcases to their rooms, and decide what to do for the rest of the day. Students should specify what city they are visiting, describe the hotel and their rooms, and explain what activities they want to do while they are visiting the city.

Pronunciación
Spanish **b** and **v**

bueno	vóleibol	biblioteca	vivir

There is no difference in pronunciation between the Spanish letters **b** and **v**. However, each letter can be pronounced two different ways, depending on which letters appear next to them.

bonito	viajar	también	investigar

B and **v** are pronounced like the English hard *b* when they appear either as the first letter of a word, at the beginning of a phrase, or after **m** or **n**.

deber	novio	abril	favor

In all other positions, **b** and **v** have a softer pronunciation, which has no equivalent in English. Unlike the hard **b**, which is produced by tightly closing the lips and stopping the flow of air, the soft **b** is produced by keeping the lips slightly open.

bola	vela	Caribe	declive

In both pronunciations, there is no difference in sound between **b** and **v**. The English *v* sound, produced by friction between the upper teeth and lower lip, does not exist in Spanish. Instead, the soft **b** comes from friction between the two lips.

Verónica y su esposo cantan boleros.

When **b** or **v** begins a word, its pronunciation depends on the previous word. At the beginning of a phrase or after a word that ends in **m** or **n**, it is pronounced as a hard **b**.

Benito es de Boquerón pero vive en Victoria.

Words that begin with **b** or **v** are pronounced with a soft **b** if they appear immediately after a word that ends in a vowel or any consonant other than **m** or **n**.

Práctica Read these words aloud to practice the **b** and the **v**.

1. hablamos	4. van	7. doble	10. nublado
2. trabajar	5. contabilidad	8. novia	11. llave
3. botones	6. bien	9. béisbol	12. invierno

Oraciones Read these sentences aloud to practice the **b** and the **v**.

1. Vamos a Guaynabo en autobús.
2. Voy de vacaciones a la Isla Culebra.
3. Tengo una habitación individual en el octavo piso.
4. Víctor y Eva van en avión al Caribe.
5. La planta baja es bonita también.
6. ¿Qué vamos a ver en Bayamón?
7. Beatriz, la novia de Víctor, es de Arecibo, Puerto Rico.

Refranes Read these sayings aloud to practice the **b** and the **v**.

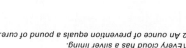

> No hay mal que por bien no venga.¹

> Hombre prevenido vale por dos.²

1 Every cloud has a silver lining.
2 An ounce of prevention equals a pound of cure.

Section Goal

In **Pronunciación**, students will be introduced to the pronunciation of **b** and **v**.

Comparisons 4.1

In-Class Tips

- Emphasize that **b** (alta/grande) and **v** (baja/chica) are pronounced identically in Spanish, but depending on the letter's position in a word, each can be pronounced two ways. Pronounce **vóleibol** and **vivir** and have students listen for the difference between the initial and medial sounds represented by **b** and **v**.
- Explain the cases in which **b** and **v** are pronounced like English *b* in *boy* and model the pronunciation of **bonito**, **viajar**, **también**, and **investigar**.
- Point out that before **b** or **v**, **n** is usually pronounced **m**.
- Explain that in all other positions, **b** and **v** are fricatives. Pronounce **deber**, **novio**, **abril**, and **cerveza** and stress that the friction is between the two lips.
- Remind the class that Spanish has no sound like the English **v**. Pronounce **vida**, **vacaciones**, **avión**, and **automóvil**.
- Explain that the same rules apply in connected speech. Practice with phrases like **de vacaciones** and **de ida y vuelta**.

TEACHING OPTIONS

Extra Practice Write some additional proverbs on the board and have the class practice saying each one. Ex: **Más vale que sobre y no que falte.** (*Better too much than too little.*) **No sólo de pan vive el hombre.** (*Man doesn't live by bread alone.*) **A caballo regalado no se le ve el colmillo.** (*Don't look a gift horse in the mouth.*) **Más vale dar que recibir.** (*It's better to give than to receive.*)

Small Groups Have students work in small groups and take turns reading aloud sentences from the **Fotonovela** on pages 158–159, focusing on the correct pronunciation of **b** and **v**. If a group member has trouble pronouncing a word that contains **b** or **v**, the rest of the group should supply the rule that explains how it should be pronounced.

EN DETALLE

Las cataratas del Iguazú

Imagine the impressive and majestic Niagara Falls, the most powerful waterfall in North America. Now, if you can, imagine a waterfall four times as wide and almost twice as tall that caused Eleanor Roosevelt to exclaim "Poor Niagara!" upon seeing it for the first time. Welcome to **las cataratas del Iguazú!**

Iguazú is located in Iguazú National Park, an area of subtropical jungle where Argentina meets Brazil. Its name comes from the indigenous Guaraní word for "great water." A UNESCO World Heritage Site, **las cataratas del Iguazú** span three kilometers and comprise 275 cascades split into two main sections by San Martín Island. Most of the falls are about 82 meters (270 feet) high. The horseshoe-shaped cataract **Garganta del Diablo** (Devil's Throat) has the greatest water flow and is considered to be the most impressive; it also marks the border between Argentina and Brazil.

Each country offers different views and tourist options. Most visitors opt to use the numerous catwalks that are available on both

Garganta del Diablo

Isla San Martín

sides; however, from the Argentinean side, tourists can get very close to the falls, whereas Brazil provides more panoramic views. If you don't mind getting wet, a jet boat tour is a good choice; those looking for wildlife—such as toucans, ocelots, butterflies, and jaguars—should head for San Martín Island. Brazil boasts less conventional ways to view the falls, such as helicopter rides and rappelling, while Argentina focuses on sustainability with its **Tren Ecológico de la Selva** (*Ecological Jungle Train*), an environmentally friendly way to reach the walkways.

No matter which way you choose to enjoy the falls, you are certain to be captivated.

Más cascadas° en Latinoamérica

Nombre	País	Altura°	Datos
Salto Ángel	Venezuela	979 metros	la más alta° del mundo°
Catarata del Gocta	Perú	771 metros	descubierta° en 2006
Piedra Volada	México	453 metros	la más alta de México

cascadas *waterfalls* Altura *Height* más alta *tallest* mundo *world* descubierta *discovered*

ACTIVIDADES

1 **¿Cierto o falso?** Indicate whether these statements are cierto or falso. Correct the false statements.

1. Iguazú Falls is located on the border of Argentina and Brazil. **Cierto.**
2. Niagara Falls is four times as wide as Iguazú Falls. **Falso.** Iguazú is four times as wide as Niagara Falls.
3. Iguazú Falls has a few cascades, each about 82 meters. **Falso.** Iguazú is composed of 275 cascades about 82 meters tall.
4. Tourists visiting Iguazú can see exotic wildlife. **Cierto.**
5. Iguazú is the Guaraní word for "blue water." **Falso.** Iguazú is the Guaraní word for "great water."
6. You can access the walkways by taking the **Garganta del Diablo**. **Falso.** One way of accessing the walkways is taking the **Tren Ecológico de la Selva**.
7. It is possible for tourists to visit Iguazú Falls by air. **Cierto.**
8. **Salto Ángel** is the tallest waterfall in the world. **Cierto.**
9. There are no waterfalls in Mexico. **Falso.** The **Piedra Volada** is in Mexico.
10. For the best views of Iguazú Falls, tourists should visit the Brazilian side. **Cierto.**

TEACHING OPTIONS

La leyenda Share this legend of the **Iguazú** Falls with students: Many ages ago, in the **Iguazú** River there lived a god-serpent, **Mboí**, to whom the **Guaraní** tribes sacrificed a young woman during their annual gathering. At one such gathering, a young man named **Tarobá** instantly fell in love with **Naipí**, who was to be sacrificed. After pleading in vain to have her spared, one night **Tarobá** took **Naipí** and tried to flee with her in his canoe.

The furious **Mboí** awoke and split the river in two, forming the waterfall and trapping the pair. He transformed **Naipí** into a rock at the base of the falls and **Tarobá** into a tree perched at the edge of the abyss. Lest the lovers try to reunite, the watchful **Mboí** keeps an eternal vigil from deep under the waters of the **Garganta del Diablo**. Now ask them to think of other creation legends they know (Ex: Paul Bunyan and the Great Lakes).

ASÍ SE DICE

Viajes y turismo

el asiento del medio, del pasillo, de la ventanilla	center, aisle, window seat
el itinerario	itinerary
media pensión	breakfast and one meal included
el ómnibus (Perú)	el autobús
pensión completa	all meals included
el puente	long weekend (lit., bridge)

EL MUNDO HISPANO

Destinos populares

- **Las playas del Parque Nacional Manuel Antonio** (Costa Rica) ofrecen° la oportunidad de nadar y luego caminar por el bosque tropical°.

- **Teotihuacán** (México) Desde antes de la época° de los aztecas, aquí se celebra el equinoccio de primavera en la Pirámide del Sol.

- **Puerto Chicama** (Perú), con sus olas° de cuatro kilómetros de largo°, es un destino para surfistas expertos.

- **Tikal** (Guatemala) Aquí puedes ver las maravillas de la selva° y ruinas de la civilización maya.

- **Las playas de Rincón** (Puerto Rico) Son ideales para descansar y observar ballenas°.

ofrecen *offer* bosque tropical *rainforest*
Desde antes de la época *Since before the time* olas *waves*
de largo *in length* selva *jungle* ballenas *whales*

PERFIL

Punta del Este

One of South America's largest and most fashionable beach resort towns is Uruguay's **Punta del Este**, a narrow strip of land containing twenty miles of pristine beaches. Its peninsular shape gives it two very different seascapes. **La Playa Mansa**, facing the bay and therefore the more protected side, has calm waters. Here, people practice water sports like swimming, water skiing, windsurfing, and diving. **La Playa Brava**, facing the east, receives the Atlantic Ocean's powerful, wave-producing winds, making it popular for surfing, body boarding, and kite surfing. Besides the beaches, posh shopping, and world-famous nightlife, **Punta** offers its 600,000 yearly visitors yacht and fishing clubs, golf courses, and excursions to observe sea lions at the **Isla de Lobos** nature reserve.

Conexión Internet

¿Cuáles son los sitios más populares para el turismo en Puerto Rico?

Use the Web to find more cultural information related to this **Cultura** section.

ACTIVIDADES

2 **Comprensión** Complete the sentences.
1. En las playas de Rincón puedes ver ___ballenas___.
2. Cerca de 600.000 turistas visitan ___Punta del Este___ cada año.
3. En el avión pides un ___asiento de la ventanilla___ si te gusta ver el paisaje.
4. En Punta del Este, la gente prefiere nadar en la Playa ___Mansa___.
5. El ___ómnibus___ es un medio de transporte en Perú.

3 **De vacaciones** Spring break is coming up, and you want to go on a short vacation with your family. Decide which of the locations featured on these pages best suits your likes and interests. Come to an agreement about how you will get there, where you prefer to stay and for how long, and what each of you will do during your free time. *Answers will vary.*

TEACHING OPTIONS

Heritage Speakers ←👤→ Ask heritage speakers to describe some popular beaches, ruins, or historical sites in their families' countries of origin. If possible, ask them to bring in a map or pictures of the locations. Have the class ask follow-up questions and compare and contrast the locations with those described on these pages.

Así se dice
- To challenge students, add these airport-related words to the list: **el/la auxiliar de vuelo** (*flight attendant*), **aterrizar** (*to land*), **el bolso de mano** (*carry-on bag*), **despegar** (*to take off*), **facturar** (*to check*), **hacer escala** (*to stop over*), **el retraso** (*delay*), **la tarjeta de embarque** (*boarding pass*).
- To practice vocabulary from the list, survey the class about their travel habits. Ex: **¿Prefieres el asiento de la ventanilla, del medio o del pasillo? ¿Por qué?**

Perfil **Punta del Este** is located 80 miles east of Uruguay's capital, Montevideo, on a small peninsula that separates the Atlantic Ocean and the **Río de la Plata** estuary. At the beginning of the nineteenth century, **Punta** was nearly deserted and only visited by fishermen and sailors. Its glamorous hotels, dining, nightlife, and beaches have earned it the nickname "the St. Tropez of South America."

El mundo hispano
- Add a visual aspect to this list by using a map to point out the locations of the different **destinos populares**.
- Ask students which destination interests them the most and why.

2 **Expansion** Ask students to write two additional cloze statements about the information on this page. Then have them exchange papers with a partner and complete the sentences.

3 **In-Class Tip** To simplify, make a list on the board of the vacation destinations mentioned on this spread. As a class, brainstorm tourist activities in Spanish for each location.

3 **Partner Chat**
👤↔👤 Available online.

Section Goals

In **Estructura 5.1**, students will learn:

• to use **estar** to describe conditions and emotions

• adjectives that describe conditions and emotions

 Comparisons 4.1

Teacher Resources

Read the front matter for suggestions on how to incorporate all the program's components. See pages 151A–151B for a detailed listing of Teacher Resources online.

In-Class Tips

• →👤← Ask students to find examples of **estar** used with adjectives in the **Fotonovela**. Have volunteers explain why **estar** instead of **ser** is used in each example.

• Remind students that adjectives agree in number and gender with the nouns they modify.

• Add a visual aspect to this grammar presentation. Bring in personal or magazine photos of people with varying facial expressions. Hold up each one and state the person's emotion. Ex: **Mi esposa y yo estamos contentos.**

• Point to objects and people and have volunteers supply the correct form of **estar** + [*adjective*]. Ex: Point to windows. (**Están abiertas.**)

• Use TPR to practice the adjectives. Have the class stand, and signal a student. Say: ____, **estás enojado/a.** (Student will make an angry face.) Vary by indicating more than one student.

• Point out the use of **de** with **enamorado/a** and **por** with **preocupado/a.** Write cloze sentences on the board and have students complete them. Ex: **Michelle Obama está ____ Barack Obama.** (**enamorada de**)

5.1 | Estar with conditions and emotions

ANTE TODO As you learned in **Lecciones 1** and **2**, the verb **estar** is used to talk about how you feel and to say where people, places, and things are located. **Estar** is also used with adjectives to talk about certain emotional and physical conditions.

▶ Use **estar** with adjectives to describe the physical condition of places and things.

La habitación **está** sucia.
The room is dirty.

La puerta **está** cerrada.
The door is closed.

▶ Use **estar** with adjectives to describe how people feel, both mentally and physically.

Yo estoy cansada.

¿Están listos para su viaje?

▶ **¡Atención!** Two important expressions with **estar** that you can use to talk about conditions and emotions are **estar de buen humor** (*to be in a good mood*) and **estar de mal humor** (*to be in a bad mood*).

CONSULTA

To review the present tense of **estar**, see **Estructura 2.3**, p. 59.
• • •
To review the present tense of **ser**, see **Estructura 1.3**, p. 20.

Adjectives that describe emotions and conditions

abierto/a	open	**contento/a**	content	**listo/a**	ready
aburrido/a	bored	**desordenado/a**	disorderly	**nervioso/a**	nervous
alegre	happy	**enamorado/a (de)**	in love (with)	**ocupado/a**	busy
avergonzado/a	embarrassed	**enojado/a**	angry	**ordenado/a**	orderly
cansado/a	tired	**equivocado/a**	wrong	**preocupado/a (por)**	worried (about)
cerrado/a	closed	**feliz**	happy	**seguro/a**	sure
cómodo/a	comfortable	**limpio/a**	clean	**sucio/a**	dirty
confundido/a	confused			**triste**	sad

¡INTÉNTALO! Provide the present tense forms of **estar**, and choose which adjective best completes the sentence.

1. La biblioteca ___está___ (cerrada / nerviosa) los domingos por la noche. *cerrada*
2. Nosotros ___estamos___ muy (ocupados / equivocados) todos los lunes. *ocupados*
3. Ellas ___están___ (alegres / confundidas) porque tienen vacaciones. *alegres*
4. Javier ___está___ (enamorado / ordenado) de Maribel. *enamorado*
5. Diana ___está___ (enojada / limpia) con su hermano. *enojada*
6. Yo ___estoy___ (nerviosa / abierta) por el viaje. *nerviosa*
7. La habitación siempre ___está___ (ordenada / segura) cuando vienen sus padres. *ordenada*
8. Ustedes no comprenden; ___están___ (equivocados / tristes). *equivocados*

TPR Call out a sentence using an adjective and have students mime the emotion or show the condition. Ex: **Sus libros están abiertos.** (Students show their open books.) **Ustedes están alegres.** (Students act happy.) Next, call on volunteers to act out an emotion or condition, and have the class tell what is going on. Ex: A student pretends to cry. (**Carlos está triste.**)

Video →👤← Replay the **Fotonovela** episode and ask comprehension questions using **estar** and adjectives expressing emotions or conditions. Ex: **¿Cómo está el hotel?** (**Está limpio y cómodo.**) **¿Está de mal humor Miguel?** (**Sí, está de mal humor.**) **¿Quién está cansado?** (**Marissa está cansada.**)

Práctica y Comunicación

1 **¿Cómo están?** Complete Martín's statements about how he and other people are feeling. In the first blank, fill in the correct form of **estar**. In the second blank, fill in the adjective that best fits the context. Some answers may vary.

AYUDA

Make sure that there is agreement between:
• Subjects and verbs in person and number
• Nouns and adjectives in gender and number
Ell**os** no est**án** enferm**os**.
They are not sick.

1. Yo ___estoy___ un poco ___nervioso___ porque tengo un examen mañana.
2. Mi hermana Patricia ___está___ muy ___contenta___ porque mañana va a hacer una excursión al campo.
3. Mis hermanos Juan y José salen de la casa a las cinco de la mañana. Por la noche, siempre ___están___ muy ___cansados___.
4. Mi amigo Ramiro ___está___ ___enamorado___; su novia se llama Adela.
5. Mi papá y sus colegas ___están___ muy ___ocupados___ hoy. ¡Hay mucho trabajo!
6. Patricia y yo ___estamos___ un poco ___preocupados___ por ellos porque trabajan mucho.
7. Mi amiga Mónica ___está___ un poco ___triste/enojada___ porque sus amigos no pueden salir esta noche.
8. Esta clase no es muy interesante. ¿Tú ___estás___ ___aburrido/a___ también?

2 **Describir** Describe these people and places. Answers will vary. Sample answers:

1. Anabela
Está contenta/alegre/feliz.

2. Juan y Luisa
Están enojados.

3. la habitación de Teresa
Está ordenada/limpia.

4. la habitación de César
Está desordenada/sucia.

3 **Situaciones** With a partner, use **estar** to talk about how you feel in these situations.
Answers will vary.

1. Cuando hace sol…
2. Cuando tomas un examen…
3. Cuando viajas en avión…
4. Cuando llueve…
5. Cuando ves una película con tu actor/actriz favorito/a…

4 **Emociones** Write an e-mail to a friend explaining what you do when you feel a certain way. Use five adjectives of emotion. Answers will vary.

> **modelo**
> *Cuando estoy preocupado, hablo por teléfono con mi madre.*
> *Cuando estoy aburrido, miro la televisión…*

---

1 In-Class Tip Have a volunteer model the first sentence by supplying the correct form of **estar** and an appropriate adjective. Ask the student to explain his or her choices.

1 Expansion Have students write five additional sentences missing **estar** and an adjective. Then have them exchange papers and complete the sentences.

2 Expansion
• Have students write a few sentences about the illustrations explaining why the people feel the way they do and why the rooms look this way.
• Have students pretend they are **Anabela, Juan,** or **Luisa** and give a short oral description of who they are and how they feel today.

3 In-Class Tip Have partners alternate completing the sentences until each has answered all items.

3 Expansion Ask students to keep a record of their partners' responses. Take a classroom poll to see what percentage of students felt a particular way for each situation.

3 Virtual Chat Available online.

4 Expansion Have pairs of students exchange e-mails, and bring their classmates' printed messages to class. Have them edit the text they received and ask volunteers to read their partner's message aloud.

TEACHING OPTIONS

Pairs Have students write a list of four questions using different conjugations of **estar** and four adjectives that have an antonym from the list on page 164. Students ask partners their questions. They respond negatively, then use the opposite adjective in an affirmative statement. Ex: **¿Está abierta la biblioteca? (No, no está abierta. Está cerrada.)**

Extra Practice For homework, have students pick eight adjectives of emotion from the list on page 164 and write sentences about what they do when they feel that way. Ex: **Cuando estoy preocupado, hablo por teléfono con mi madre…** In class, have students form small groups and share their sentences. Survey the class to see if there are any common activities.

Section Goals

In **Estructura 5.2**, students will learn:
• the present progressive of regular and irregular verbs
• the present progressive versus the simple present tense in Spanish

Comparisons 4.1

Teacher Resources

Read the front matter for suggestions on how to incorporate all the program's components. See pages 151A–151B for a detailed listing of Teacher Resources online.

In-Class Tips

• Use regular verbs to ask questions about things students are not doing. Ex: **¿Estás comiendo pizza? (No, no estoy comiendo pizza.)**
• Explain the formation of the present progressive, writing examples on the board.
• Add a visual aspect to this grammar presentation. Use photos to elicit sentences with the present progressive. Ex: **¿Qué está haciendo el hombre alto? (Está sacando fotos.)** Include present participles ending in –**yendo** as well as those with stem changes.
• Point out that the present progressive is rarely used with the verbs **ir, poder,** and **venir** since they already imply an action in progress.

5.2 # The present progressive

ANTE TODO   Both Spanish and English use the present progressive, which consists of the present tense of the verb *to be* and the present participle of another verb (the *-ing* form in English).

Las chicas están hablando con el empleado del hotel.

¿Estás estudiando en la playa?

▶ Form the present progressive with the present tense of **estar** and a present participle.

FORM OF **ESTAR** + PRESENT PARTICIPLE
Estoy   **pescando.**
I am   *fishing.*

FORM OF **ESTAR** + PRESENT PARTICIPLE
Estamos   **comiendo.**
We are   *eating.*

▶ The present participle of regular **-ar**, **-er**, and **-ir** verbs is formed as follows:

INFINITIVE	STEM	ENDING	PRESENT PARTICIPLE
hablar	habl-	**-ando**	habl**ando**
comer	com-	**-iendo**	com**iendo**
escribir	escrib-	**-iendo**	escrib**iendo**

▶ **¡Atención!** When the stem of an **-er** or **-ir** verb ends in a vowel, the present participle ends in **-yendo**.

INFINITIVE	STEM	ENDING	PRESENT PARTICIPLE
leer	le-	**-yendo**	le**yendo**
oír	o-	**-yendo**	o**yendo**
traer	tra-	**-yendo**	tra**yendo**

▶ **Ir**, **poder**, and **venir** have irregular present participles (**yendo, pudiendo, viniendo**). Several other verbs have irregular present participles that you will need to learn.

▶ **-Ir** stem-changing verbs have a stem change in the present participle.

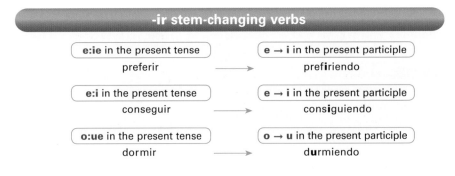

-ir stem-changing verbs

e:ie in the present tense		e → i in the present participle
preferir	⟶	prefir**iendo**

e:i in the present tense		e → i in the present participle
conseguir	⟶	consig**uiendo**

o:ue in the present tense		o → u in the present participle
dormir	⟶	d**u**rmiendo

TEACHING OPTIONS

TPR Divide the class into three groups. Appoint leaders and give them a list of verbs. Leaders call out a verb and a subject (Ex: **seguir/yo**), then toss a ball to someone in the group. That student says the appropriate present progressive form of the verb (Ex: **estoy siguiendo**) and tosses the ball back. Leaders should use all the verbs on the list and be sure to toss the ball to each member of the group.

TPR Play charades. In groups of four, have students take turns miming actions for the rest of the group to guess. Ex: Student pretends to read a newspaper. (**Estás leyendo el periódico.**) For incorrect guesses, the student should respond negatively. Ex: **No, no estoy estudiando.**

COMPARE & CONTRAST

The use of the present progressive is much more restricted in Spanish than in English. In Spanish, the present progressive is mainly used to emphasize that an action is in progress at the time of speaking.

Maru **está escuchando** música latina **ahora mismo**.
Maru is listening to Latin music right now.

Felipe y su amigo **todavía están jugando** al fútbol.
Felipe and his friend are still playing soccer.

In English, the present progressive is often used to talk about situations and actions that occur over an extended period of time or in the future. In Spanish, the simple present tense is often used instead.

Xavier **estudia** computación este semestre.
Xavier is studying computer science this semester.

Marissa **sale** mañana para los Estados Unidos.
Marissa is leaving tomorrow for the United States.

¿Está pensando en su futuro?
Nosotros, sí.

BANCO
🏛 **CONGRESO** 🏛

Preparándolo para el mañana

¡INTÉNTALO! Create complete sentences by putting the verbs in the present progressive.

1. mis amigos / descansar en la playa _Mis amigos están descansando en la playa._
2. nosotros / practicar deportes _Estamos practicando deportes._
3. Carmen / comer en casa _Carmen está comiendo en casa._
4. nuestro equipo / ganar el partido _Nuestro equipo está ganando el partido._
5. yo / leer el periódico _Estoy leyendo el periódico._
6. él / pensar comprar una bicicleta _Está pensando comprar una bicicleta._
7. ustedes / jugar a las cartas _Ustedes están jugando a las cartas._
8. José y Francisco / dormir _José y Francisco están durmiendo._
9. Marisa / leer correo electrónico _Marisa está leyendo correo electrónico._
10. yo / preparar sándwiches _Estoy preparando sándwiches._
11. Carlos / tomar fotos _Carlos está tomando fotos._
12. ¿dormir / tú? _¿Estás durmiendo?_

Práctica

1 **Completar** Alfredo's Spanish class is preparing to travel to Puerto Rico. Use the present progressive of the verb in parentheses to complete Alfredo's description of what everyone is doing.

1. Yo <u>estoy investigando</u> (investigar) la situación política de la isla (*island*).
2. La esposa del profesor <u>está haciendo</u> (hacer) las maletas.
3. Marta y José Luis <u>están buscando</u> (buscar) información sobre San Juan en Internet.
4. Enrique y yo <u>estamos leyendo</u> (leer) un correo electrónico de nuestro amigo puertorriqueño.
5. Javier <u>está aprendiendo</u> (aprender) mucho sobre la cultura puertorriqueña.
6. Y tú <u>estás practicando</u> (practicar) el español, ¿verdad?

2 **¿Qué están haciendo?** María and her friends are vacationing at a resort in San Juan, Puerto Rico. Complete her description of what everyone is doing right now.

CONSULTA

For more information about Puerto Rico, see **Panorama**, pp. 186–187.

1. Yo
estoy escribiendo una carta.

2. Javier
está buceando en el mar.

3. Alejandro y Rebeca
están jugando a las cartas.

4. Celia y yo
estamos tomando el sol.

5. Samuel
está escuchando música.

6. Lorenzo
está durmiendo.

3 **Personajes famosos** Say what these celebrities are doing right now, using the cues provided.
Answers will vary.

modelo

Shakira

Shakira está cantando una canción ahora mismo.

A		B	
Isabel Allende	Nelly Furtado	bailar	hacer
Rachael Ray	Dwight Howard	cantar	jugar
James Cameron	Las Rockettes de	correr	preparar
Venus y Serena	Nueva York	escribir	¿?
Williams	¿?	hablar	¿?
Joey Votto	¿?		

AYUDA

Isabel Allende: **novelas**

Rachael Ray: **televisión, negocios** (*business*)

James Cameron: **cine**

Venus y Serena Williams: **tenis**

Joey Votto: **béisbol**

Nelly Furtado: **canciones**

Dwight Howard: **baloncesto**

Las Rockettes de Nueva York: **baile**

1 **Expansion** Ask students comprehension questions that elicit the present progressive. Ex: **¿Quién está buscando información? (Marta y José Luis están buscando información.) ¿Qué información están buscando? (Están buscando información sobre San Juan.)**

2 **In-Class Tips**
- Use the **Lección 5 Estructura** online Resources to assist with the presentation of this activity.
- Before starting the activity, ask students questions about each drawing to elicit a description of what they see. Ex: **¿Quién está en el dibujo número 5? (Samuel está en el dibujo.) ¿Dónde está Samuel? (Está en la playa.) ¿Qué más ven en el dibujo? (Vemos una silla y el mar.)**

3 **In-Class Tip** To simplify, first read through the names in column A as a class. Point out the profession clues in the **Ayuda** box, then guide students in matching each name with an infinitive. Finally, have students form sentences.

3 **Expansion**
↔ Have students choose five more celebrities and write descriptions of what they are doing at this moment.

TEACHING OPTIONS

Pairs ↔ Have students bring in photos from a vacation. Ask them to describe the photos to a partner. Students should explain what the weather is like, who is in the photo, and what they are doing. The partner should try to guess the location the student is describing. Students can ask additional questions until they guess correctly.

Game Have the class form a circle. Appoint one student to be the starter, who will mime an action (Ex: eating) and say what he or she is doing (Ex: **Estoy comiendo.**). The next student mimes the same action, says what that person is doing (____ **está comiendo.**), and then mimes and states a different action (Ex: sleeping/**Estoy durmiendo.**). Have students continue until the chain breaks. Have students see how long the chain can get in three minutes.

Comunicación

Communication 1.1, 1.2, 1.3
Comparisons 4.1

4 **Las vacaciones** Read Elena's description of her family vacation. Then indicate whether these conclusions are **lógico** or **ilógico**, based on what you read.

> Está lloviendo. Mis tres hermanos están jugando a las cartas. Mi hermana está leyendo una revista. Mi madre está buscando la llave de la habitación. Mi padre está durmiendo. ¿Y yo? Estoy escribiendo este mensaje electrónico...

	Lógico	Ilógico
1. Hace mal tiempo.	⊘	○
2. La familia es pequeña.	○	⊘
3. La madre está contenta.	○	⊘
4. El padre está en la cama.	⊘	○
5. La familia está en un hotel.	⊘	○

4 Expansion After checking students' answers, ask volunteers to change the activities so they would be true for their family on a rainy day on vacation. Ex: **Está lloviendo. Mis hermanos están jugando a los videojuegos. Mi hermana está escuchando música en su habitación...**

5 **Preguntar** Answer your partner's questions about what you are doing at these times. *Answers will vary.*

> **modelo**
> 8:00 a.m.
> **Estudiante 1:** *Son las ocho de la mañana. ¿Qué estás haciendo?*
> **Estudiante 2:** *Estoy desayunando.*

1. 5:00 a.m.	3. 11:00 a.m.	5. 2:00 p.m.	7. 9:00 p.m.
2. 9:30 a.m.	4. 12:00 p.m.	6. 5:00 p.m.	8. 11:30 p.m.

5 Expansion
 Reverse the activity by having students state what they are doing. Their partner should guess the time of day. Alternatively, students could say that they are doing season-specific activities (Ex: **Estoy tomando el sol.**) and their partner will guess the month.

5 Virtual Chat
 Available online.

6 **Describir** Use the present progressive to write a description of what is happening in this Spanish beach scene. *Answers will vary.*

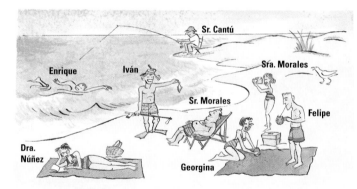

6 In-Class Tip Use the online Resources (Lección 5/ Digital Image Bank/ Estructura 5.2 Present Progressive) to assist with the presentation of this activity.

6 Expansion
 In pairs, have students write a conversation between two or more of the people in the drawing. Conversations should consist of at least three exchanges.

Síntesis

Communication 1.1

7 **¿Qué están haciendo?** With a partner, take turns asking each other what people are doing right now. You could ask about other students, professors, or even celebrities. *Answers will vary.*

bailar	comer	escribir	estudiar	leer
cantar	enseñar	escuchar	jugar	mirar

7 Expansion Divide the class in pairs and distribute the handouts for the activity **¿Qué están haciendo?** from the online Resources (Lección 5/Activity Pack/ Information Gap Activities). Ask students to read the instructions and give them ten minutes to complete the activity. Have volunteers report their findings to the class.

7 Partner Chat
 Available online.

Video Show the **Fotonovela** episode again, pausing after each exchange. Ask students to describe what each person in the shot is doing at that moment.
TPR Write sentences with the present progressive on strips of paper. Call on volunteers to draw papers out of a hat to act out. The class should guess what the sentences are. Ex: **Yo estoy durmiendo en la cama.**

Pairs Add an auditory aspect to this grammar practice. Ask students to write a short paragraph using the present progressive. Students should try to make their sentences as complex as possible. Have students dictate their sentences to a partner. After pairs have finished dictating their sentences, have them exchange papers to check for accuracy. Circulate around the room and look over students' work.

Section Goal

In **Estructura 5.3**, students will review and compare the uses of **ser** and **estar**.

Comparisons 4.1

Teacher Resources
Read the front matter for suggestions on how to incorporate all the program's components. See pages 151A–151B for a detailed listing of Teacher Resources online.

In-Class Tips
- Use the **Lección 5** Grammar Presentation Slides to assist with this presentation.
- Have pairs brainstorm as many uses of **ser** with examples as they can. Compile a list on the board, and repeat for **estar**.
- Divide the board into two columns. In column one, write sentences using **ser** and **estar** in random order (Ex: **Miguel es de España.**). In column two, write the uses of **ser** and **estar** taught so far, also in random order (Ex: place of origin). Ask volunteers to match the sentence with its corresponding use.
- Write cloze sentences on the board. Ask students to supply the correct form of **ser** or **estar**. Ex: **Mi casa ____ lejos de aquí.** (estar, location; **está**) If either **ser** or **estar** could be used, ask students to explain how the meaning of the sentence would change.
- →🔳← Contrast the uses of **ser** and **estar** by talking about celebrities. Ex: **Shakira es colombiana y su familia es de origen libanés. Es bonita y delgada. Es cantante. Ella está en los Estados Unidos ahora. Está haciendo una gira de conciertos. Tiene un concierto hoy; es a las ocho. El concierto es en un estadio. El estadio está en Miami.** Pause after each sentence and have students identify the use(s).

5.3 Ser and estar

ANTE TODO You have already learned that **ser** and **estar** both mean *to be* but are used for different purposes. These charts summarize the key differences in usage between **ser** and **estar**.

Uses of ser

1. **Nationality and place of origin** . . . . Juan Carlos **es** argentino.
   Es de Buenos Aires.

2. **Profession or occupation** . . . . Adela **es** agente de viajes.
   Francisco **es** médico.

3. **Characteristics of people and things** . . . José y Clara **son** simpáticos.
   El clima de Puerto Rico **es** agradable.

4. **Generalizations** . . . . ¡**Es** fabuloso viajar!
   Es difícil estudiar a la una de la mañana.

5. **Possession** . . . . **Es** la pluma de Jimena.
   Son las llaves del señor Díaz.

6. **What something is made of** . . . . La bicicleta **es** de metal.
   Los pasajes **son** de papel.

7. **Time and date** . . . . Hoy **es** martes. **Son** las dos.
   Hoy **es** el primero de julio.

8. **Where or when an event takes place** . . . El partido **es** en el estadio Santa Fe.
   La conferencia **es** a las siete.

Ellos son mis amigos.

Miguel está enojado conmigo.

Uses of estar

1. **Location or spatial relationships** . . . . . El aeropuerto **está** lejos de la ciudad.
   Tu habitación **está** en el tercer piso.

2. **Health** . . . . ¿Cómo **estás**?
   Estoy bien, gracias.

3. **Physical states and conditions** . . . . El profesor **está** ocupado.
   Las ventanas **están** abiertas.

4. **Emotional states** . . . . Marissa **está** feliz hoy.
   Estoy muy enojado con Maru.

5. **Certain weather expressions** . . . . **Está** lloviendo.
   Está nublado.

6. **Ongoing actions (progressive tenses)** . . **Estamos** estudiando para un examen.
   Ana **está** leyendo una novela.

TEACHING OPTIONS

Extra Practice Add an auditory aspect to this grammar presentation. Call out sentences containing forms of **ser** or **estar**. Ask students to identify the use of the verb.
Extra Practice ←🔳→ Ask students to write a postcard to a friend or family member about a vacation in Puerto Rico, incorporating as many of the uses of **ser** and **estar** as they can.

Game Divide the class into two teams. Call out a use of **ser** or **estar**. The first member of each team runs to the board and writes a sample sentence. The first student to finish a sentence correctly earns a point for his or her team. Practice all uses of each verb and make sure each team member has at least two turns. Then tally the points to see which team wins.

Ser and estar with adjectives

▶ With many descriptive adjectives, **ser** and **estar** can both be used, but the meaning will change.

Juan **es** delgado.
Juan is thin.

Juan **está** más delgado hoy.
Juan looks thinner today.

Ana **es** nerviosa.
Ana is a nervous person.

Ana **está** nerviosa por el examen.
Ana is nervous because of the exam.

▶ In the examples above, the statements with **ser** are general observations about the inherent qualities of Juan and Ana. The statements with **estar** describe conditions that are variable.

▶ Here are some adjectives that change in meaning when used with **ser** and **estar**.

With ser	With estar
El chico **es listo**. *The boy is smart.*	El chico **está listo**. *The boy is ready.*
La profesora **es mala**. *The professor is bad.*	La profesora **está mala**. *The professor is sick.*
Jaime **es aburrido**. *Jaime is boring.*	Jaime **está aburrido**. *Jaime is bored.*
Las peras **son verdes**. *Pears are green.*	Las peras **están verdes**. *The pears are not ripe.*
El gato **es muy vivo**. *The cat is very clever.*	El gato **está vivo**. *The cat is alive.*
Iván **es un hombre seguro**. *Iván is a confident man.*	Iván no **está seguro**. *Iván is not sure.*

¡INTÉNTALO!   Form complete sentences by using the correct form of **ser** or **estar** and making any other necessary changes.

1. Alejandra / cansado
   Alejandra está cansada.

2. ellos / pelirrojo
   Ellos son pelirrojos.

3. Carmen / alto
   Carmen es alta.

4. yo / la clase de español
   Estoy en la clase de español.

5. película / a las once
   La película es a las once.

6. hoy / viernes
   Hoy es viernes.

7. nosotras / enojado
   Nosotras estamos enojadas.

8. Antonio / médico
   Antonio es médico.

9. Romeo y Julieta / enamorado
   Romeo y Julieta están enamorados.

10. libros / de Ana
    Los libros son de Ana.

11. Marisa y Juan / estudiando
    Marisa y Juan están estudiando.

12. partido de baloncesto / gimnasio
    El partido de baloncesto es en el gimnasio.

Práctica

1 In-Class Tip Have students identify the use(s) of **ser** or **estar** for each item.

1 Expansion To challenge students, ask them to use each adjective in a sentence. If the adjective can take both verbs, have them provide two sentences.

2 In-Class Tip To simplify, ask students to point out context clues that will help them determine whether to use **ser** or **estar**. Ex: The word **hoy** in line 2 suggests that **guapo** is a variable physical state.

2 Expansion
←👤→ Have pairs write a continuation of the conversation and then present it to the class.

3 In-Class Tip Use the **Lección 5 Estructura** online Resources to assist with the presentation of this activity.

3 Expansion
←👤→ Add another visual aspect to this grammar practice. Bring in photos or magazine pictures that show many different people performing a variety of activities. Have students use **ser** and **estar** to write short descriptions of the scenes.

1 ¿Ser o estar? Indicate whether each adjective takes **ser** or **estar**. ¡Ojo! Three of them can take both verbs.

	ser	estar		ser	estar
1. delgada	☑	☑	5. seguro	☑	☑
2. canadiense	☑	○	6. enojada	○	☑
3. enamorado	○	☑	7. importante	☑	○
4. lista	☑	☑	8. avergonzada	○	☑

2 Completar Complete this conversation with the appropriate forms of **ser** and **estar**.

EDUARDO ¡Hola, Ceci! ¿Cómo (1)___estás___?

CECILIA Hola, Eduardo. Bien, gracias. ¡Qué guapo (2)___estás___ hoy!

EDUARDO Gracias. (3)___Eres___ muy amable. Oye, ¿qué (4)___estás___ haciendo? (5)¿___Estás___ ocupada?

CECILIA No, sólo le (6)___estoy___ escribiendo una carta a mi prima Pilar.

EDUARDO ¿De dónde (7)___es___ ella?

CECILIA Pilar (8)___es___ de Ecuador. Su papá (9)___es___ médico en Quito. Pero ahora Pilar y su familia (10)___están___ de vacaciones en Ponce, Puerto Rico.

EDUARDO Y... ¿cómo (11)___es___ Pilar?

CECILIA (12)___Es___ muy lista. Y también (13)___es___ alta, rubia y muy bonita.

3 En el parque Describe the people in the drawing. Your descriptions should answer the questions provided. Answers will vary.

1. ¿Quiénes son?
2. ¿Dónde están?
3. ¿Cómo son?
4. ¿Cómo están?
5. ¿Qué están haciendo?
6. ¿Qué estación es?
7. ¿Qué tiempo hace?
8. ¿Quiénes están de vacaciones?

TEACHING OPTIONS

Extra Practice ←👤→ Have students write a paragraph about a close friend, including the person's physical appearance, general disposition, place of birth, birthday, profession, and where the friend is now. Ask volunteers to share their descriptions with the class.

Pairs 👤↔👤 Ask pairs to role-play this scenario: Student A is at the beach with some friends while Student B is at home. Student A calls Student B, trying to convince him or her to come to the beach. Students should try to employ as many uses of **ser** and **estar** in their scenario as possible. After acting out the scene once, have students switch roles.

Comunicación

4 Ponce Listen to Carolina's description of her vacation. Then indicate whether the following conclusions are **lógico** or **ilógico**, based on what you heard.

	Lógico	Ilógico
1. Carolina es una turista.	⊘	○
2. Carolina prefiere acampar.	○	⊘
3. A Carolina no le gusta ir a la playa.	○	⊘
4. Carolina vive en Ponce.	○	⊘
5. A Carolina le gustan los museos.	⊘	○

5 Una persona famosa Describe a celebrity using these items as a guide. Answers will vary.

- descripción física
- origen
- qué está haciendo ahora
- cómo está ahora
- dónde está ahora
- profesión u ocupación

6 En el aeropuerto With a partner, take turns assuming the identity of a character from this drawing. Your partner will ask you questions using **ser** and **estar** to figure out who you are.   Answers will vary.

> **modelo**
> **Estudiante 2:** ¿Dónde estás?
> **Estudiante 1:** Estoy cerca de la puerta.
> **Estudiante 2:** ¿Qué estás haciendo?
> **Estudiante 1:** Estoy escuchando a otra persona.
> **Estudiante 2:** ¿Eres uno de los pasajeros?
> **Estudiante 1:** No, soy empleado del aeropuerto.
> **Estudiante 2:** ¿Eres Camilo?

Síntesis

7 Un hotel magnífico Write a radio ad for a vacation resort somewhere in the Spanish-speaking world. Use **ser** and **estar** in as many different ways as you can. Answers will vary.

---

4 In-Class Tip Have students listen to the audio once and ask for the global idea of the text (Ex: **Se trata de Carolina, una turista que está de vacaciones en la ciudad de Ponce**). Then, ask more specific questions, such as: **¿Qué va a hacer Carolina en Ponce? ¿Cómo se llama el museo que va a visitar?**

4 Script *See the script for this activity on Interleaf page 151B.*

5 In-Class Tip Have students work in pairs and take turns describing the celebrity without mentioning names. Model the activity for the class and tell students to use **una persona** to create ambiguity in their descriptions. Ex: **Es una persona alta…**

6 In-Class Tip Use the online Resources (Lección 5/ Digital Image Bank/ Estructura 5.3 **Ser** and **estar**) to assist with the presentation of this activity.

6 Expansion Have students pick one of the individuals pictured and write a one-paragraph description, employing as many different uses of **ser** and **estar** as possible.

6 Partner Chat Available online.

Communication 1.3
Cultures 2.1
Comparisons 4.1, 4.2

7 Expansion Have students record their radio ads, and listen to them in class.

The Affective Dimension Encourage students to consider pair and group activities as a cooperative venture in which group members support and motivate each other.

Small Groups Have students work in small groups to write a television commercial for a vacation resort in the Spanish-speaking world. Ask them to employ as many uses of **ser** and **estar** as they can. If possible, after they have written the commercial, have them tape it to show to the class.

TPR Call on a volunteer and whisper the name of a celebrity in his or her ear. The volunteer acts out verbs and characteristics and uses props to elicit descriptions from the class. Ex: The volunteer points to the U.S. on a map. (**Es de los Estados Unidos.**) He or she then indicates a tall, thin man. (**Es un hombre atlético y delgado.**) He or she acts out swimming. (**Está nadando. ¿Es Michael Phelps?**)

Section Goals

In **Estructura 5.4**, students will study:
• direct object nouns
• the personal **a**
• direct object pronouns

 Comparisons 4.1

Teacher Resources
Read the front matter for suggestions on how to incorporate all the program's components. See pages 151A–151B for a detailed listing of Teacher Resources online.

In-Class Tips
• Write these sentences on the board: —**¿Quién tiene el pasaporte? —Juan lo tiene.** Underline **pasaporte** and explain that it is a direct object noun. Then underline **lo** and explain that it is the masculine singular direct object pronoun. Translate both sentences. Continue with: —**¿Quién saca fotos? —Simón las saca. —¿Quién tiene la llave? —Pilar la tiene.**
• Read this exchange aloud: —**¿Haces las maletas? —No, no hago las maletas. —¿Por qué no haces las maletas? —No hago las maletas porque las maletas no están aquí.** Ask students if the exchange sounds natural to them. Then write it on the board and ask students to use direct object pronouns to avoid repetition. If students try to say **no las están** in the last sentence, point out that direct object pronouns cannot replace the subject of a verb. The only option is to eliminate the subject: **no están.**
• Ask individuals questions to elicit the personal a: **¿Visitas a tu abuela los fines de semana? ¿Llamas a tu padre los sábados?**
• Ask questions to elicit third-person direct object pronouns. Ex: **¿Quién ve el lápiz de Marcos? ¿Quién quiere estos diccionarios?**

5.4 Direct object nouns and pronouns

SUBJECT	VERB	DIRECT OBJECT NOUN
Juan Carlos y Jimena	están tomando	fotos.
Juan Carlos and Jimena	*are taking*	*photos.*

▶ A direct object noun receives the action of the verb directly and generally follows the verb. In the example above, the direct object noun answers the question *What are Juan Carlos and Jimena taking?*

▶ When a direct object noun in Spanish is a person or a pet, it is preceded by the word **a**. This is called the personal **a**; there is no English equivalent for this construction.

Mariela mira **a** Carlos.   Mariela mira televisión.
Mariela is watching Carlos.   *Mariela is watching TV.*

▶ In the first sentence above, the personal **a** is required because the direct object is a person. In the second sentence, the personal **a** is not required because the direct object is a thing, not a person.

No tenemos tablas de windsurf.

Miguel no me perdona.

El botones las puede conseguir para ustedes.

▶ Direct object pronouns are words that replace direct object nouns. Like English, Spanish uses a direct object pronoun to avoid repeating a noun already mentioned.

DIRECT OBJECT		DIRECT OBJECT PRONOUN		
Maribel hace	las maletas.	Maribel	las	hace.
Felipe compra	el sombrero.	Felipe	lo	compra.
Vicky tiene	la llave.	Vicky	la	tiene.

Direct object pronouns

SINGULAR		PLURAL	
me	me	**nos**	us
te	you (fam.)	**os**	you (fam.)
lo	you (m., form.)	**los**	you (m.)
	him; it (m.)		them (m.)
la	you (f., form.)	**las**	you (f.)
	her; it (f.)		them (f.)

TEACHING OPTIONS

TPR Call out a series of sentences with direct object nouns, some of which require the personal **a** and some of which do not. Ex: **Visito muchos museos. Visito a mis tíos.** Have students raise their hands if the personal **a** is used.

Extra Practice Write six sentences on the board that have direct object nouns. Use two verbs in the simple present tense, two in the present progressive, and two using **ir a** + [*infinitive*]. Draw a line through the direct objects as students call them out. Have students state which pronouns to write to replace them. Then, draw an arrow from each pronoun to where it goes in the sentence, as indicated by students.

▶ In affirmative sentences, direct object pronouns generally appear before the conjugated verb. In negative sentences, the pronoun is placed between the word **no** and the verb.

Adela practica **el tenis.**
Adela **lo** practica.

Gabriela no tiene **las llaves.**
Gabriela **no las** tiene.

Carmen compra **los pasajes.**
Carmen **los** compra.

Diego no hace **las maletas.**
Diego **no las** hace.

▶ When the verb is an infinitive construction, such as **ir a** + [*infinitive*], the direct object pronoun can be placed before the conjugated form or attached to the infinitive.

Ellos van a escribir **unas postales.** ⟨ Ellos **las** van a escribir.
Ellos van a escribir**las.**

Lidia quiere ver **una película.** ⟨ Lidia **la** quiere ver.
Lidia quiere ver**la.**

▶ When the verb is in the present progressive, the direct object pronoun can be placed before the conjugated form or attached to the present participle. **¡Atención!** When a direct object pronoun is attached to the present participle, an accent mark is added to maintain the proper stress.

CONSULTA

To learn more about accents, see **Lección 4, Pronunciación**, p. 123.

Gerardo está leyendo **la lección.** ⟨ Gerardo **la** está leyendo.
Gerardo está leyéndo**la.**

Toni está mirando **el partido.** ⟨ Toni **lo** está mirando.
Toni está mirándo**lo.**

¡INTÉNTALO!   Choose the correct direct object pronoun for each sentence.

1. Tienes el libro de español. c
   a. La tienes.   b. Los tienes.   c. Lo tienes.
2. Voy a ver el partido de baloncesto. a
   a. Voy a verlo.   b. Voy a verte.   c. Voy a vernos.
3. El artista quiere dibujar a Luisa y a su mamá. c
   a. Quiere dibujarme.   b. Quiere dibujarla.   c. Quiere dibujarlas.
4. Marcos busca la llave. b
   a. Me busca.   b. La busca.   c. Las busca.
5. Rita me lleva al aeropuerto y también lleva a Tomás. a
   a. Nos lleva.   b. Las lleva.   c. Te lleva.
6. Puedo oír a Gerardo y a Miguel. b
   a. Puedo oírte.   b. Puedo oírlos.   c. Puedo oírlo.
7. Quieren estudiar la gramática. c
   a. Quieren estudiarnos.   b. Quieren estudiarlo.   c. Quieren estudiarla.
8. ¿Practicas los verbos irregulares? a
   a. ¿Los practicas?   b. ¿Las practicas?   c. ¿Lo practicas?
9. Ignacio ve la película. a
   a. La ve.   b. Lo ve.   c. Las ve.
10. Sandra va a invitar a Mario a la excursión. También me va a invitar a mí. c
    a. Los va a invitar.   b. Lo va a invitar.   c. Nos va a invitar.

TEACHING OPTIONS

Large Group Make a list of 20 questions requiring direct object pronouns in the answer. Arrange students in two concentric circles. Students in the center circle ask questions from the list to those in the outer circle until you say stop (**¡Paren!**). The outer circle moves one person to the right and the questions begin again. Continue for five minutes, then have the students in the outer circle ask the questions.

Pairs ↔ Have students write ten sentences about a vacation they want to take using direct object nouns. Their sentences should also include a mixture of verbs in the present progressive, simple present, and **ir a** + [*infinitive*]. Ask students to exchange their sentences with a partner, who will rewrite them using direct object pronouns. Students should check their partner's work.

In-Class Tips

• Play a memory game. In view of the class, quickly distribute various items in quantities of either one or two to many different students, then tell them to hide the objects in their bag or backpack. Ask the class who has what. Ex: **¿Quién tiene las plumas? (David las tiene.) ¿Quién tiene el iPod? (Jessica lo tiene.)**

• Elicit first- and second-person direct object pronouns by asking questions first of individual students and then groups of students. Ex: **¿Quién te invita a almorzar con frecuencia? (Mi papá me invita a almorzar con frecuencia.) ¿Quién te comprende? (Mi amigo me comprende.)**

• Ask questions directed at the class as a whole to elicit first-person plural direct object pronouns. Ex: **¿Quiénes los llaman los fines de semana? (Nuestros padres nos llaman.) ¿Quiénes los esperan después de la clase? (Los amigos nos esperan.)**

• Add a visual aspect to this grammar presentation. Use magazine pictures to practice the third-person direct object pronouns with infinitives and the present progressive. Ex: **¿Quién está practicando el tenis? (Rafael Nadal lo está practicando./Rafael Nadal está practicándolo.) ¿Quién va a mirar la televisión? (El hombre pelirrojo la va a mirar./El hombre pelirrojo va a mirarla.)**

• Point out that the direct object pronoun **los** refers to both masculine and mixed groups. **Las** refers only to feminine groups.

Práctica

1 **Simplificar** Professor Vega's class is planning a trip to Costa Rica. Describe their preparations by changing the direct object nouns into direct object pronouns.

> *modelo*
>
> La profesora Vega tiene su pasaporte.
>
> *La profesora Vega lo tiene.*

1. Gustavo y Héctor confirman las reservaciones. Gustavo y Héctor las confirman.
2. Nosotros leemos los folletos (*brochures*). Nosotros los leemos.
3. Ana María estudia el mapa. Ana María lo estudia.
4. Yo aprendo los nombres de los monumentos de San José. Yo los aprendo.
5. Alicia escucha a la profesora. Alicia la escucha.
6. Miguel escribe las instrucciones para ir al hotel. Miguel las escribe.
7. Esteban busca el pasaje. Esteban lo busca.
8. Nosotros planeamos una excursión. Nosotros la planeamos.

2 **Vacaciones** Ramón is going to San Juan, Puerto Rico, with his friends, Javier and Marcos. Express his thoughts more succinctly using direct object pronouns.

> *modelo*
>
> Quiero hacer una excursión.
>
> *Quiero hacerla./La quiero hacer.*

1. Voy a hacer mi maleta. Voy a hacerla./La voy a hacer.
2. Necesitamos llevar los pasaportes. Necesitamos llevarlos./Los necesitamos llevar.
3. Marcos está pidiendo el folleto turístico. Marcos está pidiéndolo./Marcos lo está pidiendo.
4. Javier debe llamar a sus padres. Javier debe llamarlos./Javier los debe llamar.
5. Ellos desean visitar el Viejo San Juan. Ellos desean visitarlo./Ellos lo desean visitar.
6. Puedo llamar a Javier por la mañana. Puedo llamarlo./Lo puedo llamar.
7. Prefiero llevar mi cámara. Prefiero llevarla./La prefiero llevar.
8. No queremos perder nuestras reservaciones de hotel. No queremos perderlas./No las queremos perder.

3 **¿Quién?** The Garza family is preparing to go on a vacation to Puerto Rico. Based on the clues, answer the questions. Use direct object pronouns in your answers.

> *modelo*
>
> ¿Quién hace las reservaciones para el hotel? (el Sr. Garza)
>
> *El Sr. Garza las hace.*

1. ¿Quién compra los pasajes para el vuelo (*flight*)? (la Sra. Garza)
   La Sra. Garza los compra.
2. ¿Quién tiene que hacer las maletas de los niños? (María)
   María tiene que hacerlas./María las tiene que hacer.
3. ¿Quiénes buscan los pasaportes? (Antonio y María)
   Antonio y María los buscan.
4. ¿Quién va a confirmar las reservaciones de hotel? (la Sra. Garza)
   La Sra. Garza va a confirmarlas./La Sra. Garza las va a confirmar.
5. ¿Quién busca la cámara? (María)
   María la busca.
6. ¿Quién compra un mapa de Puerto Rico? (Antonio)
   Antonio lo compra.

---

1 **In-Class Tip** To simplify, ask individual students to identify the direct object in each sentence before beginning the activity.

2 **Expansion** Ask questions (using direct objects) about the people in the activity to elicit **Sí/No** answers. Ex: **¿Tiene Ramón reservaciones en el hotel? (Sí, las tiene.) ¿Tiene su mochila? (No, no la tiene.)**

3 **Expansion**
- Ask students questions about who does what in the activity. Ex: **¿La señora Garza busca la cámara? (No, María la busca.)**
- Ask additional questions about the family's preparations, allowing students to decide who does what. Ex: **¿Quién compra una revista para leer en el avión? ¿Quién llama al taxi? ¿Quién practica el español?**

¡LENGUA VIVA!

There are many Spanish words that correspond to *ticket*. **Billete** and **pasaje** usually refer to a ticket for travel, such as an airplane ticket. **Entrada** refers to a ticket to an event, such as a concert or a movie. **Boleto** can be used in either case.

NOTA CULTURAL

Puerto Rico is a U.S. territory, so people do not need travel documents when traveling to and from Puerto Rico from the U.S. mainland. However, everyone must meet all requirements for entering the U.S. when traveling directly to Puerto Rico from abroad.

TEACHING OPTIONS

Small Groups Split the class into small groups. Have students take turns asking the group who does these activities: **leer revistas, practicar el ciclismo, ganar todos los partidos, visitar a sus padres durante las vacaciones, leer el periódico, escribir cartas, escuchar a sus profesores, practicar la natación.** Ex: —**¿Quién lee revistas? —Yo las leo.**

Heritage Speakers Pair heritage speakers with other students. Ask the pairs to create a dialogue between a travel agent and client. Assign the role of traveler to the heritage speaker, who would like to visit his or her family's home country. Encourage both students to draw on their experiences from past vacations and trips to Spanish-speaking countries. Have students role-play their dialogues for the class.

Comunicación

4 **Escuchar** Listen to Mercedes and Gabriel, two students in Chicago, talk about their winter break. Then indicate whether the following conclusions are **lógico** or **ilógico**, based on what you heard.

	Lógico	Ilógico
1. Gabriel va a la playa.	☑	○
2. Gabriel está listo para salir.	○	☑
3. Va a hacer frío en Chicago.	☑	○
4. Gabriel viaja a España.	○	☑
5. Mercedes va a viajar también.	○	☑

5 **Entrevista** Answer your partner's questions. Use direct object pronouns. *Answers will vary.*

1. ¿Ves mucho la televisión?
2. ¿Cuándo vas a ver tu programa favorito?
3. ¿Quién prepara la comida (*food*) en tu casa?
4. ¿Te visita mucho tu familia?
5. ¿Visitas mucho a tus abuelos?
6. ¿Nos entienden nuestros padres a nosotros?
7. ¿Cuándo ves a tus amigos/as?
8. ¿Cuándo te llaman tus amigos/as?

6 **De mal humor** The weather has ruined your plans to go to the beach. Using words from the list, your partner offers some suggestions to cheer you up. Use direct object pronouns in your responses. *Answers will vary.*

> **modelo**
>
> **Estudiante 1:** ¿Quieres ver la película de Ryan Gosling?
> **Estudiante 2:** No la quiero ver.

computadora	fotos	libro
película	revista	videojuegos

Síntesis

7 **Adivinanzas** Write five riddles with descriptions of people, places, or things. Follow the model. Then see whether your teacher can solve your riddles. *Answers will vary.*

> **modelo**
>
> Lo uso para (*I use it to*) escribir en mi cuaderno.
> No es muy grande y tiene borrador. ¿Qué es?

TEACHING OPTIONS

Game Play a game of **20 Preguntas**. Divide the class into two teams. Think of an object in the room and alternate calling on teams to ask questions. Once a team knows the answer, the team captain should raise his or her hand. If right, the team gets a point. If wrong, the team loses a point. Play until one team has earned five points.

Pairs Have students create five questions that include the direct object pronouns **me**, **te**, and **nos**. Then have them ask their partners the questions on their list. Ex: —¿Quién te llama mucho? —Mi mejor amiga me llama mucho. —¿Quién nos escucha cuando hacemos preguntas en español? —El/La profesor(a) y los estudiantes nos escuchan.

Section Goal

In **Recapitulación**, students will review the grammar concepts from this lesson.

1 Expansion Create a list of present participles and have students supply the infinitive.
Ex: **durmiendo (dormir)**

2 In-Class Tip Ask students to explain why they chose **ser** or **estar** for each item.

2 Expansion
←👤→ Have students use **ser** and **estar** to write a brief paragraph describing **Julia's** first few days in Paris.

3 In-Class Tip To simplify, have students begin by underlining the direct object nouns and identifying the corresponding direct object pronouns.

Recapitulación

Review the grammar concepts you have learned in this lesson by completing these activities.

1 Completar Complete the chart with the correct present participle of these verbs. **16 pts.**

Infinitive	Present participle	Infinitive	Present participle
hacer	haciendo	**estar**	estando
acampar	acampando	**ser**	siendo
tener	teniendo	**vivir**	viviendo
venir	viniendo	**estudiar**	estudiando

2 Vacaciones en París Complete this paragraph about Julia's trip to Paris with the correct form of **ser** or **estar**. **24 pts.**

Hoy (1) __es__ (es/está) el 3 de julio y voy a París por tres semanas. (Yo) (2) __Estoy__ (Soy/Estoy) muy feliz porque voy a ver a mi mejor amiga. Ella (3) __es__ (es/está) de Puerto Rico, pero ahora (4) __está__ (es/está) viviendo en París. También (yo) (5) __estoy__ (soy/estoy) un poco nerviosa porque (6) __es__ (es/está) mi primer viaje a Francia. El vuelo (*flight*) (7) __es__ (es/está) hoy por la tarde, pero ahora (8) __está__ (es/está) lloviendo. Por eso (9) __estamos__ (somos/estamos) preocupadas, porque probablemente el avión va a salir tarde. Mi equipaje ya (10) __está__ (es/está) listo. (11) __Es__ (Es/Está) tarde y me tengo que ir. ¡Va a (12) __ser__ (ser/estar) un viaje fenomenal!

3 ¿Qué hacen? Respond to these questions by indicating what people do with the items mentioned. Use direct object pronouns. **20 pts.**

> *modelo*
> ¿Qué hacen ellos con la película? (ver)
> La ven.

1. ¿Qué haces tú con el libro de viajes? (leer) __Lo leo.__
2. ¿Qué hacen los turistas en la ciudad? (explorar) __La exploran.__
3. ¿Qué hace el botones con el equipaje? (llevar) __Lo lleva (a la habitación).__
4. ¿Qué hace la agente con las reservaciones? (confirmar) __Las confirma.__
5. ¿Qué hacen ustedes con los pasaportes? (mostrar) __Los mostramos.__

RESUMEN GRAMATICAL

5.1 Estar with conditions and emotions *p. 164*

► Yo est**oy** aburrido/a, feliz, nervioso/a.
► El cuarto **está** desordenado, limpio, ordenado.
► Estos libros **están** abiertos, cerrados, sucios.

5.2 The present progressive *pp. 166–167*

► The present progressive is formed with the present tense of estar plus the present participle.

Forming the present participle

infinitive	stem	ending	present participle
hablar	habl-	-ando	hablando
comer	com-	-iendo	comiendo
escribir	escrib-	-iendo	escribiendo

-ir stem-changing verbs

	infinitive	present participle
e:ie	preferir	prefiriendo
e:i	conseguir	consiguiendo
o:ue	dormir	durmiendo

► Irregular present participles: **yendo** (ir), **pudiendo** (poder), **viniendo** (venir)

5.3 Ser and estar *pp. 170–171*

► Uses of **ser**: nationality, origin, profession or occupation, characteristics, generalizations, possession, what something is made of, time and date, time and place of events
► Uses of **estar**: location, health, physical states and conditions, emotional states, weather expressions, ongoing actions
► Many adjectives can be used with both **ser** and **estar**, but the meaning of the adjectives will change.

Juan **es** delgado.	Juan **está** más delgado hoy.
Juan is thin.	*Juan looks thinner today.*

Extra Practice Add an auditory aspect to this grammar review. Go around the room and read a sentence with a direct object. Each student must repeat the sentence using a direct object pronoun. Ex: **María y Jennifer están comprando sus libros para la clase. (María y Jennifer los están comprando./María y Jennifer están comprándolos.)**
TPR Divide the board into two columns, with the heads **ser**

and **estar**. Ask a volunteer to stand in front of each verb. The rest of the class should take turns calling out a use of **ser** or **estar**. The volunteer standing in front of the correct verb should step forward and give an example sentence. Ex: nationality or origin (**Soy norteamericano/a.**) After each volunteer has given two sentences, call on different students to take their places. Continue this way until everyone has had a turn.

4 **Opuestos** Complete these sentences with the appropriate form of the verb **estar** and an antonym for the underlined adjective. **20 pts.**

> *modelo*
>
> Mis respuestas están <u>bien</u>, pero las de Susana *están mal*.

1. Las tiendas están <u>abiertas</u>, pero la agencia de viajes <u>está</u> <u>cerrada</u>.
2. No me gustan las habitaciones <u>desordenadas</u>. Incluso (*Even*) mi habitación de hotel <u>está</u> <u>ordenada</u>.
3. Nosotras estamos <u>tristes</u> cuando trabajamos. Hoy comienzan las vacaciones y <u>estamos</u> <u>contentas/alegres/felices</u>.
4. En esta ciudad los autobuses están <u>sucios</u>, pero los taxis <u>están</u> <u>limpios</u>.
5. —El avión sale a las 5:30, ¿verdad? —No, estás <u>confundida</u>. Yo <u>estoy</u> <u>seguro/a</u> de que el avión sale a las 5:00.

5.4 **Direct object nouns and pronouns** *pp. 174–175*

Direct object pronouns

Singular		Plural	
me	lo	nos	los
te	la	os	las

In affirmative sentences:
Adela practica el tenis. → Adela **lo** practica.

In negative sentences: Adela **no lo** practica.

With an infinitive:
Adela **lo** va a practicar./Adela va a practicar**lo**.

With the present progressive:
Adela **lo** está practicando./Adela está practicándo**lo**.

5 **En la playa** Describe what these people are doing. Complete the sentences using the present progressive tense. **16 pts.**

1. El Sr. Camacho <u>está pescando</u>.
2. Felicia <u>está paseando en barco</u>.
3. Leo <u>está montando a caballo</u>.
4. Nosotros <u>estamos jugando a las cartas</u>.

6 **Refrán** Complete this Spanish saying by filling in the missing present participles. Refer to the translation and the drawing. **4 pts.**

¡LA CIUDAD ESTÁ MUY SUCIA!

❝ Se consigue más

<u>haciendo</u> que <u>diciendo</u> . ❞

(You can accomplish more by doing than by saying.)

4 Expansion
👥 Have students create three sentences about their own lives, using antonyms. Ex: **Mi hermano es desordenado, pero yo soy muy ordenado.** Tell them to make one of the sentences false. Then, in pairs, have students read their sentences aloud. Their partner should try to guess which statement is false.

5 Expansion To challenge students, have them imagine that the people in the illustration are now in a hotel. Ask students to say what they are doing. Ex: **Leo está mirando un programa sobre caballos.**

6 In-Class Tip Explain the use of the impersonal **se** and explain that **Se consigue** means *You can accomplish* (as in the translation) or *One can accomplish*. Students will learn the impersonal **se** in **Senderos, nivel 2.**

6 Expansion
👥 To challenge students, have them work in pairs to create a short dialogue that ends with this saying. Encourage them to be creative.

TEACHING OPTIONS

TPR 👥 Prepare five anonymous descriptions of easily recognizable people, using **ser** and **estar**. Write each name on a separate card and give each student a set of cards. Read the descriptions aloud and have students hold up the corresponding name. Ex: **Es cantante y compositora. Es rubia. No es delgada. Es inglesa. Está muy ocupada. (Adele)**

Extra Practice Give students these items to make sentences with the present progressive. **1. con / madre / hablar / yo / mi / estar (Yo estoy hablando con mi madre.) 2. nuestro / equipaje / buscar / nosotros / estar (Nosotros estamos buscando nuestro equipaje.) 3. ¿ / llover / playa / la / estar / en / ? (¿Está lloviendo en la playa?) 4. el / Nueva York / pasaje / ella / para / comprar / estar (Ella está comprando el pasaje para Nueva York.)**

Section Goals

In **Lectura**, students will:
- learn the strategy of scanning to find specific information in reading matter
- read a brochure about ecotourism in Puerto Rico

Communication 1.1, 1.2
Cultures 2.1, 2.2, 2.3
Connections 3.1, 3.2
Comparisons 4.2

 Pre-AP®

Interpretive Reading: Estrategia
Explain to students that a good way to improve reading comprehension and to get an idea of what an article or other text is about is to scan it before reading. Scanning means running one's eyes over a text in search of specific information that can be used to infer the content of the text.

The Affective Dimension
Point out to students that becoming familiar with cognates will help them feel less overwhelmed when they encounter new Spanish texts.

Examinar el texto Do the activity orally as a class. Some cognates that give a clue to the content of the text are: **turismo ecológico, teléfono, TV por cable, Internet, hotel, aire acondicionado, perfecto, Parque Nacional Foresta, Museo de Arte Nativo, Reserva, Biosfera, Santuario.** These clues should tell a reader scanning the text that it is about a hotel promoting ecotourism.

Preguntas Ask the questions orally of the class. Possible responses: 1. travel brochure 2. Puerto Rico 3. photos of beautiful tropical beaches, bays, and forests; The document is trying to attract the reader. 4. **Hotel Vistahermosa** in Lajas, Puerto Rico; attract guests

Lectura

Antes de leer

Estrategia
Scanning

Scanning involves glancing over a document in search of specific information. For example, you can scan a document to identify its format, to find cognates, to locate visual clues about the document's content, or to find specific facts. Scanning allows you to learn a great deal about a text without having to read it word for word.

Examinar el texto

Scan the reading selection for cognates and write down a few of them. Answers will vary.

1. _____   4. _____
2. _____   5. _____
3. _____   6. _____

Based on the cognates you found, what do you think this document is about?

_____

Preguntas

Read these questions. Then scan the document again to look for answers. Answers will vary.

1. What is the format of the reading selection?
   _____

2. Which place is the document about?
   _____

3. What are some of the visual cues this document provides? What do they tell you about the content of the document?
   _____

4. Who produced the document, and what do you think it is for?
   _____

Turismo ecológico en Puerto Rico

Hotel Vistahermosa
~ Lajas, Puerto Rico ~

- 40 habitaciones individuales
- 15 habitaciones dobles
- Teléfono / TV por cable / Internet
- Aire acondicionado
- Restaurante (Bar)
- Piscina
- Área de juegos
- Cajero automático°

El hotel está situado en Playa Grande, un pequeño pueblo de pescadores del mar Caribe. Es el lugar perfecto para el viajero que viene de vacaciones. Las playas son seguras y limpias, ideales para tomar el sol, descansar, tomar fotografías y nadar. Está abierto los 365 días del año. Hay una rebaja° especial para estudiantes universitarios.

DIRECCIÓN: Playa Grande 406, Lajas, PR 00667, cerca del Parque Nacional Foresta.

Cajero automático *ATM* rebaja *discount*

Atracciones cercanas

Playa Grande ¿Busca la playa perfecta? Playa Grande es la playa que está buscando. Usted puede pescar, sacar fotos, nadar y pasear en bicicleta. Playa Grande es un paraíso para el turista que quiere practicar deportes acuáticos. El lugar es bonito e interesante y usted va a tener muchas oportunidades para descansar y disfrutar en familia.

Valle Niebla Ir de excursión, tomar café, montar a caballo, caminar, hacer picnics. Más de cien lugares para acampar.

Bahía Fosforescente Sacar fotos, salidas de noche, excursión en barco. Una maravillosa experiencia llena de luz°.

Arrecifes de Coral Sacar fotos, bucear, explorar. Es un lugar único en el Caribe.

Playa Vieja Tomar el sol, pasear en bicicleta, jugar a las cartas, escuchar música. Ideal para la familia.

Parque Nacional Foresta Sacar fotos, visitar el Museo de Arte Nativo. Reserva Mundial de la Biosfera.

Santuario de las Aves Sacar fotos, observar aves°, seguir rutas de excursión.

llena de luz *full of light*   aves *birds*

Después de leer

Listas
Which amenities of Hotel Vistahermosa would most interest these potential guests? Explain your choices. Answers will vary.

1. dos padres con un hijo de seis años y una hija de ocho años

   _____

2. un hombre y una mujer en su luna de miel (*honeymoon*)

   _____

3. una persona en un viaje de negocios (*business trip*)

   _____

Conversaciones
Answer your partner's questions. Answers will vary.

1. ¿Quieres visitar el Hotel Vistahermosa? ¿Por qué?
2. Tienes tiempo de visitar sólo tres de las atracciones turísticas que están cerca del hotel. ¿Cuáles vas a visitar? ¿Por qué?
3. ¿Qué prefieres hacer en Valle Niebla? ¿En Playa Vieja? ¿En el Parque Nacional Foresta?

Situaciones
You have just arrived at Hotel Vistahermosa. Your partner is the concierge. Use the phrases below to express your interests and ask for suggestions about where to go. Answers will vary.

1. montar a caballo
2. bucear
3. pasear en bicicleta
4. pescar
5. observar aves

Contestar
Answer these questions. Answers will vary.

1. ¿Quieres visitar Puerto Rico? Explica tu respuesta.

   _____

2. ¿Adónde quieres ir de vacaciones el verano que viene? Explica tu respuesta.

   _____

Listas
- Ask these comprehension questions. **1. ¿El Hotel Vistahermosa está situado cerca de qué mar? (el mar Caribe) 2. ¿Qué playa es un paraíso para el turista? (la Playa Grande) 3. ¿Dónde puedes montar a caballo? (en el Valle Niebla)**
- 👥↔👥 Encourage discussion of each of the items by asking questions such as: **En tu opinión, ¿qué tipo de atracciones buscan los padres con hijos de seis y ocho años? ¿Qué esperan de un hotel? Y una pareja en su luna de miel, ¿qué tipo de atracciones espera encontrar en un hotel? En tu opinión, ¿qué busca una persona en un viaje de negocios?**

Conversaciones Ask individuals about what their partners said. Ex: **¿Por qué (no) quiere _____ visitar el Hotel Vistahermosa? ¿Qué atracciones quiere ver?** Ask other students: **Y tú, ¿quieres visitar el Parque Nacional Foresta o prefieres visitar otro lugar?**

Conversaciones
👥↔👥 Available online as **Virtual Chat**

Situaciones
- Give students a couple of minutes to review **Más vocabulario** on page 152 and **Expresiones útiles** on page 159.
- To challenge students, add to the list activities such as **sacar fotos, correr, nadar,** and **ir de excursión.**

Situaciones
👥↔👥 Available online as **Partner Chat**

Contestar Have volunteers explain how the reading selection might influence their choice of a vacation destination for next summer.

TEACHING OPTIONS

Pairs Have pairs of students work together to read the brochure aloud and write three questions about it. After they have finished, ask pairs to exchange papers with another pair, who will work together to answer them. Alternatively, you might pick pairs to read their questions to the class. Ask volunteers to answer them.

Small Groups →👤← To practice scanning written material to infer its content, bring in short, simple Spanish-language magazine or newspaper articles you have read. Have small groups scan the articles to determine what they are about. Have them write down all the clues that help them. When each group has come to a decision, ask it to present its findings to the class. Confirm the accuracy of the inferences.

Section Goals

Section Goals

In **Escritura**, students will:
- write a brochure for a hotel or resort
- integrate travel-related vocabulary and structures taught in **Lección 5**

 Communication 1.3

 Pre-AP®

Interpersonal Writing: Estrategia
Explain that outlines are a great way for a writer to think about what a piece of writing will be like before actually expending much time and effort on writing. An outline is also a great way of keeping a writer on track while composing the piece and helps the person keep the whole project in mind as he or she focuses on a specific part.

Tema Discuss the hotel or resort brochure students are to write. Go over the list of information that they might include. You might indicate a specific number of the points that should be included in the brochure. Tell students that the brochure for **Hotel Vistahermosa** in **Lectura**, pages 180–181, can serve as a model for their writing. Remind them that they are writing with the purpose of attracting guests to the hotel or resort. Suggest that, as they begin to think about writing, students should brainstorm as many details as they can remember about the hotel they are going to describe. Tell them to do this in Spanish.

In-Class Tip Have students write each of the individual items of their brainstorm lists on index cards so that they can arrange and rearrange them into different idea maps as they plan their brochures.

Escritura

Estrategia
Making an outline

When we write to share information, an outline can serve to separate topics and subtopics, providing a framework for the presentation of data. Consider the following excerpt from an outline of the tourist brochure on pages 180–181.

IV. Descripción del sitio (con foto)
   A. Playa Grande
      1. Playas seguras y limpias
      2. Ideal para tomar el sol, descansar, tomar fotografías, nadar
   B. El hotel
      1. Abierto los 365 días del año
      2. Rebaja para estudiantes universitarios

Mapa de ideas

Idea maps can be used to create outlines. The major sections of an idea map correspond to the Roman numerals in an outline. The minor idea map sections correspond to the outline's capital letters, and so on. Examine the idea map that led to the outline above.

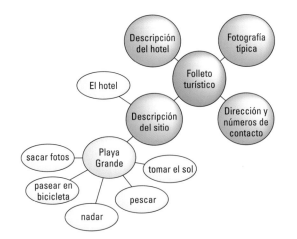

Tema
Escribir un folleto

Write a tourist brochure for a hotel or resort you have visited. If you wish, you may write about an imaginary location. You may want to include some of this information in your brochure:

▶ the name of the hotel or resort

▶ phone and fax numbers that tourists can use to make contact

▶ the hotel website that tourists can consult

▶ an e-mail address that tourists can use to request information

▶ a description of the exterior of the hotel or resort

▶ a description of the interior of the hotel or resort, including facilities and amenities

▶ a description of the surrounding area, including its climate

▶ a listing of nearby scenic natural attractions

▶ a listing of nearby cultural attractions

▶ a listing of recreational activities that tourists can pursue in the vicinity of the hotel or resort

EVALUATION: Folleto

Criteria	Scale
Appropriate details	1 2 3 4 5
Organization	1 2 3 4 5
Use of vocabulary	1 2 3 4 5
Grammatical accuracy	1 2 3 4 5

Scoring	
Excellent	18–20 points
Good	14–17 points
Satisfactory	10–13 points
Unsatisfactory	< 10 points

Escuchar

Estrategia

Listening for key words

By listening for key words or phrases, you can identify the subject and main ideas of what you hear, as well as some of the details.

 To practice this strategy, you will now listen to a short paragraph. As you listen, jot down the key words that help you identify the subject of the paragraph and its main ideas.

Preparación

Based on the illustration, who do you think Hernán Jiménez is, and what is he doing? What key words might you listen for to help you understand what he is saying?

Ahora escucha

Now you are going to listen to a weather report by Hernán Jiménez. Note which phrases are correct according to the key words and phrases you hear.

Santo Domingo

1. hace sol ✔
2. va a hacer frío
3. una mañana de mal tiempo
4. va a estar nublado ✔
5. buena tarde para tomar el sol
6. buena mañana para la playa ✔

San Francisco de Macorís

1. hace frío ✔
2. hace sol
3. va a nevar
4. va a llover ✔
5. hace calor
6. mal día para excursiones ✔

Comprensión

¿Cierto o falso?

Indicate whether each statement is **cierto** or **falso**, based on the weather report. Correct the false statements.

1. Según el meteorólogo, la temperatura en Santo Domingo es de 26 grados.
   Cierto.

2. La temperatura máxima en Santo Domingo hoy va a ser de 30 grados.
   Cierto.

3. Está lloviendo ahora en Santo Domingo.
   Falso. Hace sol.

4. En San Francisco de Macorís la temperatura mínima de hoy va a ser de 20 grados.
   Falso. La temperatura mínima va a ser de 18 grados.

5. Va a llover mucho hoy en San Francisco de Macorís.
   Cierto.

Preguntas

Answer these questions about the weather report.

1. ¿Hace viento en Santo Domingo ahora?
   Sí, hace viento en Santo Domingo.
2. ¿Está nublado en Santo Domingo ahora?
   No, no está nublado ahora en Santo Domingo.
3. ¿Está nevando ahora en San Francisco de Macorís?
   No, no está nevando ahora en San Francisco de Macorís.
4. ¿Qué tiempo hace en San Francisco de Macorís?
   Hace frío.

18 grados. Va a llover casi todo el día. ¡No es buen día para excursiones a las montañas!

Hasta el noticiero del mediodía, me despido de ustedes. ¡Que les vaya bien!

Section Goals

In **Escuchar**, students will:
- learn the strategy of listening for key words
- listen to a short paragraph and note the key words
- answer questions based on the content of a recorded conversation

Communication 1.2

Estrategia
Script Aquí está la foto de mis vacaciones en la playa. Ya lo sé; no debo pasar el tiempo tomando el sol. Es que vivo en una ciudad donde llueve casi todo el año y mis actividades favoritas son bucear, pescar en el mar y nadar.

In-Class Tip Have students look at the drawing and describe what they see. Guide them in saying what **Hernán Jiménez** is like and what he is doing.

Preguntas
Available online as **Virtual Chat**

Ahora escucha
Script Buenos días, queridos televidentes, les saluda el meteorólogo Hernán Jiménez, con el pronóstico del tiempo para nuestra bella isla.

Hoy, 17 de octubre, a las diez de la mañana, la temperatura en Santo Domingo es de 26 grados. Hace sol con viento del este a 10 kilómetros por hora.

En la tarde, va a estar un poco nublado con la posibilidad de lluvia. La temperatura máxima del día va a ser de 30 grados. Es una buena mañana para ir a la playa.

En las montañas hace bastante frío ahora, especialmente en el área de San Francisco de Macorís. La temperatura mínima de estas 24 horas va a ser de

(Script continues at far left in the bottom panels.)

Section Goals

In **En pantalla**, students will:
• read about airline travel in Latin America
• watch an ad for **LANPASS**, a Chilean airline loyalty program

 Communication 1.1, 1.2, 1.3
Cultures 2.2
Connections 3.2
Comparisons 4.2
Communities 5.2

Teacher Resources
Read the front matter for suggestions on how to incorporate all the program's components. See pages 151A–151B for a detailed listing of Teacher Resources online.

El arte de viajar Check comprehension: 1. How will airline travel evolve in Latin America by the year 2034? 2. What is LAN? 3. What is LANPASS and what is its goal?

 Pre-AP®

Audiovisual Interpretive Communication
Antes de ver **Strategy**
Remind students to focus first on familiar words to identify the purpose of the video.

Comprensión Once students have marked the items they hear in the ad, ask them to make a list of other ways everyday life is different when we travel.

Aplicación Encourage students to use photos or videos of their own family trips when presenting their ad to the class.

Preparación

Answer these questions in Spanish. Answers will vary.

1. ¿Te gusta viajar? ¿Por qué? ¿Adónde te gusta viajar?
2. ¿Qué te gusta hacer cuando estás de vacaciones?
3. ¿Qué modo de transporte prefieres usar? ¿Por qué?

El arte de viajar

Millions of people travel on airlines every year for business and pleasure. The number of airline passengers is expected to double between 2014 and 2034 worldwide. This is true for Latin America, too, as airlines are looking at how to attract all those customers to their planes. The airline of Chile, LAN, has partnered with the international bank Santander to create the loyalty program LANPASS to encourage frequent travel on LAN. What does an airline say to travelers that captures their attention and makes their business seem like your pleasure?

importa *matters*

Comprensión

Mark an X next to the phrases you hear in the ad.
Irse es volver a....

x cambiar de piel
x desconectarnos
_ estudiar mucho
x un mundo sin Internet

_ trabajar
x castillos de arena
_ destinos exóticos
x la esencia de todo

_ la oficina
x sentirse vivo
x las siestas
_ tiempo en familia

Conversación

Answers will vary.

Answer these questions with a classmate.

1. Según el anuncio, ¿cuáles son algunas cosas positivas de viajar?
2. ¿Cuáles de estas cosas positivas son importantes para ti? ¿Por qué?
3. Para tener experiencias positivas, ¿a dónde viajas tú? ¿A dónde viaja tu familia? ¿Y tus amigos?

Anuncio de Santander LANPASS

Con lo que realmente nos importa°.

Vocabulario útil

arena	sand
cambiar	to change
destino	destination
medir	to measure
mismo/a	itself
piel	skin
puestas de sol	sunsets
recuerdos	memories
sentirse	to feel
sino	but

Aplicación

With a classmate, prepare an ad inviting other people to travel to a special place. Explain why it is a perfect or ideal place. What evocative words and images will you use? Present your ad to the class. Answers will vary.

EXPANSION

Culture Note Although airline travel is becoming more popular throughout Latin America, in some countries people still use other means of transportation for their trips, especially intercity buses. This is in part a custom and in part due to the high costs of airline tickets. However, low-cost airlines have recently started operations in some countries.

Small Groups Have small groups of students research and create an oral presentation about other big airline companies in the Spanish-speaking world. Encourage them to include information on the alliances they have with other companies and the way they attract customers.

Between 1438 and 1533, when the vast and powerful Incan Empire was at its height, the Incas built an elaborate network of **caminos** (*trails*) that traversed the Andes Mountains and converged on the empire's capital, Cuzco. Today, hundreds of thousands of tourists come to Peru annually to walk the surviving trails and enjoy the spectacular scenery. The most popular trail, **el Camino Inca**, leads from Cuzco to **Intipunku** (*Sun Gate*), the entrance to the ancient mountain city of Machu Picchu.

¡Vacaciones en Perú!

Machu Picchu [...] se encuentra aislada sobre° esta montaña...

... siempre he querido° venir [...] Me encantan° las civilizaciones antiguas°.

Somos una familia francesa [...] Perú es un país muy, muy bonito de verdad.

Vocabulario útil

ciudadela	citadel
de cultivo	farming
el/la guía	guide
maravilla	wonder
quechua	Quechua (indigenous Peruvian)
sector (urbano)	(urban) sector

Preparación

Have you ever visited an archeological or historic site? Where? Why did you go there? Answers will vary.

Completar

Complete these sentences. Make the necessary changes.

1. Las ruinas de Machu Picchu son una antigua __ciudadela__ inca.

2. La ciudadela estaba (*was*) dividida en tres sectores: __urbano__ , religioso y de cultivo.

3. Cada año los __guías__ reciben a cientos (*hundreds*) de turistas de diferentes países.

4. Hoy en día, la cultura __quechua__ está presente en las comunidades andinas (*Andean*) de Perú.

se encuentra aislada sobre *it is isolated on* siempre he querido *I have always wanted* Me encantan *I love* antiguas *ancient*

Puerto Rico

El país en cifras

▶ **Área:** 8.959 km² (3.459 millas²)
menor° que el área de Connecticut
▶ **Población:** 3.667.084
Puerto Rico es una de las islas más densamente pobladas° del mundo. Más de la mitad de la población vive en San Juan, la capital.
▶ **Capital:** San Juan—2.730.000
▶ **Ciudades principales:** Arecibo, Bayamón, Fajardo, Mayagüez, Ponce
▶ **Moneda:** dólar estadounidense
▶ **Idiomas:** español (oficial); inglés (oficial)
Aproximadamente la cuarta parte de la población puertorriqueña habla inglés, pero en las zonas turísticas este porcentaje es mucho más alto. El uso del inglés es obligatorio para documentos federales.

Bandera de Puerto Rico

Puertorriqueños célebres
▶ **Raúl Juliá,** actor (1940–1994)
▶ **Roberto Clemente,** beisbolista (1934–1972)
▶ **Julia de Burgos,** escritora (1914–1953)
▶ **Benicio del Toro,** actor y productor (1967–)
▶ **Rosie Pérez,** actriz y bailarina (1964–)
▶ **José Rivera,** dramaturgo y guionista (1955–)

menor *less* pobladas *populated* río subterráneo *underground river* más largo *longest* cuevas *caves* bóveda *vault* fortaleza *fort* caber *fit*

Playa en San Juan

Faro en Arecibo

Océano Atlántico

Arecibo

San Juan

Bayamón

Río Grande de Añasco

Mayagüez

Cordillera Central

Sierra de Cayey

Ponce

Mar Caribe

Iglesia en Ponce

Pescadores en Mayagüez

OCÉANO ATLÁNTICO

PUERTO RI[CO]

OCÉANO PACÍFICO

¡Increíble pero cierto!
El río Camuy es el tercer río subterráneo° más largo° del mundo y tiene el sistema de cuevas° más grande del hemisferio occidental.
La Cueva de los Tres Pueblos es una gigantesca bóveda°, tan grande que toda la fortaleza° del Morro puede caber° en su interior.

Lugares • El Morro

El Morro es una fortaleza que se construyó para proteger° la bahía° de San Juan desde principios del siglo° XVI hasta principios del siglo XX. Hoy día muchos turistas visitan este lugar, convertido en un museo. Es el sitio más fotografiado de Puerto Rico. La arquitectura de la fortaleza es impresionante. Tiene misteriosos túneles, oscuras mazmorras° y vistas fabulosas de la bahía.

Artes • Salsa

La salsa, un estilo musical de origen puertorriqueño y cubano, nació° en el barrio latino de la ciudad de Nueva York. Dos de los músicos de salsa más famosos son Tito Puente y Willie Colón, los dos de Nueva York. Las estrellas° de la salsa en Puerto Rico son Felipe Rodríguez y Héctor Lavoe. Hoy en día, Puerto Rico es el centro internacional de este estilo musical. El Gran Combo de Puerto Rico es una de las orquestas de salsa más famosas del mundo°.

Isla de Culebra

Fajardo

Isla de Vieques

Ciencias • El Observatorio de Arecibo

El Observatorio de Arecibo tiene uno de los radiotelescopios más grandes del mundo. Gracias a este telescopio, los científicos° pueden estudiar las propiedades de la Tierra°, la Luna° y otros cuerpos celestes. También pueden analizar fenómenos celestiales como los quasares y pulsares, y detectar emisiones de radio de otras galaxias, en busca de inteligencia extraterrestre.

Historia • Relación con los Estados Unidos

Puerto Rico pasó a ser° parte de los Estados Unidos después de° la guerra° de 1898 y se hizo° un estado libre asociado en 1952. Los puertorriqueños, ciudadanos° estadounidenses desde° 1917, tienen representación política en el Congreso, pero no votan en las elecciones presidenciales y no pagan impuestos° federales. Hay un debate entre los puertorriqueños: ¿debe la isla seguir como estado libre asociado, hacerse un estado como los otros° o volverse° independiente?

¿Qué aprendiste? Contesta las preguntas con una oración completa.

1. ¿Cuál es la moneda de Puerto Rico? La moneda de Puerto Rico es el dólar estadounidense.
2. ¿Qué idiomas se hablan (*are spoken*) en Puerto Rico? Se hablan español e inglés en Puerto Rico.
3. ¿Cuál es el sitio más fotografiado de Puerto Rico? El Morro es el sitio más fotografiado de Puerto Rico.
4. ¿Qué es el Gran Combo? Es una orquesta de Puerto Rico.
5. ¿Qué hacen los científicos en el Observatorio de Arecibo? Los científicos estudian las propiedades de la Tierra y la Luna y detectan emisiones de otras galaxias.

Conexión Internet Investiga estos temas en Internet.

1. Describe a dos puertorriqueños famosos. ¿Cómo son? ¿Qué hacen? ¿Dónde viven? ¿Por qué son célebres?
2. Busca información sobre lugares en los que se puede hacer ecoturismo en Puerto Rico.

proteger *protect* bahía *bay* siglo *century* mazmorras *dungeons* nació *was born* estrellas *stars* mundo *world* científicos *scientists* Tierra *Earth* Luna *Moon* pasó a ser *became* después de *after* guerra *war* se hizo *became* ciudadanos *citizens* desde *since* pagan impuestos *pay taxes* otros *others* volverse *to become*

TEACHING OPTIONS

Variación léxica When the first Spanish colonists arrived on the island they were to name Puerto Rico, they found it inhabited by the Taínos, who called the island **Boriquen**. Puerto Ricans still use **Borinquen** to refer to the island, and they frequently call themselves **boricuas**. The Puerto Rican national anthem is ***La borinqueña***. Some other Taíno words that have entered Spanish (and English) are **huracán**, **hamaca**, **canoa**, and **iguana**. **Juracán** was the name of the

Taíno god of the winds whose anger stirred up the great storms that periodically devastated the island. The hammock, of course, was the device the Taínos slept in, and canoes were the boats made of great hollowed-out logs with which they paddled between islands. The Taíno language also survives in many Puerto Rican place names: **Arecibo**, **Bayamón**, **Guayama**, **Sierra de Cayey**, **Yauco**, and **Coamo**.

El Morro
- Remind students that at the time **El Morro** was built, piracy was a major concern for Spain and its Caribbean colonies. If possible, show other photos of **El Morro**, San Juan Bay, and **Viejo San Juan**.
- For additional information about **El Morro** and **Viejo San Juan**, you may want to play the *Panorama cultural* video footage for this lesson.

Salsa With students, listen to **salsa** or **merengue** from the Dominican Republic, and **rumba** or **mambo** from Cuba. Encourage them to identify common elements in the music (strong percussion patterns rooted in African traditions, alternating structure of soloist and ensemble, incorporation of Western instruments and musical vocabulary). Then, have them point out contrasts.

El Observatorio de Arecibo The Arecibo Ionospheric Observatory has the world's most sensitive radio telescope. It can detect objects up to 13 billion light years away. The telescope dish is 1,000 feet in diameter and covers 20 acres. The dish is made of about 40,000 aluminum mesh panels. The Arecibo Observatory celebrated its 50th anniversary in 2013.

Relación con los Estados Unidos Point out that only Puerto Ricans living on the island vote in plebiscites (or referenda) on the question of the island's political relationship with the United States.

Comparisons 4.1

Teacher Resources
Read the front matter for suggestions on how to incorporate all the program's components. See pages 151A–151B for a detailed listing of Teacher Resources online.

In-Class Tip Ask students to prepare a list of the three products or perspectives they learned about in this lesson to share with the class. You may ask them to focus specifically on the **Cultura** and **Panorama** sections.

Los viajes y las vacaciones

acampar	to camp
confirmar una reservación	to confirm a reservation
estar de vacaciones (*f. pl.*)	to be on vacation
hacer las maletas	to pack (one's suitcases)
hacer un viaje	to take a trip
hacer (wind)surf	to (wind)surf
ir de compras (*f. pl.*)	to go shopping
ir de vacaciones	to go on vacation
ir en autobús (*m.*), auto(móvil) (*m.*), avión (*m.*), barco (*m.*), moto(cicleta) (*f.*), taxi (*m.*)	to go by bus, car, plane, boat, motorcycle, taxi
jugar a las cartas	to play cards
montar a caballo (*m.*)	to ride a horse
pescar	to fish
sacar/tomar fotos (*f. pl.*)	to take photos
el/la agente de viajes	travel agent
el/la inspector(a) de aduanas	customs inspector
el/la viajero/a	traveler
el aeropuerto	airport
la agencia de viajes	travel agency
el campo	countryside
el equipaje	luggage
la estación de autobuses, del metro, de tren	bus, subway, train station
la llegada	arrival
el mar	sea
el paisaje	landscape
el pasaje (de ida y vuelta)	(round-trip) ticket
el pasaporte	passport
la playa	beach
la salida	departure; exit
la tabla de (wind)surf	surfboard/sailboard

El hotel

el ascensor	elevator
la cama	bed
el/la empleado/a	employee
la habitación individual, doble	single, double room
el hotel	hotel
el/la huésped	guest
la llave	key
el piso	floor (of a building)
la planta baja	ground floor

Adjetivos

abierto/a	open
aburrido/a	bored; boring
alegre	happy
amable	nice; friendly
avergonzado/a	embarrassed
cansado/a	tired
cerrado/a	closed
cómodo/a	comfortable
confundido/a	confused
contento/a	content
desordenado/a	disorderly
enamorado/a (de)	in love (with)
enojado/a	angry
equivocado/a	wrong
feliz	happy
limpio/a	clean
listo/a	ready; smart
nervioso/a	nervous
ocupado/a	busy
ordenado/a	orderly
preocupado/a (por)	worried (about)
seguro/a	sure; safe; confident
sucio/a	dirty
triste	sad

Los números ordinales

primer, primero/a	first
segundo/a	second
tercer, tercero/a	third
cuarto/a	fourth
quinto/a	fifth
sexto/a	sixth
séptimo/a	seventh
octavo/a	eighth
noveno/a	ninth
décimo/a	tenth

Palabras adicionales

ahora mismo	right now
el año	year
¿Cuál es la fecha (de hoy)?	What is the date (today)?
de buen/mal humor	in a good/bad mood
la estación	season
el mes	month
todavía	yet; still

Seasons, months, and dates	See page 154.
Weather expressions	See page 154.
Direct object pronouns	See page 174.
Expresiones útiles	See page 159.

Lección 6: Teacher Resources

There is a wealth of resources online to support instruction using **Senderos**. For details on how to integrate these Teacher Resources into your lessons, see the front matter of this Teacher's Edition on pages T16 to T48.

Presentation	Practice & Communicate	Assess*	Scripts and Translations	

• Digital Images:
  • **¡De compras!**
  • **Los colores**
	• Information Gap Activity*
	• Activity Pack Practice Activities (with Answer Key): **Contextos**
	• Additional Vocabulary (**Más vocabulario para ir de compras**)
	• Digital Image Bank (Shopping)
		• Vocabulary Quiz (with Answer Key)		**contextos**

		• **Fotonovela** Optional Testing Sections (with Answer Key)	• **Fotonovela** Videoscript • **Fotonovela** English Translation	**fotonovela**
• **Estructura 6.1** Grammar Slides	• Information Gap Activity* • Activity Pack Practice Activities (with Answer Key): **Saber** and **conocer** • Surveys: Worksheet for survey	• Grammar 6.1 Quiz (with Answer Key)	• Tutorial Script: **Saber** and **conocer**	
• **Estructura 6.2** Grammar Slides	• Activity Pack Practice Activities (with Answer Key): Indirect object pronouns • Surveys: Worksheet for classroom survey	• Grammar 6.2 Quiz (with Answer Key)	• Tutorial Script: Indirect object pronouns	**estructura**
• **Estructura 6.3** Grammar Slides	• Activity Pack Practice Activities (with Answer Key): Preterite tense of regular verbs	• Grammar 6.3 Quiz (with Answer Key)	• Tutorial Script: Preterite tense of regular verbs	
• **Estructura 6.4** Grammar Slides	• Activity Pack Practice Activities (with Answer Key): Demonstrative adjectives and pronouns	• Grammar 6.4 Quiz (with Answer Key)	• Tutorial Script: Demonstrative adjectives and pronouns	
			• **En pantalla** Videoscript • **En pantalla** English Translation	En pantalla
		• **Flash cultura** Optional Testing Sections (with Answer Key)	• **Flash cultura** Videoscript • **Flash cultura** English Translation	Flash cultura
Digital Images: • **Cuba**		• **Panorama** Optional Testing Sections (with Answer Key) • **Panorama cultural** (video)	• **Panorama cultural** Videoscript • **Panorama cultural** English Translation	Panorama

*Can also be assigned online.

Lección 6: Teacher Resources

Pulling It All Together

Practice and Communicate
- Role-plays
- Activity Pack Practice Activities (**¡A repasar!**) (with Answer Key)

Assessment

Tests and Exams*
- **Prueba A** with audio
- **Prueba B** with audio
- **Prueba C** with audio
- **Prueba D** with audio
- **Prueba E** with audio
- **Prueba F** with audio
- Tests Answer Key
- Oral Testing Suggestions

- **Examen A** with audio (lessons 4-6)
- **Examen B** with audio (lessons 4-6)
- Exams Answer Key

Audioscripts
- Tests and Exams Audioscripts
- Alternative Listening Sections Audioscript

Additional Tools for Planning and Teaching

- Essential Questions
- I Can Worksheets
- IPAs & Rubrics
- Lesson Plans
- Middle School Activity Pack
- Pacing Guides

Audio MP3s for Classroom Activities

- **Contextos**. Activities 1 and 2 (p. 191)
- **Contextos**. Comunicación: Activity 7 (p.193)
- **Estructura 6.1. Comunicación**: Activity 3 (p. 173)
- **Estructura 6.3. Comunicación**: Activity 4 (p. 209)
- **Estructura 6.4. Comunicación**: Activity 4 (p. 213)
- **Escuchar** (p. 219)

Script for Comunicación: Actividad 7 (p. 193)

Juan Manuel	¿Quieres ir al gimnasio ahora?
Victoria	Ahora no puedo. Tengo que ir a la tienda a comprar unos regalos para mi familia. ¡Hoy hay rebaja!
Juan Manuel	¿Qué piensas comprar?
Victoria	A mi mamá le voy a comprar un traje de baño y a mi papá le voy a comprar una corbata.
Juan Manuel	¿Y a tu hermano qué le vas a comprar?
Victoria	No estoy segura.
Juan Manuel	¿Tiene pasatiempos?
Victoria	¡Sí! Juega al tenis los fines de semana.

Script for Comunicación: Actividad 3 (p. 201)

Conozco a Laura, mi mejor amiga, desde el primer día de escuela. Es una chica genial porque sabe hacer muchas cosas. Sabe cantar y bailar y habla español, francés e inglés. A Laura le gusta ir de compras, especialmente cuando hay rebajas. ¡Sabe regatear y siempre encuentra las mejores gangas! Y ella también practica muchos deportes. Sabe esquiar y patinar en línea. Para ella es fácil conocer gente nueva y hacer amigos.

Script for Comunicación: Actividad 4 (p. 209)

Matilde	Hola, Hernán. ¿Ya estás listo para tu viaje a Cuba?
Hernán	Sí, Matilde, creo que sí.
Matilde	Vamos a ver… ¿Ya compraste el pasaje de avión?
Hernán	Sí, Matilde. Lo compré la semana pasada.
Matilde	Bueno. ¿Confirmaste la reservación para el hotel?
Hernán	No, voy a hablar con la agente de viajes esta tarde.
Matilde	¿Ya encontraste tu pasaporte?
Hernán	Acabo de encontrarlo.
Matilde	¿Ya preparaste la maleta?
Hernán	Sí, la preparé anoche.
Matilde	¿Decidiste llevar tu mochila o no?
Hernán	Decidí no llevarla.
Matilde	¿Leíste tu libro sobre Cuba?
Hernán	No. Pienso leerlo en el avión.

Script for Comunicación: Actividad 4 (p. 213)

Alejandra	Me gusta esta falda azul.
Dependienta	Sí, es muy elegante. Acaba de llegar al almacén.
Alejandra	No es muy cara… La voy a comprar.
Dependienta	¿Y le gusta esta blusa blanca? Hace juego con la falda.
Alejandra	Tengo muchas blusas blancas. Pero… ¿y esa blusa gris? ¿Cuánto cuesta?
Dependienta	¿Esta blusa gris? Cuesta treinta pesos. Es una blusa muy bonita.
Alejandra	También necesito un cinturón. ¿Cuánto cuesta aquél negro?
Dependienta	Sólo cuesta diez pesos.
Alejandra	Voy a comprar el cinturón también, pero ya no quiero ver más cosas porque voy a gastar mucho dinero.

*Tests and Exams can also be assigned online.

¡De compras!

6

A PRIMERA VISTA

- ¿Está comprando algo la chica?
- ¿Crees que busca una maleta o una blusa?
- ¿Está contenta o enojada?
- ¿Cómo es la chica?

Lesson Goals

In **Lección 6**, students will be introduced to the following:

- terms for clothing and shopping
- colors
- open-air markets
- Venezuelan clothing designer **Carolina Herrera**
- the verbs **saber** and **conocer**
- indirect object pronouns
- preterite tense of regular verbs
- demonstrative adjectives and pronouns
- skimming a document
- how to report an interview
- writing a report
- listening for linguistic cues
- a television commercial for the Spanish toy store **Juguettos**
- a video about open-air markets
- cultural, geographic, economic, and historical information about Cuba

A primera vista Here are some additional questions you can ask to personalize the photo: **¿Te gusta ir de compras? ¿Por qué? ¿Estás de buen humor cuando vas de compras? ¿Piensas ir de compras este fin de semana? ¿Adónde? ¿Qué compras cuando estás de vacaciones?**

Teaching Tip Look for these icons for additional communicative practice:

→👤←	Interpretive communication
←👤→	Presentational communication
👤↔👤	Interpersonal communication

SUPPORT FOR BACKWARD DESIGN

Lección 6 Essential Questions

1. How do people talk about shopping and describe clothing?
2. How do people talk about events in the past?
3. What types of markets are common in the Spanish-speaking world and why?

Lección 6 Integrated Performance Assessment

Before teaching this chapter, review the Integrated Performance Assessment (IPA) and its accompanying scoring rubric. Use the IPA to assess students' progress toward proficiency targets at the end of the chapter. **IPA Context:** You are traveling to Colombia. Two of your friends have given you money to bring back clothing for them because they are interested in getting something unique from the Spanish-speaking world. Each of your friends, one male and one female, has given you $25, so you'll need to check the current exchange rate to find out how many pesos you have to spend.

VOICE BOARD

Voice boards online allow you and your students to record and share up to five minutes of audio. Use voice boards for presentations, oral assessments, discussions, directions, etc.

Section Goals

In **Contextos**, students will learn and practice:
- clothing vocabulary
- vocabulary to use while shopping
- colors

Communication 1.2
Comparisons 4.1

Teacher Resources
Read the front matter for suggestions on how to incorporate all the program's components. See pages 189A–189B for a detailed listing of Teacher Resources online.

In-Class Tips
- Use the **Lección 6 Contextos** vocabulary presentation online or the digital images in the Resources online to assist with this presentation.
- Ask volunteers about shopping preferences and habits. Ex: **¿Qué te gusta comprar? ¿Música? ¿Libros? ¿Ropa?** (Point to your own clothing.) **¿Adónde vas para comprar esas cosas? ¿Las compras en una tienda o en Internet?** (Pretend to reach in your pocket and pay for something.) **¿Cuánto dinero gastas normalmente?** Ask another student: **¿Adónde va de compras ____? (Va a ____.) ¿Y qué compra allí? (Compra ____.)**
- Have students guess the meanings of **damas** and **caballeros**. As they refer to the scene, make true/false statements. Ex: **El hombre paga con tarjeta de crédito. (Cierto.) No venden zapatos en la tienda. (Falso.) Se puede regatear en el almacén. (Falso.)** Use as many clothing items and verbs from **Más vocabulario** as you can.

Note: At this point you may want to present *Vocabulario adicional: Más vocabulario para ir de compras* from the online Resources.

¡De compras!

Más vocabulario

el abrigo	*coat*
los calcetines (el calcetín)	*sock(s)*
el cinturón	*belt*
las gafas (de sol)	*(sun)glasses*
los guantes	*gloves*
el impermeable	*raincoat*
la ropa	*clothes*
la ropa interior	*underwear*
las sandalias	*sandals*
el traje	*suit*
el vestido	*dress*
los zapatos de tenis	*sneakers*
el regalo	*gift*
el almacén	*department store*
el centro comercial	*shopping mall*
el mercado (al aire libre)	*(open-air) market*
el precio (fijo)	*(fixed; set) price*
la rebaja	*sale*
la tienda	*store*
costar (o:ue)	*to cost*
gastar	*to spend (money)*
pagar	*to pay*
regatear	*to bargain*
vender	*to sell*
hacer juego (con)	*to match (with)*
llevar	*to wear; to take*
usar	*to wear; to use*

Variación léxica

calcetines	⟷	medias (*Amér. L.*)
cinturón	⟷	correa (*Col., Venez.*)
gafas/lentes	⟷	espejuelos (*Cuba, P.R.*), anteojos (*Arg., Chile*)
zapatos de tenis	⟷	zapatillas de deporte (*Esp.*), zapatillas (*Arg., Perú*)

Labels in image: Damas · los pantalones cortos · el traje de baño · los pantalones · la camiseta · el dependiente/el vendedor · la camisa · la clienta · el dinero en efectivo · la blusa · la bolsa · el suéter · la falda · las medias

TPR Call out a list of clothing items at random. Have students raise their right hand if they hear an item they associate with summer (Ex: **los pantalones cortos**), their left hand if they associate the item with winter (Ex: **el abrigo**), or both hands if the item can be worn in both seasons (Ex: **el cinturón**).
Variación léxica Point out that, although terms for clothing vary widely throughout the Spanish-speaking world, speakers in different regions can mutually understand each other.
TPR Have students stand in a circle. Name a sport, place, or activity and toss a ball to a student, who has three seconds to name a clothing item that goes with it. That student then names another sport, place, or activity and tosses the ball to another student. If a student cannot think of an item in time, he or she is eliminated. The last person standing wins.

Práctica

1 Escuchar Listen to Juanita and Vicente talk about what they're packing for their vacations. Indicate who is packing each item. If both are packing an item, write both names. If neither is packing an item, write an **X**.

1. abrigo _Vicente_
2. zapatos de tenis _Juanita, Vicente_
3. impermeable ___X___
4. chaqueta _Vicente_
5. sandalias _Juanita_
6. bluejeans _Juanita, Vicente_
7. gafas de sol _Vicente_
8. camisetas _Juanita, Vicente_
9. traje de baño _Juanita_
10. botas _Vicente_
11. pantalones cortos _Juanita_
12. suéter _Vicente_

2 ¿Lógico o ilógico? Listen to Guillermo and Ana talk about vacation destinations. Indicate whether each statement is **lógico** or **ilógico**.

1. _ilógico_
2. _lógico_
3. _ilógico_
4. _lógico_

3 Completar Anita is talking about going shopping. Complete each sentence with the correct word(s), adding definite or indefinite articles when necessary.

caja	medias	tarjeta de crédito
centro comercial	par	traje de baño
dependientas	ropa	vendedores

1. Hoy voy a ir de compras al _centro comercial_.
2. Voy a ir a la tienda de ropa para mujeres. Siempre hay muchas rebajas y las _dependientas_ son muy simpáticas.
3. Necesito comprar _un par_ de zapatos.
4. Y tengo que comprar _un traje de baño_ porque el sábado voy a la playa con mis amigos.
5. También voy a comprar unas _medias_ para mi mamá.
6. Voy a pagar todo (*everything*) en _la caja_.
7. Pero hoy no tengo dinero. Voy a tener que usar mi _tarjeta de crédito_.
8. Mañana voy al mercado al aire libre. Me gusta regatear con los _vendedores_.

4 Escoger Choose the item in each group that does not belong.

1. almacén • centro comercial • mercado • (sombrero)
2. camisa • camiseta • blusa • (botas)
3. jeans • (bolsa) • falda • pantalones
4. abrigo • suéter • (corbata) • chaqueta
5. mercado • tienda • almacén • (cartera)
6. (pagar) • llevar • hacer juego (con) • usar
7. botas • sandalias • zapatos • (traje)
8. vender • regatear • (ropa interior) • gastar

Labels (illustration):
- el sombrero
- un par de zapatos
- los zapatos
- la chaqueta
- la caja
- la cartera
- la dependienta/la vendedora
- la corbata
- la tarjeta de crédito
- los (blue)jeans
- la bota
- Caballeros

---

1 Expansion 👥↔👥 Have students form pairs and discuss what the weather will be like at each destination. Then have them name three more articles that each person should pack.

1 Script JUANITA: Hola. Me llamo Juanita. Mi familia y yo salimos de vacaciones mañana y estoy haciendo mis maletas. Para nuestra excursión al campo ya tengo bluejeans, camisetas y zapatos de tenis. También vamos a la playa… ¡no puedo esperar! *Script continues on page 192.*

2 In-Class Tip You may want to do this activity as a TPR exercise. Have students raise their right hands if they hear a logical statement and their left hands if they hear an illogical statement.

2 Script 1. Este verano quiero ir de vacaciones a un lugar caliente, con playas y mucho, mucho sol; por eso, necesito comprar un abrigo y botas. 2. A mí me gustaría visitar Costa Rica en la estación de lluvias. Hace mucho calor, pero llueve muchísimo. Voy a necesitar mi impermeable todo el tiempo. 3. Mi lugar favorito para ir de vacaciones es Argentina en invierno. Me gusta esquiar en las montañas. No puedo ir sin mis sandalias ni mi traje de baño. 4. En mi opinión, el lugar ideal para ir de vacaciones es mi club. Allí juego mi deporte favorito, el tenis, y también asisto a fiestas elegantes. Por eso siempre llevo mis zapatos de tenis y a veces traje y corbata.

3 Expansion Ask students to write three additional fill-in-the-blank sentences for a partner to complete.

4 Expansion Go over the answers quickly in class. After each answer, have volunteers indicate why a particular item does not belong. Ex: **1. Un sombrero no es un lugar donde compras cosas.**

TEACHING OPTIONS

Extra Practice Suggest a vacation spot and then ask students at random what clothing they need to take. Make it a continuing narration whereby the next student must say all of the items of clothing that came before and add one. Ex: **Vas a la playa. ¿Qué vas a llevar? (E1: Voy a llevar un traje de baño. E2: Voy a llevar un traje de baño y gafas de sol. E3: Voy a llevar un traje de baño, gafas de sol y…)**

TPR Play a game of *Simon Says* (**Simón dice…**). Write on the board **levántense** and **siéntense** and explain that they mean *stand up* and *sit down,* respectively. Then start by saying: **Simón dice… los que llevan jeans, levántense.** Students wearing jeans should stand up and remain standing until further instruction. Work through various articles of clothing. Be sure to give some instructions without saying **Simón dice**.

1 Script (continued)
Para ir a la playa necesito un traje de baño, pantalones cortos y sandalias. ¿Qué más necesito? Creo que es todo. VICENTE: Buenos días. Soy Vicente. Estoy haciendo mis maletas porque mi familia y yo vamos a las montañas a esquiar. Los primeros dos días vamos a hacer una excursión por las montañas. Necesito zapatos de tenis, camisetas, una chaqueta y bluejeans. El tercer día vamos a esquiar. Necesito un abrigo, un suéter y botas… y gafas de sol.

In-Class Tips

- Read the color words aloud, slowly, one at a time. Point to each drawing and ask: **¿De qué color es esta camiseta?** Ask about combinations. Ex: **Si combino rojo y azul, ¿qué color resulta? (morado)**
- Point to objects in the classroom and clothes you and students are wearing to elicit color words.
- Give dates and have students name the colors that they associate with each one. Ex: **el 14 de febrero (rojo, rosado); el 31 de octubre (negro, anaranjado)** You may want to repeat the process with brand names. Ex: FedEx **(anaranjado, morado, blanco)**
- Point out that color words are adjectives and agree in number and gender with the nouns they modify.

5 Expansion Add a visual aspect to this activity. Show magazine pictures of various products (cars, computers, etc.) and ask questions. Ex: **¿Es cara o barata esta computadora? (Es barata.)**

6 Expansion Point to individuals and ask other students what color of clothing each is wearing. Ex: ____, **¿de qué color es la falda de ____? (Es ____.)**

Los colores

amarillo/a	anaranjado/a	azul

blanco/a	gris	marrón, café	morado/a	negro/a

rojo/a	rosado/a	verde

¡LENGUA VIVA!

The names of colors vary throughout the Spanish-speaking world. For example, in some countries, **anaranjado/a** may be referred to as **naranja**, **morado/a** as **púrpura**, and **rojo/a** as **colorado/a**.

Other terms that will prove helpful include **claro** (*light*) and **oscuro** (*dark*): **azul claro, azul oscuro**.

Adjetivos

barato/a	*cheap*
bueno/a	*good*
cada	*each*
caro/a	*expensive*
corto/a	*short (in length)*
elegante	*elegant*
hermoso/a	*beautiful*
largo/a	*long*
loco/a	*crazy*
nuevo/a	*new*
otro/a	*other; another*
pobre	*poor*
rico/a	*rich*

5 Contrastes Complete each phrase with the opposite of the underlined word.

1. una corbata <u>barata</u> • unas camisas… caras
2. unas vendedoras <u>malas</u> • unos dependientes… buenos
3. un vestido <u>corto</u> • una falda… larga
4. un hombre muy <u>pobre</u> • una mujer muy… rica
5. una cartera <u>nueva</u> • un cinturón… viejo
6. unos trajes <u>hermosos</u> • unos jeans… feos
7. un impermeable <u>caro</u> • unos suéteres… baratos
8. unos calcetines <u>blancos</u> • unas medias… negras

6 Preguntas Answer these questions.

1. ¿De qué color es la rosa de Texas? Es amarilla.
2. ¿De qué color es la bandera (*flag*) de Canadá? Es roja y blanca.
3. ¿De qué color es la casa donde vive el presidente de los EE.UU.? Es blanca.
4. ¿De qué color es el océano Atlántico? Es azul.
5. ¿De qué color es la nieve? Es blanca.
6. ¿De qué color es el café? Es marrón./Es café.
7. ¿De qué color es el dólar de los EE.UU.? Es verde y blanco.
8. ¿De qué color es la cebra (*zebra*)? Es negra y blanca.

CONSULTA

Like other adjectives you have seen, colors must agree in gender and number with the nouns they modify.

Ex: **las camisas verdes, el vestido amarillo.**

For a review of descriptive adjectives, see **Estructura 3.1**, pp. 88–89.

TEACHING OPTIONS

Pairs Ask student pairs to write a physical description of a well-known TV or cartoon character. Then have them read their descriptions for the rest of the class to guess. Ex: **Soy bajo y un poco gordo. Llevo pantalones cortos azules y una camiseta roja. Tengo el pelo amarillo. También soy amarillo. ¿Quién soy? (Bart Simpson)**

Game Add a visual aspect to this vocabulary practice by playing

Concentración. On eight cards, write descriptions of clothing, including colors. Ex: **unos pantalones negros** On another eight cards, draw pictures that match the descriptions. Shuffle the cards and place them face-down in four rows of four. In pairs, students select two cards. If the cards match, the pair keeps them. If the cards do not match, students replace them in their original position. The pair with the most cards at the end wins.

Communication 1.1, 1.2, 1.3

Comunicación

7 **Los regalos** Listen to the conversation between Victoria and her friend Juan Manuel. Then indicate whether the following conclusions are **lógico** or **ilógico**, based on what you heard.

	Lógico	Ilógico
1. Juan Manuel quiere ir de compras.	○	●
2. A la mamá de Victoria le gusta nadar.	●	○
3. El papá de Victoria usa camisas.	●	○
4. Victoria va a regatear.	○	●
5. Victoria le va a comprar a su hermano unas botas.	○	●

8 **Preferencias** Answer your partner's questions. Answers will vary.

1. ¿Adónde vas a comprar ropa? ¿Por qué?
2. ¿Qué tipo de ropa prefieres? ¿Por qué?
3. ¿Cuáles son tus colores favoritos?
4. En tu opinión, ¿es importante comprar ropa nueva frecuentemente? ¿Por qué?
5. ¿Gastas mucho dinero en ropa cada mes? ¿Buscas rebajas?
6. ¿Regateas cuando compras ropa? ¿Usas tarjetas de crédito?

9 **El viaje** Write an e-mail to a relative about a trip you are taking with your family this summer. Include where you are going, what the weather is going to be like, what activities you are going to do, and what clothes you are taking. Answers will vary.

10 **Las maletas** With a partner, take turns asking questions about the drawings. Include the topics from the list to talk about Carmela's vacation and Pepe's trip to Bariloche. Answers will vary.

- ropa
- color
- lugar
- tiempo
- actividades

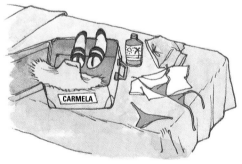
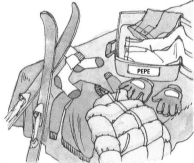

NOTA CULTURAL

Bariloche is a popular resort for skiing in South America. Located in Argentina's Patagonia region, the town is also known for its chocolate factories and its beautiful lakes, mountains, and forests.

CONSULTA

To review weather, see **Lección 5, Contextos**, p. 154.

TEACHING OPTIONS

Pairs ♟↔♟ Have students form pairs, and tell them they are going on a shopping spree. On paper strips, write varying dollar amounts, from ten dollars to three thousand, and distribute them. Have pairs discuss what they will buy. Encourage creativity. Ex: **Tenemos quince dólares y vamos a _Old Navy_. Ella va a comprar medias amarillas. Yo voy a comprar un sombrero en rebaja.**
Extra Practice →♟← Add an auditory aspect to this vocabulary

practice. Ask students to write an anonymous description of the article of clothing or outfit that best defines them. Collect the papers, shuffle them, and read the descriptions aloud for the class to guess.
Pairs ♟↔♟ Have pairs take turns describing classmates' clothing and guessing the person. Ex: **Esta persona lleva jeans y una blusa marrón. Lleva sandalias blancas. (Es _____.)**

---

7 **In-Class Tip** Before playing the audio, have pairs predict the conversation by writing a dialogue between Victoria and Juan Manuel in eight lines. Let them share their dialogues with the class before proceeding.

7 **Script** *See the script for this activity on Interleaf page 189B.*

8 **Expansion**
♟↔♟ Have students work with different partners. Tell students to assume the identity of a famous person and explain their clothing preferences, using questions similar to those in **Actividad 8**.

8 **Virtual Chat**
♟↔♟ Available online.

9 **Expansion**
♟↔♟ Have groups of three students discuss where they are going and draw three suitcases. Ask them to write on each one what clothing each person is taking and what items they need for their trip. Have them present their drawings to the class and answer these questions:
¿Adónde van?
¿Qué tiempo va a hacer allí?
¿Qué van a hacer allí?
¿Qué hay en sus maletas?
¿De qué color es la ropa que llevan?

10 **Expansion**
• ♟↔♟ In pairs, have students discuss what essential items might be missing from the suitcases. Ex:
—**Pepe debe llevar unas botas y unas gafas de sol.**
—**Sí, Pepe necesita unas botas para esquiar.**
• Ask volunteers what kind of clothing they would take with them to these destinations: **Seattle en la primavera, la Florida en el verano, Toronto en el invierno.**

10 **Partner Chat**
♟↔♟ Available online.

Section Goals

In **Fotonovela**, students will:
- receive comprehensible input from free-flowing discourse
- learn functional phrases involving clothing and how much things cost

Communication 1.2
Cultures 2.1, 2.2

Teacher Resources

Read the front matter for suggestions on how to incorporate all the program's components. See pages 189A–189B for a detailed listing of Teacher Resources online.

Video Recap: Lección 5

Before doing this **Fotonovela** section, review the previous episode with these questions:

1. **¿Qué problema hay cuando hablan con el empleado?** (El empleado no encuentra la reservación.)

2. **¿Qué piensa Felipe del hotel?** (Piensa que no está nada mal; es limpio y cómodo.)

3. **¿Qué deporte quieren hacer Miguel y Maru en la playa?** (Quieren hacer windsurf.)

4. **¿Quién consigue las tablas de windsurf para Maru y Miguel?** (El botones las consigue.)

5. **¿Quiénes nadan?** (Juan Carlos y Jimena nadan.)

Video Synopsis

The friends are back in **Mérida** where they go to the market to do some shopping. They split into two teams, the boys versus the girls, to see who is better at bargaining. Who will get the best deal?

In-Class Tips

- Have students scan the **Fotonovela** captions for vocabulary related to clothing or colors.
- Point out the clothing that a few individual students are wearing and ask them some questions about it.

    Ex: **Me gusta esa camisa azul.**
    ¿Es de algodón?
    ¿Dónde la compraste?

En el mercado

Los chicos van de compras al mercado. ¿Quién hizo la mejor compra?

PERSONAJES FELIPE JUAN CARLOS

MARISSA Oigan, vamos al mercado.

JUAN CARLOS ¡Sí! Los chicos en un equipo y las chicas en otro.

FELIPE Tenemos dos horas para ir de compras.

MARU Y don Guillermo decide quién gana.

JIMENA Esta falda azul es muy elegante.

MARISSA ¡Sí! Además, este color está de moda.

MARU Éste rojo es de algodón.

(*Las chicas encuentran unas bolsas.*)

VENDEDOR Ésta de rayas cuesta 190 pesos, ésta 120 pesos y ésta 220 pesos.

MARISSA ¿Me das aquella blusa rosada? Me parece que hace juego con esta falda, ¿no? ¿No tienen otras tallas?

JIMENA Sí, aquí. ¿Qué talla usas?

MARISSA Uso talla 4.

JIMENA La encontré. ¡Qué ropa más bonita!

(*En otra parte del mercado*)

FELIPE Juan Carlos compró una camisa de muy buena calidad.

MIGUEL (*a la vendedora*) ¿Puedo ver ésos, por favor?

VENDEDORA Sí, señor. Le doy un muy buen precio.

VENDEDOR Son 530 por las tres bolsas. Pero como ustedes son tan bonitas, son 500 pesos.

MARU Señor, no somos turistas ricas. Somos estudiantes pobres.

VENDEDOR Bueno, son 480 pesos.

TEACHING OPTIONS

Video Tips General suggestions for using video clips in the classroom can be found in the front matter of this Teacher's Edition.

En el mercado → Photocopy the **Fotonovela** Videoscript (Supersite) and white out 7–10 words in order to create a master for a cloze activity. Distribute photocopies of the master and have students fill in the missing words as they watch the **En el mercado** episode. You may want students to work in small groups and help each other fill in any gaps.

MARISSA **JIMENA** **MARU** **MIGUEL** **DON GUILLERMO** **VENDEDORA** **VENDEDOR**

JUAN CARLOS Miren, mi nueva camisa. Elegante, ¿verdad?

FELIPE A ver, Juan Carlos... te queda bien.

MARU ¿Qué compraste?

MIGUEL Sólo esto.

MARU ¡Qué bonitos aretes! Gracias, mi amor.

JUAN CARLOS Y ustedes, ¿qué compraron?

JIMENA Bolsas.

MARU Acabamos de comprar tres bolsas por sólo 480 pesos. ¡Una ganga!

FELIPE Don Guillermo, usted tiene que decidir quién gana. ¿Los chicos o las chicas?

DON GUILLERMO El ganador es... Miguel. ¡Porque no compró nada para él, sino para su novia!

Expresiones útiles

Talking about clothing

¡Qué ropa más bonita!
What nice clothing!
Esta falda azul es muy elegante.
This blue skirt is very elegant.
Está de moda.
It's in style.
Éste rojo es de algodón/lana.
This red one is cotton/wool.
Ésta de rayas/lunares/cuadros es de seda.
This striped / polka-dotted / plaid one is silk.
Es de muy buena calidad.
It's very good quality.
¿Qué talla usas/llevas?
What size do you wear?
Uso/Llevo talla 4.
I wear a size 4.
¿Qué número calza?
What size shoe do you wear?
Yo calzo siete.
I wear a size seven.

Negotiating a price

¿Cuánto cuesta?
How much does it cost?
Demasiado caro/a.
Too expensive.
Es una ganga.
It's a bargain.

Saying what you bought

¿Qué compraste?/¿Qué compró usted?
What did you buy?
Sólo compré esto.
I only bought this.
¡Qué bonitos aretes!
What beautiful earrings!
Y ustedes, ¿qué compraron?
And you guys, what did you buy?

Additional vocabulary

híjole *wow*

Expresiones útiles
- Point out the verb forms **compraste, compró, compré,** and **compraron.** Tell the class that these are forms of the verb **comprar** in the preterite tense, which is used to talk about events in the past. Tell them that **Esta** is an example of a demonstrative adjective, which is used to single out particular nouns; explain that the accented forms, **Éste** and **Ésta**, are pronouns. Tell students that **esto** is one of three neuter demonstrative pronouns. Have students scan the **Fotonovela** captions for other demonstratives. Also point out the captions for stills 3 and 4 and explain that **Me** and **Le** are examples of indirect object pronouns, which show *to whom* or *for whom* an action is done. Tell students that they will learn more about these concepts in **Estructura.**
- Help students with adjective placement and agreement when talking about clothing. Ask them to translate these phrases: 1. a white tie with gray and brown stripes (**una corbata blanca con rayas grises y marrones**) 2. black wool pants (**unos pantalones negros de lana**) 3. a yellow cotton shirt with purple polka dots (**una camisa amarilla de algodón con lunares morados**) 4. a red silk dress (**un vestido rojo de seda**) Discuss different possibilities for adjective placement and how it affects agreement. Ex: **Un vestido rojo de seda** versus **Un vestido de seda roja.**

Nota cultural When bargaining in open-air markets, one can typically expect to arrive at an agreed price of about 10 to 20% lower than the original. Bargaining is usually a friendly, pleasant experience and an expected and welcome ritual.

TEACHING OPTIONS

TPR Ask students to write **clientes** and **vendedores** on separate sheets on paper. Read aloud phrases from **Expresiones útiles** and have them hold up the paper(s) that correspond(s) to the people that would say that expression. Ex: **¿Qué número calza usted? (vendedores)**

Small Groups Have the class work in small groups to write statements about the **Fotonovela**. Then ask groups to exchange papers and write out a question that would have elicited each statement. Ex: **Miguel compra unos aretes para su novia. (¿Qué compra Miguel para su novia?)**

1 Expansion
👤↔👤 Once statements have been corrected, ask pairs to find the places in the episode that support their answers. Have pairs role-play the scenes for the class. Ask comprehension questions as a follow-up.

2 Expansion Give students these statements as items 7–9:
7. Somos estudiantes y por eso no tenemos mucho dinero. (M)
8. La ropa que compró Juan Carlos le queda muy bien. (F)
9. Don Guillermo debe decidir el ganador. (M)

3 Expansion Ask pairs to write two additional questions. Then have pairs exchange papers and answer each other's questions.

Nota cultural Shoe sizes in Mexico are different from the U.S. and Canada. Men's sizes in Mexico are 2 numbers smaller, and women's, 3 sizes smaller. For example, a man's size 11 shoe in the U.S. and Canada would be a size 9 in Mexico, and a woman's size 7.5 would be a 4.5.

4 Possible Conversation
E1: Buenas tardes.
E2: Buenas tardes. ¿Qué desea?
E1: Estoy buscando una camisa.
E2: Pues, tengo estas camisas de algodón y estas camisas de seda. ¿Cuál prefiere usted?
E1: Busco una camisa blanca o azul de algodón. Uso talla mediana.
E2: Las camisas de algodón son de talla mediana. Tengo esta camisa azul de algodón.
E1: Quiero comprarla, pero no soy rico/a. ¿Cuánto cuesta?
E2: Veinte dólares. Pero para usted... sólo diecisiete dólares.
E1: Muy bien. La compro, pero sólo tengo quince dólares.
E2: Está bien. Muchas gracias.

4 Partner Chat
👤↔👤 Available online.

¿Qué pasó?

1 **¿Cierto o falso?** Indicate whether each sentence is **cierto** or **falso**. Correct the false statements.

	Cierto	Falso
1. Jimena dice que la falda azul no es elegante.	○	☑ Jimena dice que la falda azul es muy elegante.
2. Juan Carlos compra una camisa.	☑	○
3. Marissa dice que el azul es un color que está de moda.	☑	○
4. Miguel compra unas sandalias para Maru.	○	☑ Miguel compra unos aretes para Maru.

2 **Identificar** Provide the first initial of the person who would make each statement.

M 1. ¿Te gusta cómo se me ven mis nuevos aretes?
F 2. Juan Carlos compró una camisa de muy buena calidad.
M 3. No podemos pagar 500, señor, eso es muy caro.
J 4. Aquí tienen ropa de muchas tallas.
J 5. Esta falda me gusta mucho, el color azul es muy elegante.
F 6. Hay que darnos prisa, sólo tenemos dos horas para ir de compras.

MARU
FELIPE
JIMENA

3 **Completar** Answer the questions using the information in the **Fotonovela**.
1. ¿Qué talla es Marissa? Marissa usa talla 4.
2. ¿Cuánto les pide el vendedor por las tres bolsas? Las bolsas cuestan 500 pesos.
3. ¿Cuál es el precio que pagan las tres amigas por las bolsas? El precio que pagan es 480 pesos.
4. ¿Qué dice Juan Carlos sobre su nueva camisa? Juan Carlos dice que su nueva camisa es elegante.
5. ¿Quién ganó al hacer las compras? ¿Por qué? Ganó Miguel porque le compró unos aretes su novia.

4 **Conversar** With a partner, role-play a conversation between a customer and a salesperson in an open-air market. Use these expressions and also look at **Expresiones útiles** on the previous page.
Answers will vary.

¿Qué desea?	Estoy buscando...	Prefiero el/la rojo/a.
What would you like?	*I'm looking for...*	*I prefer the red one.*

Cliente/a
Say good afternoon.
Explain that you are looking for a particular item of clothing.
Discuss colors and sizes.
Ask for the price and begin bargaining.
Settle on a price and purchase the item.

Vendedor(a)
Greet the customer and ask what he/she would like.
Show him/her some items and ask what he/she prefers.
Discuss colors and sizes.
Tell him/her a price. Negotiate a price.
Accept a price and say thank you.

NOTA CULTURAL
Las guayaberas are a popular men's shirt worn in hot climates. They are usually made of cotton, linen, or silk and decorated with pleats, pockets, and sometimes embroidery. They can be worn instead of a jacket to formal occasions or as everyday clothing.

AYUDA
When discussing prices, it's important to keep in mind singular and plural forms of verbs.
La camisa cuesta diez dólares.
Las botas cuestan sesenta dólares.
El precio de las botas **es** sesenta dólares.
Los precios de la ropa **son** altos.

TEACHING OPTIONS

Extra Practice Have the class answer questions about the **Fotonovela**. Ex: **1. ¿Quién piensa que el color azul está de moda? (Marissa) 2. ¿Quiénes regatean por tres bolsas? (Maru, Jimena y Marissa) 3. ¿Qué acaba de comprar Miguel? (Acaba de comprar unos aretes para Maru.)**
Pairs 👤↔👤 Divide the class into pairs. Tell them to imagine that they are awards show commentators on the red carpet (**la**

alfombra roja). Ask each pair to choose six celebrities and write a description of their outfits. Encourage creativity, and provide additional vocabulary if needed. Then have pairs read their descriptions for the class. Ex: **Aquí estamos en la alfombra roja de los *Video Music Awards*. Ahora viene Beyoncé con Jay-Z. Ella lleva un vestido azul de seda y sandalias grises. ¡Qué ropa tan bonita! Jay-Z usa jeans y...**

Pronunciación
The consonants **d** and **t**

¿Dónde?	vender	nadar	verdad

Like **b** and **v**, the Spanish **d** can have a hard sound or a soft sound, depending on which letters appear next to it.

Don	dinero	tienda	falda

At the beginning of a phrase and after **n** or **l**, the letter **d** is pronounced with a hard sound. This sound is similar to the English *d* in *dog*, but a little softer and duller. The tongue should touch the back of the upper teeth, not the roof of the mouth.

medias	verde	vestido	huésped

In all other positions, **d** has a soft sound. It is similar to the English *th* in *there*, but a little softer.

Don Diego no tiene el diccionario

When **d** begins a word, its pronunciation depends on the previous word. At the beginning of a phrase or after a word that ends in **n** or **l**, it is pronounced as a hard **d**.

Doña Dolores es de la capital

Words that begin with **d** are pronounced with a soft **d** if they appear immediately after a word that ends in a vowel or any consonant other than **n** or **l**.

traje	pantalones	tarjeta	tienda

When pronouncing the Spanish **t**, the tongue should touch the back of the upper teeth, not the roof of the mouth. Unlike the English *t*, no air is expelled from the mouth.

Práctica   Read these phrases aloud to practice the **d** and the **t**.

1. Hasta pronto.
2. De nada.
3. Mucho gusto.
4. Lo siento.
5. No hay de qué.
6. ¿De dónde es usted?
7. ¡Todos a bordo!
8. No puedo.
9. Es estupendo.
10. No tengo computadora.
11. ¿Cuándo vienen?
12. Son las tres y media.

Oraciones   Read these sentences aloud to practice the **d** and the **t**.

1. Don Teodoro tiene una tienda en un almacén en La Habana.
2. Don Teodoro vende muchos trajes, vestidos y zapatos todos los días.
3. Un día un turista, Federico Machado, entra en la tienda para comprar un par de botas.
4. Federico regatea con don Teodoro y compra las botas y también un par de sandalias.

Refranes   Read these sayings aloud to practice the **d** and the **t**.

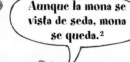

En la variedad está el gusto.[1]

Aunque la mona se vista de seda, mona se queda.[2]

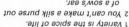

[2] *You can't make a silk purse out of a sow's ear.*
[1] *Variety is the spice of life.*

Section Goal

In **Pronunciación**, students will be introduced to the pronunciation of the letters **d** and **t**.

Comparisons 4.1

In-Class Tips

• Explain that **d** has a hard sound at the beginning of a phrase or after **n** or **l**. Write **don, dinero, tienda,** and **falda** on the board and have the class pronounce them.

• Explain that **d** has a soft sound in all other positions. Pronounce **medias, verde, vestido,** and **huésped** and have the class repeat.

• Point out that within phrases, **d** at the beginning of a word has a hard or soft sound depending on the last sound of the preceding word. Read the examples aloud and have the class repeat.

• Explain that **t** is pronounced with the tongue at the back of the upper teeth and that, unlike English, no air is expelled from the mouth. Pronounce **traje, pantalones, tarjeta,** and **tienda** and have the class repeat. Then pronounce pairs of similar-sounding Spanish and English words, having students focus on the difference between the **t** sounds: ti/*tea*; tal/*tall*; todo/*toad*; tema/*tame*; tela/*tell*.

TEACHING OPTIONS

Extra Practice   Write some additional proverbs on the board and have the class practice saying each one. Ex: **De tal padre, tal hijo.** (*Like father, like son.*) **El que tiene tejado de cristal no tira piedras al vecino.** (*People who live in glass houses shouldn't throw stones.*) **Cuatro ojos ven más que dos.** (*Two heads are better than one.*) **Donde come uno, comen dos, y donde comen dos, comen todos.** (*There's always room for one more at the table.*)

Extra Practice   Write on the board the names of these famous Cuban literary figures: **José Martí, Julián del Casal, Gertrudis Gómez de Avellaneda,** and **Dulce María Loynaz.** Say the names aloud and have the class repeat. Then ask volunteers to explain the pronunciation of each **d** and **t** in these names.

Section Goals

In **Cultura**, students will:
- read about open-air markets
- learn clothing-related terms
- read about Venezuelan clothing designer **Carolina Herrera**
- read about the fashions of Hispanic designers

Communication 1.1, 1.2
Cultures 2.1, 2.2
Connections 3.1, 3.2
Comparisons 4.2

En detalle
Antes de leer
👥↔👤 Lead a discussion about open-air markets, such as a flea market. Have students share their experiences, including the market's location, goods sold there, and prices.

Lectura
- Explain that open-air markets that specialize in second-hand or low-priced goods are often referred to as **mercados de pulgas** (*flea markets*).
- Point out that many local artists take advantage of open-air markets to sell their pieces or display new works.
- Explain that **la ñapa** can be considered similar to the Anglo tradition of a baker's dozen.

Después de leer Ask students what facts are new or surprising to them.

1 Expansion Give students these statements as items 9–11: 9. The **Tianguis Cultural del Chopo** is not a good place to go if you are interested in Mexican crafts and art. (**Falso**. The **Tianguis Cultural del Chopo** has crafts and art.) 10. Market stands are referred to as **puestos**. (**Cierto**.) 11. Bargaining often raises the price of an item significantly. (**Falso**. It usually lowers the price significantly.)

Los mercados al aire libre

Mercados al aire libre are an integral part of commerce and culture in the Spanish-speaking world. Whether they take place daily or weekly, these markets are an important forum where tourists, locals, and vendors interact. People come to the marketplace to shop, socialize, taste local foods, and watch street performers. Wandering from one **puesto** (*stand*) to the next, one can browse for fresh fruits and vegetables, clothing, CDs and DVDs, and **artesanías** (*crafts*). Some markets offer a mix of products, while others specialize in food, fashion, or used merchandise, such as antiques and books.

When shoppers see an item they like, they can bargain with the vendor. Friendly bargaining is an expected ritual and may result in a significantly lower price. When selling food, vendors may give the customer a little extra of what they purchase; this free addition is known as **la ñapa**.

Many open-air markets are also tourist attractions. The market in Otavalo, Ecuador, is world-famous and has taken place every Saturday since pre-Incan times. This market is well-known for the colorful textiles woven by the **otavaleños**, the indigenous people of the area. One can also find leather goods and wood carvings from nearby towns. Another popular market is **El Rastro**, held every Sunday in Madrid, Spain. Sellers set up **puestos** along the streets to display their wares, which range from local artwork and antiques to inexpensive clothing and electronics.

Mercado de Otavalo

Otros mercados famosos

Mercado	Lugar	Productos
Feria Artesanal de Recoleta	Buenos Aires, Argentina	artesanías
Mercado Central	Santiago, Chile	mariscos°, pescado°, frutas, verduras°
Tianguis Cultural del Chopo	Ciudad de México, México	ropa, música, revistas, libros, arte, artesanías
El mercado de Chichicastenango	Chichicastenango, Guatemala	frutas y verduras, flores°, cerámica, textiles

mariscos *seafood* pescado *fish* verduras *vegetables* flores *flowers*

1 **¿Cierto o falso?** Indicate whether these statements are cierto or falso. Correct the false statements.

1. Generally, open-air markets specialize in one type of goods. **Falso**. They sell a variety of goods.
2. Bargaining is commonplace at outdoor markets. **Cierto**.
3. Only new goods can be found at open-air markets. **Falso**. They sell both new and used goods.
4. A Spaniard in search of antiques could search at **El Rastro**. Cierto.
5. If you are in Guatemala and want to buy ceramics, you can go to Chichicastenango. **Cierto**.
6. A **ñapa** is a tax on open-air market goods. **Falso**. A **ñapa** is a free addition sometimes given to customers.
7. The **otavaleños** weave colorful textiles to sell on Saturdays. **Cierto**.
8. Santiago's **Mercado Central** is known for books and music. **Falso**. It's known for seafood, fish, fruits, and vegetables.

TEACHING OPTIONS

TPR Create a series of true/false statements about goods one can purchase at the open-air markets mentioned in **En detalle**. Tell students to raise their right hand if a statement is true or their left hand if it is false. Ex: **Compro mariscos en El Rastro.** (left hand) **Compro flores en el mercado de Chichicastenango.** (right hand)

Small Groups ↤👤→ Have students work in groups of three. For homework, have them research another famous open-air market in the Spanish-speaking world. Ex: **Pisac** (Peru), **La Romana** (Dominican Republic), **La Cancha** (Bolivia). In class, have each group present the location of the market, how often it takes place, what is sold, and any other significant information. Encourage students to bring in photos.

ASÍ SE DICE

La ropa

la chamarra (Méx.)	la chaqueta
de manga corta/larga	*short/long-sleeved*
los mahones (P. Rico); el pantalón de mezclilla (Méx.); los tejanos (Esp.); los vaqueros (Arg., Cuba, Esp., Uru.)	los bluejeans
la marca	*brand*
la playera (Méx.); la remera (Arg.)	la camiseta

EL MUNDO HISPANO

Diseñadores de moda

- **Adolfo Domínguez** (España) Su ropa tiene un estilo minimalista y práctico. Usa telas° naturales y cómodas en sus diseños.

- **Silvia Tcherassi** (Colombia) Los colores vivos y las líneas asimétricas de sus vestidos y trajes muestran influencias tropicales.

- **Óscar de la Renta** (República Dominicana) Diseñó ropa opulenta para la mujer clásica.

- **Narciso Rodríguez** (EE.UU.) En sus diseños delicados y finos predominan los colores blanco y negro. Hizo° el vestido de boda° de Carolyn Bessette Kennedy. También diseñó varios vestidos para Michelle Obama.

telas *fabrics* Hizo *He made* de boda *wedding*

PERFIL

Carolina Herrera

In 1980, at the urging of some friends, **Carolina Herrera** created a fashion collection as a "test." The Venezuelan designer received such a favorable response that within one year she moved her family from Caracas to New York City and created her own label, Carolina Herrera, Ltd.

"I love elegance and intricacy, but whether it is in a piece of clothing or a fragrance, the intricacy must appear as simplicity," Herrera once stated. She quickly found that many sophisticated women agreed; from the start,

her sleek and glamorous designs have been in constant demand. Over the years, Herrera has grown her brand into a veritable fashion empire that encompasses her fashion and bridal collections, cosmetics, perfume, and accessories that are sold around the globe.

Conexión Internet

¿Qué marcas de ropa son populares en el mundo hispano?

Use the Web to find more cultural information related to this **Cultura** section.

ACTIVIDADES

2 **Comprensión** Complete these sentences.
1. Adolfo Domínguez usa telas __naturales__ y __cómodas__ en su ropa.
2. Si hace fresco en el D.F., puedes llevar una __chamarra__.
3. La diseñadora __Carolina Herrera__ hace ropa, perfumes y más.
4. La ropa de __Silvia Tcherassi__ muestra influencias tropicales.
5. Los __mahones__ son una ropa casual en Puerto Rico.

3 **Mi ropa favorita** Write a brief description of your favorite article of clothing. Mention what store it is from, the brand, colors, fabric, style, and any other information.
Answers will vary.

6.1 Saber and conocer

ANTE TODO Spanish has two verbs that mean *to know*: **saber** and **conocer**. They cannot be used interchangeably. Note the irregular **yo** forms.

The verbs saber and conocer

		saber *(to know)*	conocer *(to know)*
SINGULAR FORMS	yo	sé	conozco
	tú	sabes	conoces
	Ud./él/ella	sabe	conoce
PLURAL FORMS	nosotros/as	sabemos	conocemos
	vosotros/as	sabéis	conocéis
	Uds./ellos/ellas	saben	conocen

▶ **Saber** means *to know a fact or piece(s) of information* or *to know how to do something*.

No **sé** tu número de teléfono.
I don't know your telephone number.

Mi hermana **sabe** hablar francés.
My sister knows how to speak French.

▶ **Conocer** means *to know* or *be familiar/acquainted* with a person, place, or thing.

¿**Conoces** la ciudad de Nueva York?
Do you know New York City?

No **conozco** a tu amigo Esteban.
I don't know your friend Esteban.

▶ When the direct object of **conocer** is a person or pet, the personal **a** is used.

¿Conoces La Habana?   *but*   ¿Conoces **a** Celia Cruz?
Do you know Havana?   *Do you know Celia Cruz?*

▶ **¡Atención!** **Parecer** (*to seem*) and **ofrecer** (*to offer*) are conjugated like **conocer**.

▶ **¡Atención!** **Conducir** (*to drive*) and **traducir** (*to translate*) also have an irregular **yo** form, but since they are **-ir** verbs, they are conjugated differently from **conocer**.

conducir	conduzco, conduces, conduce, conducimos, conducís, conducen
traducir	traduzco, traduces, traduce, traducimos, traducís, traducen

¡INTÉNTALO! Provide the appropriate forms of these verbs.

saber

1. José no ___sabe___ la hora.
2. Sara y yo ___sabemos___ jugar al tenis.
3. ¿Por qué no ___sabes___ tú estos verbos?
4. Mis padres ___saben___ hablar japonés.
5. Yo ___sé___ a qué hora es la clase.
6. Usted no ___sabe___ dónde vivo.
7. Mi hermano no ___sabe___ nadar.
8. Nosotros ___sabemos___ muchas cosas.

conocer

1. Usted y yo ___conocemos___ bien Miami.
2. ¿Tú ___conoces___ a mi amigo Manuel?
3. Sergio y Taydé ___conocen___ mi pueblo.
4. Emiliano ___conoce___ a mis padres.
5. Yo ___conozco___ muy bien el centro.
6. ¿Ustedes ___conocen___ la tienda Gigante?
7. Nosotras ___conocemos___ una playa hermosa.
8. ¿Usted ___conoce___ a mi profesora?

Práctica y Comunicación

1 **Completar** Indicate the correct verb for each sentence.

1. Mis hermanos (conocen/saben) conducir, pero yo no (sé/conozco).
2. —¿(Conocen/Saben) ustedes dónde está el estadio? —No, no lo (conocemos/sabemos).
3. —¿(Conoces/Sabes) a Lady Gaga? —Bueno, (sé/conozco) quién es, pero no la (conozco/sé).
4. Mi profesora (sabe/conoce) Cuba y también (conoce/sabe) bailar salsa.

2 **Combinar** Combine elements from each column to create sentences. Answers will vary.

A	B	C
Shakira	(no) conocer	Jimmy Fallon
los Yankees	(no) saber	cantar y bailar
el primer ministro		La Habana Vieja
de Canadá		muchas personas importantes
mis amigos y yo		hablar dos lenguas extranjeras
tú		jugar al béisbol

3 **Mi compañera de cuarto** Listen as Jennifer describes her roommate. Then indicate whether the following conclusions are **lógico** or **ilógico**, based on what you heard.

	Lógico	Ilógico
1. Jennifer y Laura son amigas.	⦿	◯
2. Laura es antipática.	◯	⦿
3. A Laura le gustan las lenguas extranjeras.	⦿	◯
4. Laura prefiere comprar ropa cara.	◯	⦿
5. Laura no tiene pasatiempos.	◯	⦿
6. Laura conoce a muchas personas.	⦿	◯

4 **Preguntas** Answer your partner's questions. Use complete sentences. Answers will vary.

1. ¿Conoces a un(a) cantante famoso/a? ¿Te gusta cómo canta?
2. En tu familia, ¿quién sabe cantar bien? ¿Tu opinión es objetiva?
3. Y tú, ¿conduces bien o mal? ¿Y tus amigos?
4. Si un(a) amigo/a no conduce muy bien, ¿le ofreces crítica constructiva?
5. ¿Cómo parecen estar tus amigos hoy?

5 **Conocimientos** Tell about three things you know how to do, three places you are familiar with, and three people you know. Answers will vary.

6 **Anuncio** Write an advertisement using two examples each of **saber** and **conocer**. Answers will vary.

1 In-Class Tip To challenge students, write this activity on the board as cloze sentences.

2 In-Class Tip To simplify, before beginning the activity, read through column C and have students determine whether each item takes the verb **saber** or **conocer**.

2 Expansion Add more elements to column A (Ex: **yo, mis padres, mi profesor(a) de español**) and continue the activity.

3 Script *See the Script for this activity on Interleaf page 189B.*

3 Expansion Have students write a list of the qualities their best friend should have and share their ideas with the class.

4 Expansion In pairs, have students create three additional questions using the verbs **conducir, ofrecer,** and **traducir**. Then have pairs join other pairs to ask and answer their questions.

4 Virtual Chat Available online.

5 In-Class Tip Have small groups of students find out what they have in common.

6 Expansion Ask students to design a poster for their advertisement. Transform the classroom into a gallery where students can present their posters to their classmates.

TEACHING OPTIONS

Extra Practice Use the Internet to research advertising slogans that use verbs from **Estructura 6.1**. In groups, have students guess the company or product for each slogan. Ex: **Sabemos por qué vuelas. (American Airlines)**
Small Groups Ask students to write down four sentences (two true, two false) using **saber** and **conocer**. In groups of three, have them read their sentences aloud. The

group should ask questions to guess if the person is lying or telling the truth.
Large Group Ask students to write down six things they know how to do. Have them circulate around the room to find out who else knows how to do those things, jotting down the names of those that answer **sí**. Have students report back to the class. Ex: **Keisha y yo sabemos tocar el piano.**

6.2 Indirect object pronouns

ANTE TODO   In **Lección 5**, you learned that a direct object receives the action of the verb directly. In contrast, an indirect object receives the action of the verb indirectly.

SUBJECT	I.O. PRONOUN	VERB	DIRECT OBJECT	INDIRECT OBJECT
Roberto	**le**	presta	cien pesos	**a Luisa.**
Roberto		*lends*	*100 pesos*	*to Luisa.*

An indirect object is a noun or pronoun that answers the question *to whom* or *for whom* an action is done. In the preceding example, the indirect object answers this question:
¿A quién le presta Roberto cien pesos? *To whom does Roberto lend 100 pesos?*

Indirect object pronouns

Singular forms		Plural forms	
me	(to, for) *me*	**nos**	(to, for) *us*
te	(to, for) *you* (fam.)	**os**	(to, for) *you* (fam.)
le	(to, for) *you* (form.)	**les**	(to, for) *you*
	(to, for) *him; her*		(to, for) *them*

▶ **¡Atención!** The forms of indirect object pronouns for the first and second persons (**me, te, nos, os**) are the same as the direct object pronouns. Indirect object pronouns agree in number with the corresponding nouns, but not in gender.

Bueno, le doy un descuento.

Acabo de mostrarles que sí sabemos regatear.

Using indirect object pronouns

▶ Spanish speakers commonly use both an indirect object pronoun and the noun to which it refers in the same sentence. This is done to emphasize and clarify to whom the pronoun refers.

I.O. PRONOUN	INDIRECT OBJECT	I.O. PRONOUN	INDIRECT OBJECT
Ella **le** vende la ropa	**a Elena.**	**Les** prestamos el dinero	**a Inés y a Álex.**

▶ Indirect object pronouns are also used without the indirect object noun when the person for whom the action is being done is known.

Ana **le** presta la falda **a Elena.**
Ana lends her skirt to Elena.

También **le** presta unos jeans.
She also lends her a pair of jeans.

▶ Indirect object pronouns are usually placed before the conjugated form of the verb. In negative sentences the pronoun is placed between **no** and the conjugated verb.

Martín **me** compra un regalo.	Eva **no me** escribe cartas.
Martín is buying me a gift.	*Eva doesn't write me letters.*

CONSULTA

For more information on accents, see **Lección 4, Pronunciación**, p. 123.

▶ When a conjugated verb is followed by an infinitive or the present progressive, the indirect object pronoun may be placed before the conjugated verb or attached to the infinitive or present participle. **¡Atención!** When an indirect object pronoun is attached to a present participle, an accent mark is added to maintain the proper stress.

Él no quiere **pagarte**./	Él está **escribiéndole** una postal a ella./
Él no **te** quiere pagar.	Él **le** está escribiendo una postal a ella.
He does not want to pay you.	*He is writing a postcard to her.*

▶ Because the indirect object pronouns **le** and **les** have multiple meanings, Spanish speakers often clarify to whom the pronouns refer with the preposition **a** + [*pronoun*] or **a** + [*noun*].

UNCLARIFIED STATEMENTS	CLARIFIED STATEMENTS
Yo **le** compro un abrigo.	Yo **le** compro un abrigo **a usted/él/ella**.
Ella **le** describe un libro.	Ella **le** describe un libro **a Juan**.

UNCLARIFIED STATEMENTS	CLARIFIED STATEMENTS
Él **les** vende unos sombreros.	Él **les** vende unos sombreros **a ustedes/ellos/ellas**.
Ellos **les** hablan muy claro.	Ellos **les** hablan muy claro **a los clientes**.

▶ The irregular verbs **dar** (*to give*) and **decir** (*to say; to tell*) are often used with indirect object pronouns.

The verbs dar and decir

	Singular forms			Plural forms	
	dar	**decir**		**dar**	**decir**
yo	**doy**	**digo**	nosotros/as	**damos**	**decimos**
tú	**das**	**dices**	vosotros/as	**dais**	**decís**
Ud./él/ella	**da**	**dice**	Uds./ellos/ellas	**dan**	**dicen**

Me dan una fiesta cada año.	**Te digo** la verdad.
They give (throw) me a party every year.	*I'm telling you the truth.*
Voy a **darle** consejos.	No **les digo** mentiras a mis padres.
I'm going to give her advice.	*I don't tell lies to my parents.*

¡INTÉNTALO!   Use the cues in parentheses to provide the correct indirect object pronoun for each sentence.

1. Juan ___le___ quiere dar un regalo. (*to Elena*)
2. María ___nos___ prepara un café. (*for us*)
3. Beatriz y Felipe ___me___ escriben desde (*from*) Cuba. (*to me*)
4. Marta y yo ___les___ compramos unos guantes. (*for them*)
5. Los vendedores ___te___ venden ropa. (*to you, fam. sing.*)
6. La dependienta ___nos___ muestra los guantes. (*to us*)

In-Class Tips

• Point out that the position of indirect object pronouns in a sentence is the same as that of direct object pronouns.

• 👤↔👤 Ask individuals questions using indirect object pronouns. Ex: **¿A quién le ofreces ayuda? ¿Les das consejos a tus amigos? ¿Qué te dicen tus padres que no debes hacer? ¿Les dices mentiras a tus padres? ¿Cuándo vas a escribirles a tus abuelos?** Have students respond with complete sentences and ask follow-up questions if necessary.

• After going over the **¡Inténtalo!** orally with the class, ask students which items might require clarification (items 1 and 4). Ask them what they would add to each sentence in order to clarify **le** or **les**.

• As a comprehension check, have students write answers to these questions: 1. **Es el cumpleaños de tu mejor amigo. ¿Qué vas a comprarle?** 2. **¿A quiénes les hablas todos los días?** 3. **¿Quién te presta dinero cuando lo necesitas?** 4. **¿Quién les está enseñando español a ustedes?**

• 👤↔👤 In pairs, have students write the dialogue of an argument between two roommates, using **dar** and **decir**. Have volunteers role-play their conversations for the class. Encourage them to be creative and act out the argument with props, if possible.

TEACHING OPTIONS

Video →👤← Replay the **Fotonovela**. Ask students to note each time an indirect object pronoun is used. Then, have students find each use of **le** and state to whom it refers.

Game Give each student an envelope and a sheet of paper. Ask them to write a sentence using an indirect object pronoun, cut the paper into strips (one word per strip), shuffle them, and place them in the envelope. Then have students pass their envelopes to the person sitting behind them. Allow thirty seconds for them to unscramble the sentence and write it down, before placing the shuffled strips back into the envelope and passing it on. After three minutes, the row with the most correctly deciphered sentences wins.

Práctica

1 In-Class Tip Before beginning the activity, have students identify the indirect object in each sentence.

1 Expansion
Have students write four sentences about themselves, leaving out the indirect object pronoun. Ex: **Yo ____ doy un regalo a mis padres. Mi tío ____ compra una moto a mí…** Then have them exchange papers with a classmate and complete the sentences.

1 **Completar** Fill in the blanks with the correct pronouns to complete Mónica's description of her family's holiday shopping.

1. Juan y yo _____le_____ damos una blusa a nuestra hermana Gisela.
2. Mi tía _____nos_____ da a nosotros una mesa para la casa.
3. Gisela _____le_____ da dos corbatas a su papá.
4. A mi mamá yo _____le_____ doy un par de guantes negros.
5. A mi profesora _____le_____ doy dos libros de José Martí.
6. Juan _____les_____ da un regalo a mis padres.
7. Mis padres _____me_____ dan un traje nuevo a mí.
8. Y a ti, yo _____te_____ doy un regalo también. ¿Quieres verlo?

2 In-Class Tips
• To simplify, read through the cues for each item and have students identify the indirect object pronoun that is needed. Then have them write the complete sentences.
• Point out that students will need to add articles to some sentences.

2 **En La Habana** Describe what happens on Pascual's trip to Cuba based on the cues provided.

1. ellos / cantar / canción / (mí)
Ellos me cantan una canción (a mí).

2. él / comprar / libros / (sus hijos) / Plaza de Armas
Él les compra libros (a sus hijos) en la Plaza de Armas.

3. yo / preparar el almuerzo (*lunch*) / (ti)
Yo te preparo el almuerzo (a ti).

4. él / explicar cómo llegar / (conductor)
Él le explica cómo llegar (al conductor).

5. mi novia / sacar / foto / (nosotros)
Mi novia nos saca una foto (a nosotros).

6. el guía (*guide*) / mostrar / catedral de San Cristóbal / (ustedes)
El guía les muestra la catedral de San Cristóbal (a ustedes).

2 Expansion
Divide the class into small groups. Have each student pick a photo (photos 1, 2, 4, and 5 are most appropriate) to present to the group as a verbal portrait, including an introductory sentence that sets the scene, followed by a body and conclusion. The verbal portrait should answer the questions *who, what, where, when,* and *why* with regard to what is seen in the photo. After each group member has presented his or her photo, the group chooses one to present to the class.

3 **Combinar** Use an item from each column and an indirect object pronoun to create logical sentences. Answers will vary.

> **modelo**
> Mis padres les dan regalos a mis primos.

A	B	C	D
yo	comprar	mensajes electrónicos	mí
el dependiente	dar	corbata	ustedes
el profesor Arce	decir	dinero en efectivo	clienta
la vendedora	escribir	tarea	novia
mis padres	explicar	problemas	primos
tú	pagar	regalos	ti
nosotros/as	prestar	ropa	nosotros
¿?	vender	¿?	¿?

3 Expansion Have students convert three of their statements into questions, using **¿Quién?, ¿A quién?,** and **¿Qué?** Have pairs take turns asking and answering their questions. Ex: **¿Quién les vende la ropa? (el dependiente) ¿A quiénes les das regalos? (a mis primos) ¿Qué te explican tus padres? (los problemas)**

Comunicación

4   **Días locos** Gabriela is e-mailing her friend Sandra about her semester. Indicate whether the following conclusions are **lógico** or **ilógico**, based on what you read.

De:	Gabriela
Para:	Sandra
Asunto:	Días locos

Los profesores nos dan mucha tarea. ¡Vivo en la biblioteca! Mi mamá me escribe mensajes electrónicos cada dos horas. Obviamente, yo no tengo tiempo de contestarle, pero ¡ella no me entiende! Rodrigo, el hermano menor de Ana, viene a visitarme todo el tiempo y me da regalos. ¡También me canta! Le tengo que decir la verdad: ¡No quiero su atención!

		Lógico	Ilógico
1.	Gabriela tiene muchos ratos libres.	○	⊘
2.	La mamá de Gabriela está enojada con ella.	⊘	○
3.	Rodrigo está enamorado de Gabriela.	⊘	○
4.	Gabriela está enamorada de Rodrigo.	○	⊘
5.	Rodrigo le debe dar más regalos a Gabriela.	○	⊘

5   **Entrevista** Answer your partner's questions.   Answers will vary.

1. ¿Qué tiendas, almacenes o centros comerciales prefieres?
2. ¿A quién le compras regalos cuando hay rebajas?
3. ¿A quién le prestas dinero cuando lo necesita?
4. ¿Me explicas cómo regatear?
5. ¿Te dan tus padres su tarjeta de crédito cuando vas de compras?

6   **¡Somos ricos!** You and another student chipped in on a lottery ticket and you won! Now you want to spend money on your loved ones. Write a paragraph telling what you plan to buy for your family and your friends.   Answers will vary.

> **modelo**
> *Quiero comprarle un vestido de Carolina Herrera a mi madre...*

Síntesis

7   **Minidrama** With a partner, role-play a conversation between a customer and a clerk in a clothing store. The customer should talk about the clothes he/she is looking for and for whom he/she is buying the clothes. The clerk should recommend different items based on the customer's descriptions. Use these expressions and also look at **Expresiones útiles** on page 195.   Answers will vary.

Me queda grande/pequeño. *It's big/small on me.*	**¿Está en rebaja?** *Is it on sale?*
¿Tiene otro color? *Do you have another color?*	**También estoy buscando...** *I'm also looking for...*

Small Groups ←🛉→ Have students write a conversation. One friend tries to convince the other to go shopping with him or her this weekend. The other friend explains that he or she cannot and lists all the things he or she is going to do. Students should include as many different indirect object pronouns as possible. **Pairs** Ask students to imagine that they are going on an extended trip. Have them make a list of five things they are

going to do (e.g., things they are going to buy for themselves or others) before leaving. Ex: **Voy a comprarme unos zapatos.** **Extra Practice** ←🛉→ Add a visual aspect to this grammar practice. Bring in personal or magazine photos that elicit statements with indirect object pronouns. Have students write descriptions of what is happening in each image. Ex: **La mujer está diciéndole a su hijo que tiene que comer el brócoli....**

Section Goals

In **Estructura 6.3**, students will learn:

• the preterite of regular verbs
• spelling changes in the preterite for different verbs
• words commonly used with the preterite tense

 Comparisons 4.1

Teacher Resources
Read the front matter for suggestions on how to incorporate all the program's components. See pages 189A–189B for a detailed listing of Teacher Resources online.

In-Class Tips

• →👤← Introduce the preterite by describing some things you did yesterday, using the first-person preterite of known regular verbs. Use adverbs that signal the preterite (page 207). Ex: **Ayer compré una chaqueta nueva. Bueno, entré en el almacén y compré una. Y de repente, vi un sombrero. Decidí comprarlo también.** Each time you introduce a preterite form, write it on the board.

• After you have used several regular first-person preterites, expand by asking students questions. Ex: **Ayer compré un sombrero. Y tú, _____, ¿qué compraste ayer? (Compré un libro.)** Ask other students about their classmates' answers. Ex: **¿Qué compró _____ ayer? (Compró un libro.)**

6.3 Preterite tense of regular verbs

ANTE TODO   In order to talk about events in the past, Spanish uses two simple tenses: the preterite and the imperfect. In this lesson, you will learn how to form the preterite tense, which is used to express actions or states completed in the past.

Preterite of regular -ar, -er, and -ir verbs

		-ar verbs	-er verbs	-ir verbs
		comprar	**vender**	**escribir**
SINGULAR FORMS	yo	compr**é** / *bought*	vend**í** / *sold*	escrib**í** / *wrote*
	tú	compr**aste**	vend**iste**	escrib**iste**
	Ud./él/ella	compr**ó**	vend**ió**	escrib**ió**
PLURAL FORMS	nosotros/as	compr**amos**	vend**imos**	escrib**imos**
	vosotros/as	compr**asteis**	vend**isteis**	escrib**isteis**
	Uds./ellos/ellas	compr**aron**	vend**ieron**	escrib**ieron**

▶ **¡Atención!** The **yo** and **Ud./él/ella** forms of all three conjugations have written accents on the last syllable to show that it is stressed.

▶ As the chart shows, the endings for regular **-er** and **-ir** verbs are identical in the preterite.

¿Qué compraste?

Compré estos aretes.

▶ Note that the **nosotros/as** forms of regular **-ar** and **-ir** verbs in the preterite are identical to the present tense forms. Context will help you determine which tense is being used.

En invierno **compramos** ropa.   Anoche **compramos** unos zapatos.
In the winter, we buy clothes.   *Last night we bought some shoes.*

▶ **-Ar** and **-er** verbs that have a stem change in the present tense are regular in the preterite. They do *not* have a stem change.

	PRESENT	PRETERITE
cerrar (e:ie)	La tienda **cierra** a las seis.	La tienda **cerró** a las seis.
volver (o:ue)	Carlitos **vuelve** tarde.	Carlitos **volvió** tarde.
jugar (u:ue)	Él **juega** al fútbol.	Él **jugó** al fútbol.

▶ **¡Atención!** **-Ir** verbs that have a stem change in the present tense also have a stem change in the preterite.

TEACHING OPTIONS

Extra Practice For practice with discrimination between preterite forms, call out preterite forms of regular verbs and point to individuals to provide the corresponding subject pronoun. Ex: **comimos (nosotros/as), creyeron (ustedes/ellos/ ellas), llegué (yo), leíste (tú).**

Pairs 👤↔👤 Tell students to have a conversation about what they did last weekend. Make sure they include things they did by themselves and with others. Then, in groups of four, have them share their partner's weekend activities.

Small Groups Give each group of five a list of verbs, including some with spelling changes. Student A chooses a verb from the list and gives the **yo** form. Student B gives the **tú** form, and so on. Students work their way down the list, alternating who begins the conjugation chain.

▶ Verbs that end in **-car**, **-gar**, and **-zar** have a spelling change in the first person singular (**yo** form) in the preterite.

bus**car**	▶	bus**c-**	▶	**qu-**	▶ yo bus**qué**
lle**gar**		lle**g-**		**gu-**	yo lle**gué**
empe**zar**		empe**z-**		**c-**	yo empe**cé**

▶ Except for the **yo** form, all other forms of **-car**, **-gar**, and **-zar** verbs are regular in the preterite.

▶ Three other verbs—**creer**, **leer**, and **oír**—have spelling changes in the preterite. The **i** of the verb endings of **creer**, **leer**, and **oír** carries an accent in the **yo**, **tú**, **nosotros/as**, and **vosotros/as** forms, and changes to **y** in the **Ud./él/ella** and **Uds./ellos/ellas forms**.

creer	▶	cre-	▶	creí, creíste, creyó, creímos, creísteis, creyeron
leer		le-		leí, leíste, leyó, leímos, leísteis, leyeron
oír		o-		oí, oíste, oyó, oímos, oísteis, oyeron

▶ **Ver** is regular in the preterite, but none of its forms has an accent.

ver ⟶ vi, viste, vio, vimos, visteis, vieron

Words commonly used with the preterite

anoche	*last night*	**pasado/a (*adj.*)**	*last; past*
anteayer	*the day before yesterday*	**el año pasado**	*last year*
		la semana pasada	*last week*
ayer	*yesterday*	**una vez**	*once*
de repente	*suddenly*	**dos veces**	*twice*
desde... hasta...	*from... until...*	**ya**	*already*

Ayer llegué a Santiago de Cuba.
Yesterday I arrived in Santiago de Cuba.

Anoche oí un ruido extraño.
Last night I heard a strange noise.

▶ **Acabar de** + [*infinitive*] is used to say that something has just occurred. Note that **acabar** is in the present tense in this construction.

Acabo de comprar una falda.
I just bought a skirt.

Acabas de ir de compras.
You just went shopping.

¡INTÉNTALO! Provide the appropriate preterite forms of the verbs.

	comer	salir	comenzar	leer
1. ellas	comieron	salieron	comenzaron	leyeron
2. tú	comiste	saliste	comenzaste	leíste
3. usted	comió	salió	comenzó	leyó
4. nosotros	comimos	salimos	comenzamos	leímos
5. yo	comí	salí	comencé	leí

Práctica

■ **In-Class Tip** To simplify, tell students to read through the items once and circle the correct infinitive for each sentence. Then ask them to read the sentences a second time and underline the subject for each verb. Finally, have them conjugate the infinitives.

■ **Expansion**
🔊↔🔊 Ask questions about **Andrea's** weekend. Have students answer with complete sentences. Ex: **¿Quién asistió a una reunión? ¿Qué compraron los amigos?**

2 **Expansion** Have students repeat the activity, using **ustedes** as the subject of the questions and **nosotros** in the answers.

2 **Partner Chat**
🔊↔🔊 Available online.

1 **Completar** Andrea is talking about what happened last weekend. Complete each sentence by choosing the correct verb and putting it in the preterite.

1. El viernes a las cuatro de la tarde, la profesora Mora ___asistió___ (asistir, costar, usar) a una reunión (*meeting*) de profesores.
2. A la una, yo ___llegué___ (llegar, bucear, llevar) a la tienda con mis amigos.
3. Mis amigos y yo ___compramos___ (comprar, regatear, gastar) dos o tres cosas.
4. Yo ___compré___ (costar, comprar, escribir) unos pantalones negros y mi amigo Mateo ___compró___ (gastar, pasear, comprar) una camisa azul.
5. Después, nosotros ___comimos___ (llevar, vivir, comer) cerca de un mercado.
6. A las tres, Pepe ___habló___ (hablar, pasear, nadar) con su amiga por teléfono.
7. El sábado por la tarde, mi mamá ___escribió___ (escribir, beber, vivir) una carta.
8. El domingo mi tía ___decidió___ (decidir, salir, escribir) comprarme un traje.
9. A las cuatro de la tarde, mi tía ___encontró___ (beber, salir, encontrar) el traje y después nosotras ___vimos___ (acabar, ver, salir) una película.

2 **Preguntas** Imagine that you have a pesky friend who keeps asking you questions. Respond that you already did or have just done what he/she asks. Make sure you and your partner take turns playing the role of the pesky friend and responding to his/her questions.

modelo
leer la lección
Estudiante 1: ¿Leíste la lección?
Estudiante 2: Sí, ya la leí./Sí, acabo de leerla.

1. escribir el mensaje electrónico
2. lavar (*to wash*) la ropa
3. oír las noticias (*news*)
4. comprar pantalones cortos
5. practicar los verbos
6. pagar la cuenta (*bill*)
7. empezar la composición
8. ver la película *Diarios de motocicleta*

1. E1: ¿Escribiste el mensaje electrónico?
   E2: Sí, ya lo escribí./Acabo de escribirlo.
2. E1: ¿Lavaste la ropa?
   E2: Sí, ya la lavé./Acabo de lavarla.
3. E1: ¿Oíste las noticias?
   E2: Sí, ya las oí./Acabo de oírlas.
4. E1: ¿Compraste pantalones cortos?
   E2: Sí, ya los compré./Acabo de comprarlos.
5. E1: ¿Practicaste los verbos?
   E2: Sí, ya los practiqué./Acabo de practicarlos.
6. E1: ¿Pagaste la cuenta?
   E2: Sí, ya la pagué./Acabo de pagarla.
7. E1: ¿Empezaste la composición?
   E2: Sí, ya la empecé./Acabo de empezarla.
8. E1: ¿Viste la película *Diarios de motocicleta*?
   E2: Sí, ya la vi./Acabo de verla.

NOTA CULTURAL

Based on Ernesto "Che" Guevara's diaries, *Diarios de motocicleta* (2004) traces the road trip of Che (played by Gael García Bernal) with his friend Alberto Granado (played by Rodrigo de la Serna) through Argentina, Chile, Peru, Colombia, and Venezuela.

3 **In-Class Tips**
• To simplify, have students work with a partner to quickly review the preterite forms of the verbs in the activity.
• 🔊↔🔊 After students have completed item 7, discuss **las tres bes.** Ask students which one is most important to them when they go shopping.

3 **Expansion**
🔊↔🔊 Have students share their responses with a partner, who will ask follow-up questions. Ex: —**Mis padres vieron una película la semana pasada.** —**¿Qué película vieron?** —**Vieron** *Gravity.* —**¿Qué les pareció?** —**Les pareció muy buena.**

3 **¿Cuándo?** Use the time expressions from the word bank to talk about when you and others did the activities listed. Answers will vary.

anoche	anteayer	el mes pasado	una vez
ayer	la semana pasada	el año pasado	dos veces

1. mi maestro/a: llegar tarde a clase
2. mi mejor (*best*) amigo/a: salir con un(a) chico/a guapo/a
3. mis padres: ver una película
4. yo: llevar un traje/vestido
5. el presidente/primer ministro de mi país: asistir a una conferencia internacional
6. mis amigos y yo: comer en un restaurante
7. ¿?: comprar algo (*something*) bueno, bonito y barato

TEACHING OPTIONS

TPR Have students stand in a circle. Begin by tossing a ball to a student and naming an infinitive and subject pronoun (Ex: **cerrar/tú**). The student who catches the ball has four seconds to provide the correct preterite form, toss the ball to another student, and name another infinitive and pronoun.
Extra Practice 🔊↔🔊 Ask students to imagine they have just visited an open-air market for the first time. Have them write a letter to a

friend describing what they saw and did there. Then, ask students to exchange their letters with a classmate, who will respond.
Small Groups In groups of three, have students write down three sentences using verbs in the preterite. Then ask each group to act out its sentences for the class. When someone guesses the action, the group writes the sentence on the board.

Comunicación

4 **¿Estás listo?** Listen to the conversation between Matilde and Hernán. Then indicate whether the following conclusions are **lógico** or **ilógico**, based on what you heard.

	Lógico	Ilógico
1. Hernán compró un pasaje de ida y vuelta.	◉	○
2. Matilde va a viajar con Hernán.	○	◉
3. Hernán buscó su pasaporte.	◉	○
4. Los documentos personales de Hernán están en su mochila.	○	◉
5. Hernán tiene mucho equipaje.	○	◉

5 **Ayer** Tell your partner at what time you did these activities yesterday. Answers will vary.

1. desayunar
2. salir de la casa
3. almorzar
4. ver a un(a) amigo/a
5. volver a la casa
6. cenar

6 **Las vacaciones** Imagine that you took these photos on a vacation with friends. Use the pictures to describe the trip. Answers will vary.

7 **Mi última compra** Write a short paragraph describing the last time you went shopping. Use at least four verbs in the preterite tense. Answers will vary.

Síntesis

8 **Conversación** With a partner, talk about what you did last week. Don't forget to include school activities, shopping, and pastimes. Answers will vary.

TEACHING OPTIONS

Large Group Have students stand up. Tell them to create a story chain about a student who had a very bad day. Begin the story by saying: **Ayer, Rigoberto pasó un día desastroso.** In order to sit down, students must contribute to the story. Call on a student to tell how **Rigoberto** began his day. The second person tells what happened next, and so on, until only one student remains. That person must conclude the story.

Extra Practice For homework, have students make a "to do" list at the beginning of their day. Then, ask students to return to their lists at the end of the day and write sentences stating which activities they completed. Ex: **limpiar mi habitación; No, no limpié mi habitación.**

Communication 1.1, 1.2, 1.3

4 **In-Class Tip** Before doing the activity, confirm students know the meaning of the following words. Ask volunteers to use each in a sentence:
anoche
avión
confirmar
encontrar
estar listo
mochila
pasaje de ida y vuelta

4 **Script** *See the script for this activity on Interleaf page 189B.*

5 **In-Class Tips**
• After forming pairs, model question formation and possible responses for the first two items.
• 🧍↔🧍 Encourage students to ask follow-up questions. Ex: **1.** **¿Dónde desayunaste, en casa o en la cafetería? ¿Qué comiste?**

5 **Virtual Chat**
🧍↔🧍 Available online.

6 **Expansion**
←🧍→ After completing the activity orally, have students write a paragraph about their vacation, basing their account on the photos.

7 **In-Class Tip** Before assigning the activity, provide an example of the last time you yourself went shopping, asking the students to help you write it in the board. Focus on the use of verbs in the preterite tense and the vocabulary taught in the lesson.

Communication 1.1

8 **In-Class Tips**
• ←🧍→ Have volunteers rehearse their conversation, then present it to the class.
• Have volunteers report to the class what their partners did last week.

8 **Partner Chat**
🧍↔🧍 Available online.

Section Goal

In **Estructura 6.4**, students will learn to use demonstrative adjectives and pronouns.

Comparisons 4.1

Teacher Resources
Read the front matter for suggestions on how to incorporate all the program's components. See pages 189A–189B for a detailed listing of Teacher Resources online.

In-Class Tips
- Point to the book on your desk. Say: **Este libro está en la mesa.** Point to a book on a student's desk. Say: **Ese libro está encima del escritorio de ____**. Then point to a book on the window ledge. Say: **Aquel libro está cerca de la ventana.** Repeat the procedure with **tiza, papeles,** and **plumas**.
- Point out that although the masculine singular forms **este** and **ese** do not end in –o, their plural forms end in –os: **estos, esos**.
- Hold up or point to objects and have students give the plural: **este libro, esta mochila, este traje, este zapato.** Repeat with forms of **ese** and **aquel** with other nouns.
- You may want to have students associate **este** with **aquí, ese** with **allí,** and **aquel** with **allá**.

6.4 Demonstrative adjectives and pronouns

Demonstrative adjectives

ANTE TODO   In Spanish, as in English, demonstrative adjectives are words that "demonstrate" or "point out" nouns. Demonstrative adjectives precede the nouns they modify and, like other Spanish adjectives you have studied, agree with them in gender and number. Observe these examples and then study the chart below.

esta camisa	**ese** vendedor	**aquellos** zapatos
this shirt	*that salesman*	*those shoes (over there)*

Demonstrative adjectives

	Singular		Plural		
	MASCULINE	FEMININE	MASCULINE	FEMININE	
	este	**esta**	**estos**	**estas**	*this; these*
	ese	**esa**	**esos**	**esas**	*that; those*
	aquel	**aquella**	**aquellos**	**aquellas**	*that; those (over there)*

▶ There are three sets of demonstrative adjectives. To determine which one to use, you must establish the relationship between the speaker and the noun(s) being pointed out.

▶ The demonstrative adjectives **este, esta, estos,** and **estas** are used to point out things that are close to the speaker and the listener.

Me gustan estos zapatos.

▶ The demonstrative adjectives **ese, esa, esos,** and **esas** are used to point out things that are not close in space and time to the speaker. They may, however, be close to the listener.

Prefiero esos zapatos.

TEACHING OPTIONS

Extra Practice Hold up one or two items of clothing or classroom objects. Have students write all three forms of the demonstrative pronouns that would apply. Ex: **estos zapatos, esos zapatos, aquellos zapatos.**

Pairs 👥 Refer students to **Contextos** illustration on pages 190–191. Have them work with a partner to comment on the articles of clothing pictured. Ex: **Este suéter es bonito, ¿no? (No, ese suéter no es bonito. Es feo.) Aquella camiseta es muy cara. (Sí, aquella camiseta es cara.)**

▶ The demonstrative adjectives **aquel**, **aquella**, **aquellos**, and **aquellas** are used to point out things that are far away from the speaker and the listener.

Aquel auto es de mi hermana.

Demonstrative pronouns

▶ Demonstrative pronouns are identical to their corresponding demonstrative adjectives, with the exception that they traditionally carry an accent mark on the stressed vowel. The **Real Academia** no longer requires this accent, but it is still commonly used.

Demonstrative pronouns

Singular		Plural	
MASCULINE	FEMININE	MASCULINE	FEMININE
éste	**ésta**	**éstos**	**éstas**
ése	**ésa**	**ésos**	**ésas**
aquél	**aquélla**	**aquéllos**	**aquéllas**

—¿Quieres comprar **este suéter**?
Do you want to buy this sweater?

—No, no quiero **éste**. Quiero **ése**.
No, I don't want this one. I want that one.

—¿Vas a leer **estas revistas**?
Are you going to read these magazines?

—Sí, voy a leer **éstas**. También voy a leer **aquéllas**.
Yes, I'm going to read these. I'll also read those (over there).

▶ **¡Atención!** Like demonstrative adjectives, demonstrative pronouns agree in gender and number with the corresponding noun.

    Este libro es de Pablito.   **Éstos** son de Juana.

▶ There are three neuter demonstrative pronouns: **esto**, **eso**, and **aquello**. These forms refer to unidentified or unspecified things, situations, ideas, and concepts. They do not change in gender or number and never carry an accent mark.

—¿Qué es **esto**?
What's this?

—**Eso** es interesante.
That's interesting.

—**Aquello** es bonito.
That's pretty.

¡INTÉNTALO!   Provide the correct form of the demonstrative adjective for these nouns.

1. la falda / este _____ esta falda
2. los estudiantes / este _____ estos estudiantes
3. los países / aquel _____ aquellos países
4. la ventana / ese _____ esa ventana
5. los periodistas / ese _____ esos periodistas
6. el chico / aquel _____ aquel chico
7. las sandalias / este _____ estas sandalias
8. las chicas / aquel _____ aquellas chicas

Práctica

1 Expansion To challenge students, ask them to expand each sentence with a phrase that includes a demonstrative pronoun. Ex: **Aquellos sombreros son muy elegantes, pero éstos son más baratos.**

1 Cambiar Make the singular sentences plural and the plural sentences singular.

> **modelo**
> Estas camisas son blancas.
> *Esta camisa es blanca.*

1. Aquellos sombreros son muy elegantes. Aquel sombrero es muy elegante.
2. Ese abrigo es muy caro. Esos abrigos son muy caros.
3. Estos cinturones son hermosos. Este cinturón es hermoso.
4. Esos precios son muy buenos. Ese precio es muy bueno.
5. Estas faldas son muy cortas. Esta falda es muy corta.
6. ¿Quieres ir a aquel almacén? ¿Quieres ir a aquellos almacenes?
7. Esas blusas son baratas. Esa blusa es barata.
8. Esta corbata hace juego con mi traje. Estas corbatas hacen juego con mis trajes.

2 In-Class Tips
- To simplify, have students underline the nouns that will be replaced by demonstrative pronouns.
- As you go over the activity, write each demonstrative pronoun on the board so students may verify that they have placed the accent marks correctly. You may choose to have your students leave out the accents.

2 Completar Here are some things people might say while shopping. Complete the sentences with the correct demonstrative pronouns.

1. No me gustan esos zapatos. Voy a comprar ___éstos___. (*these*)
2. ¿Vas a comprar ese traje o ___éste___? (*this one*)
3. Esta guayabera es bonita, pero prefiero ___ésa___. (*that one*)
4. Estas corbatas rojas son muy bonitas, pero ___ésas___ son fabulosas. (*those*)
5. Estos cinturones cuestan demasiado. Prefiero ___aquéllos___. (*those over there*)
6. ¿Te gustan esas botas o ___éstas___? (*these*)
7. Esa bolsa roja es bonita, pero prefiero ___aquélla___. (*that one over there*)
8. No voy a comprar estas botas; voy a comprar ___aquéllas___. (*those over there*)
9. ¿Prefieres estos pantalones o ___ésos___? (*those*)
10. Me gusta este vestido, pero voy a comprar ___ése___. (*that one*)
11. Me gusta ese almacén, pero ___aquél___ es mejor (*better*). (*that one over there*)
12. Esa blusa es bonita, pero cuesta demasiado. Voy a comprar ___ésta___. (*this one*)

3 Expansion
Ask students to find a photo featuring different articles of clothing or to draw several articles of clothing. Have them write five statements like that of the model in the activity. Emphasize the need to use both demonstrative adjectives and pronouns. Ex: **Esta camisa es verde. Aquel pantalón es azul. Ésta es verde. Aquél es azul.**

3 Describir Look for two items that are one of these colors: **amarillo, azul, blanco, marrón, negro, verde, rojo**. Point them out, first using demonstrative adjectives, and then demonstrative pronouns. Answers will vary.

> **modelo**
> azul
> *Esta silla es azul. Aquella mochila es azul.*
> *Ésta es azul. Aquélla es azul.*

TEACHING OPTIONS

Pairs Have pairs role-play a dialogue between friends shopping for clothes. Student A tries to convince the friend that the clothes he or she wants to buy are not attractive. Student A suggests other items of clothing, but the friend does not agree. Students should use as many demonstrative adjectives and pronouns as possible.
Game Divide the class into two teams. Post pictures of different versions of the same object (Ex: sedan, sports car, all-terrain vehicle) on the board. Assign each a dollar figure, but do not share the prices with the class. Team A guesses the price of each object, using demonstrative adjectives and pronouns. Team B either agrees or guesses a higher or lower price. The team that guesses the closest price, wins. Ex: **Este carro cuesta $20.000, ése cuesta $35.000 y aquél cuesta $18.000.**

Comunicación

4 🔊 **De compras** Listen to the conversation between Alejandra and a clerk. Then indicate whether the following conclusions are **lógico** or **ilógico**, based on what you heard.

	Lógico	Ilógico
1. A Alejandra no le gusta llevar faldas.	○	☑
2. Alejandra va a comprar la blusa blanca.	○	☑
3. La dependienta trabaja en un almacén.	☑	○
4. A Alejandra le gustan los colores azul y gris.	☑	○
5. El cinturón negro es muy caro.	○	☑
6. Alejandra va a comprar una cartera también.	○	☑

5 👥 **En una tienda** Imagine that you and a partner are in Madrid shopping at Zara. Study the floor plan, then have a conversation about your surroundings. Use demonstrative adjectives and pronouns.

Answers will vary.

> **modelo**
> **Estudiante 1:** Me gusta este suéter azul.
> **Estudiante 2:** Yo prefiero aquella chaqueta.

Síntesis

6 **En el café** Write a conversation between two people sitting at a busy sidewalk café. Use as many demonstrative adjectives and pronouns as possible to describe the people and things around them.

Answers will vary.

> **modelo**
> Carmen: Esa corbata es fea, ¿no?
> Susana: Sí. No me gustan las corbatas rosadas y verdes. Y ese traje...

Recapitulación

Section Goal

In **Recapitulación**, students will review the grammar concepts from this lesson.

1 In-Class Tips

- Before beginning the activity, ask students which preterite forms usually require accent marks.
- Ask a volunteer to identify which verbs have a spelling change in the preterite (**pagar, leer**).

1 Expansion Ask students to provide the **tú** and **nosotros** forms for these verbs.

2 In-Class Tip To simplify this activity, have students start by identifying whether a blank needs an adjective or a pronoun. If the blank requires an adjective, have them underline the corresponding noun. If the blank calls for a pronoun, have them identify the noun it replaces.

2 Expansion

👥↔👤 Have students write their own dialogue in a department store using Activity 2 as a model. Have them role-play the conversations for the class, and encourage them to ad-lib new material as they go along.

Review the grammar concepts you have learned in this lesson by completing these activities.

1 **Completar** Complete the chart with the correct preterite or infinitive form of the verbs. **30 pts.**

Infinitive	yo	ella	ellos
tomar	tomé	tomó	**tomaron**
abrir	abrí	**abrió**	abrieron
comprender	comprendí	comprendió	comprendieron
leer	**leí**	leyó	leyeron
pagar	pagué	pagó	pagaron

2 **En la tienda** Look at the drawing and complete the conversation with demonstrative adjectives and pronouns. **14 pts.**

CLIENTE Buenos días, señorita. Deseo comprar (1) ___esta___ corbata.

VENDEDORA Muy bien, señor. ¿No le interesa mirar (2) ___aquellos___ trajes que están allá? Hay unos que hacen juego con la corbata.

CLIENTE (3) ___Aquéllos___ de allá son de lana, ¿no? Prefiero ver (4) ___ese___ traje marrón que está detrás de usted.

VENDEDORA Estupendo. Como puede ver, es de seda. Cuesta seiscientos cincuenta dólares.

CLIENTE Ah... eh... no, creo que sólo voy a comprar la corbata, gracias.

VENDEDORA Bueno... si busca algo más económico, hay rebaja en (5) ___aquellos___ sombreros. Cuestan sólo treinta dólares.

CLIENTE ¡Magnífico! Me gusta (6) ___aquél___, el blanco que está hasta arriba (*at the top*). Y quiero pagar todo con (7) ___esta___ tarjeta.

VENDEDORA Sí, señor. Ahora mismo le traigo el sombrero.

RESUMEN GRAMATICAL

6.1 **Saber and conocer** *p. 200*

saber	conocer
sé	conozco
sabes	conoces
sabe	conoce
sabemos	conocemos
sabéis	conocéis
saben	conocen

▶ **saber** = to know facts/how to do something

▶ **conocer** = to know a person, place, or thing

6.2 **Indirect object pronouns** *pp. 202–203*

Indirect object pronouns

Singular	Plural
me	nos
te	os
le	les

▶ **dar** = doy, das, da, damos, dais, dan

▶ **decir** (e:i) = digo, dices, dice, decimos, decís, dicen

6.3 **Preterite tense of regular verbs** *pp. 206–207*

comprar	vender	escribir
compré	vendí	escribí
compraste	vendiste	escribiste
compró	vendió	escribió
compramos	vendimos	escribimos
comprasteis	vendisteis	escribisteis
compraron	vendieron	escribieron

Verbs with spelling changes in the preterite

▶ **-car:** buscar → yo busqué

▶ **-gar:** llegar → yo llegué

▶ **-zar:** empezar → yo empecé

▶ **creer:** creí, creíste, creyó, creímos, creísteis, creyeron

▶ **leer:** leí, leíste, leyó, leímos, leísteis, leyeron

▶ **oír:** oí, oíste, oyó, oímos, oísteis, oyeron

▶ **ver:** vi, viste, vio, vimos, visteis, vieron

Game Divide the class into two teams. Indicate a team member. Give an infinitive and a subject, and have the team member supply the correct preterite form. Award one point for each correct answer. Award a bonus point for correctly writing the verb on the board. The team with the most points wins.

TPR Write **presente** and **pretérito** on the board and have a volunteer stand in front of each word. Call out sentences

using the present or the preterite. The student whose tense corresponds to the sentence has three seconds to step forward.

Ex: **Compramos una chaqueta anteayer. (pretérito)**

Small Groups ↔👤→ Ask students to write a description of a famous person, using **saber, conocer**, and one verb in the preterite. In small groups, have students read their descriptions aloud for the group to guess.

3 **¿Saber o conocer?** Complete each dialogue with the correct form of **saber** or **conocer**. **20 pts.**

1. —¿Qué <u>sabes</u> hacer tú?
   —(Yo) <u>Sé</u> jugar al fútbol.
2. —¿<u>Conoces</u> tú esta tienda de ropa?
   —No, (yo) no la <u>conozco</u>. ¿Es buena?
3. —¿Tus amigos no <u>conocen</u> a tu hermana?
   —No, ¡ellos no <u>saben</u> que tengo una hermana!
4. —Mi maestra todavía no me <u>conoce</u> bien.
   —Y tú, ¿la quieres <u>conocer</u> a ella?
5. —¿<u>Saben</u> ustedes dónde está el mercado?
   —No, nosotros no <u>conocemos</u> bien esta ciudad.

4 **Oraciones** Form complete sentences using the information provided. Use indirect object pronouns and the present tense of the verbs. **32 pts.**

1. Javier / prestar / el abrigo / a Maripili
   Javier le presta el abrigo a Maripili.
2. nosotros / vender / ropa / a los clientes
   Nosotros les vendemos ropa a los clientes.
3. el vendedor / traer / las camisetas / a mis amigos y a mí
   El vendedor nos trae las camisetas (a mis amigos y a mí).
4. yo / querer dar / consejos / a ti
   Yo quiero darte consejos (a ti)./Yo te quiero dar consejos (a ti).
5. ¿tú / ir a comprar / un regalo / a mí?
   ¿Tú vas a comprarme un regalo (a mí)?/¿Tú me vas a comprar un regalo (a mí)?
6. el dependiente / mostrar / las corbatas / a Santiago
   El dependiente le muestra las corbatas a Santiago.
7. los hijos / pedir / dinero / a sus padres
   Los hijos les piden dinero a sus padres.
8. la profesora / escribir / mensajes electrónicos / a nosotros
   La profesora nos escribe mensajes electrónicos (a nosotros).

5 **Poema** Write the missing words to complete the excerpt from the poem *Romance sonámbulo* by Federico García Lorca. **4 pts.**

❝ Verde que <u>te</u> quiero verde.
Verde viento. Verdes ramas°.
El barco sobre la mar
y el caballo en la montaña, [...]
Verde que te quiero <u>verde</u> (*green*). **❞**

ramas *branches*

6.4 **Demonstrative adjectives and pronouns** *pp. 210–211*

Demonstrative adjectives

Singular		Plural	
Masc.	**Fem.**	**Masc.**	**Fem.**
este	esta	estos	estas
ese	esa	esos	esas
aquel	aquella	aquellos	aquellas

Demonstrative pronouns

Singular		Plural	
Masc.	**Fem.**	**Masc.**	**Fem.**
éste	ésta	éstos	éstas
ése	ésa	ésos	ésas
aquél	aquélla	aquéllos	aquéllas

---

3 **In-Class Tip** Ask students to explain why they chose **saber** or **conocer** in each case.

3 **Expansion**
Have students choose one dialogue from this activity and write a continuation. Encourage them to use at least one more example each of **saber** and **conocer**.

4 **In-Class Tips**
• Ask a volunteer to model the first sentence for the class.
• Before forming sentences, have students identify the indirect object in each item.
• Remind students of the possible positions for indirect object pronouns when using an infinitive.

4 **Expansion**
• Ask students to create three dehydrated sentences similar to those in **Actividad 4**. Have them exchange papers with a classmate and form complete sentences.
• For items 1–4, have students write questions that would elicit these statements. Ex: **1. ¿A quién le presta el abrigo Javier?/¿Qué le presta Javier a Maripili?** For item 5, have them write a response.

5 **In-Class Tips**
• Tell students to read through the whole excerpt before filling in the blanks.
• Have a volunteer read the excerpt aloud.

Extra Practice Add an auditory aspect to this grammar review. Read each of these sentences twice, pausing after the second time for students to write: **1. Ayer empecé a leer sobre los diseñadores hispanos. 2. Ellas buscaron unas bolsas en el mercado al aire libre. 3. El dependiente vendió cinco camisetas. 4. Nosotras oímos una explosión. 5. El joven le leyó el libro a su hermanito. 6. Raúl vio una película anoche.**

Game Divide the class into two teams. Indicate a member of each team and call out a color. The first student to find an object or article of clothing in the room, point to it, and use the correct form of a demonstrative adjective earns a point for their team. Ex: **¡Aquella camiseta es morada!** The team with the most points at the end wins.

Lectura

Antes de leer

Estrategia

Skimming

Skimming involves quickly reading through a document to absorb its general meaning. This allows you to understand the main ideas without having to read word for word. When you skim a text, you might want to look at its title and subtitles. You might also want to read the first sentence of each paragraph.

Examinar el texto

Look at the format of the reading selection. How is it organized? What does the organization of the document tell you about its content?

Buscar cognados

Scan the reading selection to locate at least five cognates. Based on the cognates, what do you think the reading selection is about? Answers will vary. Suggested answers for 1–5: elegancia, blusas, accesorios, pantalones, precio.

1. _____ 4. _____
2. _____ 5. _____
3. _____

The reading selection is about _a sale in a store_.

Impresiones generales

Now skim the reading selection to understand its general meaning. Jot down your impressions. What new information did you learn about the document by skimming it? Based on all the information you now have, answer these questions in Spanish.

1. Who created this document? un almacén/una tienda
2. What is its purpose? vender ropa
3. Who is its intended audience? gente que quiere comprar ropa

---

🔲 Corona

◀ ▶ ↻ http://corona.cl

Corona
¡Corona tiene las ofertas más locas del verano!

La tienda más elegante de la ciudad con precios increíbles

niños | **mujeres** | casa | baño | equipaje

Faldas largas
ROPA BONITA
Algodón. De distintos colores
Talla mediana
Precio especial: 8.000 pesos

Blusas de seda
BAMBÚ
De cuadros y de lunares
Ahora: 21.000 pesos
40% de rebaja

Vestido de algodón
PANAMÁ
Colores blanco, azul y verde
Ahora: 18.000 pesos
30% de rebaja

Accesorios
BELLEZA
Cinturones, gafas de sol, sombreros, medias
Diversos estilos
Todos con un 40% de rebaja

Carteras
ELEGANCIA
Colores anaranjado, blanco, rosado y amarillo
Ahora: 15.000 pesos
50% de rebaja

Sandalias de playa
GINO
Números del 35 al 38
A sólo 12.000 pesos
50% de descuento

Lunes a sábado de 9 a 21 horas.
Domingo de 10 a 14 horas.

Real° Liquidación° **¡Grandes rebajas!**

¡La rebaja está de moda en Corona!

y con la tarjeta de crédito más conveniente del mercado.

bebé | **hombres** | jardín | joyas | electrónica

Chaquetas CASINO
Microfibra. Colores negro, café y gris
Tallas: P, M, G, XG
Ahora: 22.500 pesos

Traje inglés GALES
Modelos originales
Ahora: 105.000 pesos
30% de rebaja

Pantalones OCÉANO
Colores negro, gris y café
Ahora: 11.500 pesos
30% de rebaja

Accesorios GUAPO
Gafas de sol, corbatas, cinturones, calcetines
Diversos estilos
Todos con un 40% de rebaja

Zapatos COLOR
Italianos y franceses
Números del 40 al 45
A sólo 20.000 pesos

Ropa interior ATLÁNTICO
Tallas: P, M, G
Colores blanco, negro y gris
40% de rebaja

Real *Royal* Liquidación *Clearance sale*

Por la compra de 40.000 pesos, puede llevar un regalo gratis.
• Un hermoso cinturón de mujer
• Un par de calcetines
• Una corbata de seda
• Una bolsa para la playa
• Una mochila
• Unas medias

Después de leer

Completar

Complete this paragraph about the reading selection with the correct forms of the words from the word bank.

almacén	hacer juego	tarjeta de crédito
caro	increíble	tienda
dinero	pantalones	verano
falda	rebaja	zapato

En este anuncio, el ___almacén___ Corona anuncia la liquidación de ___verano___ con grandes ___rebajas___. Con muy poco ___dinero___ usted puede conseguir ropa fina y elegante. Si no tiene dinero en efectivo, puede utilizar su ___tarjeta de crédito___ y pagar luego. Para el caballero con gustos refinados, hay ___zapatos___ importados de París y Roma. La señora elegante puede encontrar blusas de seda que ___hacen juego___ con todo tipo de ___pantalones/faldas___ o ___faldas/pantalones___. Los precios de esta liquidación son realmente ___increíbles___.

¿Cierto o falso?

Indicate whether each statement is **cierto** or **falso**. Correct the false statements.

1. Hay sandalias de playa. Cierto.
2. Las corbatas tienen una rebaja del 30%. Falso. Tienen una rebaja del 40%.
3. El almacén Corona tiene un departamento de zapatos. Cierto.
4. Normalmente las sandalias cuestan 22.000 pesos. Falso. Normalmente cuestan 24.000 pesos.
5. Cuando gastas 30.000 pesos en la tienda, llevas un regalo gratis. Falso. Cuando gastas 40.000 pesos en la tienda, llevas un regalo gratis.
6. Tienen carteras amarillas. Cierto.

Preguntas

Answer these questions. Answers will vary.

1. Imagina que vas a ir a la tienda Corona. ¿Qué departamentos vas a visitar? ¿El departamento de ropa para señoras, el departamento de ropa para caballeros...?
2. ¿Qué vas a buscar en Corona?
3. ¿Hay tiendas similares a la tienda Corona en tu pueblo o ciudad? ¿Cómo se llaman? ¿Tienen muchas gangas?

Section Goals

In **Escritura**, students will:
- conduct an interview
- integrate vocabulary and structures taught in **Lección 6** into a written report
- report on an interview

 Communication 1.3

Estrategia Model an interview for students by asking a volunteer a few of the questions on this page. Then model how to report on an interview by transcribing verbatim a section of the dialogue on the board. Then give an example each of summarizing and summarizing but quoting occasionally.

Tema Tell students that they may interview a classmate or another Spanish-speaking student they know. Encourage them to take notes as they conduct the interview or record it. They might want to brainstorm additional questions with a classmate that they are not planning to interview. Introduce terms such as **entrevista, entrevistar, diálogo,** and **citas** as you present the activity.

Escritura

Estrategia

How to report an interview

There are several ways to prepare a written report about an interview. For example, you can transcribe the interview verbatim, you can simply summarize it, or you can summarize it but quote the speakers occasionally. In any event, the report should begin with an interesting title and a brief introduction, which may include the five Ws (*what, where, when, who, why*) and the H (*how*) of the interview. The report should end with an interesting conclusion. Note that when you transcribe dialogue in Spanish, you should pay careful attention to format and punctuation.

Writing dialogue in Spanish

- If you need to transcribe an interview verbatim, you can use speakers' names to indicate a change of speaker.

> **CARMELA**   ¿Qué compraste? ¿Encontraste muchas gangas?
>
> **ROBERTO**   Sí, muchas. Compré un suéter, una camisa y dos corbatas. Y tú, ¿qué compraste?
>
> **CARMELA**   Una blusa y una falda muy bonitas. ¿Cuánto costó tu camisa?
>
> **ROBERTO**   Sólo diez dólares. ¿Cuánto costó tu blusa?
>
> **CARMELA**   Veinte dólares.

- You can also use a dash (*raya*) to mark the beginning of each speaker's words.

> —¿Qué compraste?
>
> —Un suéter y una camisa muy bonitos. Y tú, ¿encontraste muchas gangas?
>
> —Sí... compré dos blusas, tres camisetas y un par de zapatos.
>
> —¡A ver!

Tema

Escribe un informe

Write a report for the school newspaper about an interview you conducted with a student about his or her shopping habits and clothing preferences. First, brainstorm a list of interview questions. Then conduct the interview using the questions below as a guide, but feel free to ask other questions as they occur to you.

Examples of questions:

▶ ¿Cuándo vas de compras?

▶ ¿Adónde vas de compras?

▶ ¿Con quién vas de compras?

▶ ¿Qué tiendas, almacenes o centros comerciales prefieres?

▶ ¿Compras ropa de catálogos o por Internet?

▶ ¿Prefieres comprar ropa cara o barata? ¿Por qué? ¿Te gusta buscar gangas?

▶ ¿Qué ropa llevas cuando vas a clase?

▶ ¿Qué ropa llevas cuando sales a bailar?

▶ ¿Qué ropa llevas cuando practicas un deporte?

▶ ¿Cuáles son tus colores favoritos? ¿Compras mucha ropa de esos colores?

▶ ¿Les das ropa a tu familia o a tus amigos/as?

EVALUATION: Informe

Criteria	Scale
Content	1 2 3 4 5
Organization	1 2 3 4 5
Accuracy	1 2 3 4 5
Creativity	1 2 3 4 5

Scoring	
Excellent	18–20 points
Good	14–17 points
Satisfactory	10–13 points
Unsatisfactory	< 10 points

Escuchar

Estrategia
Listening for linguistic cues

You can enhance your listening comprehension by listening for specific linguistic cues. For example, if you listen for the endings of conjugated verbs, or for familiar constructions, such as **acabar de** + [*infinitive*] or **ir a** + [*infinitive*], you can find out whether an event already took place, is taking place now, or will take place in the future. Verb endings also give clues about who is participating in the action.

🔊 To practice listening for linguistic cues, you will now listen to four sentences. As you listen, note whether each sentence refers to a past, present, or future action. Also jot down the subject of each sentence.

Preparación

Based on the photograph, what do you think Marisol has recently done? What do you think Marisol and Alicia are talking about? What else can you guess about their conversation from the visual clues in the photograph?

Ahora escucha

Now you are going to hear Marisol and Alicia's conversation. Make a list of the clothing items that each person mentions. Then put a check mark after the item if the person actually purchased it.

Marisol		Alicia	
1.	pantalones ✔	1.	falda
2.	blusa ✔	2.	blusa
3.	_____	3.	zapatos
4.	_____	4.	cinturón

Comprensión

¿Cierto o falso?

Indicate whether each statement is **cierto** or **falso.** Then correct the false statements.

1. Marisol y Alicia acaban de ir de compras juntas (*together*). Falso. Marisol acaba de ir de compras.
2. Marisol va a comprar unos pantalones y una blusa mañana. Falso. Marisol ya los compró.
3. Marisol compró una blusa de cuadros. Cierto.
4. Alicia compró unos zapatos nuevos hoy. Falso. Alicia va a comprar unos zapatos nuevos.
5. Alicia y Marisol van a ir al café. Cierto.
6. Marisol gastó todo el dinero de la semana en ropa nueva. Cierto.

Preguntas

Answer the following questions. Be sure to explain your answers. Answers will vary.

1. ¿Crees que Alicia y Marisol son buenas amigas? ¿Por qué?
2. ¿Cuál de las dos estudiantes es más ahorradora (*frugal*)? ¿Por qué?
3. ¿Crees que a Alicia le gusta la ropa que Marisol compró?
4. ¿Crees que la moda es importante para Alicia? ¿Para Marisol? ¿Por qué?
5. ¿Es importante para ti estar a la moda? ¿Por qué?

A: ¡Ay, chica! Fui al centro comercial el mes pasado y encontré unos zapatos muy, pero muy de moda. Muy caros... pero buenos. No me los compré porque no los tenían en mi número. Voy a comprarlos cuando lleguen más... el vendedor me va a llamar.

M: Ajá... ¿Y va a invitarte a salir con él?
A: ¡Ay! ¡No seas así! Ven, vamos al café. Te ves muy bien y no hay que gastar eso aquí.
M: De acuerdo. Vamos.

Section Goals

In **Escuchar**, students will:
- listen for specific linguistic cues in oral sentences
- answer questions based on a recorded conversation

Communication 1.2

Estrategia
Script 1. Acabamos de pasear por la ciudad y encontramos unos monumentos fenomenales. 2. Estoy haciendo las maletas. 3. Carmen y Alejandro decidieron ir a un restaurante. 4. Mi familia y yo vamos a ir a la playa.

In-Class Tip Ask students to look at the photo of **Marisol** and **Alicia** and predict what they are talking about.

Ahora escucha
Script MARISOL: Oye, Alicia, ¿qué estás haciendo?
ALICIA: Estudiando no más. ¿Qué hay de nuevo?
M: Acabo de comprarme esos pantalones que andaba buscando.
A: ¿Los encontraste en el centro comercial? ¿Y cuánto te costaron?
M: Míralos. ¿Te gustan? En el almacén Melo tienen tremenda rebaja. Como estaban baratos me compré una blusa también. Es de cuadros, pero creo que hace juego con los pantalones por el color rojo. ¿Qué piensas?
A: Es de los mismos colores que la falda y la blusa que llevaste cuando fuimos al cine anoche. La verdad es que te quedan muy bien esos colores. ¿No encontraste unos zapatos y un cinturón para completar el juego?
M: No lo digas ni de chiste. Mi tarjeta de crédito está que no aguanta más. Y trabajé poco la semana pasada. ¡Acabo de gastar todo el dinero para la semana!

(Script continues at far left in the bottom panels.)

Section Goals

In **En pantalla**, students will:
• read about a toy store in Spain
• watch a television commercial for **Juguettos**, a Spanish toy store

 Communication 1.1, 1.2, 1.3
Cultures 2.1, 2.2
Connections 3.1, 3.2
Comparisons 4.2

Teacher Resources
Read the front matter for suggestions on how to incorporate all the program's components. See pages 189A–189B for a detailed listing of Teacher Resources online.

Vocabulario útil
Guide students to identify the infinitives **ser** and **pedir** in the phrases **sean como sean** and **pidan lo que pidan**. Then ask them what is different about how they are conjugated. Briefly share that this "unexpected grammar" signals a mood of possibility called the subjunctive.

 Pre-AP®

Audiovisual Interpretive Communication
Antes de ver **Strategy**
• Read through the **Vocabulario útil** with students. Model the pronunciation.
• Have students predict what is happening based on the photo.

Aplicación Have students do their own quote exploration using such key search phrases as **citas sobre la imaginación** and **citas sobre las posesiones**. Which ones do they find especially provocative or insightful? How might they restate the quotes in their own words, illustrate them, or act them out?

Anuncio de juguetería Juguettos

generosa

Me lo pido.

Preparación
Answer these questions in Spanish. Answers will vary.
1. ¿Cómo eres? Escribe tres adjetivos que te describan.
2. ¿Qué actividades ilustran (*illustrates*) tu personalidad?

El País de Siempre Jugar
Juguettos, first established in Villena (Comunidad de Valencia), Spain, in the 1980s, now has chain stores all over the country. Juguettos offers both brand-name toys you would recognize (and maybe own) and those that specifically cater to a child's life and cultural experiences in Spain. When children dreaming of the perfect toy look in a Juguettos catalog, they may be looking for Legos® but also for Nenittos® or Hazlo tú®. But children's toys, like their imaginations, are very similar throughout the world. Indeed, the company declares it has founded its own "country," el País de Siempre Jugar.

Vocabulario útil
copionas	copycats
despistado/a	distracted
sean	they may be
pidan	they may ask for

Comprensión
Match the personality trait with its visual representation in the ad.

__e__ 1. valiente
__c__ 2. galáctico/a
__d__ 3. artista
__b__ 4. generoso/a
__a__ 5. intrépido/a

a. Tienen una batalla (*battle*) imaginaria.
b. Le compra juguetes a su mascota (*pet*).
c. Está en un cartón con forma de nave espacial (*spaceship*).
d. Hacen música con parte de una basurera (*trashcan*).
e. Imagina que puede volar (*fly*).

Conversación
Answer these questions with a classmate. Answers will vary.
1. ¿Qué quieres hacer ahora en tu vida que no haces? ¿Por qué lo quieres hacer?
2. ¿Por qué es importante la imaginación en la vida de los niños?
3. ¿Qué importancia tiene la imaginación en la vida de los adultos?

Aplicación
The Spanish poet Gustavo Adolfo Bécquer wrote, **"Él que tiene imaginación, con qué facilidad saca de la nada un mundo."** Working with a partner, discuss your understanding of the quote. Then prepare and present a skit in Spanish that illustrates its point.
Answers will vary.

TEACHING OPTIONS

Discussion While being aware of your students' diverse economic situations, ask questions that explore the relationship between possessions and identity. Examples: **¿Cómo te describen tus posesiones? ¿Cómo se relacionan nuestra identidad y nuestras posesiones? ¿Es posible tener demasiadas posesiones? ¿Por qué? ¿Cómo se relacionan la imaginación y las posesiones?**

Heritage Learners Invite heritage students to share about toys in their cultures of origin. Where do children get the toys they play with? What are the roles of special stores and places dedicated to children's play? What similarities and differences do they see in the role of toys between their culture of origin and the United States? What about the role of imagination in play?

In the Spanish-speaking world, most city dwellers shop at large supermarkets and little stores that specialize in just one item, such as a butcher shop (**carnicería**), vegetable market (**verdulería**), perfume shop (**perfumería**), or hat shop (**sombrerería**). In small towns where supermarkets are less common, many people rely exclusively on specialty shops. This requires shopping more frequently—often every day or every other day for perishable items—but also means that the foods they consume are fresher and the goods are usually locally produced. Each neighborhood generally has its own shops, so people don't have to walk far to find fresh bread (at a **panadería**) for the midday meal.

Vocabulario útil

colones (pl.)	*currency from Costa Rica*
¿Cuánto vale?	**¿Cuánto cuesta?**
descuento	*discount*
disculpe	*excuse me*
¿Dónde queda...?	*Where is... located?*
los helados	*ice cream*
el regateo	*bargaining*

Preparación

Have you ever been to an open-air market? What did you buy? Have you ever negotiated a price? What did you say? Answers will vary.

Comprensión

Select the option that best summarizes this episode.

a.) Randy Cruz va al mercado al aire libre para comprar papayas. Luego va al Mercado Central. Él les pregunta a varios clientes qué compran, prueba (*tastes*) platos típicos y busca la heladería.

b. Randy Cruz va al mercado al aire libre para comprar papayas y pedir un descuento. Luego va al Mercado Central para preguntarles a los clientes qué compran en los mercados.

Comprar en los mercados

Trescientos colones.

... pero me hace un buen descuento.

¿Qué compran en el Mercado Central?

Section Goals

In **Flash cultura**, students will:
- read about specialty shops in Spanish-speaking countries
- watch a video about open-air markets

Communication 1.2
Cultures 2.1, 2.2
Comparisons 4.2

Teacher Resources
Read the front matter for suggestions on how to incorporate all the program's components. See pages 189A–189B for a detailed listing of Teacher Resources online.

Introduction To check comprehension, have students indicate whether these statements are true or false. 1. Supermarkets do not exist in Spanish-speaking countries. (False.) 2. In general, people that live in small towns only shop at specialty shops. (True.) 3. Specialty shops usually sell just one type of food or merchandise. (True.)

Antes de ver
- Read through the **Vocabulario útil** and model pronunciation. Present mini-conversations with these words, using contexts that are familiar to students. Ex: —**Disculpe, ¿me puede decir dónde queda la residencia estudiantil Evans? —Sí, claro. Está al lado de la cafetería.**
- Assure students that they do not need to understand every Spanish word they hear in the video. Tell them to rely on visual cues and to listen for words from **Vocabulario útil**.

Preparación Ask students if they have ever held a yard sale or garage sale. Did the buyers try to bargain?

Comprensión
↔👤↔ To challenge students, have them write a summary of the episode in their own words.

Cuba

El país en cifras

▶ **Área:** 110.860 km² (42.803 millas²), *aproximadamente el área de Pensilvania*
▶ **Población:** 11.061.886
▶ **Capital:** La Habana—2.116.000

La Habana Vieja fue declarada° Patrimonio° Cultural de la Humanidad por la UNESCO en 1982. Este distrito es uno de los lugares más fascinantes de Cuba. En La Plaza de Armas, se puede visitar el majestuoso Palacio de Capitanes Generales, que ahora es un museo. En la calle° Obispo, frecuentada por el autor Ernest Hemingway, hay hermosos cafés, clubes nocturnos y tiendas elegantes.

▶ **Ciudades principales:** Santiago de Cuba; Camagüey; Holguín; Guantánamo
▶ **Moneda:** peso cubano
▶ **Idiomas:** español (oficial)

Bandera de Cuba

Cubanos célebres

▶ **Carlos Finlay,** doctor y científico (1833–1915)
▶ **José Martí,** político y poeta (1853–1895)
▶ **Fidel Castro,** ex primer ministro, ex comandante en jefe° de las fuerzas armadas (1926–)
▶ **Zoé Valdés,** escritora (1959–)
▶ **Ibrahim Ferrer,** músico (1927–2005)
▶ **Carlos Acosta,** bailarín (1973–)

fue declarada *was declared* Patrimonio *Heritage* calle *street* comandante en jefe *commander in chief* liviano *light* colibrí abeja *bee hummingbird* ave *bird* mundo *world* miden *measure* pesan *weigh*

Golfo de México

Gran Teatro de La Habana

ESTADOS UNIDOS

Océano Atlántico

Los coco taxis son un medio de transporte cubano muy popular.

Plaza del Capitolio

La Habana

Cordillera de los Órganos

ESTADOS UNIDOS
OCÉANO PACÍFICO
CUBA
OCÉANO ATLÁNTICO
AMÉRICA DEL SUR

Isla de la Juventud

Mar Caribe

Camagüey

La música es parte esencial de la vida en Cuba.

¡Increíble pero cierto!

Pequeño y liviano°, el colibrí abeja° de Cuba es una de las más de 320 especies de colibrí y es también el ave° más pequeña del mundo°. Menores que muchos insectos, estas aves minúsculas miden° 5 centímetros y pesan° sólo 1,95 gramos.

Baile • Ballet Nacional de Cuba

La bailarina Alicia Alonso fundó el Ballet Nacional de Cuba en 1948, después de° convertirse en una estrella° internacional en el Ballet de Nueva York y en Broadway. El Ballet Nacional de Cuba es famoso en todo el mundo por su creatividad y perfección técnica.

Economía • La caña de azúcar y el tabaco

La caña de azúcar° es el producto agrícola° que más se cultiva en la isla y su exportación es muy importante para la economía del país. El tabaco, que se usa para fabricar los famosos puros° cubanos, es otro cultivo° de mucha importancia.

Gente • Población

La población cubana tiene raíces° muy heterogéneas. La inmigración a la isla fue determinante° desde la colonia hasta mediados° del siglo° XX. Los cubanos de hoy son descendientes de africanos, europeos, chinos y antillanos, entre otros.

Música • Buena Vista Social Club

En 1997 nace° el fenómeno musical conocido como *Buena Vista Social Club*. Este proyecto reúne° a un grupo de importantes músicos de Cuba, la mayoría ya mayores, con una larga trayectoria interpretando canciones clásicas del son° cubano. Ese mismo año ganaron un *Grammy*. Hoy en día estos músicos son conocidos en todo el mundo, y personas de todas las edades bailan al ritmo° de su música.

Holguín
Santiago de Cuba
Guantánamo
Sierra Maestra

¿Qué aprendiste? Responde a las preguntas con una oración completa.

1. ¿Qué autor está asociado con la Habana Vieja? Ernest Hemingway está asociado con la Habana Vieja.
2. ¿Por qué es famoso el Ballet Nacional de Cuba? Es famoso por su creatividad y perfección técnica.
3. ¿Cuáles son los dos cultivos más importantes para la economía cubana? Los cultivos más importantes son la caña de azúcar y el tabaco.
4. ¿Qué fabrican los cubanos con la planta del tabaco? Los cubanos fabrican puros.
5. ¿De dónde son muchos de los inmigrantes que llegaron a Cuba? Son de África, de Europa, de China y de las Antillas, entre otros lugares.
6. ¿En qué año ganó un *Grammy* el disco *Buena Vista Social Club*? Ganó un *Grammy* en 1997.

Conexión Internet Investiga estos temas en Internet.

1. Busca información sobre un(a) cubano/a célebre. ¿Por qué es célebre? ¿Qué hace? ¿Todavía vive en Cuba?
2. Busca información sobre una de las ciudades principales de Cuba. ¿Qué atracciones hay en esta ciudad?

después de *after* estrella *star* caña de azúcar *sugar cane* agrícola *farming* puros *cigars* cultivo *crop* raíces *roots* determinante *deciding* mediados *halfway through* siglo *century* nace *is born* reúne *gets together* son *Cuban musical genre* ritmo *rhythm*

Ballet Nacional de Cuba
Although the **Ballet Nacional de Cuba** specializes in classical dance, Cuban popular dances (**habanera, mambo, rumba**) have gained worldwide popularity. Students can interview grandparents or other adults to see what they remember about Cuban dances.

La caña de azúcar y el tabaco
With the collapse of the Soviet bloc and the end of subsidies, Cuba's economy suffered. In 1990, Cuba entered **el período especial en tiempo de paz**. Government planners have developed tourism, which formerly was seen as bourgeois and corrupting, as a means of gaining badly needed foreign currency.

Población
↤👤→ Have students pick an immigrant group and research its history in Cuba. Have them note general dates of arrival, what their community contributed to Cuban culture, and current demographics.

Buena Vista Social Club
If students are not familiar with the film or the music of *Buena Vista Social Club*, play some songs from the sound track for students to hear. Read some song titles and have students make predictions about the music before they listen.

In-Class Tip You may want to wrap up this section by playing the *Panorama cultural* video footage for this lesson.

Language Notes Some Cuban songs mention beings with names that do not sound Spanish, such as **Obatalá, Elegguá,** and **Babaluayé**. These are divinities (**orichas**) of the Afro-Cuban religion, which has its origins in Yoruba-speaking West Africa. Forcibly converted to Catholicism upon their arrival in Cuba, Africans developed a syncretized religion in which they worshiped the gods they had brought from Africa in the form of Catholic saints. **Babaluayé,** for instance, is worshiped as **San Lázaro**. **Obatalá** is **Nuestra Señora de las Mercedes**. Cuban popular music is deeply rooted in the songs and dances with which Afro-Cubans expressed their devotion to the **orichas**.

Comparisons 4.1

Teacher Resources
Read the front matter for suggestions on how to incorporate all the program's components. See pages 189A–189B for a detailed listing of Teacher Resources online.

In-Class Tip Ask students to prepare a list of the three products or perspectives they learned about in this lesson to share with the class. You may ask them to focus specifically on the **Cultura** and **Panorama** sections.

La ropa

el abrigo	coat
los (blue)jeans	jeans
la blusa	blouse
la bolsa	purse; bag
la bota	boot
los calcetines (el calcetín)	sock(s)
la camisa	shirt
la camiseta	t-shirt
la cartera	wallet
la chaqueta	jacket
el cinturón	belt
la corbata	tie
la falda	skirt
las gafas (de sol)	(sun)glasses
los guantes	gloves
el impermeable	raincoat
las medias	pantyhose; stockings
los pantalones	pants
los pantalones cortos	shorts
la ropa	clothes
la ropa interior	underwear
las sandalias	sandals
el sombrero	hat
el suéter	sweater
el traje	suit
el traje de baño	bathing suit
el vestido	dress
los zapatos de tenis	sneakers

Verbos

conducir	to drive
conocer	to know; to be acquainted with
dar	to give
ofrecer	to offer
parecer	to seem
saber	to know; to know how
traducir	to translate

Ir de compras

el almacén	department store
la caja	cash register
el centro comercial	shopping mall
el/la cliente/a	customer
el/la dependiente/a	clerk
el dinero	money
(en) efectivo	cash
el mercado (al aire libre)	(open-air) market
un par (de zapatos)	a pair (of shoes)
el precio (fijo)	(fixed; set) price
la rebaja	sale
el regalo	gift
la tarjeta de crédito	credit card
la tienda	store
el/la vendedor(a)	salesperson
costar (o:ue)	to cost
gastar	to spend (money)
hacer juego (con)	to match (with)
llevar	to wear; to take
pagar	to pay
regatear	to bargain
usar	to wear; to use
vender	to sell

Adjetivos

barato/a	cheap
bueno/a	good
cada	each
caro/a	expensive
corto/a	short (in length)
elegante	elegant
hermoso/a	beautiful
largo/a	long
loco/a	crazy
nuevo/a	new
otro/a	other; another
pobre	poor
rico/a	rich

Los colores

el color	color
amarillo/a	yellow
anaranjado/a	orange
azul	blue
blanco/a	white
gris	gray
marrón, café	brown
morado/a	purple
negro/a	black
rojo/a	red
rosado/a	pink
verde	green

Palabras adicionales

acabar de (+ *inf.*)	to have just done something
anoche	last night
anteayer	the day before yesterday
ayer	yesterday
de repente	suddenly
desde	from
dos veces	twice
hasta	until
pasado/a (*adj.*)	last; past
el año pasado	last year
la semana pasada	last week
prestar	to lend; to loan
una vez	once
ya	already

Indirect object pronouns	See page 202.
Demonstrative adjectives and pronouns	See page 210.
Expresiones útiles	See page 195.

Guide to Vocabulary

Note on alphabetization

For purposes of alphabetization, **ch** and **ll** are not treated as separate letters, but **ñ** follows **n**. Therefore, in this glossary you will find that **año**, for example, appears after **anuncio**.

Abbreviations used in this glossary

adj.	adjective	*form.*	formal	*pl.*	plural
adv.	adverb	*indef.*	indefinite	*poss.*	possessive
art.	article	*interj.*	interjection	*prep.*	preposition
conj.	conjunction	*i.o.*	indirect object	*pron.*	pronoun
def.	definite	*m.*	masculine	*ref.*	reflexive
d.o.	direct object	*n.*	noun	*sing.*	singular
f.	feminine	*obj.*	object	*sub.*	subject
fam.	familiar	*p.p.*	past participle	*v.*	verb

Spanish–English

A

a *prep.* at; to 1.1
  ¿A qué hora...? At what time...? 1.1
  a bordo aboard
  a dieta on a diet 3.3
  a la derecha de to the right of 1.2
  a la izquierda de to the left of 1.2
  a la plancha grilled 2.2
  a la(s) + *time* at + *time* 1.1
  a menos que *conj.* unless 3.1
  a menudo *adv.* often 2.4
  a nombre de in the name of 1.5
  a plazos in installments 3.2
  A sus órdenes. At your service.
  a tiempo *adv.* on time 2.4
  a veces *adv.* sometimes 2.4
  a ver let's see
abeja *f.* bee
abierto/a *adj.* open 1.5, 3.2
abogado/a *m., f.* lawyer 3.4
abrazar(se) *v.* to hug; to embrace (each other) 2.5
abrazo *m.* hug
abrigo *m.* coat 1.6
abril *m.* April 1.5
abrir *v.* to open 1.3
abuelo/a *m., f.* grandfather/ grandmother 1.3
abuelos *pl.* grandparents 1.3
aburrido/a *adj.* bored; boring 1.5
aburrir *v.* to bore 2.1
aburrirse *v.* to get bored 3.5
acabar de (+ *inf.*) *v.* to have just *done something* 1.6
acampar *v.* to camp 1.5
accidente *m.* accident 2.4
acción *f.* action 3.5
  de acción action (genre) 3.5

aceite *m.* oil 2.2
aceptar: ¡Acepto casarme contigo! I'll marry you! 3.5
acompañar *v.* to accompany 3.2
aconsejar *v.* to advise 2.6
acontecimiento *m.* event 3.6
acordarse (de) (o:ue) *v.* to remember 2.1
acostarse (o:ue) *v.* to go to bed 2.1
activo/a *adj.* active 3.3
actor *m.* actor 3.4
actriz *f.* actress 3.4
actualidades *f., pl.* news; current events 3.6
adelgazar *v.* to lose weight; to slim down 3.3
además (de) *adv.* furthermore; besides 2.4
adicional *adj.* additional
adiós *m.* goodbye 1.1
adjetivo *m.* adjective
administración de empresas *f.* business administration 1.2
adolescencia *f.* adolescence 2.3
¿adónde? *adv.* where (to)? (destination) 1.2
aduana *f.* customs
aeróbico/a *adj.* aerobic 3.3
aeropuerto *m.* airport 1.5
afectado/a *adj.* affected 3.1
afeitarse *v.* to shave 2.1
aficionado/a *m., f.* fan 1.4
afirmativo/a *adj.* affirmative
afuera *adv.* outside 1.5
afueras *f., pl.* suburbs; outskirts 2.6
agencia de viajes *f.* travel agency 1.5
agente de viajes *m., f.* travel agent 1.5
agosto *m.* August 1.5
agradable *adj.* pleasant
agua *f.* water 2.2
  agua mineral mineral water 2.2

aguantar *v.* to endure, to hold up 3.2
ahora *adv.* now 1.2
  ahora mismo right now 1.5
ahorrar *v.* to save (money) 3.2
ahorros *m., pl.* savings 3.2
aire *m.* air 3.1
ajo *m.* garlic 2.2
al (*contraction of* **a + el**) 1.4
  al aire libre open-air 1.6
  al contado in cash 3.2
  (al) este (to the) east 3.2
  al lado de next to; beside 1.2
  (al) norte (to the) north 3.2
  (al) oeste (to the) west 3.2
  (al) sur (to the) south 3.2
alcoba *f.* bedroom
alcohol *m.* alcohol 3.3
alcohólico/a *adj.* alcoholic 3.3
alegrarse (de) *v.* to be happy 3.1
alegre *adj.* happy; joyful 1.5
alegría *f.* happiness 2.3
alemán, alemana *adj.* German 1.3
alérgico/a *adj.* allergic 2.4
alfombra *f.* carpet; rug 2.6
algo *pron.* something; anything 2.1
algodón *m.* cotton 1.6
alguien *pron.* someone; somebody; anyone 2.1
algún, alguno/a(s) *adj.* any; some 2.1
alimento *m.* food
  alimentación *f.* diet
aliviar *v.* to reduce 3.3
  aliviar el estrés/la tensión to reduce stress/tension 3.3
allá *adv.* over there 1.2
allí *adv.* there 1.2
alma *f.* soul 2.3
almacén *m.* department store 1.6
almohada *f.* pillow 2.6
almorzar (o:ue) *v.* to have lunch 1.4

almuerzo *m.* lunch **1.4, 2.2**
aló *interj.* hello (*on the telephone*) **2.5**
alquilar *v.* to rent **2.6**
alquiler *m.* rent (payment) **2.6**
altar *m.* altar **2.3**
altillo *m.* attic **2.6**
alto/a *adj.* tall **1.3**
aluminio *m.* aluminum **3.1**
ama de casa *m., f.* housekeeper; caretaker **2.6**
amable *adj.* nice; friendly **1.5**
amarillo/a *adj.* yellow **1.6**
amigo/a *m., f.* friend **1.3**
amistad *f.* friendship **2.3**
amor *m.* love **2.3**
   amor a primera vista love at first sight **2.3**
anaranjado/a *adj.* orange **1.6**
ándale *interj.* come on **3.2**
andar *v.* **en patineta** to skateboard **1.4**
ángel *m.* angel **2.3**
anillo *m.* ring **3.5**
animal *m.* animal **3.1**
aniversario (de bodas) *m.* (wedding) anniversary **2.3**
anoche *adv.* last night **1.6**
anteayer *adv.* the day before yesterday **1.6**
antes *adv.* before **2.1**
   antes (de) que *conj.* before **3.1**
   antes de *prep.* before **2.1**
antibiótico *m.* antibiotic **2.4**
antipático/a *adj.* unpleasant **1.3**
anunciar *v.* to announce; to advertise **3.6**
anuncio *m.* advertisement **3.4**
año *m.* year **1.5**
   año pasado last year **1.6**
apagar *v.* to turn off **2.5**
aparato *m.* appliance
apartamento *m.* apartment **2.6**
apellido *m.* last name **1.3**
apenas *adv.* hardly; scarcely **2.4**
aplaudir *v.* to applaud **3.5**
aplicación *f.* app **2.5**
apreciar *v.* to appreciate **3.5**
aprender (a + *inf.*) *v.* to learn **1.3**
apurarse *v.* to hurry; to rush **3.3**
aquel, aquella *adj.* that (over there) **1.6**
aquél, aquélla *pron.* that (over there) **1.6**
aquello *neuter, pron.* that; that thing; that fact **1.6**
aquellos/as *pl. adj.* those (over there) **1.6**
aquéllos/as *pl. pron.* those (ones) (over there) **1.6**
aquí *adv.* here **1.1**
   Aquí está(n)... Here is/are... **1.5**
árbol *m.* tree **3.1**
archivo *m.* file **2.5**
arete *m.* earring **1.6**
argentino/a *adj.* Argentine **1.3**
armario *m.* closet **2.6**

arqueología *f.* archeology **1.2**
arqueólogo/a *m., f.* archeologist **3.4**
arquitecto/a *m., f.* architect **3.4**
arrancar *v.* to start (*a car*) **2.5**
arreglar *v.* to fix; to arrange **2.5**; to neaten; to straighten up **2.6**
arreglarse *v.* to get ready **2.1**; to fix oneself (*clothes, hair, etc. to go out*) **2.1**
arroba *f.* @ symbol **2.5**
arroz *m.* rice **2.2**
arte *m.* art **1.2**
artes *f., pl.* arts **3.5**
artesanía *f.* craftsmanship; crafts **3.5**
artículo *m.* article **3.6**
artista *m., f.* artist **1.3**
artístico/a *adj.* artistic **3.5**
arveja *f.* pea **2.2**
asado/a *adj.* roast **2.2**
ascenso *m.* promotion **3.4**
ascensor *m.* elevator **1.5**
así *adv.* like this; so (*in such a way*) **2.4**
asistir (a) *v.* to attend **1.3**
aspiradora *f.* vacuum cleaner **2.6**
aspirante *m., f.* candidate; applicant **3.4**
aspirina *f.* aspirin **2.4**
atún *m.* tuna **2.2**
aumentar *v.* to grow; to get bigger **3.1**
aumentar *v.* **de peso** to gain weight **3.3**
aumento *m.* increase
   aumento de sueldo pay raise **3.4**
aunque although
autobús *m.* bus **1.1**
automático/a *adj.* automatic
auto(móvil) *m.* auto(mobile) **1.5**
autopista *f.* highway **2.5**
ave *f.* bird **3.1**
avenida *f.* avenue
aventura *f.* adventure **3.5**
   de aventuras adventure (genre) **3.5**
avergonzado/a *adj.* embarrassed **1.5**
avión *m.* airplane **1.5**
¡Ay! *interj.* Oh!
   ¡Ay, qué dolor! Oh, what pain!
ayer *adv.* yesterday **1.6**
ayudar(se) *v.* to help (each other) **2.5**
azúcar *m.* sugar **2.2**
azul *adj. m., f.* blue **1.6**

B

bailar *v.* to dance **1.2**
bailarín/bailarina *m., f.* dancer **3.5**
baile *m.* dance **3.5**
bajar(se) de *v.* to get off of/out of (a vehicle) **2.5**

bajo/a *adj.* short (*in height*) **1.3**
balcón *m.* balcony **2.6**
balde *m.* bucket **1.5**
ballena *f.* whale **3.1**
baloncesto *m.* basketball **1.4**
banana *f.* banana **2.2**
banco *m.* bank **3.2**
banda *f.* band **3.5**
bandera *f.* flag
bañarse *v.* to bathe; to take a bath **2.1**
baño *m.* bathroom **2.1**
barato/a *adj.* cheap **1.6**
barco *m.* boat **1.5**
barrer *v.* to sweep **2.6**
   barrer el suelo *v.* to sweep the floor **2.6**
barrio *m.* neighborhood **2.6**
bastante *adv.* enough; rather **2.4**
basura *f.* trash **2.6**
baúl *m.* trunk **2.5**
beber *v.* to drink **1.3**
bebida *f.* drink **2.2**
   bebida alcohólica *f.* alcoholic beverage **3.3**
béisbol *m.* baseball **1.4**
bellas artes *f., pl.* fine arts **3.5**
belleza *f.* beauty **3.2**
beneficio *m.* benefit **3.4**
besar(se) *v.* to kiss (each other) **2.5**
beso *m.* kiss **2.3**
biblioteca *f.* library **1.2**
bicicleta *f.* bicycle **1.4**
bien *adv.* well **1.1**
bienestar *m.* well-being **3.3**
bienvenido(s)/a(s) *adj.* welcome **1.1**
billete *m.* paper money; ticket
billón *m.* trillion
biología *f.* biology **1.2**
bisabuelo/a *m., f.* great-grandfather/great-grandmother **1.3**
bistec *m.* steak **2.2**
blanco/a *adj.* white **1.6**
blog *m.* blog **2.5**
(blue)jeans *m., pl.* jeans **1.6**
blusa *f.* blouse **1.6**
boca *f.* mouth **2.4**
boda *f.* wedding **2.3**
boleto *m.* ticket **1.2, 3.5**
bolsa *f.* purse, bag **1.6**
bombero/a *m., f.* firefighter **3.4**
bonito/a *adj.* pretty **1.3**
borrador *m.* eraser **1.2**
borrar *v.* to erase **2.5**
bosque *m.* forest **3.1**
   bosque tropical tropical forest; rain forest **3.1**
bota *f.* boot **1.6**
botella *f.* bottle **2.3**
   botella de vino bottle of wine **2.3**
botones *m., f. sing.* bellhop **1.5**
brazo *m.* arm **2.4**
brindar *v.* to toast (*drink*) **2.3**
bucear *v.* to scuba dive **1.4**

buen, bueno/a *adj.* good 1.3, 1.6
   buena forma good shape (*physical*) 3.3
   Buenas noches. Good evening; Good night. 1.1
   Buenas tardes. Good afternoon. 1.1
   Bueno. Hello. (*on telephone*) 2.5
   Buenos días. Good morning. 1.1
bulevar *m.* boulevard
buscador *m.* browser 2.5
buscar *v.* to look for 1.2
buzón *m.* mailbox 3.2

C

caballero *m.* gentleman, sir 2.2
caballo *m.* horse 1.5
cabe: no cabe duda de there's no doubt 3.1
cabeza *f.* head 2.4
cada *adj. m., f.* each 1.6
caerse *v.* to fall (down) 2.4
café *m.* café 1.4; *adj. m., f.* brown 1.6; *m.* coffee 2.2
cafeína *f.* caffeine 3.3
cafetera *f.* coffee maker 2.6
cafetería *f.* cafeteria 1.2
caído/a *p.p.* fallen 3.2
caja *f.* cash register 1.6
cajero/a *m., f.* cashier
   cajero automático *m.* ATM 3.2
calavera de azúcar *f.* skull made out of sugar 2.3
calcetín (calcetines) *m.* sock(s) 1.6
calculadora *f.* calculator 1.2
calentamiento global *m.* global warming 3.1
calentarse (e:ie) *v.* to warm up 3.3
calidad *f.* quality 1.6
calle *f.* street 2.5
calor *m.* heat
caloría *f.* calorie 3.3
calzar *v.* to take size... shoes 1.6
cama *f.* bed 1.5
cámara de video *f.* video camera 2.5
cámara digital *f.* digital camera 2.5
camarero/a *m., f.* waiter/ waitress 2.2
camarón *m.* shrimp 2.2
cambiar (de) *v.* to change 2.3
cambio: de cambio in change 1.2
cambio *m.* **climático** climate change 3.1
cambio *m.* **de moneda** currency exchange
caminar *v.* to walk 1.2
camino *m.* road
camión *m.* truck; bus

camisa *f.* shirt 1.6
camiseta *f.* t-shirt 1.6
campo *m.* countryside 1.5
canadiense *adj.* Canadian 1.3
canal *m.* (TV) channel 2.5; 3.5
canción *f.* song 3.5
candidato/a *m., f.* candidate 3.6
canela *f.* cinnamon 2.4
cansado/a *adj.* tired 1.5
cantante *m., f.* singer 3.5
cantar *v.* to sing 1.2
capital *f.* capital city
capó *m.* hood 2.5
cara *f.* face 2.1
caramelo *m.* caramel 2.3
cargador *m.* charger 2.5
carne *f.* meat 2.2
   carne de res *f.* beef 2.2
carnicería *f.* butcher shop 3.2
caro/a *adj.* expensive 1.6
carpintero/a *m., f.* carpenter 3.4
carrera *f.* career 3.4
carretera *f.* highway; (main) road 2.5
carro *m.* car; automobile 2.5
carta *f.* letter 1.4; (playing) card 1.5
cartel *m.* poster 2.6
cartera *f.* wallet 1.4, 1.6
cartero *m.* mail carrier 3.2
casa *f.* house; home 1.2
casado/a *adj.* married 2.3
casarse (con) *v.* to get married (to) 2.3
casi *adv.* almost 2.4
catorce fourteen 1.1
cazar *v.* to hunt 3.1
cebolla *f.* onion 2.2
cederrón *m.* CD-ROM
celebrar *v.* to celebrate 2.3
cementerio *m.* cemetery 2.3
cena *f.* dinner 2.2
cenar *v.* to have dinner 1.2
centro *m.* downtown 1.4
   centro comercial shopping mall 1.6
cepillarse los dientes/el pelo *v.* to brush one's teeth/one's hair 2.1
cerámica *f.* pottery 3.5
cerca de *prep.* near 1.2
cerdo *m.* pork 2.2
cereales *m., pl.* cereal; grains 2.2
cero *m.* zero 1.1
cerrado/a *adj.* closed 1.5
cerrar (e:ie) *v.* to close 1.4
cerveza *f.* beer 2.2
césped *m.* grass
ceviche *m.* marinated fish dish 2.2
   ceviche de camarón *m.* lemon-marinated shrimp 2.2
chaleco *m.* vest
champán *m.* champagne 2.3
champiñón *m.* mushroom 2.2
champú *m.* shampoo 2.1
chaqueta *f.* jacket 1.6

chatear *v.* to chat 2.5
chau *fam. interj.* bye 1.1
cheque *m.* (bank) check 3.2
   cheque (de viajero) *m.* (traveler's) check 3.2
chévere *adj., fam.* terrific
chico/a *m., f.* boy/girl 1.1
chino/a *adj.* Chinese 1.3
chocar (con) *v.* to run into
chocolate *m.* chocolate 2.3
choque *m.* collision 3.6
chuleta *f.* chop (*food*) 2.2
   chuleta de cerdo *f.* pork chop 2.2
cibercafé *m.* cybercafé 2.5
ciclismo *m.* cycling 1.4
cielo *m.* sky 3.1
cien(to) one hundred 1.2
ciencias *f., pl.* sciences 1.2
   ciencias ambientales environmental science 1.2
   de ciencia ficción *f.* science fiction (genre) 3.5
científico/a *m., f.* scientist 3.4
cierto/a *adj.* certain 3.1
   es cierto it's certain 3.1
   no es cierto it's not certain 3.1
cima *f.* top, peak 3.3
cinco five 1.1
cincuenta fifty 1.2
cine *m.* movie theater 1.4
cinta *f.* (audio)tape
cinta caminadora *f.* treadmill 3.3
cinturón *m.* belt 1.6
circulación *f.* traffic 2.5
cita *f.* date; appointment 2.3
ciudad *f.* city
ciudadano/a *m., f.* citizen 3.6
Claro (que sí). *fam.* Of course.
clase *f.* class 1.2
   clase de ejercicios aeróbicos *f.* aerobics class 3.3
clásico/a *adj.* classical 3.5
cliente/a *m., f.* customer 1.6
clínica *f.* clinic 2.4
cobrar *v.* to cash (a check) 3.2
coche *m.* car; automobile 2.5
cocina *f.* kitchen; stove 2.3, 2.6
cocinar *v.* to cook 2.6
cocinero/a *m., f.* cook, chef 3.4
cofre *m.* hood 3.2
cola *f.* line 3.2
colesterol *m.* cholesterol 3.3
color *m.* color 1.6
comedia *f.* comedy; play 3.5
comedor *m.* dining room 2.6
comenzar (e:ie) *v.* to begin 1.4
comer *v.* to eat 1.3
comercial *adj.* commercial; business-related 3.4
comida *f.* food; meal 1.4, 2.2
como like; as 2.2
¿cómo? what?; how? 1.1, 1.2
   ¿Cómo es...? What's... like?
   ¿Cómo está usted? *form.* How are you? 1.1

¿Cómo estás? *fam.* How are you? 1.1
¿Cómo se llama usted? *(form.)* What's your name? 1.1
¿Cómo te llamas? *fam.* What's your name? 1.1
cómoda *f.* chest of drawers 2.6
cómodo/a *adj.* comfortable 1.5
compañero/a de clase *m., f.* classmate 1.2
compañero/a de cuarto *m., f.* roommate 1.2
compañía *f.* company; firm 3.4
compartir *v.* to share 1.3
compositor(a) *m., f.* composer 3.5
comprar *v.* to buy 1.2
compras *f., pl.* purchases
  ir de compras to go shopping 1.5
comprender *v.* to understand 1.3
comprobar *v.* to check
comprometerse (con) *v.* to get engaged (to) 2.3
computación *f.* computer science 1.2
computadora *f.* computer 1.1
computadora portátil *f.* portable computer; laptop 2.5
comunicación *f.* communication 3.6
comunicarse (con) *v.* to communicate (with) 3.6
comunidad *f.* community 1.1
con *prep.* with 1.2
  Con él/ella habla. Speaking. *(on telephone)* 2.5
  con frecuencia *adv.* frequently 2.4
  Con permiso. Pardon me; Excuse me. 1.1
  con tal (de) que *conj.* provided (that) 3.1
concierto *m.* concert 3.5
concordar *v.* to agree
concurso *m.* game show; contest 3.5
conducir *v.* to drive 1.6, 2.5
conductor(a) *m., f.* driver 1.1
conexión *f.* **inalámbrica** wireless connection 2.5
confirmar *v.* to confirm 1.5
confirmar *v.* **una reservación** *f.* to confirm a reservation 1.5
confundido/a *adj.* confused 1.5
congelador *m.* freezer 2.6
congestionado/a *adj.* congested; stuffed-up 2.4
conmigo *pron.* with me 1.4, 2.3
conocer *v.* to know; to be acquainted with 1.6
conocido/a *adj.; p.p.* known
conseguir (e:i) *v.* to get; to obtain 1.4
consejero/a *m., f.* counselor; advisor 3.4
consejo *m.* advice
conservación *f.* conservation 3.1

conservar *v.* to conserve 3.1
construir *v.* to build
consultorio *m.* doctor's office 2.4
consumir *v.* to consume 3.3
contabilidad *f.* accounting 1.2
contador(a) *m., f.* accountant 3.4
contaminación *f.* pollution 3.1
  contaminación del aire/del agua air/water pollution 3.1
contaminado/a *adj.* polluted 3.1
contaminar *v.* to pollute 3.1
contar (o:ue) *v.* to count; to tell 1.4
contento/a *adj.* content 1.5
contestadora *f.* answering machine
contestar *v.* to answer 1.2
contigo *fam. pron.* with you 1.5, 2.3
contratar *v.* to hire 3.4
control *m.* **remoto** remote control 2.5
controlar *v.* to control 3.1
conversación *f.* conversation 1.1
conversar *v.* to converse, to chat 1.2
copa *f.* wineglass; goblet 2.6
corazón *m.* heart 2.4
corbata *f.* tie 1.6
corredor(a) *m., f.* **de bolsa** stockbroker 3.4
correo *m.* mail; post office 3.2
  correo de voz *m.* voice mail 2.5
  correo electrónico *m.* e-mail 1.4
correr *v.* to run 1.3
cortesía *f.* courtesy
cortinas *f., pl.* curtains 2.6
corto/a *adj.* short *(in length)* 1.6
cosa *f.* thing 1.1
costar (o:ue) *v.* to cost 1.6
costarricense *adj.* Costa Rican 1.3
cráter *m.* crater 3.1
creer *v.* to believe 1.3, 3.1
  creer (en) *v.* to believe (in) 1.3
  no creer *v.* not to believe 3.1
creído/a *adj., p.p.* believed 3.2
crema de afeitar *f.* shaving cream 1.5, 2.1
crimen *m.* crime; murder 3.6
cruzar *v.* to cross 3.2
cuaderno *m.* notebook 1.1
cuadra *f.* (city) block 3.2
¿cuál(es)? which?; which one(s)? 1.2
  ¿Cuál es la fecha de hoy? What is today's date? 1.5
cuadro *m.* picture 2.6
cuando *conj.* when 2.1; 3.1
¿cuándo? when? 1.2
¿cuánto(s)/a(s)? how much/how many? 1.1, 1.2
  ¿Cuánto cuesta...? How much does... cost? 1.6
  ¿Cuántos años tienes? How old are you?
cuarenta forty 1.2
cuarto de baño *m.* bathroom 2.1
cuarto *m.* room 1.2; 2.1

cuarto/a *adj.* fourth 1.5
  menos cuarto quarter to (time) 1.1
  y cuarto quarter after (time) 1.1
cuatro four 1.1
cuatrocientos/as four hundred 1.2
cubano/a *adj.* Cuban 1.3
cubiertos *m., pl.* silverware
cubierto/a *p.p.* covered
cubrir *v.* to cover
cuchara *f.* (table or large) spoon 2.6
cuchillo *m.* knife 2.6
cuello *m.* neck 2.4
cuenta *f.* bill 2.2; account 3.2
  cuenta corriente *f.* checking account 3.2
  cuenta de ahorros *f.* savings account 3.2
cuento *m.* short story 3.5
cuerpo *m.* body 2.4
cuidado *m.* care
cuidar *v.* to take care of 3.1
cultura *f.* culture 1.2, 3.5
cumpleaños *m., sing.* birthday 2.3
cumplir años *v.* to have a birthday
cuñado/a *m., f.* brother-in-law/ sister-in-law 1.3
currículum *m.* résumé 3.4
curso *m.* course 1.2

D

danza *f.* dance 3.5
dañar *v.* to damage; to break down 2.4
dar *v.* to give 1.6
  dar un consejo *v.* to give advice
  darse con *v.* to bump into; to run into (something) 2.4
  darse prisa *v.* to hurry; to rush 3.3
de *prep.* of; from 1.1
  ¿De dónde eres? *fam.* Where are you from? 1.1
  ¿De dónde es usted? *form.* Where are you from? 1.1
  ¿De parte de quién? Who is speaking/calling? *(on telephone)* 2.5
  ¿de quién...? whose...? *(sing.)* 1.1
  ¿de quiénes...? whose...? *(pl.)* 1.1
  de algodón (made) of cotton 1.6
  de aluminio (made) of aluminum 3.1
  de buen humor in a good mood 1.5
  de compras shopping 1.5
  de cuadros plaid 1.6
  de excursión hiking 1.4
  de hecho in fact
  de ida y vuelta roundtrip 1.5
  de la mañana in the morning; A.M. 1.1
  de la noche in the evening; at night; P.M. 1.1

de la tarde in the afternoon; in the early evening; P.M. 1.1
de lana (made) of wool 1.6
de lunares polka-dotted 1.6
de mal humor in a bad mood 1.5
de moda in fashion 1.6
De nada. You're welcome. 1.1
de niño/a as a child 2.4
de parte de on behalf of 2.5
de plástico (made) of plastic 3.1
de rayas striped 1.6
de repente suddenly 1.6
de seda (made) of silk 1.6
de vaqueros western (genre) 3.5
de vez en cuando from time to time 2.4
de vidrio (made) of glass 3.1
debajo de *prep.* below; under 1.2
deber (+ *inf.*) *v.* should; must; ought to 1.3
deber *m.* responsibility; obligation 3.6
debido a due to (the fact that)
débil *adj.* weak 3.3
decidir (+ *inf.*) *v.* to decide 1.3
décimo/a *adj.* tenth 1.5
decir (e:i) *v.* (**que**) to say (that); to tell (that) 1.4
    decir la respuesta to say the answer 1.4
    decir la verdad to tell the truth 1.4
    decir mentiras to tell lies 1.4
declarar *v.* to declare; to say 3.6
dedo *m.* finger 2.4
dedo del pie *m.* toe 2.4
deforestación *f.* deforestation 3.1
dejar *v.* to let; to quit; to leave behind 3.4
    dejar de (+ *inf.*) *v.* to stop (*doing something*) 3.1
    dejar una propina *v.* to leave a tip
del (*contraction of* **de + el**) of the; from the 1.1
delante de *prep.* in front of 1.2
delgado/a *adj.* thin; slender 1.3
delicioso/a *adj.* delicious 2.2
demás *adj.* the rest
demasiado *adv.* too much 1.6
dentista *m., f.* dentist 2.4
dentro de (diez años) within (ten years) 3.4; inside
dependiente/a *m., f.* clerk 1.6
deporte *m.* sport 1.4
deportista *m.* sports person
deportivo/a *adj.* sports-related 1.4
depositar *v.* to deposit 3.2
derecha *f.* right 1.2
    a la derecha de to the right of 1.2
derecho *adv.* straight (ahead) 3.2
derechos *m., pl.* rights 3.6
desarrollar *v.* to develop 3.1

desastre (natural) *m.* (natural) disaster 3.6
desayunar *v.* to have breakfast 1.2
desayuno *m.* breakfast 2.2
descafeinado/a *adj.* decaffeinated 3.3
descansar *v.* to rest 1.2
descargar *v.* to download 2.5
descompuesto/a *adj.* not working; out of order 2.5
describir *v.* to describe 1.3
descrito/a *p.p.* described 3.2
descubierto/a *p.p.* discovered 3.2
descubrir *v.* to discover 3.1
desde *prep.* from 1.6
desear *v.* to wish; to desire 1.2
desempleo *m.* unemployment 3.6
desierto *m.* desert 3.1
desigualdad *f.* inequality 3.6
desordenado/a *adj.* disorderly 1.5
despacio *adv.* slowly 2.4
despedida *f.* farewell; goodbye
despedir (e:i) *v.* to fire 3.4
despedirse (de) (e:i) *v.* to say goodbye (to) 3.6
despejado/a *adj.* clear (*weather*)
despertador *m.* alarm clock 2.1
despertarse (e:ie) *v.* to wake up 2.1
después *adv.* afterwards; then 2.1
    después de after 2.1
    después de que *conj.* after 3.1
destruir *v.* to destroy 3.1
detrás de *prep.* behind 1.2
día *m.* day 1.1
    día de fiesta holiday 2.3
diario *m.* diary 1.1; newspaper 3.6
diario/a *adj.* daily 2.1
dibujar *v.* to draw 1.2
dibujo *m.* drawing
    dibujos animados *m., pl.* cartoons 3.5
diccionario *m.* dictionary 1.1
dicho/a *p.p.* said 3.2
diciembre *m.* December 1.5
dictadura *f.* dictatorship 3.6
diecinueve nineteen 1.1
dieciocho eighteen 1.1
dieciséis sixteen 1.1
diecisiete seventeen 1.1
diente *m.* tooth 2.1
dieta *f.* diet 3.3
    comer una dieta equilibrada to eat a balanced diet 3.3
diez ten 1.1
difícil *adj.* difficult; hard 1.3
Diga. Hello. (*on telephone*) 2.5
diligencia *f.* errand 3.2
dinero *m.* money 1.6
dirección *f.* address 3.2
    dirección electrónica *f.* e-mail address 2.5
director(a) *m., f.* director; (*musical*) conductor 3.5
dirigir *v.* to direct 3.5

disco compacto compact disc (CD) 2.5
discriminación *f.* discrimination 3.6
discurso *m.* speech 3.6
diseñador(a) *m., f.* designer 3.4
diseño *m.* design
disfraz *m.* costume 2.3
disfrutar (de) *v.* to enjoy; to reap the benefits (of) 3.3
disminuir *v.* to reduce 3.4
diversión *f.* fun activity; entertainment; recreation 1.4
divertido/a *adj.* fun
divertirse (e:ie) *v.* to have fun 2.3
divorciado/a *adj.* divorced 2.3
divorciarse (de) *v.* to get divorced (from) 2.3
divorcio *m.* divorce 2.3
doblar *v.* to turn 3.2
doble *adj.* double 1.5
doce twelve 1.1
doctor(a) *m., f.* doctor 1.3; 2.4
documental *m.* documentary 3.5
documentos de viaje *m., pl.* travel documents
doler (o:ue) *v.* to hurt 2.4
dolor *m.* ache; pain 2.4
    dolor de cabeza *m.* headache 2.4
doméstico/a *adj.* domestic 2.6
domingo *m.* Sunday 1.2
don *m.* Mr.; sir 1.1
doña *f.* Mrs.; ma'am 1.1
donde *adv.* where
    ¿Dónde está...? Where is...? 1.2
    ¿dónde? where? 1.1, 1.2
dormir (o:ue) *v.* to sleep 1.4
dormirse (o:ue) *v.* to go to sleep; to fall asleep 2.1
dormitorio *m.* bedroom 2.6
dos two 1.1
    dos veces *f.* twice; two times 1.6
doscientos/as two hundred 1.2
drama *m.* drama; play 3.5
dramático/a *adj.* dramatic 3.5
dramaturgo/a *m., f.* playwright 3.5
droga *f.* drug 3.3
drogadicto/a *m., f.* drug addict 3.3
ducha *f.* shower 2.1
ducharse *v.* to shower; to take a shower 2.1
duda *f.* doubt 3.1
dudar *v.* to doubt 3.1
    no dudar *v.* not to doubt 3.1
dueño/a *m., f.* owner 2.2
dulces *m., pl.* sweets; candy 2.3
durante *prep.* during 2.1
durar *v.* to last 3.6

E

e *conj.* (*used instead of* **y** *before words beginning with* **i** *and* **hi**) and

echar *v.* to throw
  echar (una carta) al buzón *v.* to put (a letter) in the mailbox; to mail **3.2**
ecología *f.* ecology **3.1**
ecológico/a *adj.* ecological **3.1**
ecologista *m., f.* ecologist **3.1**
economía *f.* economics **1.2**
ecoturismo *m.* ecotourism **3.1**
ecuatoriano/a *adj.* Ecuadorian **1.3**
edad *f.* age **2.3**
edificio *m.* building **2.6**
  edificio de apartamentos apartment building **2.6**
(en) efectivo *m.* cash **1.6**
ejercer *v.* to practice/exercise (a degree/profession) **3.4**
ejercicio *m.* exercise **3.3**
  ejercicios aeróbicos aerobic exercises **3.3**
  ejercicios de estiramiento stretching exercises **3.3**
ejército *m.* army **3.6**
el *m., sing., def. art.* the **1.1**
él *sub. pron.* he **1.1**; *obj. pron.* him
elecciones *f., pl.* election **3.6**
electricista *m., f.* electrician **3.4**
electrodoméstico *m.* electric appliance **2.6**
elegante *adj. m., f.* elegant **1.6**
elegir (e:i) *v.* to elect **3.6**
ella *sub. pron.* she **1.1**; *obj. pron.* her
ellos/as *sub. pron.* they **1.1**; *obj. pron.* them
embarazada *adj.* pregnant **2.4**
emergencia *f.* emergency **2.4**
emitir *v.* to broadcast **3.6**
emocionante *adj. m., f.* exciting
empezar (e:ie) *v.* to begin **1.4**
empleado/a *m., f.* employee **1.5**
empleo *m.* job; employment **3.4**
empresa *f.* company; firm **3.4**
en *prep.* in; on **1.2**
  en casa at home
  en caso (de) que *conj.* in case (that) **3.1**
  en cuanto *conj.* as soon as **3.1**
  en efectivo in cash **3.2**
  en exceso in excess; too much **3.3**
  en línea in-line **1.4**
  en punto on the dot; exactly; sharp (*time*) **1.1**
  en qué in what; how
  ¿En qué puedo servirles? How can I help you? **1.5**
  en vivo live **2.1**
enamorado/a (de) *adj.* in love (with) **1.5**
enamorarse (de) *v.* to fall in love (with) **2.3**
encantado/a *adj.* delighted; pleased to meet you **1.1**
encantar *v.* to like very much; to love (*inanimate objects*) **2.1**

encima de *prep.* on top of **1.2**
encontrar (o:ue) *v.* to find **1.4**
encontrar(se) (o:ue) *v.* to meet (each other); to run into (each other) **2.5**
  encontrarse con to meet up with **2.1**
encuesta *f.* poll; survey **3.6**
energía *f.* energy **3.1**
  energía nuclear nuclear energy **3.1**
  energía solar solar energy **3.1**
enero *m.* January **1.5**
enfermarse *v.* to get sick **2.4**
enfermedad *f.* illness **2.4**
enfermero/a *m., f.* nurse **2.4**
enfermo/a *adj.* sick **2.4**
enfrente de *adv.* opposite; facing **3.2**
engordar *v.* to gain weight **3.3**
enojado/a *adj.* angry **1.5**
enojarse (con) *v.* to get angry (with) **2.1**
ensalada *f.* salad **2.2**
ensayo *m.* essay **1.3**
enseguida *adv.* right away
enseñar *v.* to teach **1.2**
ensuciar *v.* to get (something) dirty **2.6**
entender (e:ie) *v.* to understand **1.4**
enterarse *v.* to find out **3.4**
entonces *adv.* so, then **1.5, 2.1**
entrada *f.* entrance **2.6**; ticket
entre *prep.* between; among **1.2**
entregar *v.* to hand in **2.5**
entremeses *m., pl.* hors d'oeuvres; appetizers **2.2**
entrenador(a) *m., f.* trainer **3.3**
entrenarse *v.* to practice; to train **3.3**
entrevista *f.* interview **3.4**
entrevistador(a) *m., f.* interviewer **3.4**
entrevistar *v.* to interview **3.4**
envase *m.* container **3.1**
enviar *v.* to send; to mail **3.2**
equilibrado/a *adj.* balanced **3.3**
equipaje *m.* luggage **1.5**
equipo *m.* team **1.4**
equivocado/a *adj.* wrong **1.5**
eres *fam.* you are **1.1**
es he/she/it is **1.1**
  Es bueno que... It's good that... **2.6**
  es cierto it's certain **3.1**
  es extraño it's strange **3.1**
  es igual it's the same **1.5**
  Es importante que... It's important that... **2.6**
  es imposible it's impossible **3.1**
  es improbable it's improbable **3.1**
  Es malo que... It's bad that... **2.6**
  Es mejor que... It's better that... **2.6**

  Es necesario que... It's necessary that... **2.6**
  es obvio it's obvious **3.1**
  es posible it's possible **3.1**
  es probable it's probable **3.1**
  es ridículo it's ridiculous **3.1**
  es seguro it's certain **3.1**
  es terrible it's terrible **3.1**
  es triste it's sad **3.1**
  Es urgente que... It's urgent that... **2.6**
  Es la una. It's one o'clock. **1.1**
  es una lástima it's a shame **3.1**
  es verdad it's true **3.1**
esa(s) *f., adj.* that; those **1.6**
ésa(s) *f., pron.* that (one); those (ones) **1.6**
escalar *v.* to climb **1.4**
  escalar montañas to climb mountains **1.4**
escalera *f.* stairs; stairway **2.6**
escalón *m.* step **3.3**
escanear *v.* to scan **2.5**
escoger *v.* to choose **2.2**
escribir *v.* to write **1.3**
  escribir un mensaje electrónico to write an e-mail **1.4**
  escribir una carta to write a letter **1.4**
escrito/a *p.p.* written **3.2**
escritor(a) *m., f.* writer **3.5**
escritorio *m.* desk **1.2**
escuchar *v.* to listen (to) **1.2**
  escuchar la radio to listen to the radio **1.2**
  escuchar música to listen to music **1.2**
escuela *f.* school **1.1**
esculpir *v.* to sculpt **3.5**
escultor(a) *m., f.* sculptor **3.5**
escultura *f.* sculpture **3.5**
ese *m., sing., adj.* that **1.6**
ése *m., sing., pron.* that one **1.6**
eso *neuter, pron.* that; that thing **1.6**
esos *m., pl., adj.* those **1.6**
ésos *m., pl., pron.* those (ones) **1.6**
España *f.* Spain
español *m.* Spanish (*language*) **1.2**
español(a) *adj. m., f.* Spanish **1.3**
espárragos *m., pl.* asparagus **2.2**
especialidad: las especialidades del día today's specials **2.2**
especialización *f.* major **1.2**
espectacular *adj.* spectacular
espectáculo *m.* show **3.5**
espejo *m.* mirror **2.1**
esperar *v.* to hope; to wish **3.1**
  esperar (+ inf.) *v.* to wait (for); to hope **1.2**
esposo/a *m., f.* husband/wife; spouse **1.3**
esquí (acuático) *m.* (water) skiing **1.4**
esquiar *v.* to ski **1.4**
esquina *f.* corner **3.2**

está he/she/it is, you are
  Está bien. That's fine.
  Está (muy) despejado. It's (very) clear. (*weather*)
  Está lloviendo. It's raining. **1.5**
  Está nevando. It's snowing. **1.5**
  Está (muy) nublado. It's (very) cloudy. (*weather*) **1.5**
esta(s) *f., adj.* this; these **1.6**
  esta noche tonight
ésta(s) *f., pron.* this (one); these (ones) **1.6**
establecer *v.* to establish **3.4**
estación *f.* station; season **1.5**
  estación de autobuses bus station **1.5**
  estación del metro subway station **1.5**
  estación de tren train station **1.5**
estacionamiento *m.* parking lot **3.2**
estacionar *v.* to park **2.5**
estadio *m.* stadium **1.2**
estado civil *m.* marital status **2.3**
Estados Unidos *m., pl.* (EE.UU.; E.U.) United States
estadounidense *adj. m., f.* from the United States **1.3**
estampilla *f.* stamp **3.2**
estante *m.* bookcase; bookshelves **2.6**
estar *v.* to be **1.2**
  estar a dieta to be on a diet **3.3**
  estar aburrido/a to be bored **1.5**
  estar afectado/a (por) to be affected (by) **3.1**
  estar cansado/a to be tired **1.5**
  estar contaminado/a to be polluted **3.1**
  estar de acuerdo to agree **3.5**
    Estoy de acuerdo. I agree. **3.5**
    No estoy de acuerdo. I don't agree. **3.5**
  estar de moda to be in fashion **1.6**
  estar de vacaciones *f., pl.* to be on vacation **1.5**
  estar en buena forma to be in good shape **3.3**
  estar enfermo/a to be sick **2.4**
  estar harto/a de... to be sick of... **3.6**
  estar listo/a to be ready **1.5**
  estar perdido/a to be lost **3.2**
  estar roto/a to be broken
  estar seguro/a to be sure **1.5**
  estar torcido/a to be twisted; to be sprained **2.4**
  No está nada mal. It's not bad at all. **1.5**
estatua *f.* statue **3.5**
este *m.* east **3.2**
este *m., sing., adj.* this **1.6**
éste *m., sing., pron.* this (one) **1.6**

estéreo *m.* stereo **2.5**
estilo *m.* style
estiramiento *m.* stretching **3.3**
esto *neuter pron.* this; this thing **1.6**
estómago *m.* stomach **2.4**
estornudar *v.* to sneeze **2.4**
estos *m., pl., adj.* these **1.6**
éstos *m., pl., pron.* these (ones) **1.6**
estrella *f.* star **3.1**
  estrella de cine *m., f.* movie star **3.5**
estrés *m.* stress **3.3**
estudiante *m., f.* student **1.1, 1.2**
estudiantil *adj. m., f.* student **1.2**
estudiar *v.* to study **1.2**
estufa *f.* stove **2.6**
estupendo/a *adj.* stupendous **1.5**
etapa *f.* stage **2.3**
evitar *v.* to avoid **3.1**
examen *m.* test; exam **1.2**
  examen médico physical exam **2.4**
excelente *adj. m., f.* excellent **1.5**
exceso *m.* excess **3.3**
excursión *f.* hike; tour; excursion **1.4**
excursionista *m., f.* hiker
éxito *m.* success
experiencia *f.* experience
explicar *v.* to explain **1.2**
explorar *v.* to explore
expresión *f.* expression
extinción *f.* extinction **3.1**
extranjero/a *adj.* foreign **3.5**
extrañar *v.* to miss **3.4**
extraño/a *adj.* strange **3.1**

F

fábrica *f.* factory **3.1**
fabuloso/a *adj.* fabulous **1.5**
fácil *adj.* easy **1.3**
falda *f.* skirt **1.6**
faltar *v.* to lack; to need **2.1**
familia *f.* family **1.3**
famoso/a *adj.* famous
farmacia *f.* pharmacy **2.4**
fascinar *v.* to fascinate **2.1**
favorito/a *adj.* favorite **1.4**
fax *m.* fax (machine)
febrero *m.* February **1.5**
fecha *f.* date **1.5**
¡Felicidades! Congratulations! **2.3**
¡Felicitaciones! Congratulations! **2.3**
feliz *adj.* happy **1.5**
  ¡Feliz cumpleaños! Happy birthday! **2.3**
fenomenal *adj.* great, phenomenal **1.5**
feo/a *adj.* ugly **1.3**
festival *m.* festival **3.5**
fiebre *f.* fever **2.4**
fiesta *f.* party **2.3**
fijo/a *adj.* fixed, set **1.6**

fin *m.* end **1.4**
  fin de semana weekend **1.4**
finalmente *adv.* finally
firmar *v.* to sign (*a document*) **3.2**
física *f.* physics **1.2**
flan (de caramelo) *m.* baked (caramel) custard **2.3**
flexible *adj.* flexible **3.3**
flor *f.* flower **3.1**
folclórico/a *adj.* folk; folkloric **3.5**
folleto *m.* brochure
forma *f.* shape **3.3**
formulario *m.* form **3.2**
foto(grafía) *f.* photograph **1.1**
francés, francesa *adj. m., f.* French **1.3**
frecuentemente *adv.* frequently
frenos *m., pl.* brakes
frente (frío) *m.* (cold) front **1.5**
fresco/a *adj.* cool
frijoles *m., pl.* beans **2.2**
frío/a *adj.* cold
frito/a *adj.* fried **2.2**
fruta *f.* fruit **2.2**
frutería *f.* fruit store **3.2**
fuera *adv.* outside
fuerte *adj. m., f.* strong **3.3**
fumar *v.* to smoke **3.3**
  (no) fumar *v.* (not) to smoke **3.3**
funcionar *v.* to work **2.5**; to function
fútbol *m.* soccer **1.4**
fútbol americano *m.* football **1.4**
futuro/a *adj.* future
  en el futuro in the future

G

gafas (de sol) *f., pl.* (sun)glasses **1.6**
gafas (oscuras) *f., pl.* (sun)glasses
galleta *f.* cookie **2.3**
ganar *v.* to win **1.4**; to earn (*money*) **3.4**
ganga *f.* bargain **1.6**
garaje *m.* garage; (mechanic's) repair shop **2.5**; garage (*in a house*) **2.6**
garganta *f.* throat **2.4**
gasolina *f.* gasoline **2.5**
gasolinera *f.* gas station **2.5**
gastar *v.* to spend (*money*) **1.6**
gato *m.* cat **3.1**
gemelo/a *m., f.* twin **1.3**
genial *adj.* great **3.4**
gente *f.* people **1.3**
geografía *f.* geography **1.2**
gerente *m., f.* manager **2.2, 3.4**
gimnasio *m.* gymnasium **1.4**
gobierno *m.* government **3.1**
golf *m.* golf **1.4**
gordo/a *adj.* fat **1.3**
grabar *v.* to record **2.5**
gracias *f., pl.* thank you; thanks **1.1**
  Gracias por invitarme. Thanks for inviting me. **2.3**
graduarse (de/en) *v.* to graduate (from/in) **2.3**

grande *adj.* big; large **1.3**
grasa *f.* fat **3.3**
gratis *adj. m., f.* free of charge **3.2**
grave *adj.* grave; serious **2.4**
gripe *f.* flu **2.4**
gris *adj. m., f.* gray **1.6**
gritar *v.* to scream, to shout
grito *m.* scream **1.5**
guantes *m., pl.* gloves **1.6**
guapo/a *adj.* handsome; good-looking **1.3**
guardar *v.* to save (on a computer) **2.5**
guerra *f.* war **3.6**
guía *m., f.* guide
gustar *v.* to be pleasing to; to like **1.2**
  Me gustaría... I would like...
gusto *m.* pleasure **1.1**
  El gusto es mío. The pleasure is mine. **1.1**
  Mucho gusto. Pleased to meet you. **1.1**
  ¡Qué gusto verlo/la! *(form.)* *How nice to see you!* **3.6**
  ¡Qué gusto verte! *(fam.) How nice to see you!* **3.6**

H

haber *(auxiliar) v.* to have (done something) **3.3**
habitación *f.* room **1.5**
  habitación doble double room **1.5**
  habitación individual single room **1.5**
hablar *v.* to talk; to speak **1.2**
hacer *v.* to do; to make **1.4**
  Hace buen tiempo. The weather is good. **1.5**
  Hace (mucho) calor. It's (very) hot. *(weather)* **1.5**
  Hace fresco. It's cool. *(weather)* **1.5**
  Hace (mucho) frío. It's (very) cold. *(weather)* **1.5**
  Hace mal tiempo. The weather is bad. **1.5**
  Hace (mucho) sol. It's (very) sunny. *(weather)* **1.5**
  Hace (mucho) viento. It's (very) windy. *(weather)* **1.5**
hacer cola to stand in line **3.2**
hacer diligencias to run errands **3.2**
hacer ejercicio to exercise **3.3**
hacer ejercicios aeróbicos to do aerobics **3.3**
hacer ejercicios de estiramiento to do stretching exercises **3.3**
hacer el papel (de) to play the role (of) **3.5**
hacer gimnasia to work out **3.3**
hacer juego (con) to match (with) **1.6**

hacer la cama to make the bed **2.6**
hacer las maletas to pack (one's) suitcases **1.5**
hacer quehaceres domésticos to do household chores **2.6**
hacer (wind)surf to (wind) surf **1.5**
hacer turismo to go sightseeing
hacer un viaje to take a trip **1.5**
¿Me harías el honor de casarte conmigo? Would you do me the honor of marrying me? **3.5**
hacia *prep.* toward **3.2**
hambre *f.* hunger
hamburguesa *f.* hamburger **2.2**
hasta *prep.* until **1.6**; toward
  Hasta la vista. See you later. **1.1**
  Hasta luego. See you later. **1.1**
  Hasta mañana. See you tomorrow. **1.1**
  Hasta pronto. See you soon. **1.1**
hasta que *conj.* until **3.1**
hay there is; there are **1.1**
  Hay (mucha) contaminación. It's (very) smoggy.
  Hay (mucha) niebla. It's (very) foggy.
  Hay que It is necessary that
  No hay de qué. You're welcome. **1.1**
  No hay duda de There's no doubt **3.1**
hecho/a *p.p.* done **3.2**
heladería *f.* ice cream shop **3.2**
helado/a *adj.* iced **2.2**
helado *m.* ice cream **2.3**
hermanastro/a *m., f.* stepbrother/stepsister **1.3**
hermano/a *m., f.* brother/sister **1.3**
hermano/a mayor/menor *m., f.* older/younger brother/sister **1.3**
hermanos *m., pl.* siblings (brothers and sisters) **1.3**
hermoso/a *adj.* beautiful **1.6**
hierba *f.* grass **3.1**
hijastro/a *m., f.* stepson/stepdaughter **1.3**
hijo/a *m., f.* son/daughter **1.3**
  hijo/a único/a *m., f.* only child **1.3**
  hijos *m., pl.* children **1.3**
híjole *interj.* wow **1.6**
historia *f.* history **1.2**; story **3.5**
hockey *m.* hockey **1.4**
hola *interj.* hello; hi **1.1**
hombre *m.* man **1.1**
  hombre de negocios *m.* businessman **3.4**
hora *f.* hour **1.1**; the time
horario *m.* schedule **1.2**
horno *m.* oven **2.6**
  horno de microondas *m.* microwave oven **2.6**

horror *m.* horror **3.5**
  de horror horror (genre) **3.5**
hospital *m.* hospital **2.4**
hotel *m.* hotel **1.5**
hoy *adv.* today **1.2**
  hoy día *adv.* nowadays
  Hoy es... Today is... **1.2**
hueco *m.* hole **1.4**
huelga *f.* strike (*labor*) **3.6**
hueso *m.* bone **2.4**
huésped *m., f.* guest **1.5**
huevo *m.* egg **2.2**
humanidades *f., pl.* humanities **1.2**
huracán *m.* hurricane **3.6**

I

ida *f.* one way (*travel*)
idea *f.* idea **3.6**
iglesia *f.* church **1.4**
igualdad *f.* equality **3.6**
igualmente *adv.* likewise **1.1**
impermeable *m.* raincoat **1.6**
importante *adj. m., f.* important **1.3**
importar *v.* to be important to; to matter **2.1**
imposible *adj. m., f.* impossible **3.1**
impresora *f.* printer **2.5**
imprimir *v.* to print **2.5**
improbable *adj. m., f.* improbable **3.1**
impuesto *m.* tax **3.6**
incendio *m.* fire **3.6**
increíble *adj. m., f.* incredible **1.5**
indicar cómo llegar *v.* to give directions **3.2**
individual *adj.* single (*room*) **1.5**
infección *f.* infection **2.4**
informar *v.* to inform **3.6**
informe *m.* report; paper (*written work*) **3.6**
ingeniero/a *m., f.* engineer **1.3**
inglés *m.* English (*language*) **1.2**
inglés, inglesa *adj.* English **1.3**
inodoro *m.* toilet **2.1**
insistir (en) *v.* to insist (on) **2.6**
inspector(a) de aduanas *m., f.* customs inspector **1.5**
inteligente *adj. m., f.* intelligent **1.3**
intento *m.* attempt **2.5**
intercambiar *v.* to exchange
interesante *adj. m., f.* interesting **1.3**
interesar *v.* to be interesting to; to interest **2.1**
internacional *adj. m., f.* international **3.6**
Internet Internet **2.5**
inundación *f.* flood **3.6**
invertir (e:ie) *v.* to invest **3.4**
invierno *m.* winter **1.5**
invitado/a *m., f.* guest **2.3**
invitar *v.* to invite **2.3**
inyección *f.* injection **2.4**
ir *v.* to go **1.4**
  ir a (+ *inf.*) to be going to do something **1.4**

ir de compras to go shopping 1.5
ir de excursión (a las montañas) to go on a hike (in the mountains) 1.4
ir de pesca to go fishing
ir de vacaciones to go on vacation 1.5
ir en autobús to go by bus 1.5
ir en auto(móvil) to go by auto(mobile); to go by car 1.5
ir en avión to go by plane 1.5
ir en barco to go by boat 1.5
ir en metro to go by subway 1.5
ir en moto(cicleta) to go by motorcycle 1.5
ir en taxi to go by taxi 1.5
ir en tren to go by train
irse *v.* to go away; to leave 2.1
italiano/a *adj.* Italian 1.3
izquierda *f.* left 1.2
   a la izquierda de to the left of 1.2

J

jabón *m.* soap 2.1
jamás *adv.* never; not ever 2.1
jamón *m.* ham 2.2
japonés, japonesa *adj.* Japanese 1.3
jardín *m.* garden; yard 2.6
jefe, jefa *m., f.* boss 3.4
jengibre *m.* ginger 2.4
joven *adj. m., f., sing.* (**jóvenes** *pl.*) young 1.3
   joven *m., f., sing.* (**jóvenes** *pl.*) young person 1.1
joyería *f.* jewelry store 3.2
jubilarse *v.* to retire (*from work*) 2.3
juego *m.* game
jueves *m., sing.* Thursday 1.2
jugador(a) *m., f.* player 1.4
jugar (u:ue) *v.* to play 1.4
   jugar a las cartas *f., pl.* to play cards 1.5
jugo *m.* juice 2.2
   jugo de fruta *m.* fruit juice 2.2
julio *m.* July 1.5
jungla *f.* jungle 3.1
junio *m.* June 1.5
juntos/as *adj.* together 2.3
juventud *f.* youth 2.3

K

kilómetro *m.* kilometer 2.5

L

la *f., sing., def. art.* the 1.1; *f., sing., d.o. pron.* her, it, *form.* you 1.5
laboratorio *m.* laboratory 1.2
lago *m.* lake 3.1
lámpara *f.* lamp 2.6

lana *f.* wool 1.6
langosta *f.* lobster 2.2
lápiz *m.* pencil 1.1
largo/a *adj.* long 1.6
las *f., pl., def. art.* the 1.1; *f., pl., d.o. pron.* them; you 1.5
lástima *f.* shame 3.1
lastimarse *v.* to injure oneself 2.4
   lastimarse el pie to injure one's foot 2.4
lata *f.* (*tin*) can 3.1
lavabo *m.* sink 2.1
lavadora *f.* washing machine 2.6
lavandería *f.* laundromat 3.2
lavaplatos *m., sing.* dishwasher 2.6
lavar *v.* to wash 2.6
   lavar (el suelo, los platos) to wash (the floor, the dishes) 2.6
lavarse *v.* to wash oneself 2.1
   lavarse la cara to wash one's face 2.1
   lavarse las manos to wash one's hands 2.1
le *sing., i.o. pron.* to/for him, her, *form.* you 1.6
   Le presento a... *form.* I would like to introduce you to (name). 1.1
lección *f.* lesson 1.1
leche *f.* milk 2.2
lechuga *f.* lettuce 2.2
leer *v.* to read 1.3
   leer el correo electrónico to read e-mail 1.4
   leer un periódico to read a newspaper 1.4
   leer una revista to read a magazine 1.4
leído/a *p.p.* read 3.2
lejos de *prep.* far from 1.2
lengua *f.* language 1.2
   lenguas extranjeras *f., pl.* foreign languages 1.2
lentes de contacto *m., pl.* contact lenses
   lentes (de sol) (sun)glasses
lento/a *adj.* slow 2.5
les *pl., i.o. pron.* to/for them, you 1.6
letrero *m.* sign 3.2
levantar *v.* to lift 3.3
   levantar pesas to lift weights 3.3
levantarse *v.* to get up 2.1
ley *f.* law 3.1
libertad *f.* liberty; freedom 3.6
libre *adj. m., f.* free 1.4
librería *f.* bookstore 1.2
libro *m.* book 1.2
licencia de conducir *f.* driver's license 2.5
limón *m.* lemon 2.2
limpiar *v.* to clean 2.6
   limpiar la casa *v.* to clean the house 2.6

limpio/a *adj.* clean 1.5
línea *f.* line 1.4
listo/a *adj.* ready; smart 1.5
literatura *f.* literature 1.2
llamar *v.* to call 2.5
   llamar por teléfono to call on the phone
llamarse *v.* to be called; to be named 2.1
llanta *f.* tire 2.5
llave *f.* key 1.5; wrench 2.5
llegada *f.* arrival 1.5
llegar *v.* to arrive 1.2
llenar *v.* to fill 2.5, 3.2
   llenar el tanque to fill the tank 2.5
   llenar (un formulario) to fill out (a form) 3.2
lleno/a *adj.* full 2.5
llevar *v.* to carry 1.2; to wear; to take 1.6
   llevar una vida sana to lead a healthy lifestyle 3.3
   llevarse bien/mal (con) to get along well/badly (with) 2.3
llorar *v.* to cry 3.3
llover (o:ue) *v.* to rain 1.5
   Llueve. It's raining. 1.5
lluvia *f.* rain
lo *m., sing. d.o. pron.* him, it, *form.* you 1.5
   ¡Lo he pasado de película! I've had a fantastic time! 3.6
   lo mejor the best (thing)
   lo que that which; what 2.6
   Lo siento. I'm sorry. 1.1
loco/a *adj.* crazy 1.6
locutor(a) *m., f.* (TV or radio) announcer 3.6
lodo *m.* mud
los *m., pl., def. art.* the 1.1; *m. pl., d.o. pron.* them, you 1.5
luchar (contra/por) *v.* to fight; to struggle (against/for) 3.6
luego *adv.* then 2.1; later 1.1
lugar *m.* place 1.2, 1.4
luna *f.* moon 3.1
lunares *m.* polka dots
lunes *m., sing.* Monday 1.2
luz *f.* light; electricity 2.6

M

madrastra *f.* stepmother 1.3
madre *f.* mother 1.3
madurez *f.* maturity; middle age 2.3
maestro/a *m., f.* teacher 3.4
magnífico/a *adj.* magnificent 1.5
maíz *m.* corn 2.2
mal, malo/a *adj.* bad 1.3
maleta *f.* suitcase 1.1
mamá *f.* mom
mandar *v.* to order 2.6; to send; to mail 3.2
manejar *v.* to drive 2.5

manera *f.* way
mano *f.* hand 1.1
manta *f.* blanket 2.6
mantener *v.* to maintain 3.3
  mantenerse en forma to stay in shape 3.3
mantequilla *f.* butter 2.2
manzana *f.* apple 2.2
mañana *f.* morning, a.m. 1.1; tomorrow 1.1
mapa *m.* map 1.1, 1.2
maquillaje *m.* makeup 2.1
maquillarse *v.* to put on makeup 2.1
mar *m.* sea 1.5
maravilloso/a *adj.* marvelous 1.5
mareado/a *adj.* dizzy; nauseated 2.4
margarina *f.* margarine 2.2
mariscos *m., pl.* shellfish 2.2
marrón *adj. m., f.* brown 1.6
martes *m., sing.* Tuesday 1.2
marzo *m.* March 1.5
más *adv.* more 1.2
  más de (+ *number*) more than 2.2
  más tarde later (on) 2.1
  más... que more... than 2.2
masaje *m.* massage 3.3
matemáticas *f., pl.* mathematics 1.2
materia *f.* course 1.2
matrimonio *m.* marriage 2.3
máximo/a *adj.* maximum 2.5
mayo *m.* May 1.5
mayonesa *f.* mayonnaise 2.2
mayor *adj.* older 1.3
  el/la mayor *adj.* oldest 2.2
me *sing., d.o. pron.* me 1.5; *sing. i.o. pron.* to/for me 1.6
  Me gusta... I like... 1.2
  Me gustaría(n)... I would like... 3.3
  Me llamo... My name is... 1.1
  Me muero por... I'm dying to (for)...
mecánico/a *m., f.* mechanic 2.5
mediano/a *adj.* medium
medianoche *f.* midnight 1.1
medias *f., pl.* pantyhose, stockings 1.6
medicamento *m.* medication 2.4
medicina *f.* medicine 2.4
médico/a *m., f.* doctor 1.3; *adj.* medical 2.4
medio/a *adj.* half 1.3
  medio ambiente *m.* environment 3.1
  medio/a hermano/a *m., f.* half-brother/half-sister 1.3
  mediodía *m.* noon 1.1
  medios de comunicación *m., pl.* means of communication; media 3.6
  y media thirty minutes past the hour (time) 1.1

mejor *adj.* better 2.2
  el/la mejor *m., f.* the best 2.2
mejorar *v.* to improve 3.1
melocotón *m.* peach 2.2
menor *adj.* younger 1.3
  el/la menor *m., f.* youngest 2.2
menos *adv.* less 2.4
  menos cuarto..., menos quince... quarter to... (*time*) 1.1
  menos de (+ *number*) fewer than 2.2
  menos... que less... than 2.2
mensaje *m.* **de texto** text message 2.5
mensaje electrónico *m.* e-mail message 1.4
mentira *f.* lie 1.4
menú *m.* menu 2.2
mercado *m.* market 1.6
  mercado al aire libre open-air market 1.6
merendar (e:ie) *v.* to snack 2.2; to have an afternoon snack
merienda *f.* afternoon snack 3.3
mes *m.* month 1.5
mesa *f.* table 1.2
mesita *f.* end table 2.6
  mesita de noche night stand 2.6
meterse en problemas *v.* to get into trouble 3.1
metro *m.* subway 1.5
mexicano/a *adj.* Mexican 1.3
mí *pron., obj. of prep.* me 2.3
mi(s) *poss. adj.* my 1.3
microonda *f.* microwave 2.6
  horno de microondas *m.* microwave oven 2.6
miedo *m.* fear
miel *f.* honey 2.4
mientras *conj.* while 2.4
miércoles *m., sing.* Wednesday 1.2
mil *m.* one thousand 1.2
  mil millones billion
milla *f.* mile
millón *m.* million 1.2
millones (de) *m.* millions (of)
mineral *m.* mineral 3.3
minuto *m.* minute
mío(s)/a(s) *poss.* my; (of) mine 2.5
mirar *v.* to look (at); to watch 1.2
  mirar (la) televisión to watch television 1.2
mismo/a *adj.* same 1.3
mochila *f.* backpack 1.2
moda *f.* fashion 1.6
moderno/a *adj.* modern 3.5
molestar *v.* to bother; to annoy 2.1
monitor *m.* (computer) monitor 2.5
  monitor(a) *m., f.* trainer
mono *m.* monkey 3.1
montaña *f.* mountain 1.4
montar *v.* **a caballo** to ride a horse 1.5

montón: un montón de a lot of 1.4
monumento *m.* monument 1.4
morado/a *adj.* purple 1.6
moreno/a *adj.* brunet(te) 1.3
morir (o:ue) *v.* to die 2.2
mostrar (o:ue) *v.* to show 1.4
moto(cicleta) *f.* motorcycle 1.5
motor *m.* motor
muchacho/a *m., f.* boy/girl 1.3
mucho/a *adj.*, a lot of; much; many 1.3
  (Muchas) gracias. Thank you (very much); Thanks (a lot). 1.1
  muchas veces *adv.* a lot; many times 2.4
  Mucho gusto. Pleased to meet you. 1.1
mudarse *v.* to move (from one house to another) 2.6
muebles *m., pl.* furniture 2.6
muerte *f.* death 2.3
muerto/a *p.p.* died 3.2
mujer *f.* woman 1.1
  mujer de negocios *f.* business woman 3.4
  mujer policía *f.* female police officer
multa *f.* fine
mundial *adj. m., f.* worldwide
mundo *m.* world 2.2
muro *m.* wall 3.3
músculo *m.* muscle 3.3
museo *m.* museum 1.4
música *f.* music 1.2, 3.5
musical *adj. m., f.* musical 3.5
músico/a *m., f.* musician 3.5
muy *adv.* very 1.1
  (Muy) bien, gracias. (Very) well, thanks. 1.1

N

nacer *v.* to be born 2.3
nacimiento *m.* birth 2.3
nacional *adj. m., f.* national 3.6
nacionalidad *f.* nationality 1.1
nada nothing 1.1; not anything 2.1
  nada mal not bad at all 1.5
nadar *v.* to swim 1.4
nadie *pron.* no one, nobody, not anyone 2.1
naranja *f.* orange 2.2
nariz *f.* nose 2.4
natación *f.* swimming 1.4
natural *adj. m., f.* natural 3.1
naturaleza *f.* nature 3.1
navegador *m.* **GPS** GPS 2.5
navegar (en Internet) *v.* to surf (the Internet) 2.5
Navidad *f.* Christmas 2.3
necesario/a *adj.* necessary 2.6
necesitar (+ *inf.*) *v.* to need 1.2
negar (e:ie) *v.* to deny 3.1
  no negar (e:ie) *v.* not to deny 3.1

negocios *m.*, *pl.* business; commerce **3.4**
negro/a *adj.* black **1.6**
nervioso/a *adj.* nervous **1.5**
nevar (e:ie) *v.* to snow **1.5**
  Nieva. It's snowing. **1.5**
ni…ni neither… nor **2.1**
niebla *f.* fog
nieto/a *m.*, *f.* grandson/ granddaughter **1.3**
nieve *f.* snow
ningún, ninguno/a(s) *adj.* no; none; not any **2.1**
niñez *f.* childhood **2.3**
niño/a *m.*, *f.* child **1.3**
no no; not **1.1**
  ¿no? right? **1.1**
  no cabe duda de there is no doubt **3.1**
  no es seguro it's not certain **3.1**
  no es verdad it's not true **3.1**
  No está nada mal. It's not bad at all. **1.5**
  no estar de acuerdo to disagree
  No estoy seguro. I'm not sure.
  no hay there is not; there are not **1.1**
  No hay de qué. You're welcome. **1.1**
  no hay duda de there is no doubt **3.1**
  ¡No me diga(s)! You don't say!
  No me gustan nada. I don't like them at all. **1.2**
  no muy bien not very well **1.1**
  No quiero. I don't want to. **1.4**
  No sé. I don't know.
  No te preocupes. (*fam.*) Don't worry. **2.1**
  no tener razón to be wrong **1.3**
noche *f.* night **1.1**
nombre *m.* name **1.1**
norte *m.* north **3.2**
norteamericano/a *adj.* (North) American **1.3**
nos *pl.*, *d.o. pron.* us **1.5**; *pl.*, *i.o. pron.* to/for us **1.6**
  Nos vemos. See you. **1.1**
nosotros/as *sub. pron.* we **1.1**; *obj. pron.* us
noticia *f.* news **2.5**
noticias *f.*, *pl.* news **3.6**
noticiero *m.* newscast **3.6**
novecientos/as nine hundred **1.2**
noveno/a *adj.* ninth **1.5**
noventa ninety **1.2**
noviembre *m.* November **1.5**
novio/a *m.*, *f.* boyfriend/ girlfriend **1.3**
nube *f.* cloud **3.1**
nublado/a *adj.* cloudy **1.5**
  Está (muy) nublado. It's very cloudy. **1.5**
nuclear *adj. m. f.* nuclear **3.1**

nuera *f.* daughter-in-law **1.3**
nuestro(s)/a(s) *poss. adj.* our **1.3**; our, (of) ours **2.5**
nueve nine **1.1**
nuevo/a *adj.* new **1.6**
número *m.* number **1.1**; (shoe) size **1.6**
nunca *adv.* never; not ever **2.1**
nutrición *f.* nutrition **3.3**
nutricionista *m.*, *f.* nutritionist **3.3**

O

o or **2.1**
o… o; either… or **2.1**
obedecer *v.* to obey **3.6**
obra *f.* work (*of art, literature, music, etc.*) **3.5**
  obra maestra *f.* masterpiece **3.5**
obtener *v.* to obtain; to get **3.4**
obvio/a *adj.* obvious **3.1**
océano *m.* ocean
ochenta eighty **1.2**
ocho eight **1.1**
ochocientos/as eight hundred **1.2**
octavo/a *adj.* eighth **1.5**
octubre *m.* October **1.5**
ocupación *f.* occupation **3.4**
ocupado/a *adj.* busy **1.5**
ocurrir *v.* to occur; to happen **3.6**
odiar *v.* to hate **2.3**
oeste *m.* west **3.2**
oferta *f.* offer
oficina *f.* office **2.6**
oficio *m.* trade **3.4**
ofrecer *v.* to offer **1.6**
oído *m.* (sense of) hearing; inner ear **2.4**
oído/a *p.p.* heard **3.2**
oír *v.* to hear **1.4**
ojalá (que) *interj.* I hope (that); I wish (that) **3.1**
ojo *m.* eye **2.4**
olvidar *v.* to forget **2.4**
once eleven **1.1**
ópera *f.* opera **3.5**
operación *f.* operation **2.4**
ordenado/a *adj.* orderly **1.5**
ordinal *adj.* ordinal (*number*)
oreja *f.* (outer) ear **2.4**
organizarse *v.* to organize oneself **2.6**
orquesta *f.* orchestra **3.5**
ortografía *f.* spelling
ortográfico/a *adj.* spelling
os *fam.*, *pl. d.o. pron.* you **1.5**; *fam.*, *pl. i.o. pron.* to/for you **1.6**
otoño *m.* autumn **1.5**
otro/a *adj.* other; another **1.6**
  otra vez again

P

paciente *m.*, *f.* patient **2.4**
padrastro *m.* stepfather **1.3**
padre *m.* father **1.3**
padres *m.*, *pl.* parents **1.3**

pagar *v.* to pay **1.6**
  pagar a plazos to pay in installments **3.2**
  pagar al contado to pay in cash **3.2**
  pagar en efectivo to pay in cash **3.2**
  pagar la cuenta to pay the bill
página *f.* page **2.5**
  página principal *f.* home page **2.5**
país *m.* country **1.1**
paisaje *m.* landscape **1.5**
pájaro *m.* bird **3.1**
palabra *f.* word **1.1**
paleta helada *f.* popsicle **1.4**
pálido/a *adj.* pale **3.2**
pan *m.* bread **2.2**
  pan tostado *m.* toasted bread **2.2**
panadería *f.* bakery **3.2**
pantalla *f.* screen **2.5**
  pantalla táctil *f.* touch screen
pantalones *m.*, *pl.* pants **1.6**
  pantalones cortos *m.*, *pl.* shorts **1.6**
pantuflas *f.* slippers **2.1**
papa *f.* potato **2.2**
  papas fritas *f.*, *pl.* fried potatoes; French fries **2.2**
papá *m.* dad
  papás *m.*, *pl.* parents
papel *m.* paper **1.2**; role **3.5**
papelera *f.* wastebasket **1.2**
paquete *m.* package **3.2**
par *m.* pair **1.6**
  par de zapatos pair of shoes **1.6**
para *prep.* for; in order to; by; used for; considering **2.5**
  para que *conj.* so that **3.1**
parabrisas *m.*, *sing.* windshield **2.5**
parar *v.* to stop **2.5**
parecer *v.* to seem **1.6**
pared *f.* wall **2.6**
pareja *f.* (married) couple; partner **2.3**
parientes *m.*, *pl.* relatives **1.3**
parque *m.* park **1.4**
párrafo *m.* paragraph
parte: de parte de on behalf of **2.5**
partido *m.* game; match (*sports*) **1.4**
pasado/a *adj.* last; past **1.6**
  pasado *p.p.* passed
pasaje *m.* ticket **1.5**
  pasaje de ida y vuelta *m.* roundtrip ticket **1.5**
pasajero/a *m.*, *f.* passenger **1.1**
pasaporte *m.* passport **1.5**
pasar *v.* to go through
  pasar la aspiradora to vacuum **2.6**
  pasar por la aduana to go through customs
  pasar tiempo to spend time
  pasarlo bien/mal to have a good/bad time **2.3**

pasatiempo *m.* pastime; hobby **1.4**

pasear *v.* to take a walk; to stroll **1.4**

   pasear en bicicleta to ride a bicycle **1.4**

   pasear por to walk around

pasillo *m.* hallway **2.6**

pasta *f.* **de dientes** toothpaste **2.1**

pastel *m.* cake; pie **2.3**

   pastel de chocolate *m.* chocolate cake **2.3**

   pastel de cumpleaños *m.* birthday cake

pastelería *f.* pastry shop **3.2**

pastilla *f.* pill; tablet **2.4**

patata *f.* potato **2.2**

   patatas fritas *f., pl.* fried potatoes; French fries **2.2**

patinar (en línea) *v.* to (inline) skate **1.4**

patineta *f.* skateboard **1.4**

patio *m.* patio; yard **2.6**

pavo *m.* turkey **2.2**

paz *f.* peace **3.6**

pedir (e:i) *v.* to ask for; to request **1.4**; to order (*food*) **2.2**

   pedir prestado *v.* to borrow **3.2**

   pedir un préstamo *v.* to apply for a loan **3.2**

   Todos me dijeron que te pidiera una disculpa de su parte. They all told me to ask you to excuse them/forgive them. **3.6**

peinarse *v.* to comb one's hair **2.1**

película *f.* movie **1.4**

peligro *m.* danger **3.1**

peligroso/a *adj.* dangerous **3.6**

pelirrojo/a *adj.* red-haired **1.3**

pelo *m.* hair **2.1**

pelota *f.* ball **1.4**

peluquería *f.* beauty salon **3.2**

peluquero/a *m., f.* hairdresser **3.4**

penicilina *f.* penicillin

pensar (e:ie) *v.* to think **1.4**

   pensar (+ *inf.*) *v.* to intend to; to plan to (*do something*) **1.4**

   pensar en *v.* to think about **1.4**

pensión *f.* boardinghouse

peor *adj.* worse **2.2**

   el/la peor *adj.* the worst **2.2**

pequeño/a *adj.* small **1.3**

pera *f.* pear **2.2**

perder (e:ie) *v.* to lose; to miss **1.4**

perdido/a *adj.* lost **3.1, 3.2**

Perdón. Pardon me.; Excuse me. **1.1**

perezoso/a *adj.* lazy

perfecto/a *adj.* perfect **1.5**

periódico *m.* newspaper **1.4**

periodismo *m.* journalism **1.2**

periodista *m., f.* journalist **1.3**

permiso *m.* permission

pero *conj.* but **1.2**

perro *m.* dog **3.1**

persona *f.* person **1.3**

personaje *m.* character **3.5**

   personaje principal *m.* main character **3.5**

pesas *f. pl.* weights **3.3**

pesca *f.* fishing

pescadería *f.* fish market **3.2**

pescado *m.* fish (*cooked*) **2.2**

pescar *v.* to fish **1.5**

peso *m.* weight **3.3**

pez *m., sing.* (**peces** *pl.*) fish (*live*) **3.1**

pie *m.* foot **2.4**

piedra *f.* stone **3.1**

pierna *f.* leg **2.4**

pimienta *f.* black pepper **2.2**

pintar *v.* to paint **3.5**

pintor(a) *m., f.* painter **3.4**

pintura *f.* painting; picture **2.6, 3.5**

piña *f.* pineapple

piscina *f.* swimming pool **1.4**

piso *m.* floor (*of a building*) **1.5**

pizarra *f.* blackboard **1.2**

placer *m.* pleasure

planchar la ropa *v.* to iron the clothes **2.6**

planes *m., pl.* plans

planta *f.* plant **3.1**

   planta baja *f.* ground floor **1.5**

plástico *m.* plastic **3.1**

plato *m.* dish (*in a meal*) **2.2**; *m.* plate **2.6**

   plato principal *m.* main dish **2.2**

playa *f.* beach **1.5**

plaza *f.* city or town square **1.4**

plazos *m., pl.* periods; time **3.2**

pluma *f.* pen **1.2**

plumero *m.* duster **2.6**

población *f.* population **3.1**

pobre *adj. m., f.* poor **1.6**

pobrecito/a *adj.* poor thing **1.3**

pobreza *f.* poverty

poco *adv.* little **1.5, 2.4**

poder (o:ue) *v.* to be able to; can **1.4**

   ¿Podría pedirte algo? Could I ask you something? **3.5**

   ¿Puedo dejar un recado? May I leave a message? **2.5**

poema *m.* poem **3.5**

poesía *f.* poetry **3.5**

poeta *m., f.* poet **3.5**

policía *f.* police (force) **2.5**

política *f.* politics **3.6**

político/a *m., f.* politician **3.4**; *adj.* political **3.6**

pollo *m.* chicken **2.2**

   pollo asado *m.* roast chicken **2.2**

poner *v.* to put; to place **1.4**; to turn on (*electrical appliances*) **2.5**

   poner la mesa to set the table **2.6**

   poner una inyección to give an injection **2.4**

   ponerle el nombre to name someone/something **2.3**

ponerse (+ *adj.*) *v.* to become (+ *adj.*) **2.1**; to put on **2.1**

por *prep.* in exchange for; for; by; in; through; around; along; during; because of; on account of; on behalf of; in search of; by way of; by means of **2.5**

   por aquí around here **2.5**

   por ejemplo for example **2.5**

   por eso that's why; therefore **2.5**

   por favor please **1.1**

   por fin finally **2.5**

   por la mañana in the morning **2.1**

   por la noche at night **2.1**

   por la tarde in the afternoon **2.1**

   por lo menos *adv.* at least **2.4**

   ¿por qué? why? **1.2**

   Por supuesto. Of course.

   por teléfono by phone; on the phone

   por último finally **2.1**

porque *conj.* because **1.2**

portátil *adj.* portable **2.5**

portero/a *m., f.* doorman/ doorwoman **1.1**

porvenir *m.* future **3.4**

   por el porvenir for/to the future **3.4**

posesivo/a *adj.* possessive

posible *adj.* possible **3.1**

   es posible it's possible **3.1**

   no es posible it's not possible **3.1**

postal *f.* postcard

postre *m.* dessert **2.3**

practicar *v.* to practice **1.2**

   practicar deportes *m., pl.* to play sports **1.4**

precio (fijo) *m.* (fixed; set) price **1.6**

preferir (e:ie) *v.* to prefer **1.4**

pregunta *f.* question

preguntar *v.* to ask (*a question*) **1.2**

premio *m.* prize; award **3.5**

prender *v.* to turn on **2.5**

prensa *f.* press **3.6**

preocupado/a (por) *adj.* worried (about) **1.5**

preocuparse (por) *v.* to worry (about) **2.1**

preparar *v.* to prepare **1.2**

preposición *f.* preposition

presentación *f.* introduction

presentar *v.* to introduce; to present **3.5**; to put on (*a performance*) **3.5**

   Le presento a... I would like to introduce you to (name). (*form.*) **1.1**

   Te presento a... I would like to introduce you to (name). (*fam.*) **1.1**

presiones *f., pl.* pressures 3.3
prestado/a *adj.* borrowed
préstamo *m.* loan 3.2
prestar *v.* to lend; to loan 1.6
primavera *f.* spring 1.5
primer, primero/a *adj.* first 1.5
primero *adv.* first 1.2
primo/a *m., f.* cousin 1.3
principal *adj. m., f.* main 2.2
prisa *f.* haste
  darse prisa *v.* to hurry; to rush 3.3
probable *adj. m., f.* probable 3.1
  es probable it's probable 3.1
  no es probable it's not probable 3.1
probar (o:ue) *v.* to taste; to try 2.2
probarse (o:ue) *v.* to try on 2.1
problema *m.* problem 1.1
profesión *f.* profession 1.3; 3.4
profesor(a) *m., f.* teacher 1.1, 1.2
programa *m.* program 1.1
  programa de computación *m.* software 2.5
  programa de entrevistas *m.* talk show 3.5
  programa de realidad *m.* reality show 3.5
programador(a) *m., f.* computer programmer 1.3
prohibir *v.* to prohibit 2.4; to forbid
pronombre *m.* pronoun
pronto *adv.* soon 2.4
propina *f.* tip 2.2
propio/a *adj.* own
proteger *v.* to protect 3.1
proteína *f.* protein 3.3
próximo/a *adj.* next 1.3, 3.4
proyecto *m.* project 2.5
prueba *f.* test; quiz 1.2
psicología *f.* psychology 1.2
psicólogo/a *m., f.* psychologist 3.4
publicar *v.* to publish 3.5
público *m.* audience 3.5
pueblo *m.* town
puerta *f.* door 1.2
puertorriqueño/a *adj.* Puerto Rican 1.3
pues *conj.* well
puesto *m.* position; job 3.4
puesto/a *p.p.* put 3.2
puro/a *adj.* pure 3.1

Q

que *pron.* that; which; who 2.6
  ¿En qué...? In which...?
  ¡Qué...! How...!
  ¡Qué dolor! What pain!
  ¡Qué ropa más bonita! What pretty clothes! 1.6
  ¡Qué sorpresa! What a surprise!
  ¿qué? what? 1.1, 1.2

¿Qué día es hoy? What day is it? 1.2
¿Qué hay de nuevo? What's new? 1.1
¿Qué hora es? What time is it? 1.1
¿Qué les parece? What do you (*pl.*) think?
¿Qué onda? What's up? 3.2
¿Qué pasa? What's happening? What's going on? 1.1
¿Qué pasó? What happened?
¿Qué precio tiene? What is the price?
¿Qué tal...? How are you?; How is it going? 1.1
¿Qué talla lleva/usa? What size do you wear? 1.6
¿Qué tiempo hace? How's the weather? 1.5
quedar *v.* to be left over; to fit (*clothing*) 2.1; to be located 3.2
quedarse *v.* to stay; to remain 2.1
quehaceres domésticos *m., pl.* household chores 2.6
quemar (un CD/DVD) *v.* to burn (a CD/DVD)
querer (e:ie) *v.* to want; to love 1.4
queso *m.* cheese 2.2
quien(es) *pron.* who; whom; that 2.6
¿quién(es)? who?; whom? 1.1, 1.2
  ¿Quién es...? Who is...? 1.1
  ¿Quién habla? Who is speaking/calling? (*telephone*) 2.5
química *f.* chemistry 1.2
quince fifteen 1.1
  menos quince quarter to (time) 1.1
  y quince quarter after (time) 1.1
quinceañera *f.* young woman celebrating her fifteenth birthday 2.3
quinientos/as five hundred 1.2
quinto/a *adj.* fifth 1.5
quisiera *v.* I would like
quitar el polvo *v.* to dust 2.6
quitar la mesa *v.* to clear the table 2.6
quitarse *v.* to take off 2.1
quizás *adv.* maybe 1.5

R

racismo *m.* racism 3.6
radio *f.* radio (*medium*) 1.2; *m.* radio (set) 2.5
radiografía *f.* X-ray 2.4
rápido *adv.* quickly 2.4
ratón *m.* mouse 2.5
ratos libres *m., pl.* spare (free) time 1.4
raya *f.* stripe
razón *f.* reason
rebaja *f.* sale 1.6
receta *f.* prescription 2.4
recetar *v.* to prescribe 2.4

recibir *v.* to receive 1.3
reciclaje *m.* recycling 3.1
reciclar *v.* to recycle 3.1
recién casado/a *m., f.* newlywed 2.3
recoger *v.* to pick up 3.1
recomendar (e:ie) *v.* to recommend 2.2, 2.6
recordar (o:ue) *v.* to remember 1.4
recorrer *v.* to tour an area
recorrido *m.* tour 3.1
recuperar *v.* to recover 2.5
recurso *m.* resource 3.1
  recurso natural *m.* natural resource 3.1
red *f.* network; Web 2.5
reducir *v.* to reduce 3.1
refresco *m.* soft drink 2.2
refrigerador *m.* refrigerator 2.6
regalar *v.* to give (a gift) 2.3
regalo *m.* gift 1.6
regatear *v.* to bargain 1.6
región *f.* region; area
regresar *v.* to return 1.2
regular *adv.* so-so; OK 1.1
reído *p.p.* laughed 3.2
reírse (e:i) *v.* to laugh 2.3
relaciones *f., pl.* relationships
relajarse *v.* to relax 2.3
reloj *m.* clock; watch 1.2
renovable *adj.* renewable 3.1
renunciar (a) *v.* to resign (from) 3.4
repetir (e:i) *v.* to repeat 1.4
reportaje *m.* report 3.6
reportero/a *m., f.* reporter 3.4
representante *m., f.* representative 3.6
reproductor de CD *m.* CD player 2.5
reproductor de DVD *m.* DVD player 2.5
reproductor de MP3 *m.* MP3 player 2.5
resfriado *m.* cold (*illness*) 2.4
residencia estudiantil *f.* dormitory 1.2
resolver (o:ue) *v.* to resolve; to solve 3.1
respirar *v.* to breathe 3.1
responsable *adj.* responsible 2.2
respuesta *f.* answer
restaurante *m.* restaurant 1.4
resuelto/a *p.p.* resolved 3.2
reunión *f.* meeting 3.4
revisar *v.* to check 2.5
  revisar el aceite *v.* to check the oil 2.5
revista *f.* magazine 1.4
rico/a *adj.* rich 1.6; *adj.* tasty; delicious 2.2
ridículo/a *adj.* ridiculous 3.1
río *m.* river 3.1
rodilla *f.* knee 2.4
rogar (o:ue) *v.* to beg; to plead 2.6

rojo/a *adj.* red 1.6
romántico/a *adj.* romantic 3.5
romper *v.* to break 2.4
   romperse la pierna *v.* to break one's leg 2.4
   romper (con) *v.* to break up (with) 2.3
ropa *f.* clothing; clothes 1.6
   ropa interior *f.* underwear 1.6
rosado/a *adj.* pink 1.6
roto/a *adj.* broken 3.2
rubio/a *adj.* blond(e) 1.3
ruso/a *adj.* Russian 1.3
rutina *f.* routine 2.1
   rutina diaria *f.* daily routine 2.1

S

sábado *m.* Saturday 1.2
saber *v.* to know; to know how 1.6
   saber a to taste like 2.2
sabrosísimo/a *adj.* extremely delicious 2.2
sabroso/a *adj.* tasty; delicious 2.2
sacar *v.* to take out
   sacar buenas notas to get good grades 1.2
   sacar fotos to take photos 1.5
   sacar la basura to take out the trash 2.6
   sacar(se) un diente to have a tooth removed 2.4
sacudir *v.* to dust 2.6
   sacudir los muebles to dust the furniture 2.6
sal *f.* salt 2.2
sala *f.* living room 2.6; room
   sala de emergencia(s) emergency room 2.4
salario *m.* salary 3.4
salchicha *f.* sausage 2.2
salida *f.* departure; exit 1.5
salir *v.* to leave 1.4; to go out
   salir con to go out with; to date 1.4, 2.3
   salir de to leave from 1.4
   salir para to leave for (*a place*) 1.4
salmón *m.* salmon 2.2
salón de belleza *m.* beauty salon 3.2
salud *f.* health 2.4
saludable *adj.* healthy 2.4
saludar(se) *v.* to greet (each other) 2.5
saludo *m.* greeting 1.1
   saludos a... greetings to... 1.1
sandalia *f.* sandal 1.6
sandía *f.* watermelon
sándwich *m.* sandwich 2.2
sano/a *adj.* healthy 2.4

se *ref. pron.* himself, herself, itself, *form.* yourself, themselves, yourselves 2.1
se *impersonal* one 2.4
   Se hizo... He/she/it became...
secadora *f.* clothes dryer 2.6
secarse *v.* to dry (oneself) 2.1
sección de (no) fumar *f.* (non) smoking section 2.2
secretario/a *m., f.* secretary 3.4
secuencia *f.* sequence
sed *f.* thirst
seda *f.* silk 1.6
sedentario/a *adj.* sedentary; related to sitting 3.3
seguir (e:i) *v.* to follow; to continue 1.4
según according to
segundo/a *adj.* second 1.5
seguro/a *adj.* sure; safe; confident 1.5
seis six 1.1
seiscientos/as six hundred 1.2
sello *m.* stamp 3.2
selva *f.* jungle 3.1
semáforo *m.* traffic light 3.2
semana *f.* week 1.2
   fin *m.* **de semana** weekend 1.4
   semana *f.* **pasada** last week 1.6
semestre *m.* semester 1.2
sendero *m.* trail; path 3.1
sentarse (e:ie) *v.* to sit down 2.1
sentir (e:ie) *v.* to be sorry; to regret 3.1
sentirse (e:ie) *v.* to feel 2.1
señor (Sr.); don *m.* Mr.; sir 1.1
señora (Sra.); doña *f.* Mrs.; ma'am 1.1
señorita (Srta.) *f.* Miss 1.1
separado/a *adj.* separated 2.3
separarse (de) *v.* to separate (from) 2.3
septiembre *m.* September 1.5
séptimo/a *adj.* seventh 1.5
ser *v.* to be 1.1
   ser aficionado/a (a) to be a fan (of)
   ser alérgico/a (a) to be allergic (to) 2.4
   ser gratis to be free of charge 3.2
serio/a *adj.* serious
servicio *m.* service 3.3
servilleta *f.* napkin 2.6
servir (e:i) *v.* to serve 2.2; to help 1.5
sesenta sixty 1.2
setecientos/as seven hundred 1.2
setenta seventy 1.2
sexismo *m.* sexism 3.6
sexto/a *adj.* sixth 1.5
sí *adv.* yes 1.1
si *conj.* if 1.4
SIDA *m.* AIDS 3.6
siempre *adv.* always 2.1
siete seven 1.1

silla *f.* seat 1.2
sillón *m.* armchair 2.6
similar *adj. m., f.* similar
simpático/a *adj.* nice; likeable 1.3
sin *prep.* without 3.1
   sin duda without a doubt
   sin embargo however
   sin que *conj.* without 3.1
sino but (rather) 2.1
síntoma *m.* symptom 2.4
sitio *m.* place 1.3
sitio *m.* **web** website 2.5
situado/a *p.p.* located
sobre *m.* envelope 3.2; *prep.* on; over 1.2
   sobre todo above all 3.1
(sobre)población *f.* (over)population 3.1
sobrino/a *m., f.* nephew/niece 1.3
sociología *f.* sociology 1.2
sofá *m.* couch; sofa 2.6
sol *m.* sun 3.1
solar *adj. m., f.* solar 3.1
soldado *m., f.* soldier 3.6
soleado/a *adj.* sunny
solicitar *v.* to apply (*for a job*) 3.4
solicitud (de trabajo) *f.* (job) application 3.4
sólo *adv.* only 1.6
solo/a *adj.* alone
soltero/a *adj.* single 2.3
solución *f.* solution 3.1
sombrero *m.* hat 1.6
Son las dos. It's two o'clock. 1.1
sonar (o:ue) *v.* to ring 2.5
sonreído *p.p.* smiled 3.2
sonreír (e:i) *v.* to smile 2.3
sopa *f.* soup 2.2
sorprender *v.* to surprise 2.3
sorpresa *f.* surprise 2.3
sótano *m.* basement; cellar 2.6
soy I am 1.1
   Soy de... I'm from... 1.1
su(s) *poss. adj.* his; her; its; *form.* your; their 1.3
subir(se) a *v.* to get on/into (*a vehicle*) 2.5
sucio/a *adj.* dirty 1.5
sudar *v.* to sweat 3.3
suegro/a *m., f.* father-in-law/ mother-in-law 1.3
sueldo *m.* salary 3.4
suelo *m.* floor 2.6
sueño *m.* sleep
suerte *f.* luck
suéter *m.* sweater 1.6
sufrir *v.* to suffer 2.4
   sufrir muchas presiones to be under a lot of pressure 3.3
   sufrir una enfermedad to suffer an illness 2.4
sugerir (e:ie) *v.* to suggest 2.6
supermercado *m.* supermarket 3.2
suponer *v.* to suppose 1.4
sur *m.* south 3.2

sustantivo *m.* noun
suyo(s)/a(s) *poss.* (of) his/her; (of) hers; its; *form.* your, (of) yours, (of) theirs, their **2.5**

T

tabla de (wind)surf *f.* surf board/sailboard **1.5**
tal vez *adv.* maybe **1.5**
talentoso/a *adj.* talented **3.5**
talla *f.* size **1.6**
　talla grande *f.* large
taller *m.* **mecánico** garage; mechanic's repair shop **2.5**
también *adv.* also; too **1.2; 2.1**
tampoco *adv.* neither; not either **2.1**
tan *adv.* so **1.5**
　tan... como as... as **2.2**
　tan pronto como *conj.* as soon as **3.1**
tanque *m.* tank **2.5**
tanto *adv.* so much
　tanto... como as much... as **2.2**
tantos/as... como as many... as **2.2**
tarde *adv.* late **2.1**; *f.* afternoon; evening; P.M. **1.1**
tarea *f.* homework **1.2**
tarjeta *f.* (post) card
tarjeta de crédito *f.* credit card **1.6**
tarjeta postal *f.* postcard
taxi *m.* taxi **1.5**
taza *f.* cup **2.6**
te *sing., fam., d.o. pron.* you **1.5**; *sing., fam., i.o. pron.* to/for you **1.6**
　Te presento a... *fam.* I would like to introduce you to (name). **1.1**
　¿Te gustaría? Would you like to?
　¿Te gusta(n)...? Do you like...? **1.2**
té *m.* tea **2.2**
　té helado *m.* iced tea **2.2**
teatro *m.* theater **3.5**
teclado *m.* keyboard **2.5**
técnico/a *m., f.* technician **3.4**
tejido *m.* weaving **3.5**
teleadicto/a *m., f.* couch potato **3.3**
(teléfono) celular *m.* (cell) phone **2.5**
telenovela *f.* soap opera **3.5**
teletrabajo *m.* telecommuting **3.4**
televisión *f.* television **1.2**
televisión por cable *f.* cable television
televisor *m.* television set **2.5**
temer *v.* to fear; to be afraid **3.1**
temperatura *f.* temperature **2.4**
temporada *f.* period of time **1.5**
temprano *adv.* early **2.1**

tenedor *m.* fork **2.6**
tener *v.* to have **1.3**
　tener... años to be... years old **1.3**
　tener (mucho) calor to be (very) hot **1.3**
　tener (mucho) cuidado to be (very) careful **1.3**
　tener dolor to have pain **2.4**
　tener éxito to be successful **3.4**
　tener fiebre to have a fever **2.4**
　tener (mucho) frío to be (very) cold **1.3**
　tener ganas de (+ inf.) to feel like (*doing something*) **1.3**
　tener (mucha) hambre *f.* to be (very) hungry **1.3**
　tener (mucho) miedo (de) to be (very) afraid (of); to be (very) scared (of) **1.3**
　tener miedo (de) que to be afraid that
　tener planes *m., pl.* to have plans
　tener (mucha) prisa to be in a (big) hurry **1.3**
　tener que (+ inf.) *v.* to have to (*do something*) **1.3**
　tener razón *f.* to be right **1.3**
　tener (mucha) sed *f.* to be (very) thirsty **1.3**
　tener (mucho) sueño to be (very) sleepy **1.3**
　tener (mucha) suerte to be (very) lucky **1.3**
　tener tiempo to have time **3.2**
　tener una cita to have a date; to have an appointment **2.3**
tenis *m.* tennis **1.4**
tensión *f.* tension **3.3**
tercer, tercero/a *adj.* third **1.5**
terco/a *adj.* stubborn **2.4**
terminar *v.* to end; to finish **1.2**
　terminar de (+ inf.) *v.* to finish (*doing something*)
terremoto *m.* earthquake **3.6**
terrible *adj. m., f.* terrible **3.1**
ti *obj. of prep., fam.* you **2.3**
tiempo *m.* time **3.2**; weather **1.5**
　tiempo libre free time
tienda *f.* store **1.6**
tierra *f.* land; soil **3.1**
tinto/a *adj.* red (wine) **2.2**
tío/a *m., f.* uncle/aunt **1.3**
tíos *m., pl.* aunts and uncles **1.3**
título *m.* title **3.4**
tiza *f.* chalk **1.2**
toalla *f.* towel **2.1**
tobillo *m.* ankle **2.4**
tocar *v.* to play (*a musical instrument*) **3.5**; to touch **3.5**
todavía *adv.* yet; still **1.3, 1.5**
todo *m.* everything **1.5**
todo(s)/a(s) *adj.* all
todos *m., pl.* all of us; *m., pl.* everybody; everyone
todos los días *adv.* every day **2.4**

tomar *v.* to take; to drink **1.2**
　tomar clases *f., pl.* to take classes **1.2**
　tomar el sol to sunbathe **1.4**
　tomar en cuenta to take into account
　tomar fotos *f., pl.* to take photos **1.5**
　tomar la temperatura to take someone's temperature **2.4**
　tomar una decisión to make a decision **3.3**
tomate *m.* tomato **2.2**
tonto/a *adj.* foolish **1.3**
torcerse (o:ue) (el tobillo) *v.* to sprain (one's ankle) **2.4**
tormenta *f.* storm **3.6**
tornado *m.* tornado **3.6**
tortuga (marina) *f.* (sea) turtle **3.1**
tos *f., sing.* cough **2.4**
toser *v.* to cough **2.4**
tostado/a *adj.* toasted **2.2**
tostadora *f.* toaster **2.6**
trabajador(a) *adj.* hard-working **1.3**
trabajar *v.* to work **1.2**
trabajo *m.* job; work **3.4**
traducir *v.* to translate **1.6**
traer *v.* to bring **1.4**
tráfico *m.* traffic **2.5**
tragedia *f.* tragedy **3.5**
traído/a *p.p.* brought **3.2**
traje *m.* suit **1.6**
　traje de baño *m.* bathing suit **1.6**
trajinera *f.* type of barge **1.3**
tranquilo/a *adj.* calm; quiet **3.3**
　Tranquilo/a. Relax. **2.1**
　Tranquilo/a, cariño. Relax, sweetie. **2.5**
transmitir *v.* to broadcast **3.6**
tratar de (+ inf.) *v.* to try (*to do something*) **3.3**
trece thirteen **1.1**
treinta thirty **1.1, 1.2**
　y treinta thirty minutes past the hour (time) **1.1**
tren *m.* train **1.5**
tres three **1.1**
trescientos/as three hundred **1.2**
trimestre *m.* trimester; quarter **1.2**
triste *adj.* sad **1.5**
tú *fam. sub. pron.* you **1.1**
tu(s) *fam. poss. adj.* your **1.3**
turismo *m.* tourism
turista *m., f.* tourist **1.1**
turístico/a *adj.* touristic
tuyo(s)/a(s) *fam. poss. pron.* your; (of) yours **2.5**

U

Ud. *form. sing.* you **1.1**
Uds. *pl.* you **1.1**

último/a *adj.* last 2.1
  la última vez the last time 2.1
un, uno/a *indef. art.* a; one 1.1
  a la una at one o'clock 1.1
  una vez once 1.6
  una vez más one more time
uno one 1.1
único/a *adj.* only 1.3; unique 2.3
universidad *f.* university;
  college 1.2
unos/as *m., f., pl. indef. art.*
  some 1.1
urgente *adj.* urgent 2.6
usar *v.* to wear; to use 1.6
usted (Ud.) *form. sing.* you 1.1
ustedes (Uds.) *pl.* you 1.1
útil *adj.* useful
uva *f.* grape 2.2

V

vaca *f.* cow 3.1
vacaciones *f. pl.* vacation 1.5
valle *m.* valley 3.1
vamos let's go 1.4
vaquero *m.* cowboy 3.5
  de vaqueros *m., pl.* western
  (genre) 3.5
varios/as *adj. m. f., pl.* various;
  several
vaso *m.* glass 2.6
veces *f., pl.* times 1.6
vecino/a *m., f.* neighbor 2.6
veinte twenty 1.1
veinticinco twenty-five 1.1
veinticuatro twenty-four 1.1
veintidós twenty-two 1.1
veintinueve twenty-nine 1.1
veintiocho twenty-eight 1.1
veintiséis twenty-six 1.1
veintisiete twenty-seven 1.1
veintitrés twenty-three 1.1
veintiún, veintiuno/a *adj.*
  twenty-one 1.1
veintiuno twenty-one 1.1

vejez *f.* old age 2.3
velocidad *f.* speed 2.5
  velocidad máxima *f.* speed
  limit 2.5
vencer *v.* to expire 3.2
vendedor(a) *m., f.*
  salesperson 1.6
vender *v.* to sell 1.6
venir *v.* to come 1.3
ventana *f.* window 1.2
ver *v.* to see 1.4
  a ver *v.* let's see
  ver películas *f., pl.* to see
  movies 1.4
verano *m.* summer 1.5
verbo *m.* verb
verdad *f.* truth 1.4
  (no) es verdad it's (not)
  true 3.1
  ¿verdad? right? 1.1
verde *adj., m. f.* green 1.6
verduras *pl., f.* vegetables 2.2
vestido *m.* dress 1.6
vestirse (e:i) *v.* to get dressed 2.1
vez *f.* time 1.6
viajar *v.* to travel 1.2
viaje *m.* trip 1.5
viajero/a *m., f.* traveler 1.5
vida *f.* life 2.3
video *m.* video 1.1
videoconferencia *f.*
  videoconference 3.4
videojuego *m.* video game 1.4
vidrio *m.* glass 3.1
viejo/a *adj.* old 1.3
viento *m.* wind
viernes *m., sing.* Friday 1.2
vinagre *m.* vinegar 2.2
vino *m.* wine 2.2
  vino blanco *m.* white wine 2.2
  vino tinto *m.* red wine 2.2
violencia *f.* violence 3.6
visitar *v.* to visit 1.4
  visitar monumentos *m., pl.*
  to visit monuments 1.4

visto/a *p.p.* seen 3.2
vitamina *f.* vitamin 3.3
viudo/a *adj.* widower/widow 2.3
vivienda *f.* housing 2.6
vivir *v.* to live 1.3
vivo/a *adj.* clever; living
volante *m.* steering wheel 2.5
volcán *m.* volcano 3.1
vóleibol *m.* volleyball 1.4
volver (o:ue) *v.* to return 1.4
volver a ver(te, lo, la) *v.* to see
  (you, him, her) again
vos *pron.* you
vosotros/as *fam., pl.* you 1.1
votar *v.* to vote 3.6
vuelta *f.* return trip
vuelto/a *p.p.* returned 3.2
vuestro(s)/a(s) *poss. adj.*
  your 1.3; your, (of) yours
  fam., pl. 2.5

Y

y *conj.* and 1.1
  y cuarto quarter after (time) 1.1
  y media half-past (time) 1.1
  y quince quarter after (time) 1.1
  y treinta thirty (minutes past
  the hour) 1.1
  ¿Y tú? *fam.* And you? 1.1
  ¿Y usted? *form.* And you? 1.1
ya *adv.* already 1.6
yerno *m.* son-in-law 1.3
yo *sub. pron.* I 1.1
yogur *m.* yogurt 2.2

Z

zanahoria *f.* carrot 2.2
zapatería *f.* shoe store 3.2
zapatos de tenis *m., pl.* tennis
  shoes, sneakers 1.6

English–Spanish

A

a **un/a** *m., f., sing.; indef. art.* 1.1
@ (*symbol*) **arroba** *f.* 2.5
a.m. **de la mañana** *f.* 1.1
able: be able to **poder (o:ue)** *v.* 1.4
aboard **a bordo**
above all **sobre todo** 3.1
accident **accidente** *m.* 2.4
accompany **acompañar** *v.* 3.2
account **cuenta** *f.* 3.2
   on account of **por** *prep.* 2.5
accountant **contador(a)** *m., f.* 3.4
accounting **contabilidad** *f.* 1.2
ache **dolor** *m.* 2.4
acquainted: be acquainted with
   conocer *v.* 1.6
action (genre) **de acción** *f.* 3.5
active **activo/a** *adj.* 3.3
actor **actor** *m.,* **actriz** *f.* 3.4
addict (*drug*) **drogadicto/a**
   m., f. 3.3
additional **adicional** *adj.*
address **dirección** *f.* 3.2
adjective **adjetivo** *m.*
adolescence **adolescencia** *f.* 2.3
adventure (genre) **de aventuras**
   f. 3.5
advertise **anunciar** *v.* 3.6
advertisement **anuncio** *m.* 3.4
advice **consejo** *m.*
   give advice **dar consejos** 1.6
advise **aconsejar** *v.* 2.6
advisor **consejero/a** *m., f.* 3.4
aerobic **aeróbico/a** *adj.* 3.3
   aerobics class **clase de**
     ejercicios aeróbicos 3.3
   to do aerobics **hacer ejercicios**
     aeróbicos 3.3
affected **afectado/a** *adj.* 3.1
   be affected (by) **estar** *v.*
     afectado/a (por) 3.1
affirmative **afirmativo/a** *adj.*
afraid: be (very) afraid (of) **tener**
   (mucho) miedo (de) 1.3
   be afraid that **tener miedo**
     (de) que
after **después de** *prep.* 2.1;
   después de que *conj.* 3.1
afternoon **tarde** *f.* 1.1
afterward **después** *adv.* 2.1
again **otra vez**
age **edad** *f.* 2.3
agree **concordar** *v.*
agree **estar** *v.* **de acuerdo** 3.5
   I agree. **Estoy de acuerdo.** 3.5
   I don't agree. **No estoy de**
     acuerdo. 3.5
agreement **acuerdo** *m.*
AIDS **SIDA** *m.* 3.6
air **aire** *m.* 3.1
   air pollution **contaminación**
     del aire 3.1
airplane **avión** *m.* 1.5
airport **aeropuerto** *m.* 1.5
alarm clock **despertador** *m.* 2.1

alcohol **alcohol** *m.* 3.3
   to consume alcohol **consumir**
     alcohol 3.3
alcoholic **alcohólico/a** *adj.* 3.3
all **todo(s)/a(s)** *adj.*
   all of us **todos**
allergic **alérgico/a** *adj.* 2.4
   be allergic (to) **ser alérgico/a**
     (a) 2.4
alleviate **aliviar** *v.*
almost **casi** *adv.* 2.4
alone **solo/a** *adj.*
along **por** *prep.* 2.5
already **ya** *adv.* 1.6
also **también** *adv.* 1.2; 2.1
altar **altar** *m.* 2.3
aluminum **aluminio** *m.* 3.1
   (made) of aluminum **de**
     aluminio 3.1
always **siempre** *adv.* 2.1
American (*North*)
   norteamericano/a *adj.* 1.3
among **entre** *prep.* 1.2
amusement **diversión** *f.*
and **y** 1.1, **e** (*before words*
   beginning with i *or* hi)
   And you? **¿Y tú?** *fam.* 1.1;
     ¿Y usted? *form.* 1.1
angel **ángel** *m.* 2.3
angry **enojado/a** *adj.* 1.5
   get angry (with) **enojarse** *v.*
     (con) 2.1
animal **animal** *m.* 3.1
ankle **tobillo** *m.* 2.4
anniversary **aniversario** *m.* 2.3
   (wedding) anniversary
     aniversario *m.* **(de**
     bodas) 2.3
announce **anunciar** *v.* 3.6
announcer (*TV/radio*) **locutor(a)**
   m., f. 3.6
annoy **molestar** *v.* 2.1
another **otro/a** *adj.* 1.6
answer **contestar** *v.* 1.2;
   respuesta *f.*
answering machine **contestadora** *f.*
antibiotic **antibiótico** *m.* 2.4
any **algún, alguno/a(s)** *adj.* 2.1
anyone **alguien** *pron.* 2.1
anything **algo** *pron.* 2.1
apartment **apartamento** *m.* 2.6
apartment building **edificio de**
   apartamentos 2.6
app **aplicación** *f.* 2.5
appear **parecer** *v.*
appetizers **entremeses** *m., pl.* 2.2
applaud **aplaudir** *v.* 3.5
apple **manzana** *f.* 2.2
appliance (electric)
   electrodoméstico *m.* 2.6
applicant **aspirante** *m., f.* 3.4
application **solicitud** *f.* 3.4
   job application **solicitud de**
     trabajo 3.4
apply (*for a job*) **solicitar** *v.* 3.4
   apply for a loan **pedir (e:i)** *v.*
     un préstamo 3.2
appointment **cita** *f.* 2.3
   have an appointment **tener** *v.*
     una cita 2.3

appreciate **apreciar** *v.* 3.5
April **abril** *m.* 1.5
archeologist **arqueólogo/a**
   m., f. 3.4
archeology **arqueología** *f.* 1.2
architect **arquitecto/a** *m., f.* 3.4
area **región** *f.*
Argentine **argentino/a** *adj.* 1.3
arm **brazo** *m.* 2.4
armchair **sillón** *m.* 2.6
army **ejército** *m.* 3.6
around **por** *prep.* 2.5
   around here **por aquí** 2.5
arrange **arreglar** *v.* 2.5
arrival **llegada** *f.* 1.5
arrive **llegar** *v.* 1.2
art **arte** *m.* 1.2
   (fine) arts **bellas artes** *f.,*
     pl. 3.5
article **artículo** *m.* 3.6
artist **artista** *m., f.* 1.3
artistic **artístico/a** *adj.* 3.5
arts **artes** *f., pl.* 3.5
as **como** 2.2
   as a child **de niño/a** 2.4
   as... as **tan... como** 2.2
   as many... as **tantos/as...**
     como 2.2
   as much... as **tanto... como** 2.2
   as soon as **en cuanto** *conj.* 3.1;
     tan pronto como *conj.* 3.1
ask (*a question*) **preguntar** *v.* 1.2
   ask for **pedir (e:i)** *v.* 1.4
asparagus **espárragos** *m., pl.* 2.2
aspirin **aspirina** *f.* 2.4
at **a** *prep.* 1.1; **en** *prep.* 1.2
   at + *time* **a la(s)** + *time* 1.1
   at home **en casa**
   at least **por lo menos** 2.4
   at night **por la noche** 2.1
   At what time...? **¿A qué**
     hora...? 1.1
   At your service. **A sus**
     órdenes.
ATM **cajero automático** *m.* 3.2
attempt **intento** *m.* 2.5
attend **asistir (a)** *v.* 1.3
attic **altillo** *m.* 2.6
audience **público** *m.* 3.5
August **agosto** *m.* 1.5
aunt **tía** *f.* 1.3
   aunts and uncles **tíos** *m., pl.* 1.3
automobile **automóvil** *m.* 1.5;
   carro *m.;* **coche** *m.* 2.5
autumn **otoño** *m.* 1.5
avenue **avenida** *f.*
avoid **evitar** *v.* 3.1
award **premio** *m.* 3.5

B

backpack **mochila** *f.* 1.2
bad **mal, malo/a** *adj.* 1.3
   It's bad that... **Es malo**
     que... 2.6
   It's not bad at all. **No está**
     nada mal. 1.5
bag **bolsa** *f.* 1.6

bakery **panadería** *f.* 3.2
balanced **equilibrado/a** *adj.* 3.3
　to eat a balanced diet **comer
　una dieta equilibrada** 3.3
balcony **balcón** *m.* 2.6
ball **pelota** *f.* 1.4
banana **banana** *f.* 2.2
band **banda** *f.* 3.5
bank **banco** *m.* 3.2
bargain **ganga** *f.* 1.6; **regatear**
　v. 1.6
baseball (*game*) **béisbol** *m.* 1.4
basement **sótano** *m.* 2.6
basketball (*game*) **baloncesto**
　m. 1.4
bathe **bañarse** *v.* 2.1
bathing suit **traje** *m.* **de baño** 1.6
bathroom **baño** *m.* 2.1; **cuarto
　de baño** *m.* 2.1
be **ser** *v.* 1.1; **estar** *v.* 1.2
　be… years old **tener… años** 1.3
　be sick of… **estar harto/a
　de…** 3.6
beach **playa** *f.* 1.5
beans **frijoles** *m., pl.* 2.2
beautiful **hermoso/a** *adj.* 1.6
beauty **belleza** *f.* 3.2
　beauty salon **peluquería** *f.* 3.2;
　salón *m.* **de belleza** 3.2
because **porque** *conj.* 1.2
　because of **por** *prep.* 2.5
become (+ *adj.*) **ponerse (+
　adj.)** 2.1; **convertirse** *v.*
bed **cama** *f.* 1.5
　go to bed **acostarse (o:ue)**
　v. 2.1
bedroom **alcoba** *f.*, **recámara** *f.*;
　dormitorio *m.* 2.6
beef **carne de res** *f.* 2.2
beer **cerveza** *f.* 2.2
before **antes** *adv.* 2.1; **antes de**
　prep. 2.1; **antes (de) que**
　conj. 3.1
beg **rogar (o:ue)** *v.* 2.6
begin **comenzar (e:ie)** *v.* 1.4;
　empezar (e:ie) *v.* 1.4
behalf: on behalf of **de parte
　de** 2.5
behind **detrás de** *prep.* 1.2
believe (in) **creer** *v.* **(en)** 1.3;
　creer *v.* 3.1
　not to believe **no creer** 3.1
believed **creído/a** *p.p.* 3.2
bellhop **botones** *m., f. sing.* 1.5
below **debajo de** *prep.* 1.2
belt **cinturón** *m.* 1.6
benefit **beneficio** *m.* 3.4
beside **al lado de** *prep.* 1.2
besides **además (de)** *adv.* 2.4
best **mejor** *adj.*
　the best **el/la mejor** *m., f.* 2.2
　lo mejor *neuter*
better **mejor** *adj.* 2.2
　It's better that… **Es mejor
　que…** 2.6
between **entre** *prep.* 1.2
beverage **bebida** *f.* 2.2
　alcoholic beverage **bebida
　alcohólica** *f.* 3.3

bicycle **bicicleta** *f.* 1.4
big **grande** *adj.* 1.3
bill **cuenta** *f.* 2.2
billion **mil millones**
biology **biología** *f.* 1.2
bird **ave** *f.* 3.1; **pájaro** *m.* 3.1
birth **nacimiento** *m.* 2.3
birthday **cumpleaños** *m.,
　sing.* 2.3
　have a birthday **cumplir
　v. años**
black **negro/a** *adj.* 1.6
blackboard **pizarra** *f.* 1.2
blanket **manta** *f.* 2.6
block (city) **cuadra** *f.* 3.2
blog **blog** *m.* 2.5
blond(e) **rubio/a** *adj.* 1.3
blouse **blusa** *f.* 1.6
blue **azul** *adj. m., f.* 1.6
boarding house **pensión** *f.*
boat **barco** *m.* 1.5
body **cuerpo** *m.* 2.4
bone **hueso** *m.* 2.4
book **libro** *m.* 1.2
bookcase **estante** *m.* 2.6
bookshelves **estante** *m.* 2.6
bookstore **librería** *f.* 1.2
boot **bota** *f.* 1.6
bore **aburrir** *v.* 2.1
bored **aburrido/a** *adj.* 1.5
　be bored **estar** *v.*
　aburrido/a 1.5
　get bored **aburrirse** *v.* 3.5
boring **aburrido/a** *adj.* 1.5
born: be born **nacer** *v.* 2.3
borrow **pedir (e:i)** *v.*
　prestado 3.2
borrowed **prestado/a** *adj.*
boss **jefe** *m.*, **jefa** *f.* 3.4
bother **molestar** *v.* 2.1
bottle **botella** *f.* 2.3
　bottle of wine **botella de
　vino** 2.3
bottom **fondo** *m.*
boulevard **bulevar** *m.*
boy **chico** *m.* 1.1; **muchacho**
　m. 1.3
boyfriend **novio** *m.* 1.3
brakes **frenos** *m., pl.*
bread **pan** *m.* 2.2
break **romper** *v.* 2.4
　break (one's leg) **romperse
　(la pierna)** 2.4
　break down **dañar** *v.* 2.4
　break up (with) **romper** *v.*
　(con) 2.3
breakfast **desayuno** *m.* 2.2
　have breakfast **desayunar** *v.* 1.2
breathe **respirar** *v.* 3.1
bring **traer** *v.* 1.4
broadcast **transmitir** *v.* 3.6;
　emitir *v.* 3.6
brochure **folleto** *m.*
broken **roto/a** *adj.* 3.2
　be broken **estar roto/a**
brother **hermano** *m.* 1.3
brother-in-law **cuñado** *m.* 1.3

brothers and sisters **hermanos** *m.,
　pl.* 1.3
brought **traído/a** *p.p.* 3.2
brown **café** *adj.* 1.6; **marrón**
　adj. 1.6
browser **buscador** *m.* 2.5
brunet(te) **moreno/a** *adj.* 1.3
brush **cepillar(se)** *v.* 2.1
　brush one's hair **cepillarse el
　pelo** 2.1
　brush one's teeth **cepillarse los
　dientes** 2.1
bucket **balde** *m.* 1.5
build **construir** *v.*
building **edificio** *m.* 2.6
bump into (*something accidentally*)
　darse con 2.4; (*someone*)
　encontrarse *v.* 2.5
burn (a CD/DVD) **quemar** *v.*
　(un CD/DVD)
bus **autobús** *m.* 1.1
　bus station **estación** *f.* **de
　autobuses** 1.5
business **negocios** *m. pl.* 3.4
　business administration
　administración *f.* **de
　empresas** 1.2
　business-related **comercial**
　adj. 3.4
businessperson **hombre** *m.* **/
　mujer** *f.* **de negocios** 3.4
busy **ocupado/a** *adj.* 1.5
but **pero** *conj.* 1.2; (*rather*) **sino**
　conj. (*in negative sentences*) 2.1
butcher shop **carnicería** *f.* 3.2
butter **mantequilla** *f.* 2.2
buy **comprar** *v.* 1.2
by **por** *prep.* 2.5; **para** *prep.* 2.5
　by means of **por** *prep.* 2.5
　by phone **por teléfono**
　by plane **en avión** 1.5
　by way of **por** *prep.* 2.5
bye **chau** *interj. fam.* 1.1

C

cable television **televisión** *f.*
　por cable *m.*
café **café** *m.* 1.4
cafeteria **cafetería** *f.* 1.2
caffeine **cafeína** *f.* 3.3
cake **pastel** *m.* 2.3
　chocolate cake **pastel de
　chocolate** *m.* 2.3
calculator **calculadora** *f.* 1.2
call **llamar** *v.* 2.5
　be called **llamarse** *v.* 2.1
　call on the phone **llamar por
　teléfono**
calm **tranquilo/a** *adj.* 3.3
calorie **caloría** *f.* 3.3
camera **cámara** *f.* 2.5
camp **acampar** *v.* 1.5
can (*tin*) **lata** *f.* 3.1
can **poder (o:ue)** *v.* 1.4
　Could I ask you something?
　¿Podría pedirte algo? 3.5

Canadian **canadiense** *adj.* 1.3
candidate **aspirante** *m.*, *f.* 3.4; **candidato/a** *m.*, *f.* 3.6
candy **dulces** *m.*, *pl.* 2.3
capital city **capital** *f.*
car **coche** *m.* 2.5; **carro** *m.* 2.5; **auto(móvil)** *m.* 1.5
caramel **caramelo** *m.* 2.3
card **tarjeta** *f.*; (*playing*) **carta** *f.* 1.5
care **cuidado** *m.*
    take care of **cuidar** *v.* 3.1
career **carrera** *f.* 3.4
careful: be (very) careful **tener** *v.* **(mucho) cuidado** 1.3
caretaker **ama** *m.*, *f.* **de casa** 2.6
carpenter **carpintero/a** *m.*, *f.* 3.4
carpet **alfombra** *f.* 2.6
carrot **zanahoria** *f.* 2.2
carry **llevar** *v.* 1.2
cartoons **dibujos** *m*, *pl.* **animados** 3.5
case: in case (that) **en caso (de) que** 3.1
cash (a check) **cobrar** *v.* 3.2; cash **(en) efectivo** 1.6
    cash register **caja** *f.* 1.6
    pay in cash **pagar** *v.* **al contado** 3.2; **pagar en efectivo** 3.2
cashier **cajero/a** *m.*, *f.*
cat **gato** *m.* 3.1
CD **disco compacto** *m.* 2.5
CD player **reproductor de CD** *m.* 2.5
CD-ROM **cederrón** *m.*
celebrate **celebrar** *v.* 2.3
celebration **celebración** *f.*
cellar **sótano** *m.* 2.6
(cell) phone **(teléfono) celular** *m.* 2.5
cemetery **cementerio** *m.* 2.3
cereal **cereales** *m.*, *pl.* 2.2
certain **cierto/a** *adj.*; **seguro/a** *adj.* 3.1
    it's (not) certain **(no) es cierto/seguro** 3.1
chalk **tiza** *f.* 1.2
champagne **champán** *m.* 2.3
change **cambiar** *v.* **(de)** 2.3
change: in change **de cambio** 1.2
channel (*TV*) **canal** *m.* 2.5; 3.5
character (*fictional*) **personaje** *m.* 3.5
    (main) character *m.* **personaje (principal)** 3.5
charger **cargador** *m.* 2.5
chat **conversar** *v.* 1.2; **chatear** *v.* 2.5
cheap **barato/a** *adj.* 1.6
check **comprobar (o:ue)** *v.*; **revisar** *v.* 2.5; (*bank*) **cheque** *m.* 3.2
    check the oil **revisar el aceite** 2.5
checking account **cuenta** *f.* **corriente** 3.2
cheese **queso** *m.* 2.2
chef **cocinero/a** *m.*, *f.* 3.4
chemistry **química** *f.* 1.2

chest of drawers **cómoda** *f.* 2.6
chicken **pollo** *m.* 2.2
child **niño/a** *m.*, *f.* 1.3
childhood **niñez** *f.* 2.3
children **hijos** *m.*, *pl.* 1.3
Chinese **chino/a** *adj.* 1.3
chocolate **chocolate** *m.* 2.3
    chocolate cake **pastel** *m.* **de chocolate** 2.3
cholesterol **colesterol** *m.* 3.3
choose **escoger** *v.* 2.2
chop (*food*) **chuleta** *f.* 2.2
Christmas **Navidad** *f.* 2.3
church **iglesia** *f.* 1.4
cinnamon **canela** *f.* 2.4
citizen **ciudadano/a** *m.*, *f.* 3.6
city **ciudad** *f.*
class **clase** *f.* 1.2
    take classes **tomar clases** 1.2
classical **clásico/a** *adj.* 3.5
classmate **compañero/a** *m.*, *f.* **de clase** 1.2
clean **limpio/a** *adj.* 1.5; **limpiar** *v.* 2.6
    clean the house *v.* **limpiar la casa** 2.6
clear (*weather*) **despejado/a** *adj.*
    clear the table **quitar la mesa** 2.6
    It's (very) clear. (*weather*) **Está (muy) despejado.**
clerk **dependiente/a** *m.*, *f.* 1.6
climate change **cambio climático** *m.* 3.1
climb **escalar** *v.* 1.4
    climb mountains **escalar montañas** 1.4
clinic **clínica** *f.* 2.4
clock **reloj** *m.* 1.2
close **cerrar (e:ie)** *v.* 1.4
closed **cerrado/a** *adj.* 1.5
closet **armario** *m.* 2.6
clothes **ropa** *f.* 1.6
    clothes dryer **secadora** *f.* 2.6
clothing **ropa** *f.* 1.6
cloud **nube** *f.* 3.1
cloudy **nublado/a** *adj.* 1.5
    It's (very) cloudy. **Está (muy) nublado.** 1.5
coat **abrigo** *m.* 1.6
coffee **café** *m.* 2.2
    coffee maker **cafetera** *f.* 2.6
cold **frío** *m.* 1.5; (*illness*) **resfriado** *m.* 2.4
    be (*feel*) (very) cold **tener (mucho) frío** 1.3
    It's (very) cold. (*weather*) **Hace (mucho) frío.** 1.5
college **universidad** *f.* 1.2
collision **choque** *m.* 3.6
color **color** *m.* 1.6
comb one's hair **peinarse** *v.* 2.1
come **venir** *v.* 1.3
come on **ándale** *interj.* 3.2
comedy **comedia** *f.* 3.5
comfortable **cómodo/a** *adj.* 1.5
commerce **negocios** *m.*, *pl.* 3.4
commercial **comercial** *adj.* 3.4
communicate (with) **comunicarse** *v.* **(con)** 3.6

communication **comunicación** *f.* 3.6
    means of communication **medios** *m. pl.* **de comunicación** 3.6
community **comunidad** *f.* 1.1
company **compañía** *f.* 3.4; **empresa** *f.* 3.4
comparison **comparación** *f.*
composer **compositor(a)** *m.*, *f.* 3.5
computer **computadora** *f.* 1.1
    computer disc **disco** *m.*
    computer monitor **monitor** *m.* 2.5
    computer programmer **programador(a)** *m.*, *f.* 1.3
    computer science **computación** *f.* 1.2
concert **concierto** *m.* 3.5
conductor (*musical*) **director(a)** *m.*, *f.* 3.5
confident **seguro/a** *adj.* 1.5
confirm **confirmar** *v.* 1.5
    confirm a reservation **confirmar una reservación** 1.5
confused **confundido/a** *adj.* 1.5
congested **congestionado/a** *adj.* 2.4
Congratulations! **¡Felicidades!**; **¡Felicitaciones!** *f.*, *pl.* 2.3
conservation **conservación** *f.* 3.1
conserve **conservar** *v.* 3.1
considering **para** *prep.* 2.5
consume **consumir** *v.* 3.3
container **envase** *m.* 3.1
contamination **contaminación** *f.*
content **contento/a** *adj.* 1.5
contest **concurso** *m.* 3.5
continue **seguir (e:i)** *v.* 1.4
control **control** *m.*; **controlar** *v.* 3.1
conversation **conversación** *f.* 1.1
converse **conversar** *v.* 1.2
cook **cocinar** *v.* 2.6; **cocinero/a** *m.*, *f.* 3.4
cookie **galleta** *f.* 2.3
cool **fresco/a** *adj.* 1.5
    It's cool. (*weather*) **Hace fresco.** 1.5
corn **maíz** *m.* 2.2
corner **esquina** *f.* 3.2
cost **costar (o:ue)** *v.* 1.6
Costa Rican **costarricense** *adj.* 1.3
costume **disfraz** *m.* 2.3
cotton **algodón** *f.* 1.6
    (made of) cotton **de algodón** 1.6
couch **sofá** *m.* 2.6
couch potato **teleadicto/a** *m.*, *f.* 3.3
cough **tos** *f.* 2.4; **toser** *v.* 2.4
counselor **consejero/a** *m.*, *f.* 3.4
count **contar (o:ue)** *v.* 1.4
country (*nation*) **país** *m.* 1.1
countryside **campo** *m.* 1.5
(married) couple **pareja** *f.* 2.3
course **curso** *m.* 1.2; **materia** *f.* 1.2
courtesy **cortesía** *f.*
cousin **primo/a** *m.*, *f.* 1.3
cover **cubrir** *v.*
covered **cubierto/a** *p.p.*

cow **vaca** *f.* 3.1
crafts **artesanía** *f.* 3.5
craftsmanship **artesanía** *f.* 3.5
crater **cráter** *m.* 3.1
crazy **loco/a** *adj.* 1.6
create **crear** *v.*
credit **crédito** *m.* 1.6
   credit card **tarjeta** *f.* **de crédito** 1.6
crime **crimen** *m.* 3.6
cross **cruzar** *v.* 3.2
cry **llorar** *v.* 3.3
Cuban **cubano/a** *adj.* 1.3
culture **cultura** *f.* 1.2, 3.5
cup **taza** *f.* 2.6
currency exchange **cambio** *m.* **de moneda**
current events **actualidades** *f., pl.* 3.6
curtains **cortinas** *f., pl.* 2.6
custard (*baked*) **flan** *m.* 2.3
custom **costumbre** *f.*
customer **cliente/a** *m., f.* 1.6
customs **aduana** *f.*
   customs inspector **inspector(a)** *m., f.* **de aduanas** 1.5
cybercafé **cibercafé** *m.* 2.5
cycling **ciclismo** *m.* 1.4

D

dad **papá** *m.*
daily **diario/a** *adj.* 2.1
   daily routine **rutina** *f.* **diaria** 2.1
damage **dañar** *v.* 2.4
dance **bailar** *v.* 1.2; **danza** *f.* 3.5; **baile** *m.* 3.5
dancer **bailarín/bailarina** *m., f.* 3.5
danger **peligro** *m.* 3.1
dangerous **peligroso/a** *adj.* 3.6
date (*appointment*) **cita** *f.* 2.3; (*calendar*) **fecha** *f.* 1.5; (*someone*) **salir** *v.* **con (alguien)** 2.3
   have a date **tener una cita** 2.3
daughter **hija** *f.* 1.3
daughter-in-law **nuera** *f.* 1.3
day **día** *m.* 1.1
   day before yesterday **anteayer** *adv.* 1.6
death **muerte** *f.* 2.3
decaffeinated **descafeinado/a** *adj.* 3.3
December **diciembre** *m.* 1.5
decide **decidir** *v.* (+ *inf.*) 1.3
declare **declarar** *v.* 3.6
deforestation **deforestación** *f.* 3.1
delicious **delicioso/a** *adj.* 2.2; **rico/a** *adj.* 2.2; **sabroso/a** *adj.* 2.2
delighted **encantado/a** *adj.* 1.1
dentist **dentista** *m., f.* 2.4
deny **negar (e:ie)** *v.* 3.1
   not to deny **no negar** 3.1
department store **almacén** *m.* 1.6
departure **salida** *f.* 1.5

deposit **depositar** *v.* 3.2
describe **describir** *v.* 1.3
described **descrito/a** *p.p.* 3.2
desert **desierto** *m.* 3.1
design **diseño** *m.*
designer **diseñador(a)** *m., f.* 3.4
desire **desear** *v.* 1.2
desk **escritorio** *m.* 1.2
dessert **postre** *m.* 2.3
destroy **destruir** *v.* 3.1
develop **desarrollar** *v.* 3.1
diary **diario** *m.* 1.1
dictatorship **dictadura** *f.* 3.6
dictionary **diccionario** *m.* 1.1
die **morir (o:ue)** *v.* 2.2
died **muerto/a** *p.p.* 3.2
diet **dieta** *f.* 3.3; **alimentación**
   balanced diet **dieta equilibrada** 3.3
   be on a diet **estar a dieta** 3.3
difficult **difícil** *adj. m., f.* 1.3
digital camera **cámara** *f.* **digital** 2.5
dining room **comedor** *m.* 2.6
dinner **cena** *f.* 2.2
   have dinner **cenar** *v.* 1.2
direct **dirigir** *v.* 3.5
director **director(a)** *m., f.* 3.5
dirty **ensuciar** *v.*; **sucio/a** *adj.* 1.5
   get (something) dirty **ensuciar** *v.* 2.6
disagree **no estar de acuerdo**
disaster **desastre** *m.* 3.6
discover **descubrir** *v.* 3.1
discovered **descubierto/a** *p.p.* 3.2
discrimination **discriminación** *f.* 3.6
dish **plato** *m.* 2.2, 2.6
   main dish *m.* **plato principal** 2.2
dishwasher **lavaplatos** *m., sing.* 2.6
disk **disco** *m.*
disorderly **desordenado/a** *adj.* 1.5
divorce **divorcio** *m.* 2.3
divorced **divorciado/a** *adj.* 2.3
   get divorced (from) **divorciarse** *v.* **(de)** 2.3
dizzy **mareado/a** *adj.* 2.4
do **hacer** *v.* 1.4
   do aerobics **hacer ejercicios aeróbicos** 3.3
   do household chores **hacer quehaceres domésticos** 2.6
   do stretching exercises **hacer ejercicios de estiramiento** 3.3
   (I) don't want to. **No quiero.** 1.4
doctor **doctor(a)** *m., f.* 1.3; 2.4; **médico/a** *m., f.* 1.3
documentary (*film*) **documental** *m.* 3.5
dog **perro** *m.* 3.1
domestic **doméstico/a** *adj.*
   domestic appliance **electrodoméstico** *m.*
done **hecho/a** *p.p.* 3.2
door **puerta** *f.* 1.2
doorman/doorwoman **portero/a** *m., f.* 1.1
dormitory **residencia** *f.* **estudiantil** 1.2

double **doble** *adj.* 1.5
   double room **habitación** *f.* **doble** 1.5
doubt **duda** *f.* 3.1; **dudar** *v.* 3.1
   not to doubt **no dudar** 3.1
   there is no doubt that **no cabe duda de** 3.1; **no hay duda de** 3.1
download **descargar** *v.* 2.5
downtown **centro** *m.* 1.4
drama **drama** *m.* 3.5
dramatic **dramático/a** *adj.* 3.5
draw **dibujar** *v.* 1.2
drawing **dibujo** *m.*
dress **vestido** *m.* 1.6
   get dressed **vestirse (e:i)** *v.* 2.1
drink **beber** *v.* 1.3; **bebida** *f.* 2.2; **tomar** *v.* 1.2
drive **conducir** *v.* 1.6; **manejar** *v.* 2.5
driver **conductor(a)** *m., f.* 1.1
drug **droga** *f.* 3.3
   drug addict **drogadicto/a** *m., f.* 3.3
dry (oneself) **secarse** *v.* 2.1
during **durante** *prep.* 2.1; **por** *prep.* 2.5
dust **sacudir** *v.* 2.6; **quitar** *v.* **el polvo** 2.6
   dust the furniture **sacudir los muebles** 2.6
duster **plumero** *m.* 2.6
DVD player **reproductor** *m.* **de DVD** 2.5

E

each **cada** *adj.* 1.6
ear (outer) **oreja** *f.* 2.4
early **temprano** *adv.* 2.1
earn **ganar** *v.* 3.4
earring **arete** *m.* 1.6
earthquake **terremoto** *m.* 3.6
ease **aliviar** *v.*
east **este** *m.* 3.2
   to the east **al este** 3.2
easy **fácil** *adj. m., f.* 1.3
eat **comer** *v.* 1.3
ecological **ecológico/a** *adj.* 3.1
ecologist **ecologista** *m., f.* 3.1
ecology **ecología** *f.* 3.1
economics **economía** *f.* 1.2
ecotourism **ecoturismo** *m.* 3.1
Ecuadorian **ecuatoriano/a** *adj.* 1.3
effective **eficaz** *adj. m., f.*
egg **huevo** *m.* 2.2
eight **ocho** 1.1
eight hundred **ochocientos/as** 1.2
eighteen **dieciocho** 1.1
eighth **octavo/a** 1.5
eighty **ochenta** 1.2
either... or **o... o** *conj.* 2.1
elect **elegir (e:i)** *v.* 3.6
election **elecciones** *f. pl.* 3.6
electric appliance **electrodoméstico** *m.* 2.6
electrician **electricista** *m., f.* 3.4
electricity **luz** *f.* 2.6

elegant **elegante** *adj. m., f.* 1.6
elevator **ascensor** *m.* 1.5
eleven **once** 1.1
e-mail **correo** *m.*
  electrónico 1.4
  e-mail address **dirección** *f.*
    electrónica 2.5
  e-mail message **mensaje** *m.*
    electrónico 1.4
  read e-mail **leer** *v.* **el correo**
    electrónico 1.4
embarrassed **avergonzado/a**
  adj. 1.5
embrace (each other) **abrazar(se)**
  v. 2.5
emergency **emergencia** *f.* 2.4
  emergency room **sala** *f.* **de**
    emergencia(s) 2.4
employee **empleado/a** *m., f.* 1.5
employment **empleo** *m.* 3.4
end **fin** *m.* 1.4; **terminar** *v.* 1.2
  end table **mesita** *f.* 2.6
endure **aguantar** *v.* 3.2
energy **energía** *f.* 3.1
engaged: get engaged (to)
  comprometerse *v.* **(con)** 2.3
engineer **ingeniero/a** *m., f.* 1.3
English (*language*) **inglés** *m.* 1.2;
  inglés, inglesa *adj.* 1.3
enjoy **disfrutar** *v.* **(de)** 3.3
enough **bastante** *adv.* 2.4
entertainment **diversión** *f.* 1.4
entrance **entrada** *f.* 2.6
envelope **sobre** *m.* 3.2
environment **medio ambiente**
  m. 3.1
environmental science **ciencias**
  ambientales 1.2
equality **igualdad** *f.* 3.6
erase **borrar** *v.* 2.5
eraser **borrador** *m.* 1.2
errand **diligencia** *f.* 3.2
essay **ensayo** *m.* 1.3
establish **establecer** *v.* 3.4
evening **tarde** *f.* 1.1
event **acontecimiento** *m.* 3.6
every day **todos los días** 2.4
everything **todo** *m.* 1.5
exactly **en punto** 1.1
exam **examen** *m.* 1.2
excellent **excelente** *adj.* 1.5
excess **exceso** *m.* 3.3
  in excess **en exceso** 3.3
exchange **intercambiar** *v.*
  in exchange for **por** 2.5
exciting **emocionante** *adj. m., f.*
excursion **excursión** *f.*
excuse **disculpar** *v.*
Excuse me. (*May I?*) **Con**
  permiso. 1.1; (*I beg your*
  pardon.) **Perdón.** 1.1
exercise **ejercicio** *m.* 3.3;
  hacer *v.* **ejercicio** 3.3; (*a*
  degree/profession) **ejercer** *v.* 3.4
exit **salida** *f.* 1.5
expensive **caro/a** *adj.* 1.6
experience **experiencia** *f.*
expire **vencer** *v.* 3.2
explain **explicar** *v.* 1.2
explore **explorar** *v.*

expression **expresión** *f.*
extinction **extinción** *f.* 3.1
eye **ojo** *m.* 2.4

F

fabulous **fabuloso/a** *adj.* 1.5
face **cara** *f.* 2.1
facing **enfrente de** *prep.* 3.2
fact: in fact **de hecho**
factory **fábrica** *f.* 3.1
fall (down) **caerse** *v.* 2.4
  fall asleep **dormirse (o:ue)** *v.* 2.1
  fall in love (with) **enamorarse**
    v. **(de)** 2.3
fall (season) **otoño** *m.* 1.5
fallen **caído/a** *p.p.* 3.2
family **familia** *f.* 1.3
famous **famoso/a** *adj.*
fan **aficionado/a** *m., f.* 1.4
  be a fan (of) **ser aficionado/a (a)**
far from **lejos de** *prep.* 1.2
farewell **despedida** *f.*
fascinate **fascinar** *v.* 2.1
fashion **moda** *f.* 1.6
  be in fashion **estar de**
    moda 1.6
fast **rápido/a** *adj.*
fat **gordo/a** *adj.* 1.3; **grasa** *f.* 3.3
father **padre** *m.* 1.3
father-in-law **suegro** *m.* 1.3
favorite **favorito/a** *adj.* 1.4
fax (machine) *fax m.*
fear **miedo** *m.*; **temer** *v.* 3.1
February **febrero** *m.* 1.5
feel **sentir(se) (e:ie)** *v.* 2.1
  feel like (*doing something*) **tener**
    ganas de (+ *inf.*) 1.3
festival **festival** *m.* 3.5
fever **fiebre** *f.* 2.4
  have a fever **tener** *v.* **fiebre** 2.4
few **pocos/as** *adj. pl.*
  fewer than **menos de**
    (+ *number*) 2.2
field: major field of study
  especialización *f.*
fifteen **quince** 1.1
  fifteen-year-old girl celebrating her
    birthday **quinceañera** *f.*
fifth **quinto/a** 1.5
fifty **cincuenta** 1.2
fight (for/against) **luchar** *v.* **(por/**
  contra) 3.6
figure (*number*) **cifra** *f.*
file **archivo** *m.* 2.5
fill **llenar** *v.* 2.5
  fill out (a form) **llenar (un**
    formulario) 3.2
  fill the tank **llenar el**
    tanque 2.5
finally **finalmente** *adv.*; **por**
  último 2.1; **por fin** 2.5
find **encontrar (o:ue)** *v.* 1.4
  find (each other) **encontrar(se)**
  find out **enterarse** *v.* 3.4

fine **multa** *f.*
  That's fine. **Está bien.**
(fine) arts **bellas artes** *f., pl.* 3.5
finger **dedo** *m.* 2.4
finish **terminar** *v.* 1.2
  finish (*doing something*)
    terminar *v.* **de (+ *inf.*)**
fire **incendio** *m.* 3.6; **despedir**
  (e:i) *v.* 3.4
firefighter **bombero/a** *m., f.* 3.4
firm **compañía** *f.* 3.4; **empresa**
  f. 3.4
first **primer, primero/a** 1.2, 1.5
fish (*food*) **pescado** *m.* 2.2;
  pescar *v.* 1.5; (*live*) **pez** *m.,*
  sing. (**peces** *pl.*) 3.1
  fish market **pescadería** *f.* 3.2
fishing **pesca** *f.*
fit (*clothing*) **quedar** *v.* 2.1
five **cinco** 1.1
five hundred **quinientos/as** 1.2
fix (*put in working order*) **arreglar**
  v. 2.5; (*clothes, hair, etc. to*
  go out) **arreglarse** *v.* 2.1
fixed **fijo/a** *adj.* 1.6
flag **bandera** *f.*
flexible **flexible** *adj.* 3.3
flood **inundación** *f.* 3.6
floor (*of a building*) **piso** *m.* 1.5;
  suelo *m.* 2.6
  ground floor **planta baja** *f.* 1.5
  top floor **planta** *f.* **alta**
flower **flor** *f.* 3.1
flu **gripe** *f.* 2.4
fog **niebla** *f.*
folk **folclórico/a** *adj.* 3.5
follow **seguir (e:i)** *v.* 1.4
food **comida** *f.* 1.4, 2.2
foolish **tonto/a** *adj.* 1.3
foot **pie** *m.* 2.4
football **fútbol** *m.*
  americano 1.4
for **para** *prep.* 2.5; **por** *prep.* 2.5
  for example **por ejemplo** 2.5
  for me **para mí** 2.2
forbid **prohibir** *v.*
foreign **extranjero/a** *adj.* 3.5
  foreign languages **lenguas**
    f., pl. **extranjeras** 1.2
forest **bosque** *m.* 3.1
forget **olvidar** *v.* 2.4
fork **tenedor** *m.* 2.6
form **formulario** *m.* 3.2
forty **cuarenta** 1.2
four **cuatro** 1.1
four hundred
  cuatrocientos/as 1.2
fourteen **catorce** 1.1
fourth **cuarto/a** *m., f.* 1.5
free **libre** *adj. m., f.* 1.4
  be free (of charge) **ser gratis** 3.2
  free time **tiempo libre**; spare
    (free) time **ratos libres** 1.4
freedom **libertad** *f.* 3.6
freezer **congelador** *m.* 2.6

French **francés, francesa** *adj.* 1.3
  French fries **papas** *f., pl.*
    fritas 2.2; **patatas** *f., pl.*
    fritas 2.2
frequently **frecuentemente** *adv.;*
  con frecuencia *adv.* 2.4
Friday **viernes** *m., sing.* 1.2
fried **frito/a** *adj.* 2.2
  fried potatoes **papas** *f., pl.*
    fritas 2.2; **patatas** *f., pl.*
    fritas 2.2
friend **amigo/a** *m., f.* 1.3
friendly **amable** *adj. m., f.* 1.5
friendship **amistad** *f.* 2.3
from **de** *prep.* 1.1; **desde** *prep.* 1.6
  from the United States
    estadounidense *m., f. adj.* 1.3
  from time to time **de vez en**
    cuando 2.4
  I'm from… **Soy de…** 1.1
front: (cold) front **frente (frío)**
  m. 1.5
fruit **fruta** *f.* 2.2
  fruit juice **jugo** *m.* **de fruta** 2.2
  fruit store **frutería** *f.* 3.2
full **lleno/a** *adj.* 2.5
fun **divertido/a** *adj.*
  fun activity **diversión** *f.* 1.4
  have fun **divertirse (e:ie)** *v.* 2.3
function **funcionar** *v.*
furniture **muebles** *m., pl.* 2.6
furthermore **además (de)** *adv.* 2.4
future **porvenir** *m.* 3.4
  for/to the future **por el**
    porvenir 3.4
  in the future **en el futuro**

G

gain weight **aumentar** *v.* **de**
  peso 3.3; **engordar** *v.* 3.3
game **juego** *m.;* (*match*)
  partido *m.* 1.4
  game show **concurso** *m.* 3.5
garage (*in a house*) **garaje** *m.* 2.6;
  garaje *m.* 2.5; **taller**
  (mecánico) 2.5
garden **jardín** *m.* 2.6
garlic **ajo** *m.* 2.2
gas station **gasolinera** *f.* 2.5
gasoline **gasolina** *f.* 2.5
gentleman **caballero** *m.* 2.2
geography **geografía** *f.* 1.2
German **alemán, alemana**
  adj. 1.3
get **conseguir(e:i)** *v.* 1.4;
  obtener *v.* 3.4
  get along well/badly (with)
    llevarse bien/mal (con) 2.3
  get bigger **aumentar** *v.* 3.1
  get bored **aburrirse** *v.* 3.5
  get good grades **sacar buenas**
    notas 1.2
  get into trouble **meterse en**
    problemas *v.* 3.1

get off of (a vehicle) **bajar(se)** *v.*
  de 2.5
get on/into (a vehicle) **subir(se)**
  v. **a** 2.5
get out of (a vehicle) **bajar(se)**
  v. **de** 2.5
get ready **arreglarse** *v.* 2.1
get up **levantarse** *v.* 2.1
gift **regalo** *m.* 1.6
ginger **jengibre** *m.* 2.4
girl **chica** *f.* 1.1; **muchacha** *f.* 1.3
girlfriend **novia** *f.* 1.3
give **dar** *v.* 1.6; (*as a gift*)
  regalar 2.3
  give directions **indicar cómo**
    llegar 3.2
glass (*drinking*) **vaso** *m.* 2.6;
  vidrio *m.* 3.1
  (made) of glass **de vidrio** 3.1
glasses **gafas** *f., pl.* 1.6
  sunglasses **gafas** *f., pl.*
    de sol 1.6
global warming **calentamiento**
  global *m.* 3.1
gloves **guantes** *m., pl.* 1.6
go **ir** *v.* 1.4
  go away **irse** 2.1
  go by boat **ir en barco** 1.5
  go by bus **ir en autobús** 1.5
  go by car **ir en auto(móvil)** 1.5
  go by motorcycle **ir en**
    moto(cicleta) 1.5
  go by plane **ir en avión** 1.5
  go by taxi **ir en taxi** 1.5
  go down **bajar(se)** *v.*
  go on a hike **ir de excursión** 1.4
  go out (with) **salir** *v.* **(con)** 2.3
  go up **subir** *v.*
  Let's go. **Vamos.** 1.4
goblet **copa** *f.* 2.6
going to: be going to (*do*
  something) **ir a (+ inf.)** 1.4
golf **golf** *m.* 1.4
good **buen, bueno/a** *adj.* 1.3, 1.6
  Good afternoon. **Buenas**
    tardes. 1.1
  Good evening. **Buenas**
    noches. 1.1
  Good morning. **Buenos días.** 1.1
  Good night. **Buenas noches.** 1.1
  It's good that… **Es bueno**
    que… 2.6
goodbye **adiós** *m.* 1.1
  say goodbye (to) **despedirse** *v.*
    (de) (e:i) 3.6
good-looking **guapo/a** *adj.* 1.3
government **gobierno** *m.* 3.1
GPS **navegador GPS** *m.* 2.5
graduate (from/in) **graduarse** *v.*
  (de/en) 2.3
grains **cereales** *m., pl.* 2.2
granddaughter **nieta** *f.* 1.3
grandfather **abuelo** *m.* 1.3
grandmother **abuela** *f.* 1.3
grandparents **abuelos** *m., pl.* 1.3

grandson **nieto** *m.* 1.3
grape **uva** *f.* 2.2
grass **hierba** *f.* 3.1
grave **grave** *adj.* 2.4
gray **gris** *adj. m., f.* 1.6
great **fenomenal** *adj. m., f.* 1.5;
  genial *adj.* 3.4
great-grandfather **bisabuelo** *m.* 1.3
great-grandmother **bisabuela** *f.* 1.3
green **verde** *adj. m., f.* 1.6
greet (each other) **saludar(se)**
  v. 2.5
greeting **saludo** *m.* 1.1
  Greetings to… **Saludos a…** 1.1
grilled **a la plancha** 2.2
ground floor **planta baja** *f.* 1.5
grow **aumentar** *v.* 3.1
guest (*at a house/hotel*) **huésped**
  m., f. 1.5 (*invited to a function*)
  invitado/a *m., f.* 2.3
guide **guía** *m., f.*
gymnasium **gimnasio** *m.* 1.4

H

hair **pelo** *m.* 2.1
hairdresser **peluquero/a** *m., f.* 3.4
half **medio/a** *adj.* 1.3
  half-brother **medio**
    hermano *m.* 1.3
  half-past… (*time*) **…y media** 1.1
  half-sister **media hermana** *f.* 1.3
hallway **pasillo** *m.* 2.6
ham **jamón** *m.* 2.2
hamburger **hamburguesa** *f.* 2.2
hand **mano** *f.* 1.1
hand in **entregar** *v.* 2.5
handsome **guapo/a** *adj.* 1.3
happen **ocurrir** *v.* 3.6
happiness **alegría** *v.* 2.3
Happy birthday!
  ¡Feliz cumpleaños! 2.3
happy **alegre** *adj.* 1.5; **contento/a**
  adj. 1.5; **feliz** *adj. m., f.* 1.5
  be happy **alegrarse** *v.* **(de)** 3.1
hard **difícil** *adj. m., f.* 1.3
hard-working **trabajador(a)** *adj.* 1.3
hardly **apenas** *adv.* 2.4
hat **sombrero** *m.* 1.6
hate **odiar** *v.* 2.3
have **tener** *v.* 1.3
  have time **tener tiempo** 3.2
  have to (*do something*) **tener**
    que (+ inf.) 1.3
  have a tooth removed **sacar(se)**
    un diente 2.4
he **él** 1.1
head **cabeza** *f.* 2.4
headache **dolor** *m.* **de cabeza** 2.4
health **salud** *f.* 2.4
healthy **saludable** *adj. m., f.* 2.4;
  sano/a *adj.* 2.4
  lead a healthy lifestyle **llevar** *v.*
    una vida sana 3.3
hear **oír** *v.* 1.4
heard **oído/a** *p.p.* 3.2

hearing: sense of hearing **oído** *m.* 2.4
heart **corazón** *m.* 2.4
heat **calor** *m.*
Hello. **Hola.** 1.1; (*on the telephone*) **Aló.** 2.5; **Bueno.** 2.5; **Diga.** 2.5
help **ayudar** *v.*; **servir (e:i)** *v.* 1.5
  help each other **ayudarse** *v.* 2.5
her **su(s)** *poss. adj.* 1.3; (*of*) hers **suyo(s)/a(s)** *poss.* 2.5
  her **la** *f., sing., d.o. pron.* 1.5
  to/for her **le** *f., sing., i.o. pron.* 1.6
here **aquí** *adv.* 1.1
  Here is/are... **Aquí está(n)...** 1.5
Hi. **Hola.** 1.1
highway **autopista** *f.* 2.5; **carretera** *f.* 2.5
hike **excursión** *f.* 1.4
  go on a hike **ir de excursión** 1.4
hiker **excursionista** *m., f.*
hiking **de excursión** 1.4
him *m., sing., d.o. pron.* **lo** 1.5; to/for him **le** *m., sing., i.o. pron.* 1.6
hire **contratar** *v.* 3.4
his **su(s)** *poss. adj.* 1.3; (*of*) his **suyo(s)/a(s)** *poss. pron.* 2.5
history **historia** *f.* 1.2; 3.5
hobby **pasatiempo** *m.* 1.4
hockey **hockey** *m.* 1.4
hold up **aguantar** *v.* 3.2
hole **hueco** *m.* 1.4
holiday **día** *m.* **de fiesta** 2.3
home **casa** *f.* 1.2
  home page **página** *f.* **principal** 2.5
homework **tarea** *f.* 1.2
honey **miel** *f.* 2.4
hood **capó** *m.* 2.5; **cofre** *m.* 2.5
hope **esperar** *v.* (+ *inf.*) 1.2; **esperar** *v.* 3.1
  I hope (that) **ojalá (que)** 3.1
horror (genre) **de horror** *m.* 3.5
hors d'oeuvres **entremeses** *m., pl.* 2.2
horse **caballo** *m.* 1.5
hospital **hospital** *m.* 2.4
hot: be (*feel*) (very) hot **tener (mucho) calor** 1.3
  It's (very) hot. **Hace (mucho) calor.** 1.5
hotel **hotel** *m.* 1.5
hour **hora** *f.* 1.1
house **casa** *f.* 1.2
household chores **quehaceres** *m. pl.* **domésticos** 2.6
housekeeper **ama** *m., f.* **de casa** 2.6
housing **vivienda** *f.* 2.6
How...! **¡Qué...!**
  how **¿cómo?** *adv.* 1.1, 1.2
  How are you? **¿Qué tal?** 1.1
  How are you? **¿Cómo estás?** *fam.* 1.1
  How are you? **¿Cómo está usted?** *form.* 1.1

How can I help you? **¿En qué puedo servirles?** 1.5
How is it going? **¿Qué tal?** 1.1
How is the weather? **¿Qué tiempo hace?** 1.5
How much/many? **¿Cuánto(s)/a(s)?** 1.1
How much does... cost? **¿Cuánto cuesta...?** 1.6
How old are you? **¿Cuántos años tienes?** *fam.*
however **sin embargo**
hug (each other) **abrazar(se)** *v.* 2.5
humanities **humanidades** *f., pl.* 1.2
hundred **cien, ciento** 1.2
hunger **hambre** *f.*
hungry: be (very) hungry **tener** *v.* **(mucha) hambre** 1.3
hunt **cazar** *v.* 3.1
hurricane **huracán** *m.* 3.6
hurry **apurarse** *v.* 3.3; **darse prisa** *v.* 3.3
  be in a (big) hurry **tener** *v.* **(mucha) prisa** 1.3
hurt **doler (o:ue)** *v.* 2.4
husband **esposo** *m.* 1.3

I

I **yo** 1.1
  I hope (that) **Ojalá (que)** *interj.* 3.1
  I wish (that) **Ojalá (que)** *interj.* 3.1
ice cream **helado** *m.* 2.3
  ice cream shop **heladería** *f.* 3.2
iced **helado/a** *adj.* 2.2
  iced tea **té** *m.* **helado** 2.2
idea **idea** *f.* 3.6
if **si** *conj.* 1.4
illness **enfermedad** *f.* 2.4
important **importante** *adj.* 1.3
  be important to **importar** *v.* 2.1
  It's important that... **Es importante que...** 2.6
impossible **imposible** *adj.* 3.1
  it's impossible **es imposible** 3.1
improbable **improbable** *adj.* 3.1
  it's improbable **es improbable** 3.1
improve **mejorar** *v.* 3.1
in **en** *prep.* 1.2; **por** *prep.* 2.5
  in the afternoon **de la tarde** 1.1; **por la tarde** 2.1
  in a bad mood **de mal humor** 1.5
  in the direction of **para** *prep.* 2.5
  in the early evening **de la tarde** 1.1
  in the evening **de la noche** 1.1; **por la tarde** 2.1
  in a good mood **de buen humor** 1.5
  in the morning **de la mañana** 1.1; **por la mañana** 2.1

in love (with) **enamorado/a (de)** 1.5
in search of **por** *prep.* 2.5
in front of **delante de** *prep.* 1.2
increase **aumento** *m.*
incredible **increíble** *adj.* 1.5
inequality **desigualdad** *f.* 3.6
infection **infección** *f.* 2.4
inform **informar** *v.* 3.6
injection **inyección** *f.* 2.4
  give an injection *v.* **poner una inyección** 2.4
injure (oneself) **lastimarse** 2.4
  injure (one's foot) **lastimarse** *v.* **(el pie)** 2.4
inner ear **oído** *m.* 2.4
inside **dentro** *adv.*
insist (on) **insistir** *v.* **(en)** 2.6
installments: pay in installments **pagar** *v.* **a plazos** 3.2
intelligent **inteligente** *adj.* 1.3
intend to **pensar** *v.* (+ *inf.*) 1.4
interest **interesar** *v.* 2.1
interesting **interesante** *adj.* 1.3
  be interesting to **interesar** *v.* 2.1
international **internacional** *adj. m., f.* 3.6
Internet **Internet** 2.5
interview **entrevista** *f.* 3.4; interview **entrevistar** *v.* 3.4
interviewer **entrevistador(a)** *m., f.* 3.4
introduction **presentación** *f.*
  I would like to introduce you to (name). **Le presento a...** *form.* 1.1; **Te presento a...** *fam.* 1.1
invest **invertir (e:ie)** *v.* 3.4
invite **invitar** *v.* 2.3
iron (clothes) **planchar** *v.* **la ropa** 2.6
it **lo/la** *sing., d.o., pron.* 1.5
Italian **italiano/a** *adj.* 1.3
its **su(s)** *poss. adj.* 1.3; **suyo(s)/a(s)** *poss. pron.* 2.5
it's the same **es igual** 1.5

J

jacket **chaqueta** *f.* 1.6
January **enero** *m.* 1.5
Japanese **japonés, japonesa** *adj.* 1.3
jeans **(blue)jeans** *m., pl.* 1.6
jewelry store **joyería** *f.* 3.2
job **empleo** *m.* 3.4; **puesto** *m.* 3.4; **trabajo** *m.* 3.4
  job application **solicitud** *f.* **de trabajo** 3.4
jog **correr** *v.*
journalism **periodismo** *m.* 1.2
journalist **periodista** *m., f.* 1.3
joy **alegría** *f.* 2.3
juice **jugo** *m.* 2.2
July **julio** *m.* 1.5

June **junio** *m.* 1.5
jungle **selva, jungla** *f.* 3.1
just **apenas** *adv.*
   have just done something
     acabar de (+ *inf.*) 1.6

K

key **llave** *f.* 1.5
keyboard **teclado** *m.* 2.5
kilometer **kilómetro** *m.* 2.5
kiss **beso** *m.* 2.3
   kiss each other **besarse** *v.* 2.5
kitchen **cocina** *f.* 2.3, 2.6
knee **rodilla** *f.* 2.4
knife **cuchillo** *m.* 2.6
know **saber** *v.* 1.6; **conocer**
   v. 1.6
know how **saber** *v.* 1.6

L

laboratory **laboratorio** *m.* 1.2
lack **faltar** *v.* 2.1
lake **lago** *m.* 3.1
lamp **lámpara** *f.* 2.6
land **tierra** *f.* 3.1
landscape **paisaje** *m.* 1.5
language **lengua** *f.* 1.2
laptop (computer) **computadora**
   f. portátil 2.5
large **grande** *adj.* 1.3
large (*clothing size*) **talla grande**
last **durar** *v.* 3.6; **pasado/a**
   adj. 1.6; **último/a** *adj.* 2.1
   last name **apellido** *m.* 1.3
   last night **anoche** *adv.* 1.6
   last week **semana** *f.*
     pasada 1.6
   last year **año** *m.* **pasado** 1.6
   the last time **la última vez** 2.1
late **tarde** *adv.* 2.1
later (on) **más tarde** 2.1
   See you later. **Hasta la vista.** 1.1;
     Hasta luego. 1.1
laugh **reírse (e:i)** *v.* 2.3
laughed **reído** *p.p.* 3.2
laundromat **lavandería** *f.* 3.2
law **ley** *f.* 3.1
lawyer **abogado/a** *m., f.* 3.4
lazy **perezoso/a** *adj.*
learn **aprender** *v.* **(a + *inf.*)** 1.3
least, at **por lo menos** *adv.* 2.4
leave **salir** *v.* 1.4; **irse** *v.* 2.1
   leave a tip **dejar una**
     propina
   leave behind **dejar** *v.* 3.4
   leave for (*a place*) **salir para**
   leave from **salir de**
left **izquierda** *f.* 1.2
   be left over **quedar** *v.* 2.1
   to the left of **a la izquierda**
     de 1.2
leg **pierna** *f.* 2.4
lemon **limón** *m.* 2.2
lend **prestar** *v.* 1.6

less **menos** *adv.* 2.4
   less... than **menos... que** 2.2
   less than **menos de** (+ *number*)
lesson **lección** *f.* 1.1
let **dejar** *v.*
let's see **a ver**
letter **carta** *f.* 1.4, 3.2
lettuce **lechuga** *f.* 2.2
liberty **libertad** *f.* 3.6
library **biblioteca** *f.* 1.2
license (*driver's*) **licencia** *f.* **de**
   conducir 2.5
lie **mentira** *f.* 1.4
life **vida** *f.* 2.3
lifestyle: lead a healthy lifestyle
   llevar una vida sana 3.3
lift **levantar** *v.* 3.3
   lift weights **levantar pesas** 3.3
light **luz** *f.* 2.6
like **como** *prep.* 2.2; **gustar** *v.* 1.2
   I like... **Me gusta(n)...** 1.2
   like this **así** *adv.* 2.4
   like very much **encantar** *v.*;
     fascinar *v.* 2.1
   Do you like...? **¿Te**
     gusta(n)...? 1.2
likeable **simpático/a** *adj.* 1.3
likewise **igualmente** *adv.* 1.1
line **línea** *f.* 1.4; **cola** (*queue*)
   f. 3.2
listen (to) **escuchar** *v.* 1.2
   listen to music **escuchar**
     música 1.2
   listen to the radio **escuchar la**
     radio 1.2
literature **literatura** *f.* 1.2
little (*quantity*) **poco** *adv.* 2.4
live **vivir** *v.* 1.3; **en vivo** *adj.* 2.1
living room **sala** *f.* 2.6
loan **préstamo** *m.* 3.2; **prestar**
   v. 1.6, 3.2
lobster **langosta** *f.* 2.2
located **situado/a** *adj.*
   be located **quedar** *v.* 3.2
long **largo/a** *adj.* 1.6
look (at) **mirar** *v.* 1.2
look for **buscar** *v.* 1.2
lose **perder (e:ie)** *v.* 1.4
   lose weight **adelgazar** *v.* 3.3
lost **perdido/a** *adj.* 3.1, 3.2
   be lost **estar perdido/a** 3.2
lot, a **muchas veces** *adv.* 2.4
lot of, a **mucho/a** *adj.* 1.3;
   un montón de 1.4
love (*another person*) **querer**
   (e:ie) *v.* 1.4; (*inanimate objects*)
   encantar *v.* 2.1; **amor** *m.* 2.3
   in love **enamorado/a** *adj.* 1.5
   love at first sight **amor a**
     primera vista 2.3
luck **suerte** *f.*
lucky: be (very) lucky **tener**
   (mucha) suerte 1.3
luggage **equipaje** *m.* 1.5
lunch **almuerzo** *m.* 1.4, 2.2
   have lunch **almorzar (o:ue)**
     v. 1.4

M

ma'am **señora (Sra.); doña** *f.* 1.1
mad **enojado/a** *adj.* 1.5
magazine **revista** *f.* 1.4
magnificent **magnífico/a** *adj.* 1.5
mail **correo** *m.* 3.2; **enviar** *v.*,
   mandar *v.* 3.2; **echar (una**
   carta) al buzón 3.2
   mail carrier **cartero** *m.* 3.2
mailbox **buzón** *m.* 3.2
main **principal** *adj. m., f.* 2.2
maintain **mantener** *v.* 3.3
major **especialización** *f.* 1.2
make **hacer** *v.* 1.4
   make a decision **tomar una**
     decisión 3.3
   make the bed **hacer la cama** 2.6
makeup **maquillaje** *m.* 2.1
   put on makeup **maquillarse**
     v. 2.1
man **hombre** *m.* 1.1
manager **gerente** *m., f.* 2.2, 3.4
many **mucho/a** *adj.* 1.3
   many times **muchas veces** 2.4
map **mapa** *m.* 1.1, 1.2
March **marzo** *m.* 1.5
margarine **margarina** *f.* 2.2
marinated fish **ceviche** *m.* 2.2
   lemon-marinated shrimp
     ceviche *m.* **de camarón** 2.2
marital status **estado** *m.* **civil** 2.3
market **mercado** *m.* 1.6
   open-air market **mercado al**
     aire libre 1.6
marriage **matrimonio** *m.* 2.3
married **casado/a** *adj.* 2.3
   get married (to) **casarse** *v.*
     (con) 2.3
   I'll marry you! **¡Acepto**
     casarme contigo! 3.5
marvelous **maravilloso/a** *adj.* 1.5
massage **masaje** *m.* 3.3
masterpiece **obra maestra** *f.* 3.5
match (*sports*) **partido** *m.* 1.4
match (with) **hacer** *v.*
   juego (con) 1.6
mathematics **matemáticas**
   f., pl. 1.2
matter **importar** *v.* 2.1
maturity **madurez** *f.* 2.3
maximum **máximo/a** *adj.* 2.5
May **mayo** *m.* 1.5
May I leave a message? **¿Puedo**
   dejar un recado? 2.5
maybe **tal vez** 1.5; **quizás** 1.5
mayonnaise **mayonesa** *f.* 2.2
me **me** *sing., d.o. pron.* 1.5
   to/for me **me** *sing., i.o. pron.* 1.6
meal **comida** *f.* 2.2
means of communication **medios**
   m., pl. **de comunicación** 3.6
meat **carne** *f.* 2.2
mechanic **mecánico/a** *m., f.* 2.5
   mechanic's repair shop **taller**
     mecánico 2.5

media **medios** *m.*, *pl.* **de comunicación** 3.6
medical **médico/a** *adj.* 2.4
medication **medicamento** *m.* 2.4
medicine **medicina** *f.* 2.4
medium **mediano/a** *adj.*
meet (each other) **encontrar(se)** *v.* 2.5; **conocer(se)** *v.* 2.2
   meet up with **encontrarse con** 2.1
meeting **reunión** *f.* 3.4
menu **menú** *m.* 2.2
message **mensaje** *m.*
Mexican **mexicano/a** *adj.* 1.3
microwave **microonda** *f.* 2.6
   microwave oven **horno** *m.* **de microondas** 2.6
middle age **madurez** *f.* 2.3
midnight **medianoche** *f.* 1.1
mile **milla** *f.*
milk **leche** *f.* 2.2
million **millón** *m.* 1.2
   million of **millón de** 1.2
mine **mío(s)/a(s)** *poss.* 2.5
mineral **mineral** *m.* 3.3
   mineral water **agua** *f.* **mineral** 2.2
minute **minuto** *m.*
mirror **espejo** *m.* 2.1
Miss **señorita (Srta.)** *f.* 1.1
miss **perder (e:ie)** *v.* 1.4; **extrañar** *v.* 3.4
mistaken **equivocado/a** *adj.*
modern **moderno/a** *adj.* 3.5
mom **mamá** *f.*
Monday **lunes** *m.*, *sing.* 1.2
money **dinero** *m.* 1.6
monitor **monitor** *m.* 2.5
monkey **mono** *m.* 3.1
month **mes** *m.* 1.5
monument **monumento** *m.* 1.4
moon **luna** *f.* 3.1
more **más** 1.2
   more... than **más... que** 2.2
   more than **más de** (+ *number*) 2.2
morning **mañana** *f.* 1.1
mother **madre** *f.* 1.3
mother-in-law **suegra** *f.* 1.3
motor **motor** *m.*
motorcycle **moto(cicleta)** *f.* 1.5
mountain **montaña** *f.* 1.4
mouse **ratón** *m.* 2.5
mouth **boca** *f.* 2.4
move (*from one house to another*) **mudarse** *v.* 2.6
movie **película** *f.* 1.4
   movie star **estrella** *f.* **de cine** 3.5
   movie theater **cine** *m.* 1.4
MP3 player **reproductor** *m.* **de MP3** 2.5
Mr. **señor (Sr.)**; **don** *m.* 1.1
Mrs. **señora (Sra.)**; **doña** *f.* 1.1
much **mucho/a** *adj.* 1.3
mud **lodo** *m.*

murder **crimen** *m.* 3.6
muscle **músculo** *m.* 3.3
museum **museo** *m.* 1.4
mushroom **champiñón** *m.* 2.2
music **música** *f.* 1.2, 3.5
musical **musical** *adj.*, *m.*, *f.* 3.5
musician **músico/a** *m.*, *f.* 3.5
must **deber** *v.* (+ *inf.*) 1.3
my **mi(s)** *poss. adj.* 1.3; **mío(s)/a(s)** *poss. pron.* 2.5

N

name **nombre** *m.* 1.1
   be named **llamarse** *v.* 2.1
   in the name of **a nombre de** 1.5
   last name **apellido** *m.* 1.3
   My name is... **Me llamo...** 1.1
   name someone/something **ponerle el nombre** 2.3
napkin **servilleta** *f.* 2.6
national **nacional** *adj. m.*, *f.* 3.6
nationality **nacionalidad** *f.* 1.1
natural **natural** *adj. m.*, *f.* 3.1
   natural disaster **desastre** *m.* **natural** 3.6
   natural resource **recurso** *m.* **natural** 3.1
nature **naturaleza** *f.* 3.1
nauseated **mareado/a** *adj.* 2.4
near **cerca de** *prep.* 1.2
neaten **arreglar** *v.* 2.6
necessary **necesario/a** *adj.* 2.6
   It is necessary that... **Es necesario que...** 2.6
neck **cuello** *m.* 2.4
need **faltar** *v.* 2.1; **necesitar** *v.* (+ *inf.*) 1.2
neighbor **vecino/a** *m.*, *f.* 2.6
neighborhood **barrio** *m.* 2.6
neither **tampoco** *adv.* 2.1
neither... nor **ni... ni** *conj.* 2.1
nephew **sobrino** *m.* 1.3
nervous **nervioso/a** *adj.* 1.5
network **red** *f.* 2.5
never **nunca** *adj.* 2.1; **jamás** 2.1
new **nuevo/a** *adj.* 1.6
newlywed **recién casado/a** *m.*, *f.* 2.3
news **noticias** *f.*, *pl.* 3.6; **actualidades** *f.*, *pl.* 3.6; **noticia** *f.* 2.5
newscast **noticiero** *m.* 3.6
newspaper **periódico** 1.4; **diario** *m.* 3.6
next **próximo/a** *adj.* 1.3, 3.4
   next to **al lado de** *prep.* 1.2
nice **simpático/a** *adj.* 1.3; **amable** *adj.* 1.5
niece **sobrina** *f.* 1.3
night **noche** *f.* 1.1
   night stand **mesita** *f.* **de noche** 2.6

nine **nueve** 1.1
nine hundred **novecientos/as** 1.2
nineteen **diecinueve** 1.1
ninety **noventa** 1.2
ninth **noveno/a** 1.5
no **no** 1.1; **ningún, ninguno/a(s)** *adj.* 2.1
   no one **nadie** *pron.* 2.1
nobody **nadie** 2.1
none **ningún, ninguno/a(s)** *adj.* 2.1
noon **mediodía** *m.* 1.1
nor **ni** *conj.* 2.1
north **norte** *m.* 3.2
   to the north **al norte** 3.2
nose **nariz** *f.* 2.4
not **no** 1.1
   not any **ningún, ninguno/a(s)** *adj.* 2.1
   not anyone **nadie** *pron.* 2.1
   not anything **nada** *pron.* 2.1
   not bad at all **nada mal** 1.5
   not either **tampoco** *adv.* 2.1
   not ever **nunca** *adv.* 2.1; **jamás** *adv.* 2.1
   not very well **no muy bien** 1.1
   not working **descompuesto/a** *adj.* 2.5
notebook **cuaderno** *m.* 1.1
nothing **nada** 1.1; 2.1
noun **sustantivo** *m.*
November **noviembre** *m.* 1.5
now **ahora** *adv.* 1.2
nowadays **hoy día** *adv.*
nuclear **nuclear** *adj. m.*, *f.* 3.1
   nuclear energy **energía nuclear** 3.1
number **número** *m.* 1.1
nurse **enfermero/a** *m.*, *f.* 2.4
nutrition **nutrición** *f.* 3.3
nutritionist **nutricionista** *m.*, *f.* 3.3

O

o'clock: It's... o'clock **Son las...** 1.1
   It's one o'clock. **Es la una.** 1.1
obey **obedecer** *v.* 3.6
obligation **deber** *m.* 3.6
obtain **conseguir (e:i)** *v.* 1.4; **obtener** *v.* 3.4
obvious **obvio/a** *adj.* 3.1
   it's obvious **es obvio** 3.1
occupation **ocupación** *f.* 3.4
occur **ocurrir** *v.* 3.6
October **octubre** *m.* 1.5
of **de** *prep.* 1.1
   Of course. **Claro que sí.**; **Por supuesto.**
offer **oferta** *f.*; **ofrecer (c:zc)** *v.* 1.6
office **oficina** *f.* 2.6
   doctor's office **consultorio** *m.* 2.4

often **a menudo** *adv.* 2.4
Oh! **¡Ay!**
oil **aceite** *m.* 2.2
OK **regular** *adj.* 1.1
  It's okay. **Está bien.**
old **viejo/a** *adj.* 1.3
old age **vejez** *f.* 2.3
older **mayor** *adj. m., f.* 1.3
  older brother, sister **hermano/a mayor** *m., f.* 1.3
oldest **el/la mayor** 2.2
on **en** *prep.* 1.2; **sobre** *prep.* 1.2
  on behalf of **por** *prep.* 2.5
  on the dot **en punto** 1.1
  on time **a tiempo** 2.4
  on top of **encima de** 1.2
once **una vez** 1.6
one **uno** 1.1
  one hundred **cien(to)** 1.2
  one million **un millón** *m.* 1.2
  one more time **una vez más**
  one thousand **mil** 1.2
  one time **una vez** 1.6
onion **cebolla** *f.* 2.2
only **sólo** *adv.* 1.6; **único/a** *adj.* 1.3
  only child **hijo/a único/a** *m., f.* 1.3
open **abierto/a** *adj.* 1.5, 3.2; **abrir** *v.* 1.3
open-air **al aire libre** 1.6
opera **ópera** *f.* 3.5
operation **operación** *f.* 2.4
opposite **enfrente de** *prep.* 3.2
or **o** *conj.* 2.1
orange **anaranjado/a** *adj.* 1.6; **naranja** *f.* 2.2
orchestra **orquesta** *f.* 3.5
order **mandar** 2.6; *(food)* **pedir (e:i)** *v.* 2.2
  in order to **para** *prep.* 2.5
orderly **ordenado/a** *adj.* 1.5
ordinal *(numbers)* **ordinal** *adj.*
organize oneself **organizarse** *v.* 2.6
other **otro/a** *adj.* 1.6
ought to **deber** *v.* **(+ inf.)** *adj.* 1.3
our **nuestro(s)/a(s)** *poss. adj.* 1.3; *poss. pron.* 2.5
out of order **descompuesto/a** *adj.* 2.5
outside **afuera** *adv.* 1.5
outskirts **afueras** *f., pl.* 2.6
oven **horno** *m.* 2.6
over **sobre** *prep.* 1.2
(over)population **(sobre)población** *f.* 3.1
over there **allá** *adv.* 1.2
own **propio/a** *adj.*
owner **dueño/a** *m., f.* 2.2

P

p.m. **de la tarde, de la noche** *f.* 1.1
pack (one's suitcases) **hacer** *v.* **las maletas** 1.5

package **paquete** *m.* 3.2
page **página** *f.* 2.5
pain **dolor** *m.* 2.4
  have pain **tener** *v.* **dolor** 2.4
paint **pintar** *v.* 3.5
painter **pintor(a)** *m., f.* 3.4
painting **pintura** *f.* 2.6, 3.5
pair **par** *m.* 1.6
  pair of shoes **par** *m.* **de zapatos** 1.6
pale **pálido/a** *adj.* 3.2
pants **pantalones** *m., pl.* 1.6
pantyhose **medias** *f., pl.* 1.6
paper **papel** *m.* 1.2; *(report)* **informe** *m.* 3.6
Pardon me. *(May I?)* **Con permiso.** 1.1; *(Excuse me.)* Pardon me. **Perdón.** 1.1
parents **padres** *m., pl.* 1.3; **papás** *m., pl.*
park **estacionar** *v.* 2.5; **parque** *m.* 1.4
parking lot **estacionamiento** *m.* 3.2
partner *(one of a married couple)* **pareja** *f.* 2.3
party **fiesta** *f.* 2.3
passed **pasado/a** *p.p.*
passenger **pasajero/a** *m., f.* 1.1
passport **pasaporte** *m.* 1.5
past **pasado/a** *adj.* 1.6
pastime **pasatiempo** *m.* 1.4
pastry shop **pastelería** *f.* 3.2
path **sendero** *m.* 3.1
patient **paciente** *m., f.* 2.4
patio **patio** *m.* 2.6
pay **pagar** *v.* 1.6
  pay in cash **pagar** *v.* **al contado; pagar en efectivo** 3.2
  pay in installments **pagar** *v.* **a plazos** 3.2
  pay the bill **pagar la cuenta**
pea **arveja** *m.* 2.2
peace **paz** *f.* 3.6
peach **melocotón** *m.* 2.2
peak **cima** *f.* 3.3
pear **pera** *f.* 2.2
pen **pluma** *f.* 1.2
pencil **lápiz** *m.* 1.1
penicillin **penicilina** *f.*
people **gente** *f.* 1.3
pepper *(black)* **pimienta** *f.* 2.2
per **por** *prep.* 2.5
perfect **perfecto/a** *adj.* 1.5
period of time **temporada** *f.* 1.5
person **persona** *f.* 1.3
pharmacy **farmacia** *f.* 2.4
phenomenal **fenomenal** *adj.* 1.5
photograph **foto(grafía)** *f.* 1.1
physical (exam) **examen** *m.* **médico** 2.4
physician **doctor(a), médico/a** *m., f.* 1.3
physics **física** *f. sing.* 1.2
pick up **recoger** *v.* 3.1
picture **cuadro** *m.* 2.6; **pintura** *f.* 2.6
pie **pastel** *m.* 2.3

pill (tablet) **pastilla** *f.* 2.4
pillow **almohada** *f.* 2.6
pineapple **piña** *f.*
pink **rosado/a** *adj.* 1.6
place **lugar** *m.* 1.2, 1.4; **sitio** *m.* 1.3; **poner** *v.* 1.4
plaid **de cuadros** 1.6
plans **planes** *m., pl.*
  have plans **tener planes**
plant **planta** *f.* 3.1
plastic **plástico** *m.* 3.1
  (made) of plastic **de plástico** 3.1
plate **plato** *m.* 2.6
play **drama** *m.* 3.5; **comedia** *f.* 3.5 **jugar (u:ue)** *v.* 1.4; *(a musical instrument)* **tocar** *v.* 3.5; *(a role)* **hacer el papel de** 3.5; *(cards)* **jugar a (las cartas)** 1.5; *(sports)* **practicar deportes** 1.4
player **jugador(a)** *m., f.* 1.4
playwright **dramaturgo/a** *m., f.* 3.5
plead **rogar (o:ue)** *v.* 2.6
pleasant **agradable** *adj.*
please **por favor** 1.1
Pleased to meet you. **Mucho gusto.** 1.1; **Encantado/a.** *adj.* 1.1
pleasing: be pleasing to **gustar** *v.* 2.1
pleasure **gusto** *m.* 1.1; **placer** *m.* The pleasure is mine. **El gusto es mío.** 1.1
poem **poema** *m.* 3.5
poet **poeta** *m., f.* 3.5
poetry **poesía** *f.* 3.5
police (force) **policía** *f.* 2.5
political **político/a** *adj.* 3.6
politician **político/a** *m., f.* 3.4
politics **política** *f.* 3.6
polka-dotted **de lunares** 1.6
poll **encuesta** *f.* 3.6
pollute **contaminar** *v.* 3.1
polluted **contaminado/a** *m., f.* 3.1
  be polluted **estar contaminado/a** 3.1
pollution **contaminación** *f.* 3.1
pool **piscina** *f.* 1.4
poor **pobre** *adj., m., f.* 1.6
  poor thing **pobrecito/a** *adj.* 1.3
popsicle **paleta helada** *f.* 1.4
population **población** *f.* 3.1
pork **cerdo** *m.* 2.2
  pork chop **chuleta** *f.* **de cerdo** 2.2
portable **portátil** *adj.* 2.5
  portable computer **computadora** *f.* **portátil** 2.5
position **puesto** *m.* 3.4
possessive **posesivo/a** *adj.*
possible **posible** *adj.* 3.1
  it's (not) possible **(no) es posible** 3.1
post office **correo** *m.* 3.2
postcard **postal** *f.*
poster **cartel** *m.* 2.6
potato **papa** *f.* 2.2; **patata** *f.* 2.2

pottery **cerámica** *f.* 3.5
practice **entrenarse** *v.* 3.3;
 practicar *v.* 1.2; (a degree/
 profession) **ejercer** *v.* 3.4
prefer **preferir (e:ie)** *v.* 1.4
pregnant **embarazada** *adj. f.* 2.4
prepare **preparar** *v.* 1.2
preposition **preposición** *f.*
prescribe (*medicine*) **recetar** *v.* 2.4
prescription **receta** *f.* 2.4
present **regalo** *m.*; **presentar**
 v. 3.5
press **prensa** *f.* 3.6
pressure **presión** *f.*
 be under a lot of pressure **sufrir**
 muchas presiones 3.3
pretty **bonito/a** *adj.* 1.3
price **precio** *m.* 1.6
 (fixed, set) price **precio** *m.*
 fijo 1.6
print **imprimir** *v.* 2.5
printer **impresora** *f.* 2.5
prize **premio** *m.* 3.5
probable **probable** *adj.* 3.1
 it's (not) probable **(no) es**
 probable 3.1
problem **problema** *m.* 1.1
profession **profesión** *f.* 1.3; 3.4
professor **profesor(a)** *m., f.*
program **programa** *m.* 1.1
programmer **programador(a)**
 m., f. 1.3
prohibit **prohibir** *v.* 2.4
project **proyecto** *m.* 2.5
promotion (*career*)
 ascenso *m.* 3.4
pronoun **pronombre** *m.*
protect **proteger** *v.* 3.1
protein **proteína** *f.* 3.3
provided (that) **con tal (de) que**
 conj. 3.1
psychologist **psicólogo/a**
 m., f. 3.4
psychology **psicología** *f.* 1.2
publish **publicar** *v.* 3.5
Puerto Rican **puertorriqueño/a**
 adj. 1.3
purchases **compras** *f., pl.*
pure **puro/a** *adj.* 3.1
purple **morado/a** *adj.* 1.6
purse **bolsa** *f.* 1.6
put **poner** *v.* 1.4; **puesto/a** *p.p.* 3.2
 put (a letter) in the mailbox
 echar (una carta) al
 buzón 3.2
 put on (*a performance*)
 presentar *v.* 3.5
 put on (*clothing*) **ponerse** *v.* 2.1
 put on makeup **maquillarse**
 v. 2.1

quality **calidad** *f.* 1.6
quarter (*academic*) **trimestre** *m.* 1.2
 quarter after (*time*) **y cuarto**
 1.1; **y quince** 1.1

quarter to (*time*) **menos cuarto**
 1.1; **menos quince** 1.1
question **pregunta** *f.*
quickly **rápido** *adv.* 2.4
quiet **tranquilo/a** *adj.* 3.3
quit **dejar** *v.* 3.4
quiz **prueba** *f.* 1.2

racism **racismo** *m.* 3.6
radio (*medium*) **radio** *f.* 1.2
 radio (set) **radio** *m.* 2.5
rain **llover (o:ue)** *v.* 1.5; **lluvia** *f.*
 It's raining. **Llueve.** 1.5; **Está**
 lloviendo. 1.5
raincoat **impermeable** *m.* 1.6
rain forest **bosque** *m.* **tropical** 3.1
raise (*salary*) **aumento de**
 sueldo 3.4
rather **bastante** *adv.* 2.4
read **leer** *v.* 1.3; **leído/a** *p.p.* 3.2
 read e-mail **leer el correo**
 electrónico 1.4
 read a magazine **leer una**
 revista 1.4
 read a newspaper **leer un**
 periódico 1.4
ready **listo/a** *adj.* 1.5
reality show **programa de**
 realidad *m.* 3.5
reap the benefits (of) *v.* **disfrutar**
 v. **(de)** 3.3
receive **recibir** *v.* 1.3
recommend **recomendar (e:ie)**
 v. 2.2; 2.6
record **grabar** *v.* 2.5
recover **recuperar** *v.* 2.5
recreation **diversión** *f.* 1.4
recycle **reciclar** *v.* 3.1
recycling **reciclaje** *m.* 3.1
red **rojo/a** *adj.* 1.6
red-haired **pelirrojo/a** *adj.* 1.3
reduce **reducir** *v.* 3.1; **disminuir**
 v. 3.4
 reduce stress/tension **aliviar el**
 estrés/la tensión 3.3
refrigerator **refrigerador** *m.* 2.6
region **región** *f.*
regret **sentir (e:ie)** *v.* 3.1
relatives **parientes** *m., pl.* 1.3
relax **relajarse** *v.* 2.3
 Relax. **Tranquilo/a.** 2.1
 Relax, sweetie. **Tranquilo/a,**
 cariño. 2.5
remain **quedarse** *v.* 2.1
remember **acordarse (o:ue)** *v.*
 (de) 2.1; **recordar (o:ue)**
 v. 1.4
remote control **control remoto**
 m. 2.5
renewable **renovable** *adj.* 3.1
rent **alquilar** *v.* 2.6; (payment)
 alquiler *m.* 2.6
repeat **repetir (e:i)** *v.* 1.4

report **informe** *m.* 3.6; **reportaje**
 m. 3.6
reporter **reportero/a** *m., f.* 3.4
representative **representante** *m.,*
 f. 3.6
request **pedir (e:i)** *v.* 1.4
reservation **reservación** *f.* 1.5
resign (from) **renunciar (a)** *v.* 3.4
resolve **resolver (o:ue)** *v.* 3.1
resolved **resuelto/a** *p.p.* 3.2
resource **recurso** *m.* 3.1
responsibility **deber** *m.* 3.6;
 responsabilidad *f.*
responsible **responsable** *adj.* 2.2
rest **descansar** *v.* 1.2
restaurant **restaurante** *m.* 1.4
résumé **currículum** *m.* 3.4
retire (from work) **jubilarse**
 v. 2.3
return **regresar** *v.* 1.2; **volver**
 (o:ue) *v.* 1.4
returned **vuelto/a** *p.p.* 3.2
rice **arroz** *m.* 2.2
rich **rico/a** *adj.* 1.6
ride a bicycle **pasear** *v.* **en**
 bicicleta 1.4
ride a horse **montar** *v.* **a**
 caballo 1.5
ridiculous **ridículo/a** *adj.* 3.1
 it's ridiculous **es ridículo** 3.1
right **derecha** *f.* 1.2
 be right **tener razón** 1.3
 right? (*question tag*) **¿no?** 1.1;
 ¿verdad? 1.1
 right away **enseguida** *adv.*
 right now **ahora mismo** 1.5
 to the right of **a la**
 derecha de 1.2
rights **derechos** *m.* 3.6
ring **anillo** *m.* 3.5
ring (*a doorbell*) **sonar (o:ue)**
 v. 2.5
river **río** *m.* 3.1
road **carretera** *f.* 2.5; **camino** *m.*
roast **asado/a** *adj.* 2.2
roast chicken **pollo** *m.* **asado** 2.2
rollerblade **patinar en línea** *v.*
romantic **romántico/a** *adj.* 3.5
room **habitación** *f.* 1.5; **cuarto**
 m. 1.2; 2.1
 living room **sala** *f.* 2.6
roommate **compañero/a**
 m., f. **de cuarto** 1.2
roundtrip **de ida y vuelta** 1.5
 roundtrip ticket **pasaje** *m.* **de**
 ida y vuelta 1.5
routine **rutina** *f.* 2.1
rug **alfombra** *f.* 2.6
run **correr** *v.* 1.3
 run errands **hacer**
 diligencias 3.2
 run into (*have an accident*)
 chocar (con) *v.*; (*meet*
 accidentally) **encontrar(se)**
 (o:ue) *v.* 2.5; (*run into*
 something) **darse (con)** 2.4

run into (each other)
  encontrar(se) (o:ue) *v.* 2.5
rush **apurarse, darse prisa**
  v. 3.3
Russian **ruso/a** *adj.* 1.3

S

sad **triste** *adj.* 1.5; 3.1
  it's sad **es triste** 3.1
safe **seguro/a** *adj.* 1.5
said **dicho/a** *p.p.* 3.2
sailboard **tabla de windsurf** *f.* 1.5
salad **ensalada** *f.* 2.2
salary **salario** *m.* 3.4; **sueldo**
  m. 3.4
sale **rebaja** *f.* 1.6
salesperson **vendedor(a)** *m.,*
  f. 1.6
salmon **salmón** *m.* 2.2
salt **sal** *f.* 2.2
same **mismo/a** *adj.* 1.3
sandal **sandalia** *f.* 1.6
sandwich **sándwich** *m.* 2.2
Saturday **sábado** *m.* 1.2
sausage **salchicha** *f.* 2.2
save (*on a computer*) **guardar**
  v. 2.5; save (money) **ahorrar**
  v. 3.2
savings **ahorros** *m.* 3.2
  savings account **cuenta** *f.* **de**
    ahorros 3.2
say **decir** *v.* 1.4; **declarar** *v.* 3.6
say (that) **decir (que)** *v.* 1.4
  say the answer **decir la**
    respuesta 1.4
scan **escanear** *v.* 2.5
scarcely **apenas** *adv.* 2.4
scared: be (very) scared (of) **tener**
  (mucho) miedo (de) 1.3
schedule **horario** *m.* 1.2
school **escuela** *f.* 1.1
sciences *f., pl.* **ciencias** 1.2
science fiction (genre) **de**
  ciencia ficción *f.* 3.5
scientist **científico/a** *m., f.* 3.4
scream **grito** *m.* 1.5; **gritar** *v.*
screen **pantalla** *f.* 2.5
scuba dive **bucear** *v.* 1.4
sculpt **esculpir** *v.* 3.5
sculptor **escultor(a)** *m., f.* 3.5
sculpture **escultura** *f.* 3.5
sea **mar** *m.* 1.5
  (sea) turtle **tortuga (marina)**
    f. 3.1
season **estación** *f.* 1.5
seat **silla** *f.* 1.2
second **segundo/a** 1.5
secretary **secretario/a** *m., f.* 3.4
sedentary **sedentario/a** *adj.* 3.3
see **ver** *v.* 1.4
  see (you, him, her) again **volver**
    a ver(te, lo, la)
  see movies **ver películas** 1.4
  See you. **Nos vemos.** 1.1
  See you later. **Hasta la vista.**
    1.1; **Hasta luego.** 1.1
  See you soon. **Hasta pronto.** 1.1
  See you tomorrow. **Hasta**
    mañana. 1.1

seem **parecer** *v.* 1.6
seen **visto/a** *p.p.* 3.2
sell **vender** *v.* 1.6
semester **semestre** *m.* 1.2
send **enviar; mandar** *v.* 3.2
separate (from) **separarse** *v.*
  (de) 2.3
separated **separado/a** *adj.* 2.3
September **septiembre** *m.* 1.5
sequence **secuencia** *f.*
serious **grave** *adj.* 2.4
serve **servir (e:i)** *v.* 2.2
service **servicio** *m.* 3.3
set (*fixed*) **fijo/a** *adj.* 1.6
  set the table **poner la mesa** 2.6
seven **siete** 1.1
seven hundred **setecientos/as** 1.2
seventeen **diecisiete** 1.1
seventh **séptimo/a** 1.5
seventy **setenta** 1.2
several **varios/as** *adj. pl.*
sexism **sexismo** *m.* 3.6
shame **lástima** *f.* 3.1
  it's a shame **es una lástima** 3.1
shampoo **champú** *m.* 2.1
shape **forma** *f.* 3.3
  be in good shape **estar en**
    buena forma 3.3
  stay in shape **mantenerse en**
    forma 3.3
share **compartir** *v.* 1.3
sharp (*time*) **en punto** 1.1
shave **afeitarse** *v.* 2.1
shaving cream **crema** *f.* **de**
  afeitar 1.5, 2.1
she **ella** 1.1
shellfish **mariscos** *m., pl.* 2.2
ship **barco** *m.*
shirt **camisa** *f.* 1.6
shoe **zapato** *m.* 1.6
  shoe size **número** *m.* 1.6
  shoe store **zapatería** *f.* 3.2
    tennis shoes **zapatos** *m., pl.*
      de tenis 1.6
shop **tienda** *f.* 1.6
shopping, to go **ir de compras** 1.5
  shopping mall **centro**
    comercial *m.* 1.6
short (*in height*) **bajo/a** *adj.* 1.3;
  (*in length*) **corto/a** *adj.* 1.6
short story **cuento** *m.* 3.5
shorts **pantalones cortos**
  m., pl. 1.6
should (*do something*) **deber** *v.*
  (+ inf.) 1.3
shout **gritar** *v.*
show **espectáculo** *m.* 3.5;
  mostrar (o:ue) *v.* 1.4
  game show **concurso** *m.* 3.5
shower **ducha** *f.* 2.1; **ducharse**
  v. 2.1
shrimp **camarón** *m.* 2.2
siblings **hermanos/as** *pl.* 1.3
sick **enfermo/a** *adj.* 2.4
  be sick **estar enfermo/a** 2.4
  get sick **enfermarse** *v.* 2.4
sign **firmar** *v.* 3.2; **letrero** *m.* 3.2
silk **seda** *f.* 1.6
  (made of) silk **de seda** 1.6
since **desde** *prep.*
sing **cantar** *v.* 1.2

singer **cantante** *m., f.* 3.5
single **soltero/a** *adj.* 2.3
  single room **habitación** *f.*
    individual 1.5
sink **lavabo** *m.* 2.1
sir **señor (Sr.), don** *m.* 1.1;
  caballero *m.* 2.2
sister **hermana** *f.* 1.3
sister-in-law **cuñada** *f.* 1.3
sit down **sentarse (e:ie)** *v.* 2.1
six **seis** 1.1
six hundred **seiscientos/as** 1.2
sixteen **dieciséis** 1.1
sixth **sexto/a** 1.5
sixty **sesenta** 1.2
size **talla** *f.* 1.6
  shoe size *m.* **número** 1.6
(in-line) skate **patinar (en**
  línea) 1.4
skateboard **andar en patineta**
  v. 1.4
ski **esquiar** *v.* 1.4
skiing **esquí** *m.* 1.4
  water-skiing **esquí** *m.*
    acuático 1.4
skirt **falda** *f.* 1.6
skull made out of sugar **calavera**
  de azúcar *f.* 2.3
sky **cielo** *m.* 3.1
sleep **dormir (o:ue)** *v.* 1.4;
  sueño *m.*
  go to sleep **dormirse**
    (o:ue) *v.* 2.1
sleepy: be (very) sleepy **tener**
  (mucho) sueño 1.3
slender **delgado/a** *adj.* 1.3
slim down **adelgazar** *v.* 3.3
slippers **pantuflas** *f.* 2.1
slow **lento/a** *adj.* 2.5
slowly **despacio** *adv.* 2.4
small **pequeño/a** *adj.* 1.3
smart **listo/a** *adj.* 1.5
smile **sonreír (e:i)** *v.* 2.3
smiled **sonreído** *p.p.* 3.2
smoggy: It's (very) smoggy. **Hay**
  (mucha) contaminación.
smoke **fumar** *v.* 3.3
  (not) to smoke **(no) fumar** 3.3
smoking section **sección** *f.* **de**
  fumar 2.2
  (non) smoking section *f.* **sección**
    de (no) fumar 2.2
snack **merendar (e:ie)** *v.* 2.2
  afternoon snack **merienda** *f.* 3.3
  have a snack **merendar** *v.* 2.2
sneakers **los zapatos de**
  tenis 1.6
sneeze **estornudar** *v.* 2.4
snow **nevar (e:ie)** *v.* 1.5; **nieve** *f.*
snowing: It's snowing. **Nieva.** 1.5;
  Está nevando. 1.5
so (*in such a way*) **así** *adv.* 2.4;
  tan *adv.* 1.5
  so much **tanto** *adv.*
  so-so **regular** 1.1
  so that **para que** *conj.* 3.1
soap **jabón** *m.* 2.1
soap opera **telenovela** *f.* 3.5
soccer **fútbol** *m.* 1.4
sociology **sociología** *f.* 1.2
sock(s) **calcetín (calcetines)** *m.* 1.6

sofa **sofá** *m.* 2.6
soft drink **refresco** *m.* 2.2
software **programa** *m.* **de computación** 2.5
soil **tierra** *f.* 3.1
solar **solar** *adj., m., f.* 3.1
   solar energy **energía solar** 3.1
soldier **soldado** *m., f.* 3.6
solution **solución** *f.* 3.1
solve **resolver (o:ue)** *v.* 3.1
some **algún, alguno/a(s)** *adj.* 2.1; **unos/as** *indef. art.* 1.1
somebody **alguien** *pron.* 2.1
someone **alguien** *pron.* 2.1
something **algo** *pron.* 2.1
sometimes **a veces** *adv.* 2.4
son **hijo** *m.* 1.3
song **canción** *f.* 3.5
son-in-law **yerno** *m.* 1.3
soon **pronto** *adv.* 2.4
   See you soon. **Hasta pronto.** 1.1
sorry: be sorry **sentir (e:ie)** *v.* 3.1
   I'm sorry. **Lo siento.** 1.1
soul **alma** *f.* 2.3
soup **sopa** *f.* 2.2
south **sur** *m.* 3.2
   to the south **al sur** 3.2
Spain **España** *f.*
Spanish (*language*) **español** *m.* 1.2; **español(a)** *adj.* 1.3
spare (free) time **ratos libres** 1.4
speak **hablar** *v.* 1.2
   Speaking. (*on the telephone*) **Con él/ella habla.** 2.5
special: today's specials **las especialidades del día** 2.2
spectacular **espectacular** *adj. m., f.*
speech **discurso** *m.* 3.6
speed **velocidad** *f.* 2.5
   speed limit **velocidad** *f.* **máxima** 2.5
spelling **ortografía** *f.,* **ortográfico/a** *adj.*
spend (*money*) **gastar** *v.* 1.6
spoon (*table or large*) **cuchara** *f.* 2.6
sport **deporte** *m.* 1.4
   sports-related **deportivo/a** *adj.* 1.4
spouse **esposo/a** *m., f.* 1.3
sprain (one's ankle) **torcerse (o:ue)** *v.* **(el tobillo)** 2.4
spring **primavera** *f.* 1.5
(city or town) square **plaza** *f.* 1.4
stadium **estadio** *m.* 1.2
stage **etapa** *f.* 2.3
stairs **escalera** *f.* 2.6
stairway **escalera** *f.* 2.6
stamp **estampilla** *f.* 3.2; **sello** *m.* 3.2
stand in line **hacer** *v.* **cola** 3.2
star **estrella** *f.* 3.1
start (*a vehicle*) **arrancar** *v.* 2.5
station **estación** *f.* 1.5
statue **estatua** *f.* 3.5
status: marital status **estado** *m.* **civil** 2.3

stay **quedarse** *v.* 2.1
   stay in shape **mantenerse en forma** 3.3
steak **bistec** *m.* 2.2
steering wheel **volante** *m.* 2.5
step **escalón** *m.* 3.3
stepbrother **hermanastro** *m.* 1.3
stepdaughter **hijastra** *f.* 1.3
stepfather **padrastro** *m.* 1.3
stepmother **madrastra** *f.* 1.3
stepsister **hermanastra** *f.* 1.3
stepson **hijastro** *m.* 1.3
stereo **estéreo** *m.* 2.5
still **todavía** *adv.* 1.5
stockbroker **corredor(a)** *m., f.* **de bolsa** 3.4
stockings **medias** *f., pl.* 1.6
stomach **estómago** *m.* 2.4
stone **piedra** *f.* 3.1
stop **parar** *v.* 2.5
   stop (*doing something*) **dejar de (+ *inf.*)** 3.1
store **tienda** *f.* 1.6
storm **tormenta** *f.* 3.6
story **cuento** *m.* 3.5; **historia** *f.* 3.5
stove **cocina, estufa** *f.* 2.6
straight **derecho** *adv.* 3.2
   straight (ahead) **derecho** 3.2
straighten up **arreglar** *v.* 2.6
strange **extraño/a** *adj.* 3.1
   it's strange **es extraño** 3.1
street **calle** *f.* 2.5
stress **estrés** *m.* 3.3
stretching **estiramiento** *m.* 3.3
   do stretching exercises **hacer ejercicios** *m. pl.* **de estiramiento** 3.3
strike (*labor*) **huelga** *f.* 3.6
striped **de rayas** 1.6
stroll **pasear** *v.* 1.4
strong **fuerte** *adj. m., f.* 3.3
struggle (for/against) **luchar** *v.* **(por/contra)** 3.6
student **estudiante** *m., f.* 1.1; 1.2; **estudiantil** *adj.* 1.2
study **estudiar** *v.* 1.2
stupendous **estupendo/a** *adj.* 1.5
style **estilo** *m.*
suburbs **afueras** *f., pl.* 2.6
subway **metro** *m.* 1.5
   subway station **estación** *f.* **del metro** 1.5
success **éxito** *m.*
successful: be successful **tener éxito** 3.4
such as **tales como**
suddenly **de repente** *adv.* 1.6
suffer **sufrir** *v.* 2.4
   suffer an illness **sufrir una enfermedad** 2.4
sugar **azúcar** *m.* 2.2
suggest **sugerir (e:ie)** *v.* 2.6
suit **traje** *m.* 1.6
suitcase **maleta** *f.* 1.1
summer **verano** *m.* 1.5
sun **sol** *m.* 3.1
sunbathe **tomar** *v.* **el sol** 1.4

Sunday **domingo** *m.* 1.2
(sun)glasses **gafas** *f., pl.* **(de sol)** 1.6
sunny: It's (very) sunny. **Hace (mucho) sol.** 1.5
supermarket **supermercado** *m.* 3.2
suppose **suponer** *v.* 1.4
sure **seguro/a** *adj.* 1.5
   be sure **estar seguro/a** 1.5
surf **hacer** *v.* **surf** 1.5; (*the Internet*) **navegar** *v.* **(en Internet)** 2.5
surfboard **tabla de surf** *f.* 1.5
surprise **sorprender** *v.* 2.3; **sorpresa** *f.* 2.3
survey **encuesta** *f.* 3.6
sweat **sudar** *v.* 3.3
sweater **suéter** *m.* 1.6
sweep the floor **barrer el suelo** 2.6
sweets **dulces** *m., pl.* 2.3
swim **nadar** *v.* 1.4
swimming **natación** *f.* 1.4
   swimming pool **piscina** *f.* 1.4
symptom **síntoma** *m.* 2.4

T

table **mesa** *f.* 1.2
tablespoon **cuchara** *f.* 2.6
tablet (*pill*) **pastilla** *f.* 2.4
take **tomar** *v.* 1.2; **llevar** *v.* 1.6
   take care of **cuidar** *v.* 3.1
   take someone's temperature **tomar** *v.* **la temperatura** 2.4
   take (*wear*) a shoe size **calzar** *v.* 1.6
   take a bath **bañarse** *v.* 2.1
   take a shower **ducharse** *v.* 2.1
   take off **quitarse** *v.* 2.1
   take out the trash *v.* **sacar la basura** 2.6
   take photos **tomar** *v.* **fotos** 1.5; **sacar** *v.* **fotos** 1.5
talented **talentoso/a** *adj.* 3.5
talk **hablar** *v.* 1.2
   talk show **programa** *m.* **de entrevistas** 3.5
tall **alto/a** *adj.* 1.3
tank **tanque** *m.* 2.5
taste **probar (o:ue)** *v.* 2.2
   taste like **saber a** 2.2
tasty **rico/a** *adj.* 2.2; **sabroso/a** *adj.* 2.2
tax **impuesto** *m.* 3.6
taxi **taxi** *m.* 1.5
tea **té** *m.* 2.2
teach **enseñar** *v.* 1.2
teacher **profesor(a)** *m., f.* 1.1, 1.2; **maestro/a** *m., f.* 3.4
team **equipo** *m.* 1.4
technician **técnico/a** *m., f.* 3.4
telecommuting **teletrabajo** *m.* 3.4
telephone **teléfono** 2.5
television **televisión** *f.* 1.2
   television set **televisor** *m.* 2.5
tell **contar** *v.* 1.4; **decir** *v.* 1.4

tell (that) **decir** *v.* **(que)** 1.4
  tell lies **decir mentiras** 1.4
  tell the truth **decir la
    verdad** 1.4
temperature **temperatura** *f.* 2.4
ten **diez** 1.1
tennis **tenis** *m.* 1.4
  tennis shoes **zapatos** *m., pl.*
    de tenis 1.6
tension **tensión** *f.* 3.3
tent **tienda** *f.* **de campaña**
tenth **décimo/a** 1.5
terrible **terrible** *adj. m., f.* 3.1
  it's terrible **es terrible** 3.1
terrific **chévere** *adj.*
test **prueba** *f.* 1.2; **examen** *m.* 1.2
text message **mensaje** *m.* **de
  texto** 2.5
Thank you. **Gracias.** *f., pl.* 1.1
  Thank you (very much).
    (Muchas) gracias. 1.1
  Thanks (a lot). **(Muchas)
    gracias.** 1.1
  Thanks for inviting me. **Gracias
    por invitarme.** 2.3
that **que, quien(es)** *pron.* 2.6
  that (one) **ése, ésa, eso**
    pron. 1.6; **ese, esa,** *adj.* 1.6
  that (*over there*) **aquél,
    aquélla, aquello** *pron.* 1.6;
    aquel, aquella *adj.* 1.6
  that which **lo que** 2.6
  that's why **por eso** 2.5
the **el** *m.,* **la** *f. sing.,* **los** *m.,*
  las *f., pl.* 1.1
theater **teatro** *m.* 3.5
their **su(s)** *poss. adj.* 1.3;
  suyo(s)/a(s) *poss. pron.* 2.5
them **los/las** *pl., d.o. pron.* 1.5
  to/for them **les** *pl., i.o. pron.* 1.6
then (*afterward*) **después**
  adv. 2.1; (*as a result*) **entonces**
  adv. 1.5, 2.1; (*next*) **luego**
  adv. 2.1
there **allí** *adv.* 1.2
  There is/are... **Hay...** 1.1
  There is/are not... **No hay...** 1.1
therefore **por eso** 2.5
these **éstos, éstas** *pron.* 1.6;
  estos, estas *adj.* 1.6
they **ellos** *m.,* **ellas** *f. pron.* 1.1
  They all told me to ask you to
    excuse them/forgive them.
    **Todos me dijeron que te
    pidiera una disculpa de su
    parte.** 3.6
thin **delgado/a** *adj.* 1.3
thing **cosa** *f.* 1.1
think **pensar (e:ie)** *v.* 1.4;
  (*believe*) **creer** *v.*
  think about **pensar en** *v.* 1.4
third **tercero/a** 1.5
thirst **sed** *f.*
thirsty: be (very) thirsty **tener
  (mucha) sed** 1.3
thirteen **trece** 1.1
thirty **treinta** 1.1; thirty (*minutes
  past the hour*) **y treinta; y
  media** 1.1
this **este, esta** *adj.;* **éste, ésta,
  esto** *pron.* 1.6

those **ésos, ésas** *pron.* 1.6; **esos,
  esas** *adj.* 1.6
those (over there) **aquéllos,
  aquéllas** *pron.* 1.6; **aquellos,
  aquellas** *adj.* 1.6
thousand **mil** *m.* 1.2
three **tres** 1.1
three hundred **trescientos/as** 1.2
throat **garganta** *f.* 2.4
through **por** *prep.* 2.5
Thursday **jueves** *m., sing.* 1.2
thus (*in such a way*) **así** *adv.*
ticket **boleto** *m.* 1.2, 3.5;
  pasaje *m.* 1.5
tie **corbata** *f.* 1.6
time **vez** *f.* 1.6; **tiempo** *m.* 3.2
  have a good/bad time **pasarlo
    bien/mal** 2.3
  I've had a fantastic time. **Lo
    he pasado de película.** 3.6
  What time is it? **¿Qué hora
    es?** 1.1
  (At) What time...? **¿A qué
    hora...?** 1.1
times **veces** *f., pl.* 1.6
  many times **muchas
    veces** 2.4
  two times **dos veces** 1.6
tip **propina** *f.* 2.2
tire **llanta** *f.* 2.5
tired **cansado/a** *adj.* 1.5
  be tired **estar cansado/a** 1.5
title **título** *m.* 3.4
to **a** *prep.* 1.1
toast (*drink*) **brindar** *v.* 2.3
  toast **pan** *m.* **tostado** 2.2
toasted **tostado/a** *adj.* 2.2
  toasted bread **pan tostado**
    m. 2.2
toaster **tostadora** *f.* 2.6
today **hoy** *adv.* 1.2
  Today is... **Hoy es...** 1.2
toe **dedo** *m.* **del pie** 2.4
together **juntos/as** *adj.* 2.3
toilet **inodoro** *m.* 2.1
tomato **tomate** *m.* 2.2
tomorrow **mañana** *f.* 1.1
  See you tomorrow. **Hasta
    mañana.** 1.1
tonight **esta noche** *adv.*
too **también** *adv.* 1.2; 2.1
  too much **demasiado** *adv.* 1.6;
    en exceso 3.3
tooth **diente** *m.* 2.1
toothpaste **pasta** *f.* **de
  dientes** 2.1
top **cima** *f.* 3.3
tornado **tornado** *m.* 3.6
touch **tocar** *v.* 3.5
touch screen **pantalla táctil** *f.*
tour **excursión** *f.* 1.4; **recorrido**
  m. 3.1
tour an area **recorrer** *v.*
tourism **turismo** *m.*
tourist **turista** *m., f.* 1.1;
  turístico/a *adj.*
toward **hacia** *prep.* 3.2;
  para *prep.* 2.5
towel **toalla** *f.* 2.1
town **pueblo** *m.*

trade **oficio** *m.* 3.4
traffic **circulación** *f.* 2.5; **tráfico**
  m. 2.5
  traffic light **semáforo** *m.* 3.2
tragedy **tragedia** *f.* 3.5
trail **sendero** *m.* 3.1
train **entrenarse** *v.* 3.3; **tren** *m.* 1.5
  train station **estación** *f.* **de
    tren** *m.* 1.5
trainer **entrenador(a)** *m., f.* 3.3
translate **traducir** *v.* 1.6
trash **basura** *f.* 2.6
travel **viajar** *v.* 1.2
  travel agency **agencia** *f.* **de
    viajes** 1.5
  travel agent **agente** *m., f.*
    de viajes 1.5
traveler **viajero/a** *m., f.* 1.5
  (traveler's) check **cheque (de
    viajero)** 3.2
treadmill **cinta caminadora**
  f. 3.3
tree **árbol** *m.* 3.1
trillion **billón** *m.*
trimester **trimestre** *m.* 1.2
trip **viaje** *m.* 1.5
  take a trip **hacer un viaje** 1.5
tropical forest **bosque** *m.*
  tropical 3.1
true: it's (not) true **(no) es
  verdad** 3.1
trunk **baúl** *m.* 2.5
truth **verdad** *f.* 1.4
try **intentar** *v.;* **probar (o:ue)**
  v. 2.2
  try (*to do something*) **tratar de
    (+ inf.)** 3.3
  try on **probarse (o:ue)** *v.* 2.1
t-shirt **camiseta** *f.* 1.6
Tuesday **martes** *m., sing.* 1.2
tuna **atún** *m.* 2.2
turkey **pavo** *m.* 2.2
turn **doblar** *v.* 3.2
  turn off (*electricity/appliance*)
    apagar *v.* 2.5
  turn on (*electricity/appliance*)
    poner *v.* 2.5; **prender** *v.* 2.5
twelve **doce** 1.1
twenty **veinte** 1.1
twenty-eight **veintiocho** 1.1
twenty-five **veinticinco** 1.1
twenty-four **veinticuatro** 1.1
twenty-nine **veintinueve** 1.1
twenty-one **veintiuno** 1.1;
  veintiún, veintiuno/a *adj.* 1.1
twenty-seven **veintisiete** 1.1
twenty-six **veintiséis** 1.1
twenty-three **veintitrés** 1.1
twenty-two **veintidós** 1.1
twice **dos veces** 1.6
twin **gemelo/a** *m., f.* 1.3
two **dos** 1.1
  two hundred **doscientos/as** 1.2
  two times **dos veces** 1.6

U

ugly **feo/a** *adj.* 1.3
uncle **tío** *m.* 1.3

under **debajo de** *prep.* 1.2
understand **comprender** *v.* 1.3; **entender (e:ie)** *v.* 1.4
underwear **ropa interior** 1.6
unemployment **desempleo** *m.* 3.6
unique **único/a** *adj.* 2.3
United States **Estados Unidos (EE.UU.)** *m. pl.*
university **universidad** *f.* 1.2
unless **a menos que** *conj.* 3.1
unmarried **soltero/a** *adj.* 2.3
unpleasant **antipático/a** *adj.* 1.3
until **hasta** *prep.* 1.6; **hasta que** *conj.* 3.1
urgent **urgente** *adj.* 2.6
  It's urgent that... **Es urgente que...** 2.6
us **nos** *pl., d.o. pron.* 1.5
  to/for us **nos** *pl., i.o. pron.* 1.6
use **usar** *v.* 1.6
used for **para** *prep.* 2.5
useful **útil** *adj. m., f.*

vacation **vacaciones** *f., pl.* 1.5
  be on vacation **estar de vacaciones** 1.5
  go on vacation **ir de vacaciones** 1.5
vacuum **pasar** *v.* **la aspiradora** 2.6
  vacuum cleaner **aspiradora** *f.* 2.6
valley **valle** *m.* 3.1
various **varios/as** *adj. m., f. pl.*
vegetables **verduras** *pl., f.* 2.2
verb **verbo** *m.*
very **muy** *adv.* 1.1
  (Very) well, thank you. **(Muy) bien, gracias.** 1.1
video **video** *m.* 1.1
  video camera **cámara** *f.* **de video** 2.5
  video game **videojuego** *m.* 1.4
videoconference **videoconferencia** *f.* 3.4
vinegar **vinagre** *m.* 2.2
violence **violencia** *f.* 3.6
visit **visitar** *v.* 1.4
  visit monuments **visitar monumentos** 1.4
vitamin **vitamina** *f.* 3.3
voice mail **correo de voz** *m.* 2.5
volcano **volcán** *m.* 3.1
volleyball **vóleibol** *m.* 1.4
vote **votar** *v.* 3.6

wait (for) **esperar** *v.* **(+** *inf.***)** 1.2
waiter/waitress **camarero/a** *m., f.* 2.2

wake up **despertarse (e:ie)** *v.* 2.1
walk **caminar** *v.* 1.2
  take a walk **pasear** *v.* 1.4
  walk around **pasear por** 1.4
wall **pared** *f.* 2.6; **muro** *m.* 3.3
wallet **cartera** *f.* 1.4, 1.6
want **querer (e:ie)** *v.* 1.4
war **guerra** *f.* 3.6
warm up **calentarse (e:ie)** *v.* 3.3
wash **lavar** *v.* 2.6
  wash one's face/hands **lavarse la cara/las manos** 2.1
  wash (the floor, the dishes) **lavar (el suelo, los platos)** 2.6
  wash oneself **lavarse** *v.* 2.1
washing machine **lavadora** *f.* 2.6
wastebasket **papelera** *f.* 1.2
watch **mirar** *v.* 1.2; **reloj** *m.* 1.2
  watch television **mirar (la) televisión** 1.2
water **agua** *f.* 2.2
  water pollution **contaminación del agua** 3.1
  water-skiing **esquí** *m.* **acuático** 1.4
way **manera** *f.*
we **nosotros(as)** *m., f.* 1.1
weak **débil** *adj. m., f.* 3.3
wear **llevar** *v.* 1.6; **usar** *v.* 1.6
weather **tiempo** *m.*
  The weather is bad. **Hace mal tiempo.** 1.5
  The weather is good. **Hace buen tiempo.** 1.5
weaving **tejido** *m.* 3.5
Web **red** *f.* 2.5
website **sitio** *m.* **web** 2.5
wedding **boda** *f.* 2.3
Wednesday **miércoles** *m., sing.* 1.2
week **semana** *f.* 1.2
weekend **fin** *m.* **de semana** 1.4
weight **peso** *m.* 3.3
  lift weights **levantar** *v.* **pesas** *f., pl.* 3.3
welcome **bienvenido(s)/a(s)** *adj.* 1.1
well: (Very) well, thanks. **(Muy) bien, gracias.** 1.1
well-being **bienestar** *m.* 3.3
well organized **ordenado/a** *adj.* 1.5
west **oeste** *m.* 3.2
  to the west **al oeste** 3.2
western (*genre*) **de vaqueros** 3.5
whale **ballena** *f.* 3.1
what **lo que** *pron.* 2.6
what? **¿qué?** 1.1
  At what time...? **¿A qué hora...?** 1.1
  What a pleasure to...! **¡Qué gusto (+** *inf.***)...!** 3.6
  What day is it? **¿Qué día es hoy?** 1.2
  What do you guys think? **¿Qué les parece?**
  What happened? **¿Qué pasó?**

What is today's date? **¿Cuál es la fecha de hoy?** 1.5
What nice clothes! **¡Qué ropa más bonita!** 1.6
What size do you wear? **¿Qué talla lleva (usa)?** 1.6
What time is it? **¿Qué hora es?** 1.1
What's going on? **¿Qué pasa?** 1.1
What's happening? **¿Qué pasa?** 1.1
What's... like? **¿Cómo es...?**
What's new? **¿Qué hay de nuevo?** 1.1
What's the weather like? **¿Qué tiempo hace?** 1.5
What's up? **¿Qué onda?** 3.2
What's wrong? **¿Qué pasó?**
What's your name? **¿Cómo se llama usted?** *form.* 1.1; **¿Cómo te llamas (tú)?** *fam.* 1.1
when **cuando** *conj.* 2.1; 3.1
When? **¿Cuándo?** 1.2
where **donde**
where (to)? (*destination*) **¿adónde?** 1.2; (*location*) **¿dónde?** 1.1, 1.2
  Where are you from? **¿De dónde eres (tú)?** (*fam.*) 1.1; **¿De dónde es (usted)?** (*form.*) 1.1
  Where is...? **¿Dónde está...?** 1.2
which **que** *pron.*, **lo que** *pron.* 2.6
which? **¿cuál?** 1.2; **¿qué?** 1.2
  In which...? **¿En qué...?**
  which one(s)? **¿cuál(es)?** 1.2
while **mientras** *conj.* 2.4
white **blanco/a** *adj.* 1.6
  white wine **vino blanco** 2.2
who **que** *pron.* 2.6; **quien(es)** *pron.* 2.6
who? **¿quién(es)?** 1.1, 1.2
  Who is...? **¿Quién es...?** 1.1
  Who is speaking/calling? (*on telephone*) **¿De parte de quién?** 2.5
  Who is speaking? (*on telephone*) **¿Quién habla?** 2.5
whole **todo/a** *adj.*
whom **quien(es)** *pron.* 2.6
whose? **¿de quién(es)?** 1.1
why? **¿por qué?** 1.2
widower/widow **viudo/a** *adj.* 2.3
wife **esposa** *f.* 1.3
win **ganar** *v.* 1.4
wind **viento** *m.*
window **ventana** *f.* 1.2
windshield **parabrisas** *m., sing.* 2.5
windsurf **hacer** *v.* **windsurf** 1.5
windy: It's (very) windy. **Hace (mucho) viento.** 1.5
wine **vino** *m.* 2.2
  red wine **vino tinto** 2.2
  white wine **vino blanco** 2.2
wineglass **copa** *f.* 2.6
winter **invierno** *m.* 1.5

wireless connection **conexión inalámbrica** *f.* 2.5
wish **desear** *v.* 1.2; **esperar** *v.* 3.1
 I wish (that) **ojalá (que)** 3.1
with **con** *prep.* 1.2
 with me **conmigo** 1.4; 2.3
 with you **contigo** *fam.* 1.5, 2.3
within (ten years) **dentro de (diez años)** *prep.* 3.4
without **sin** *prep.* 1.2; **sin que** *conj.* 3.1
woman **mujer** *f.* 1.1
wool **lana** *f.* 1.6
 (made of) wool **de lana** 1.6
word **palabra** *f.* 1.1
work **trabajar** *v.* 1.2; **funcionar** *v.* 2.5; **trabajo** *m.* 3.4
 work (of art, literature, music, etc.) **obra** *f.* 3.5
 work out **hacer gimnasia** 3.3
world **mundo** *m.* 2.2
worldwide **mundial** *adj. m., f.*
worried (about) **preocupado/a (por)** *adj.* 1.5
worry (about) **preocuparse** *v.* **(por)** 2.1
 Don't worry. **No te preocupes.** *fam.* 2.1
worse **peor** *adj. m., f.* 2.2
worst **el/la peor** 2.2
Would you like to...? **¿Te gustaría...?** *fam.*
Would you do me the honor of marrying me? **¿Me harías el honor de casarte conmigo?** 3.5

wow **híjole** *interj.* 1.6
wrench **llave** *f.* 2.5
write **escribir** *v.* 1.3
 write a letter/an e-mail **escribir una carta/un mensaje electrónico** 1.4
writer **escritor(a)** *m., f* 3.5
written **escrito/a** *p.p.* 3.2
wrong **equivocado/a** *adj.* 1.5
 be wrong **no tener razón** 1.3

X

X-ray **radiografía** *f.* 2.4

Y

yard **jardín** *m.* 2.6; **patio** *m.* 2.6
year **año** *m.* 1.5
 be... years old **tener... años** 1.3
yellow **amarillo/a** *adj.* 1.6
yes **sí** *interj.* 1.1
yesterday **ayer** *adv.* 1.6
yet **todavía** *adv.* 1.5
yogurt **yogur** *m.* 2.2
you **tú** *fam.* **usted (Ud.)** *form. sing.* **vosotros/as** *m., f. fam. pl.* **ustedes (Uds.)** *pl.* 1.1; (to, for) you *fam. sing.* **te** *pl.* **os** 1.6; *form. sing.* **le** *pl.* **les** 1.6
you **te** *fam., sing.,* **lo/la** *form., sing.,* **os** *fam., pl.,* **los/las** *pl, d.o. pron.* 1.5

You don't say! **¡No me digas!** *fam.;* **¡No me diga!** *form.*
You're welcome. **De nada.** 1.1; **No hay de qué.** 1.1
young **joven** *adj., sing.* (**jóvenes** *pl.*) 1.3
 young person **joven** *m., f., sing.* (**jóvenes** *pl.*) 1.1
 young woman **señorita (Srta.)** *f.*
younger **menor** *adj. m., f.* 1.3
younger: younger brother, sister *m., f.* **hermano/a menor** 1.3
youngest **el/la menor** *m., f.* 2.2
your **su(s)** *poss. adj. form.* 1.3; **tu(s)** *poss. adj. fam. sing.* 1.3; **vuestro/a(s)** *poss. adj. fam. pl.* 1.3
your(s) *form.* **suyo(s)/a(s)** *poss. pron. form.* 2.5; **tuyo(s)/a(s)** *poss. fam. sing.* 2.5; **vuestro(s)/a(s)** *poss. fam.* 2.5
youth *f.* **juventud** 2.3

Z

zero **cero** *m.* 1.1

MATERIAS / ACADEMIC SUBJECTS

MATERIAS	ACADEMIC SUBJECTS
la administración de empresas	business administration
la agronomía	agriculture
el alemán	German
el álgebra	algebra
la antropología	anthropology
la arqueología	archaeology
la arquitectura	architecture
el arte	art
la astronomía	astronomy
la biología	biology
la bioquímica	biochemistry
la botánica	botany
el cálculo	calculus
el chino	Chinese
las ciencias políticas	political science
la computación	computer science
las comunicaciones	communications
la contabilidad	accounting
la danza	dance
el derecho	law
la economía	economics
la educación	education
la educación física	physical education
la enfermería	nursing
el español	Spanish
la filosofía	philosophy
la física	physics
el francés	French
la geografía	geography
la geología	geology
el griego	Greek
el hebreo	Hebrew
la historia	history
la informática	computer science
la ingeniería	engineering
el inglés	English
el italiano	Italian
el japonés	Japanese
el latín	Latin
las lenguas clásicas	classical languages
las lenguas romances	Romance languages
la lingüística	linguistics
la literatura	literature
las matemáticas	mathematics
la medicina	medicine
el mercadeo/ la mercadotecnia	marketing
la música	music
los negocios	business
el periodismo	journalism
el portugués	Portuguese
la psicología	psychology
la química	chemistry
el ruso	Russian
los servicios sociales	social services
la sociología	sociology
el teatro	theater
la trigonometría	trigonometry

LOS ANIMALES / ANIMALS

LOS ANIMALES	ANIMALS
la abeja	bee
la araña	spider
la ardilla	squirrel
el ave (f.), el pájaro	bird
la ballena	whale
el burro	donkey
la cabra	goat
el caimán	alligator
el camello	camel
la cebra	zebra
el ciervo, el venado	deer
el cochino, el cerdo, el puerco	pig
el cocodrilo	crocodile
el conejo	rabbit
el coyote	coyote
la culebra, la serpiente, la víbora	snake
el elefante	elephant
la foca	seal
la gallina	hen
el gallo	rooster
el gato	cat
el gorila	gorilla
el hipopótamo	hippopotamus
la hormiga	ant
el insecto	insect
la jirafa	giraffe
el lagarto	lizard
el león	lion
el lobo	wolf
el loro, la cotorra, el papagayo, el perico	parrot
la mariposa	butterfly
el mono	monkey
la mosca	fly
el mosquito	mosquito
el oso	bear
la oveja	sheep
el pato	duck
el perro	dog
el pez	fish
la rana	frog
el ratón	mouse
el rinoceronte	rhinoceros
el saltamontes, el chapulín	grasshopper
el tiburón	shark
el tigre	tiger
el toro	bull
la tortuga	turtle
la vaca	cow
el zorro	fox

EL CUERPO HUMANO Y LA SALUD

THE HUMAN BODY AND HEALTH

El cuerpo humano

The human body

la barba	beard
el bigote	mustache
la boca	mouth
el brazo	arm
la cabeza	head
la cadera	hip
la ceja	eyebrow
el cerebro	brain
la cintura	waist
el codo	elbow
el corazón	heart
la costilla	rib
el cráneo	skull
el cuello	neck
el dedo	finger
el dedo del pie	toe
la espalda	back
el estómago	stomach
la frente	forehead
la garganta	throat
el hombro	shoulder
el hueso	bone
el labio	lip
la lengua	tongue
la mandíbula	jaw
la mejilla	cheek
el mentón, la barba, la barbilla	chin
la muñeca	wrist
el músculo	muscle
el muslo	thigh
las nalgas, el trasero, las asentaderas	buttocks
la nariz	nose
el nervio	nerve
el oído	(inner) ear
el ojo	eye
el ombligo	navel, belly button
la oreja	(outer) ear
la pantorrilla	calf
el párpado	eyelid
el pecho	chest
la pestaña	eyelash
el pie	foot
la piel	skin
la pierna	leg
el pulgar	thumb
el pulmón	lung
la rodilla	knee
la sangre	blood
el talón	heel
el tobillo	ankle
el tronco	torso, trunk
la uña	fingernail
la uña del dedo del pie	toenail
la vena	vein

Los cinco sentidos

The five senses

el gusto	taste
el oído	hearing
el olfato	smell
el tacto	touch
la vista	sight

La salud

Health

el accidente	accident
alérgico/a	allergic
el antibiótico	antibiotic
la aspirina	aspirin
el ataque cardiaco, el ataque al corazón	heart attack
el cáncer	cancer
la cápsula	capsule
la clínica	clinic
congestionado/a	congested
el consultorio	doctor's office
la curita	adhesive bandage
el/la dentista	dentist
el/la doctor(a), el/la médico/a	doctor
el dolor (de cabeza)	(head)ache, pain
embarazada	pregnant
la enfermedad	illness, disease
el/la enfermero/a	nurse
enfermo/a	ill, sick
la erupción	rash
el examen médico	physical exam
la farmacia	pharmacy
la fiebre	fever
la fractura	fracture
la gripe	flu
la herida	wound
el hospital	hospital
la infección	infection
el insomnio	insomnia
la inyección	injection
el jarabe	(cough) syrup
mareado/a	dizzy, nauseated
el medicamento	medication
la medicina	medicine
las muletas	crutches
la operación	operation
el/la paciente	patient
el/la paramédico/a	paramedic
la pastilla, la píldora	pill, tablet
los primeros auxilios	first aid
la pulmonía	pneumonia
los puntos	stitches
la quemadura	burn
el quirófano	operating room
la radiografía	x-ray
la receta	prescription
el resfriado	cold (illness)
la sala de emergencia(s)	emergency room
saludable	healthy, healthful
sano/a	healthy
el seguro médico	medical insurance
la silla de ruedas	wheelchair
el síntoma	symptom
el termómetro	thermometer
la tos	cough
la transfusión	transfusion

la vacuna	vaccination
la venda	bandage
el virus	virus

_____

cortar(se)	to cut (oneself)
curar	to cure, to treat
desmayar(se)	to faint
enfermarse	to get sick
enyesar	to put in a cast
estornudar	to sneeze
guardar cama	to stay in bed
hinchar(se)	to swell
internar(se) en el hospital	to check into the hospital
lastimarse (el pie)	to hurt (one's foot)
mejorar(se)	to get better; to improve
operar	to operate
quemar(se)	to burn
respirar (hondo)	to breathe (deeply)
romperse (la pierna)	to break (one's leg)
sangrar	to bleed
sufrir	to suffer
tomarle la presión a alguien	to take someone's blood pressure
tomarle el pulso a alguien	to take someone's pulse
torcerse (el tobillo)	to sprain (one's ankle)
vendar	to bandage

EXPRESIONES ÚTILES PARA LA CLASE
USEFUL CLASSROOM EXPRESSIONS

Palabras útiles
Useful words

ausente	absent
el departamento	department
el dictado	dictation
la conversación, las conversaciones	conversation(s)
la expresión, las expresiones	expression(s)
el examen, los exámenes	test(s), exam(s)
la frase	sentence

la hoja de actividades	activity sheet
el horario de clases	class schedule
la oración, las oraciones	sentence(s)
el párrafo	paragraph
la persona	person
presente	present
la prueba	test, quiz
siguiente	following
la tarea	homework

Expresiones útiles
Useful expressions

Abra(n) su(s) libro(s).	Open your book(s).
Cambien de papel.	Change roles.
Cierre(n) su(s) libro(s).	Close your book(s).
¿Cómo se dice ___ en español?	How do you say ___ in Spanish?
¿Cómo se escribe ___ en español?	How do you write ___ in Spanish?
¿Comprende(n)?	Do you understand?
(No) comprendo.	I (don't) understand.
Conteste(n) las preguntas.	Answer the questions.
Continúe(n), por favor.	Continue, please.
Escriba(n) su nombre.	Write your name.
Escuche(n) el audio.	Listen to the audio.
Estudie(n) la Lección tres.	Study Lesson three.
Haga(n) la actividad (el ejercicio) número cuatro.	Do activity (exercise) number four.
Lea(n) la oración en voz alta.	Read the sentence aloud.
Levante(n) la mano.	Raise your hand(s).
Más despacio, por favor.	Slower, please.
No sé.	I don't know.
Páse(n)me los exámenes.	Pass me the tests.
¿Qué significa ___?	What does ___ mean?
Repita(n), por favor.	Repeat, please.
Siénte(n)se, por favor.	Sit down, please.
Siga(n) las instrucciones.	Follow the instructions.
¿Tiene(n) alguna pregunta?	Do you have any questions?
Vaya(n) a la página dos.	Go to page two.

COUNTRIES & NATIONALITIES
PAÍSES Y NACIONALIDADES

North America
Norteamérica

Canada	Canadá	canadiense
Mexico	México	mexicano/a
United States	Estados Unidos	estadounidense

Central America
Centroamérica

Belize	Belice	beliceño/a
Costa Rica	Costa Rica	costarricense
El Salvador	El Salvador	salvadoreño/a
Guatemala	Guatemala	guatemalteco/a
Honduras	Honduras	hondureño/a
Nicaragua	Nicaragua	nicaragüense
Panama	Panamá	panameño/a

The Caribbean	El Caribe	
Cuba	**Cuba**	*cubano/a*
Dominican Republic	**República Dominicana**	*dominicano/a*
Haiti	**Haití**	*haitiano/a*
Puerto Rico	**Puerto Rico**	*puertorriqueño/a*

South America	Suramérica	
Argentina	**Argentina**	*argentino/a*
Bolivia	**Bolivia**	*boliviano/a*
Brazil	**Brasil**	*brasileño/a*
Chile	**Chile**	*chileno/a*
Colombia	**Colombia**	*colombiano/a*
Ecuador	**Ecuador**	*ecuatoriano/a*
Paraguay	**Paraguay**	*paraguayo/a*
Peru	**Perú**	*peruano/a*
Uruguay	**Uruguay**	*uruguayo/a*
Venezuela	**Venezuela**	*venezolano/a*

Europe	Europa	
Armenia	**Armenia**	*armenio/a*
Austria	**Austria**	*austríaco/a*
Belgium	**Bélgica**	*belga*
Bosnia	**Bosnia**	*bosnio/a*
Bulgaria	**Bulgaria**	*búlgaro/a*
Croatia	**Croacia**	*croata*
Czech Republic	**República Checa**	*checo/a*
Denmark	**Dinamarca**	*danés, danesa*
England	**Inglaterra**	*inglés, inglesa*
Estonia	**Estonia**	*estonio/a*
Finland	**Finlandia**	*finlandés, finlandesa*
France	**Francia**	*francés, francesa*
Germany	**Alemania**	*alemán, alemana*
Great Britain (United Kingdom)	**Gran Bretaña (Reino Unido)**	*británico/a*
Greece	**Grecia**	*griego/a*
Hungary	**Hungría**	*húngaro/a*
Iceland	**Islandia**	*islandés, islandesa*
Ireland	**Irlanda**	*irlandés, irlandesa*
Italy	**Italia**	*italiano/a*
Latvia	**Letonia**	*letón, letona*
Lithuania	**Lituania**	*lituano/a*
Netherlands (Holland)	**Países Bajos (Holanda)**	*holandés, holandesa*
Norway	**Noruega**	*noruego/a*
Poland	**Polonia**	*polaco/a*
Portugal	**Portugal**	*portugués, portuguesa*
Romania	**Rumania**	*rumano/a*
Russia	**Rusia**	*ruso/a*
Scotland	**Escocia**	*escocés, escocesa*
Serbia	**Serbia**	*serbio/a*
Slovakia	**Eslovaquia**	*eslovaco/a*
Slovenia	**Eslovenia**	*esloveno/a*
Spain	**España**	*español(a)*
Sweden	**Suecia**	*sueco/a*
Switzerland	**Suiza**	*suizo/a*
Ukraine	**Ucrania**	*ucraniano/a*
Wales	**Gales**	*galés, galesa*

Asia	Asia	
Bangladesh	**Bangladés**	*bangladesí*
Cambodia	**Camboya**	*camboyano/a*
China	**China**	*chino/a*
India	**India**	*indio/a*
Indonesia	**Indonesia**	*indonesio/a*
Iran	**Irán**	*iraní*
Iraq	**Iraq, Irak**	*iraquí*

Israel	**Israel**	*israelí*
Japan	**Japón**	*japonés, japonesa*
Jordan	**Jordania**	*jordano/a*
Korea	**Corea**	*coreano/a*
Kuwait	**Kuwait**	*kuwaití*
Lebanon	**Líbano**	*libanés, libanesa*
Malaysia	**Malasia**	*malasio/a*
Pakistan	**Pakistán**	*pakistaní*
Russia	**Rusia**	*ruso/a*
Saudi Arabia	**Arabia Saudí**	*saudí*
Singapore	**Singapur**	*singapurés, singapuresa*
Syria	**Siria**	*sirio/a*
Taiwan	**Taiwán**	*taiwanés, taiwanesa*
Thailand	**Tailandia**	*tailandés, tailandesa*
Turkey	**Turquía**	*turco/a*
Vietnam	**Vietnam**	*vietnamita*

Africa	**África**	
Algeria	**Argelia**	*argelino/a*
Angola	**Angola**	*angoleño/a*
Cameroon	**Camerún**	*camerunés, camerunesa*
Congo	**Congo**	*congolés, congolesa*
Egypt	**Egipto**	*egipcio/a*
Equatorial Guinea	**Guinea Ecuatorial**	*ecuatoguineano/a*
Ethiopia	**Etiopía**	*etíope*
Ivory Coast	**Costa de Marfil**	*marfileño/a*
Kenya	**Kenia, Kenya**	*keniano/a, keniata*
Libya	**Libia**	*libio/a*
Mali	**Malí**	*maliense*
Morocco	**Marruecos**	*marroquí*
Mozambique	**Mozambique**	*mozambiqueño/a*
Nigeria	**Nigeria**	*nigeriano/a*
Rwanda	**Ruanda**	*ruandés, ruandesa*
Somalia	**Somalia**	*somalí*
South Africa	**Sudáfrica**	*sudafricano/a*
Sudan	**Sudán**	*sudanés, sudanesa*
Tunisia	**Tunicia, Túnez**	*tunecino/a*
Uganda	**Uganda**	*ugandés, ugandesa*
Zambia	**Zambia**	*zambiano/a*
Zimbabwe	**Zimbabue**	*zimbabuense*

Australia and the Pacific	**Australia y el Pacífico**	
Australia	**Australia**	*australiano/a*
New Zealand	**Nueva Zelanda**	*neozelandés, neozelandesa*
Philippines	**Filipinas**	*filipino/a*

MONEDAS DE LOS PAÍSES HISPANOS
CURRENCIES OF HISPANIC COUNTRIES

País / Country	Moneda / Currency
Argentina	el peso
Bolivia	el boliviano
Chile	el peso
Colombia	el peso
Costa Rica	el colón
Cuba	el peso
Ecuador	el dólar estadounidense
El Salvador	el dólar estadounidense
España	el euro
Guatemala	el quetzal
Guinea Ecuatorial	el franco
Honduras	el lempira
México	el peso
Nicaragua	el córdoba
Panamá	el balboa, el dólar estadounidense
Paraguay	el guaraní
Perú	el nuevo sol
Puerto Rico	el dólar estadounidense
República Dominicana	el peso
Uruguay	el peso
Venezuela	el bolívar

EXPRESIONES Y REFRANES

EXPRESSIONS AND SAYINGS

Expresiones y refranes con partes del cuerpo

Expressions and sayings with parts of the body

A cara o cruz	Heads or tails
A corazón abierto	Open heart
A ojos vistas	Clearly, visibly
Al dedillo	Like the back of one's hand
¡Choca/Vengan esos cinco!	Put it there!/Give me five!
Codo con codo	Side by side
Con las manos en la masa	Red-handed
Costar un ojo de la cara	To cost an arm and a leg
Darle a la lengua	To chatter/To gab
De rodillas	On one's knees
Duro de oído	Hard of hearing
En cuerpo y alma	In body and soul
En la punta de la lengua	On the tip of one's tongue
En un abrir y cerrar de ojos	In a blink of the eye
Entrar por un oído y salir por otro	In one ear and out the other
Estar con el agua al cuello	To be up to one's neck with/in
Estar para chuparse los dedos	To be delicious/To be finger-licking good
Hablar entre dientes	To mutter/To speak under one's breath
Hablar por los codos	To talk a lot/To be a chatterbox
Hacer la vista gorda	To turn a blind eye on something
Hombro con hombro	Shoulder to shoulder
Llorar a lágrima viva	To sob/To cry one's eyes out
Metérsele (a alguien) algo entre ceja y ceja	To get an idea in your head
No pegar ojo	Not to sleep a wink
No tener corazón	Not to have a heart
No tener dos dedos de frente	Not to have an ounce of common sense
Ojos que no ven, corazón que no siente	Out of sight, out of mind
Perder la cabeza	To lose one's head
Quedarse con la boca abierta	To be thunderstruck
Romper el corazón	To break someone's heart
Tener buen/mal corazón	Have a good/bad heart
Tener un nudo en la garganta	Have a knot in your throat
Tomarse algo a pecho	To take something too seriously
Venir como anillo al dedo	To fit like a charm/To suit perfectly

Expresiones y refranes con animales

Expressions and sayings with animals

A caballo regalado no le mires el diente.	Don't look a gift horse in the mouth.
Comer como un cerdo	To eat like a pig
Cuando menos se piensa, salta la liebre.	Things happen when you least expect it.
Llevarse como el perro y el gato	To fight like cats and dogs
Perro ladrador, poco mordedor./Perro que ladra no muerde.	His/her bark is worse than his/her bite.
Por la boca muere el pez.	Talking too much can be dangerous.
Poner el cascabel al gato	To stick one's neck out
Ser una tortuga	To be a slowpoke

Expresiones y refranes con alimentos

Expressions and sayings with food

Agua que no has de beber, déjala correr.	If you're not interested, don't ruin it for everybody else.
Con pan y vino se anda el camino.	Things never seem as bad after a good meal.
Contigo pan y cebolla.	You are all I need.
Dame pan y dime tonto.	I don't care what you say, as long as I get what I want.
Descubrir el pastel	To let the cat out of the bag
Dulce como la miel	Sweet as honey
Estar como agua para chocolate	To furious/To be at the boiling point
Estar en el ajo	To be in the know
Estar en la higuera	To have one's head in the clouds
Estar más claro que el agua	To be clear as a bell
Ganarse el pan	To earn a living/To earn one's daily bread
Llamar al pan, pan y al vino, vino.	Not to mince words.
No hay miel sin hiel.	Every rose has its thorn./There's always a catch.
No sólo de pan vive el hombre.	Man doesn't live by bread alone.
Pan con pan, comida de tontos.	Variety is the spice of life.
Ser agua pasada	To be water under the bridge
Ser más bueno que el pan	To be kindness itself
Temblar como un flan	To shake/tremble like a leaf

Expresiones y refranes con colores

Expressions and sayings with colors

Estar verde	To be inexperienced/wet behind the ears
Poner los ojos en blanco	To roll one's eyes
Ponerle a alguien un ojo morado	To give someone a black eye
Ponerse rojo	To turn red/To blush
Ponerse rojo de ira	To turn red with anger
Ponerse verde de envidia	To be green with envy
Quedarse en blanco	To go blank
Verlo todo de color de rosa	To see the world through rose-colored glasses

Refranes	**Sayings**
A buen entendedor, pocas palabras bastan.	A word to the wise is enough.
Ande o no ande, caballo grande.	Bigger is always better.
A quien madruga, Dios le ayuda.	The early bird catches the worm.
Cuídate, que te cuidaré.	Take care of yourself, and then I'll take care of you.
De tal palo tal astilla.	A chip off the old block.
Del dicho al hecho hay mucho trecho.	Easier said than done.
Dime con quién andas y te diré quién eres.	A man is known by the company he keeps.
El saber no ocupa lugar.	One never knows too much.
Lo que es moda no incomoda.	You have to suffer in the name of fashion.
Más vale maña que fuerza.	Brains are better than brawn.
Más vale prevenir que curar.	Prevention is better than cure.
Más vale solo que mal acompañado.	Better alone than with people you don't like.
Más vale tarde que nunca.	Better late than never.
No es oro todo lo que reluce.	All that glitters is not gold.
Poderoso caballero es don Dinero.	Money talks.

COMMON FALSE FRIENDS

False friends are Spanish words that look similar to English words but have very different meanings. While recognizing the English relatives of unfamiliar Spanish words you encounter is an important way of constructing meaning, there are some Spanish words whose similarity to English words is deceptive. Here is a list of some of the most common Spanish false friends.

actualmente ≠ actually
actualmente = nowadays, currently
actually = **de hecho, en realidad, en efecto**

argumento ≠ argument
argumento = plot
argument = **discusión, pelea**

armada ≠ army
armada = navy
army = **ejército**

balde ≠ bald
balde = pail, bucket
bald = **calvo/a**

batería ≠ battery
batería = drum set
battery = **pila**

bravo ≠ brave
bravo = wild; fierce
brave = **valiente**

cándido/a ≠ candid
cándido/a = innocent
candid = **sincero/a**

carbón ≠ carbon
carbón = coal
carbon = **carbono**

casual ≠ casual
casual = accidental, chance
casual = **informal, despreocupado/a**

casualidad ≠ casualty
casualidad = chance, coincidence
casualty = **víctima**

colegio ≠ college
colegio = school
college = **universidad**

collar ≠ collar (of a shirt)
collar = necklace
collar = **cuello (de camisa)**

comprensivo/a ≠ comprehensive
comprensivo/a = understanding
comprehensive = **completo, extensivo**

constipado ≠ constipated
estar constipado/a = to have a cold
to be constipated = **estar estreñido/a**

crudo/a ≠ crude
crudo/a = raw, undercooked
crude = **burdo/a, grosero/a**

divertir ≠ to divert
divertirse = to enjoy oneself
to divert = **desviar**

educado/a ≠ educated
educado/a = well-mannered
educated = **culto/a, instruido/a**

embarazada ≠ embarrassed
estar embarazada = to be pregnant
to be embarrassed = **estar avergonzado/a; dar/tener vergüenza**

eventualmente ≠ eventually
eventualmente = possibly
eventually = **finalmente, al final**

éxito ≠ exit
éxito = success
exit = **salida**

físico/a ≠ physician
físico/a = physicist
physician = **médico/a**

fútbol ≠ football
fútbol = soccer
football = **fútbol americano**

lectura ≠ lecture
lectura = reading
lecture = **conferencia**

librería ≠ library
librería = bookstore
library = **biblioteca**

máscara ≠ mascara
máscara = mask
mascara = **rímel**

molestar ≠ to molest
molestar = to bother, to annoy
to molest = **abusar**

oficio ≠ office
oficio = trade, occupation
office = **oficina**

rato ≠ rat
rato = while, time
rat = **rata**

realizar ≠ to realize
realizar = to carry out; to fulfill
to realize = **darse cuenta de**

red ≠ red
red = net
red = **rojo/a**

revolver ≠ revolver
revolver = to stir, to rummage through
revolver = **revólver**

sensible ≠ sensible
sensible = sensitive
sensible = **sensato/a, razonable**

suceso ≠ success
suceso = event
success = **éxito**

sujeto ≠ subject (topic)
sujeto = fellow; individual
subject = **tema, asunto**

LOS ALIMENTOS / FOODS

Frutas / Fruits

la aceituna	olive
el aguacate	avocado
el albaricoque, el damasco	apricot
la banana, el plátano	banana
la cereza	cherry
la ciruela	plum
el dátil	date
la frambuesa	raspberry
la fresa, la frutilla	strawberry
el higo	fig
el limón	lemon; lime
el melocotón, el durazno	peach
la mandarina	tangerine
el mango	mango
la manzana	apple
la naranja	orange
la papaya	papaya
la pera	pear
la piña	pineapple
el pomelo, la toronja	grapefruit
la sandía	watermelon
las uvas	grapes

Vegetales / Vegetables

la alcachofa	artichoke
el apio	celery
la arveja, el guisante	pea
la berenjena	eggplant
el brócoli	broccoli
la calabaza	squash; pumpkin
la cebolla	onion
el champiñón, la seta	mushroom
la col, el repollo	cabbage
la coliflor	cauliflower
los espárragos	asparagus
las espinacas	spinach
los frijoles, las habichuelas	beans
las habas	fava beans
las judías verdes, los ejotes	string beans, green beans
la lechuga	lettuce
el maíz, el choclo, el elote	corn
la papa, la patata	potato
el pepino	cucumber
el pimentón	bell pepper
el rábano	radish
la remolacha	beet
el tomate, el jitomate	tomato
la zanahoria	carrot

El pescado y los mariscos / Fish and shellfish

la almeja	clam
el atún	tuna
el bacalao	cod
el calamar	squid
el cangrejo	crab
el camarón, la gamba	shrimp
la langosta	lobster
el langostino	prawn
el lenguado	sole; flounder
el mejillón	mussel
la ostra	oyster
el pulpo	octopus
el salmón	salmon
la sardina	sardine
la vieira	scallop

La carne / Meat

la albóndiga	meatball
el bistec	steak
la carne de res	beef
el chorizo	hard pork sausage
la chuleta de cerdo	pork chop
el cordero	lamb
los fiambres	cold cuts, food served cold
el filete	fillet
la hamburguesa	hamburger
el hígado	liver
el jamón	ham
el lechón	suckling pig, roasted pig
el pavo	turkey
el pollo	chicken
el cerdo	pork
la salchicha	sausage
la ternera	veal
el tocino	bacon

Otras comidas / Other foods

el ajo	garlic
el arroz	rice
el azúcar	sugar
el batido	milkshake
el budín	pudding
el cacahuete, el maní	peanut
el café	coffee
los fideos	noodles, pasta
la harina	flour
el huevo	egg
el jugo, el zumo	juice
la leche	milk
la mermelada	marmalade, jam
la miel	honey
el pan	bread
el queso	cheese
la sal	salt
la sopa	soup
el té	tea
la tortilla	omelet (Spain), tortilla (Mexico)
el yogur	yogurt

Cómo describir la comida / Ways to describe food

a la plancha, a la parrilla	grilled
ácido/a	sour
al horno	baked
amargo/a	bitter
caliente	hot
dulce	sweet
duro/a	tough
frío/a	cold
frito/a	fried
fuerte	strong, heavy
ligero/a	light
picante	spicy
sabroso/a	tasty
salado/a	salty

DÍAS FESTIVOS

HOLIDAYS

enero

Año Nuevo (1)
Día de los Reyes Magos (6)
Día de Martin Luther King, Jr.

January

New Year's Day
Three Kings Day (Epiphany)

Martin Luther King, Jr. Day

febrero

Día de San Blas (Paraguay) (3)
Día de San Valentín, Día de los Enamorados (14)
Día de los Presidentes
Carnaval

February

St. Blas Day (Paraguay)

Valentine's Day

Presidents' Day
Carnival (Mardi Gras)

marzo

Día de San Patricio (17)
Nacimiento de Benito Juárez (México) (21)

March

St. Patrick's Day
Benito Juárez's Birthday (Mexico)

abril

Semana Santa
Pésaj
Pascua
Declaración de la Independencia de Venezuela (19)
Día de la Tierra (22)

April

Holy Week
Passover
Easter
Declaration of Independence of Venezuela
Earth Day

mayo

Día del Trabajo (1)
Cinco de Mayo (5) (México)
Día de las Madres
Independencia Patria (Paraguay) (15)
Día Conmemorativo

May

Labor Day
Cinco de Mayo (May 5th) (Mexico)
Mother's Day
Independence Day (Paraguay)

Memorial Day

junio

Día de los Padres
Día de la Bandera (14)
Día del Indio (Perú) (24)

June

Father's Day
Flag Day
Native People's Day (Peru)

julio

Día de la Independencia de los Estados Unidos (4)
Día de la Independencia de Venezuela (5)
Día de la Independencia de la Argentina (9)
Día de la Independencia de Colombia (20)

July

Independence Day (United States)

Independence Day (Venezuela)
Independence Day (Argentina)

Independence Day (Colombia)

(continued)

Nacimiento de Simón Bolívar (24)
Día de la Revolución (Cuba) (26)
Día de la Independencia del Perú (28)

Simón Bolívar's Birthday

Revolution Day (Cuba)

Independence Day (Peru)

agosto

Día de la Independencia de Bolivia (6)
Día de la Independencia del Ecuador (10)
Día de San Martín (Argentina) (17)
Día de la Independencia del Uruguay (25)

August

Independence Day (Bolivia)

Independence Day (Ecuador)

San Martín Day (anniversary of his death) (Argentina)
Independence Day (Uruguay)

septiembre

Día del Trabajo (EE. UU.)
Día de la Independencia de Costa Rica, El Salvador, Guatemala, Honduras y Nicaragua (15)
Día de la Independencia de México (16)
Día de la Independencia de Chile (18)
Año Nuevo Judío
Día de la Virgen de las Mercedes (Perú) (24)

September

Labor Day (U.S.)
Independence Day (Costa Rica, El Salvador, Guatemala, Honduras, Nicaragua)

Independence Day (Mexico)

Independence Day (Chile)

Jewish New Year
Day of the Virgin of Mercedes (Peru)

octubre

Día de la Raza (12)
Noche de Brujas (31)

October

Columbus Day
Halloween

noviembre

Día de los Muertos (2)
Día de los Veteranos (11)
Día de la Revolución Mexicana (20)
Día de Acción de Gracias
Día de la Independencia de Panamá (28)

November

All Souls Day
Veterans' Day
Mexican Revolution Day

Thanksgiving
Independence Day (Panama)

diciembre

Día de la Virgen (8)
Día de la Virgen de Guadalupe (México) (12)
Januká
Nochebuena (24)
Navidad (25)
Año Viejo (31)

December

Day of the Virgin
Day of the Virgin of Guadalupe (Mexico)
Chanukah
Christmas Eve
Christmas
New Year's Eve

NOTE: In Spanish, dates are written with the day first, then the month. Christmas Day is **el 25 de diciembre**. In Latin America and in Europe, abbreviated dates also follow this pattern. Halloween, for example, falls on 31/10. You may also see the numbers in dates separated by periods: 27.4.16. When referring to centuries, roman numerals are always used. The 16th century, therefore, is **el siglo XVI**.

PESOS Y MEDIDAS

WEIGHTS AND MEASURES

Longitud
Length

El sistema métrico
Metric system

El equivalente estadounidense
U.S. equivalent

milímetro = 0,001 metro
millimeter = 0.001 meter
= 0.039 inch
centímetro = 0,01 metro
centimeter = 0.01 meter
= 0.39 inch
decímetro = 0,1 metro
decimeter = 0.1 meter
= 3.94 inches
metro
meter
= 39.4 inches
decámetro = 10 metros
dekameter = 10 meters
= 32.8 feet
hectómetro = 100 metros
hectometer = 100 meters
= 328 feet
kilómetro = 1.000 metros
kilometer = 1,000 meters
= .62 mile
U.S. system
Metric equivalent
El sistema estadounidense
El equivalente métrico
inch
= 2.54 centimeters
pulgada
= 2,54 centímetros
foot = 12 inches
= 30.48 centimeters
pie = 12 pulgadas
= 30,48 centímetros
yard = 3 feet
= 0.914 meter
yarda = 3 pies
= 0,914 metro
mile = 5,280 feet
= 1.609 kilometers
milla = 5.280 pies
= 1,609 kilómetros

Superficie
Surface Area

El sistema métrico
Metric system

El equivalente estadounidense
U.S. equivalent

metro cuadrado
square meter
= 10.764 square feet
área = 100 metros cuadrados
area = 100 square meters
= 0.025 acre
hectárea = 100 áreas
hectare = 100 ares
= 2.471 acres
U.S. system
Metric equivalent
El sistema estadounidense
El equivalente métrico

yarda cuadrada = 9 pies cuadrados = 0,836 metros cuadrados
square yard = 9 square feet = 0.836 square meters
acre = 4.840 yardas cuadradas = 0,405 hectáreas
acre = 4,840 square yards = 0.405 hectares

Capacidad
Capacity

El sistema métrico
Metric system

El equivalente estadounidense
U.S. equivalent

mililitro = 0,001 litro
milliliter = 0.001 liter
= 0.034 ounces
centilitro = 0,01 litro
centiliter = 0.01 liter
= 0.34 ounces
decilitro = 0,1 litro
deciliter = 0.1 liter
= 3.4 ounces
litro
liter
= 1.06 quarts
decalitro = 10 litros
dekaliter = 10 liters
= 2.64 gallons
hectolitro = 100 litros
hectoliter = 100 liters
= 26.4 gallons
kilolitro = 1.000 litros
kiloliter = 1,000 liters
= 264 gallons
U.S. system
Metric equivalent
El sistema estadounidense
El equivalente métrico
ounce
= 29.6 milliliters
onza
= 29,6 mililitros
cup = 8 ounces
= 236 milliliters
taza = 8 onzas
= 236 mililitros
pint = 2 cups
= 0.47 liters
pinta = 2 tazas
= 0,47 litros
quart = 2 pints
= 0.95 liters
cuarto = 2 pintas
= 0,95 litros
gallon = 4 quarts
= 3.79 liters
galón = 4 cuartos
= 3,79 litros

Peso
Weight

El sistema métrico
Metric system

El equivalente estadounidense
U.S. equivalent

miligramo = 0,001 gramo
milligram = 0.001 gram
gramo
gram
= 0.035 ounce
decagramo = 10 gramos
dekagram = 10 grams
= 0.35 ounces
hectogramo = 100 gramos
hectogram = 100 grams
= 3.5 ounces
kilogramo = 1.000 gramos
kilogram = 1,000 grams
= 2.2 pounds
tonelada (métrica) = 1.000 kilogramos
metric ton = 1,000 kilograms
= 1.1 tons
U.S. system
Metric equivalent
El sistema estadounidense
El equivalente métrico
ounce
= 28.35 grams
onza
= 28,35 gramos
pound = 16 ounces
= 0.45 kilograms
libra = 16 onzas
= 0,45 kilogramos
ton = 2,000 pounds
= 0.9 metric tons
tonelada = 2.000 libras
= 0,9 toneladas métricas

Temperatura
Temperature

Grados centígrados
Degrees Celsius
To convert from Celsius to Fahrenheit, multiply by $\frac{9}{5}$ and add 32.

Grados Fahrenheit
Degrees Fahrenheit
To convert from Fahrenheit to Celsius, subtract 32 and multiply by $\frac{5}{9}$.

NÚMEROS

Números ordinales

primer, primero/a	**1º/1ª**
segundo/a	**2º/2ª**
tercer, tercero/a	**3º/3ª**
cuarto/a	**4º/4ª**
quinto/a	**5º/5ª**
sexto/a	**6º/6ª**
séptimo/a	**7º/7ª**
octavo/a	**8º/8ª**
noveno/a	**9º/9ª**
décimo/a	**10º/10ª**

Fracciones

$\frac{1}{2}$	**un medio, la mitad**
$\frac{1}{3}$	**un tercio**
$\frac{1}{4}$	**un cuarto**
$\frac{1}{5}$	**un quinto**
$\frac{1}{6}$	**un sexto**
$\frac{1}{7}$	**un séptimo**
$\frac{1}{8}$	**un octavo**
$\frac{1}{9}$	**un noveno**
$\frac{1}{10}$	**un décimo**
$\frac{2}{3}$	**dos tercios**
$\frac{3}{4}$	**tres cuartos**
$\frac{5}{8}$	**cinco octavos**

Decimales

un décimo	**0,1**
un centésimo	**0,01**
un milésimo	**0,001**

NUMBERS

Ordinal numbers

first	1st
second	2nd
third	3rd
fourth	4th
fifth	5th
sixth	6th
seventh	7th
eighth	8th
ninth	9th
tenth	10th

Fractions

one half
one third
one fourth (quarter)
one fifth
one sixth
one seventh
one eighth
one ninth
one tenth
two thirds
three fourths (quarters)
five eighths

Decimals

one tenth	0.1
one hundredth	0.01
one thousandth	0.001

OCUPACIONES OCCUPATIONS

el/la abogado/a	lawyer
el actor, la actriz	actor
el/la administrador(a) de empresas	business administrator
el/la agente de bienes raíces	real estate agent
el/la agente de seguros	insurance agent
el/la agricultor(a)	farmer
el/la arqueólogo/a	archaeologist
el/la arquitecto/a	architect
el/la artesano/a	artisan
el/la auxiliar de vuelo	flight attendant
el/la basurero/a	garbage collector
el/la bibliotecario/a	librarian
el/la bombero/a	firefighter
el/la cajero/a	bank teller, cashier
el/la camionero/a	truck driver
el/la cantinero/a	bartender
el/la carnicero/a	butcher
el/la carpintero/a	carpenter
el/la científico/a	scientist
el/la cirujano/a	surgeon
el/la cobrador(a)	bill collector
el/la cocinero/a	cook, chef
el/la comprador(a)	buyer
el/la consejero/a	counselor, advisor
el/la contador(a)	accountant
el/la corredor(a) de bolsa	stockbroker
el/la diplomático/a	diplomat
el/la diseñador(a) (gráfico/a)	(graphic) designer
el/la electricista	electrician
el/la empresario/a de pompas fúnebres	funeral director
el/la especialista en dietética	dietician
el/la fisioterapeuta	physical therapist
el/la fotógrafo/a	photographer
el/la higienista dental	dental hygienist
el hombre/la mujer de negocios	businessperson
el/la ingeniero/a en computación	computer engineer
el/la intérprete	interpreter
el/la juez(a)	judge
el/la maestro/a	elementary school teacher
el/la marinero/a	sailor
el/la obrero/a	manual laborer
el/la obrero/a de la construcción	construction worker
el/la oficial de prisión	prision guard
el/la optometrista	optometrist
el/la panadero/a	baker
el/la paramédico/a	paramedic
el/la peluquero/a	hairdresser
el/la piloto	pilot
el/la pintor(a)	painter
el/la plomero/a	plumber
el/la político/a	politician
el/la programador(a)	computer programer
el/la psicólogo/a	psychologist
el/la quiropráctico/a	chiropractor
el/la redactor(a)	editor
el/la reportero/a	reporter
el/la sastre	tailor
el/la secretario/a	secretary
el/la supervisor(a)	supervisor
el/la técnico/a (en computación)	(computer) technician
el/la vendedor(a)	sales representative
el/la veterinario/a	veterinarian

Comic Credits

page 30 © Joaquin Salvador Lavado (QUINO) Toda Mafalda - Ediciones de La Flor, 1993.

TV Clip Credits

page 34   Courtesy of Mastercard. WARNER CHAPPELL MUSIC ARGENTINA (SADAIC) All Rights Reserved.
page 72   Courtesy of Cencosud Supermercados.
page 110   Courtesy of Banco Galicia/Mercado McCann.
page 146   Courtesy of ContentLine.
page 184   Courtesy of Santander Chile.
page 220   Courtesy of Juguettos.

Photography Credits

Cover: Jose Manuel Trujillo/500PX.

Front matter (SE): xiv: (l) Bettmann/Corbis; (r) Florian Biamm/123RF; **xv:** (l) Lawrence Manning/Corbis; (r) Design Pics Inc/Alamy; **xvi:** Jose Blanco; **xvii:** (l) Digital Vision/Getty Images; (r) Andres/Big Stock Photo; **xviii:** Fotolia IV/Fotolia; **xix:** (l) Goodshoot/Corbis; (r) Tyler Olson/Shutterstock; **xx:** Shelly Wall/Shutterstock; **xxi:** (t) Colorblind/Corbis; (b) Moodboard/Fotolia; **xxii:** (t) Digital Vision/Getty Images; (b) Purestock/Getty Images.

Front matter (TE): T4: Teodor Cucu/500PX; **T14:** Asiseeit/iStockphoto; **T35:** Corbis Photography/Veer; (inset) Fancy Photography/Veer; **T47:** Imgorthand/iStockphoto.

Lesson 1: 1: Paula Díez; **2:** John Henley/Getty Images; **3:** Martín Bernetti; **4:** Martín Bernetti; **10:** (l) Rachel Distler; (r) Ali Burafi; **11:** (l) Chris Pizzello/AP Images; (tr) Hans Georg Roth/Getty Images; (br) Paola Ríos-Schaaf; **12:** (l) Janet Dracksdorf; (r) Tom Grill/Corbis; **16:** (l) José Girarte/iStockphoto; (r) Blend Images/Alamy; **19:** (l) Buzzshotz/Alamy; (m) Anne Loubet; (r) Shutterstock; **27:** Martín Bernetti; **28:** (all) Martín Bernetti; **31:** (tl) Ana Cabezas Martín; (tmr) Kadmy/Fotolia; (tr) Vanessa Bertozzi; (bl) Corey Hochachka/Design Pics/Corbis; (bm) Sanek70974/Fotolia; (br) Ramiro Isaza/Fotocolombia; **32:** Carolina Zapata; **33:** Paula Díez; **36:** (t) Robert Holmes/Getty Images; (m) Jon Arnold Images/Alamy; (b) Andres R/Shutterstock; **37:** (tl) PhotoLink/Getty Images; (tr) Tony Arruza/Getty Images; (bl) A. Katz/Shutterstock; (br) Torontonian/Alamy.

Lesson 2: 39: Pamela Moore/iStockphoto; **42:** Martín Bernetti; **43:** Chris Schmidt/iStockphoto; **48:** (l) Hill Street Studios/AGE Fotostock; (r) David Ashley/Corbis; **49:** Guayo Fuentes/Shutterstock; **57:** Chris Schmidt/iStockphoto; **59:** (l) Paola Rios-Schaaf; (r) Image Source/Corbis; **67:** (l) Rick Gomez/Corbis; (r) Hola Images/Workbook.com; **68:** PigProx/Fotolia; **69:** Andres Benitez/Media Bakery; **70:** (t) Sam Edwards/Media Bakery; (b) Zdyma4/Fotolia; **71:** Kadmy/Fotolia; **74:** (tl) José Blanco; (tr) José Blanco; (m) Jack Q/Shutterstock; (b) Andrew Innerarity/Reuters/Newscom; **75:** (t) Courtesy of Charles Ommanney; (ml) José Blanco; (mr) José Blanco; (bl) Iconotec/Fotosearch; (br) VHL.

Lesson 3: 77: Paul Bradbury/Age Fotostock; **79:** Martín Bernetti; **80:** (tl) Anne Loubet; (tr) Blend Images/Alamy; (mtl) Ana Cabezas Martín; (mtr) Maskot/Media Bakery; (mbl) Martín Bernetti; (mbr) Martín Bernetti; (bl) Himchenko/Fotolia; (br) Martín Bernetti; **86:** (tl) Minerva Studio/Fotolia; (tr) Mangostock/Shutterstock; (b) John Roman Images/Shutterstock; **87:** (t) Robin Utrecht/Sipa Press/Newscom; (b) DPA Picture Alliance/Alamy; **90:** (l) Martín Bernetti; (r) José Blanco; **92:** Andres Rodriguez/Alamy; **95:** Monkey Business Images/Shutterstock; **97:** (l) Tyler Olson/Fotolia; (r) Michael Puche/Bigstock; **98:** Martín Bernetti; **103:** Fotoluminate/123RF; **106:** (t) Martín Bernetti; (m) Martín Bernetti; (b) Martín Bernetti; **107:** (t) Nora y Susana/Fotocolombia; (m) Monkey Business Images/Fotolia; (b) Martín Bernetti; **108:** Tom & Dee Ann McCarthy/Getty Images; **109:** AGE Fotostock RF; **112:** (t) Martín Bernetti; (ml) Martín Bernetti; (mm) Iván Mejía; (mr) Lauren Krolick; (b) Martín Bernetti; **113:** (tl) Martín Bernetti; (tr) Pablo Corral V/Getty Images; (ml) Martín Bernetti; (mr) Gerardo Mora; (b) Martín Bernetti.

Lesson 4: 115: Franz Faltermaier/AGE Fotostock; **117:** George Shelley/Getty Images; **124:** (l) Javier Soriano/AFP/Getty Images; (r) Fernando Bustamante/AP Images; **125:** (t) Photo Works/Shutterstock; (b) Zuma Press/Alamy; **128:** Jacek Chabraszewski/Fotolia; **139:** Mat Hayward/Fotolia; **142:** Martín Bernetti; **143:** Fernando Llano/AP Images; **144:** JGI/Jamie Grill/Media Bakery; **145:** Rick Gomez/Getty Images; **148:** (tl) Sorincolac/Fotolia; (tr) Albright Knox Art Gallery/Art Resource; (ml) Ruben Varela; (mr) Carolina Zapata; (b) Brian Overcast/Alamy; **149:** (tl) Radius Images/Alamy; (tr) Bettmann/Getty Images; (m) Corel/Corbis; (b) David R. Frazier Photolibrary/Alamy.

Lesson 5: 151: Gavin Hellier/Getty Images; **157:** Jeff Greenberg/Alamy; **162:** Gary Cook/Alamy; **163:** (t) AFP/Getty Images; (b) Mark A. Johnson/Getty Images; **167:** Ronnie Kaufman/Getty Images; **177:** Blend Images/Fotolia; **180:** Carlos Gaudier; **181:** (all) Corel/Corbis; **182:** Carolina Zapata; **186:** (tl) Bryan Mullennix/Alamy; (tr) José Blanco; (ml) Carlos Gaudier; (mr) Capricornis Photographic/Shutterstock; (b) Dave G. Houser/Getty Images; **187:** (tl) Carlos Gaudier; (tr) Lawrence Manning/Getty Images; (m) Stocktrek/Getty Images; (b) Carlos Gaudier.

Lesson 6: 189: Asiapix RF/Inmagine; **198:** (l) Jose Caballero Digital Press Photos/Newscom; (r) Janet Dracksdorf; **199:** (t) Carlos Alvarez/Getty Images; (bl) Guiseppe Carace/Getty Images; (br) Mark Mainz/Getty Images; **204:** (all) Pascal Pernix; **209:** (all) Martín Bernetti; **210:** (all) Paula Díez; **211:** Paula Díez; **216-217:** VHL and Shutterstock; **218:** Chris Schmidt/iStockphoto; **219:** John Henley/Media Bakery; **222:** (t) Pascal Pernix; (tml) Pascal Pernix; (tmr) Pascal Pernix; (mb) Pascal Pernix; (b) PhotoLink/Getty Images; **223:** (tl) Don Emmert/AFP/Getty Images; (tr) Pascal Pernix; (bl) Pascal Pernix; (br) The Kobal Collection at Art Resource, NY.